Building Low Latency Applications with C++

Develop a complete low latency trading ecosystem from scratch using modern C++

Sourav Ghosh

<packt>

BIRMINGHAM—MUMBAI

Building Low Latency Applications with C++

Copyright © 2023 Packt Publishing

All rights reserved. No part of this book may be reproduced, stored in a retrieval system, or transmitted in any form or by any means, without the prior written permission of the publisher, except in the case of brief quotations embedded in critical articles or reviews.

Every effort has been made in the preparation of this book to ensure the accuracy of the information presented. However, the information contained in this book is sold without warranty, either express or implied. Neither the author, nor Packt Publishing or its dealers and distributors, will be held liable for any damages caused or alleged to have been caused directly or indirectly by this book.

Packt Publishing has endeavored to provide trademark information about all of the companies and products mentioned in this book by the appropriate use of capitals. However, Packt Publishing cannot guarantee the accuracy of this information.

Group Product Manager: Gebin George
Publishing Product Manager: Kunal Sawant
Senior Editor: Nithya Sadanandan
Technical Editor: Shruti Thingalaya
Copy Editor: Safis Editing
Project Coordinator: Manisha Singh
Proofreader: Safis Editing
Indexer: Sejal Dsilva
Production Designer: Shyam Sundar Korumilli
Marketing Coordinator: Sonia Chauhan
Business Development Executive: Kriti Sharma

First published: July 2023

Production reference: 1300623

Published by Packt Publishing Ltd.
Livery Place
35 Livery Street
Birmingham
B3 2PB, UK.

ISBN 978-1-83763-935-9

www.packtpub.com

This book took a very long time and a tremendous amount of effort, and I would like to thank my wife, Alexis Raphael, for supporting me through this endeavor. I would also like to thank every mentor and colleague that I have ever had the privilege of working with, throughout my career with C++ in the low latency electronic trading business.

– Sourav Ghosh

Contributors

About the author

Sourav Ghosh has worked in several proprietary, high-frequency algorithmic trading firms over the last decade. He has built and deployed extremely low latency, high-throughput automated trading systems for trading exchanges around the world, across multiple asset classes. He specializes in statistical arbitrage market-making and pairs trading strategies with the most liquid global futures contracts. He is currently the vice president at an investment bank based in São Paulo, Brazil. He holds a master's in computer science from the University of Southern California. His areas of interest include computer architecture, FinTech, probability theory and stochastic processes, statistical learning and inference methods, and natural language processing.

About the reviewers

Anthony Weston is the software development manager at HCTech, a proprietary trading firm that specializes in futures and FX low latency trading. Anthony has over 20 years of experience in FinTech, working with C++, Python, C#, and VB.Net across several companies in NYC and Chicago, where he currently resides.

Hai-Ha Do is a finance and C++ veteran with over eight years of experience. Early in her career, she developed low latency, high throughput data feeds used by well-known investment banks and trading firms. After leaving Activ Financial, she worked in the equity derivative team at Morgan Stanley. There, she led a New York/London/Budapest collaboration, parallelizing risk calculations for exotic derivative products. Subsequently, she worked at leading UK options market maker Mako Trading on its trading signal GUI. She holds a master's degree in computer science from the University of Birmingham and a master's degree in financial engineering from WorldQuant University.

Simone Angeloni is a skilled software engineer with over 17 years of industry experience, specializing in software development and team management. He possesses extensive expertise in architecting and implementing high-performance, multithreading, and low-latency cross-platform applications. Throughout his career, Simone has worked in various technical domains, including game development, networking, motion control, and embedded systems. He is also an experienced build and release engineer, capable of implementing efficient deployment automations. Currently employed as a staff software engineer at Rocksteady, a subsidiary of Warner Bros. Discovery, Simone focuses on developing internal tools and overseeing company-wide DevOps practices.

Table of Contents

Preface — xv

Part 1: Introducing C++ Concepts and Exploring Important Low-Latency Applications

1

Introducing Low Latency Application Development in C++ — 3

Understanding requirements for latency-sensitive applications	4
Understanding latency-sensitive versus latency-critical applications	5
Measuring latency	5
Differentiating between latency metrics	7
Requirements of latency-sensitive applications	8
Understanding why C++ is the preferred programming language	**9**
Compiled language	10
Closer to hardware – low-level language	10
Deterministic usage of resources	11
Speed and high performance	11
Language constructs and features	11
Mature and large community support	15
Language under active development	15
Introducing some important low latency applications	**17**
Lower-level low latency applications	17
Higher-level low latency applications	19
Internet of Things and machine-to-machine applications	21
Summary	**22**

2

Designing Some Common Low Latency Applications in C++ — 23

Understanding low latency performance in live video streaming applications	23
Defining important concepts in low latency streaming	24
Understanding sources of latency in video streaming applications	25

Measuring latencies in low latency video streaming ... 27
Understanding the impact of high latencies ... 28
Exploring technologies for low latency video streaming ... 29
Exploring solutions and platforms for low latency streaming ... 32

Understanding what low latency constraints matter in gaming applications ... 34
Concepts in low latency gaming applications ... 35
Improving gaming application performance ... 38

Discussing the design of IoT and retail analytics systems ... 44
Ensuring low latency in IoT devices ... 45

Exploring low latency electronic trading ... 49
Understanding the need for low latency in modern electronic trading ... 49
Achieving the lowest latencies in electronic trading ... 50

Summary ... 53

3

Exploring C++ Concepts from A Low-Latency Application's Perspective ... 55

Technical requirements ... 55
Approaching low-latency application development in C++ ... 56
Coding for correctness first, optimizing second ... 56
Designing optimal data structures and algorithms ... 56
Being mindful of the processor ... 57
Understanding the cache and memory access costs ... 57
Understanding how C++ features work under the hood ... 58
Leveraging the C++ compiler ... 59
Measuring and improving performance ... 59

Avoiding pitfalls and leveraging C++ features to minimize application latency ... 60
Choosing storage ... 60
Choosing data types ... 61
Using casting and conversion operations ... 61
Optimizing numerical operations ... 62
Optimizing boolean and bitwise operations ... 63
Initializing, destroying, copying, and moving objects ... 64
Using references and pointers ... 64
Optimizing jumping and branching ... 66
Calling functions efficiently ... 67
Using bitfields ... 70
Using runtime polymorphism ... 70
Using compile-time polymorphism ... 71
Using additional compile-time processing ... 73
Handling exceptions ... 74
Accessing cache and memory ... 74
Dynamically allocating memory ... 77
Multi-threading ... 78

Maximizing C++ compiler optimization parameters ... 78
Understanding how compilers optimize ... 78
Understanding when compilers fail to optimize ... 89
Learning about compiler optimization flags ... 90

Summary ... 96

4

Building the C++ Building Blocks for Low Latency Applications 97

Technical requirements	97	Consuming elements from the queue	114
C++ threading for multi-threaded low latency applications	98	Using the lock-free queue	115
		Building a low latency logging framework	**117**
Defining some useful macros and functions	98	Designing utility methods for time	117
Creating and launching a new thread	100	Designing the low latency logger	118
Setting thread affinity	101	Defining some logger structures	118
Building an example	102	Initializing the logger data structures	120
Designing C++ memory pools to avoid dynamic memory allocations	**103**	Creating the logger and launching the logger thread	120
Understanding the definition of a memory pool	103	Pushing data to the logger queue	122
Understanding the use cases of a memory pool	104	Adding a useful and generic log function	124
Designing the memory pool storage	104	Learning how to use the logger with an example	125
Initializing the memory pool	107		
Serving new allocation requests	108	**C++ network programming using sockets**	**126**
Handling deallocations	109	Building a basic socket API	127
Using the memory pool with an example	110	Implementing a sender/receiver TCP socket	134
Transferring data using lock-free queues	**111**	Building a TCP server component	139
Communicating between threads and processes	111	Building an example of the TCP server and clients	147
Designing lock-free queue storage	112		
Initializing the lock-free queue	113	**Summary**	**151**
Adding elements to the queue	113		

Part 2: Building a Live Trading Exchange in C++

5

Designing Our Trading Ecosystem 155

Understanding the layout of the electronic trading ecosystem	**156**	Introducing the components of the electronic trading ecosystem	157
Defining the topology of the electronic trading ecosystem	156	**Designing the C++ matching engine in a trading exchange**	**159**

Understanding the purpose of the matching engine	159	Understanding the market data consumer infrastructure	172
Understanding the exchange order book	159	Designing the market data consumer	174
Matching participant orders	162	Understanding the order gateway client infrastructure	176
Designing our matching engine	163	Designing the order gateway client infrastructure	177

Understanding how an exchange publishes information to participants 164

Designing a framework for low-latency C++ trading algorithms 178

Communicating market events through markets data	165	Building the order book	178
Designing the market data publisher	168	Building a feature engine	179
Notifying market participants through the order gateway interfaces	170	Developing the execution logic	179
		Understanding the risk management systems	179
Designing the order gateway server	171	Designing our trading strategy framework	182

Building a market participant's interface to the exchange 172

Summary 184

6

Building the C++ Matching Engine 187

Technical requirements	187	Publishing to the market data publisher queue	212
Defining the operations and interactions in our matching engine	188	Building the exchange application binary	213
		Running the exchange application binary	215
Defining some types and constants	188		
Designing the matching engine	193	**Building the order book and matching orders**	**215**
Designing the exchange order book	201	Building the internal data structures	216
Building the matching engine and exchanging external data	**206**	Handling new passive orders	219
		Handling order cancellation requests	225
Building the matching engine	207	Matching aggressive orders and updating the order book	228
Consuming from and publishing to the order gateway queue	211	**Summary**	**232**

7

Communicating with Market Participants 235

Technical requirements	235	sequencer	248
Defining the market data protocol		Sending client responses	251
and order data protocol	236	**Building the market data publisher**	**253**
Designing the market data protocol	236	Defining the data members in the market	
Designing the order data protocol	239	data publisher	254
Building the order gateway server	**241**	Initializing the market data publisher	255
Defining the data members in the order		Publishing order book updates	257
gateway server	242	Synthesizing and publishing snapshots	259
Initializing the order gateway server	243	**Building the main exchange**	
Handling incoming client requests	245	**application**	**268**
Processing requests fairly using the FIFO		**Summary**	**273**

Part 3: Building Real-Time C++ Algorithmic Trading Systems

8

Processing Market Data and Sending Orders to the Exchange in C++ 277

Technical requirements	277	Defining the structures for the market	
Subscribing to market data and		order book	295
decoding the market data protocol	**278**	Defining the data members in the order book	300
Defining the data members in the market		Initializing the order book	302
data consumer	279	Processing market updates and updating the	
Initializing the market data consumer	281	order book	303
Running the market data consumer main loop	284	Revisiting the generic utility methods for	
Processing market data updates and handling		order book management	308
packet drops	284	**Connecting to the exchange and**	
Synchronizing with the snapshot stream	288	**sending and receiving order flow**	**309**
Building order books from		Defining the data members in the order	
market data	**295**	gateway client	309

Initializing the order gateway client	311	Processing order responses from the exchange	313
Sending order requests to the exchange	312	**Summary**	**315**

9

Building the C++ Trading Algorithm's Building Blocks — 317

Technical requirements	**317**	Defining the OMOrder struct and its related types	334
Reacting to executions and managing positions, PnLs, and risk	**318**	Designing the OrderManager class	337
Building the feature and computing complex features	**320**	Defining the data members in OrderManager	337
		Initializing OrderManager	338
Defining the data members in the feature engine	320	Sending new orders from OrderManager	339
Initializing the feature engine	321	Cancelling orders from OrderManager	340
Computing the feature on order book changes	321	Adding methods to simplify order management	341
Computing the feature on trade events	322	Handling order updates and updating orders	343
Using executions to update positions and PnLs	**323**	**Computing and managing risk**	**345**
		Defining the RiskCfg structure	345
Declaring the data members in PositionInfo	323	Defining the TradeEngineCfg structure	346
Handling order executions in PositionInfo	325	Declaring the RiskCheckResult enumeration	347
Handling order book changes in PositionInfo	330	Defining the RiskInfo structure	349
Designing PositionKeeper	332	Performing risk checks in RiskInfo	350
Initializing PositionKeeper	333	Designing the data members in RiskManager	351
Handling order executions and market updates in PositionKeeper	333	Initializing our RiskManager class	351
		Performing risk checks in RiskManager	351
Sending and managing orders	**334**	**Summary**	**352**

10

Building the C++ Market Making and Liquidity Taking Algorithms — 353

Technical requirements	**353**	Inspecting market making mechanics with an example	355
Understanding the behavior of our trading algorithms	**354**	Understanding the liquidity taking trading algorithm	357
Understanding the market making trading algorithm	354	Adding an enumeration to define the type of algorithm	359

Managing the passive liquidity provided in the order book	360	Building the trade engine framework	370
Defining the data members in the MarketMaker algorithm	360	Defining the data members in the trade engine	370
Initializing the MarketMaker algorithm	361	Initializing the trade engine	374
Handling order book updates and trade events	363	Sending client requests	377
Handling order updates in the MarketMaker algorithm	365	Processing market data updates and client responses	378
Opening and closing positions aggressively	365	Handling order book, trade, and order response updates	379
Defining the data members in the LiquidityTaker algorithm	365	Adding some miscellaneous methods	380
Initializing the LiquidityTaker trading algorithm	366	Building and running the main trading application	381
Handling trade events and order book updates	367	Building the main trading application	381
Handling order updates in the LiquidityTaker algorithm	369	Running the final trading ecosystem	387
		Inspecting the output of a run	389
		Summary	395

Part 4: Analyzing and Improving Performance

11

Adding Instrumentation and Measuring Performance 399

Technical requirements	399	Measuring the latencies inside the matching engine and order book	410
Adding an instrumentation system to measure system performance	400	Measuring latencies in the trading engine	414
Adding utilities for performance measurement using RDTSC	400	Measuring the latencies inside the market data consumer	417
Updating our previous time utilities	402	Measuring the latencies inside the order gateway	417
Understanding some issues with measurement systems in practice	403	Measuring the latencies inside the trading engine	419
Measuring latencies at the exchange	404	Running the entire ecosystem with the new instrumentation system	426
Measuring the latencies inside the market data publisher	407	Summary	427
Measuring the latencies inside the order server	408		

12

Analyzing and Optimizing the Performance of Our C++ System — 429

Technical requirements	429	Inspecting the impact of these optimizations	447
Analyzing the performance of our trading ecosystem	430	Thinking about the future of our trading ecosystem	453
Revisiting the latencies we measure	430	Growing containers dynamically	453
Analyzing the performance	431	Growing and enhancing the hash maps	453
Understanding the output of our analysis	434	Optimizing snapshot messages	460
Discussing tips and techniques for optimizing our C++ trading system	442	Adding authentication and rejection messages to the Order protocol	461
Optimizing the release build	443	Supporting modify messages in the Order protocol	462
Setting thread affinity correctly	444	Enhancing trade engine components	463
Optimizing Logger for strings	445	**Summary**	**463**
Eliminating the use of std::function instances	446		

Index — 465

Other Books You May Enjoy — 482

Preface

A theoretical knowledge of C++ is not sufficient for building practical low latency applications. The C++ programming language is also quite feature-rich, so it can be difficult to decide which features to use and which ones to avoid for ultra-low latency applications. This book dives into the technical details of the features available in the C++ programming language as well as C++ compilers, from the perspective of low latency performance optimization.

Low latency trading system development in C++ is a highly sought-after skill in quantitative finance. Designing and building a low latency electronic trading ecosystem from scratch in C++ can be daunting, which this book will present in detail. It builds a complete low latency trading ecosystem completely from scratch so that you can learn by following the development and evolution of a trading system. We will learn the important details when building low latency applications in C++ using step-by-step examples and explanations.

Additionally, measuring and optimizing performance is a continuous evolution of all low latency systems, which will also be covered in this book. By the end of this book, you will have a very good understanding of low latency trading systems as well as C++ features and techniques to focus on low latency development.

Who this book is for

This book is for beginner or intermediate-level C++ developers who want to learn how to build low latency systems. This book is also for C++ developers who are especially interested in learning about low latency electronic trading systems in C++.

What this book covers

Chapter 1, Introducing Low Latency Application Development in C++, introduces the desired behavior and performance profile of low latency applications. It also discusses what attributes of the C++ programming language have made it the preferred language for low latency application development. This chapter also discusses some of the most important low latency applications in different business areas.

Chapter 2, Designing Some Common Low Latency Applications in C++, dives into a discussion of the technical details driving some important low latency applications in practice. This chapter explores the details of low latency applications, such as live video streaming, online and offline gaming applications, **Internet of Things (IoT)** applications, and low latency electronic trading.

Chapter 3, Exploring C++ Concepts from a Low Latency Application's Perspective, jumps into the details of the C++ programming language from the perspective of low latency application development. It will discuss how to approach the design and development of these applications in C++ and best practices.

It will discuss the technical details of the C++ programming language itself and discuss which features are particularly helpful for low latency applications, along with which features to avoid when trying to boost performance. This chapter will also dive into all the modern compiler optimization techniques employed by modern C++ compilers, as well as the optimization parameters and flags supported in the GCC compiler.

Chapter 4, Building the C++ Building Blocks for Low Latency Applications, implements some of the basic C++ building blocks that find use in a lot of low latency applications. The first component built in this chapter is a threading library to support multi-threaded processing in low latency applications. The second component is a memory pool abstraction that avoids dynamic memory allocations, which are extremely slow. This chapter then builds a low latency lock-free queue to transfer generic data between threads without the use of locks, which are too slow for many low latency applications. The chapter also builds a flexible and low latency logging framework. Finally, this chapter will build a library of utilities and classes to support TCP and UDP network socket operations.

Chapter 5, Designing Our Trading Ecosystem, discusses the theory, requirements, and design of a full electronic trading ecosystem and all the components that we will build from scratch in C++ over the next few chapters. This chapter will describe the requirements and design of the matching engine at the trading exchange, which is responsible for executing orders against each other. We will also describe the order server and market data publisher components, which communicate with market participants. We will also discuss the requirements and design of the order gateway client and market data consumer components that exist in trading clients' systems to communicate with the exchange. This chapter concludes by describing and designing the trade engine framework used to build and run different trading algorithms in the clients' systems.

Chapter 6, Building the C++ Matching Engine, describes the details behind the design of the matching engine component at the exchange, which is responsible for building the limit order book and performing matching between client orders. The limit order book tracks all orders sent by all market participants. The chapter then fully implements the matching engine and limit order book components in C++ with all the functionality they need.

Chapter 7, Communicating with Market Participants, describes the details behind the design of the market data publisher and order server components at the exchange, which are responsible for publishing market data updates and communicating with the trading clients. It then fully implements these two components in C++ with all the functionality they need. This chapter concludes by building the binary to be used as the electronic trading exchange, tying together components from *Chapter 6* and *Chapter 7*.

Chapter 8, Processing Market Data and Sending Orders to the Exchange in C++, describes the details behind the design of the market data consumer and the limit order book in the trading strategy framework, which are responsible for consuming market data updates and building order books in clients' systems. This chapter will also discuss the order gateway in the trading clients' systems that is used to communicate with the exchange and send orders. This chapter then fully implements these three components in C++ with all the needed functionality.

Chapter 9, *Building the C++ Trading Algorithm Building Blocks*, describes the design of the trading strategy framework and its sub-components, which will be used to run the trading algorithms. We will implement the full framework in C++, including all the components to track positions, profits, and losses, compute trading features/signals to build intelligence, send and manage live orders in the market, and perform risk management.

Chapter 10, *Building the C++ Market Making and Liquidity Taking Algorithms*, completes the C++ implementation of the entire electronic trading ecosystem. This chapter builds the market-making and liquidity-taking trading algorithms in the framework we built in the previous chapter. Before we implement the trading algorithms, we will discuss the trading behavior of these algorithms, the motivation behind building them, and how these strategies aim to profit. This chapter also builds the trade engine framework needed to build the final trading client application, tying together components from *Chapter 8*, *Chapter 9*, and *Chapter 10*. This chapter concludes by running a fully electronic trading ecosystem and understanding the interactions between the different exchange and trading client components.

Chapter 11, *Adding Instrumentation and Measuring Performance*, creates a system to measure the performance of our low latency components at a higher granularity level. We will also add a system to timestamp order and market data events through our system as they move from component to component. This chapter concludes by rerunning our electronic trading ecosystem with the performance measurement system, generating performance data.

Chapter 12, *Analyzing and Optimizing the Performance of Our C++ System*, starts off by analyzing and visualizing the performance data from the previous chapter. It then presents specific tips and techniques that can be used to optimize the performance of our electronic trading components and the overall ecosystem. It implements some of the performance optimization ideas and benchmarks the performance improvements. This chapter concludes by presenting a couple of possible future enhancements to the electronic trading system that was built in this book, and implements and benchmarks one such idea.

To get the most out of this book

You need to have at least beginner-level experience with the C++ programming language and have a basic level of comfort when it comes to compiling, building, and running C++ code in a Linux environment. Prior knowledge of low latency applications and electronic trading is a plus but not required, since all of the information relevant to that will be covered.

Software/hardware covered in the book	Operating system requirements
C++ 20	Linux
GCC 11.3.0	Linux

This book was developed on a `Linux 5.19.0-41-generic #42~22.04.1-Ubuntu x86_64 x86_64 x86_64 GNU/Linux` operating system. It uses `CMake 3.23.2` and `Ninja 1.10.2` as the build systems. However, the source code presented in this book is expected to work on all Linux distributions that have at least the `GCC 11.3.0` compiler.

If you are using the digital version of this book, we advise you to type the code yourself or access the code from the book's GitHub repository (a link is available in the next section). Doing so will help you avoid any potential errors related to the copying and pasting of code.

Download the example code files

You can download the example code files for this book from GitHub at `https://github.com/PacktPublishing/Building-Low-Latency-Applications-with-CPP`. If there's an update to the code, it will be updated in the GitHub repository.

We also have other code bundles from our rich catalog of books and videos available at `https://github.com/PacktPublishing/`. Check them out!

Download the color images

We also provide a PDF file that has color images of the screenshots and diagrams used in this book. You can download it here: `https://packt.link/ulPYN`.

Conventions used

There are a number of text conventions used throughout this book.

`Code in text`: Indicates code words in text, database table names, folder names, filenames, file extensions, pathnames, dummy URLs, user input, and Twitter handles. Here is an example: "The `-Werror` parameter turns these warnings into errors and will force the developer to inspect and fix each case that generates a compiler warning before compilation can succeed."

A block of code is set as follows:

```
if(!a && !b) {}
```

When we wish to draw your attention to a particular part of a code block, the relevant lines or items are set in bold:

```
main:
.LFB1
    Movl    $100, %edi
    Call    _Z9factorialj
```

Any command-line input or output is written as follows:

```
SpecificRuntimeExample::placeOrder()
SpecificCRTPExample::actualPlaceOrder()
```

> **Tips or important notes**
> Appear like this.

Get in touch

Feedback from our readers is always welcome.

General feedback: If you have questions about any aspect of this book, email us at `customercare@packtpub.com` and mention the book title in the subject of your message.

Errata: Although we have taken every care to ensure the accuracy of our content, mistakes do happen. If you have found a mistake in this book, we would be grateful if you would report this to us. Please visit `www.packtpub.com/support/errata` and fill in the form.

Piracy: If you come across any illegal copies of our works in any form on the internet, we would be grateful if you would provide us with the location address or website name. Please contact us at `copyright@packt.com` with a link to the material.

If you are interested in becoming an author: If there is a topic that you have expertise in and you are interested in either writing or contributing to a book, please visit `authors.packtpub.com`.

Share Your Thoughts

Once you've read *Building Low Latency Applications with C++*, we'd love to hear your thoughts! Scan the QR code below to go straight to the Amazon review page for this book and share your feedback.

`https://packt.link/r/1837639353`

Your review is important to us and the tech community and will help us make sure we're delivering excellent quality content.

Download a free PDF copy of this book

Thanks for purchasing this book!

Do you like to read on the go but are unable to carry your print books everywhere? Is your eBook purchase not compatible with the device of your choice?

Don't worry, now with every Packt book you get a DRM-free PDF version of that book at no cost.

Read anywhere, any place, on any device. Search, copy, and paste code from your favorite technical books directly into your application.

The perks don't stop there, you can get exclusive access to discounts, newsletters, and great free content in your inbox daily

Follow these simple steps to get the benefits:

1. Scan the QR code or visit the link below

https://packt.link/free-ebook/9781837639359

2. Submit your proof of purchase
3. That's it! We'll send your free PDF and other benefits to your email directly

Part 1: Introducing C++ Concepts and Exploring Important Low-Latency Applications

In this part, we will introduce low-latency applications as well as the proper approach toward low-latency application development in C++. We will discuss the technical details of some common low-latency applications in different business areas. We will discuss some details relevant to low-latency application development and how C++ concepts and techniques fit into that. We will also write some C++ code to implement the different low-latency components we introduced previously from the perspective of an electronic trading exchange.

This part contains the following chapters:

- *Chapter 1, Introducing Low-Latency Application Development in C++*
- *Chapter 2, Designing Some Common Low-Latency Applications in C++*
- *Chapter 3, Exploring C++ Concepts from a Low-Latency Application's Perspective*
- *Chapter 4, Building the C++ Building Blocks for Low-Latency Applications*

1
Introducing Low Latency Application Development in C++

Let us kick off our journey with low latency applications by introducing them in this first chapter. In this chapter, we will first understand the behavior and requirements of latency-sensitive and latency-critical applications. We will understand the huge business impact that application latencies have for businesses that rely on quick and strict response times.

We will also discuss why C++ is one of the most preferred programming languages when it comes to low latency application development. We will spend a large part of this book building an entire low latency electronic trading system from scratch in C++. So, this will serve as a good chapter for you to understand the motivation for using C++ as well as what makes it the most popular language for low latency applications.

We will also present some of the important low latency applications in different business areas. Part of the motivation is to make you understand that latencies are indeed very critical in different business areas for use cases that are sensitive to response times. The other part of the motivation is to identify the similarities in the behavior, expectations, design, and implementation of these applications. Even though they solve different business problems, the low latency requirements of these applications are often built on similar technical design and implementation principles.

In this chapter, we will cover the following topics:

- Understanding the requirements for latency-sensitive applications
- Understanding why C++ is the preferred programming language
- Introducing some important low latency applications

In order to build ultra-low latency applications effectively, we should first understand the terms and concepts we will refer to throughout the rest of this book. We should also understand why C++ has emerged as the clear choice for most low latency application development. It is also important to always keep the business impact of low latencies in mind because the aim is to build low latency applications to benefit the business's bottom line. This chapter discusses these ideas so that you can build a good foundation before we dive into the technical details in the rest of this book.

Understanding requirements for latency-sensitive applications

In this section, we will discuss some concepts that are required to build an understanding of what metrics matter for latency-sensitive applications. First, let's define clearly what latency means and what latency-sensitive applications are.

Latency is defined as the time delay between when a task is started to the time when the task is finished. By definition, any processing or work will incur some overhead or latency – that is, no system has zero latency unless the system does absolutely no work. The important detail here is that some systems might have latency that is an infinitesimal fraction of a millisecond and the tolerance for an additional microsecond there might be low.

Low latency applications are applications that execute tasks and respond or return results as quickly as possible. The point here is that reaction latency is an important criterion for such applications where higher latencies can degrade performance or even render an application completely useless. On the other hand, when such applications perform with the low latencies that are expected of them, they can beat the competition, run at maximum speed, achieve maximum throughput, or increase productivity and improve the user experience – depending on the application and business.

Low latency can be thought of as both a quantitative as well as a qualitative term. The quantitative aspect is pretty obvious, but the qualitative aspect might not necessarily be obvious. Depending on the context, architects and developers might be willing to accept higher latencies in some cases but be unwilling to accept an extra microsecond in some contexts. For instance, if a user refreshes a web page or they wait for a video to load, a few seconds of latency is quite acceptable. However, once the video loads and starts playing, it can no longer incur a few seconds of latency to render or display without negatively impacting the user experience. An extreme example is high-speed financial trading systems where a few extra microseconds can make a huge difference between a profitable firm and a firm that cannot compete at all.

In the following subsections, we will present some nomenclature that applies to low latency applications. It is important to understand these terms well so that we can continue our discussion on low latency applications, as we will refer to these concepts frequently. The concepts and terms we will discuss next are used to differentiate between different latency-sensitive applications, the measurement of latencies, and the requirements of these applications.

Understanding latency-sensitive versus latency-critical applications

There is a subtle but important difference between the terms **latency-sensitive applications** and **latency-critical applications**. A latency-sensitive application is one in which, as performance latencies are reduced, it improves the business impact or profitability. So, the system might still be functional and possibly profitable at higher performance latencies but can be significantly more profitable if latencies are reduced. Examples of such applications would be operating systems (OSes), web browsers, databases, and so on.

A latency-critical application, on the other hand, is one that fails completely if performance latency is higher than a certain threshold. The point here is that while latency-sensitive applications might only lose part of their profitability at higher latencies, latency-critical applications fail entirely at high enough latencies. Examples of such applications are traffic control systems, financial trading systems, autonomous vehicles, and some medical appliances.

Measuring latency

In this section, we will discuss different methods of measuring latency. The real difference between these methods comes down to what is considered the beginning of the processing task and what is the end of the processing task. Another approach would be the units of what we are measuring – time is the most common one but in some cases, CPU clock cycles can also be used if it comes down to instruction-level measurements. Let's look at the different measurements next, but first, we present a diagram of a generic server-client system without diving into the specifics of the use case or transport protocols. This is because measuring latency is generic and applies to many different applications with this kind of server-client setup.

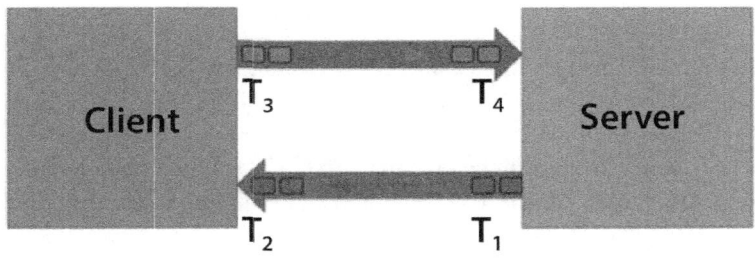

T_1: Time server puts first byte of packet on the wire.
T_2: Time client reads first byte of packet from the wire.
T_3: Time client puts a packet containing a response on the wire.
T_4: Time server reads first byte of packet containing the response from the wire.

Figure 1.1 – A general server-client system with timestamps between different hops

We present this diagram here because, in the next few subsections, we will define and understand latencies between the different hops on the round-trip path from the server client and back to the server.

Time to first byte

Time to first byte is measured as the time elapsed from when the sender sends the first byte of a request (or response) to the moment when the receiver receives the first byte. This typically (but not necessarily) applies to network links or systems where there are data transfer operations that are latency-sensitive. In *Figure 1.1*, time to first byte would be the difference between T_4 and T_3

Round-trip time

Round-trip time (**RTT**) is the sum of the time it takes for a packet to travel from one process to another and then the time it takes for the response packet to reach the original process. Again, this is typically (but not necessarily) used for network traffic going back and forth between server and client processes, but can also be used for two processes communicating in general.

RTT, by default, includes the time taken by the server process to read, process, and respond to the request sent by the sender – that is, RTT generally includes server processing times. In the context of electronic trading, the true RTT latency is based on three components:

- First, the time it takes for information from the exchange to reach the participant
- Second, the time it takes for the execution of the algorithms to analyze the information and make a decision
- Finally, the time it take for the decision to reach the exchange and get processed by the matching engine

We will discuss this more in the last section of this book, *Analyzing and improving performance*.

Tick-to-trade

Tick-to-trade (**TTT**) is similar to RTT and is a term most commonly used in electronic trading systems. TTT is defined as the time from when a packet (usually a market data packet) first hits a participant's infrastructure (trading server) to the time when the participant is done processing the packet and sends a packet out (order request) to the trading exchange. So, TTT includes the time spent by the trading infrastructure to read the packet, process it, calculate trading signals, generate an order request in reaction to that, and *put it on the wire*. **Putting it on the wire** typically means writing something to a network socket. We will revisit this topic and explore it in greater detail in the last section of this book, *Analyzing and improving performance*. In *Figure 1.1*, TTT would be the difference between T_3 and T_2.

CPU clock cycles

CPU clock cycles are basically the smallest increment of work that can be done by the CPU processor. In reality, they are the amount of time between two pulses of the oscillator that drives the CPU processor. Measuring CPU clock cycles is typically used to measure latency at the instruction level – that is, at an extremely low level at the processor level. C++ is both a low-level as well as a high-level language; it lets you get as close to the hardware as needed and also provides higher-level abstractions such as classes, templates, and so on. But generally, C++ developers do not spend a lot of time dealing with extremely low-level or possibly assembly code. This means that the compiled machine code might not be exactly what a C++ developer expects. Additionally, depending on the compiler versions, the processor architectures, and so on, there may be even more sources of differences. So, for extremely performance-sensitive low latency code, it is often not uncommon for engineers to measure how many instructions are executed and how many CPU clock cycles are required to do so. This level of optimization is typically the highest level of optimization possible, alongside kernel-level optimizations.

Now that we have seen some different methods of measuring latencies in different applications, in the next section, we will look at some latency summary metrics and how each one of them can be important under different scenarios.

Differentiating between latency metrics

The relative importance of a specific latency metric over the other depends on the application and the business itself. As an example, a latency-critical application such as an autonomous vehicle software system cares about peak latency much more than the mean latency. Low latency electronic trading systems typically care more about mean latency and smaller latency variance than they do about peak latency. Video streaming and playback applications might generally prioritize high throughput over lower latency variance due to the nature of the application and the consumers.

Throughput versus latency

Before we look at the metrics themselves, first, we need to clearly understand the difference between two terms – **throughput** and **latency** – which are very similar to each other and often used interchangeably but should not be. Throughput is defined as how much work gets done in a certain period of time, and latency is how quickly a single task is completed. To improve throughput, the usual approach is to introduce parallelism and add additional computing, memory, and networking resources. Note that each individual task might not be processed as quickly as possible, but overall, more tasks will be completed after a certain amount of time. This is because, while being processed individually, each task might take longer than in a low latency setup, but the parallelism boosts throughput over a set of tasks. Latency, on the other hand, is measured for each individual task from beginning to finish, even if fewer tasks are executed overall.

Mean latency

Mean latency is basically the expected average response time of a system. It is simply the average of all the latency measurement observations. This metric includes large outliers, so can be a noisy metric for systems that experience a large range of performance latencies.

Median latency

Median latency is typically a better metric for the expected response time of a system. Since it is the median of the latency measurement observations, it excludes the impact of large outliers. Due to this, it is sometimes preferred over the mean latency metric.

Peak latency

Peak latency is an important metric for systems where a single large outlier in performance can have a devastating impact on the system. Large values of peak latency can also significantly influence the mean latency metric of the system.

Latency variance

For systems that require a latency profile that is as deterministic as possible, the actual **variance** of the performance latency is an important metric. This is typically important where the expected latencies are quite predictable. For systems with low latency variance, the mean, median, and peak latencies are all expected to be quite close to each other.

Requirements of latency-sensitive applications

In this section, we will formally describe the behavior of latency-sensitive applications and the performance profile that these applications are expected to adhere to. Obviously, latency-sensitive applications need low latency performance, but here we will try to explore minor subtleties in the term *low latency* and discuss some different ways of looking at it.

Correctness and robustness

When we think of latency-sensitive applications, it is often the case that we think low latency is the single most important aspect of such applications. But in reality, a huge requirement of such applications is correctness and we mean very high levels of robustness and fault tolerance. Intuitively, this idea should make complete sense; these applications require very low latency to be successful, which then should tell you that these applications also have very high throughput and need to process huge amounts of inputs and produce a large number of outputs. Hence, the system needs to achieve very close to 100% correctness and be very robust as well for the application to be successful in their business area. Additionally, the correctness and robustness requirements need to be maintained as the application grows and changes during its lifetime.

Low latencies on average

This is the most obvious requirement when we think about latency-sensitive applications. The expected reaction or processing latency needs to be as low as possible for the application or business overall to succeed. Here, we care about the mean and median performance latency and need it to be as low as possible. By design, this means the system cannot have too many outliers or very high peaks in performance latency.

Capped peak latency

We use the term **capped peak latency** to refer to the requirement that there needs to be a well-defined upper threshold for the maximum possible latency the application can ever encounter. This behavior is important for all latency-sensitive applications, but most important for latency-critical applications. But even in the general case, applications that have extremely high-performance latency for a handful of cases will typically destroy the performance of the system. What this really means is that the application needs to handle any input, scenario, or sequence of events and do so within a low latency period. Of course, the performance to handle a very rare and specific scenario can possibly be much higher than the most likely case, but the point here is that it cannot be unbounded or unacceptable.

Predictable latency – low latency variance

Some applications prefer that the expected performance latency is predictable, even if that means sacrificing latency a little bit if the average latency metric is higher than it could be. What this really means is that such applications will make sure that the expected performance latency for all kinds of different inputs or events has as little variance as possible. It is impossible to achieve zero latency variance, but some choices can be made in data structures, algorithms, code implementation, and setup to try to minimize this as much as possible.

High throughput

As mentioned before, low latency and throughput are related but not identical. For that reason, sometimes some applications that need the highest throughput possible might have some differences in design and implementation to maximize throughput. The point is that maximizing throughput might come at the cost of sacrificing average performance latencies or increasing peak latencies to achieve that.

In this section, we introduced the concepts that apply to low latency application performance and the business impact of those metrics. We will need these concepts in the rest of the book when we refer to the performance of the applications we build. Next, we will move the conversation forward and explore the programming languages available for low latency application development. We will discuss the characteristics of the languages that support low latency applications and understand why C++ has risen to the top of the list when it comes to developing and improving latency-sensitive applications.

Understanding why C++ is the preferred programming language

There are several high-level language choices when it comes to low latency applications – Java, Scala, Go, and C++. In this section, we will discuss why C++ is one of the most popular languages when it comes to low latency applications. We will discuss several characteristics of the C++ language that support the high-level language constructs to support large code bases. The power of C++ is that it also provides very low-level access, similar to the C programming language, to support a very high level of control and optimization.

Compiled language

C++ is a compiled language and not an interpreted language. A **compiled language** is a programming language where the source code is translated into a machine code binary that is ready to run on a specific architecture. Examples of compiled languages are C, C++, Erlang, Haskell, Rust, and Go. The alternative to compiled languages is interpreted languages. **Interpreted languages** are different in the sense that the program is run by an interpreter, which runs through the source line by line and executes each command. Some examples of interpreted languages are Ruby, Python, and JavaScript.

Interpreted languages are inherently slower than compiled languages because, unlike compiled languages where the translation into machine instructions is done at compile time, here the interpretation to machine instructions is done at runtime. However, with the development of just-in-time compilation, interpreted languages are not tremendously slower. For compiled languages, the code is already pre-built for the target hardware so there is no extra interpretation step at runtime. Since C++ is a compiled language, it gives the developers a lot of control over the hardware. This means competent developers can optimize things such as memory management, CPU usage, cache performance, and so on. Additionally, since compiled languages are converted into machine code for specific hardware at compile time, it can be optimized to a large degree. Hence, compiled languages in general, and especially C++, are faster and more efficient to execute.

Closer to hardware – low-level language

Compared to other popular programming languages such as Python, Java, and so on, C++ is low level so it's extremely close to the hardware. This is especially useful when the software is tightly coupled with the target hardware it runs on and possibly even in cases where low-level support is required. Being extremely close to the hardware also means that there is a significant speed advantage when building systems in C++. Especially in low latency applications such as **high-frequency trading** (**HFT**) where a few microseconds can make a huge difference, C++ is generally the established gold standard in the industry.

We will discuss an example of how being closer to the hardware helps boost C++ performance over another language such as Java. A C/C++ pointer is the actual address of an object in memory. So, the software can access memory and objects in memory directly without needing extra abstractions that would slow it down. This, however, does mean that the application developer will often have to explicitly manage the creation, ownership, destruction, and lifetime of objects instead of relying on the programming language to manage things for you as in Python or Java. An extreme case of C++ being close to the hardware is that it is possible to call assembly instructions straight from C++ statements – we will see an example of this in later chapters.

Deterministic usage of resources

It is critical for low latency applications to use resources very efficiently. Embedded applications (which are also often used in real-time applications) are especially limited in time and memory resources. In languages such as Java and Python that rely on automatic garbage collection, there is an element of non-determinism – that is, the garbage collector can introduce large latencies in performance unpredictably. Additionally, for systems that are very limited in memory, low-level languages such as C and C++ can do special things such as placing data at custom sections or addresses in memory through pointers. In languages such as C and C++, the programmer is in charge of explicit creation, management, and deallocation of memory resources, allowing for deterministic and efficient use of resources.

Speed and high performance

C++ is faster than most other programming languages for the reasons we have already discussed. It also provides excellent concurrency and multithreading support. Obviously, this is another good feature when it comes to developing low latency applications that are latency-sensitive or even latency-critical. Such requirements are also often found in applications around servers that are under heavy load such as web servers, application servers, database servers, trading servers, and so on.

Another advantage of C++ is due to its compile-time optimization ability. C and C++ support features such as macros or pre-processor directives, a `constexpr` specifier, and template metaprogramming. These allow us to move a large part of the processing from runtime to compile time. Basically, this means we minimize the work done during runtime on the critical code path by moving a lot of the processing to the compilation step when building the machine code binary. We will discuss these features heavily in later chapters when we build a complete electronic trading system, and their benefits will become very clear at that point.

Language constructs and features

The C++ language itself is a perfect combination of flexibility and feature richness. It allows a lot of freedom for the developers, who can leverage it to tune applications down to a very low level. However, it also provides a lot of higher-level abstractions, which can be used to build very large, feature-rich, versatile, and scalable applications, while still being extremely low latency when required. In this section, we will explore some of those C++-specific language features that put it in a unique position of low-level control and high-level abstraction features.

Portability

First off, C++ is highly portable and can build applications that can be compiled for a lot of different operating systems, platforms, CPU architecture, and so on. Since it does not require a runtime interpreter that differs for different platforms, all that is required to do is build the correct binaries at compile time, which is relatively straightforward, and the final deployed binary can just run on any platform. Additionally, some of the other features we have already discussed (such as the ability to run in low-memory and weaker CPU architectures combined with the lack of garbage collection requirements) make it even more portable than some of the other high-level languages.

Compiler optimizations

We have discussed that C++ is a compiled language, which makes it inherently faster than interpreted languages since it does not incur additional runtime costs. Since the developer's complete source code is compiled into the final executable binary, compilers have an opportunity to holistically analyze all the objects and code paths. This leads to the possibility of very high levels of optimization at compile times. Modern compilers work closely with modern hardware to produce some surprisingly optimized machine code. The point here is that developers can focus on solving business problems and, assuming the C++ developers are competent, the compiled program is still extremely optimized without requiring a lot of the developer's time and effort. Since C++ allows you to directly inline assembly code as well, it gives the developers an even greater chance to work with the compiler and produce highly optimized executables.

Statically typed

When it comes to type systems in programming languages, there are two options – **statically typed language** and **dynamically typed language**. A statically typed language performs checks around data types (integers, floats, doubles, structures, and classes) and interactions between these types during the compilation process. A dynamically typed language performs these type checks at runtime. Examples of statically typed languages are C++ and Java, and examples of dynamically typed languages are Python, Perl, and JavaScript.

One big benefit of statically typed languages is that since all the type-checking is done at compile time, it gives us the opportunity to find and eliminate many bugs before the program is even run. Obviously, type checking alone cannot find all possible bugs, but the point we're trying to make here is that statically typed languages do a significantly better job at finding errors and bugs related to types at compile time. This is especially true for low latency applications that are highly numerical in nature.

Another huge benefit of statically typed languages, especially when it comes to low latency applications, is that since the type-checking is done at compile time, there is an additional opportunity for the compiler to optimize the types and type interactions at compile time. In fact, a large part of the reason that compiled languages are much faster is due to the static versus dynamic type-checking system itself. This is also a big reason why, for a dynamically typed language such as Python, high-performance libraries such as NumPy require types when creating arrays and matrices.

Multiple paradigms

Unlike some other languages, C++ does not force the developer to follow a specific programming paradigm. It supports a lot of different programming paradigms such as monolithic, procedural, **object-oriented programming** (**OOP**), generic programming, and so on. This makes it a good fit for a wide range of applications because it gives the developer the flexibility to design their program in a way that facilitates maximum optimization and lowest latencies instead of forcing a programming paradigm onto that application.

Libraries

Out of the box, C++ already comes with a large C and C++ library, which provides a lot of data structures, algorithms, and abstractions for tasks such as the following:

- Network programming
- Dynamic memory management
- Numeric operations
- Error and exception handling
- String operations
- Commonly needed algorithms
- **Input/output** (**I/O**) operations including file operations
- Multithreading support

Additionally, the huge community of C++ developers has built and open-sourced a lot of the libraries; we will discuss some of the most popular ones in the following subsections.

Standard Template Library

Standard Template Library (**STL**) is a very popular and widely used templatized and header-only library containing data structures and containers, iterators and allocators for these containers, and algorithms for tasks such as sorting, searching, algorithms for the containers, and so on.

Boost

Boost is a large C++ library that provides support for multithreading, network operations, image processing, **regular expressions** (**regex**), linear algebra, unit testing, and so on.

Asio

Asio (**asynchronous input/output**) is another well-known and widely used library that comes in two versions: **non-Boost** and one that is part of the Boost library. It provides support for multithreading concurrency and for implementing and using the asynchronous I/O model and is portable to all major platforms.

GNU Scientific Library

GNU Scientific Library (**GSL**) provides support for a wide range of mathematical concepts and operations such as complex numbers, matrices, and calculus, and manages other functions.

Active Template Library

Active Template Library (**ATL**) is a template-heavy C++ library to help program the **Component Object Model** (**COM**). It replaces the previous **Microsoft Foundation Classes** (**MFC**) library and improves upon it. It is developed by Microsoft and is open source and heavily uses an important low latency C++ feature, the **Curiously Recurring Template Pattern** (**CRTP**), which we will also explore and use heavily in this book. It supports COM features such as dual interfaces, ActiveX controls, connection points, tear-off interfaces, COM enumerator interfaces, and a lot more.

Eigen

Eigen is a powerful C++ library for mathematical and scientific applications. It has functions for linear algebra, numerical methods and solvers, numeric types such as complex numbers, features and operations for geometry, and much more.

LAPACK

Linear Algebra Package (**LAPACK**) is another large and extremely powerful C++ library specifically for linear algebra and linear equations and to support routines for large matrices. It implements a lot of functionality such as solving simultaneous linear equations, least squares methods, eigenvalues, **singular value decomposition** (**SVD**), and many more applications.

OpenCV

Open Source Computer Vision (**OpenCV**) is one of the most well-known C++ libraries when it comes to computer graphics and vision-related applications. It is also available for Java and Python and provides many algorithms for face and object recognition, 3D models, machine learning, deep learning, and more.

mlpack

mlpack is a super-fast, header-only C++ library for a wide variety of machine learning models and the mathematical operations related to them. It also has support for other languages such as Go, Julia, R, and Python.

QT

QT is by far the most popular library when it comes to building cross-platform graphical programs in C++. It works on Windows, Linux, macOS, and even platforms such as Android and embedded systems. It is open source and is used to build GUI widgets.

Crypto++

Crypto++ is a free open source C++ library to support algorithms, operations, and utilities for cryptography. It has many cryptographic algorithms, random number generators, block ciphers, functions, public-key operations, secret sharing, and more across many platforms such as Linux, Windows, macOS, iOS, and Android.

Suitable for big projects

In the previous section, we discussed the design and a lot of features of C++ that make it a great fit for low latency applications. Another aspect of C++ is that because of the flexibility it provides to the developer and all the high-level abstractions it allows you to build, it is actually very well suited to very large real-world projects. Huge projects such as compilers, cloud processing and storage systems, and **OSes** are built in C++ for these reasons. We will dive into these and many other applications that try to strike a balance between low latency performance, feature richness, and different business cases, and quite often, C++ is the perfect fit for developing such systems.

Mature and large community support

The C programming language was originally created in 1972, and then C++ (originally referred to as C with classes) was created in 1983. C++ is a very mature language and is embedded extensively into many applications in many different business areas. Some examples are the Unix operating system, Oracle MySQL, the Linux kernel, Microsoft Office, and Microsoft Visual Studio – these were all written in C++. The fact that C++ has been around for 40 years means that most software problems have been encountered and solutions have been designed and implemented. C++ is also very popular and taught as part of most computer science degrees and, additionally, has a huge library of developer tools, third-party components, open source projects, libraries, manuals, tutorials, books, and so on dedicated to it. The bottom line is that there is a large amount of documentation, examples, and community support backing up new C++ developers and new C++ projects.

Language under active development

Even though C++ is 40 years old, it is still very much under active development. Ever since the first C++ version was commercially released in 1985, there have been multiple improvements and enhancements to the C++ standard and the language. In chronological order, C++ 98, C++ 03, C++ 0X, C++ 11, C++ 14, C++ 17, and C++ 20 have been released, and C++ 23 is being developed. Each version comes with improvements and new features. So, C++ is a powerful language and is constantly evolving with time and adding modern features. Here is a diagram showing the evolution of C++ over the years:

History of C++

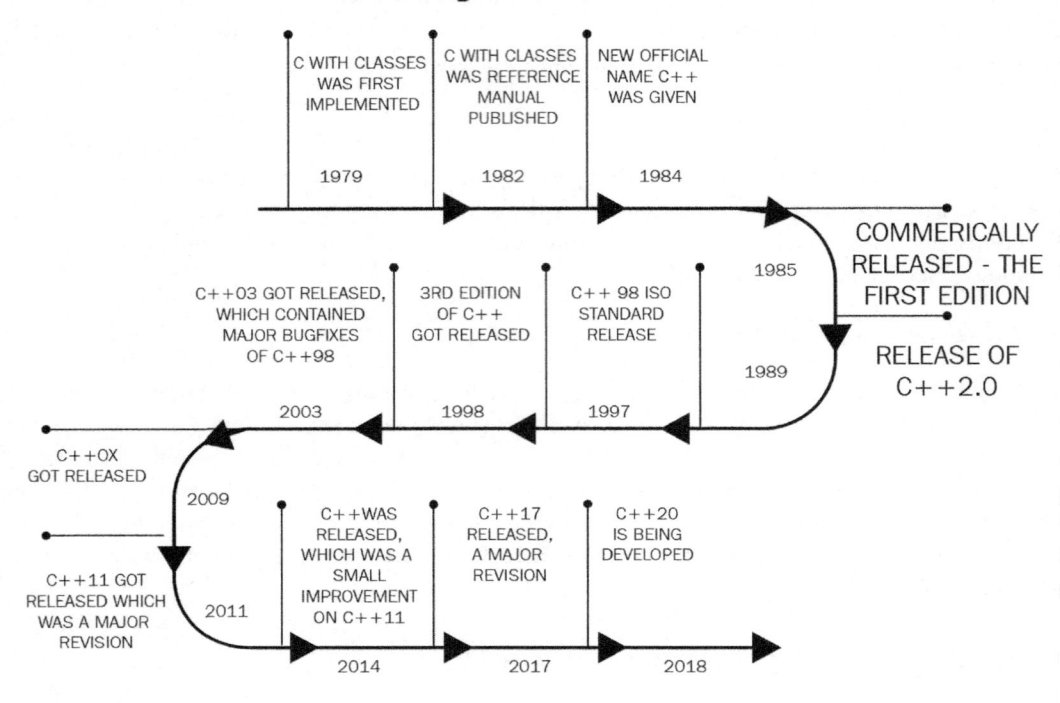

Figure 1.2 – Evolution of C++

Given the already mature state of the C++ programming language, super-fast speed, perfect combination of high-level abstractions and low-level hardware access and control, huge knowledge base, and developer community along with best practices, libraries, and tools, C++ is a clear pick for low latency application development.

In this section, we looked at the choice of the C++ programming language for low latency application development. We discussed the various characteristics, features, libraries, and community support that make it a great fit for these applications. It is no surprise that C++ is deeply embedded into most applications that have strict performance requirements. In the next section, we will look at a lot of different low latency applications in different business areas with the goal of understanding the similarities that such applications share.

Introducing some important low latency applications

In this section, we will explore some common low latency applications in different business areas in order to familiarize ourselves with different kinds of latency-sensitive applications and how latency plays an important part in their performance. Additionally, discussing these applications will reveal some similarities in the nature and design of these applications.

Lower-level low latency applications

First, we will start with applications that would be considered extremely low-level, meaning very close to the hardware. Note that all low latency applications have at least some portion of the application that is low-level since, by definition, that is how low latency performance is achieved. These applications, however, have large portions of the entire application dealing with mostly low-level details; let us discuss those next.

Telecommunications

We already discussed that C++ is one of the fastest programming languages out there. It is used a lot in building telephone switches, routers, internet, space probes, and various other parts of telecommunications infrastructure. These applications are required to handle a large number of simultaneous connections and facilitate communication between them. These applications need to perform these tasks with speed and efficiency, making them a good example of low latency applications.

Embedded systems

Since C++ is closer to the hardware compared to other high-level programming languages, it is used in latency-sensitive embedded systems. Some examples of these would be machines used in the field of medicine, surgical tools, smart watches, and so on. C++ is usually the language of choice for medical applications such as MRI machines, lab testing systems, and systems to manage patient information. Additionally, there are use cases to model medical data, run simulations for research, and so on.

Compilers

Interestingly, compilers for various programming languages use C and C++ to build the compilers for those languages. The reason for this is, again, that C and C++ are low-level languages closer to the hardware and can build these compilers efficiently. The compiler applications themselves are able to optimize the code for the programming language to a very large degree and produce low latency machine code.

Operating systems

From Microsoft Windows to macOS to Linux itself, all the major OSes are built in C++ – yet again, another example of a low latency application where the fact that C++ is a low-level language makes it an ideal fit. OSes are extremely large and extremely complex. In addition to that, they have to have low latency and be highly performant to be a competitive modern OS.

For instance, Linux is typically the OS of choice for many high-load servers as well as servers designed for low latency applications, so the OS itself needs to have very high performance. In addition to traditional OSes, C and C++ are also heavily used to build mobile OSes such as iOS, Android, and Windows phone kernels. In summary, OSes need to be extremely fast and efficient at managing all the system and hardware resources. C++ developers building OSes can leverage the language's abilities to build super-low-latency OSes.

Cloud/distributed systems

Organizations that develop and use cloud and distributed storage and processing systems have very low latency requirements. For this reason, they rely heavily on a programming language such as C++. Distributed storage systems have to support very fast and very efficient filesystem operations, so need to be close to the hardware. Additionally, distributed processing generally means high levels of concurrency, reliance on low latency multithreading libraries, as well as high load tolerance and scalability optimization requirements.

Databases

Databases are another good example of applications that need low latencies and high levels of concurrency and parallelism. Databases are also critical components in many different applications in many different business areas. Postgres, MySQL, and MongoDB (which are by far the most popular database systems right now) are written in C and C++ – yet another example of why C++ is the preferred language for low latency applications. C++ is also ideal for designing and structuring databases to optimize storage efficiency.

Flight software and traffic control

Flight software for commercial airplanes and military aircraft is a class of latency-critical applications. Here, not only is it important that the code follow very strict guidelines, be extremely robust, and be very well tested but the applications also need to respond and react to events predictably and within strict latency thresholds.

Traffic control software depends on many sensors, which need to monitor the speed, location, and volume of vehicles and transmit them to the central software. The software then uses the information to control traffic signs, maps, and traffic lights. Obviously, for such real-time applications, there is a requirement for it to be low latency and easily able to handle the large volume of data quickly and efficiently.

Higher-level low latency applications

In this subsection, we will discuss what many might consider slightly higher-level low latency applications. These are the applications people typically think of when trying to solve business problems; however, one thing to keep in mind is that these applications still have to implement and use lower-level optimization techniques to provide the performance that is required of them.

Graphics and video game applications

Graphics applications require super-fast rendering performance and serve as another example of a low latency application. Graphics software employs techniques from computer vision, image processing, and so on, which typically involves a lot of very fast and very efficient matrix operations on numerous large matrices. When it comes to graphics rendering in video games, there are even more stringent requirements for low latency performance since these are interactive applications, and speed and responsiveness are critical to the user experience. Nowadays, video games are typically made available on multiple platforms to reach a larger target audience. What this means is that these applications, or slightly stripped-down versions of these applications, need to run on low-end devices, which might not have a lot of computation and memory resources available. Video games overall have a lot of resource-intensive operations – rendering graphics, handling multiple players simultaneously, fast responsiveness to user inputs, and so on. C++ is a very good fit for all these applications and has been used to create a lot of well-known games such as Counter-Strike, Starcraft, and Warcraft, and game engines such as Unreal Engine. C++ is also a good fit for different gaming platforms – Windows PCs, Nintendo Switch, Xbox, and PlayStation.

Augmented reality and virtual reality applications

Augmented reality (**AR**) and **virtual reality** (**VR**) are both technologies that augment and enhance a real-life environment or create a whole new virtual environment. While AR just augments the environment by adding digital elements to our live view, VR creates a completely new simulated environment. So, these applications take graphics rendering and video game applications to a whole new level.

AR and VR technology has found a lot of different business use cases, such as design and construction, maintenance and repairs, training and education, healthcare, retail and marketing, and even in the field of technology itself. AR and VR applications have similar requirements as video game applications and need to handle large amounts of data from various sources in real time, as well as handle user interactions seamlessly and smoothly. The technical challenges for these applications are handling limited processing capability and available memory, possibly limited mobile bandwidth, and maintaining low latency and real-time performance to not hurt the user experience.

Browsers

Web browsers are often more complicated than they might appear. There are rendering engines in a web browser that require low latencies and efficient processing. Additionally, there are often interactions with databases and interactive rendering code so that users do not have to wait a long time for the content to update or for interactive content to respond. Due to the low latency requirements of web browsers, it is no surprise that C++ is often the preferred language for this application as well. In fact, some of the most popular web browsers (Google Chrome, Mozilla Firefox, Safari, Opera, etc.) heavily employ C++.

Search engines

Search engines are another use case that requires low latency and highly efficient data structures, algorithms, and code bases. Modern search engines such as Google use techniques such as internet crawling technology, indexing infrastructures, page rank algorithms, and other complex algorithms including machine learning. Google's search engine relies on C++ to implement all these requirements in a highly low latency and efficient fashion.

Libraries

Many high-level libraries often have stringent performance requirements and can be regarded as low latency applications themselves but usually, they are key components in larger low latency applications and businesses. These libraries cover different areas – network programming, data structures, faster algorithms, databases, multithreading, mathematical libraries (for example, machine learning), and many more. Such libraries require very low latency and high-performance processing such as computations that involve many matrix operations on a large number of matrices, a lot of which can also be very large in size.

It should be clear here that performance is critical in such applications – another area where C++ is often used quite heavily. Even though a lot of these libraries such as TensorFlow are available in Python, under the hood, the core machine learning mathematical operations are actually implemented in C++ to power these machine learning methods on huge datasets.

Banking and financial applications

Banking applications are another class of low latency applications that need to process millions of transactions every day and require low latency, high concurrency, and robustness. Large banks have millions of clients and hundreds of millions of transactions that all need to be executed correctly and quickly and be able to scale up to handle the client load and thus database and server loads. C++ is automatically the choice here for a lot of these banking applications for the reasons we have discussed before.

When it comes to applications such as financial modeling, electronic trading systems, and trading strategies, low latency is more critical than in any other field. The speed and deterministic performance of C++ make it ideal for processing billions of market updates. sending millions of orders, and transacting at the exchange, especially when it comes to HFT. Since markets update very quickly, trading applications need the right data very quickly to execute trades extremely quickly. Large latencies in this system can cause losses that destroy a significant amount of trading profits, or worse. On the research and development side of things, simulations over many trading instruments across multiple exchanges also need large-scale low latency distributed processing to be done quickly and efficiently. The quantitative development and research and risk analysis libraries are also written in C++ because they need to process massive amounts of data as quickly as possible. One of the best examples of this would be the pricing and risk libraries that calculate fair trading prices for options products and run many simulations to assess options risk, as the search space is enormous.

Mobile phone applications

Modern mobile phone applications are quite feature-rich. Additionally, they have to run on platforms with very limited hardware resources. This makes it even more important that the implementation of these applications be very low latency and highly efficient in how they use the limited resources they have. However, these applications still need to be extremely quick to respond to user interactions, possibly handle backend connectivity, and render high-quality graphics on mobile devices. Mobile platforms such as Android and the Windows OS, browsers such as Google Chrome and Firefox, and apps such as YouTube have a lot of C++ involvement.

Internet of Things and machine-to-machine applications

Internet of Things (**IoT**) and **machine-to-machine** (**M2M**) applications are based on connecting devices to collect, store and exchange data with each other automatically. Overall, while IoT and M2M are similar in nature, there are some differences around aspects such as networks, scalability, interoperability, and human interactions.

IoT is a broad term that refers to connecting different physical devices together. IoT devices are generally actuators and sensors that are embedded inside other larger devices such as smart thermostats, refrigerators, doorbells, cars, smart watches, TVs, and medical devices. These devices operate on platforms with limited computing resources, power requirements, and minimal available memory resources.

M2M is a communication method where multiple machines interact with each other using wired or wireless connections without any human oversight or interaction. The point here is that internet connectivity is not necessary for M2M. So IoT is a subset of M2M, but M2M is a broader universe of M2M communication-based systems. M2M technology is used in different applications such as security, tracking and tracing, automation, manufacturing, and facility management.

We have already discussed these applications before, but to summarize again here, IoT and M2M technology are used in applications such as telecommunications, medical and healthcare, pharmaceuticals, automotive and aerospace industries, retail and logistics and supply chain management, manufacturing, and military satellite data analysis systems.

This section was all about different business areas and use cases where low latency applications thrive and, in some cases, are a necessity for the business. Our hope is that you understand that low latency applications are used in many different areas, even though it might not be immediately obvious. The other objective here was to establish similarities that these applications share, even though they are designed to solve different business problems.

Summary

In this chapter, we provided an introduction to low latency applications. First, we defined latency-sensitive and latency-critical applications and different measures of latency. We then discussed different metrics that are important in low latency applications and other considerations that define the requirements of low latency applications.

We spent a section of this chapter understanding why C++ is most frequently chosen for low latency applications across different businesses. Specifically, we discussed the features of the language itself and also the flexibility and low-level nature of the language, which makes C++ a perfect fit when it comes to low latency applications.

Finally, we looked at many different examples of low latency applications across different businesses and the similarities they share. The point of that discussion is that even though the business cases are different, these applications share a lot of common requirements and features. Again, here, C++ is a good fit for most (if not all) of these low latency applications in different business areas.

In the next chapter, we will discuss some of the most popular low latency applications in much greater detail. In this book, we will be using low latency electronic trading as a case study to understand and apply C++ low latency techniques. However, before we do that, we will explore other low latency applications such as real-time video streaming, real-time offline and online video gaming applications, and IoT applications as well.

2
Designing Some Common Low Latency Applications in C++

In this chapter, we will look at some applications in different fields from video streaming, online gaming, real-time data analysis, and electronic trading. We will understand their behavior, and what features need to be executed in real time under extremely low-latency considerations. We will introduce the electronic trading ecosystem, since we will use that as a case study in the rest of the book, and build a system from scratch in C++, with a focus on understanding and using low latency ideas.

In this chapter, we will cover the following topics:

- Understanding low latency performance in live video streaming applications
- Understanding which low latency constraints matter in gaming applications
- Discussing the design of Internet-of-Things (IoT) and retail analytics systems
- Exploring low latency electronic trading

This chapter's goal is to dig into some of the technical aspects of low latency applications in different business areas. By the end of this chapter, you should be able to understand and appreciate the technical challenges that applications such as real-time video streaming, offline and online gaming applications, IoT machines and applications, and electronic trading face. You will be able to understand the different solutions that advancements in technology provide to solve these problems and make these businesses viable and profitable.

Understanding low latency performance in live video streaming applications

In this section, we will first discuss the details behind low latency performance in the context of video streaming applications. We will define the important concepts and terms relevant to live video streaming to build an understanding of the field and business use cases. We will understand what causes latencies in these applications and the business impact of those. Finally, we will discuss technologies, platforms, and solutions to build and support low latency video streaming applications.

Defining important concepts in low latency streaming

Here, we will first define a few important concepts and terms when it comes to low latency streaming applications. Let us get started with a few basics and build up from there into more complex concepts.

Latency in video streaming

Video streaming is defined as audio-video content delivered in real time or near real time. Latency in general refers to the time delay between an input event and the output event. In the context of live video streaming applications, latency refers specifically to the time from when a live video stream hits the camera on the recording device and then gets transported to the target audience's screens and gets rendered and displayed there. It should be easy to intuitively understand why this is also referred to as **glass-to-glass latency** in the context of live video streaming applications. Glass-to-glass latency in video streaming applications is quite important regardless of the actual application, whether it be a video call, live video streams for other applications, or online video game rendering. In live streaming, video latency is basically the delay between when the video frame captures at the recorder's side to when the video frame is displayed at the viewer's side. Another commonly encountered term is **lag**, which often just refers to a higher-than-expected glass-to-glass latency, which the user may perceive as reduced or jittery performance.

Video distribution services and content delivery networks

Video distribution service (**VDS**) is a fancy term for a relatively easy-to-understand concept. A VDS basically means the system responsible for taking multiple incoming streams of video and audio from the sources and presenting them to the viewers. One of the most well-known examples of a VDS would be a **content delivery network** (**CDN**). A CDN is a means of efficiently distributing context across the globe.

Transcoding, transmuxing, and transrating

Let us discuss three concepts that relate to encoding the audio-video stream:

- **Transcoding** refers to the process of decoding a media stream from one format (so lower-level details such as codec, video size, sampling rates, encoder formats, etc.) and possibly recoding it in a different format or with different parameters.
- **Transmuxing** is similar to transcoding but here, the delivery format changes without any changes to the encoding, as in the case of transcoding.
- **Transrating** is also similar to transcoding, but we change the video bitrate; usually, it is compressed to a lower value. The video bitrate is the number of bits (or kilobits) being transferred per second and captures the information and quality in the video stream.

- In the next section, we will understand the sources of latencies in low latency video streaming applications.

Understanding sources of latency in video streaming applications

Let us look at the details of what happens in the glass-to-glass journey. Our ultimate motivation in this section is to understand the sources of latencies in video streaming applications. This figure describes at a high level what happens in the glass-to-glass journey from the camera to the display:

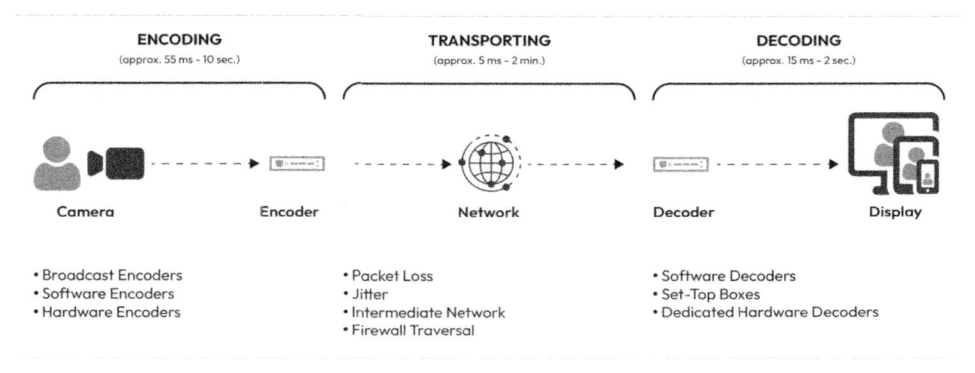

Figure 2.1 – Glass-to-glass journey in live video streaming applications

Discussing the steps in the glass-to-glass journey

We will begin by understanding all the steps and components involved in the glass-to-glass journey of low latency video streaming applications. There are two forms of latency – the initial startup latency and then the lag between video frames once the live stream starts. Typically for the user experience, a slightly longer startup latency is much preferred over lag between video frames, but there is usually a trade-off in trying to reduce one latency over the other. So, we need to understand which metric is more important for a specific use case and adjust the design and technical details appropriately. The following are the steps in the glass-to-glass journey from the broadcaster to the receivers:

1. Camera capturing and processing the audio and video at the broadcaster
2. Video consumption and packaging at the broadcaster
3. Encoders transcoding, transmuxing, and transrating the content
4. Sending the data over the network over the appropriate protocol(s)
5. Distribution over a VDS such as a CDN
6. Reception at the receivers and buffering
7. Decoding the content on the viewer's device
8. Dealing with packet drops, network changes, and so on at the receiver end

9. Rendering of the audio-video content on the viewer's device of choice
10. Possibly collecting interactive inputs (selections, audio, video, etc.) from the viewer for interactive applications and sending them back to the broadcaster where needed

Now that we have described the details behind content delivery from the sender to the receiver and possibly back to the sender, in the next section, we will describe where we have possibilities of latencies on that path. Typically, each step does not take a long time, but higher latencies in multiple components can accumulate and cause significant degradation in user performance.

Describing possibilities of high latencies on the path

We will look at the reasons for high latencies in low latency video streaming applications. There are numerous reasons for this on each of the components of the glass-to-glass path we discussed in the previous subsection.

Physical distance, server load, and internet quality

- This is an obvious one: the physical distance between the source and destination will affect the glass-to-glass latency. This is sometimes very obvious when streaming videos from a different country.
- In addition to the distance, the quality of the internet connection itself can affect the streaming latency. Slow or limited bandwidth connections lead to instability, buffering, and lags.

Depending on how many users are simultaneously streaming the videos and how much load that puts on the servers involved in the streaming path, the latency and user experience can vary. Overloaded servers lead to slower response times, higher latencies, buffering, and lag and can even make the streaming come to a grinding halt.

Capture equipment and hardware

The video and audio capture devices have a big impact on the glass-to-glass latencies. Taking an audio and video frame and turning it into digital signals takes time. Advanced systems such as recorders, encoders, processors, re-encoders, decoders, and re-transmitters have a significant impact on the final user experience. The capture equipment and hardware will determine the latency values.

Streaming protocol, transmission, and jitter buffer

Given the availability of different streaming protocols (as we will discuss shortly), the final choice can determine the latency of video streaming applications. If the protocol is not optimized for dynamic adaptive streaming, it can increase delays. Overall, there are two categories of protocols for live video streaming – HTTP-based and non-HTTP-based – and there are differences in latencies and scalability between the two broad options, which will change the performance of the final system.

The internet routes chosen on the way through the VDS can change the glass-to-glass latency. These routes can also change over time, and packets can be queued on some hops and can even arrive out of order at the receiver. The software that handles these issues is known as a **jitter buffer**. If the CDN has issues, that can also cause additional delays. Then, there are constraints such as the encoded bitrate (lower bitrates mean less data being transferred per unit time and lead to lower latencies), which can change the latencies encountered.

Encoding – transcoding and transrating

The encoding process determines the compression, format, and so on of the final video output, and the choice and quality of encoding protocols will have a huge impact on the performance. Also, there are many options for viewer devices (TVs, phones, PCs, Macs, etc.) and networks (3G, 4G, 5G, LAN, Wi-Fi, etc.) and a streaming provider needs to implement **adaptive bitrate** (**ABR**) to handle these efficiently. The computer or server running the encoder needs to have adequate CPU and memory resources for the encoding process to keep up with the incoming audio-video data. Whether we use encoding software on a computer or encoding hardware such as *BoxCaster* or *Teradek*, we incur processing latencies ranging from a few milliseconds to seconds. The tasks that the encoder needs to perform are to ingest the raw video data, buffer the content, and decode, process, and re-encode it before forwarding it.

Decoded and played on the viewer's device

Assuming the content makes it to the viewer's device without incurring noticeable latencies, the client still must decode, playback, and render the content. Video players do not render video segments one at a time as they receive them, but instead, have a buffer of received segments, usually in memory. This means several segments are buffered before the video begins to play and, depending on the actual size of the segment chosen, can cause latency on the end user side. For instance, if we choose a segment length that contains 10 seconds of video, the player at the end user must at least receive a complete segment before it can play it and will introduce an extra 10-second delay between the sender and receiver. Typically, these segments are between 2 and 10 seconds, trying to balance between optimizing network efficiency and glass-to-glass latency. Obviously, factors such as the viewer's device, platform, hardware, CPU, memory, and player efficiency can add to the glass-to-glass latencies.

Measuring latencies in low latency video streaming

Measuring latencies in low latency video streaming applications is not extremely complicated, since the latency range we care about should at least be a few seconds to be perceptible to the end user as a delay or lag. The easiest ways to measure end-to-end video latency are the following:

- The first place to start would be to use a **clapperboard** application. A clapperboard is a tool used to synchronize video and audio during filmmaking, and apps are available to detect synchronization issues between two streams due to latency.
- Another option is to publish the video stream back to yourself to measure whether there are any latencies in the capturing, encoding, decoding, and rendering steps by taking the network out of it.

- An obvious solution is to take a screenshot of two screens running the same live stream to spot differences.
- The best solution to measure live video streaming latencies is to add a timestamp to the video stream itself at the source and then the receiver can use that to determine the glass-to-glass latencies. Obviously, the clocks used by the sender and the receiver need to be synchronized with each other reasonably well.

Understanding the impact of high latencies

Before we understand the impact of high latencies on low latency video streaming applications, first, we need to define what the acceptable latency is for different applications. For video streaming applications that do not require a lot of real-time interactions, anything up to 5 seconds is acceptable. For streaming applications that need to support live and interactive use cases, anything up to 1 second is enough for the users. Obviously, for video-on-demand, latency is not an issue since it is pre-recorded and there is no live-streaming component. Overall, high latency in real-time live-streaming applications negatively impacts an end user's experience. The key motivation for real time is that viewers want to feel connected and get the feeling of being in person. Large delays in receiving and rendering the content destroy the feeling of watching something in real time. One of the most annoying experiences occurs when a real-time video regularly pauses and buffers due to latencies.

Let us briefly discuss the main negative impacts of real-time video streaming applications due to latency.

Low audio-video quality

If the components of the streaming system cannot achieve real-time latencies, that usually leads to higher levels of compression. Due to the high levels of compression on the audio-video data, the audio quality can sound scrambled and scratchy at times and the video quality can be blurry and pixelated, so it's just a worse user experience overall.

Buffering pauses and delays

Buffering is one of the worst things that can ruin the user experience since the viewer experiences a jittery performance with constant pauses instead of having a smooth experience. This is very frustrating for viewers if a video keeps pausing to buffer and catch up, and will likely lead to the viewer quitting the video, the platform, or the business itself and never returning.

Audio-video synchronization issues

In many implementations of real-time audio-video streaming applications, the audio data is sent separately from the video data and thus the audio data can reach the receiver faster than the video data. This is because by its nature, audio data is smaller in size than video data, and due to high latencies, video data might lag behind audio data at the receiver's end. This leads to problems with synchronization and hurts the viewer's experience with real-time video streaming.

Playback – rewinding and fast-forwarding

High latencies can cause issues with rewinding and fast-forwarding, even when the applications aren't necessarily in 100% real time. This is because the audio-video data will have to be resent so that the end user's player can re-sync with the newly selected location.

Exploring technologies for low latency video streaming

In this section, we will look at different technology protocols that apply to the encoding, decoding, streaming, and distribution of audio-video data. These protocols are specially designed for low latency video streaming applications and platforms. These protocols fall into one of two broad categories – HTTP-based protocols and non-HTTP-based protocols – but for low latency video streaming, typically, HTTP-based protocols are the way to go, as we will see in this section.

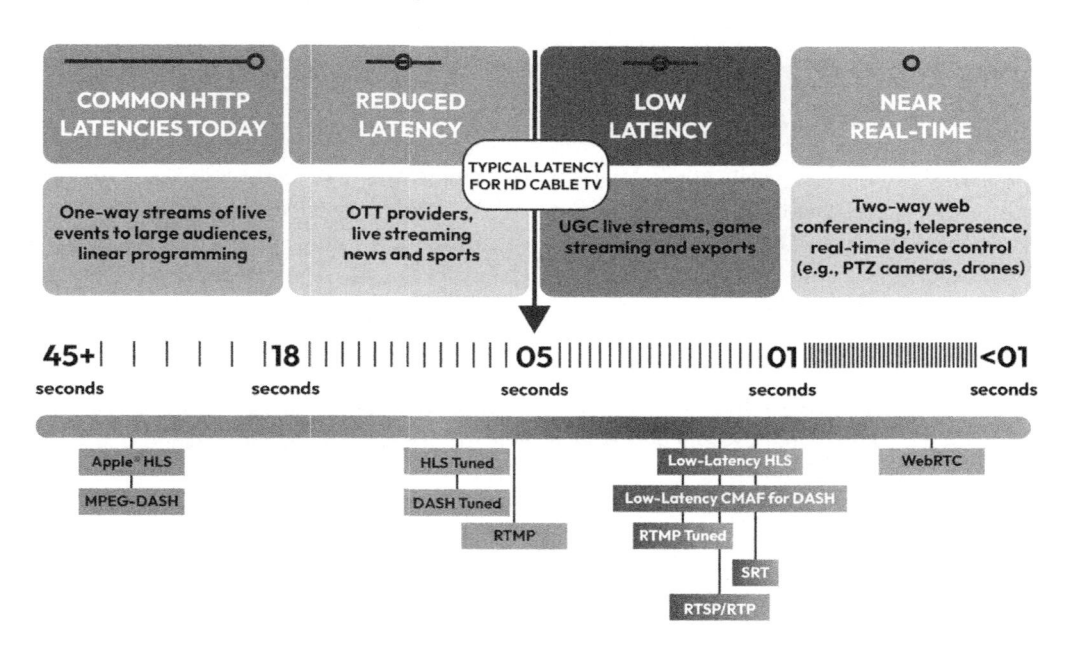

Figure 2.2 – Live video streaming latencies and technologies

Non-HTTP-based protocols

Non-HTTP-based protocols use a combination of **User Datagram Protocol** (**UDP**) and **Transmission Control Protocol** (**TCP**) to transfer data from the sender to the receiver. These protocols can be used for low latency applications, but many do not have advanced support for adaptive streaming technology and suffer from limited scalability. Two examples of these protocols are **Real-Time Streaming Protocol** (**RTSP**) and **Real-Time Messaging Protocol** (**RTMP**), which we will discuss next.

RTSP

RTSP is an application layer protocol that was used for the low latency streaming of videos. It also has playback capabilities to allow playing and pausing the video content and can handle multiple data streams. This, however, is no longer popular today and has been replaced by other more modern protocols, which we will see in later sections. RTSP was replaced by modern protocols such as HLS and DASH because a lot of receivers did not support RTSP; it was incompatible with HTTP and lost popularity with the advent of web-based streaming applications.

Flash and RTMP

Flash-based applications were very popular once upon a time. They use RTMP and work well for low latency streaming use cases. However, Flash as a technology has declined a lot in popularity for many reasons, mostly security-related. Web browsers as well as CDNs have removed support for RTMP because it did not scale too well as demand grew. RTMP is a streaming protocol that accomplishes low latencies in streaming but, as mentioned before, is being replaced by other technologies now.

HTTP-based protocols

HTTP-based protocols typically break down the continuous stream of audio-video data into small segments of 2 to 10 seconds in length. These segments are then transported through a CDN or a web service. These are the preferred protocols for low latency live streaming applications since they are still acceptably low latency but also feature-rich and scale better. These protocols, however, do have a disadvantage that we have mentioned before: the latency incurred depends on the length of the segments. The minimum latency is at least the length of the segment because the receiver needs to receive at least one full segment before it can play it. In some cases, the latency can be in the order of multiples of segment length depending on the video player devices' implementation. For example, iOS buffers at least three to five segments before playing the first segment to ensure smooth rendering.

Some examples of HTTP-based protocols are as follows:

- **HTTP Live Streaming (HLS)**
- **HTTP Dynamic Streaming (HDS)**
- **Microsoft Smooth Streaming (MSS)**
- **Dynamic Adaptive Streaming over HTTP (DASH)**
- **Common Media Application Format (CMAF)**
- **High-Efficiency Stream Protocol (HESP)**

We will discuss some of these protocols in this section to understand how they work and how they achieve low latency performance in real-time video streaming applications. Overall, these protocols are designed to scale to millions of simultaneous receivers and support adaptive streaming and playback. HTTP-based streaming protocols use communication over standard HTTP protocol and require a server for distribution. In contrast to that, **Web Real-Time Communication (WebRTC)**, which we will explore later, is a **Peer-to-Peer (P2P)** protocol that can technically establish direct communication between two machines and skip the need for an intermediate machine or server.

HLS

HLS is used both for real-time and on-demand audio-video content delivery and can scale tremendously well. HLS is generally converted from RTMP by the video delivery platform. Using both RTMP and HLS is the best way to achieve low latency and stream to all devices. There is a variant of **Low Latency HLS (LL-HLS)** that can get latencies down to under 2 seconds, but it is still experimental. LL-HLS enables low latency audio-video real-time streaming by exploiting the ability to stream and render partial segments instead of requiring a full segment. The success of HLS and LL-HLS as the most widely used ABR streaming protocols comes from scalability to many users and compatibility with most kinds of devices, browsers, and players.

CMAF

CMAF is relatively new; strictly speaking, it is not really a new format but instead packages and delivers various forms of protocols for video streaming. It works with HTTP-based protocols such as HLS and DASH to encode, package, and decode video segments. This typically helps businesses by reducing storage costs and audio-video streaming latencies.

DASH

DASH was created from the work of the **Moving Picture Experts Group (MPEG)** and is an alternative to the HLS protocol we discussed before. It is quite similar to HLS because it prepares different quality levels of the audio-video content and divides them into small segments to enable ABR streaming. Under the hood, DASH still relies on CMAF and, to be specific, one of the features it relies on is **chunked encoding**, which facilitates breaking a segment into even smaller subsegments of a few milliseconds. The other feature it relies on is **chunked transfer encoding**, which takes these subsegments sent to the distribution layer and distributes them in real time.

HESP

HESP is another ABR HTTP-based streaming protocol. This protocol has the ambitious goals of ultra-low latencies, increasing scalability, supporting currently popular CDNs, reducing bandwidth requirements, and reducing times to switch between streams (i.e., the latency to start a new audio video stream). Since it is extremely low latency (<500 milliseconds) it is a competitor to the WebRTC protocol, but HESP can be expensive since it is not an open source protocol.

Fundamentally, the major difference in HESP relative to other protocols is that HESP relies on two streams rather than one. One of the streams (which only contains keyframes or snapshot frames) is known as the **initialization stream**. The other stream contains data that applies incremental changes to the frames in the initialization stream, and this stream is known as the **continuation stream**. So, while the keyframes from the initialization stream contain snapshot data and require higher bandwidth, they support the ability to quickly seek various locations in the video during playback. But the continuation stream is lower-bandwidth since it only contains changes and can be used to quickly play back once the receiver video player synchronizes with the initialization stream.

While, on paper, HESP might sound perfect, it has a few drawbacks such as higher costs for encoding and storing two streams instead of one, the need to encode and distribute two streams instead of one, and the need to update the players on the receivers' platforms to decode and render the two streams.

WebRTC

WebRTC is regarded as the new standard in the real-time video streaming industry and allows subsecond latencies so can be played back on most platforms and almost every browser (such as Safari, Chrome, Opera, Firefox, etc.). It is a P2P protocol (i.e., it creates a direct communication channel between devices or streaming applications). A big advantage of WebRTC is that it does not need additional plugins to support audio-video streaming and playback. It also supports ABR and adaptive video quality changes for bi-directional and real-time audio-video streaming. Even though WebRTC uses a P2P protocol and so can establish a direct connection for conferencing, the performance is still dependent on the hardware and network quality because that is still a consideration for all protocols, regardless of whether they're P2P or not.

WebRTC does have some challenges, such as needing its own multimedia server infrastructure, the need to encrypt data that is exchanged, security protocols to handle the gaps in UDP, trying to scale worldwide cost-effectively, and the engineering complexity that comes with dealing with the several protocols that WebRTC is a combination of.

Exploring solutions and platforms for low latency streaming

In this section, we will explore some of the most popular solutions and commercially available platforms for low latency video streaming. These platforms build on all the technologies we discussed in the previous section to solve a lot of the business problems associated with high latencies in real-time audio-video streaming applications. Note that a lot of these platforms support and use multiple underlying streaming protocols, but we will mention the ones that are primarily used for these platforms.

Twitch

Twitch is a very popular online platform, mostly used by video gamers who want to live-stream their gameplay in real time as well as interact with their target audience via chats, comments, donations, and so on. It goes without saying, but this requires low latency streaming as well as the ability to scale to a large community, which Twitch provides. Twitch uses RTMP for its broadcasting needs.

Zoom

Zoom is one of the real-time video conferencing platforms that exploded in popularity during the COVID pandemic and working-from-home era. Zoom provides real-time low latency audio and video conferencing with little delays and supports many simultaneous users. It also provides features such as screen sharing and group chats while on video conferencing. Zoom primarily uses the WebRTC streaming protocol technology.

Dacast

Dacast is a platform for broadcasting events, and even though it is not as low latency as some other real-time streaming applications, it still has acceptable performance when it comes to broadcasting purposes. It is affordable and works well but does not allow for a lot of interactive workflows. Dacast uses the RTMP streaming protocol as well.

Ant Media Server

Ant Media Server uses WebRTC technology to provide an extremely low latency video streaming platform and is intended to be used at an enterprise level on-premises or on the cloud. It is also used for live video monitoring and surveillance-based applications that require real-time video streaming at their core.

Vimeo

Vimeo is another very popular video streaming platform that, while not the fastest in the business, is still used quite extensively. It is mostly used to house real-time live event broadcasts and on-demand video distribution applications. Vimeo uses RTMP streaming by default but also supports others, including HLS.

Wowza

Wowza has been around for a long time in the field of online real-time video streaming and is quite reliable and widely used. It is used by many large corporations such as Sony, Vimeo, and Facebook and focuses on providing video streaming services at a commercial and enterprise level on a very large scale. Wowza is another platform that uses RTMP streaming protocol technology.

Evercast

Evercast is an ultra-low latency streaming platform that has found a lot of uses for collaborative content creation and editing applications, as well as live streaming applications. Since it can support ultra-low latency performance, multiple collaborators are able to stream their workspaces and create an environment of real-time and collaborative editing. The demand for such use cases has exploded in recent years due to the COVID pandemic, remote work and collaboration, and online collaboration education systems. Evercast primarily uses WebRTC on its streaming servers.

CacheFly

CacheFly is another platform that provides live video streaming for live event broadcast purposes. It provides an acceptably low latency of single digit seconds and scales very well for real-time audio-video broadcasting applications. CacheFly uses a custom Websocket-based end-to-end streaming solution.

Vonage Video API

Vonage Video API (previously known as **TokBox**) is another platform that provides live video streaming capabilities and targets large corporations to support enterprise-level applications. It supports data encryption, which is what makes it a preferred choice for enterprises, corporations, and healthcare companies looking for audio-video conferencing, meetings, and training online. Vonage uses RTMP as well as HLS as its broadcasting technologies.

Open Broadcast Software (OBS)

OBS is another low latency video streaming platform that is also open source, which makes it popular in a lot of circles where enterprise-level solutions might be a deterrent. Many live streamers who stream several types of content use OBS, and even some platforms such as Facebook Live and Twitch use some parts of OBS. OBS supports multiple protocols such as RTMP and **Secure Reliable Transport** (**SRT**).

Here, we conclude our discussion of low latency considerations for live video streaming applications. Next, we will transition into video gaming applications, which share some common traits when compared to live video streaming applications, especially when it comes to online video games.

Understanding what low latency constraints matter in gaming applications

Video gaming has evolved greatly since it was first born in the 1960s and, these days, video games are not about playing alone or even playing along with or against the person physically next to you. These days, gaming involves many players all over the globe, and even the quality and complexity of these games have increased tremendously. It is no surprise that ultra-low latency and high scalability are non-negotiable requirements when it comes to modern gaming applications. With new technologies such as AR and VR, this only further increases the need for ultra-low latency performance. Additionally, with the advent of mobile gaming combined with online gaming, complex gaming applications have been ported to smartphones and need ultra-low latency content delivery systems, multiplayer systems, and super-fast processing speeds.

In the previous section, we discussed low latency real-time video streaming applications in detail, including streaming applications that are interactive. In this section, we will look at low latency considerations, high-latency impact, and techniques to facilitate low latency performance in video gaming applications. Since a lot of modern video games are either online or in the cloud, or have a strong online presence due to multiplayer features, a lot of what we learned in the previous section is still important here. Streaming and rendering video games in real time, preventing lag, and responding to player interactions quickly and efficiently are necessities when it comes to gaming applications. Additionally, there are some extra concepts, considerations, and techniques to maximize low latency gaming performance.

Concepts in low latency gaming applications

Before we understand the impact of high latency in gaming applications and how to improve the latencies in these applications, we will define and explain a few concepts related to gaming applications and their performance. When it comes to low latency gaming applications, the most important concepts are the **refresh rate**, **response time**, and **input lag**. The main goal of these applications is to minimize the delay between the player and the character on screen that the player controls. Really, what this means is that any user input reflects the impact on the screen right away, and any changes to the character due to the gameplay environment are rendered on the screen right away. The optimal user experience is achieved when the gameplay feels very smooth, and the player feels like they really are inside the game world being rendered on screen. Now, let us jump into a discussion of the important concepts with regard to low latency gaming applications.

Ping

In computer science and online video gaming applications, **ping** is the latency from when data is sent from the user's computer to a server (or possibly a different player's computer) until when the data is received back at the original user's computer. Typically, the magnitude of the ping latency depends on the application; for low latency electronic trading, this will be in hundreds of microseconds, and for gaming applications, it is usually tens to hundreds of milliseconds. Ping latency basically measures how fast a server and client communicate with each other in the absence of any processing delays at the server or client machines.

The closer to real-time the requirements for the gaming application are, the lower the ping times need to be. This is typically required for games such as **first-person shooters** (**FPS**) and sports and racing games, while other games such as **massive multiplayer online** (**MMO**) games and some **real-time strategy** (**RTS**) games can tolerate higher ping latencies. It is common for the game interface itself to have a ping functionality or display ping statistics in real time. In general, 50 to 100 milliseconds is an acceptable ping time, above 100 milliseconds can cause noticeable delays during gameplay, and any higher than that degrades the player's experience too much to be viable. Typically, less than 25 milliseconds is the ideal ping latency for good responsiveness, crisp rendering of visuals, and no gameplay lags.

Frames per second (FPS)

FPS (not to be confused with *first-person shooters*) is another important concept when it comes to online gaming applications. FPS measures how many frames or images can be rendered each second by the graphics card. FPS can also be measured for the monitor hardware itself instead of the graphics card (i.e., how many frames can be displayed or updated by the monitor hardware itself). Higher FPS typically leads to the smoother rendering of game worlds and the user experience feels more responsive to inputs and gameplay events. Lower FPS leads to the gameplay and rendering feeling like it is rigid, stuttering, and flickering, and overall, just leads to significantly reduced enjoyment and adoption.

For a game to be functional or even playable, 30 FPS is the bare minimum necessity, and this can support console games and some PC games. As long as the FPS stays above 20 FPS, these games can continue to be playable without any noticeable lag and degradation. For most games, 60 FPS or more is the ideal performance range that is easily supported by most graphics cards, PCs, monitors, and TVs. Beyond 60 FPS, the next milestone is 120 FPS, which is only needed and available for high-end gaming hardware connected to monitors that support at least 144-Hz refresh rates. Beyond this, 240 FPS is the maximum frame rate achievable and needs to be paired with 240-Hz refresh rate monitors. This high-end configuration is typically only needed for the biggest gaming enthusiasts out there.

Refresh rate

The refresh rate is a concept that is very closely related to FPS, and even though technically they are slightly different, they do impact each other. The refresh rate also measures how quickly the screen refreshes and impacts the maximum possible FPS that hardware can support. Like FPS, the higher the refresh rate, the smoother the rendering transition when animating motion during gameplay on the screen. The maximum refresh rate controls the maximum FPS achievable because even though the graphics card can render faster than a monitor screen can refresh, the bottleneck then becomes the monitor screen refresh rate. When there are cases where the FPS exceeds the refresh rate, one of the display artifacts that we encounter is called **screen tearing**. Screen tearing is when the graphics card (GPU) is not synchronized with the monitor, so there are cases where the monitor paints an incomplete frame on top of the current frame, resulting in horizontal or vertical splits where the partial and full frames overlap on the screen. This does not completely break down the gameplay but, at the very least, can be distracting if it happens rarely, all the way to completely ruining the visual quality of the gameplay if quite frequent. There are various techniques to deal with screen tearing, which we will look at shortly, such as **vertical synchronization** (**V-Sync**), **adaptive sync**, **FreeSync**, **Fast Sync**, **G-Sync**, and **variable refresh rate** (**VRR**).

Input lag

Input lag measures the latency between when a user generates an input (such as a keystroke, mouse movement, or a mouse click) to when the response to that input is rendered on the screen. This is basically the responsiveness of the hardware and the game to user inputs and interactions. Obviously, for all games, this is a non-zero value and is the sum of the hardware itself (the controller, mouse, keyboard, internet connection, processor, display monitor, etc.) or the game software itself (processing input, updating the game and character states, dispatching the graphics updates, rendering them via the graphics card, and refreshing the monitor). When there is high input lag, the game feels unresponsive and lagging, which can affect the player's performance during multiplayer or online gameplay and even ruin the game completely for the user.

Response time

Response time is often mistaken for input lag, but they are different terms. Response time refers to the pixel response time, which basically means the time it takes for pixels to change colors. While input lag impacts the gameplay's responsiveness, response time impacts the blurriness of rendered animations on the screen. Intuitively, if the pixel response time is high, the pixels take longer to change colors when rendering motion or animation on screen, thus causing blurriness. Lower pixel response times (1 millisecond or lower) lead to crisp and sharp image and animation quality, even for games that have fast camera movements. Good examples of such games would be first-person shooters and racing games. In cases where the response time is high, we encounter an artifact known as **ghosting**, which refers to trails and artifacts slowly fading off the screen when there is motion. Usually, ghosting and high pixel response times are not a problem, and modern hardware can easily provide response times of less than 5 milliseconds and render sharp animations.

Network bandwidth

Network bandwidth affects online gaming applications in the same way as it would affect real-time video streaming applications. Bandwidth measures how many megabits per second can be uploaded to or downloaded from the gaming application server. Bandwidth is also affected by packet losses, which we will look at next, and varies depending on the location of the players and the gaming server they connect to. **Contention** is another term to think about when it comes to network bandwidth. Contention is a measure of how many simultaneous users are trying to access the same server or shared resource and whether that causes the server to be overloaded or not.

Network packet loss and jitter

Network packet loss is an inescapable fact of transmitting packets over the network. Network packet loss reduces the effective bandwidth and causes retransmission and recovery protocols, which introduce additional delays. Some packet losses are tolerable, but when the network packet losses are very high, they can degrade the user experience of online gaming applications and can even bring it to a grinding halt. **Jitter** is like packet losses except, in this case, packets arrive out of order. This introduces additional delays as the game software is on the user's end because the receiver must save the out-of-order packets and wait for packets that have not arrived yet and then process the packets in order.

Networking protocols

When it comes to networking protocols, there are broadly two protocols to transfer data across the internet: **TCP** and **UDP**. TCP provides a reliable transport protocol by tracking packets successfully delivered to the receiver and having mechanisms to retransmit lost packets. The advantage here is obvious where applications cannot operate with packet and information losses. The disadvantage here is that these additional mechanisms to detect and handle packet drops cause additional latencies (additional milliseconds) and use the available bandwidth less effectively. Examples of applications that must rely on TCP are online shopping and online banking, where it is critical to make sure the data is delivered correctly, even if it is delivered late. UDP instead focuses on making sure that the data is delivered as quickly as possible and with greater bandwidth effectiveness. However, it does so at the cost of not guaranteeing delivery or even guaranteeing in-order delivery of packets since it does not have mechanisms to retransmit dropped packets. UDP works well for applications that can tolerate some packet losses without completely breaking down and some dropped information is preferred over delayed information. Some examples of such applications are real-time video streaming and some components of online gaming applications. For instance, some video components or rendering components in online video games can be transported over UDP, but some components such as user input and game and player state updates need to be sent over TCP.

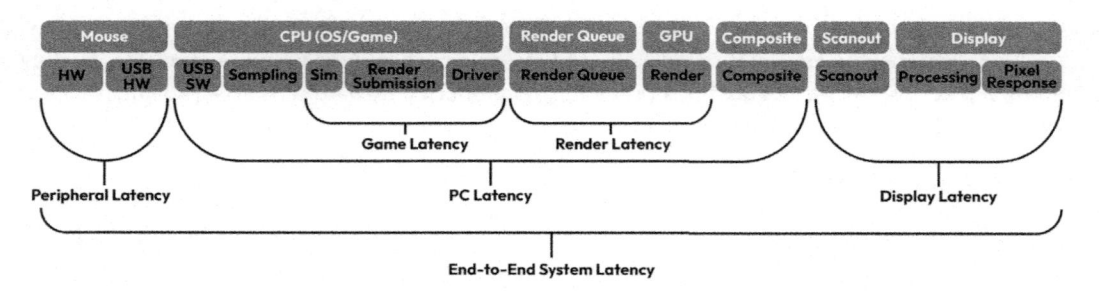

Figure 2.3 – Components in an end-to-end video gaming system

Improving gaming application performance

In the previous section, we discussed some concepts that apply to low latency gaming applications and their impact on the application and the user experience. In this section, we will explore additional details about the sources of high latency in gaming applications and discuss the steps we can take to improve gaming application latencies and performance and thus improve the user experience.

Approaching gaming application optimization from the developer's perspective

First, we look at the approach and techniques that game developers use to optimize gaming application performance. Let us quickly describe a few optimization techniques employed by developers – some that apply to all applications and some that only apply to gaming applications.

Managing memory, optimizing cache access, and optimizing the hot path

Gaming applications, like other low latency applications, must use the available resources efficiently and maximize runtime performance. This includes managing the memory correctly to avoid memory leaks and pre-allocating and pre-initializing as many things as possible. Avoiding mechanisms such as garbage collection and dynamic memory allocations and deallocation on the critical path are also important to meet a certain runtime performance expectation. This is especially relevant to gaming applications because there are many objects in video games, especially ones that create and deal with large worlds.

Another important aspect of most low latency applications is using the data and instruction cache as efficiently as possible. Gaming applications are no different, especially given the large amount of data that they must deal with.

A lot of applications, including gaming applications, spend a lot of their time in a critical loop. For gaming applications, this can be a loop that checks for inputs, updates the game state, character states, and so on based on the physics engine ,and renders on screen, as well as generates audio output. Gaming developers typically spend a lot of time focusing on the operations performed in this critical path, like what we would do with any low latency application running in a tight loop.

Frustum culling

In computer graphics, the term view **frustum** refers to the part of the game world that is currently visible on the screen. **Frustum culling** is a term that refers to the technique of determining which objects are visible on the screen and only rendering those objects on the screen. Another way to think about this is that most game engines minimize the amount of processing power being directed toward off-screen objects. This is typically achieved by separating the display or rendering functionality of an object from its data and logic management, such as the location, state, next move, and so on. Eliminating the overhead of rendering objects not currently on the screen reduces the processing cost to a fraction of what it would be. Another way to introduce this separation would be to have an update method that is used when the object is on screen and another update method to be used when the object is off-screen.

Caching calculations and using mathematical approximations

This is an easy-to-understand optimization technique that applies to applications that need to perform a lot of expensive mathematical computations. Gaming applications especially are heavy on mathematical computations in their physics engines, especially for 3D games with large worlds and lots of objects in the world. Optimization techniques such as caching values instead of recomputing them each time, using lookup tables to trade memory usage for CPU usage to lookup values, and using mathematical approximations instead of extremely accurate but expensive expressions are used in such cases. These optimization techniques have been used for a very long time in the world of video games because, for a long time, hardware resources were extremely limited, and developing such systems needed to rely on these techniques.

The raycasting engine from **id Software** (which pioneered and powered games such as Wolfenstein, Doom, Quake, etc.) is an impressive masterpiece of low latency software development from back in the old days. Another example would be cases where we have side scrollers or top-down shooters where there are a lot of enemies on screen but a lot of them have similar movement patterns and can be reused instead of being recalculated.

Prioritizing critical tasks and leveraging CPU idle time

A game engine that deals with many objects in a huge game world typically has many objects that update frequently. Instead of updating every object on every frame update, a game engine needs to prioritize tasks that need to be performed in the critical section (for example, objects whose visual properties have changed since the last frame). A simple implementation would be to have a member method for each object that the game engine can use to check whether it has changed since the last frame and prioritize the updates for those objects. For instance, some game components such as the scenery (stationary environment objects, weather, lighting, etc.) and **heads-up display** (**HUD**) do not change very frequently and typically have extremely limited animation sequences. The tasks related to updating these components are slightly lower-priority than some other game components.

Classifying tasks into high-priority and low-priority tasks also means that the game engine has the option of guaranteeing a good gameplay experience by making sure high-priority tasks are performed in all hardware and game settings. If the game engine detects a lot of CPU idle time, it can add additional low-priority features (such as particle engines, lighting, shading, atmospheric effects, etc.).

Ordering draw calls depending on layer, depth, and texture

A game engine needs to determine which rendering or draw calls to issue to the graphics card. To optimize performance, the goal here is to not only minimize the number of draw calls issued but also to order and group these draw calls to perform them optimally. When rendering objects to the screen, we must think about the following layers or considerations:

- **The fullscreen layer**: This comprises the HUD, the game layer, the translucent effects layer, and so on
- **The viewport layer**: These exist if there are mirrors, portals, split screens, and so on
- **Depth considerations**: We need to draw objects in back-to-front order or farthest-to-closest order
- **Texturing considerations**: These comprise textures, shading, lighting, and so on

There are various decisions to be made about the ordering of these different layers and components and in which order the draw calls are sent to the graphics card. An example would be in cases where translucent objects might be ordered back-to-front (i.e., sorted by depth first and texture second). For opaque objects, it might sort by texture first and eliminate draw calls for objects that are behind opaque objects.

Approaching gaming application optimization from the gamer's perspective

For gaming applications, a lot of the performance depends on the end user's hardware, OS, and game settings. This section describes a few things that end users can do to maximize gaming performance under different settings and different resource availability.

Upgrading hardware

The first obvious method to improve gaming application performance is to improve the hardware the end user's game runs on. Some important candidates would be the gaming monitor, mouse, keyboard, and controllers used. Gaming monitors with higher refresh rates (such as 360-Hz monitors that support 1920 x 1080p (pixels) resolution and 240-Hz monitors that support 2560 x 1440p resolution) can provide high-quality rendering and fluid animations and enhance gameplay. We can also use a mouse with an extremely high polling rate, which allows for clicks and movements to be registered faster than before and reduce latency and lag. Similarly, for keyboards, gaming keyboards have much higher polling rates and can improve response times, especially for games where there are a lot of constant keystrokes, which can often be the case for RTS games. Another important point to mention here would be that using official and reputable controllers for specific consoles and platforms usually results in the best performance.

Gaming monitor refresh rates

We have discussed this aspect a few times before but with the rise of very high-quality images and animations, the quality and capacity of gaming monitors themselves have become quite important. Here, the key is to have a high refresh rate monitor that also has a low pixel response time so that animations can be rendered and updated quickly as well as smoothly. The configuration must also avoid the screen-tearing, ghosting, and blurring artifacts that we discussed before.

Upgrading your graphics card

Upgrading the graphics card is another option that can result in significant improvements by increasing the frame rate and thus improving the gaming performance. NVIDIA found that upgrading the graphics card and the GPU drivers can help improve gaming performance by more than 20% in some cases. NVIDIA GeForce, ATI Radeon, Intel HD graphics, and so on are popular vendors that provide updated and optimized drivers that can be used to boost your gaming performance depending on which graphics cards are installed on the user's platform.

Overclocking the graphics card

Another possible area of improvement instead of, or in addition to, upgrading the GPU is attempting to overclock the GPU with the aim of adding FPS. **Overclocking** the GPU works by increasing the frequency of the GPU and ultimately increasing the FPS output of the GPU. The one drawback of overclocking the GPU is increased internal temperatures, which can lead to overheating in extreme cases. So, when overclocking, you should monitor the increase in temperatures, increase the overclock levels gradually, monitor along the way, and make sure that the PC, laptop, or console has sufficient cooling in place. GPU overclocking can yield a performance boost of around 10%.

Upgrading your RAM

This is another obvious general-purpose improvement technique that applies to low latency gaming applications as well. Adding additional RAM to the PC, smartphone, tablet, or console gives the game applications and graphics rendering tasks to perform their best. Thankfully, RAM costs have dropped tremendously over the last decade, so this is an easy way to boost the performance of gaming applications and is highly recommended.

Tweaking the hardware, OS, and game settings

In the previous subsection, we discussed some options for upgrading the hardware resources that lead to improved gaming applications performance. In this subsection, we will discuss settings that can be optimized for the hardware, the platform, the OS, and the game settings themselves to further push gaming application performance.

Enabling game mode

Game mode is a setting available for displays such as high-end TVs and similar high-end display monitors. Enabling game mode disables extra functionality in the display, which improves image and animation quality but comes at the price of higher latency. Enabling game mode will cause a slight deterioration in image quality but can help improve the low latency gaming application end user experience by reducing rendering latencies. An example of game mode is the Windows game mode on Windows 10, which optimizes gaming performance when enabled.

Using high-performance mode

The high-performance mode we discuss here refers to power settings. Different power settings try to optimize between battery usage and performance; high-performance mode drains battery power faster and possibly raises the internal temperature more than low-performance mode but it boosts the performance of the applications running.

Delaying automatic updates

Automatic updates are a feature most notably available in Windows, which downloads and installs security fixes automatically. While this is typically not a major problem, if a particularly large automatic update download and install starts while we are in the middle of an online gaming session, then it can affect the gaming performance and experience. Automatic updates can spike processor usage and bandwidth consumption if this coincides with a gaming session utilizing high processor usage and bandwidth, and can degrade the gaming performance. So, turning off or delaying automatic Windows updates is usually a good idea when running latency-sensitive and resource-intensive gaming applications.

Turning off background services

This is another option similar to delaying automatic updates we just discussed. Here, we find and turn off apps and services that might be running in the background but are not necessarily needed for a low latency gaming session to function properly. In fact, turning these off prevents these applications from consuming hardware resources unexpectedly and non-deterministically during gaming sessions. This maximizes the low latency gaming application performance by making the maximum amount of resources available to that application.

Meeting or exceeding refresh rates

We have discussed the concept of screen tearing before, so we at least need a system where the FPS meets or exceeds the refresh rate to prevent it. Technologies such as FreeSync and G-Sync facilitate smooth rendering without any screen tearing while still providing low latency performance. When frame rates exceed refresh rates, the latency continues to remain low, but if frame rates start exceeding refresh rates by a large magnitude, screen tearing can show up again. This can be addressed by using V-Sync technology or limiting FPS intentionally. FreeSync and G-Sync need hardware support, so you need a compatible GPU to use these technologies. But the upside with FreeSync and G-Sync is that you can completely disable V-Sync, which introduces latencies, and instead have a low latency and tear-free rendering experience as long as you have the hardware support for it.

Disabling triple buffering and V-Sync and running exclusively in full-screen mode

We have explained before that V-Sync can introduce additional latency due to the need to synchronize the frames rendered by the GPU with the display device. **Triple buffering** is just another form of V-Sync and has the same goal of reducing screen tearing. Triple buffering especially comes into play when running a game in windowed mode, in which the game runs inside a window instead of full screen. The key takeaway here is that to disable V-Sync and triple buffering to improve latency and performance, we have to run exclusively in full-screen mode.

Optimizing game settings for low latency and high frame rate

Modern games come with a plethora of options and settings designed to maximize performance (sometimes at the cost of rendering quality), and the end user can optimize these parameters for their target hardware, platform, network resources, and performance requirements. Reducing settings such as **anti-aliasing** would be an example, and reducing resolution is another option. Finally, adjusting settings related to the viewing distance, texture rendering, shadows, and lighting can also maximize performance at the cost of lower rendering quality. Anti-aliasing seeks to render smooth edges instead of jagged edges when we try to render high-resolution images in low-resolution environments, so turning it down deteriorates image smoothness but accelerates low latency performance. Advanced rendering effects such as fire, water, motion blur, and lens flares can also be turned down if additional performance is required.

Further optimizing your hardware

In the last two subsections, we discussed options for optimizing low latency gaming applications by upgrading hardware resources and tweaking the hardware, OS, and game settings. In this final subsection, we will discuss how to squeeze the performance even further and what our options are to further optimize online low latency gaming application performance.

Installing DirectX 12 Ultimate

DirectX is a Windows graphics and gaming API developed by Microsoft. Upgrading DirectX to the latest version means the gaming platform gets access to the latest fixes and improvements and better performance. At this time, DirectX 12 Ultimate is the latest version, with DirectX 13 expected to be released at the end of 2022 or early 2023.

Defragmenting and optimizing disks

Defragmentation of disks occurs as files are created and deleted on the hard disk and the free and used disk space blocks are spread out or fragmented causing lower driver performance. **Hard Disk Drives (HDD)** and **Solid State Drives (SSD)** are typically the two commonly used storage options for most gaming platforms. SSDs are significantly faster than HDDs and do not typically suffer from a lot of fragmentation-related issues but can still become suboptimal over time. Windows, for instance, has a defragmentation and optimization application to optimize the performance of the drives, which can improve gaming application performance as well.

Ensuring the laptop cools optimally

When under heavy loads due to high processor, network, memory, and disk usage, the internal temperatures of the laptop or PC are raised. Other than being dangerous, it also forces the laptop to try and cool itself down by limiting resource consumption and thus, ultimately, performance. We mention laptops specifically to explain this issue because PCs typically have better airflow and cooling abilities than laptops. Ensuring that laptops cool effectively by clearing the vents and fans, removing dirt and dust, placing them on a hard, smooth, and flat surface, using an external power supply to not drain the battery, and possibly even using additional cooling stands can boost gaming performance on laptops.

Using NVIDIA Reflex low latency technology

NVIDIA Reflex low latency technology seeks to minimize the input lag measured from the moment the user clicks the mouse or hits a key on the keyboard or controller to the time at which the impact of that action is rendered on screen. We have already discussed the sources of latency here, and NVIDIA breaks this down into nine chunks from the input device to the processors and the display. The NVIDIA Reflex software speeds up this critical path performance by improving communication paths between CPUs and GPUs, optimizing frame delivery and rendering by skipping unnecessary tasks and pauses, and accelerating the GPU rendering time. NVIDIA also provides an NVIDIA Reflex Latency Analyzer to measure the speed-up achieved by using these low latency enhancements.

Discussing the design of IoT and retail analytics systems

In the previous chapter, we discussed **IoT** and retail analytics and many of the different use cases that they create. Our focus in this section will be to have a brief discussion about the technologies being used to achieve low latency performance for these applications and use cases. Note that IoT is a technology space that is still actively growing and evolving, so there are going to be a lot of breakthroughs and advancements in the coming years. Let us quickly recap some important use cases of IoT and retail data analytics. A lot of these new applications and future possibilities are fueled by the research and advancements in 5G wireless technology, **edge computing**, and **artificial intelligence** (**AI**). We will look at those aspects in the next section, along with other technologies that facilitate applications using low latency IoT and retail data analytics.

A lot of applications fall under the remote inspection/analysis category, where drones can replace humans when it comes to being the first line of defense in fields such as remote technicians, monitoring infrastructure such as bridges, tunnels, railways, highways, and waterways, and even things such as transformers, utility wires, gas pipelines, and electricity and telephone lines. Incorporating AI into such applications enhances the complexity of the data analysis possible and thus creates new opportunities and use cases. Incorporating AR technology also increases the possibilities. Modern automobiles collect large amounts of data and, with the possibility of having autonomous driving vehicles at some point, the use cases for IoT only expand further. Automation in agriculture, shipping and logistics, supply chain management, inventory, and warehouse management, and managing fleets of vehicles creates numerous additional use cases for IoT technology and analyzes data generated from and collected by these devices.

Ensuring low latency in IoT devices

In this section, we will look at some considerations to facilitate low latency performance in IoT applications and retail analytics. Note that a lot of the considerations we discussed for real-time video streaming and online video gaming use cases apply here as well, such as hardware resources, encoding and decoding data streams, content delivery mechanisms, and hardware and system-level optimizations. We will not repeat those techniques here in the interest of brevity, but we will present additional low latency considerations that apply specifically to IoT and retail data analysis.

P2P connectivity

P2P connectivity for IoT devices establishes direct connectivity between different IoT devices or between an IoT device and the end user application. The user's input from their device is directly sent to the IoT device that it is meant for without any third-party service or server in between to minimize latencies. Similarly, data from the IoT devices is streamed back to the other devices directly from the device. The P2P approach is an alternative to connecting to the IoT device through a cloud, which has extra latencies due to additional server databases, cloud worker instances, and so on. P2P is also referred to as a decentralized **Application Enablement Platform** (**AEP**) for IoT, which is an alternative to the cloud-based AEPs.

Using fifth-generation wireless (5G)

5G wireless technology delivers higher bandwidth, ultra-low latency, reliability, and scalability. Not only do the end users benefit from 5G but it also helps each step of the IoT devices and applications that require low latency and real-time data streaming and processing. 5G's low latency facilitates faster and more reliable inventory tracking, transportation services and monitoring, real-time visibility into distribution logistics, and more. The 5G network was designed keeping all the different IoT use cases in mind, so it is an excellent fit for all kinds of IoT applications and more.

Understanding edge computing

Edge computing is a distributed processing technology where the key point is to bring the processing application and the data storage components as close to the source of data as possible, which, in this case, is the IoT devices that capture the data. Edge computing breaks the older paradigm where the data is recorded by remote devices and then transferred to a central storage and processing location and then results are transported back to the devices and client applications. This exciting new technology is revolutionizing how massive amounts of data generated by a lot of IoT devices are transported, stored, and processed. The main goals for edge computing are to reduce bandwidth costs to transfer massive amounts of data across wide distances and to support ultra-low latency to facilitate real-time applications that need to process massive amounts of data as quickly and efficiently as possible. Additionally, it also reduces costs for businesses because they do not necessarily need a centralized and cloud-based storage and processing solution. This point is especially important when it comes to IoT applications because the sheer scale of how many devices generate data means the bandwidth consumption will increase exponentially.

Understanding all the details of the physical architecture of an edge computing system is difficult and outside the scope of this book. However, at a very high level, the client devices and IoT devices connect to edge modules that are available nearby. Typically, there are many gateways and servers that are deployed by service providers or enterprises looking to build their own edge network to support such edge computing operations. The devices that can use these edge modules range from IoT sensors, laptops and computers, smartphones and tablets, cameras, microphones, and anything else you can imagine.

Understanding the relationship between 5G and edge computing

We mentioned before that 5G was designed and developed keeping IoT and edge computing in mind. So IoT, 5G, and edge computing are all related to each other and work with each other to maximize the use cases and performance of these IoT applications. Theoretically, edge computing could be deployed to non-5G networks, but obviously, 5G is the preferred network. However, the reverse is not true; to leverage 5G's true power, you need an edge computing infrastructure to really maximize the use of everything 5G offers. This is intuitive because, without an edge computing infrastructure, the data from the devices must travel long distances to get processed, and then results must travel a long distance to reach the end user's applications or other devices. In those cases, even if you have a 5G network, the latency due to the data's travel distance far outweighs the latency improvements gained by using 5G. So, edge computing is necessary when it comes to IoT applications and applications that need to analyze retail data in real time.

Understanding the relationship between edge computing and AI

Data analytics techniques, machine learning, and AI have revolutionized how the retail and non-retail data collected from IoT devices is analyzed to derive meaningful insights. NVIDIA is a pioneer when it comes to developing new hardware solutions to push not only edge computing but also AI processing to the maximum. Jetson AGX Orin is a particularly good example of how NVIDIA packages AI and robotics functionality together into a single product.

We will not go into too many details about the Jetson AGX Orin since that is neither the focus nor within the scope of this book. The Jetson AGX Orin has a few qualities that make it excellent for AI, robotics, and autonomous vehicles – it is compact, enormously powerful, and energy-efficient. The power and energy efficiency allows it to be used for AI applications and enable edge computing. This latest model in particular lets developers combine AI, robotics, **natural language processing** (NLP), computer vision, and so on into a compact package, making it excellent for robotics. This device also has multiple I/O connectors and is compatible with many different sensors (MIPI, USB, cameras, etc.). There are also additional hardware expansion slots to support storage, wireless, and so on. This powerful GPU-powered device makes it perfect for deep learning (in addition to classic machine learning) and computer vision applications such as robotics.

Buying and deploying edge computing systems

When it comes to purchasing and setting up an edge computing infrastructure, businesses generally go down one of two routes: customize the components and build and manage the infrastructure in-house or use a vendor that provides and manages edge services for the enterprise.

Building and managing the edge computing infrastructure in-house needs expertise from the IT, network, and business departments. Then, they can select the edge devices from hardware vendors (such as IBM, Dell, etc.) and architect and manage the 5G network infrastructure for the specific use case. This option only makes sense for a large enterprise that sees value in customizing its edge computing infrastructure for a specific use case. When it comes to the option of having a third-party vendor facilitate and manage the edge computing infrastructure, the vendor sets up the hardware, software, and networking architecture for a fee. This leaves the management of a complicated system such as edge computing infrastructure to firms such as GE and Siemens with expertise in this field and allows the client business to focus on building on top of this infrastructure.

Leveraging proximity

We have implicitly discussed this point in the previous sections, but now we will explicitly discuss it here. A key requirement of IoT applications is achieving ultra-low latency performance, and the key to achieving that is leveraging proximity between the different devices and applications involved in the IoT use case. It is no surprise that edge computing is the key to leveraging proximity for IoT applications to minimize latencies from capturing data to processing it and sharing results with other devices or client applications. As we have seen before, the biggest bottleneck with a non-edge computing infrastructure is the distance of data centers and processing resources from the source of the data and the destination of the results. This gets worse with additional distributed data centers spread out miles away from each other, and ultimately leads to critically high latencies and lags. Clearly, placing edge computing resources closer to the data sources is the key to driving IoT adoption, IoT use cases, and scaling IoT businesses to a huge number of devices and users.

Reducing cloud costs

This is another point we have discussed before, but we will have a formal conversation about it in this section. There are billions of IoT devices out there and they generate a continuous stream of data. Any effective IoT-driven business will need to scale extremely well to large increases in the number of devices and clients involved, which leads to exponential increases in the amount of data recorded and data processed by edge computing, and the results being transferred to other devices and clients. Data-heavy infrastructures that rely on centralized cloud infrastructure cannot support IoT applications in a cost-effective manner and the data and cloud infrastructure itself becomes a significant fraction of an enterprise's expenses. The clear solution here is to find a low-cost edge solution (third-party or in-house) and use it to facilitate the IoT data capture, storage, and processing needs. This removes the costs associated with transferring data in and out of cloud solutions and can improve edge computing reliability and cut costs significantly.

We will conclude our discussion of low latency IoT applications by summarizing the current and future state of IoT applications in the following figure:

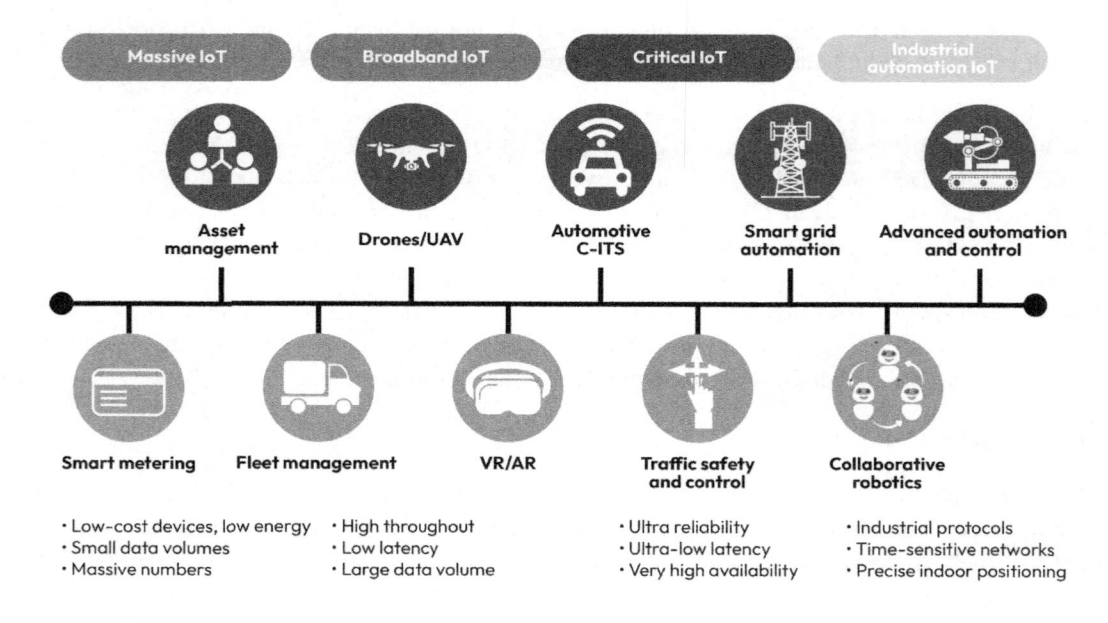

Figure 2.4 – Current and future states of IoT applications

Exploring low latency electronic trading

The final example of low latency applications is the applications used in low latency electronic trading and ultra-low latency electronic trading, also known as HFT. We will build a full end-to-end low latency electronic trading system from scratch in C++ in the rest of this book. So, in this section, we will briefly discuss the important considerations for electronic trading applications to achieve low latency performance and then build out the low-level details in the remaining chapters. *Developing High-Frequency Trading Systems* by Sebastian Donadio, Sourav Ghosh, and Romain Rossier would be an excellent book for understanding low latency electronic trading systems in greater detail for interested readers. Our focus in this book will be to design and build each component from scratch in C++ to learn about low latency application development, but that book can be used as a good reference for the additional theory behind the HFT business.

Understanding the need for low latency in modern electronic trading

With the modernization of electronic trading and the rise of HFT, low latencies are more important than ever before for these applications. In many cases, achieving lower latency leads to a direct increase in trading revenue. In some cases, there is a constant race to try and reduce latencies more and more to maintain a competitive edge in the markets. And in extreme cases, if a participant falls behind in the arms race to the lowest possible latencies, they may go out of business.

Trading opportunities in modern electronic markets are extremely short-lived, so only the market participants that can process market data and find such an opportunity and quickly send orders in reaction to this can be profitable. Failure to react quickly enough means you get a smaller piece of the opportunity, and it is common for only the fastest participant to get all the profit, and for all other slower participants to get nothing. Another nuance here is that if a participant is not quick enough to react to a market event, they can also be caught on the wrong side of the trade and lose money to people who were able to react to the event quickly enough. In such a case, trading profits are not just lower, but trading revenue can be negative (i.e., losses). To understand this better, let us present an example of something we will build in this book: market-making and liquidity-taking algorithms.

Without going into too many details, a market-making algorithm has orders in the market that other participants can trade against when needed. A market-making algorithm thus needs to constantly re-evaluate its active orders and change the prices and quantities for them depending on the market conditions. A liquidity-taking algorithm, however, does not always have active orders in the market. This algorithm instead waits for an opportunity to present itself and then trades against a market-making algorithm's active order in the book. A simple view of the HFT market would be a constant battle between market-making and liquidity-taking algorithms because they naturally take opposite sides.

In this setup, a market-making algorithm loses money when it is slow at modifying its active orders in the market. For instance, say depending on market conditions, it is quite clear that the market prices are going to go up in the short term; a market-making algorithm will try to move or cancel its sell orders if they are at risk of being executed since it no longer wants to sell at those prices. A liquidity-taking algorithm, at the same time, will try to see whether it can send a buy order to trade against a market maker's sell order at that price. In this race, if the market-making algorithm is slower than the liquidity-taking algorithms, it will not be able to modify or cancel its sell order. If the liquidity-taking algorithm is slow, it will not be able to execute against the orders it wanted to either because a different (and faster) algorithm was able to execute before it or because the market maker was able to move out of the way. This example should make it clear to you that latency directly affects trading revenue in electronic trading.

For HFT, trading applications on the client's side can receive and process market data, analyze the information, look for opportunities, and send an order out to the exchange, all within sub-10-microsecond latency, and using **Field-Programmable Gate Arrays** (**FPGAs**), can reduce that to sub-1-microsecond latency. FPGAs are special hardware chips that are re-programmable and can be used to build extremely specialized and low latency functionality directly onto the chip itself. Understanding the details and developing and using FPGAs is an advanced topic beyond this book's scope.

While we have referred to trading performance and revenue in the previous example, low latencies are also important in other aspects of electronic trading businesses that might not be immediately obvious. Obviously, trading revenues and performance are still the primary focus for trading applications; another important requirement for long-term business continuity is real-time risk management. Since each electronic market has many trading instruments and each of those continuously changes prices throughout the day, there is a tremendous amount of data that the risk management system needs to keep up with, across all the exchanges and all the products available throughout the day.

Additionally, since a firm employs HFT strategies across all these products and exchanges, the firm's position on each of these products changes rapidly all day long. A real-time risk management system needs to evaluate the firm's constantly evolving exposure across all these products against market prices to track profits and losses and risk throughout the day. The risk evaluation metrics and systems can themselves be quite complicated; for instance, in options trading, it is common to run Monte Carlo simulations to try and find worst-case risk evaluations in real time or very close to real time. Some risk management systems are also in charge of shutting down automated trading strategies if they exceed any of their risk limits. These risk systems are often added to multiple components – a central risk system, the order gateways, and the trading strategies themselves – but we will understand these details later in this book.

Achieving the lowest latencies in electronic trading

In this section, we will briefly discuss some of the higher-level ideas and concepts when it comes to implementing low latency electronic trading systems. We will, of course, revisit these with examples in greater detail as we work on building our electronic trading ecosystem in the coming chapters.

Optimizing trading server hardware

Getting powerful trading servers to support the low latency trading operations is a first step. Typically, the processing power of these servers depends on the architecture of the trading system processes, such as how many processes we expect to run, how many network resources we expect to consume, and how much memory we expect these applications to consume. Typically, low latency trading applications have high CPU usage, low kernel usage (system calls), low memory consumption, and relatively high network resource usage during busy trading periods. CPU registers, cache architecture, and capacity matter as well, and typically, we try to get larger sizes, if possible, but these can be quite expensive. Advanced considerations such as **Non-Uniform Memory Access (NUMA)**, processor instruction sets, instruction pipelines and instruction parallelism, cache hierarchy architecture details, hyperthreading, and overclocked CPUs are often considered, but those are extremely advanced optimization techniques and outside the scope of this book.

Network Interface Cards, switches, and kernel bypass

Trading servers that need to support ultra-low latency trading applications (especially ones that must read massive amounts of market data, update packets from the network, and process them) need specialized **Network Interface Cards (NICs)** and switches. The NICs preferred for such applications need to have very low latency performance, low jitter, and large buffer capacities to handle market data bursts without dropping packets. Also, optimal NICs for modern electronic trading applications support an especially low-latency path that avoids system calls and buffer copies, known as **kernel bypass**. One example is **Solarflare**, which provides **OpenOnload** and APIs such as **ef_vi** and **TCPDirect, which** bypass the kernel when using their NICs; **Exablaze** is another example of a specialized NIC that supports kernel bypass. Network switches show up in various places in the network topology, which support interconnectivity between trading servers and trading servers that are located far away from each other and between trading servers and electronic exchange servers. For network switches, one of the important considerations is the size of the buffer that the switch can support to buffer packets that need to be forwarded. Another important requirement is the latency between a switch receiving a packet and forwarding it to the correct interface known as **switching latency**. Switching latencies are generally very low, in the order of tens of hundreds of nanoseconds, but this applies to all inbound or outbound traffic going through the switch, so needs to be consistently low to not have a negative impact on trading performance.

Understanding multithreading, locks, context switches, and CPU scheduling

We have discussed the closely related but technically different concepts of bandwidth and low latency in the previous chapter. It is sometimes incorrectly assumed that having an architecture with a larger number of threads is always lower-latency, but this is not always true. Multithreading adds value in certain areas of low latency electronic trading systems, and we will make use of it in the system we build in this book. But the point here is that we need to be careful when using additional threads in HFT systems because, while adding threads generally boosts throughput for applications that need it, it can sometimes end up increasing latencies in applications as well. As we increase the number of threads, we must think about concurrency and thread safety, and if we need to use locks for synchronization and concurrency between threads, that adds additional latencies and context switches. Context switches are not free because the scheduler and OS must save the state of the thread or process being switched out and load the state of the thread or process that will be run next. Many lock implementations are built on top of kernel system calls, which are more expensive than user space routines, thus increasing the latencies in a heavily multithreaded application even further. For optimal performance, we try to get the CPU scheduler to do little to no work (i.e., processes and threads that are scheduled to run are never context switched out and keep running in user space). Additionally, it is quite common to pin specific threads and processes to specific CPU cores, which eliminates context switching and the OS needing to find free cores to schedule tasks, and additionally, improves memory access efficiency.

Dynamically allocating memory and managing memory

Dynamic memory allocation is a request for memory blocks of arbitrary sizes made at runtime. At a very high level, dynamic memory allocations and deallocations are handled by the OS by looking through a list of free memory blocks and trying to allocate a contiguous block as large as the program requested. Dynamic memory deallocations are handled by appending the freed blocks to the list of free blocks managed by the OS. Searching through this list can incur higher and higher latencies as the program runs through the day and memory gets increasingly fragmented. Additionally, if dynamic memory allocations and deallocations are on the same critical path, then they incur an additional overhead every single time. This is one of the major reasons we discussed before that led us to choose C++ as our preferred language for building low latency and resource-constrained applications. We will explore the performance impact of dynamic memory allocation and techniques to avoid it during later chapters in this book as we build our own trading system.

Static versus dynamic linking and compile time versus runtime

Linking is the compilation or translation step in the process of converting high-level programming language source code into machine code for the target architecture. Linking ties together pieces of code that might be in different libraries – these can be libraries internal to the code base or external standalone libraries. During the linking step, we have two choices: **static linking** or **dynamic linking**.

Dynamic linking is when the linker does not incorporate the code from libraries into the final binary at linking time. Instead, when the main application requires code from the shared libraries for the first time, then the resolution is performed at runtime. Obviously, there is a particularly large extra cost incurred at runtime the first time the shared library code is called. The bigger downside is that since the compiler and linker do not incorporate the code at compilation and linking time, they are unable to perform possible optimizations, resulting in an application that can be inefficient overall.

Static linking is when the linker arranges the application code and the code for the library dependencies into a single binary executable file. The upside here is that the libraries are already linked at compile time so there is no need for the OS to find and resolve the dependencies at runtime startup by loading the dependent libraries before the application starts executing. The even bigger upside is that this creates an opportunity for the program to be super-optimized at compile and linking time to yield lower latencies at runtime. The downside to static linking over dynamic linking is that the application binary is much larger and each application binary that relies on the same set of external libraries has a copy of all the external library code compiled and linked into the binary. It is common for ultra-low latency electronic trading systems to link all dependent libraries statically to minimize runtime performance latencies.

We have discussed compile time versus runtime processing in the previous chapter, and that approach tries to move the maximum amount of processing to the compilation step instead of at runtime. This increases compile times, but the runtime performance latencies are much lower because a lot of the work is already done at compile time. We will look at this aspect in detail specifically for C++ in the next few chapters and throughout the course of this book as we build our electronic trading system in C++.

Summary

In this chapter, we looked at different low latency applications in different business areas. The goals were to understand how low latency applications impact businesses in different areas and the similarities that some of these applications share, such as the hardware requirements and optimization, software design, performance optimization, and different revolutionary technologies being used to achieve these performance requirements.

The first applications we looked at in detail were real-time, low latency, online video streaming applications. We discussed different concepts and investigated where high latencies come from, and how that affects performance and businesses. Finally, we discussed different technologies and solutions, and platforms that facilitate low latency video streaming applications to be a success.

The next applications we looked at had a lot of overlap with video streaming applications – offline and online video gaming applications. We introduced some additional concepts and considerations that apply to offline and online gaming applications and explained their impact on the user experience and thus, ultimately, on business performance. We discussed a myriad of things to consider when trying to maximize the performance of these applications, ranging from a lot of factors that apply to live video streaming applications to additional hardware and software considerations for gaming applications.

We then briefly discussed the requirement of low latency performance when it comes to IoT devices and retail data collection and analysis applications. This is a relatively new and fast-improving technology and is likely to continue growing aggressively over the next decade. Lots of research and advancements are being made for IoT devices and we find new business ideas and use cases as we make progress here. We discussed how 5G wireless and edge computing technologies are breaking the old paradigm of central data storage and processing and why that is critical for IoT devices and applications.

The last applications we also discussed briefly in this chapter were low latency electronic trading and HFT applications. We kept the discussion short and focused on the higher-level ideas when it comes to maximizing the performance of low latency and ultra-low latency electronic trading applications. We did so because we will build a full end-to-end C++ low latency electronic trading ecosystem from scratch in the remaining chapters of this book. When we do that, we will discuss, understand, and implement all the different low latency C++ concepts and ideas with examples and performance data, so there is a lot more to come on this application.

We will move on from this discussion of different low latency applications to a more in-depth discussion of the C++ programming language. We will discuss the correct approach to using C++ for low latency performance, the different modern C++ features, and how to unleash the power of modern C++ compiler optimizations.

3

Exploring C++ Concepts from A Low-Latency Application's Perspective

In this chapter, we assume that the reader has an intermediate level of understanding of C++ programming concepts, features, and so on. We will discuss how to approach low-latency application development in C++. We will move on to discussing what C++ features to avoid specifically when it comes to low-latency applications. We will then discuss the key C++ features that make it perfect for low-latency applications and how we will use them in the rest of the book. We will conclude by discussing how to maximize compiler optimizations and which C++ compiler flags are important for low-latency applications.

In this chapter, we will cover the following topics:

- Approaching low-latency application development in C++
- Avoiding pitfalls and leveraging C++ features to minimize application latency
- Maximizing C++ compiler optimization parameters

Let us start by discussing the higher-level ideas when it comes to approaching low-latency application development in C++ in the next section.

Technical requirements

All the code for this book can be found in the GitHub repository for this book at `https://github.com/PacktPublishing/Building-Low-Latency-Applications-with-CPP`. The source code for this chapter is in the Chapter3 directory in the repository.

Approaching low-latency application development in C++

In this section, we will discuss the higher-level ideas to keep in mind when trying to build low-latency applications in C++. Overall, the ideas are to understand the architecture that your application runs on, your application use cases that are latency-sensitive, the programming language of your choice (C++ in this case), how to work with the development tools (the compiler, linker, etc.) and how to measure application performance in practice to understand which parts of the application to optimize first.

Coding for correctness first, optimizing second

For low-latency applications, correct behavior of the application under different use cases and scenarios and robust handling of edge conditions is still the primary focus. A fast application that does not do what we need is useless, so the best approach when it comes to developing a low-latency application is to first code for correctness, not speed. Once the application works correctly, only then the focus should be shifted to optimizing the critical parts of the application while maintaining correctness. This ensures that developers spend time focusing on the correct parts to optimize because it is common to find that our intuition on which pieces are critical to performance does not match what happens in practice. Optimizing the code can also take significantly longer than coding for correctness, so it is important to optimize the most important things first.

Designing optimal data structures and algorithms

Designing custom data structures that are optimal for the application's use cases is an important part of building low-latency applications. A good amount of thought needs to be put into each data structure used in the critical parts of the application in terms of scalability, robustness, and performance under the use cases and data encountered *in practice*. It is important to understand why we mention the term *in practice* here because different data structure choices will perform better under different use cases and input data even if the different data structures themselves have the same output or behavior. Before we discuss an example of different possible data structures and algorithms to solve the same problem, let us quickly review Big-O notation. Big-O notation is used to describe the asymptotic worst-case time complexity of performing a certain task. The term asymptotic here is used to describe the fact that we discuss cases where we measure the performance over a theoretically infinite (in practice an exceptionally large) number of data points. The asymptotic performance eliminates all the constant terms and describes the performance only as a function of the number of input data elements.

A simple example of using different data structures to solve the same problem would be searching for an entry in a container by a key value. We can solve this either by using a hash map implementation that has an expected *amortized* complexity of O(1) or using an array that has a complexity of O(n), where n is the number of elements in the container. While on paper it might appear that the hash map is clearly the way to go, other factors such as the number of elements, the complexity of applying the hash function to the keys, and so on might change which data structure is the way to go. In this case, for a handful of elements, the array solution is faster due to better cache performance, while for many elements, the hash map solution is better. Here, we chose a suboptimal algorithm because the underlying data structure for the suboptimal algorithm performed better in practice due to cache performance.

Another slightly different example would be using lookup tables over recomputing values for some mathematical functions, say, trigonometric functions. While it makes complete sense that looking up the result in a precomputed lookup table *should* always be faster compared to performing some calculations, this might not always be true. For instance, if the lookup table is very large, then the cost of evaluating a floating-point expression might be less than the cost of getting a cache miss and reading the lookup table value from the main memory. The overall application performance might also be better if accessing the lookup table from the main memory leads to a lot of cache pollution, leading to performance degradation in other parts of the application code.

Being mindful of the processor

Modern processors have a lot of architectural and functional details that a low-latency application developer should understand, especially a C++ developer since it allows very low-level control. Modern processors have multiple cores, larger and specialized register banks, pipelined instruction processing where instructions needed next are prefetched while executing the current one, instruction level parallelism, branch predictions, extended instruction sets to facilitate faster and specialized processing, and so on. The better the application developer understands these aspects of the processor on which their applications will run, the better they can avoid sub-optimal code and/or compilation choices and make sure that the compiled machine code is optimal for their target architecture. At the very least, the developer should instruct the compiler to output code for their specific target architecture using compiler optimization flags, but we will discuss that topic later in this chapter.

Understanding the cache and memory access costs

Typically, a lot of effort is put into the design and development of data structures and algorithms when it comes to low-latency application development from the perspective of reducing the amount of work done or the number of instructions executed. While this is the correct approach, in this section, we would like to point out that thinking about cache and memory accesses is equally important.

We saw in the previous sub-section, *Designing optimal data structures and algorithms*, that it is common for data structures and algorithms that are sub-optimal on paper to outperform ones that are optimal on paper. A large reason behind that can be the higher cache and memory access costs for the optimal solution outweighing the time saved because of the reduced number of instructions the processor needs to execute. Another way to think about this is that even though the amount of work from the perspective of the number of algorithmic steps is less, in practice, it takes longer to finish with the modern processor, cache, and memory access architectures today.

Let us quickly review the memory hierarchy in a modern computer architecture. Note that details of what we will recap here can be found in our other book, *Developing High-Frequency Trading Systems*. The key points here are that the memory hierarchy works in such a way that if the CPU cannot find the data or instruction it needs next in the register, it goes to the L0 cache, and if it cannot find it there, goes to the L1 cache, L2, other caches, and so on, then goes to the main memory in that order. Note that the storage is accessed from fastest to slowest, which also happens to be least amount of space to most amount of space. The art of effective low-latency and cache-friendly application development relies on writing code that is cognizant of code and data access patterns to maximize the likelihood of finding data in the fastest form of storage possible. This relies on maximizing the concepts of **temporal locality** and **spatial locality**. These terms mean that data accessed recently is likely to be in the cache and data next to what we just accessed is likely to be in the cache, respectively. The following diagram visually lays out the register, cache, and memory banks and provides some data on access times from the CPU. Note that there is a good amount of variability in the access times depending on the hardware and the constant improvements being made to technologies. The key takeaway here should be that there is a significant increase in access times as we go from CPU registers to cache banks to the main memory.

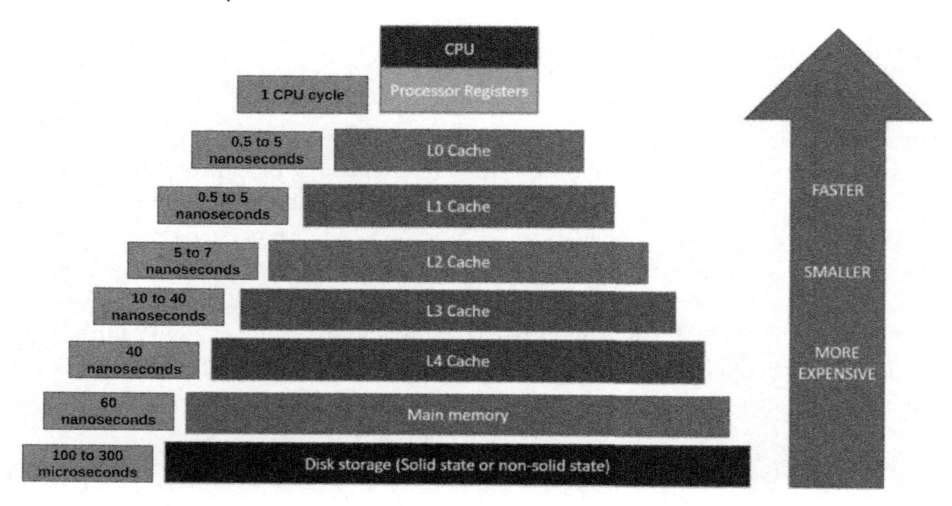

Figure 3.1 – The hierarchy of memory in modern computer architectures.

I would advise you to think carefully about the cache and memory access patterns for the algorithm locally, as well as the entire application globally, to make sure that your source code optimizes cache and memory access patterns, which will boost overall application performance. If you have a function that executes very quickly when it is called but causes a lot of cache pollution, that will degrade the complete application's performance because other components will incur additional cache miss penalties. In such a case, we have failed in our objective of having an application that performs optimally even though we might have managed to make this function perform optimally locally.

Understanding how C++ features work under the hood

When developing low-latency applications, it is very important that the developers have an extremely good understanding of how the high-level language abstractions work at a lower level or "under the hood." For applications that are not latency-sensitive, this is perhaps not as important since if the application behaves the way the developer intends it to, the extremely low-level details of how their source code achieves that is not relevant.

For low-latency applications in C++, the more knowledge the developer has of how their program gets compiled into machine code, the better they can use the programming language to achieve low-latency performance. A lot of high-level abstractions available in C++ improve the ease and speed of development, robustness and safety, maintainability, software design elegance, and so on, but not all of them might be optimal when it comes to low-latency applications.

Many C++ features, such as dynamic polymorphism, dynamic memory allocation, and exception handling, are great additions to the language for most applications. However, these are best avoided or used sparingly or used in a specific manner when it comes to low-latency applications since they have larger overheads.

Conversely, traditional programming practices suggest the developer break everything down into numerous very small functions for reusability; use recursive functions when applicable; use **Object-Oriented Programming** (**OOP**) principles, such as inheritance and virtual functions; always use smart pointers instead of raw pointers; and so on. These principles are sensible for most applications, but for low-latency applications, these need to be evaluated and used carefully because they might add non-trivial amounts of overhead and latency.

The key takeaway here is that it is important for low-latency application developers to understand each one of these C++ features very well to understand how they are implemented in machine code and what impact they have on the hardware resources and how they perform in practice.

Leveraging the C++ compiler

The modern C++ compiler is truly a fascinating piece of software. There is an immense amount of effort invested into building these compilers to be robust and correct. A lot of effort is also made to make them very intelligent in terms of the transformations and optimizations they apply to the developer's high-level source code. Understanding how the compiler translates the developer's code into machine instructions, how it tries to optimize the code, and when it fails is important for low-latency application developers looking to squeeze as much performance out of their applications as possible. We will discuss the workings of the compiler and optimization opportunities extensively in this chapter so that we can learn to work with the compiler instead of against it when it comes to optimizing our final application's representation (machine code executable).

Measuring and improving performance

We mentioned that the ideal application development journey involves first building the application for correctness and then worrying about optimizing it after that. We also mentioned that it is not uncommon for a developer's intuition to be incorrect when it comes to identifying performance bottlenecks.

Finally, we also mentioned that the task of optimizing an application can take significantly longer than the task of developing it to perform correctly. For that reason, it is advisable that before embarking on an optimization journey, the developer try to run the application under practical constraints and inputs to check performance. It is important to add instrumentation to the application in different forms to measure the performance and find bottlenecks to understand and prioritize the optimization opportunities. This is also an important step since as the application evolves, measuring and improving performance continues to be part of the workflow, that is, measuring and improving performance is a part of the application's evolution. In the last section of this book, *Analyzing and improving performance*, we will discuss this idea with a real case study to understand this better.

Avoiding pitfalls and leveraging C++ features to minimize application latency

In this section, we will look at different C++ features that, if used correctly, can minimize application latency. We will also discuss the details of using these features in a manner that optimizes application performance throughout this sub-section. Now, let us start learning about how to use these features correctly to maximize application performance and avoid the pitfalls to minimize latency. Note that all the code snippets for this chapter are in the `Chapter3` directory in the GitHub repository for this book.

Choosing storage

Local variables created within a function are stored on the stack by default and the stack memory is also used to store function return values. Assuming no large objects are created, the same range of stack storage space is reused a lot, resulting in great cache performance due to locality of reference.

Register variables are closest to the processor and are the fastest possible form of storage available. They are extremely limited, and the compiler will try to use them for the local variables that are used the most, another reason to prefer *local variables*.

Static variables are inefficient from the perspective of cache performance since that memory cannot be re-used for other variables and accessing static variables is likely a small fraction of all memory accesses. So, it is best to avoid static variables as well as global variables, which have similarly inefficient cache performance.

The `volatile` keyword instructs the compiler to disable a lot of optimizations that rely on the assumption that the variable value does not change without the compiler's knowledge. This should only ever be used carefully in multi-threaded use cases since it prevents optimizations such as storing the variables in registers and force-flushing them to the main memory from the cache every time the value changes.

Dynamically allocated memory is inefficient to allocate and deallocate and, depending on how it is used, can suffer from poor cache performance. More on dynamically allocated memory inefficiencies will be discussed later in this section in the *Dynamically allocating memory* sub-section.

An example of C++ optimization technique that leverages storage choice optimization is **Small String Optimization (SSO)**. SSO attempts to use local storage for short strings if they are smaller than a certain size (typically 32 characters) instead of the default of dynamically allocated memory for string content storage.

In summary, you should think carefully about where the data gets stored during the execution of your program, especially in the critical sections. We should try to use registers and local variables as much as possible and optimize cache performance. Use volatile, static, global, and dynamic memory only when necessary or when it does not affect performance on the critical path.

Choosing data types

C++ integer operations are typically super-fast as long as the size of the largest register is larger than the integer size. Integers smaller or larger than the register size are sometimes slightly slower than regular integers. This is because the processor must use multiple registers for a single variable and apply some carry-over logic for large integers. Conversely, handling integers smaller than a register size is usually handled by using a regular register, zeroing out the upper bits, using only the lower bits, and possibly invoking a type conversion operation. Note that the extra overhead is very small and generally not something to worry about. Signed and unsigned integers are equally fast, but in some cases unsigned integers are faster than signed integers. The only cases where signed integer operations are a tiny bit slower is where the processor needs to check and adjust for the sign bit. Again, the extra overhead is extremely small when present and not necessarily something we need to worry about in most cases. We will look at the cost of different operations – addition, subtraction, comparison, bit operations, and so on typically take a single clock cycle. Multiplication operations take longer, and division operations take longest.

Using casting and conversion operations

Converting between signed and unsigned integers is free. Converting integers from a smaller size into a larger one can take a single clock cycle but sometimes can be optimized to be free. Converting integer sizes down from a larger size into a smaller one has no additional cost.

Conversion between floats, doubles, and long doubles is typically free except under very few conditions. Conversion of signed and unsigned integers into floats or doubles takes a few clock cycles. Conversion from unsigned integers can take longer than signed integers.

Conversion from floating-point values into integers can be extremely expensive – 50 to 100 clock cycles or more. If these conversions are on the critical path, it is common for low-latency application developers to try and make these more efficient by enabling special instruction sets, avoiding or refactoring these conversions, if possible, using special assembly language rounding implementations, and so on.

Converting pointers from one type into another type is completely free; whether the conversions are safe or not is the developer's responsibility. Type-casting a pointer to an object to a pointer to a different object violates the strict aliasing rule stating that *two pointers of different types cannot point to the same memory location*, which really means that it is possible the compiler might not use the same register to store the two different pointers, even though they point to the same address. Remember that the CPU registers are the fastest form of storage available to the processor but are extremely limited in storage capacity. So, when an extra register gets used to store the same variable, it is an inefficient use of the registers and negatively impacts performance overall.

An example of type-casting a pointer to be a different object is presented here. This example uses a conversion from `double *` into `uint64_t *` and modifies the sign bit using the `uint64_t` pointer. This is nothing more than a convoluted and more efficient method of achieving `x = -std::abs(x)` but demonstrates how this violates the strict aliasing rule (`strict_alias.cpp` in `Chapter3` on GitHub):

```
#include <cstdio>
#include <cstdint>
int main() {
  double x = 100;
  const auto orig_x = x;
  auto x_as_ui = (uint64_t *) (&x);
  *x_as_ui |= 0x8000000000000000;
  printf("orig_x:%0.2f x:%0.2f &x:%p &x_as_ui:%p\n",
      orig_x, x, &x, x_as_ui);
}
```

It yields something like this:

```
orig_x:100.00 x:-100.00 &x:0x7fff1e6b00d0 &x_as_ui:0x7fff1e6b00d0
```

Using modern C++ casting operations, `const_cast`, `static_cast`, and `reinterpret_cast` do not incur any additional overhead when used. However, when it comes to `dynamic_cast`, which converts an object of a certain class into an object of a different class, this can be expensive at runtime. `dynamic_cast` checks whether the conversion is valid using **Run-Time Type Information (RTTI)**, which is slow and possibly throws an exception if the conversion is invalid – this makes it safer but increases latency.

Optimizing numerical operations

Typically, double-precision calculations take about the same time as single-precision operations. In general, for integers and floating values, additions are fast, multiplications are slightly more expensive than additions, and division is quite a bit more expensive than multiplication. Integer multiplications take around 5 clock cycles and floating-point multiplications take around 8 clock cycles. Integer additions take a single clock cycle on most processors and floating-point additions take around 2-5 clock cycles. Floating-point divisions and integer divisions both take about the same amount of time around 20-80 clock cycles, depending on the processor and depending on whether it has special floating-point operations or not.

Compilers will try to rewrite and reduce expressions wherever possible to prefer faster operations such as rewriting divisions to be multiplications by reciprocals. Multiplication and division by values that are powers of 2 are significantly faster because the compiler rewrites them to be bit-shift operations, which are much faster. There is additional overhead when the compiler uses this optimization since it must handle signs and rounding errors. Obviously, this only applies when the expressions involve values that can be determined to be powers of 2 at compile time. When dealing with multi-dimensional arrays, for instance, the compiler converts multiplications into bitwise shift operations wherever possible.

Mixing single- and double-precision operations in the same expression and expressions involving floating and integer values should be avoided because they implicitly force type conversions. We saw before that type conversions are not always free, so these expressions can take longer to compute than we would guess. For instance, when mixing single- and double-precision values in an expression, the single-precision values must first be converted into double-precision values, which can consume a few clock cycles before the expression is computed. Similarly, when mixing integers and floating-point values in an expression, either the floating-point value has to be converted into an integer or the integer must be converted into a floating-point value, which adds a few clock cycles to the final calculation time.

Optimizing boolean and bitwise operations

Boolean operations such as **logical AND** (&&) and **logical OR** (||) are evaluated such that for &&, if the first operand is false, then the second one is not evaluated, and, for ||, if the first operand is true, then the second one is not evaluated. A simple optimization technique is to order the operands of && in order from lowest to highest probability of being evaluated to true.

Similarly, for ||, ordering the operands from highest to lowest probability of being true is best. This technique is referred to as **short-circuiting** the boolean operations and it not only reduces the number of times these operands are evaluated but also improves branch prediction. This technique cannot be used if the order of the operands is important to the program, for instance, if we require that for an && boolean operation, the second operand should not be evaluated if the first one is false. Or for an || boolean operation, the second operand should not be evaluated if the first one is true, and so on.

Another aspect of using boolean variables is understanding the way they are stored. Boolean variables are stored as 8 bits and not a single bit, as might match our intuition from the way they are used. What this means is that operations involving boolean values have to be implemented such that any 8-bit values other than 0 are treated as 1, which leads to implementations with branches in them with comparisons against 0. For example, the c = a && b; expression is implemented as follows:

```
if(a != 0) {
  if(b != 0) {
    c = true;
  } else {
    c = false;
  }
}
```

```
} else {
  c = false;
}
```

If there was a guarantee that a and b could not have values other than 0 or 1, then `c = a && b;` would simply be `c = a & b;`, which is super-fast and avoids branching and branching-related overheads.

Bitwise operations can also help speed up other cases of boolean expressions by treating each bit of an integer as a single boolean variable and then rewriting expressions involving comparisons of multiple booleans with bit-masking operations. For instance, take an expression such as this, where `market_state` is `uint64_t` and `PreOpen`, `Opening`, and `Trading` are enum values that reflect different market states:

```
if(market_state == PreOpen ||
   market_state == Opening ||
   market_state == Trading) {
  // do something...
}
```

It can be rewritten as follows:

```
if(market_state & (PreOpen | Opening | Trading)) {
  // do something...
}
```

If the enum values are chosen such that each bit in the `market_state` variable represents a state of true or false, one choice would be for the `PreOpen`, `Opening`, and `Trading` enums to be set to `0x001`, `0x010`, and `0x100`.

Initializing, destroying, copying, and moving objects

Constructors and destructors for developer-defined classes should be kept as light and efficient as possible since they can be called without the developer expecting it. Keeping these methods super-simple and small also allows the compiler to *inline* these methods to improve performance. The same applies to copy and move constructors, which should be kept simple, with using move constructors preferred over using copy constructors wherever possible. In many cases where high levels of optimization are required, the developer can delete the default constructor and the copy constructor to make sure unnecessary or unexpected copies of their objects are not being made.

Using references and pointers

A lot of C++ features are built around implicitly accessing class members through the `this` pointer, so access through references and pointers occurs very frequently regardless of whether the developer explicitly does so or not. Accessing objects through pointers and references is mostly as efficient as directly accessing the objects. This is because most modern processors have support to efficiently fetch the pointer values and dereference them. The big disadvantage of using references and pointers is that they take up an extra register for the pointer themselves and the other one consists of the extra dereference instructions to access the variable pointed to by the pointer value.

Pointer arithmetic is just as fast as integer arithmetic except computing the differences between pointers requires a division by the size of the object, which can potentially be very slow. This is not necessarily a problem if the size of the type of object is a multiple of 2, which is quite often the case with primitive types and optimized structures.

Smart pointers are an important feature of modern C++ that offers safety, life cycle management, automatic memory management, and clear ownership control for dynamically allocated objects. Smart pointers such as std::unique_ptr, std::shared_ptr, and std::weak_ptr use the **Resource Acquisition is Initialization** (**RAII**) C++ paradigm. There is an extra cost associated with std::shared_ptr due to the reference counting overhead but generally, smart pointers are expected to add very little overhead to the entire program unless there are a lot of them.

Another important aspect of using pointers is that it can prevent compiler optimizations due to **Pointer Aliasing**. This is because, while it may be obvious to the user, at compile time, the compiler cannot guarantee that two pointer variables in the code will never point to the same memory address. Under those theoretical possible cases of pointer aliasing, some compiler optimizations would change the outcome of code; hence, those optimizations are disabled. For instance, the following code would prevent the compiler from applying loop-invariant code motion. This is despite there being no overlap between pointers a[0] to a[n-1] and b. That means that this optimization is valid because *b is a constant for the entire loop and can be computed once:

```
void func(int* a, int* b, int n) {
  for(int i = 0; i < n; ++i) {
    a[i] = *b;
  }
}
```

There are really two options for instructing the compiler to assume no pointer aliasing in cases where the developer is confident that there is no behavior that is dependent on the side effects of pointer aliasing. Use __restrict__, or __restrict, a similar specifier keyword, for your compiler on the function arguments or functions to specify no aliasing on the pointers. However, this is a hint, and the compiler does not guarantee that this will make a difference. The other option is to specify the -fstrict-aliasing compiler option to assume no pointer aliasing globally. The following code block demonstrates the use of the restrict specifier for the preceding func() function (pointer_alias.cpp in Chapter3 on GitHub):

```
void func(int *__restrict a, int *__restrict b, int n) {
  for (int i = 0; i < n; ++i) {
    a[i] = *b;
  }
}
```

Optimizing jumping and branching

In modern processor pipelines, instructions and data are fetched and decoded in stages. When there is a branch instruction, the processor tries to predict which of the branches will be taken and fetches and decodes instructions from that branch. However, when the processor has mispredicted the branch taken, it takes 10 or more clock cycles before it detects the misprediction. After that, it must spend a bunch of clock cycles fetching the instructions and data from the correct branch and evaluate it. The key takeaway here is that a branch misprediction wastes many clock cycles every time it happens.

Let us discuss some of the most used forms of jumps and branches in C++:

- `if-else` branching is the most common thing that comes to mind when discussing branching. Long chains of `if-else` conditionals are best avoided, if possible, because it is difficult to predict these correctly as they grow. Keeping the number of conditions small and trying to structure them so they are more predictable is the way to optimize them.
- `for` and `while` loops are also types of branching that are typically predicted well if the loop count is relatively small. This, of course, gets complicated with nested loops and loops containing hard-to-predict exit conditions.
- `switch` statements are branches with multiple jump targets, so they can be very difficult to predict. When label values are widely spread out, the compiler must use `switch` statements as a long sequence of `if-else` branching trees. An optimization technique that works well with `switch` statements is to assign case label values that increment by one and are arranged in ascending order because there is a very good chance they will get implemented as jump tables, which is significantly more efficient.

Replacing branching with table lookups containing different output values in the source code is a good optimization wherever possible. We can also create a table of function pointers indexed by jump conditions but beware that function pointers are not necessarily much more efficient than the branching itself.

Loop unrolling can also help with minimizing branching if there are branches within a loop that are difficult to predict and can lead to a lot of branch mispredictions. We will discuss loop unrolling in detail later, but for now, let us briefly introduce the idea. Loop unrolling duplicates the body of the loop multiple times in order to avoid the checks and branching that determine whether a loop should continue. The compiler will attempt to unroll loops if possible, but it is often best if the developer does it themself. For example, consider a simple loop such as this with a low loop counter (`loop_unroll.cpp` in `Chapter3` on GitHub):

```
int a[5]; a[0] = 0;
  for(int i = 1; i < 5; ++i)
    a[i] = a[i-1] + 1;
```

The compiler can unroll the loop into the following code shown here. Note that it is more than likely that for such a simple example, the compiler will use additional optimizations and reduce this loop even further. But for now, we limit ourselves to only present the impact of loop unrolling:

```
int a[5];
a[0] = 0;
a[1] = a[0] + 1; a[2] = a[1] + 1;
a[3] = a[2] + 1; a[4] = a[3] + 1;
```

Compile-time branching using an `if constexpr (condition-expression) {}` format can obviously help a lot by moving the overhead of branching to compile time, but this requires that `condition-expression` be something that can be evaluated at compile time. This is technically part of the **Compile time Polymorphism** or **Template Metaprogramming** paradigm, which we will discuss more in the *Using compile-time polymorphism* sub-section in this section.

It is possible to provide the compiler with branch prediction hints in the source code since the developer has a better idea of the expected use cases. These do not make a significant difference overall since modern processors are good at learning which branches are most likely to be taken after a few iterations through the branches. For GNU C++, these are traditionally implemented as follows using `__builtin_expect`:

```
#define LIKELY_CONDITION(x)    __builtin_expect(!!(x), 1)
#define UNLIKELY_CONDITION (x) __builtin_expect(!!(x), 0)
```

For C++ 20, these are standardized as the `[[likely]]` and `[[unlikely]]` attributes.

Calling functions efficiently

There are numerous overheads associated with calling functions – the overhead of fetching the function address and jumping to it, passing the parameters to it and returning the results, setting up the stack frame, saving and restoring registers, exception handling, possible latency in the code cache misses, and so on.

When breaking up the code base into functions, some general things to consider to maximize the performance would be the following.

Thinking before creating an excessive number of functions

Functions should only be created if there is enough re-usability to justify them. The criteria for creating functions should be logical program flow and re-usability and not the length of code because, as we saw, calling functions is not free, and creating excessive functions is not a good idea.

Grouping related functions together

Class member and non-class member functions typically get assigned memory addresses in the order in which they are created, so it is generally a good idea to group together performance-critical functions that call each other frequently or operate on the same datasets. This facilitates better code and data cache performance.

Link Time Optimization (LTO) or Whole Program Optimization (WPO)

When writing performance-critical functions, it is important to place them in the same module where they are used if possible. Doing so unlocks a lot of compiler optimizations, the most important of which is the ability to inline the function call.

Using the `static` keyword to declare a function does the equivalent of putting it in an **anonymous namespace**, which makes it local to the translation unit it is used in. Specifying the `inline` keyword achieves this as well, but we will explore that in the next section.

Specifying WPO and LTO parameters for the compiler instructs it to treat the entire code base as a single module and enable compiler optimizations across modules. Without enabling these compiler options, optimizations occur across functions in the same module but not between modules which can be quite sub-optimal for large code bases which typically have a lot of source files and modules.

Macros, inline functions, and template metaprogramming

Macro expressions are a pre-processor directive and are expanded even before compilation begins. This eliminates the overhead associated with calling and returning from functions at runtime. Macros have several disadvantages though, such as namespace collision, cryptic compilation errors, unnecessary evaluation of conditions and expressions, and so on.

Inlined functions, whether they are part of a class or not, are similar to macros but solve a lot of the problems associated with macros. Inlined functions are expanded at their usage during compilation and link times and eliminate the overhead associated with function calls.

Using template metaprogramming, it is possible to move a lot of the computation load from runtime to compile time. This involves using partial and full template specialization and recursive loop templates. However, template metaprogramming can be clumsy and difficult to use, compile, and debug and should only really be used where the performance improvements justify the increased development discomfort. We will explore templates and template metaprogramming shortly.

Avoiding function pointers

Calling a function through a function pointer has a larger overhead than directly calling the function. For one, if the pointer changes, then the compiler cannot predict which function will be called and cannot pre-fetch the instructions and data. Additionally, this also prevents a lot of compiler optimizations since these cannot be inlined at compile time.

The `std::function` is a much more powerful construct available in modern C++ but should be used only if necessary since there is potential for misuse and extra overhead of a few clock cycles compared to direct inlined functions. `std::bind` is another construct to be very careful about when using and should also only be used if absolutely necessary. If `std::function` must be used, try to see whether you can use a lambda expression instead of `std::bind` since that is typically a few clock cycles faster to invoke. Overall, be careful when using `std::function` and/or `std::bind` since a lot of developers are surprised that these constructs can perform virtual function calls and invoke dynamic memory allocations under the hood.

Passing function parameters by reference or pointers

For primitive types, passing parameters by value is super-efficient. For composite types that are function parameters, the preferred way of passing them would be const references. The **constness** means that the object cannot be modified and allows the compiler to apply optimizations based on that and the reference allows the compiler to possibly inline the object itself. If the function needs to modify the object passed to it, then obviously a non-const reference or pointer is the way to go.

Returning simple types from functions

Functions that return primitive types are very efficient. Returning composite types is much more inefficient and can lead to a couple of copies being created in some cases, which is quite sub-optimal especially if these are large and/or have slow copy constructors and assignment operators. When the compiler can apply **Return Value Optimization** (**RVO**), it can eliminate the temporary copy created and just write the result to the caller's object directly. The optimal way to return a composite type is to have the caller create an object of that type and pass it to the function using a reference or a pointer for the function to modify.

Let us look at an example to explain what happens with RVO; let us say we have the following function definition and call to the function (`rvo.cpp` in `Chapter3` on GitHub):

```cpp
#include <iostream>

struct LargeClass {
  int i;
  char c;
  double d;
};

auto rvoExample(int i, char c, double d) {
  return LargeClass{i, c, d};
}

int main() {
```

```
    LargeClass lc_obj = rvoExample(10, 'c', 3.14);
}
```

With RVO, instead of creating a temporary `LargeClass` object inside `rvoExample()` and then copying it into the `LargeClass lc_obj` object in `main()`, the `rvoExample()` function can directly update `lc_obj` and avoid the temporary object and copy.

Avoiding recursive functions or replacing them with a loop

Recursive functions are inefficient because of the overhead of calling themselves repeatedly. Additionally, recursive functions can go very deep in the stack and take up a lot of stack space, and, in worst-case scenarios, even cause a stack overflow. This causes a lot of cache misses due to the new memory areas and makes predicting the return address difficult and inefficient. In such cases, replacing recursive functions with a loop is significantly more efficient since it avoids a lot of the cache performance issues that recursive functions encounter.

Using bitfields

Bitfields are just structs where the developer controls the number of bits assigned to each member. This makes the data as compact as possible and greatly improves cache performance for many objects. Bitfield members are also usually modified using bitmask operations, which are very efficient, as we have seen before. Accessing the members of bitfields is less efficient than accessing the members of a regular structure, so it is important to carefully assess whether using bitfields and improving the cache **performance** is worthwhile.

Using runtime polymorphism

Runtime polymorphism is an elegant solution when the member function that needs to be called will be determined at runtime instead of compile time. `Virtual` functions are the key to implementing runtime polymorphism, but they have an additional overhead compared to non-virtual function calls.

Usually, the compiler cannot determine at compile time which implementation of a virtual function will be called. At runtime, this causes many branch mispredictions unless the same version of the virtual function gets called most of the time. It is possible for the compiler to determine the virtual function implementation called at compile time using **devirtualization**, but this is not possible in many cases. The primary problem with `virtual` functions is that the compiler cannot apply many of the compile-time optimizations in the presence of `virtual` functions, the most important one being inlining.

Inheritance in C++ is another important OOP concept but be careful when the inheritance structure gets too complicated since there are many subtle inefficiencies that can be introduced. Child classes inherit every single data member from their parent class, so the size of the child classes can become quite large and lead to poor cache performance.

In general, instead of inheriting from multiple parent classes, we can consider using the **Composition** paradigm, where the child class has members of different parent class types instead of inheriting from them. This avoids complications related to accessing child class objects using different parent class pointers, offsets of the data members and methods in the child classes, and so on. The following example (composition.cpp in Chapter3 on GitHub) builds OrderBook, which basically holds a vector of Order objects, in two different ways. The benefit (if used properly) of the inheritance model is that it now inherits all the methods that std::vector provides while the composition model would need to implement them. In this example, we demonstrate this by implementing a size() method in CompositionOrderBook, which calls the size() method on the std::vector object, while InheritanceOrderBook inherits it directly from std::vector:

```cpp
#include <cstdio>
#include <vector>
struct Order { int id; double price; };

class InheritanceOrderBook : public std::vector<Order> { };

class CompositionOrderBook {
  std::vector<Order> orders_;
public:
  auto size() const noexcept {
    return orders_.size();
  }
};

int main() {
  InheritanceOrderBook i_book;
  CompositionOrderBook c_book;
  printf("InheritanceOrderBook::size():%lu Composi
      tionOrderBook:%lu\n", i_book.size(), c_book.size());
}
```

C++ **RTTI** adds a bunch of extra metadata to each class object to extract and use additional information at runtime. This makes all instances of these objects inefficient, and it is best to turn off RTTI support at the compiler level for low-latency applications. If the developer needs to attach specific metadata to specific classes or objects, it is best to customize the implementation itself instead of adding overhead to the entire application. dynamic_cast, as we discussed before, usually uses the RTTI information to perform the cast and should also be avoided.

Using compile-time polymorphism

Let us discuss an alternative to using runtime polymorphism, which is to use templates to achieve compile-time polymorphism. Templates are similar to macros, meaning they are expanded before compilation, and because of this, not only is the runtime overhead eliminated but it also unlocks additional compiler optimization opportunities. Templates make the compiler machine code super-efficient but they come at the cost of additional source code complexity, as well as larger executable sizes.

The **Curiously Recurring Template Pattern** (**CRTP**) facilitates compile-time polymorphism. Note that the syntax here is more complicated than using runtime polymorphism using `virtual` functions and the base class and derived class relationships are similar but slightly different using the *CRTP*. A simple example of converting runtime polymorphism into compile-time polymorphism is shown here. In both cases, the derived classes, `SpecificRuntimeExample` and `SpecificCRTPExample`, override the `placeOrder()` method. The code discussed in this sub-section is in the `crtp.cpp` file in the GitHub repo for this book under the `Chapter3` directory.

Runtime polymorphism using virtual functions

Here, we have an example of implementing runtime polymorphism where `SpecificRuntimeExample` derives `RuntimeExample` and overrides the `placeOrder()` method:

```
#include <cstdio>
class RuntimeExample {
public:
  virtual void placeOrder() {
    printf("RuntimeExample::placeOrder()\n");
  }
};
class SpecificRuntimeExample : public RuntimeExample {
public:
  void placeOrder() override {
    printf("SpecificRuntimeExample::placeOrder()\n");
  }
};
```

Compile-time polymorphism using the CRTP

Now we implement similar functionality as discussed in the previous section, but instead of using runtime polymorphism, we use compile-time polymorphism. Here, we use the CRTP pattern and `SpecificCRTPExample` specializes/implements the `CRTPExample` interface and has a different implementation of `placeOrder()` via `actualPlaceOrder()`:

```
template <typename actual_type>
class CRTPExample {
public:
  void placeOrder() {
    static_cast<actual_type*>(this)->actualPlaceOrder();
  }
  void actualPlaceOrder() {
```

```
      printf("CRTPExample::actualPlaceOrder()\n");
   }
};
class SpecificCRTPExample : public CRTPExample<Specific
      CRTPExample> {
public:
   void actualPlaceOrder() {
      printf("SpecificCRTPExample::actualPlaceOrder()\n");
   }
};
```

Invoking polymorphic methods in the two cases

Finally, in the following snippet presented, we show how we would create `SpecificRuntimeExample` and `SpecificCRTPExample` objects. We then invoke runtime and compile-time polymorphism respectively using the `placeOrder()` method:

```
int main(int, char **) {
   RuntimeExample* runtime_example = new SpecificRuntimeEx
      ample();
   runtime_example->placeOrder();

   CRTPExample<SpecificCRTPExample> crtp_example;
   crtp_example.placeOrder();

   return 0;
}
```

Running this yields the following output, the first line using runtime polymorphism and the second line using compile time polymorphism:

```
SpecificRuntimeExample::placeOrder()
SpecificCRTPExample::actualPlaceOrder()
```

Using additional compile-time processing

Template metaprogramming is a more general term that means writing code that itself yields more code. The benefit here is also to move computations from runtime to compile time and maximize compiler optimization opportunities and runtime performance. It is possible to write almost anything with template metaprogramming, but it can get extremely complicated and difficult to understand, maintain, and debug, lead to very long compilation times, and increase the binary size to a very large size.

Handling exceptions

The C++ exception handling system is designed to detect unexpected error conditions at runtime and either gracefully recover or shut down from that point. When it comes to low-latency applications, it is important to evaluate the use of exception handling since while it is true that exception handling incurs the largest latencies during these rare error cases, there can still be some overhead even when exceptions are not raised. There is some bookkeeping overhead related to the logic used to recover gracefully when exceptions are raised under various scenarios. With nested functions, exceptions need to be propagated all the way up to the top-most caller function and each stack frame needs to be cleaned up. This is known as **stack unwinding** and requires the exception handler to track all the information it needs to walk backward during an exception.

For low-latency applications, exceptions are either disabled per function using the `throw()` or `noexcept` specifications or disabled across the entire program using compiler flags. This allows the compiler to assume that some or all methods will not throw an exception and hence the processor does not have to worry about saving and tracking recovery information. Note that using `noexcept` or disabling the C++ exception handling system is not without some disadvantages. For one, usually, the C++ exception handling system does not typically add a lot of extra overhead unless an exception is thrown, so this decision must be made with careful consideration. Another point is that if a method marked as `noexcept` throws an exception for some reason, the exception can no longer be propagated up the stack and instead the program is terminated right there. What this means is that disabling the C++ exception handling system either partially or fully makes handling failures and exceptions harder and completely the developer's responsibility. Usually, what this means is that the developer will still need to make sure that exceptional error conditions are not encountered or handled elsewhere, but the point is that now the developer has explicit control over this and can move it out of the critical hot path. For this reason, it is common that during the development and testing phases, the C++ exception handling system is not disabled, but only during the very last optimization steps do we consider removing exception handling.

Accessing cache and memory

We have frequently referred to cache performance while discussing different uses of C++ features since accessing the main memory is significantly slower than the clock cycles used to execute CPU instructions or access registers or cache storage. Here are some general points to keep in mind when trying to optimize cache and memory access.

Aligning data

Variables that are aligned, in that they are placed at memory locations that are multiples of the size of the variable, are accessed most efficiently. The term **word size** for processors describes the number of bits read by and processed by processors, which for modern processors is either 32-bits or 64-bits. This is because the processor can read a variable from memory up to the word size in a single read operation. If the variable is aligned in memory, then the processor does not have to do any extra work to get it into the required register to be processed.

For these reasons, aligned variables are more efficient to handle, and the compiler will take care of automatically aligning variables. This includes adding padding in between member variables in a class or a struct to keep those variables aligned. When adding member variables to structures where we expect to have a lot of objects, it is important to consider the extra padding added carefully because the size of the struct will be larger than expected. The extra space in each instance of this struct's or class's objects means that they can have worse cache performance if there are a lot of them. The recommended approach here would be to reorder the members of the struct so that minimal extra padding is added to keep the members aligned.

We will see an example that orders the same members inside a structure in three different ways – one where there is a lot of additional padding added to keep each variable aligned, another where the developer reorders the member variables to minimize space waste due to compiler-added padding, and, finally, where we use the `pack()` pragma to eliminate all padding. This code is available in the `Chapter3/alignment.cpp` file in the GitHub repository for this book:

```cpp
#include <cstdio>
#include <cstdint>
#include <cstddef>

struct PoorlyAlignedData {
  char c;
  uint16_t u;
  double d;
  int16_t i;
};

struct WellAlignedData {
  double d;
  uint16_t u;
  int16_t i;
  char c;
};

#pragma pack(push, 1)
struct PackedData {
  double d;
  uint16_t u;
  int16_t i;
  char c;
};
#pragma pack(pop)

int main() {
  printf("PoorlyAlignedData c:%lu u:%lu d:%lu i:%lu
```

```
            size:%lu\n",
        offsetof(struct PoorlyAlignedData,c), offsetof
            (struct PoorlyAlignedData,u), offsetof(struct
            PoorlyAlignedData,d), offsetof(struct PoorlyA
            lignedData,i), sizeof(PoorlyAlignedData));
    printf("WellAlignedData d:%lu u:%lu i:%lu c:%lu
        size:%lu\n",
        offsetof(struct WellAlignedData,d), offsetof
            (struct WellAlignedData,u), offsetof(struct
            WellAlignedData,i), offsetof(struct WellAligned
            Data,c), sizeof(WellAlignedData));
    printf("PackedData d:%lu u:%lu i:%lu c:%lu size:%lu\n",
        offsetof(struct PackedData,d), offsetof(struct
            PackedData,u), offsetof(struct PackedData,i),
            offsetof(struct PackedData,c), sizeof
            (PackedData));
}
```

This code outputs the following on my system, displaying the offsets of the different data members in each of the three designs of the same structure. Note that the first version has an extra 11 bytes of padding, the second one only has an extra 3 bytes of padding due to the reordering, and the last version has no extra padding:

```
PoorlyAlignedData c:0 u:2 d:8 i:16 size:24
WellAlignedData d:0 u:8 i:10 c:12 size:16
PackedData d:0 u:8 i:10 c:12 size:13
```

Accessing data

Cache-friendly data access (read and/or write) is when the data is accessed sequentially or somewhat sequentially. If the data is accessed backward, it is less efficient than this, and cache performance is worse if the data is accessed randomly. This is something to consider, especially when accessing multi-dimensional arrays of objects and/or objects residing in a container with a non-trivial underlying storage of the objects.

For instance, accessing elements in an array is significantly more efficient than accessing elements in a linked list, tree, or hash-map container because of the contiguous memory storage versus random memory storage locations. From the perspective of algorithmic complexity, searching linearly in an array is less efficient than using a hash map since the array search has O(n) and the hash map has O(1) theoretical algorithmic complexity. However, if the number of elements is small enough, then using the array still yields better performance, a large reason being due to cache performance and algorithm overhead.

Using large data structures

When dealing with large multi-dimensional matrix datasets, for instance, with linear algebra operations, cache access performance dominates the performance of the operation. Often, the actual algorithm implementation for matrix operations is different from that used in classic texts to reorder the matrix access operations for cache performance. The best approach here is to measure the performance of different algorithms and access patterns and find the one that performs best under different matrix dimensions, cache contention conditions, and so on.

Grouping variables together

When designing classes and method or non-method functions, grouping variables that are accessed together greatly improves cache performance by reducing the number of cache misses. We discussed that preferring local variables over global, static, and dynamically allocated memory leads to better cache performance.

Grouping functions together

Grouping class member functions and non-member functions together so that functions that are used together are close together in memory also leads to better cache performance. This is because functions are placed in memory addresses depending on where they are in the developer's source code and functions next to each other get assigned addresses close to each other.

Dynamically allocating memory

Dynamically allocated memory has several good use cases, specifically when the size of containers is not known at compile time and when they can grow or shrink in size during the application instance's life cycle. Dynamically allocated memory is also important for objects that are very large and take up a lot of stack space. Dynamically allocated memory can have a place in low-latency applications if allocation and deallocation are not done on the critical path and an allocated block of memory is used so that the cache performance is not hurt.

A disadvantage of dynamically allocated memory is that the process of allocating and deallocating memory blocks is awfully slow. The repeated allocation and deallocation of memory blocks of varied sizes fragments the heap, that is, it creates free memory blocks of different sizes interspersed with allocated memory blocks.

A fragmented heap makes the allocation and deallocation process even slower. Allocated memory blocks might not be optimally aligned unless the developer is careful about it. Dynamically allocated memory accessed through pointers causes pointer aliasing and prevents compiler optimizations, as we have seen before. There are other disadvantages of dynamically allocated memory, but these are the biggest ones for low-latency applications. Hence, it is best to avoid dynamically allocated memory completely when it comes to low-latency applications, or at the very least use it carefully and sparingly.

Multi-threading

If low-latency applications use multi-threading, the threads and the interactions between these threads should be designed carefully. Starting and stopping threads takes time, so it is best to avoid launching new threads when they are needed and instead use a thread pool of worker threads. Task switching or context switching is when one thread is paused or blocked, and another thread starts executing in its place. Context switching is very expensive since it requires the OS to save the state of the current thread, load the state of the next thread, start the processing, and so on, and is usually accompanied by memory reads and writes, cache misses, instruction pipeline stalls, and so on.

Synchronization using locks and mutexes between threads is also expensive and involves additional checks around concurrent access and context-switching overhead. When multiple threads access shared resources, they need to use the `volatile` keyword and that also prevents several compiler optimizations. Additionally, different threads can compete for the same cache lines and invalidate each other's caches and this contention leads to terrible cache performance. Each thread gets its own stack, so it's best to keep the shared data to a minimum and allocate variables locally on the thread's stack.

Maximizing C++ compiler optimization parameters

In this last section, we will understand how advanced and amazing modern C++ compilers are at optimizing the C++ code that the developers write. We will understand how compilers optimize the C++ code during the compilation, linking, and optimization stages to generate the most efficient machine code possible. We will understand how compilers optimize high-level C++ code and when they fail to do the best job. We will follow that up with a discussion on what the application developer can do to aid the compilers in their optimization task. Finally, we will look at different options available in modern C++ compilers by looking specifically at the **GNU compiler** (**GCC**). Let us start by understanding how compilers optimize our C++ program.

Understanding how compilers optimize

In this sub-section, we will understand the different compiler optimization techniques that the compiler employs during its many passes over the high-level C++ code. The compiler typically first performs local optimizations and then tries to globally optimize these smaller code sections. It does so over several passes through the translated machine code during the pre-processing, compilation, linking, and optimization stages. Broadly, most compiler optimization techniques have some common themes, some of which overlap and some of which conflict with each other, which we will look at next.

Optimizing the common cases

This concept applies to software development too and helps the compiler optimize the code better. If the compiler can understand which code paths the program execution will spend most of its time in, it can optimize the common path to be faster even if it slows down the paths that are rarely taken. This results in better performance overall, but typically this is harder for the compiler to achieve at compilation time since it is not obvious which code paths are expected to be more likely unless the developer adds directives to specify this. We will discuss the hints that a developer can provide to the compiler to help specify which code paths are expected to be more likely during runtime.

Minimizing branching

Modern processors typically prefetch data and instructions before they are required so that the processors can execute instructions as quickly as possible. However, when there are jumps and branches (conditional and unconditional), the processor cannot know which instructions and data will be needed ahead of time with 100% certainty. What this means is that sometimes the processor incorrectly predicts the branch taken and thus the instructions and data prefetched are incorrect. When this happens, there is an extra penalty incurred since now the processor must remove the instructions and data that were fetched incorrectly and replace them with the correct instructions and data and then execute them after that. Techniques such as loop unrolling, inlining, and branch prediction hints help reduce branching and the misprediction of branching and improve performance. We will explore these concepts in more detail later in this section.

There are several cases in which a developer can refactor code in such a way that they avoid branching and achieve the same behavior. Sometimes, these optimization opportunities are only available to the developer, who understands the code and behavior at a deeper level than the compiler. A very simple example of how to convert a code block that uses branching and transform it to avoid branching is presented next. Here we have an enumeration to track side for an execution and we track the last bought/sold quantity, as well as updating the position in two different ways. The first way uses a branch on the `fill_side` variable and the second method avoids that branching by assuming that the `fill_side` variable can only have BUY/SELL values and can be cast to integers to be indexed into an array. This code can be found in the `Chapter3/branch.cpp` file:

```
#include <cstdio>
#include <cstdint>
#include <cstdlib>

enum class Side : int16_t { BUY = 1, SELL = -1 };

int main() {
  const auto fill_side = (rand() % 2 ? Side::BUY : Side
      ::SELL);
  const int fill_qty = 10;
  printf("fill_side:%s fill_qty:%d.\n", (fill_side == Side
      ::BUY ? "BUY" : (fill_side == Side::SELL ? "SELL" :
      "INVALID")), fill_qty);

  { // with branching
    int last_buy_qty = 0, last_sell_qty = 0, position = 0;
```

```cpp
        if (fill_side == Side::BUY) {
          position += fill_qty; last_buy_qty = fill_qty;
        } else if (fill_side == Side::SELL) {
          position -= fill_qty; last_sell_qty = fill_qty; }

        printf("With branching - position:%d last-buy:%d last-
            sell:%d.\n", position, last_buy_qty,
            last_sell_qty);
      }

      { // without branching
        int last_qty[3] = {0, 0, 0}, position = 0;

        auto sideToInt = [](Side side) noexcept { return
            static_cast<int16_t>(side); };

        const auto int_fill_side = sideToInt(fill_side);
        position += int_fill_side * fill_qty;
        last_qty[int_fill_side + 1] = fill_qty;

        printf("Without branching - position:%d last-buy:%d
            last-sell:%d.\n", position, last_qty[sideToInt
              (Side::BUY) + 1], last_qty[side
              ToInt(Side::SELL) +
              1]);
      }
    }
```

And both the branching and branchless implementations compute the same values:

```
fill_side:BUY fill_qty:10.
With branching - position:10 last-buy:10 last-sell:0.
Without branching - position:10 last-buy:10 last-sell:0.
```

Reordering and scheduling instructions

The compiler can take advantage of advanced processors by re-ordering instructions in such a way that parallel processing can happen at the instruction, memory, and thread levels. The compiler can detect dependencies between code blocks and re-order them so that the program still works correctly but executes faster by executing instructions and processing data in parallel at the processor level. Modern processors can reorder instructions even without the compiler doing so, but it helps if the compiler can make it easier for the processors to do so as well. The main objective here is to prevent stalls and bubbles in modern processors, which have multiple pipelined processors, by choosing and ordering instructions in such a way as to preserve the original logical flow.

A simple example of how an expression can be reordered to take advantage of parallelism is shown here. Note that this is somewhat hypothetical since the actual implementation of this will vary greatly depending on the processor and the compiler:

```
x = a + b + c + d + e + f;
```

As it is written, this expression has a data dependency and would be executed sequentially, roughly as follows, and cost 5 clock cycles:

```
x = a + b;
x = x + c;
x = x + d;
x = x +e;
x = x + f;
```

It can be re-ordered into the following instructions, and assuming the advanced processor can perform two additions at a time, can be reduced to three clock cycles. This is because two operations such as x = a + b; and p = c +d; can be performed in parallel since they are independent of each other:

```
x = a + b; p = c + d;
q = e + f; x = x + p;
x = x + q;
```

Using special instructions depending on the architecture

During the compilation process, the compiler can choose which CPU instructions to use to implement the high-level program logic. When the compiler generates an executable for a specific architecture, it can use special instructions that the architecture supports. This means there is an opportunity to generate even more efficient instruction sequences, which leverage the special instructions that the architecture provides. We will look at how to specify this in the *Learning about compiler optimization flags* section.

Vectorization

Modern processors can use vector registers to perform multiple calculations on multiple pieces of data in parallel. For instance, the SSE2 instruction set has 128-bit vector registers, which can be used to perform multiple operations on multiple integers or floating values depending on the size of these types. Extending this further, the AVX2 instruction set, for example, has 256-bit vector registers and can support a higher degree of vectorized operations. This optimization can be technically considered as part of the discussion in the *Using special instructions depending on the architecture* section from before.

To understand vectorization even better, let us present the following very simple example of a loop that operates on two arrays and stores the result in another array (vector.cpp in Chapter3 in GitHub):

```
const size_t size = 1024;
float x[size], a[size], b[size];
```

```
for (size_t i = 0; i < size; ++i) {
  x[i] = a[i] + b[i];
}
```

For architectures that support special vector registers such as the SSE2 instruction set we discussed before, it can hold 4 4-byte float values simultaneously and perform 4 additions at a time. In this case, the compiler can leverage the vectorization optimization technique and re-write this as the following with loop unrolling to use the SSE2 instruction set:

```
for (size_t i = 0; i < size; i += 4) {
  x[i] = a[i] + b[i];
  x[i + 1] = a[i + 1] + b[i + 1];
  x[i + 2] = a[i + 2] + b[i + 2];
  x[i + 3] = a[i + 3] + b[i + 3];
}
```

Strength reduction

Strength reduction is a term used to describe compiler optimizations where complex operations that are quite expensive are replaced by instructions that are simpler and cheaper to improve performance. A classic example is one in which the compiler replaces operations involving division by some value with multiplication by the reciprocal of that value. Another example would be replacing multiplication by a loop index with an addition operation.

The simplest example we could think of is presented here, where we try to convert a price from its double notation into its integer notation by dividing the floating value by its minimum valid price increment. The variant that demonstrates the strength reduction that a compiler would perform is a simple multiplication instead of a division. Note that `inv_min_price_increment = 1 / min_price_increment;` is a `constexpr` expression, so it is not evaluated at runtime. This code is available in the `Chapter3/strength.cpp` file:

```
#include <cstdint>

int main() {
  const auto price = 10.125; // prices are like: 10.125,
      10.130, 10.135...
  constexpr auto min_price_increment = 0.005;
  [[maybe_unused]] int64_t int_price = 0;

  // no strength reduction
  int_price = price / min_price_increment;

  // strength reduction
  constexpr auto inv_min_price_increment = 1 /
      min_price_increment;
```

```
    int_price = price * inv_min_price_increment;
}
```

Inlining

Calling functions is expensive, as we have already seen before. There are several steps:

- Saving the current state of variables and execution
- Loading the variables and instructions from the function being called
- Executing them and possibly returning back values and resuming execution after the function call

The compiler tries to replace a call to a function with the body of the function where possible to remove this overhead associated with calling functions and optimize performance. Not only that but now that it has replaced a call to a function with the actual body of the function, that opens room for more optimizations since the compiler can inspect this new larger code block.

Constant folding and constant propagation

Constant folding is a no-brainer optimization technique and applies when there are expressions whose output can be computed entirely at compile time that do not depend on runtime branches or variables. Then, the compiler computes these expressions at compile time and replaces the evaluation of these expressions with the compile-time constant output value.

A similar and closely related compiler optimization tracks values in the code that are known to be compile-time constants and tries to propagate those constant values and unlock additional optimization opportunities. This optimization technique is known as **constant propagation**. An example would be loop unrolling if the compiler can determine the starting value, incremental value, or stopping value of the loop iterator.

Dead Code Elimination (DCE)

DCE applies when the compiler can detect code blocks that have no impact on the program behavior. This can be due to code blocks that are never needed or code blocks where the calculations do not end up being used or affect the outcome. Once the compiler detects such *dead* code blocks, it can remove them and boost program performance. Modern compilers emit warnings when the outcome of running some code ends up not being used to help developers find such cases, but the compiler cannot detect all of these cases at compile time and there are still opportunities for DOE once it is translated into machine code instructions.

Common Subexpression Elimination (CSE)

CSE is a specific optimization technique where the compiler finds duplicated sets of instructions or calculations. Here, the compiler restructures the code to remove this redundancy by computing the result only once and then using the value where it is required.

Peephole optimizations

Peephole optimization is a relatively generic compiler optimization term that refers to a compiler optimization technique where the compiler tries to search for local optimizations in short sequences of instructions. We use the term local because the compiler does not necessarily try to understand the entire program and optimize it globally. Of course, however, by repeatedly and iteratively performing peephole optimizations, the compiler can achieve a decent degree of optimization at a global scale.

Tail call optimization

We know that function calls are not cheap because they have overhead associated with passing parameters and results and affect the cache performance and processor pipeline. **Tail call optimization** refers to compiler optimization techniques in which recursive function calls are replaced by loops. This has obvious performance benefits such as eliminating function call overheads and stack operations and avoids possible stack overflow cases. The following simple example of a recursive factorial implementation. For now, you can ignore the `__attribute__ ((noinline))` attribute, which is there to explicitly prevent the compiler from inlining the `factorial()` function directly into `main()`. You can find this example in the `Chapter3/tail_call.cpp` source file on GitHub:

```
auto __attribute__ ((noinline)) factorial(unsigned n) ->
    unsigned {
  return (n ? n * factorial(n - 1) : 1);
}

int main() {
  [[maybe_unused]] volatile auto res = factorial(100);
}
```

For this implementation, we would expect that in the machine code for the `factorial()` function, we would find a call to itself, but when compiled with optimization turned on, the compiler performs tail call optimization and implements the `factorial()` function as a loop and not a recursion. To observe that machine code, you can compile this code with something like this:

```
g++ -S -Wall -O3 tail_call.cpp ; cat tail_call.s
```

And in that `tail_call.s` file, you will see the call to `factorial()` in `main()` to be something like the following example. If this is your first time looking at assembly code, then let us quickly describe the instructions you will encounter.

- The `movl` instruction moves a value into a register (100 in the following block)
- The `call` instruction calls a function (`factorial()` with name mangling (step where the C++ compiler changes the function names in intermediate code) and the parameter is passed in the `edi` register)

- The `testl` instruction compares two registers and sets the zero flag if they're equal
- `je` and `jne` check whether the zero flag is set and jump to the specified memory address if it is (`je`) or jump to the specified memory address if it is not (`jne`)
- The `ret` instruction returns from the function and the return value is in the `eax` register:

```
main:
.LFB1
    Movl     $100, %edi
    Call     _Z9factorialj
```

When you look at the `factorial()` function itself, you will find a loop (the `je` and `jne` instructions) instead of an additional `call` instruction to itself:

```
_Z9factorialj:
.LFB0:
    Movl     $1, %eax
    testl    %edi, %edi
    je       .L4
.L3:
    Imull    %edi, %eax
    subl     $1, %edi
    jne      .L3
    ret
.L4:
    ret
```

Loop unrolling

Loop unrolling duplicates the body of the loop multiple times. Sometimes, it is not possible for the compiler to know at compile time how many times the loop will be executed – in which case, it will partially unroll the loop. For loops where the loop body is small and/or where it can be determined that the number of times that the loop will execute is low, the compiler can completely unroll the loop. This avoids the need for checking the loop counters and the overhead associated with conditional branching or looping. This is like function inlining where the call to the function is replaced by the body of the function. For loop unrolling, the entire loop is rolled out and replaces the conditional loop body.

Additional loop optimizations

Loop unrolling is the primary loop-related optimization technique employed by compilers but there are additional loop optimizations:

- **Loop fission** breaks a loop down into multiple loops operating on smaller sets of data to improve cache reference locality.

- **Loop fusion** does the opposite, where if two adjacent loops are executed the same number of times, they can be merged into one to reduce the loop overhead.
- **Loop inversion** is a technique where a `while` loop is transformed into a `do-while` loop inside a conditional `if` statement. This reduces the total number of jumps by two when the loop is executed and is typically applied to loops that are expected to execute at least once.
- **Loop interchange** exchanges inner loops and outer loops especially when doing so leads to better cache reference locality – for example, in the cases of iterating over an array where accessing memory contiguously makes a huge performance difference.

Register variables

Registers are internal processor memory and are the fastest form of storage available for the processor on account of being the closest to them. Because of this, the compiler tries to store variables that have the highest number of accesses in the registers. Registers, however, are limited, so the compiler needs to choose the variables to store effectively, and the effectiveness of this choice can make a significant difference to performance. The compiler typically picks variables such as local variables, loop counter and iterator variables, function parameters, commonly used expressions, or **induction variables** (variables that change by fixed amounts on each loop iteration). There are some limitations to what the compiler can place in registers such as variables whose address needs to be taken via pointers or references that need to reside in the main memory.

Now, we present a very simple example of how a compiler will transform a loop expression using induction variables. See the following code (`Chapter3/induction.cpp` on GitHub):

```
    for(auto i = 0; i < 100; ++i)
       a[i] = i * 10 + 12;
gets transformed into something of the form presented below
      and avoids the multiplication in the loop and replaces
      it
         with an induction variable based addition.
   int temp = 12;
   for(auto i = 0; i < 100; ++i) {
      a[i] = temp;
      temp += 10;
   }
```

Live range analysis

The term **live range** describes the code block within which a variable is active or used. If there are multiple variables in the same code block with overlapping live ranges, then each variable needs a different storage location. However, if there are variables with live ranges that do not overlap, then the compiler can use the same register for multiple variables in each live range.

Rematerialization

Rematerialization is a compiler technique where the compiler chooses to re-calculate a value (assuming the calculation is trivial) instead of accessing the memory location that contains the value of this calculation already. The output value of this recalculation must be stored in registers, so this technique works in tandem with *register allocation techniques*. The main objective here is to avoid accessing the caches and main memory, which are slower to access than accessing the register storage. This, of course, depends on making sure that the recalculation takes less time than a cache or memory access.

Algebraic reductions

The compiler can find expressions that can be further reduced and simplified using algebraic laws. While software developers do not unnecessarily complicate expressions, there are cases where simpler forms of expressions exist compared to what the developer originally wrote in C++. Opportunities for algebraic reductions also show up as the compiler optimizes code iteratively due to inlining, macro expansions, constant folding, and so on.

Something to note here is that compilers do not typically apply algebraic reductions to floating-point operations because, in C++, floating-point operations are not safe to reduce due to precision issues. Flags need to be turned on to force the compiler to perform unsafe floating-point algebraic reductions, but it would be preferable for developers to reduce them explicitly and correctly.

The simplest example we can think of here is where a compiler might rewrite this expression:

```
if(!a && !b) {}
```

Here, it uses two operations instead of three previously like so:

```
if(!(a || b)) {}
```

Induction variable analysis

The idea behind **induction variable**-related compiler optimization techniques is that an expression that is a linear function of the loop counter variable can be reduced into an expression that is a simple addition to a previous value. The simplest possible example would be calculating the address of elements in an array where the next element is at a memory location equal to the current element's location plus the size of the object type. This is just a simple example since in modern compilers and processors, there are special instructions to calculate addresses of array elements and induction is not really used there, but induction variable-based optimizations are still performed for other loop expressions.

Loop invariant code movement

When the compiler can ascertain that some code and instructions within a loop are constant for the entire duration of the loop, that expression can be moved out of the loop. If there are expressions within the loop that conditionally yield one value or the other depending on branching conditions, those can also be moved out of the loop. Also, if there are expressions executed on each branch within a loop, these can be moved out of the branches and possibly the loop. There are many such optimization possibilities, but the fundamental idea is that code that does not need to be executed on each loop iteration or can be evaluated once before the loop falls under the umbrella of loop invariant code refactoring. Here is a hypothetical example of how loop invariant code movement implemented by the compiler would work. The first block is what the developer originally wrote, but the compiler can understand that the call to `doSomething()` and the expression involving the b variable are loop invariants and only need to be computed once. You will find this code in the `Chapter3/loop_invariant.cpp` file:

```cpp
#include <cstdlib>

int main() {
  auto doSomething = [](double r) noexcept { return 3.14 *
      r * r; };
  [[maybe_unused]] int a[100], b = rand();

  // original
  for(auto i = 0; i < 100; ++i)
    a[i] = (doSomething(50) + b * 2) + 1;

  // loop invariant code movement
  auto temp = (doSomething(50) + b * 2) + 1;
  for(auto i = 0; i < 100; ++i)
    a[i] = temp;
}
```

Static Single Assignment (SSA)-based optimizations

SSA is a transformed form of the original program where instructions are re-ordered such that every variable is assigned in a single place. After this transformation, the compiler can apply many additional optimizations, leveraging the property that every variable is assigned in only a single place.

Devirtualization

Devirtualization is a compiler optimization technique, especially for C++, that tries to avoid **Virtual Table (vtable)** lookups when calling virtual functions. This optimization technique boils down to the compiler figuring out the correct method to call at compile time. This can happen even when using virtual functions because in some cases, the object type is known at compile time, such as when there is only a single implementation of pure virtual functions.

Another case is where the compiler can determine that only a single derived class is created and used in some contexts or code branches, and it can replace the indirect functional call using vtable to be a direct call to the correct derived type's method.

Understanding when compilers fail to optimize

In this section, we will discuss the different scenarios under which a compiler cannot apply some of the optimization techniques we discussed in the previous section. Understanding when compilers fail to optimize will help us develop C++ code that avoids these failures so that the code can be highly optimized by the compiler to yield highly efficient machine code.

Failure to optimize across modules

When the compiler compiles the entire program, it compiles modules independently of each other on a file-by-file basis. So, the compiler does not have information about functions in a module other than the one it is currently compiling. This prevents it from being able to optimize functions across modules and a lot of the techniques we saw cannot be applied since the compiler does not understand the whole program. Modern compilers solve such issues by using **LTO**, where, after the individual modules are compiled, the linker treats the different modules as if they were part of the same translation unit at compile time. This activates all the optimizations we have discussed so far, so it is important to enable LTO when trying to optimize the entire application.

Dynamic memory allocation

We already know that dynamic memory allocation is slow at runtime and introduces non-deterministic latency into your applications. They also have another side effect and that is **pointer aliasing** in the pointers that point to these dynamically allocated memory blocks. We will look at pointer aliasing in more detail next, but with dynamically allocated memory blocks, the compiler cannot ascertain that the pointers will necessarily point to different and non-overlapping memory areas, even though for the programmer it might seem obvious. This prevents various compiler optimizations that depend on aligning data or assuming alignment, as well as pointer aliasing-related inefficiencies, which we will see next. Local storage and declarations are also more cache-efficient because the memory space gets reused frequently as new functions are called and local objects are created. Dynamically allocated memory blocks can be randomly scattered in memory and yield poor cache performance.

Pointer aliasing

When accessing variables through pointers or references, while it might be obvious to the developer which pointers point to different and non-overlapping memory locations, the compiler cannot be 100% sure. To put it another way, the compiler cannot guarantee that a pointer is not pointing to another variable in the code block or different pointers are not pointing to overlapping memory locations. Since the compiler must assume this possibility, this prevents a lot of the compiler optimizations we discussed before since they can no longer be applied safely. There are ways to specify which pointers the compiler can safely assume are not aliases in C++ code. Another way would be to instruct the compiler to assume no pointer aliasing across the entire code, but that would require the developer to analyze all pointers and references and make sure there is never any aliasing, which is not trivial to do. Finally, the last option is to optimize the code explicitly keeping these hindrances to compiler optimizations in mind, which is not trivial either.

Our advice on dealing with pointer aliasing would be to do the following:

1. Use the `__restrict` keyword in the function declarations when passing pointers to functions to instruct the compiler to assume no pointer aliasing for the pointers marked with that specifier
2. If additional optimization is required, we recommend explicitly optimizing code paths, being aware of pointer aliasing considerations
3. Finally, if additional optimizations are still required, we can instruct the compiler to assume no pointer aliasing across the entire code base, but this is a dangerous option and should only be used as a last resort

Floating-point induction variables

Compilers typically do not use induction variable optimizations for floating-point expressions and variables. This is because of the rounding errors and issues with precision that we have discussed before. This prevents compiler optimizations when dealing with floating-point expressions and values. There are compiler options that can enable unsafe floating-point optimizations, but the developer must make sure to check each expression and formulate them in such a way that these precision issues due to compiler optimizations do not have unintended side effects. This is not a trivial task; hence, developers should be careful to either optimize floating-point expressions explicitly or analyze side effects from unsafe compiler optimizations.

Virtual functions and function pointers

We have already discussed that when it comes to virtual functions and function pointers, the compiler cannot perform optimizations at compile time since in many cases it is not possible for the compiler to determine which method will be called at runtime.

Learning about compiler optimization flags

So far, we have discussed the different optimization techniques that the compiler uses, as well as the different cases where the compiler fails to optimize our C++ code. There are two fundamental keys to generating optimized low-latency code. The first is to write efficient C++ code and optimize manually in cases where the compiler might not be able to do so. Secondly, you can provide the compiler with as much visibility and information as possible so it can make the correct and best optimization decisions. We can convey our intent to the compiler through the compiler flags we use to configure it.

In this section, we will learn about the compiler flags for the GCC since that is the compiler we will use in this book. However, most modern compilers have flags to configure optimizations like the ones we will discuss in this section.

Approaching compiler optimization flags

At a high level, the general approach toward GCC compiler optimization flags is the following:

- The highest optimization level is typically preferred so -O3 is a good starting point and enables a lot of optimizations, which we will see shortly.

- Measuring the performance of the application in practice is the best way to measure and optimize the most critical code paths. GCC itself can perform **Profile-Guided Optimization** (**PGO**) when the -fprofile-generate option is enabled. The compiler determines the flow of the program and counts how many times each function and code branch is executed to find optimizations for the critical code paths.

- Enabling **LTO** is a good practice for building the lowest latency machine code due to the reasons we have discussed before and the inability of the compiler to optimize across modules without this. For GCC, the -flto parameter enables LTO for our applications. The -fwhole-program option enables **WPO** to enable inter-procedural optimizations, treating the entire code base as a whole program.

- Allowing the compiler to generate a build for a specific architecture where the application will run is a good idea. This lets the compiler use special instruction sets specific to that architecture and maximize optimization opportunities. For GCC, this is enabled using the -march parameter.

- It is recommended to disable **RTTI** because RTTI depends on figuring out the type of an object at runtime. For GCC, this is achieved using the -no-rtti parameter.

- It is possible to instruct the GCC compiler to enable fast floating-point value optimizations and even enable unsafe floating-point optimizations. GCC has the -ffp-model=fast, -funsafe-math-optimizations and -ffinite-math-only options to enable these unsafe floating-point optimizations. When using these flags, it is important that the developer carefully thinks about the order of operations and the precision resulting from these operations. When using a parameter such as -ffinite-math-only, make sure that all floating-point variables and expressions are finite because this optimization depends on that property. -fno-trapping-math and -fno-math-errno allow the compiler to vectorize loops containing floating-point operations by assuming that there will be no reliance on exception handling or the errno global variable for error signaling.

Understanding the details of GCC optimization flags

In this section, we will provide additional details on the GCC optimization flags available. The complete list of optimization flags available is exceptionally large and out of the scope of this book. First, we will describe what turning on the higher-level optimization directives, -O1, -O2, and -O3, enables in GCC, and we encourage interested readers to learn about each one of these in greater detail from the GCC manual.

Optimization level -O1

-O1 is the first level of optimization and enables the following flags presented in the following table. At this level, the compiler tries to reduce the code size and execution time without incurring a very large increase in compilation, linking, and optimization times. These are the most important levels of optimization and provide tremendous optimization opportunities based on the ones we discussed in this chapter. We will discuss a few of the flags next.

-fdce and -fdse perform DCE and **Dead Store Elimination** (DSE).

-fdelayed-branch is supported on many architectures and tries to reorder instructions to try and maximize the throughput of the pipeline after delayed branch instructions.

-fguess-branch-probability tries to guess branch probabilities based on heuristics for branches that the developer has not provided any hints.

-fif-conversion and -fif-conversion2 try to eliminate branching by changing them into branchless equivalents using tricks similar to what we discussed in this chapter.

-fmove-loop-invariants enables loop invariant code movement optimization.

If you are interested, you should investigate the details of these flags since discussing every parameter is outside the scope of this book.

-fauto-inc-dec	-fshrink-wrap
-fbranch-count-reg	-fshrink-wrap-separate
-fcombine-stack-adjustments	-fsplit-wide-types
-fcompare-elim	-fssa-backprop
-fcprop-registers	-fssa-phiopt
-fdce	-ftree-bit-ccp
-fdefer-pop	-ftree-ccp
-fdelayed-branch	-ftree-ch
-fdse	-ftree-coalesce-vars
-fforward-propagate	-ftree-copy-prop
-fguess-branch-probability	-ftree-dce
-fif-conversion	-ftree-dominator-opts
-fif-conversion2	-ftree-dse
-finline-functions-called-once	-ftree-forwprop
-fipa-modref	-ftree-fre
-fipa-profile	-ftree-phiprop
-fipa-pure-const	-ftree-pta
-fipa-reference	-ftree-scev-cprop
-fipa-reference-addressable	-ftree-sink

`-fmerge-constants162`	`-ftree-slsr`
`-fmove-loop-invariants`	`-ftree-sra`
`-fmove-loop-stores`	`-ftree-ter`
`-fomit-frame-pointer`	`-funit-at-a-time`
`-freorder-blocks`	

Table 3.1 – GCC optimization flags enabled when -O1 is enabled

Optimization level -O2

-O2 is the next optimization level and at this level, GCC will perform a lot more optimizations and will lead to longer compilation and linking times. -O2 adds the flags in the following table in addition to the flags enabled by –O1. We will quickly discuss a few of these flags and leave a detailed discussion of each flag up to interested readers to pursue.

-falign-functions, -falign-labels, and -falign-loops align the starting address of functions, jump targets, and loop locations so that the processor can access them as efficiently as possible. The principles we discussed on optimal data alignment in this chapter apply to the instruction addresses as well.

-fdelete-null-pointer-checks lets the program assume that dereferencing null pointers is not safe and leverages that assumption to perform constant folding, eliminate null pointer checks, and so on.

-fdevirtualize and -fdevirtualize-speculatively attempt to convert virtual function calls into direct function calls wherever possible. This, in turn, can lead to even more optimization due to inlining.

-fgcse enables **Global Common Subexpression Elimination** (**GCSE**) and constant propagation.

-finline-functions, -finline-functions-called-once, and -findirect-inlining increase the aggressiveness of the compiler in its attempts to inline functions and look for indirect inline opportunities due to previous optimization passes.

`-falign-functions -falign-jumps`	`-foptimize-sibling-calls`
`-falign-labels -falign-loops`	`-foptimize-strlen`
`-fcaller-saves`	`-fpartial-inlining`
`-fcode-hoisting`	`-fpeephole2`
`-fcrossjumping`	`-freorder-blocks-algorithm=stc`
`-fcse-follow-jumps -fcse-skip-blocks`	`-freorder-blocks-and-partition` `-freorder-functions`
`-fdelete-null-pointer-checks`	`-frerun-cse-after-loop`

`-fdevirtualize -fdevirtualize-speculatively`	`-fschedule-insns -fschedule-insns2`
`-fexpensive-optimizations`	`-fsched-interblock -fsched-spec`
`-ffinite-loops`	`-fstore-merging`
`-fgcse -fgcse-lm`	`-fstrict-aliasing`
`-fhoist-adjacent-loads`	`-fthread-jumps`
`-finline-functions`	`-ftree-builtin-call-dce`
`-finline-small-functions`	`-ftree-loop-vectorize`
`-findirect-inlining`	`-ftree-pre`
`-fipa-bit-cp -fipa-cp -fipa-icf`	`-ftree-slp-vectorize`
`-fipa-ra -fipa-sra -fipa-vrp`	`-ftree-switch-conversion -ftree-tail-merge`
`-fisolate-erroneous-paths-dereference`	`-ftree-vrp`
`-flra-remat`	`-fvect-cost-model=very-cheap`

Table 3.2 – GCC optimization flags enabled in addition to the ones from -O1 when -O2 is enabled

Optimization level –O3

-O3 is the most aggressive optimization option in GCC and it will optimize even when it leads to larger executable sizes as long as the program performs better. -O3 enables the following flags presented in the next table beyond -O2. We quickly discuss a few important ones first and then provide the complete list.

-fipa-cp-clone creates function clones to make interprocedural constant propagation and other forms of optimization stronger by trading execution speed at the cost of higher executable sizes.

-fsplit-loops attempts to split a loop if it can avoid branching within the loop by having the loop for one side and then the other side – for instance, in a case where we check the side of execution in a trading algorithm within a loop and execute two different code blocks within the loop.

-funswitch-loops moves loop invariant branches out of the loop to minimize branching.

`-fgcse-after-reload`	`-fsplit-paths`
`-fipa-cp-clone -floop-interchange`	`-ftree-loop-distribution`
`-floop-unroll-and-jam`	`-ftree-partial-pre`
`-fpeel-loops`	`-funswitch-loops`
`-fpredictive-commoning`	`-fvect-cost-model=dynamic`
`-fsplit-loops`	`-fversion-loops-for-strides`

Table 3.3 – GCC optimization flags enabled in addition to the ones from -O2 when -O3 is enabled

We will discuss some additional compiler optimization flags we have found useful when it comes to optimizing low-latency applications.

Static linkage

The `-l library` option is passed to the linker to specify which library to link the executables with. However, if the linker finds a static library that has a name such as `liblibrary.a` and a shared library that has a name such as `liblibrary.so`, then we must specify the `-static` parameter to prevent linking with shared libraries and opt for the static library instead. We have discussed before why static linkage is preferred over shared library linkage for low-latency applications.

Target architecture

The `-march` parameter is used to specify the target architecture for which the compiler should build the final executable binary. For example, `-march=native` specifies that the compiler should build the executable for the architecture that it is being built on. We reiterate here that when the compiler knows the target architecture that the application is being built to run on, it can leverage information about that architecture, such as extended instruction sets and so on, to improve optimization.

Warnings

The `-Wall`, `-Wextra`, and `-Wpendantic` parameters control the number of warnings that are generated by the compiler when it detects a variety of different cases that are not technically errors but could be unsafe. It is advisable to turn these on for most applications because they detect potential bugs and typos in developers' code. While these do not directly affect the compiler's ability to optimize the application, sometimes, the warnings force developers to inspect cases of ambiguity or sub-optimal code, such as unexpected or implicit type conversions, which can be inefficient. The `-Werror` parameter turns these warnings into errors and will force the developer to inspect and fix each case that generates a compiler warning before compilation can succeed.

Unsafe fast math

This category of compiler optimization flags should not be enabled without a lot of consideration and due diligence. In C++, the compiler cannot apply a lot of floating-point optimizations that depend on properties such as floating-point operations yielding valid values, floating-point expressions being associative, and so on. To recap, this is because of the way floating-point values are represented in hardware, and a lot of these optimizations can lead to precision loss and different (and possibly incorrect) results. Enabling the `-ffast-math` parameter in turn enables the following parameters:

- `-fno-math-errno`
- `-funsafe-math-optimizations`
- `-ffinite-math-only`
- `-fno-rounding-math`

- `-fno-signaling-nans`
- `-fcx-limited-range`
- `-fexcess-precision=fast`

These parameters will allow the compiler to apply optimizations to floating-point expressions even if they are unsafe. These are not automatically enabled in any of the three optimization levels because they are unsafe and should only be enabled if the developer is confident that there are no errors or side effects that show up because of these.

Summary

In this chapter, first, we discussed general advice that applies to developing low-latency applications in any programming language. We discussed the ideal software engineering approach when it comes to these applications and how to think about, design, develop, and evaluate building blocks such as the data structures and algorithms to use.

We emphasized that when it comes to low-latency application development specifically, the depth of knowledge on topics such as processor architecture, cache and memory layout and access, how the C++ programming language works under the hood, and how the compiler works to optimize your code will dictate your success. Measuring and improving performance is also a critical component for low-latency applications but we will dive into those details at the end of this book.

We spent a lot of time discussing different C++ principles, constructs, and features with the objective of understanding how they are implemented at a lower level. The goal here was to unlearn sub-optimal practices and emphasize some of the ideal aspects of using C++ for low-latency application development.

In the remainder of this book, as we build our low-latency electronic trading exchange ecosystem (collection of applications that interact with each other), we will reinforce and build on these ideas we discussed here as we avoid certain C++ features and use others instead.

In the last section of this chapter, we discussed many aspects of the C++ compiler in detail. We tried to build an understanding of how compilers optimize developers' high-level code, as in, what techniques they have at their disposal. We also investigated scenarios in which the compiler fails to optimize a developer's code. The goal there was for you to understand how to use a compiler to your advantage when trying to output the most optimal machine code possible and help the compiler help you avoid conditions where the compiler fails to optimize. Finally, we looked at the different compiler optimization flags available for the GNU GCC compiler, which is what we will use in the rest of this book.

We will put our theoretical knowledge into practice in the next chapter where we jump into implementing some common building blocks of low-latency applications in C++. We will keep our goal of building these components to be low-latency and highly performant. We will carefully use the principles and techniques we discussed in this chapter to build these high-performance components. In later chapters, we will use these components to build an electronic trading ecosystem.

4

Building the C++ Building Blocks for Low Latency Applications

In the previous chapter, we had a detailed and highly technical discussion of how to approach developing low latency applications in C++. We also investigated the technical details of the C++ programming language as well as the GCC compiler. Now, we will move from a theoretical discussion to building some practical low latency C++ components ourselves.

We will build some relatively general components that can be used in a variety of different low latency applications, such as the ones we discussed in the previous chapters. As we build these basic building blocks in this chapter, we will learn about using C++ effectively to write highly performant C++ code. We will use these components in the rest of the book to demonstrate where these components fit into the electronic trading ecosystem that we will design and build.

In this chapter, we will cover the following topics:

- C++ threading for multi-threaded low latency applications
- Designing C++ memory pools to avoid dynamic memory allocations
- Transferring data using lock-free queues
- Building a low latency logging framework
- C++ network programming using sockets

Technical requirements

All the code for this book can be found in the GitHub repository for this book at https://github.com/PacktPublishing/Building-Low-Latency-Applications-with-CPP. The source for this chapter is in the Chapter4 directory in the repository.

We expect you to have at least intermediate C++ programming experience, since we will assume you understand the widely used C++ programming features well. We also assume that you have some experience with network programming in C++, since network programming is a huge topic and cannot be covered in this book. For this book, starting with this chapter, we will use the CMake and Ninja build systems, so we expect you to either understand CMake, g++, Ninja, Make, or some such build system to be able to build the code samples for this book.

The specifications of the environment in which the source code for this book was developed are shown here. We present the details of this environment since all the C++ code presented in this book is not necessarily portable and might require some minor changes to work in your environment:

- **OS**: `Linux 5.19.0-41-generic #42~22.04.1-Ubuntu SMP PREEMPT_DYNAMIC Tue Apr 18 17:40:00 UTC 2 x86_64 x86_64 x86_64 GNU/Linux`
- **GCC**: `g++ (Ubuntu 11.3.0-1ubuntu1~22.04.1) 11.3.0`
- **CMake**: `cmake version 3.23.2`
- **Ninja**: `1.10.2`

C++ threading for multi-threaded low latency applications

The first component we will build is a very small one but still quite fundamental. This section will design and implement a method of creating and running threads of execution. These will be used in many different parts of a full low-latency system, depending on the design of the different sub-components in the system. Depending on the design of the system, different components might work together as a pipeline to facilitate parallel processing. We will use the multi-threading framework in exactly such a way in our electronic trading systems. Another use case is to pass off non-critical tasks such as logging onto disk, computing statistics, and so on to a background thread.

Before we move on to the source code that creates and manipulates threads, let us first quickly define a few useful macros. We will use these functions in many places in the source code that we will be writing in this book, starting with this chapter.

Defining some useful macros and functions

Most low latency applications run on modern pipelined processors that pre-fetch instructions and data before they need to be executed. We discussed in the previous chapter that branch mispredictions are extremely expensive and stall the pipeline, introducing bubbles into it. Therefore, an important development practice for low latency applications is to have fewer branches. Since branches are unavoidable, it is also important to try and make them as predictable as possible.

We have two simple macros that we will use to provide branching hints to the compiler. These use the `__builtin_expect` GCC built-in function that reorders the machine instructions generated by the compiler. Effectively, the compiler uses the branch prediction hints provided by the developer to generate machine code that is optimized under the assumption that a branch is more or less likely to be taken.

Note that instruction reordering is only part of the full picture when it comes to branch prediction, since there is a hardware branch predictor that the processor uses when running instructions. Note that modern hardware branch predictors are extremely good at predicting branches and jumps, especially in cases where the same branch gets taken many times and even when there are at least easily predictable branching patterns.

The two macros are the following:

```
#define LIKELY(x)   __builtin_expect(!!(x), 1)
#define UNLIKELY(x) __builtin_expect(!!(x), 0)
```

The `LIKELY(x)` macro specifies that the condition specified by x is likely to be true, and the `UNLIKELY(x)` macro does the opposite. As an example of the usage, we will use the `UNLIKELY` macro shortly in the next set of functions. In C++20, this is standardized like the `[[likely]]` and `[[unlikely]]` attributes to perform the same function in a standard and portable manner.

We will define two additional functions next, but these are simply used for assertions in our code base. These should be pretty self-explanatory; `ASSERT` logs a message and exits if the condition it is provided evaluates to `false`, and `FATAL` simply logs a message and exits. Note the use of `UNLIKELY` here to specify that we do not expect the `!cond` condition to evaluate to `true`. Also note that using the `ASSERT` method on critical code paths is not free, mostly because of the if check. This is something that we will eventually change to be optimized out of our code for release builds, but for now, we will keep it, since it should be extremely cheap to use:

```
inline auto ASSERT(bool cond, const std::string& msg)
  noexcept {
  if(UNLIKELY(!cond)) {
    std::cerr << msg << std::endl;
    exit(EXIT_FAILURE);
  }
}
inline auto FATAL(const std::string& msg) noexcept {
  std::cerr << msg << std::endl;
  exit(EXIT_FAILURE);
}
```

The code discussed in this section can be found in the `Chapter4/macros.h` source file in the GitHub repository for this book. Note that the `macros.h` header file includes the following two header files:

```
#include <cstring>
#include <iostream>
```

Now, let us jump into thread creation and manipulation functionality in the next section.

Creating and launching a new thread

The method defined in the following code block creates a new thread object, sets the thread affinity on the thread (more on this later), and forwards the function and related arguments that the thread will run during its execution. This is achieved in the `thread_body` lambda, which is passed to the constructor of `std::thread`. Note the use of *variadic template arguments* and *perfect forwarding* to allow this method to be used, running all kinds of functions, arbitrary types, and any number of arguments. After creating the thread, the method waits till the thread either starts running successfully or fails because it failed to set thread affinity, which is what the call to `t->join()` does. Ignore the call to `setThreadCore(core_id)` for now; we will discuss that in the next section:

```cpp
#pragma once

#include <iostream>
#include <atomic>
#include <thread>
#include <unistd.h>

#include <sys/syscall.h>

template<typename T, typename... A>
inline auto createAndStartThread(int core_id, const
  std::string &name, T &&func, A &&... args) noexcept {
  std::atomic<bool> running(false), failed(false);

  auto thread_body = [&] {
    if (core_id >= 0 && !setThreadCore(core_id)) {
      std::cerr << "Failed to set core affinity for " <<
        name << " " << pthread_self() << " to " << core_id
          << std::endl;
      failed = true;
      return;
    }
    std::cout << "Set core affinity for " << name << " " <<
      pthread_self() << " to " << core_id << std::endl;

    running = true;
    std::forward<T>(func)((std::forward<A>(args))...);
  };

  auto t = new std::thread(thread_body);
```

```cpp
  while (!running && !failed) {
    using namespace std::literals::chrono_literals;
    std::this_thread::sleep_for(1s);
  }

  if (failed) {
    t->join();

    delete t;
    t = nullptr;
  }

  return t;
}
```

The code discussed in this section can be found in the `Chapter4/thread_utils.h` source file in the GitHub repository for this book. Now, let us jump into the final section to set thread affinity in the `setThreadCore(core_id)` function.

Setting thread affinity

Here, we will discuss the source code to set the thread affinity for the thread creation lambda we saw in the previous section. Before we discuss the source code, remember that if there is a lot of context-switching between threads, it adds a lot of overhead to thread performance. Threads jumping between CPU cores also hurts performance for similar reasons. Setting thread affinity for performance-critical threads is very important for low latency applications to avoid these issues.

Now, let us look at how to set thread affinity in the `setThreadCore()` method. First, we use the `CPU_ZERO()` method to clear the `cpu_set_t` variable, which is just an array of flags. Then, we use the `CPU_SET()` method to enable entry for the `core_id` we are trying to pin the core to. Finally, we use the `pthread_setaffinity_np()` function to set the thread affinity and return `false` if that fails. Note the use of `pthread_self()` here to get the thread ID to use, which makes sense because this is called from within the `std::thread` instance we create in `createAndStartThread()`:

```cpp
  inline auto setThreadCore(int core_id) noexcept {
    cpu_set_t cpuset;
    CPU_ZERO(&cpuset);
    CPU_SET(core_id, &cpuset);

    return (pthread_setaffinity_np(pthread_self(), sizeof
      (cpu_set_t), &cpuset) == 0);
  }
```

The code discussed in this section can be found in the `Chapter4/thread_utils.h` source file in the GitHub repository for this book. These code blocks belong in the `Common` namespace, as you will see when you look at the `thread_utils.h` source file in the GitHub repository.

Building an example

Before we conclude this section, let us quickly look at a simple example that uses the thread utilities we just created. This example can be found in the `Chapter4/thread_example.cpp` source file in the GitHub repository for this book. Note that the library and all the examples for this chapter can be built using the `CMakeLists.txt` included in the `Chapter4` directory. We also provided two simple scripts, `build.sh` and `run_examples.sh`, to build and run these examples after setting the correct paths to the `cmake` and `ninja` binaries. Note that `cmake` and `ninja` are arbitrary build system choices here, and you can change the build system to be anything else if needed.

The example should be quite self-explanatory – we create and launch two threads with a dummy task of adding the two arguments (a and b) passed to it. Then, we wait for the threads to finish execution before exiting the program:

```cpp
#include "thread_utils.h"

auto dummyFunction(int a, int b, bool sleep) {
  std::cout << "dummyFunction(" << a << "," << b << ")" <<
    std::endl;
  std::cout << "dummyFunction output=" << a + b <<
    std::endl;

  if(sleep) {
    std::cout << "dummyFunction sleeping..." << std::endl;

    using namespace std::literals::chrono_literals;
    std::this_thread::sleep_for(5s);
  }

  std::cout << "dummyFunction done." << std::endl;
}

int main(int, char **) {
  using namespace Common;

  auto t1 = createAndStartThread(-1, "dummyFunction1",
    dummyFunction, 12, 21, false);
  auto t2 = createAndStartThread(1, "dummyFunction2",
    dummyFunction, 15, 51, true);
```

```cpp
    std::cout << "main waiting for threads to be done." <<
      std::endl;
    t1->join();
    t2->join();
    std::cout << "main exiting." << std::endl;

    return 0;
}
```

Running this example will output something like this as the program executes:

```
(base) sghosh@sghosh-ThinkPad-X1-Carbon-3rd:~/Building-Low-Latency-
Applications-with-CPP/Chapter4$ ./cmake-build-release/thread_example
Set core affinity for dummyFunction1 140124979386112 to -1
dummyFunction(12,21)
dummyFunction output=33
dummyFunction done.
Set core affinity for dummyFunction2 140124970993408 to 1
dummyFunction(15,51)
dummyFunction output=66
dummyFunction sleeping...
main waiting for threads to be done.
dummyFunction done.
main exiting.
```

Let us move on to the next section, where we will discuss how to avoid dynamic memory allocations when objects need to be created and discarded during runtime.

Designing C++ memory pools to avoid dynamic memory allocations

We have had several discussions on dynamic memory allocation, the steps the OS needs to perform, and why dynamic memory allocation is slow. Dynamic memory allocation is so slow in fact that low latency applications actively try to avoid it as much as possible on the critical path. We cannot build useful applications without creating and deleting many objects at runtime, and dynamic memory allocation is too slow for low latency applications.

Understanding the definition of a memory pool

First, let us formally define what a memory pool is and why we need one. Many applications (including low latency applications) need to be able to handle many objects and an unknown number of objects. By an unknown number of objects, we mean that the expected count of objects cannot be determined ahead of time, and it cannot be ascertained what the maximum number of objects will be. Obviously, the maximum number of objects possible is what can fit inside the system's memory. The traditional approach to handling these objects is to use dynamic memory allocations as needed. In such a case, the heap memory is considered the memory pool – that is, the pool of memory to allocate from and deallocate to. Unfortunately, these are slow, and we will control how the allocation and deallocation of memory happen in our system using our own custom memory pool. We define a memory pool as anything from which we can request additional memory or objects and return free memory or objects to. By building our own custom memory pool, we can leverage the usage patterns and control the allocation and deallocation mechanisms for optimal performance.

Understanding the use cases of a memory pool

When the exact number of objects of a certain type that will be required is known ahead of time, you can decide to create exactly that number when needed. In practice, there are many cases where the exact number of objects is not known ahead of time. This means we need to create objects on the fly using dynamic memory allocation. As mentioned previously, dynamic memory allocation is a very slow process and a problem for low latency applications. We use the term *memory pool* to describe a pool of objects of a certain type, and that is what we will build in this section. We will use the memory pool in this book to allocate and deallocate objects that we cannot predict.

The solution we will use is to pre-allocate large blocks of memory at startup and serve out required amounts at runtime – that is, do the memory allocation and deallocation steps ourselves from this storage pool. This ends up performing significantly better for a lot of different reasons, such as being able to limit the memory pool usage to certain components in our system instead of all processes running on the server. We can also control the memory storage and allocation and deallocation algorithms, tuning them to perform optimally for our specific application.

Let us start by first making some design decisions for our memory pool. All the source code for our memory pool is in the `Chapter4/mem_pool.h` source file in the GitHub repository for this book.

Designing the memory pool storage

First, we need to decide how to store the elements inside the memory pool. We have really two major choices here – store them on the stack using something like an old-style array (`T[N]`) or `std::array`, or store it on the heap using something like an old-style pointer (`T*`) or something like `std::vector`. Depending on the size of the memory pool, the usage frequency, usage patterns, and the application itself, one choice might be better than the other. For instance, it is possible that we expect to need a huge amount of memory in the memory pool, either because the objects it stores are large or there are many of them. For such a case, heap allocation would be the preferred choice to accommodate the large memory requirements without impacting the stack memory. If we expect very few objects or small objects, we should consider using the stack implementation instead. If we expect to access the objects rarely, putting them on the stack might encounter better cache performance, but for frequent access, either implementation should work equally well. As with a lot of other choices, these decisions are always made by measuring performance in practice. For our memory pool, we will use `std::vector` and heap allocation while noting that it is not thread-safe.

We also need a variable to track which blocks are free or in use. Finally, we will need one last variable to track the location of the next free block to quickly serve allocation requests. One important thing to note here is that we have two choices:

- We use two vectors – one to track the objects and one to track the free or empty markers. This solution is presented in the following diagram; note that in this example, we assume that these two vectors are in very different memory locations. The point we are trying to make here is that accessing the free or empty marker and the object itself might cause cache misses because they are far away from each other.

is_free_or_in_use_ vector Memory : 0x00AA00CC		T object vector Memory: 0xFF00EEDD	
0	is_free_ = true;	0	T object_;
1	is_free_ = false;	1	T object_;
2	is_free_ = false;	2	T object_;
3	is_free_ = false;	3	T object_;
4	is_free_ = true;	4	T object_;
...		...	
...		...	
N	is_free_ = false;	N	T object_;

Figure 4.1 – A memory pool implementation that uses two vectors to track objects and show which indices are free or in use

- We maintain a single vector of structures (a struct, a class, or primitive objects), and each structure stores both the object and variable to represent the free or empty flag.

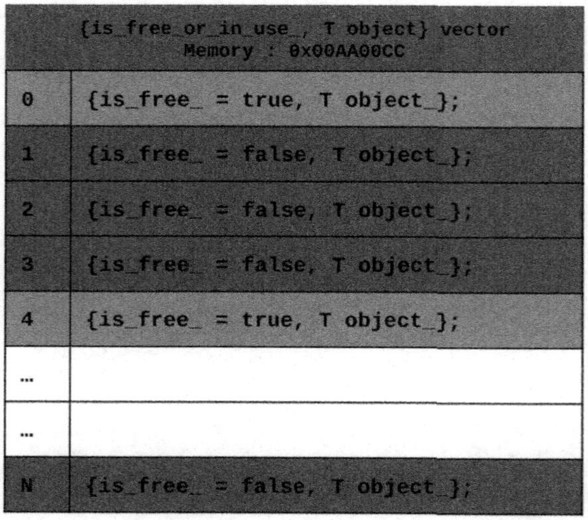

	{is_free_or_in_use_, T object} vector Memory : 0x00AA00CC
0	{is_free_ = true, T object_};
1	{is_free_ = false, T object_};
2	{is_free_ = false, T object_};
3	{is_free_ = false, T object_};
4	{is_free_ = true, T object_};
...	
...	
N	{is_free_ = false, T object_};

Figure 4.2 – A memory pool implementation that uses a single vector to track the object and see whether it is free or in use

The second choice is better from a cache performance perspective, because accessing the object and free marker placed right after the object is better than accessing two different locations in two different vectors that might be potentially far away from each other in memory. This is also because, in almost all usage patterns, if we access the object, we access the free marker and vice versa:

```
#pragma once

#include <cstdint>
#include <vector>
#include <string>

#include "macros.h"

namespace Common {
  template<typename T>
  class MemPool final {
  private:
    struct ObjectBlock {
      T object_;
      bool is_free_ = true;
    };

    std::vector<ObjectBlock> store_;
```

```
    size_t next_free_index_ = 0;
};
```

Next, we need to look at how we initialize this memory pool in the constructor and some boilerplate code for the construction and assignment tasks.

Initializing the memory pool

Initializing our memory pool is quite straightforward – we simply accept a parameter that specifies the initial size of our memory pool and initialize the vector to be large enough to accommodate that many concurrently allocated objects. In our design, we will not add functionality to resize the memory pool past its initial size, but that is a relatively straightforward extension to add if needed. Note that this initial vector initialization is the only time the memory pool allocates memory dynamically, so the memory pool should be created before the execution of the critical path starts. One thing to note here is that we add an assertion to make sure that the actual object of type T is the first one in the `ObjectBlock` struct; we will see the reason for this requirement in the *Handling deallocations* section:

```
public:
  explicit MemPool(std::size_t num_elems) :
      store_(num_elems, {T(), true}) /* pre-allocation of
        vector storage. */ {
    ASSERT(reinterpret_cast<const ObjectBlock *>
      (&(store_[0].object_)) == &(store_[0]), "T object
        should be first member of ObjectBlock.");
}
```

Now for some boilerplate code – we will delete the default constructor, the copy constructor, and the move constructor methods. We will do the same with the copy assignment operator and the move assignment operator. We do this so that these methods are not accidentally called without our knowledge. This is also the reason we made our constructor explicit – to prohibit implicit conversions where we do not expect them:

```
MemPool() = delete;
MemPool(const MemPool&) = delete;
MemPool(const MemPool&&) = delete;
MemPool& operator=(const MemPool&) = delete;
MemPool& operator=(const MemPool&&) = delete;
```

Now, let us move on to the code to serve allocation requests by providing a free object of the T-type template parameter.

Serving new allocation requests

Serving allocation requests is a simple task of finding a block that is free in our memory pool storage, which we can do easily using the `next_free_index_` tracker. Then, we update the `is_free_` marker for that block, initialize the object block of type `T` using `placement new`, and then update `next_free_index_` to point to the next available free block.

Note two things – the first is that we use `placement new` to return an object of type `T` instead of a memory block that is the same size as `T`. This is not strictly necessary and can be removed if the user of the memory pool wants to take responsibility for constructing the object from the memory block we return. `placement new` in most compiler implementations might add an extra `if` check to confirm that the memory block provided to it is not null.

The second thing, which is more of a design choice for us to make depending on the application, is that we call `updateNextFreeIndex()` to update `next_free_index_` to point to the next available free block, which can be implemented in different ways other than the provided here. To answer the question of which implementation is optimal is that it *depends* and needs to be measured in practice. Now, let us first look at the `allocate()` method where, again, we use variadic template arguments to allow arbitrary arguments to be forwarded to the constructor of `T`. Note that here we use the `placement new` operator to construct an object of type `T` with the given arguments from the memory block. Remember that `new` is an operator that can also be overridden if needed, and the `placement new` operator skips the step that allocates memory and uses the provided memory block instead:

```
template<typename... Args>
T *allocate(Args... args) noexcept {
  auto obj_block = &(store_[next_free_index_]);
  ASSERT(obj_block->is_free_, "Expected free
    ObjectBlock at index:" + std::to_string
      (next_free_index_));
  T *ret = &(obj_block->object_);
  ret = new(ret) T(args...); // placement new.
  obj_block->is_free_ = false;

  updateNextFreeIndex();

  return ret;
}
```

Let us look at the `updateNextFreeIndex()` method next. There are two things to note here – first, we have a branch for a case where the index wraps around the end. While this adds an `if` condition here, with the `UNLIKELY()` specification and the expectation of our hardware branch predictor to always predict that the branch isn't taken, this should not hurt our performance in a meaningful way. We can, of course, break up the loop into two loops and remove that `if` condition if we really want to – that is, the first loop loops till `next_free_index_ == store_.size()`, and the second loop loops from 0 onwards.

Secondly, we added a check to detect and fail if there is ever a case where the memory pool is completely full. There are obviously better ways to handle this in practice that do not involve failures, but for the sake of brevity and to stay within the scope of this book, we will just fail when this happens for now:

```cpp
private:
  auto updateNextFreeIndex() noexcept {
    const auto initial_free_index = next_free_index_;
    while (!store_[next_free_index_].is_free_) {
      ++next_free_index_;
      if (UNLIKELY(next_free_index_ == store_.size())) {
        // hardware branch predictor should almost always
          predict this to be false any ways.
        next_free_index_ = 0;
      }
      if (UNLIKELY(initial_free_index ==
        next_free_index_)) {
        ASSERT(initial_free_index != next_free_index_,
          "Memory Pool out of space.");
      }
    }
  }
}
```

The next section deals with handling deallocations or returning objects of type T back to the memory pool to reclaim them as free.

Handling deallocations

Deallocations are a simple matter of finding the correct `ObjectBlock` in our internal `store_` that corresponds to the T object being deallocated and marking the `is_free_` marker for that block to be `true`. Here, we use `reinterpret_cast` to convert `T*` to `ObjectBlock*`, which is OK to do, since object T is the first member in `ObjectBlock`. This should now explain the assertion we added to the constructor in the *Initializing the memory pool* section. We also add an assertion here to make sure that the element that the user tries to deallocate belongs to this memory pool. Again, there can be more graceful handling of such error cases, but we will leave that up to you for the sake of brevity and to keep the discussion within the scope of this book:

```cpp
auto deallocate(const T *elem) noexcept {
  const auto elem_index = (reinterpret_cast<const
    ObjectBlock *>(elem) - &store_[0]);
  ASSERT(elem_index >= 0 && static_cast<size_t>
```

```
        (elem_index) < store_.size(), "Element being
          deallocated does not belong to this Memory
            pool.");
      ASSERT(!store_[elem_index].is_free_, "Expected in-use
        ObjectBlock at index:" + std::to_string
          (elem_index));
      store_[elem_index].is_free_ = true;
    }
```

That concludes our design and implementation of memory pools. Let us look at a simple example.

Using the memory pool with an example

Let us look at a simple and self-explanatory example of the memory pool we just created. This code is in the `Chapter4/mem_pool_example.cpp` file and can be built using the `CMake` file, as previously mentioned. It creates a memory pool of a primitive `double` type and another of a custom `MyStruct` type. Then, it allocates and deallocates some elements from this memory pool and prints out the values and memory locations:

```
#include "mem_pool.h"

struct MyStruct {
  int d_[3];
};

int main(int, char **) {
  using namespace Common;

  MemPool<double> prim_pool(50);
  MemPool<MyStruct> struct_pool(50);

  for(auto i = 0; i < 50; ++i) {
    auto p_ret = prim_pool.allocate(i);
    auto s_ret = struct_pool.allocate(MyStruct{i, i+1,
      i+2});

    std::cout << "prim elem:" << *p_ret << " allocated at:"
      << p_ret << std::endl;
    std::cout << "struct elem:" << s_ret->d_[0] << "," <<
      s_ret->d_[1] << "," << s_ret->d_[2] << " allocated
        at:" << s_ret << std::endl;

    if(i % 5 == 0) {
      std::cout << "deallocating prim elem:" << *p_ret << "
```

```
                from:" << p_ret << std::endl;
        std::cout << "deallocating struct elem:" << s_ret
            ->d_[0] << "," << s_ret->d_[1] << "," << s_ret->
                d_[2] << " from:" << s_ret << std::endl;

        prim_pool.deallocate(p_ret);
        struct_pool.deallocate(s_ret);
    }
  }

  return 0;
}
```

Running this example using the following command should produce output similar to what is shown here:

```
(base) sghosh@sghosh-ThinkPad-X1-Carbon-3rd:~/Building-Low-Latency-
Applications-with-CPP/Chapter4$ ./cmake-build-release/mem_pool_example
prim elem:0 allocated at:0x5641b4d1beb0
struct elem:0,1,2 allocated at:0x5641b4d1c220
deallocating prim elem:0 from:0x5641b4d1beb0
deallocating struct elem:0,1,2 from:0x5641b4d1c220
prim elem:1 allocated at:0x5641b4d1bec0
struct elem:1,2,3 allocated at:0x5641b4d1c230
prim elem:2 allocated at:0x5641b4d1bed0
...
```

In the next section, we will build a very similar component – lock-free queues.

Transferring data using lock-free queues

In the *C++ threading for multi-threaded low latency applications* section, we hinted that one possible application of having multiple threads is to set up a pipelined system. Here, one component thread performs part of the processing and forwards the results to the next stage of the pipeline for further processing. We will be using such a design in our electronic trading system, but there'll be more on that later.

Communicating between threads and processes

There are a lot of options when it comes to transferring data between processes and/or threads. **Inter-Process Communication** (**IPC**), such as mutexes, semaphores, signals, memory-mapped files, and shared memory, can be used for these purposes. It also gets tricky when there is concurrent access to shared data and the important requirement is to avoid data corruption. Another important requirement is to make sure that the reader and writer have consistent views of the shared data. To transfer information from one thread to another (or from one process to another), the optimal way to do so is through a data queue that both threads have access to. Building a queue of data and using locks to synchronize in a concurrent access environment is an option here. Due to the concurrent access nature of this design, locks or mutexes or something similar has to be used to prevent errors. However, locks and mutexes are extremely inefficient and lead to context switches, which degrade performance tremendously for critical threads. So, what we need is a lock-free queue to facilitate communication between threads without the overhead of locks and context switches. Note that the lock-free queue we will build here is only to be used for **Single Producer Single Consumer** (**SPSC**) – that is, only one thread writes to the queue and only one thread consumes from the queue. More complex use cases for lock-free queues will require additional complexity, which is out of the scope of this book.

Designing lock-free queue storage

For lock-free queues, we again have the option of either having the storage allocated on the stack or the heap. Here, we will again choose `std::vector` and allocate memory on the heap. Additionally, we create two `std::atomic` variables – one called `next_write_index_` – to track what index the next write to the queue will go to.

The second variable, called `next_read_index_`, is used to track what index the next unread element in the queue is located in. The implementation is relatively straightforward because of our assumption that a single thread writes to the queue and a single thread reads from it. Now, let us first design and implement the internal storage of the lock-free queue data structure. The source code discussed in this section can be found in the `Chapter4/lf_queue.h` source file in the GitHub repository for this book.

A quick word on `std::atomic` – it is a modern C++ construct that allows thread-safe operations. It lets us read, update, and write variables on a shared variable without using locks or mutexes, and it does so while preserving the order of operations. A detailed discussion of `std::atomic` and memory ordering is outside the scope of this book, but you can find a reference in our other book *Developing High-Frequency Trading Systems*.

First, let us define the data members for this class in the following code snippet:

```cpp
#pragma once

#include <iostream>
#include <vector>
#include <atomic>

namespace Common {
  template<typename T>
  class LFQueue final {
  private:
    std::vector<T> store_;
```

```
    std::atomic<size_t> next_write_index_ = {0};
    std::atomic<size_t> next_read_index_  = {0};

    std::atomic<size_t> num_elements_ = {0};
  };
}
```

This class holds a `std::vector` object `store_` of a T template object type, which is the actual queue of data. A `std::atomic<size_t> next_write_index_` variable tracks the index in this vector, where the next element will be written to. Similarly, a `std::atomic<size_t> next_read_index_` variable tracks the index in this vector, where the next element to be read or consumed is available. These need to be the `std::atomic<>` type, since the reading and writing operations are performed from different threads.

Initializing the lock-free queue

The constructor for our lock-free queue is very similar to the constructor of the memory pool we saw earlier. We dynamically allocate the memory for the entire vector in the constructor. We can extend this design to allow the lock-free queue to be resized at runtime, but for now, we will stick to a fixed-size queue:

```
template<typename T>
class LFQueue final {
public:
  LFQueue(std::size_t num_elems) :
      store_(num_elems, T()) /* pre-allocation of vector
        storage. */ {
  }
```

We have similar boilerplate code here with regards to the default constructor, copy and move constructors, and assignment operators. These are deleted for the reasons we discussed before:

```
  LFQueue() = delete;
  LFQueue(const LFQueue&) = delete;
  LFQueue(const LFQueue&&) = delete;
  LFQueue& operator=(const LFQueue&) = delete;
  LFQueue& operator=(const LFQueue&&) = delete;
```

Next, we will look at the code to add new elements to the queue.

Adding elements to the queue

The code to add new elements to the queue is implemented in two parts; the first part, `getNextToWriteTo()`, returns a pointer to the next element to write new data to. The second part, `updateWriteIndex()`, increments the write index, `next_write_index_`, once the element has been written to the slot provided. We designed it in such a way that, instead of having a single `write()` function, we provide the user with a pointer to the element and if the objects are quite large then not all of it needs to be updated or overwritten. Additionally, this design makes it much easier to deal with race conditions:

```
auto getNextToWriteTo() noexcept {
  return &store_[next_write_index_];
}

auto updateWriteIndex() noexcept {
    next_write_index_ = (next_write_index_ + 1) %
      store_.size();
    num_elements_++;
}
```

In the next section, we will use a very similar design to consume elements from the queue.

Consuming elements from the queue

To consume elements from the queue, we do the opposite of what we did to add elements to the queue. Like the design we have where we split `write()` into two parts, we will have two parts to consume an element from the queue. We have a `getNextToRead()` method that returns a pointer to the next element to be consumed but does not update the read index. This method will return `nullptr` if there is no element to be consumed. The second part, `updateReadIndex()`, just updates the read index after the element is consumed:

```
auto getNextToRead() const noexcept -> const T * {
  return (next_read_index_ == next_write_index_) ?
    nullptr : &store_[next_read_index_];
}

auto updateReadIndex() noexcept {
    next_read_index_ = (next_read_index_ + 1) %
      store_.size();
    ASSERT(num_elements_ != 0, "Read an invalid element
      in:" + std::to_string(pthread_self()));
    num_elements_--;
}
```

We also define another simple method to return the number of elements in the queue:

```
auto size() const noexcept {
  return num_elements_.load();
}
```

wThis finishes our design and implementation of lock-free queues for the SPSC use case. Let us look at an example that uses this component in the next sub-section.

Using the lock-free queue

This example of how to use the lock-free data queue can be found in the `Chapter4/lf_queue_example.cpp` file and built as previously mentioned. This example creates a consumer thread and provides it with a lock-free queue instance. The producer then generates and adds some elements to that queue, and the consumer thread checks the queue and consumes the queue elements till the queue is empty. Both threads of execution – producer and consumer – wait for short periods of time between generating an element and consuming it:

```cpp
#include "thread_utils.h"
#include "lf_queue.h"

struct MyStruct {
  int d_[3];
};

using namespace Common;

auto consumeFunction(LFQueue<MyStruct>* lfq) {
  using namespace std::literals::chrono_literals;
  std::this_thread::sleep_for(5s);

  while(lfq->size()) {
    const auto d = lfq->getNextToRead();
    lfq->updateReadIndex();

    std::cout << "consumeFunction read elem:" << d->d_[0]
      << "," << d->d_[1] << "," << d->d_[2] << " lfq-size:"
        <<lfq->size() << std::endl;

    std::this_thread::sleep_for(1s);
  }

  std::cout << "consumeFunction exiting." << std::endl;
}

int main(int, char **) {
  LFQueue<MyStruct> lfq(20);

  auto ct = createAndStartThread(-1, "", consumeFunction,
```

```cpp
        &lfq);

    for(auto i = 0; i < 50; ++i) {
      const MyStruct d{i, i * 10, i * 100};
      *(lfq.getNextToWriteTo()) = d;
      lfq.updateWriteIndex();

      std::cout << "main constructed elem:" << d.d_[0] << ","
        << d.d_[1] << "," << d.d_[2] << " lfq-size:" <<
          lfq.size() << std::endl;

      using namespace std::literals::chrono_literals;
      std::this_thread::sleep_for(1s);
    }

    ct->join();

    std::cout << "main exiting." << std::endl;

    return 0;
}
```

The output of running this example program is provided as follows, which is just the producer and the consumer writing to and reading from the lock-free queue:

```
(base) sghosh@sghosh-ThinkPad-X1-Carbon-3rd:~/Building-Low-Latency-
Applications-with-CPP/Chapter4$ ./cmake-build-release/lf_queue_example
Set core affinity for  139710770276096 to -1
main constructed elem:0,0,0 lfq-size:1
main constructed elem:1,10,100 lfq-size:2
main constructed elem:2,20,200 lfq-size:3
main constructed elem:3,30,300 lfq-size:4
consumeFunction read elem:0,0,0 lfq-size:3
main constructed elem:4,40,400 lfq-size:4
consumeFunction read elem:1,10,100 lfq-size:3
main constructed elem:5,50,500 lfq-size:4
consumeFunction read elem:2,20,200 lfq-size:3
main constructed elem:6,60,600 lfq-size:4
consumeFunction read elem:3,30,300 lfq-size:3
main constructed elem:7,70,700 lfq-size:4
consumeFunction read elem:4,40,400 lfq-size:3
...
```

Next, we will build a low latency logging framework using some of the components we just built – threads and lock-free queues.

Building a low latency logging framework

Now, we will build a low latency logging framework using some of the components we just built in the previous sections. Logging is an important part of any application, whether it is logging general application behavior, warnings, errors, or even performance statistics. However, a lot of important logging output is actually from performance-critical components that are on a critical path.

A naïve logging approach would be to output to the screen, while a slightly better approach would be for logs to be saved to one or more log files. However, here we have a few problems – disk I/O is extremely slow and unpredictable, and string operations and formatting themselves are slow. For these reasons, performing these operations on a performance-critical thread is a terrible idea, so we will build a solution in this section to alleviate the downsides while preserving the ability to output logs as needed.

Before we jump into the logger class, we will define a few utility methods to fetch the current system time as well as convert them to strings for logging purposes.

Designing utility methods for time

We will define a simple utility function to fetch the current system time and some constants to make conversions from different units easier. The code for the time utilities can be found in `Chapter4/time_utils.h` in the GitHub repository for this book:

```
#pragma once

#include <chrono>
#include <ctime>

namespace Common {
  typedef int64_t Nanos;

  constexpr Nanos NANOS_TO_MICROS = 1000;
  constexpr Nanos MICROS_TO_MILLIS = 1000;
  constexpr Nanos MILLIS_TO_SECS = 1000;
  constexpr Nanos NANOS_TO_MILLIS = NANO_TO_MICROS *
    MICROS_TO_MILLIS;
  constexpr Nanos NANOS_TO_SECS = NANOS_TO_MILLIS *
    MILLIS_TO_SECS;

  inline auto getCurrentNanos() noexcept {
    return std::chrono::duration_cast
```

```
            <std::chrono::nanoseconds>(std::chrono::
              system_clock::now().time_since_epoch()).count();
  }

  inline auto& getCurrentTimeStr(std::string* time_str) {
    const auto time = std::chrono::system_clock::
      to_time_t(std::chrono::system_clock::now());
    time_str->assign(ctime(&time));
    if (!time_str->empty())
      time_str->at(time_str->length()-1) = '\0';
    return *time_str;
  }
}
```

Now, let us design the logger class itself, starting with the next section.

Designing the low latency logger

To build this low latency logging framework, we will create a background logging thread whose only task is to write log lines to a log file on disk. The idea here is to offload the slow disk I/O operations as well as the string formatting operations away from the main performance-critical thread onto this background thread. One thing to understand is that logging to disk does not have to be instantaneous – that is, most systems can tolerate some delay between an event happening and information pertinent to that event being logged to disk. We will use the multi-threading function we created in the first section of this chapter to create this logger thread and assign it the task of writing to the log file.

To publish data that needs to be logged from the main performance-critical thread to this logging thread, we will use the lock-free data queue we created in the previous section. The way the logger will work is that instead of writing information directly to the disk, the performance-sensitive threads will simply push the information to this lock-free queue. As we discussed before, a logger thread will consume from the other end of this queue and write to the disk. The source code for this component is available in the `logging.h` and `logging.cpp` files in the `Chapter4` directory in the GitHub repository for this book.

Defining some logger structures

Before we start designing the logger itself, we will first define the basic block of information that will be transferred across the lock-free queue from the performance-sensitive thread to the logger thread. In this design, we simply create a structure capable of holding the different types that we will log. First, let us define an enumeration that specifies the type of value the structure it is pointing to; we will call this enumeration `LogType`:

```
#pragma once
```

```
#include <string>
#include <fstream>
#include <cstdio>

#include "types.h"
#include "macros.h"
#include "lf_queue.h"
#include "thread_utils.h"
#include "time_utils.h"

namespace Common {
  constexpr size_t LOG_QUEUE_SIZE = 8 * 1024 * 1024;
  enum class LogType : int8_t {
    CHAR = 0,
    INTEGER = 1, LONG_INTEGER = 2, LONG_LONG_INTEGER = 3,
    UNSIGNED_INTEGER = 4, UNSIGNED_LONG_INTEGER = 5,
    UNSIGNED_LONG_LONG_INTEGER = 6,
    FLOAT = 7, DOUBLE = 8
  };
}
```

Now, we can define the `LogElement` structure that will hold the next value to push to the queue and, eventually, write logs to the file from the logger thread. This structure contains a member of type `LogType` to specify the type of value it holds. The other member in this structure is a union of the different possible primitive types. This would have been a good place to use `std::variant`, since it is a type-safe union in modern C++ with the **discriminator** (`LogType type_`, which specifies what the union contains) built into it. However, `std::variant` has worse runtime performance; hence, we choose to move forward with the old-style union here:

```
struct LogElement {
  LogType type_ = LogType::CHAR;
  union {
    char c;
    int i; long l; long long ll;
    unsigned u; unsigned long ul; unsigned long long ull;
    float f; double d;
  } u_;
};
```

With the definition of the `LogElement` structure out of the way, let us move on to defining data in the logger class.

Initializing the logger data structures

Our logger will contain a few important objects. Firstly, a `std::ofstream` file object is the log file that data is written to. Secondly, an `LFQueue<LogElement>` object is the lock-free queue to transfer data from the main thread to the logger thread. Next, `std::atomic<bool>` stops the logger thread's processing when needed, and a `std::thread` object which is the logger thread. Finally, `std::string` is the filename, which we provide purely for informational purposes:

```
class Logger final {
private:
  const std::string file_name_;
  std::ofstream file_;
  LFQueue<LogElement> queue_;
  std::atomic<bool> running_ = {true};
  std::thread *logger_thread_ = nullptr;
};
```

Now, let us move on to constructing our logger, the logger queue, and the logger thread.

Creating the logger and launching the logger thread

In the logger constructor, we will initialize the logger queue with an appropriate size, save `file_name_` for informational purposes, open the output log file object, and create and launch the logger thread. Note that here we will exit if we are unable to open the output log file or unable to create and launch the logger thread. As we've mentioned before, there are obviously more forgiving and more graceful ways to handle these failures, but we will not explore those in this book. Note here that we set the `core_id` parameter in `createAndStartThread()` to -1, to not set affinity on the thread right now. We will revisit the design of how to assign each thread to a CPU core later in the book once we understand the design of the full ecosystem, and we will tune it for performance:

```
  explicit Logger(const std::string &file_name)
      : file_name_(file_name), queue_(LOG_QUEUE_SIZE) {
    file_.open(file_name);
    ASSERT(file_.is_open(), "Could not open log file:" +
      file_name);
    logger_thread_ = createAndStartThread(-1,
      "Common/Logger", [this]() { flushQueue(); });
    ASSERT(logger_thread_ != nullptr, "Failed to start
      Logger thread.");
  }
```

We pass a method called `flushQueue()` that this logger thread will run. As the name suggests, and in line with what we discussed, this thread will empty the queue of log data and write the data to the file; we will look at that next. The implementation of `flushQueue()` is simple. If the atomic running_ Boolean is true, it runs in a loop, performing the following steps: it consumes any new elements pushed to the lock-free queue, queue_, and writes them to the file_ object we created. It unpacks the LogElement objects in the queue and writes the correct member of the union to the file, depending on the type. The thread sleeps for a millisecond when the lock-free queue is empty and then checks again to see whether there are new elements to be written to disk:

```
auto flushQueue() noexcept {
  while (running_) {
    for (auto next = queue_.getNextToRead();
      queue_.size() && next; next = queue_
        .getNextToRead()) {
      switch (next->type_) {
        case LogType::CHAR: file_ << next->u_.c; break;
        case LogType::INTEGER: file_ << next->u_.i; break;
        case LogType::LONG_INTEGER: file_ << next->u_.l; break;
        case LogType::LONG_LONG_INTEGER: file_ << next->
          u_.ll; break;
        case LogType::UNSIGNED_INTEGER: file_ << next->
          u_.u; break;
        case LogType::UNSIGNED_LONG_INTEGER: file_ <<
          next->u_.ul; break;
        case LogType::UNSIGNED_LONG_LONG_INTEGER: file_
          << next->u_.ull; break;
        case LogType::FLOAT: file_ << next->u_.f; break;
        case LogType::DOUBLE: file_ << next->u_.d; break;
      }
      queue_.updateReadIndex();
      next = queue_.getNextToRead();
    }

    using namespace std::literals::chrono_literals;
    std::this_thread::sleep_for(1ms);
  }
}
```

The destructor for our logger class is important, so let us look at what cleanup tasks it needs to perform. First, the destructor waits for the lock-free queue to be consumed by the logger thread, so it waits till it is empty. Once it is empty, it sets the running_ flag to be false so that the logger thread can finish its execution. To wait for the logger thread to finish execution – that is, return from the flushQueue() method, it calls the std::thread::join() method on the logger thread. Finally, it closes the file_ object, which writes any buffered data onto the disk, and then we are done:

```
~Logger() {
  std::cerr << "Flushing and closing Logger for " <<
```

```
      file_name_ << std::endl;

  while (queue_.size()) {
    using namespace std::literals::chrono_literals;
    std::this_thread::sleep_for(1s);
  }
  running_ = false;
  logger_thread_->join();

  file_.close();
}
```

Finally, we will add the usual boilerplate code we discussed multiple times before regarding the constructors and assignment operators:

```
Logger() = delete;
Logger(const Logger &) = delete;
Logger(const Logger &&) = delete;
Logger &operator=(const Logger &) = delete;
Logger &operator=(const Logger &&) = delete;
```

In this section, we saw the portion of the component that consumes from the queue and writes it to disk. In the next section, we will see how data gets added to the lock-free queue as part of the logging process from the performance-critical thread.

Pushing data to the logger queue

To push data to the logger queue, we will define a couple of overloaded `pushValue()` methods that handle different types of arguments. Each method does the same thing, which is to push values one by one onto the queue. One thing worthy of note here is that there are more efficient implementations for what we are about to discuss; however, they involve additional complexity, and we left them out for the sake of brevity and to limit the scope of what we can cover in this book. We will point out the areas of potential improvement when we discuss them.

First, we create a variant of `pushValue()` to push objects of type `LogElement`, which will get called from the other `pushValue()` functions we will define shortly. It basically writes to the next location in the lock-free queue and increments the write index:

```
auto pushValue(const LogElement &log_element) noexcept {
  *(queue_.getNextToWriteTo()) = log_element;
  queue_.updateWriteIndex();
}
```

The next simple variant of `pushValue()` is for a single char value, which basically just creates an object of type `LogElement`, calls the `pushValue()` method we just discussed, and passes the `LogElement` object:

```
auto pushValue(const char value) noexcept {
  pushValue(LogElement{LogType::CHAR, {.c = value}});
}
```

Now, we create a variant of `pushValue()` for `const char*` – that is, a collection of chars. This implementation loops through the characters one at a time and calls the `pushValue()` we implemented previously. This is an area of potential improvement, where we could use a single `memcpy()` to copy over all the characters in the array instead of looping through them. There are some edge cases we would need to handle around the wrapping of the indices at the end of the queue, but we will leave it up to you to explore further:

```
auto pushValue(const char *value) noexcept {
  while (*value) {
    pushValue(*value);
    ++value;
  }
}
```

Next, we create another variant of `pushValue()` for `const std::string&`, which is quite straightforward and uses `pushValue()`, which we created previously:

```
auto pushValue(const std::string &value) noexcept {
  pushValue(value.c_str());
}
```

Finally, we need to add variants of `pushValue()` for the different primitive types. They are very similar to the one we built for a single char value and are shown here:

```
auto pushValue(const int value) noexcept {
  pushValue(LogElement{LogType::INTEGER, {.i = value}});
}
auto pushValue(const long value) noexcept {
  pushValue(LogElement{LogType::LONG_INTEGER, {.l =
    value}});
}
auto pushValue(const long long value) noexcept {
  pushValue(LogElement{LogType::LONG_LONG_INTEGER, {.ll =
    value}});
}
auto pushValue(const unsigned value) noexcept {
  pushValue(LogElement{LogType::UNSIGNED_INTEGER, {.u =
```

```
        value}});
}
auto pushValue(const unsigned long value) noexcept {
  pushValue(LogElement{LogType::UNSIGNED_LONG_INTEGER,
    {.ul = value}});
}
auto pushValue(const unsigned long long value) noexcept {
  pushValue(LogElement{LogType::UNSIGNED_LONG_LONG_INTEGER,
    {.ull = value}});
}
auto pushValue(const float value) noexcept {
  pushValue(LogElement{LogType::FLOAT, {.f = value}});
}
auto pushValue(const double value) noexcept {
  pushValue(LogElement{LogType::DOUBLE, {.d = value}});
}
```

At this point, we have achieved two goals – moved the disk output operation to the background logger thread and moved the task of formatting the primitive values into string format to the background thread. Next, we will add functionality for the performance-sensitive thread to use to push data to the lock-free queue, using the `pushValue()` methods we just built.

Adding a useful and generic log function

We will define a `log()` method, which is very similar to the `printf()` function but slightly simpler. It is simpler in the sense that the format specifier is just a `%` character that is used to substitute all the different primitive types. This method uses variadic template arguments to support an arbitrary number and types of arguments. It looks for the `%` character and then substitutes the next value in its place, calling one of the overloaded `pushValue()` methods we defined in the last section. After that, it calls itself recursively, except this time, the value points to the first argument in the template parameter pack:

```
template<typename T, typename... A>
auto log(const char *s, const T &value, A... args)
  noexcept {
  while (*s) {
    if (*s == '%') {
      if (UNLIKELY(*(s + 1) == '%')) {
        ++s;
      } else {
        pushValue(value);
        log(s + 1, args...);
        return;
```

```
      }
    }
    pushValue(*s++);
  }
  FATAL("extra arguments provided to log()");
}
```

This method is meant to be called using something like this example:

```
int int_val = 10;
std::string str_val = "hello";
double dbl_val = 10.10;
log("Integer:% String:% Double:%",
    int_val, str_val, dbl_val);
```

The `log()` method we built here cannot handle a case where there are no arguments passed to it. Therefore, we need an extra overloaded `log()` method to handle the case, where a simple `const char *` is passed to it. We add an extra check here to make sure that extra arguments were not passed to this method or the aforementioned `log()` method:

```
auto log(const char *s) noexcept {
  while (*s) {
    if (*s == '%') {
      if (UNLIKELY(*(s + 1) == '%')) {
        ++s;
      } else {
        FATAL("missing arguments to log()");
      }
    }
    pushValue(*s++);
  }
}
```

This finishes the design and implementation of our low latency logging framework. Using our multi-threading routine and our lock-free queue, we created a framework where the performance-critical thread offloads the string formatting and disk file write tasks to the background logger thread. Now, let us look at a good example of how to create, configure, and use the logger we just created.

Learning how to use the logger with an example

We will present a basic example that creates a `Logger` object and configures it to write the logs to `logging_example.log`. Then, it logs a few different data types to the file through the logger. This source for this can be found in the `Chapter4/logging_example.cpp` file:

```cpp
#include "logging.h"

int main(int, char **) {
  using namespace Common;

  char c = 'd';
  int i = 3;
  unsigned long ul = 65;
  float f = 3.4;
  double d = 34.56;
  const char* s = "test C-string";
  std::string ss = "test string";

  Logger logger("logging_example.log");

  logger.log("Logging a char:% an int:% and an
    unsigned:%\n", c, i, ul);
  logger.log("Logging a float:% and a double:%\n", f, d);
  logger.log("Logging a C-string:'%'\n", s);
  logger.log("Logging a string:'%'\n", ss);

  return 0;
}
```

The output of running this can be viewed by outputting the contents of the `logging_example.log` file in the current directory, as shown here:

```
(base) sghosh@sghosh-ThinkPad-X1-Carbon-3rd:~/Building-Low-Latency-Applications-with-CPP/Chapter4$ cat logging_example.log
Logging a char:d an int:3 and an unsigned:65
Logging a float:3.4 and a double:34.56
Logging a C-string:'test C-string'
Logging a string:'test string'
```

In this framework, the only overhead that a call to `log()` invokes is the overhead of iterating through the characters in the string and pushing the characters and values onto the lock-free queue. Now, we will move our discussion to network programming and the use of sockets, which we will be using later on to facilitate communication between different processes.

C++ network programming using sockets

In this final section, we will build the last of our basic building blocks – a framework to handle network programming using Unix sockets. We will use this framework to build a server that listens for incoming TCP connections and a client that is capable of establishing a TCP connection to such a server. We will also use this framework to publish UDP traffic and consume from a stream of multicast traffic. Note that to limit the scope of this discussion, we will only discuss Unix sockets without any kernel bypass capabilities. Using kernel bypass and leveraging the kernel bypass API provided by the **Network Interface Cards** (**NICs**) that support it is outside the scope of this book. Note also that we expect you to have some basic knowledge or experience with network sockets and, ideally, programming network sockets in C++.

Building a basic socket API

Our goal here is to create a mechanism to create a network socket and initialize it with the correct parameters. This method will be used to create listener, receiver, and sender sockets to communicate over UDP and TCP protocols. Before we jump into the routine that creates the socket itself, let us first define a bunch of utility methods that we will use in our final method. All the code for the basic socket API is in `Chapter4/socket_utils.cpp` in the GitHub repository for this book. Note that before we investigate the implementation of the functionality, we will present the `Chapter4/socket_utils.h` header file, which contains all the `include` files and function signatures we will implement:

```
#pragma once

#include <iostream>
#include <string>
#include <unordered_set>
#include <sys/epoll.h>
#include <unistd.h>
#include <sys/types.h>
#include <sys/socket.h>
#include <netdb.h>
#include <netinet/in.h>
#include <netinet/tcp.h>
#include <arpa/inet.h>
#include <ifaddrs.h>
#include <sys/socket.h>
#include <fcntl.h>

#include "macros.h"

#include "logging.h"

namespace Common {
  constexpr int MaxTCPServerBacklog = 1024;

  auto getIfaceIP(const std::string &iface) -> std::string;
```

```
    auto setNonBlocking(int fd) -> bool;
    auto setNoDelay(int fd) -> bool;
    auto setSOTimestamp(int fd) -> bool;
    auto wouldBlock() -> bool;
    auto setMcastTTL(int fd, int ttl) -> bool;
    auto setTTL(int fd, int ttl) -> bool;
    auto join(int fd, const std::string &ip, const
      std::string &iface, int port) -> bool;
    auto createSocket(Logger &logger, const std::string
      &t_ip, const std::string &iface, int port, bool is_udp,
        bool is_blocking, bool is_listening, int ttl, bool
          needs_so_timestamp) -> int;
}
```

Now, let us start with the implementation of these methods, starting with the next section.

Getting interface information

The first utility method we need to build is to convert network interfaces represented in string form to a form that can be used by the lower-level socket routines we will use. We call this getIfaceIP(), and we will need this when we specify what network interfaces to listen to, connect from, or send through. We use the getifaddrs() method to fetch information about all the interfaces, which returns a linked list structure, ifaddrs, containing this information. Finally, it uses the getnameinfo() information to get the final name to be used with the rest of the methods:

```
#include "socket_utils.h"

namespace Common {
  auto getIfaceIP(const std::string &iface) -> std::string {
    char buf[NI_MAXHOST] = {'\0'};
    ifaddrs *ifaddr = nullptr;

    if (getifaddrs(&ifaddr) != -1) {
      for (ifaddrs *ifa = ifaddr; ifa; ifa = ifa->ifa_next) {
        if (ifa->ifa_addr && ifa->ifa_addr->sa_family ==
          AF_INET && iface == ifa->ifa_name) {
          getnameinfo(ifa->ifa_addr, sizeof(sockaddr_in),
            buf, sizeof(buf), NULL, 0, NI_NUMERICHOST);
          break;
        }
      }
      freeifaddrs(ifaddr);
    }
```

```
    return buf;
  }
}
```

For instance, on my system with the following network interfaces, we have the following:

```
lo: flags=73<UP,LOOPBACK,RUNNING>  mtu 65536
        inet 127.0.0.1  netmask 255.0.0.0
wlp4s0: flags=4163<UP,BROADCAST,RUNNING,MULTICAST>  mtu 1500
        inet 192.168.10.104  netmask 255.255.255.0  broadcast 192.168.10.255
```

`getIfaceIP("lo")` returns `127.0.0.1`, and `getIfaceIP("wlp4s0")` returns `192.168.10.104`.

Next, we will move on to the next important utility function we need, and this one affects the performance of applications that need network sockets.

Setting sockets to be non-blocking

The next utility function we will build is one that sets sockets as non-blocking. A blocking socket is one where a call that is read on it will block indefinitely till data is available. This is generally not a good design for extremely low latency applications for many reasons. One of the main reasons is that blocking sockets are implemented using switches between the user space and the kernel space, and that is highly inefficient. When the socket needs to be *woken up* or unblocked, there needs to be an interrupt, an interrupt handler, and so on from the kernel space to the user space to handle the event. Additionally, the performance-critical thread that gets blocked would incur context-switching costs, which, as already discussed, are detrimental to performance.

The following `setNonBlocking()` method uses the `fcntl()` routine with `F_GETFL` to first check a socket file descriptor, seeing whether it is already non-blocking. If it is not already non-blocking, then it uses the `fcntl()` routine again but this time with `F_SETFL` to add the non-blocking bit, which is set on the file descriptor. It returns `true` if the socket file descriptor was already non-blocking or the method was able to successfully make it non-blocking:

```
auto setNonBlocking(int fd) -> bool {
  const auto flags = fcntl(fd, F_GETFL, 0);
  if (flags == -1)
    return false;
  if (flags & O_NONBLOCK)
    return true;
  return (fcntl(fd, F_SETFL, flags | O_NONBLOCK) != -1);
}
```

Next, we will enable another important optimization for TCP sockets by disabling **Nagle's algorithm**.

Disabling Nagle's algorithm

Without diving into too many details, Nagle's algorithm is used to improve buffering in TCP sockets and prevent overhead associated with guaranteeing reliability on the TCP socket. This is achieved by delaying some packets instead of sending them out immediately. For many applications, it is a good feature to have, but for low latency applications, disabling the latency associated with sending packets out is imperative.

Fortunately, disabling Nagle's algorithm is a simple matter of setting a socket option, `TCP_NODELAY`, using the `setsockopt()` routine, as shown here:

```
auto setNoDelay(int fd) -> bool {
  int one = 1;
  return (setsockopt(fd, IPPROTO_TCP, TCP_NODELAY,
    reinterpret_cast<void *>(&one), sizeof(one)) != -1);
}
```

We will define a few more routines to set optional and/or additional functionality in the next section, before we finally implement the functionality to create a socket.

Setting up additional parameters

First, we will define a simple method to check whether a socket operation would block or not. This is a simple check of the global `errno` error variable against two possible values, `EWOULDBLOCK` and `EINPROGRESS`:

```
auto wouldBlock() -> bool {
  return (errno == EWOULDBLOCK || errno == EINPROGRESS);
}
```

Next, we define a method to set the **Time to Live** (**TTL**) value on our sockets. TTL is a network-level setting that controls the maximum number of hops that a packet can take from sender to receiver. We might not really need to use this, depending on the setup of our application, but it is provided here if required. Fortunately, again, all we need to do is set the `IP_TTL` socket options for non-multicast sockets and `IP_MULTICAST_TTL` for multicast sockets, using the `setsockopt()` routine, as shown here:

```
auto setTTL(int fd, int ttl) -> bool {
  return (setsockopt(fd, IPPROTO_IP, IP_TTL,
    reinterpret_cast<void *>(&ttl), sizeof(ttl)) != -1);
}
auto setMcastTTL(int fd, int mcast_ttl) noexcept -> bool {
  return (setsockopt(fd, IPPROTO_IP, IP_MULTICAST_TTL,
    reinterpret_cast<void *>(&mcast_ttl), sizeof
      (mcast_ttl)) != -1);
}
```

Finally, we define one last method that will allow us to generate software timestamps when network packets hit the network socket. Note that if we had specialized hardware (NICs) that support hardware timestamping, we would enable and use those here. However, to limit the scope of this book, we will assume that you do not have any special hardware and can only set the SO_TIMESTAMP option, using the setsockopt() method, to enable software timestamping:

```
auto setSOTimestamp(int fd) -> bool {
  int one = 1;
  return (setsockopt(fd, SOL_SOCKET, SO_TIMESTAMP,
    reinterpret_cast<void *>(&one), sizeof(one)) != -1);
}
```

This completes our discussion of socket-related utility functions, and now, we can move on to finally implementing the functionality to create generic Unix sockets.

Creating the socket

In the first section of the createSocket() method, we first check whether a non-empty t_ip has been provided, which represents the interface IP, such as 192.168.10.104, and if not, we fetch one from the interface name provided using the getIfaceIP() method we built previously. We also need to populate the addrinfo struct, based on the arguments passed in, because we will need to pass it to the getaddrinfo() routine, which will return a linked list that will finally be used to build the actual socket. Note that in the createSocket() method, anytime we fail to create the socket or initialize it with the correct parameters, we return –1 to signify the failure:

```
auto createSocket(Logger &logger, const std::string
  &t_ip, const std::string &iface, int port,
                  bool is_udp, bool is_blocking, bool
                     is_listening, int ttl, bool
                        needs_so_timestamp) -> int {
  std::string time_str;

  const auto ip = t_ip.empty() ? getIfaceIP(iface) :
    t_ip;
  logger.log("%:% %() % ip:% iface:% port:% is_udp:%
    is_blocking:% is_listening:% ttl:% SO_time:%\n",
      __FILE__, __LINE__, __FUNCTION__,
          Common::getCurrentTimeStr(&time_str), ip,
             iface, port, is_udp, is_blocking,
               is_listening, ttl, needs_so_timestamp);

  addrinfo hints{};
  hints.ai_family = AF_INET;
  hints.ai_socktype = is_udp ? SOCK_DGRAM : SOCK_STREAM;
```

```cpp
    hints.ai_protocol = is_udp ? IPPROTO_UDP : IPPROTO_TCP;
    hints.ai_flags = is_listening ? AI_PASSIVE : 0;
    if (std::isdigit(ip.c_str()[0]))
      hints.ai_flags |= AI_NUMERICHOST;
    hints.ai_flags |= AI_NUMERICSERV;

    addrinfo *result = nullptr;
    const auto rc = getaddrinfo(ip.c_str(), std::
      to_string(port).c_str(), &hints, &result);
    if (rc) {
      logger.log("getaddrinfo() failed. error:% errno:%\n",
        gai_strerror(rc), strerror(errno));
      return -1;
    }
```

The next section then checks the parameters passed to the `createSocket()` method and uses all the methods we built previously to set the correct socket parameters as needed. Note that we use the `addrinfo *` result object returned from `getaddrinfo()` to create the socket through the `socket()` routine.

First, we make the actual function call to create the socket:

```cpp
    int fd = -1;
    int one = 1;
    for (addrinfo *rp = result; rp; rp = rp->ai_next) {
      fd = socket(rp->ai_family, rp->ai_socktype, rp
        ->ai_protocol);
      if (fd == -1) {
        logger.log("socket() failed. errno:%\n",
          strerror(errno));
        return -1;
      }
```

Next, we set it to be non-blocking and disable Nagle's algorithm using the methods we defined previously:

```cpp
      if (!is_blocking) {
        if (!setNonBlocking(fd)) {
          logger.log("setNonBlocking() failed. errno:%\n",
            strerror(errno));
          return -1;
        }
        if (!is_udp && !setNoDelay(fd)) {
          logger.log("setNoDelay() failed. errno:%\n",
            strerror(errno));
          return -1;
```

```
            }
        }
```

Next, we connect the socket to the target address if it is not a listening socket:

```
        if (!is_listening && connect(fd, rp->ai_addr, rp
          ->ai_addrlen) == 1 && !wouldBlock()) {
            logger.log("connect() failed. errno:%\n",
              strerror(errno));
            return -1;
        }
```

Then, if we want to create a socket that listens for incoming connections, we set the correct parameters and bind the socket to a specific address that the client will try to connect to. We also need to call the `listen()` routine for such a socket configuration. Note that we reference a `MaxTCPServerBacklog` parameter here, which is defined as follows:

```
constexpr int MaxTCPServerBacklog = 1024;
```

Now, let us look at the code to make the socket a listening socket:

```
        if (is_listening && setsockopt(fd, SOL_SOCKET,
          SO_REUSEADDR, reinterpret_cast<const char *>(&one),
            sizeof(one)) == -1) {
            logger.log("setsockopt() SO_REUSEADDR failed.
              errno:%\n", strerror(errno));
            return -1;
        }
        if (is_listening && bind(fd, rp->ai_addr, rp->
          ai_addrlen) == -1) {
            logger.log("bind() failed. errno:%\n",
              strerror(errno));
            return -1;
        }
        if (!is_udp && is_listening && listen(fd,
          MaxTCPServerBacklog) == -1) {
            logger.log("listen() failed. errno:%\n",
              strerror(errno));
            return -1;
        }
```

Finally, we set the TTL value for the socket we just created and return the socket. We will also set the ability to fetch the data receipt timestamps from incoming packets using the `setSOTimestamp()` method we created before:

```
      if (is_udp && ttl) {
        const bool is_multicast = atoi(ip.c_str()) & 0xe0;
        if (is_multicast && !setMcastTTL(fd, ttl)) {
          logger.log("setMcastTTL() failed. errno:%\n",
            strerror(errno));
          return -1;
        }
        if (!is_multicast && !setTTL(fd, ttl)) {
          logger.log("setTTL() failed. errno:%\n",
            strerror(errno));
          return -1;
        }
      }
        if (needs_so_timestamp && !setSOTimestamp(fd)) {
          logger.log("setSOTimestamp() failed. errno:%\n",
            strerror(errno));
          return -1;
        }
    }

    if (result)
      freeaddrinfo(result);

    return fd;
}
```

Now that we have discussed and implemented the details of our lower-level socket method, we can move on to the next section and build a slightly higher-level abstraction that builds on top of this method.

Implementing a sender/receiver TCP socket

Now that we have finished our design and implementation of basic methods to create sockets and set different parameters on them, we can start using them. First, we will implement a `TCPSocket` structure that builds on top of the socket utilities we created in the previous section. `TCPSocket` can be used to both send and receive data, so it will be used both within TCP socket servers and clients.

Defining the data members of the TCP socket

Let us jump into our implementation of the `TCPSocket` structure, starting with the data members we need. Since this socket will be used to send and receive data, we will create two buffers – one to store data to be sent out and one to store data that was just read in. We will also store the file descriptor corresponding to our TCP socket in the `fd_` variable. We also create two flags: one to track if the send socket is connected and another to check whether the receive socket is connected. We will also save a reference to a `Logger` object, purely for logging purposes. Finally, we will store a `std::function` object, which we will use to dispatch callbacks to components that want to read data from this socket when there is new data available to be consumed. The code for this section is in `Chapter4/tcp_socket.h` and `Chapter4/tcp_socket.cpp` in the GitHub repository for this book:

```cpp
#pragma once

#include <functional>

#include "socket_utils.h"
#include "logging.h"

namespace Common {
  constexpr size_t TCPBufferSize = 64 * 1024 * 1024;

  struct TCPSocket {
    int fd_ = -1;

    char *send_buffer_ = nullptr;
    size_t next_send_valid_index_ = 0;
    char *rcv_buffer_ = nullptr;
    size_t next_rcv_valid_index_ = 0;

    bool send_disconnected_ = false;
    bool recv_disconnected_ = false;

    struct sockaddr_in inInAddr;

    std::function<void(TCPSocket *s, Nanos rx_time)>
      recv_callback_;

    std::string time_str_;
    Logger &logger_;
  };
}
```

We define a default receive callback we will use to initialize the `recv_callback_` data member. This method simply logs information that confirms that the callback was invoked:

```cpp
        auto defaultRecvCallback(TCPSocket *socket, Nanos
          rx_time) noexcept {
          logger_.log("%:% %() %
            TCPSocket::defaultRecvCallback() socket:% len:%
```

```
              rx:%\n", __FILE__, __LINE__, __FUNCTION__,
              Common::getCurrentTimeStr(&time_str_),
              socket->fd_, socket->
                next_rcv_valid_index_, rx_time);
}
```

Next, let us look at the constructor for the `TCPSocket` structure.

Constructing and destroying the TCP socket

For the constructor, we will create the `send_buffer_` and `rcv_buffer_` char * storage on the heap and assign the `defaultRecvCallback()` method to the `recv_callback_` member variable through a lambda method. Note that we set the socket's receive and send buffers to be of size `TCPBufferSize`, as defined here:

```
constexpr size_t TCPBufferSize = 64 * 1024 * 1024;
    explicit TCPSocket(Logger &logger)
        : logger_(logger) {
    send_buffer_ = new char[TCPBufferSize];
    rcv_buffer_ = new char[TCPBufferSize];
    recv_callback_ = [this](auto socket, auto rx_time) {
      defaultRecvCallback(socket, rx_time); };
}
```

We then create `destroy()` and a destructor to perform straightforward cleanup tasks. We will close the socket file descriptor and destroy the receive and send buffers we created in the constructor:

```
auto TCPSocket::destroy() noexcept -> void {
  close(fd_);
  fd_ = -1;
}

~TCPSocket() {
  destroy();
  delete[] send_buffer_; send_buffer_ = nullptr;
  delete[] rcv_buffer_; rcv_buffer_ = nullptr;
}
```

We define the boilerplate code we saw previously to prevent accidental or unintentional constructions, copies, or assignments:

```
// Deleted default, copy & move constructors and
  assignment-operators.
TCPSocket() = delete;
```

```
TCPSocket(const TCPSocket &) = delete;
TCPSocket(const TCPSocket &&) = delete;
TCPSocket &operator=(const TCPSocket &) = delete;
TCPSocket &operator=(const TCPSocket &&) = delete;
```

Next, let us try to perform one key operation on this socket – establishing TCP connections.

Establishing TCP connections

For this structure, we will define a `connect()` method, which is basically what creates, initializes, and connects `TCPSocket`. We will use the `createSocket()` method we created in the previous section with the correct parameters to achieve this:

```
auto TCPSocket::connect(const std::string &ip, const
  std::string &iface, int port, bool is_listening) ->
    int {
  destroy();
  fd_ = createSocket(logger_, ip, iface, port, false,
    false, is_listening, 0, true);

  inInAddr.sin_addr.s_addr = INADDR_ANY;
  inInAddr.sin_port = htons(port);
  inInAddr.sin_family = AF_INET;

  return fd_;
}
```

Next, we will move on to the next critical functionality in our socket – sending and receiving data.

Sending and receiving data

We mentioned in our discussion that when new data is available, the interested listener will be notified through the `recv_callback_ std::function` mechanism. Therefore, we just need to provide a `send()` method for the users of this structure to send data out. Note that this `send()` method simply copies the provided data into the outgoing buffer, and the actual write to the wire will be done in the `sendAndRecv()` method we will see shortly:

```
auto TCPSocket::send(const void *data, size_t len)
  noexcept -> void {
  if (len > 0) {
    memcpy(send_buffer_ + next_send_valid_index_, data,
      len);
    next_send_valid_index_ += len;
  }
}
```

Finally, we have the most important method for the `TCPSocket` structure, `sendAndRecv()`, which reads available data into `rcv_buffer_`, increments the counters, and dispatches `recv_callback_` if there is some amount of data that was read. The second half of this method does the opposite – it tries to write out data in `send_buffer_` using the `send()` routine and updates the index tracker variables:

```cpp
auto TCPSocket::sendAndRecv() noexcept -> bool {
  char ctrl[CMSG_SPACE(sizeof(struct timeval))];
  struct cmsghdr *cmsg = (struct cmsghdr *) &ctrl;

  struct iovec iov;
  iov.iov_base = rcv_buffer_ + next_rcv_valid_index_;
  iov.iov_len = TCPBufferSize - next_rcv_valid_index_;

  msghdr msg;
  msg.msg_control = ctrl;
  msg.msg_controllen = sizeof(ctrl);
  msg.msg_name = &inInAddr;
  msg.msg_namelen = sizeof(inInAddr);
  msg.msg_iov = &iov;
  msg.msg_iovlen = 1;

  const auto n_rcv = recvmsg(fd_, &msg, MSG_DONTWAIT);
  if (n_rcv > 0) {
    next_rcv_valid_index_ += n_rcv;

    Nanos kernel_time = 0;
    struct timeval time_kernel;
    if (cmsg->cmsg_level == SOL_SOCKET &&
        cmsg->cmsg_type == SCM_TIMESTAMP &&
        cmsg->cmsg_len == CMSG_LEN(sizeof(time_kernel))) {
      memcpy(&time_kernel, CMSG_DATA(cmsg),
        sizeof(time_kernel));
      kernel_time = time_kernel.tv_sec * NANOS_TO_SECS +
        time_kernel.tv_usec * NANOS_TO_MICROS;
    }

    const auto user_time = getCurrentNanos();

    logger_.log("%:% %() % read socket:% len:% utime:%
      ktime:% diff:%\n", __FILE__, __LINE__,
        __FUNCTION__,
          Common::getCurrentTimeStr(&time_str_),
            fd_, next_rcv_valid_index_, user_time,
```

```cpp
                      kernel_time, (user_time -
                        kernel_time));
    recv_callback_(this, kernel_time);
  }

  ssize_t n_send = std::min(TCPBufferSize,
    next_send_valid_index_);
  while (n_send > 0) {
    auto n_send_this_msg = std::min(static_cast<ssize_t>
      (next_send_valid_index_), n_send);
    const int flags = MSG_DONTWAIT | MSG_NOSIGNAL |
      (n_send_this_msg < n_send ? MSG_MORE : 0);
    auto n = ::send(fd_, send_buffer_, n_send_this_msg,
      flags);
    if (UNLIKELY(n < 0)) {
      if (!wouldBlock())
        send_disconnected_ = true;
      break;
    }

    logger_.log("%:% %() % send socket:% len:%\n",
        __FILE__, __LINE__, __FUNCTION__,
        Common::getCurrentTimeStr(&time_str_), fd_, n);

    n_send -= n;
    ASSERT(n == n_send_this_msg, "Don't support partial
      send lengths yet.");
  }
  next_send_valid_index_ = 0;

  return (n_rcv > 0);
}
```

This concludes our discussion of the `TCPSocket` class. Next, we will build a class that encapsulates and manages `TCPSocket` objects. It will be used to implement functionality for TCP servers in components that act as servers.

Building a TCP server component

We built a `TCPSocket` class in the previous section that can be used by components that need to connect to TCP connections and send as well as receive data. In this section, we will build a `TCPServer` component that manages several such `TCPSocket` objects internally. It also manages tasks, such as listening for, accepting, and tracking new incoming connections and sending and receiving data on this collection of sockets. All the source code for the `TCPServer` component is in the `Chapter4/tcp_server.h` and `Chapter4/tcp_server.cpp` files in the GitHub repository for this book.

Defining the data members of the TCP server

First, we will define and describe the data members that the `TCPServer` class will contain. It needs a file descriptor, `efd_`, and a corresponding `TCPSocket listener_socket_` to represent the socket on which it will be listening for new incoming connections from clients. It maintains an array of `epoll_event events_`, which will be used to monitor the listening socket file descriptor, along with socket descriptors for connected clients. It will have a few `std::vectors` of socket objects – sockets that we expect to receive data from, sockets we expect to send data on, and sockets that are disconnected. We will see how these are used shortly.

This class has two `std::function` objects – one used to dispatch callbacks when new data is received and another one that is dispatched after all callbacks in the current round of polling the sockets are completed. To explain this better, we will first use the `epoll` call to find all the sockets that have data to read, dispatch `recv_callback_` for each socket that has data, and finally, when all sockets have been notified, dispatch `recv_finished_callback_`. One more thing to note here is that the `recv_callback_` provides `TCPSocket` on which the data was received, as well as `Nanos rx_time` to specify the software receive time of the data on that socket. The receive timestamps are used to process the TCP packets in the exact order in which they were received, since the TCP server monitors and reads from many different client TCP sockets:

```
#pragma once

#include "tcp_socket.h"

namespace Common {
  struct TCPServer {
  public:
    int efd_ = -1;
    TCPSocket listener_socket_;

    epoll_event events_[1024];
    std::vector<TCPSocket *> sockets_, receive_sockets_,
      send_sockets_, disconnected_sockets_;

    std::function<void(TCPSocket *s, Nanos rx_time)>
      recv_callback_;
    std::function<void()> recv_finished_callback_;

    std::string time_str_;
    Logger &logger_;
```

```
        };
}
```

In the next section, we will look at the code to initialize these fields and de-initialize the TCP server.

Initializing and destroying the TCP server

The constructor for `TCPServer` is straightforward – it initializes `listener_socket_` and `logger_` and sets the default callback receivers, as we did with `TCPSocket`:

```
explicit TCPServer(Logger &logger)
    : listener_socket_(logger), logger_(logger) {
  recv_callback_ = [this](auto socket, auto rx_time) {
    defaultRecvCallback(socket, rx_time); };
  recv_finished_callback_ = [this]() {
    defaultRecvFinishedCallback(); };
}
```

We define the default receive callback methods here, which do not do anything except log that the callback was received. These are placeholders anyway, since we will set different ones in real applications:

```
auto defaultRecvCallback(TCPSocket *socket, Nanos
  rx_time) noexcept {
  logger_.log("%:% %() %
    TCPServer::defaultRecvCallback() socket:% len:%
      rx:%\n", __FILE__, __LINE__, __FUNCTION__,
        Common::getCurrentTimeStr(&time_str_), socket->
          fd_, socket->next_rcv_valid_index_, rx_time);
}

auto defaultRecvFinishedCallback() noexcept {
  logger_.log("%:% %() % TCPServer::
    defaultRecvFinishedCallback()\n", __FILE__,
      __LINE__, __FUNCTION__,
        Common::getCurrentTimeStr(&time_str_));
}
```

The code to destroy the sockets is quite simple as well – we close the file descriptor and destroy `TCPSocket listener_socket_`:

```
auto TCPServer::destroy() {
  close(efd_);
  efd_ = -1;
  listener_socket_.destroy();
}
```

Finally, we present the boilerplate code that we saw previously for this class:

```
TCPServer() = delete;
TCPServer(const TCPServer &) = delete;
TCPServer(const TCPServer &&) = delete;
TCPServer &operator=(const TCPServer &) = delete;
TCPServer &operator=(const TCPServer &&) = delete;
```

Next, let us understand the code that initializes the listener socket.

Starting up and listening for new connections

The method `TCPServer::listen()`, first creates a new `epoll` instance, using the `epoll_create()` Linux system call, and then saves it in the `efd_` variable. It uses the `TCPSocket::connect()` method we built earlier to initialize `listener_socket_`, but here, the important part is that we set the `listening` argument to be `true`. Finally, we add `listener_socket_` to the list of sockets to be monitored using the `epoll_add()` method, since initially, this is the only socket to monitor. We will look at this `epoll_add()` method in the next section:

```
auto TCPServer::listen(const std::string &iface, int
    port) -> void {
  destroy();
  efd_ = epoll_create(1);
  ASSERT(efd_ >= 0, "epoll_create() failed error:" +
    std::string(std::strerror(errno)));

  ASSERT(listener_socket_.connect("", iface, port, true)
    >= 0,
        "Listener socket failed to connect. iface:" +
          iface + " port:" + std::to_string(port) + "
          error:" + std::string
            (std::strerror(errno)));

  ASSERT(epoll_add(&listener_socket_), "epoll_ctl()
    failed. error:" + std::string(std::strerror(errno)));
}
```

Now, let us look at how the `epoll_add()` and the complementary `epoll_del()` methods are built in the next subsection.

Adding and removing monitored sockets

The `epoll_add()` method is used to add `TCPSocket` to the list of sockets to be monitored. It uses the `epoll_ctl()` system call with the `EPOLL_CTL_ADD` parameter to add the provided file descriptor of the socket to the `efd_` epoll class member. `EPOLLET` enabled the *edge-triggered epoll* option, which in simple terms means you are notified only once when data needs to be read instead of constant reminders. In this mode, it is up to the application developer to read the data when they want. EPOLLIN is used for notification once data is available to be read:

```
auto TCPServer::epoll_add(TCPSocket *socket) {
  epoll_event ev{};
  ev.events = EPOLLET | EPOLLIN;
  ev.data.ptr = reinterpret_cast<void *>(socket);
  return (epoll_ctl(efd_, EPOLL_CTL_ADD, socket->fd_,
    &ev) != -1);
}
```

The `epoll_del()` does the opposite of `epoll_add()` - `epoll_ctl()` is still used, but this time, the EPOLL_CTL_DEL parameter removes TCPSocket from the list of sockets being monitored:

```
auto TCPServer::epoll_del(TCPSocket *socket) {
  return (epoll_ctl(efd_, EPOLL_CTL_DEL, socket->fd_,
    nullptr) != -1);
}
```

The `del()` method we will build here removes TCPSocket from the list of sockets being monitored, as well as the different data member containers of the sockets:

```
auto TCPServer::del(TCPSocket *socket) {
  epoll_del(socket);

  sockets_.erase(std::remove(sockets_.begin(),
    sockets_.end(), socket), sockets_.end());
  receive_sockets_.erase(std::remove
    (receive_sockets_.begin(), receive_sockets_.end(),
      socket), receive_sockets_.end());
  send_sockets_.erase(std::remove(send_sockets_.begin(),
    send_sockets_.end(), socket), send_sockets_.end());
}
```

Now, we can look at the most important method in this subsection – `TCPServer::poll()`, which will be used to perform a few tasks, as listed here:

- Call `epoll_wait()`, detect whether there are any new incoming connections, and if so, add them to our containers
- From the call to `epoll_wait()`, detect sockets that have disconnected from the client's side and remove them from our containers
- From the call to `epoll_wait()`, check to see whether there are sockets with data ready to be read or with outgoing data

Let us break down the entire method into a few blocks – first, the block that calls the `epoll_wait()` method, with the `epoll` instance and the maximum number of events being the total number of sockets in our containers, with no timeout:

```
auto TCPServer::poll() noexcept -> void {
  const int max_events = 1 + sockets_.size();

  for (auto socket: disconnected_sockets_) {
    del(socket);
  }

  const int n = epoll_wait(efd_, events_, max_events, 0);
```

Next, we iterate through the `events_` array populated by the call to `epoll_wait()` if it returns a value of n greater than 0. For each `epoll_event` in the `events_` array, we use the `event.data.ptr` object and cast it to `TCPSocket*`, since that is how we set up the `events_` array in the `epoll_add()` method:

```
bool have_new_connection = false;
for (int i = 0; i < n; ++i) {
  epoll_event &event = events_[i];
  auto socket = reinterpret_cast<TCPSocket
    *>(event.data.ptr);
```

For each `epoll_event` entry, we check whether the `EPOLLIN` flag is set on the events flag, which would signify that there is a new socket with data to read from. If this socket happens to be `listener_socket_`, which is `TCPServer`'s primary socket that we configured to listen for connections on, we can see that we have a new connection to add. If this is a socket different from `listener_socket_`, then we add it to the list of `receive_sockets_` vectors if it does not already exist in the list:

```
if (event.events & EPOLLIN) {
  if (socket == &listener_socket_) {
    logger_.log("%:% %() % EPOLLIN
      listener_socket:%\n", __FILE__, __LINE__,
        __FUNCTION__,
          Common::getCurrentTimeStr(&time_str_),
            socket->fd_);
    have_new_connection = true;
    continue;
  }
  logger_.log("%:% %() % EPOLLIN socket:%\n",
    __FILE__, __LINE__, __FUNCTION__,
      Common::getCurrentTimeStr(&time_str_), socket-
```

```
            >fd_);
    if(std::find(receive_sockets_.begin(),
       receive_sockets_.end(), socket) ==
         receive_sockets_.end())
       receive_sockets_.push_back(socket);
}
```

Similarly, we check for the `EPOLLOUT` flag, which signifies there is a socket that we can send data to, and add it to the `send_sockets_` vector if it does not already exist:

```
if (event.events & EPOLLOUT) {
    logger_.log("%:% %() % EPOLLOUT socket:%\n",
       __FILE__, __LINE__, __FUNCTION__,
         Common::getCurrentTimeStr(&time_str_), socket-
            >fd_);
    if(std::find(send_sockets_.begin(),
       send_sockets_.end(), socket) ==
         send_sockets_.end())
       send_sockets_.push_back(socket);
}
```

Finally, we check whether the `EPOLLERR` or `EPOLLHUP` flags are set, which indicate an error or indicate that the socket was closed (signal `hang up`) from the other end. In this case, we add this socket to the `disconnected_sockets_` vector to be removed:

```
    if (event.events & (EPOLLERR | EPOLLHUP)) {
        logger_.log("%:% %() % EPOLLERR socket:%\n",
           __FILE__, __LINE__, __FUNCTION__,
             Common::getCurrentTimeStr(&time_str_), socket-
                >fd_);
        if(std::find(disconnected_sockets_.begin(),
           disconnected_sockets_.end(), socket) ==
             disconnected_sockets_.end())
           disconnected_sockets_.push_back(socket);
    }
}
```

Finally, in this method, we need to accept the new connection if we detected one in the previous code block. We use the `accept()` system call with the `listener_socket_` file descriptor to achieve this and fetch the file descriptor for this new socket. We also set the socket to be non-blocking and disable Nagle's algorithm, using the `setNonBlocking()` and `setNoDelay()` methods we built before:

```
while (have_new_connection) {
    logger_.log("%:% %() % have_new_connection\n",
       __FILE__, __LINE__, __FUNCTION__,
```

```
        Common::getCurrentTimeStr(&time_str_));
    sockaddr_storage addr;
    socklen_t addr_len = sizeof(addr);
    int fd = accept(listener_socket_.fd_,
        reinterpret_cast<sockaddr *>(&addr), &addr_len);
    if (fd == -1)
      break;

    ASSERT(setNonBlocking(fd) && setNoDelay(fd), "Failed
      to set non-blocking or no-delay on socket:" + std::
        to_string(fd));

    logger_.log("%:% %() % accepted socket:%\n",
        __FILE__, __LINE__, __FUNCTION__,
          Common::getCurrentTimeStr(&time_str_), fd);
```

Finally, we create a new `TCPSocket` object using this file descriptor and add the `TCPSocket` object to the `sockets_` and `receive_sockets_` containers:

```
    TCPSocket *socket = new TCPSocket(logger_);
    socket->fd_ = fd;
    socket->recv_callback_ = recv_callback_;
    ASSERT(epoll_add(socket), "Unable to add socket.
      error:" + std::string(std::strerror(errno)));

    if(std::find(sockets_.begin(), sockets_.end(),
      socket) == sockets_.end())
      sockets_.push_back(socket);
    if(std::find(receive_sockets_.begin(),
      receive_sockets_.end(), socket) ==
        receive_sockets_.end())
      receive_sockets_.push_back(socket);
  }
}
```

This concludes all the functionality we need to look for new connections and dead connections, as well as monitor existing connections to see whether there is data to be read. The next sub-section concludes our `TCPServer` class by demonstrating how to send and receive data from a list of sockets that have data to be read or sent out.

Sending and receiving data

The code to send and receive data on a list of sockets with incoming or outgoing data is shown here. The implementation is very straightforward – it simply calls the `TCPSocket::sendAndRecv()`

method on each of the sockets in `receive_sockets_` and `send_sockets_`. For incoming data, the call to `TCPSocket::sendAndRecv()` dispatches the `recv_callback_` method. One thing we need to do here is to check whether there was any data that was read this time around, and if so, we dispatch `recv_finished_callback_` after all the `recv_callback_` calls are dispatched:

```
auto TCPServer::sendAndRecv() noexcept -> void {
  auto recv = false;

  for (auto socket: receive_sockets_) {
    if(socket->sendAndRecv())
      recv = true;
  }
  if(recv)
    recv_finished_callback_();

  for (auto socket: send_sockets_) {
    socket->sendAndRecv();
  }
}
```

This concludes our implementation of the `TCPServer` class, let us wrap up our network programming discussion with a simple example of everything we built in this section.

Building an example of the TCP server and clients

In this section, we will build an example and use the `TCPSocket` and `TCPServer` classes we implemented in this section. This example can be found in the `Chapter4/socket_example.cpp` source file. This simple example creates `TCPServer`, which listens for incoming connections on the lo interface, the loopback `127.0.0.1` IP, and the listening port, `12345`. The `TCPServer` class receives data from the clients, which connect to it using the `tcpServerRecvCallback()` lambda method, and the `TCPServer` responds back to the clients with a simple response. We then create five clients using the `TCPSocket` class, each of which connects to this `TCPServer`. Finally, they each send some data to the server, which sends responses back, each of the clients repeatedly calling `sendAndRecv()` to send and receive data. `TCPServer` calls `poll()` and `sendAndRecv()` to look for connections and data and reads it.

First, the code that sets up the callback lambdas is presented here:

```
#include "time_utils.h"
#include "logging.h"
#include "tcp_server.h"

int main(int, char **) {
  using namespace Common;
```

```cpp
std::string time_str_;
Logger logger_("socket_example.log");

auto tcpServerRecvCallback = [&](TCPSocket *socket, Nanos
  rx_time)
noexcept{
    logger_.log("TCPServer::defaultRecvCallback()
      socket:% len:% rx:%\n",
                socket->fd_, socket->
                  next_rcv_valid_index_, rx_time);

    const std::string reply = "TCPServer received msg:" +
      std::string(socket->rcv_buffer_, socket->
        next_rcv_valid_index_);
    socket->next_rcv_valid_index_ = 0;

    socket->send(reply.data(), reply.length());
};

auto tcpServerRecvFinishedCallback = [&]()
noexcept{
    logger_.log("TCPServer::defaultRecvFinishedCallback()\n");
};

auto tcpClientRecvCallback = [&](TCPSocket *socket, Nanos
  rx_time)
noexcept{
    const std::string recv_msg = std::string(socket->
      rcv_buffer_, socket->next_rcv_valid_index_);
    socket->next_rcv_valid_index_ = 0;

    logger_.log("TCPSocket::defaultRecvCallback()
      socket:% len:% rx:% msg:%\n",
      socket->fd_, socket->next_rcv_valid_index_, rx_time,
      recv_msg);
};
```

Then, we create, initialize, and connect the server and the clients, as shown here:

```cpp
const std::string iface = "lo";
const std::string ip = "127.0.0.1";
const int port = 12345;

logger_.log("Creating TCPServer on iface:% port:%\n",
```

```cpp
    iface, port);
TCPServer server(logger_);
server.recv_callback_ = tcpServerRecvCallback;
server.recv_finished_callback_ =
  tcpServerRecvFinishedCallback;
server.listen(iface, port);

std::vector < TCPSocket * > clients(5);

for (size_t i = 0; i < clients.size(); ++i) {
  clients[i] = new TCPSocket(logger_);
  clients[i]->recv_callback_ = tcpClientRecvCallback;

  logger_.log("Connecting TCPClient-[%] on ip:% iface:%
    port:%\n", i, ip, iface, port);
  clients[i]->connect(ip, iface, port, false);
  server.poll();
}
```

Finally, we have the clients send data and call the appropriate polling and sending/receiving methods on the clients and the server, as shown here:

```cpp
using namespace std::literals::chrono_literals;

for (auto itr = 0; itr < 5; ++itr) {
  for (size_t i = 0; i < clients.size(); ++i) {
    const std::string client_msg = "CLIENT-[" +
      std::to_string(i) + "] : Sending " +
        std::to_string(itr * 100 + i);
    logger_.log("Sending TCPClient-[%] %\n", i,
      client_msg);
    clients[i]->send(client_msg.data(),
      client_msg.length());
    clients[i]->sendAndRecv();

    std::this_thread::sleep_for(500ms);
    server.poll();
    server.sendAndRecv();
  }
}

for (auto itr = 0; itr < 5; ++itr) {
  for (auto &client: clients)
    client->sendAndRecv();
```

```
        server.poll();
        server.sendAndRecv();
        std::this_thread::sleep_for(500ms);
    }

    return 0;
}
```

Running this example, as shown here, will output something similar to what is shown here in the log file:

```
(base) sghosh@sghosh-ThinkPad-X1-Carbon-3rd:~/Building-Low-Latency-
Applications-with-CPP/Chapter4$ ./cmake-build-release/socket_example ;
cat socket_example.log
Creating TCPServer on iface:lo port:12345
/home/sghosh/Building-Low-Latency-Applications-with-CPP/Chapter4/
socket_utils.cpp:68 createSocket() Sat Mar 25 11:32:55 2023
ip:127.0.0.1 iface:lo port:12345 is_udp:0 is_blocking:0 is_listening:1
ttl:0 SO_time:1
Connecting TCPClient-[0] on ip:127.0.0.1 iface:lo port:12345
/home/sghosh/Building-Low-Latency-Applications-with-CPP/Chapter4/
tcp_server.cpp:74 poll() Sat Mar 25 11:32:55 2023 EPOLLIN listener_
socket:5
/home/sghosh/Building-Low-Latency-Applications-with-CPP/Chapter4/tcp_
server.cpp:97 poll() Sat Mar 25 11:32:55 2023 have_new_connection
...
Sending TCPClient-[0] CLIENT-[0] : Sending 0
/home/sghosh/Building-Low-Latency-Applications-with-CPP/Chapter4/
tcp_socket.cpp:67 sendAndRecv() Sat Mar 25 11:32:55 2023 send socket:6
len:22
/home/sghosh/Building-Low-Latency-Applications-with-CPP/Chapter4/tcp_
server.cpp:78 poll() Sat Mar 25 11:32:55 2023 EPOLLIN socket:7
/home/sghosh/Building-Low-Latency-Applications-with-CPP/Chapter4/
tcp_socket.cpp:51 sendAndRecv() Sat Mar 25 11:32:55 2023 read socket:7
len:22 utime:1679761975918407366 ktime:0 diff:1679761975918407366
TCPServer::defaultRecvCallback() socket:7 len:22 rx:0
...
TCPSocket::defaultRecvCallback() socket:12 len:0
rx:1679761987425505000 msg:TCPServer received msg:CLIENT-[3] : Sending
403
/home/sghosh/Building-Low-Latency-Applications-with-CPP/Chapter4/tcp_
socket.cpp:51 sendAndRecv() Sat Mar 25 11:33:07 2023 read socket:14
len:47 utime:1679761987925931213 ktime:1679761987925816000 diff:115213
TCPSocket::defaultRecvCallback() socket:14 len:0
rx:1679761987925816000 msg:TCPServer received msg:CLIENT-[4] : Sending
404
```

This concludes our discussion of C++ network programming with sockets. We covered a lot regarding the basic low-level details of socket programming. We also designed and implemented slightly higher-level abstractions for TCP and UDP communication, both from a server's and a client's perspective.

Summary

In this chapter, we jumped into the world of low latency application C++ development. We built some relatively fundamental but extremely useful building blocks that can be used for a variety of low latency application purposes. We put into practice a lot of the theoretical discussions related to using C++ and computer architecture features effectively to build low latency and highly performant applications.

The first component was used to create new threads of execution and run the functions that different components might require. One important functionality here is being able to control the CPU core that the newly created thread gets pinned to by setting the thread affinity.

The second component we built was meant to avoid dynamic memory allocation on the critical code path. We reiterated the inefficiencies associated with dynamic memory allocation and designed a memory pool to be used to pre-allocate memory from the heap when constructed. Then, we added utility to the component to allow the allocation and deallocation of objects at runtime without relying on dynamic memory allocation.

Next, we built a lock-free, **First In First Out** (**FIFO**)-style queue to communicate between threads in an SPSC setup. The important requirement here was that a single reader and a single writer are able to access the shared data in the queue without using any locks or mutexes. The absence of locks and mutexes means the absence of context switches, which, as discussed, are a major source of inefficiencies and latencies in multi-threaded applications.

The fourth component on our list was a framework to facilitate efficient logging for latency-sensitive applications. Logging is a very important if not mandatory component of all applications, including low latency applications. However, due to issues such as disk I/O, slow string formatting, and so on, traditional logging mechanisms such as writing to a log file on disk is impractical for use with low latency applications. To build this component, we used the multi-threading mechanism we built, as well as the lock-free FIFO queue.

Finally, we had an in-depth discussion about designing our network stack – how to create network sockets, how to use them to create TCP servers and clients, and how to use them to publish and consume multicast traffic. We have not used this last component yet, but we will use this component in subsequent chapters to facilitate communication between our electronic trading exchange and different market participants.

Now, we will move on to a case study project, which we will build in the rest of this book – our electronic trading ecosystem. In the next chapter, we will first focus on designing and understanding the higher-level design of the various components in our system. We will understand the purpose of these components, the motivation behind their design choices, and how the flow of information occurs in the system. The next chapter will also see us designing the higher-level C++ interfaces that we will implement in the rest of this book.

Part 2: Building a Live Trading Exchange in C++

In this part, we will describe and design the trading applications that make up our ecosystem, which we will be building from scratch in this book – electronic trading exchanges, exchange market data dissemination, order gateways, client market data decoders, and client trading algorithm frameworks. We will implement the matching engine that tracks client orders and performs matching between them. We will also build the components that publish market data for all participants and how it handles client connections and order requests. The focus will be on very low-latency reaction times and high throughput since modern electronic exchanges have thousands of participants and a huge amount of order flow flowing through it.

This part contains the following chapters:

- *Chapter 5, Designing Our Trading Ecosystem*
- *Chapter 6, Building the C++ Matching Engine*
- *Chapter 7, Communicating with Market Participants*

5
Designing Our Trading Ecosystem

The previous chapter jumped into some hands-on, low-latency development in C++, where we built some basic building blocks to be used throughout the rest of this book. Now we are ready to start designing our electronic trading ecosystem, which will be our main project for the rest of this book, where we will learn about low-latency application development principles in practice. First, we will discuss the high-level design and architecture of the different low-latency components or applications that we will be building for the end-to-end electronic trading ecosystem. We will also design the abstractions, components, and interactions between them, which we will implement in the rest of the book.

In this chapter, we will cover the following topics:

- Understanding the layout of the electronic trading ecosystem
- Designing the C++ matching engine in a trading exchange
- Understanding how an exchange publishes information to participants
- Building a market participant's interface to the exchange
- Designing a framework for low-latency C++ trading algorithms

Let us kick off this chapter by describing the high-level topology of the electronic trading ecosystem we will design and build in the rest of this book. We will briefly introduce the different components in the next section and then have a much more detailed discussion in the rest of this chapter. One thing to keep in mind is that the electronic trading ecosystem we will be building in this book is a simplified version of what is found in practice. Not only is it a simplified version but it is also a subset of all the components you would need in practice to build and run a full electronic trading ecosystem. The components we will build in this book were chosen because they are the most latency-sensitive components, and we try to keep our focus on low-latency application development. We would like to mention that, in practice, you will find components such as historical data capture at the exchange and client ends, connections to clearing brokers, backend systems for transaction processing, accounting and reconciliation at both the exchange and trading client's ends, backtesting frameworks (testing against historical data), and many others.

Understanding the layout of the electronic trading ecosystem

First, we start by providing the higher-level layout of the electronic trading ecosystem we will be building in the rest of this book. Before we get into the details, we start with the disclaimer that this is a simplified design of what happens in practice in electronic trading markets. Simplification was necessary to limit the scope to what can be covered in this book; however, it is still an accurate but simplified representation of what you will find in practice. The other thing to note is that the goal here is to understand the design and implementation of low-latency applications, so we ask you to focus more on the application of C++ and computer science principles that we apply and less on the details of the trading ecosystem itself.

Now, let us kick off this introduction by defining and explaining the overall topology of the electronic trading ecosystem and the components involved.

Defining the topology of the electronic trading ecosystem

Let us first provide a bird's eye view of the system with the diagram presented here:

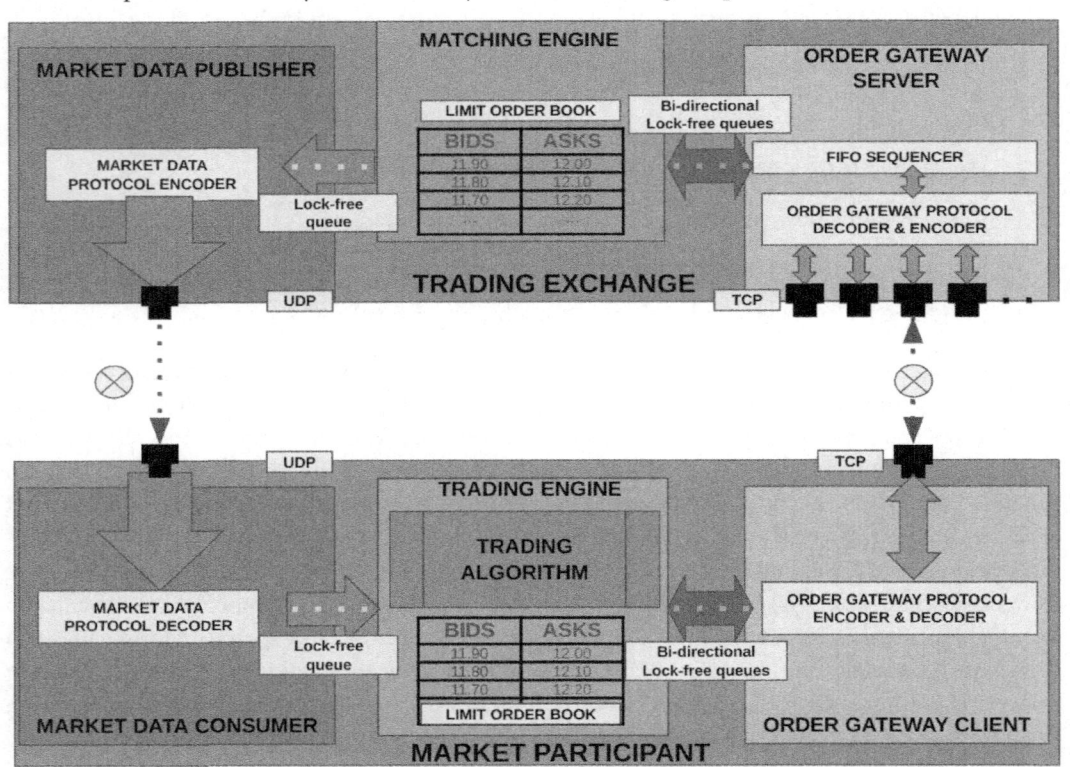

Figure 5.1 – Topology of a simple electronic trading ecosystem

The major components, as laid out in the preceding diagram, are the following, split at a high level depending on whether it belongs on the exchange side or the trading client/market-participant side.

These are the exchange components:

- Matching engine at the electronic trading exchange
- Order gateway server and protocol encoder and decoder at the trading exchange
- Market data encoder and publisher at the exchange

These are the trading client components:

- Market data consumer and decoder for a market participant interested in this market data
- Order gateway encoder and decoder client in the market participant's system
- Trading engine inside the participant's system

We will quickly introduce each one of these components in the next section and then discuss them in detail in the rest of this chapter.

Introducing the components of the electronic trading ecosystem

Here, we will quickly introduce the different components that make up the electronic trading ecosystem. One thing to keep in mind is that each one of these components in a competitive ecosystem needs to be designed such that they can process events and data with the lowest latencies possible. Also note that during periods of heightened volatility, these systems must be able to keep up with and react to large bursts in market activity.

Introducing the market data publisher

The market data publisher at the trading exchange is responsible for communicating every change to the limit order book maintained by the matching engine to the market participants. Compared to the order gateway, the difference here is that the market data publisher publishes public data meant for all participants, and it typically hides details of which order belongs to which participant to maintain fairness. Another difference is that the order gateway infrastructure only communicates order updates to the market participants whose orders were impacted by the change and not to all market participants. The market data publisher can use TCP or UDP to publish market data, but given the large volume of market data updates, UDP multicast is the preferred network-level protocol. The market data publisher is also responsible for converting the internal matching engine format into the market data format before publishing the updates.

Introducing the matching engine

The matching engine at the electronic trading exchange is the most critical piece of the trading exchange. It is responsible for handling requests from market participants for their orders and updating the limit order book that it maintains. These requests are generated when the clients want to add a new order, replace an existing order, cancel an existing order, and so on. The limit order book is a collection of all orders sent by all participants aggregated into a central single book consisting of bids (buy orders) and asks (sell orders). The matching engine is also responsible for performing matches between orders that cross in price (i.e., matching buy orders with sell orders when the buy price is higher than or equal to the sell price). During special market states such as **PreOpen** (right before the market opens), **Auction/Opening** (right at the moment at which the market opens), **PreOpenNoCancel** (orders can be entered but not canceled), and so on, the rules are slightly different, but we will not worry about those rules or implement them to keep the focus on low-latency application development.

Introducing the order gateway server at the exchange

The order gateway server at the exchange is responsible for accepting connections from market participants so that they can send requests for orders and receive notifications when there are updates to their respective orders. The order gateway server is also responsible for translating messages between the matching engine format and the order gateway messaging protocol. The network protocol used for the order gateway server is always TCP to enforce in-order delivery of messages and reliability.

Introducing the market data consumer at the market participant level

The market data consumer is the complement of the exchange market data publisher component on the market participants' side. This component is responsible for subscribing to the UDP stream or the TCP server set up by the market data publisher, consuming the market data updates, and decoding the market data protocol into an internal format used by the rest of the trading engine.

Introducing the order gateway encoder and decoder client

The order gateway client component is the complement of the exchange order gateway server on the market participants' side. The responsibility of this component is to establish and maintain TCP connections with the exchange's order gateway infrastructure. It is also responsible for encoding strategy order requests in the correct exchange order messaging protocol and decoding exchange responses into an internal format that the trading engine uses.

Introducing the trading engine in the market participants' systems

The trading engine is the brain of a market participant's trading system. This is where intelligence resides, and where the trading decisions are made. This component is responsible for consuming the normalized market data updates from the market data consumer component. It will usually also build the complete limit order book to reflect the state of the market or, at the very least, a simplified variant of the order book, depending on the requirements of the trading strategies. It usually also builds analytics on top of the liquidity and prices from the order book and makes automated trading decisions. This component uses the order gateway client component to communicate with the trading exchange.

Now that we have introduced the major components involved in our electronic trading ecosystem, we will look at these components in greater detail. First, we will start with the matching engine, which resides in the electronic trading exchange system.

Designing the C++ matching engine in a trading exchange

In this section, we will discuss the matching engine component inside the electronic trading exchange system introduced in the previous section. The first thing we will do is understand what purpose the matching engine serves and why it is needed.

Understanding the purpose of the matching engine

In the electronic trading ecosystem consisting of a single trading exchange, generally, there is a single exchange that is responsible for accepting and managing orders from numerous market participants. The matching engine in this case accepts different kinds of orders that the participants are allowed to send for any given trading instrument. An **order** is simply a request sent by any market participant to the trading exchange to convey their interest in buying or selling a tradeable product. Every time a new order is received by the matching engine from the order gateway server infrastructure, it checks to see whether this new order crosses an existing order with an opposite side to see whether a trade occurs. For this book's purposes, we will assume the market participants only send **limit orders** and specify the side of the order, quantity, and price. Limit orders are orders that can only execute at a price that is at, or better than, the price specified by the market participant.

It should be obvious by now that the matching engine performs the most critical task of performing matches between orders from different market participants and does so correctly and fairly. By fairness, we mean that the orders that reach the exchange first are processed first, and this **first in, first out** (**FIFO**) ordering is handled in the order gateway infrastructure, which we will discuss shortly. Orders that do not match immediately rest in the book and are referred to as **passive orders**. These orders are eligible for matching when new orders come in with prices that cross the passive orders. Such orders that cross the prices on passive orders are known as **aggressive orders**.

The matching engine arranges all the passive orders sent by all market participants into a data structure that is aptly named the **order book**. The details of this order book will be the topic of our next discussion.

Understanding the exchange order book

The limit order book contains all the passive limit orders across all market participants for a single trading instrument. These are typically arranged from the highest buy price to the lowest buy price for passive buy orders, and from the lowest sell price to the highest sell price for passive sell orders. This ordering is intuitive and natural because passive buy orders are matched from highest to lowest buy prices and passive sell orders are matched from lowest to highest sell prices. For orders that have the same side and the same price, they are arranged in FIFO order based on when they were sent. Note that FIFO is just one ordering criterion; modern electronic trading markets have different types of matching algorithms, such as **Pro Rata** and some mix of FIFO and Pro Rata. Pro Rata is simply a matching algorithm where larger orders get larger fills from aggressive orders regardless of where they are in the FIFO queue. For our matching engine, we will only implement the FIFO matching algorithm.

To fully understand how the order book works, we will look at a few scenarios that happen in the market and how they impact the order book. Let us first establish the starting state of the order book. Let us assume there are orders belonging to three different market participants – clients A, B, and C on the buy and sell sides.

Client A OrderId 1 BUY 20 @ 10.90	Client B OrderId 5 SELL 10 @ 11.00
Client A OrderId 2 BUY 10 @ 10.80	Client C OrderId 6 Sell 5 @ 11.00
Client B OrderId 3 BUY 5 @ 10.80	Client B OrderId 7 SELL 5 @ 11.10
Client C OrderId 4 BUY 100 @ 10.70	

Table 5.1 – Initial state of the limit order book consisting of some orders

Here, client A has 2 passive buy orders of quantities of 20 and 10 at prices of 10.90 and 10.80, respectively. Client B has a buy order of a quantity of 5 at 10.80, and 2 sell orders of quantities of 10 and 5 at prices of 11.00 and 11.10, respectively. Client C has 2 passive orders – a buy of a quantity of 5 at 10.80 and a sell of a quantity of 5 at 11.00, respectively. Now, let us assume client A sends a new buy order of a quantity of 10 at the price of 10.90 and client B sends a new sell order of a quantity of 10 at the price of 11.20. The updated order book is shown in the following table and the new orders are highlighted. Due to the FIFO ordering, the new buy order of *OrderId=8* is behind the buy order of *OrderId=1* at the same price.

Client A OrderId 1 BUY 20 @ 10.90	Client B OrderId 5 SELL 10 @ 11.00
Client A OrderId 8 BUY 10 @ 10.90	Client C OrderId 6 Sell 5 @ 11.00
Client A OrderId 2 BUY 10 @ 10.80	Client B OrderId 7 SELL 5 @ 11.10
Client B OrderId 3 BUY 5 @ 10.80	Client B OrderId 9 SELL 10 @ 11.20
Client C OrderId 4 BUY 100 @ 10.70	

Table 5.2 – Updated order book with newly added orders

Now let us assume that client A modifies the order with *OrderId=2* to go from a quantity of 10 to a quantity of 20. When an order's quantity is increased in such a manner, the order loses priority in the FIFO ordering and goes to the back of the queue at that price level. Let us also assume that client B modifies the order of *OrderId=5* to reduce the order's quantity from 10 to 1. Note that per the rules of the market, when an order's quantity is reduced, it does not lose its priority in the queue and still stays where it is. The updated order book is shown next, and the orders that are impacted are highlighted:

Client A OrderId 1 BUY 20 @ 10.90	Client B OrderId 5 SELL 1 @ 11.00
Client A OrderId 8 BUY 10 @ 10.90	Client C OrderId 6 Sell 5 @ 11.00
Client A OrderId 3 BUY 5 @ 10.80	Client B OrderId 7 SELL 5 @ 11.10
Client B OrderId 2 BUY 20 @ 10.80	Client B OrderId 9 SELL 10 @ 11.20
Client C OrderId 4 BUY 100 @ 10.70	

Table 5.3 – State of the order book after the modification of an order

Finally, let us assume that client A modifies the buy order with *OrderId=4* from a price of 10.70 to a price of 10.90 with no changes to quantity. The impact of this order action is equivalent to canceling the order and sending a new order at the new price. Let us also assume that client B decides that they no longer want the sell order of *OrderId=9* and sends a cancel for it. The updated order book due to these two actions is shown next, with the modified order highlighted and the canceled order removed from the order book:

Client A OrderId 1 BUY 20 @ 10.90	Client B OrderId 5 SELL 1 @ 11.00
Client A OrderId 8 BUY 10 @ 10.90	Client C OrderId 6 Sell 5 @ 11.00
Client C OrderId 4 BUY 100 @ 10.90	Client B OrderId 7 SELL 5 @ 11.10
Client A OrderId 3 BUY 5 @ 10.80	
Client B OrderId 2 BUY 20 @ 10.80	

Table 5.4 – Limit order book state after the modification and cancellation actions

So far in the scenarios we discussed, there has not been a trade because the order activity has been such that all buy orders have prices lower than all sell orders. Let us further this discussion in the next section and see what happens when there is an aggressive order that can cross the buy or sell order prices and what that does.

Two things to note here as far as order modification is concerned are as follows:

- When orders are modified to reduce the quantity, the priority or position of the order in the queue does not change
- When orders are modified to increase the quantity or the price of the order is modified, it has the equivalent effect of canceling the order and sending the order with the new price and quantity values (i.e., a new priority will be assigned to it)

In the next section, we will look at the next big task that a matching engine needs to perform – matching participant orders that cross each other.

Matching participant orders

In this section, we will understand what happens when a market participant modifies an existing order or sends a new order in such a way that the price on this order will cause a match against an existing passive order on the other side. In such a scenario, the matching engine matches this aggressive order against passive orders in order from most aggressive to least aggressive price. This means passive bids are matched from highest to lowest buy prices, and passive asks are matched from lowest to highest sell prices. In cases where the passive orders are not fully matched because the aggressive order has a smaller quantity than the passive liquidity available on the other side, then the remaining liquidity on the passive orders stays in the book. In cases where the aggressive order is not fully matched because the passive liquidity available on the other side is less than the quantity on the aggressive order, then the remaining quantity on the aggressive order rests in the book as a passive order.

Let us understand the different cases of matching participant orders and let us assume the state of the order book is where we left it in the last section, as shown here:

Client A OrderId 1 BUY 20 @ 10.90	Client B OrderId 5 SELL 1 @ 11.00
Client A OrderId 8 BUY 10 @ 10.90	Client C OrderId 6 Sell 5 @ 11.00
Client C OrderId 4 BUY 100 @ 10.90	Client B OrderId 7 SELL 5 @ 11.10
Client A OrderId 3 BUY 5 @ 10.80	
Client B OrderId 2 BUY 20 @ 10.80	

Table 5.5 – Starting state of the order book before any order matches

Now, let us assume client C sends a sell order of a quantity of 50 at a sell price of 10.90. This will cause the sell order to match against the buy orders with *OrderId=1* and *OrderId=8*, which are fully matched, and *OrderId=4*, which is partially matched for a quantity of 20 and has the remaining quantity of 80. The orders that are fully matched are removed from the order book and the partially-matched order is modified to the new remaining quantity. The updated order book after this matching transaction is shown here:

Client C OrderId 4 BUY 80 @ 10.90	Client B OrderId 5 SELL 1 @ 11.00
Client A OrderId 3 BUY 5 @ 10.80	Client C OrderId 6 Sell 5 @ 11.00
Client B OrderId 2 BUY 20 @ 10.80	Client B OrderId 7 SELL 5 @ 11.10

Table 5.6 – Order book reflecting the impact of the aggressive order and partial executions

Now, let us assume client A sends a buy order of a quantity of 10 at a buy price of 11.00. This fully matches the sell orders with *OrderId=5* and *OrderId=6*, and the remaining unmatched quantity on the aggressive buy order rests in the book as a passive bid order. The updated order book after this matching transaction is shown here:

Client A OrderId 9 BUY 4 @ 11.00	Client B OrderId 7 SELL 5 @ 11.10
Client C OrderId 4 BUY 80 @ 10.90	
Client A OrderId 3 BUY 5 @ 10.80	
Client B OrderId 2 BUY 20 @ 10.80	

Table 5.7 – Order book after full execution and resting quantity from the aggressor

Now that we understand a lot of the common interactions that we will encounter in the matching engine and how those are handled, as well as how they interact with the limit order book, we can design the matching engine we will build in this book.

Designing our matching engine

We will spend the rest of this book implementing each one of the C++ electronic trading ecosystem components we discussed in this chapter. However, before we get started on the next chapter, it is important to understand the architecture of these components to make the implementation details easier and clearer later on. We present only the matching engine component from *Figure 5.1* here so we can discuss the design of our matching engine in a little more detail:

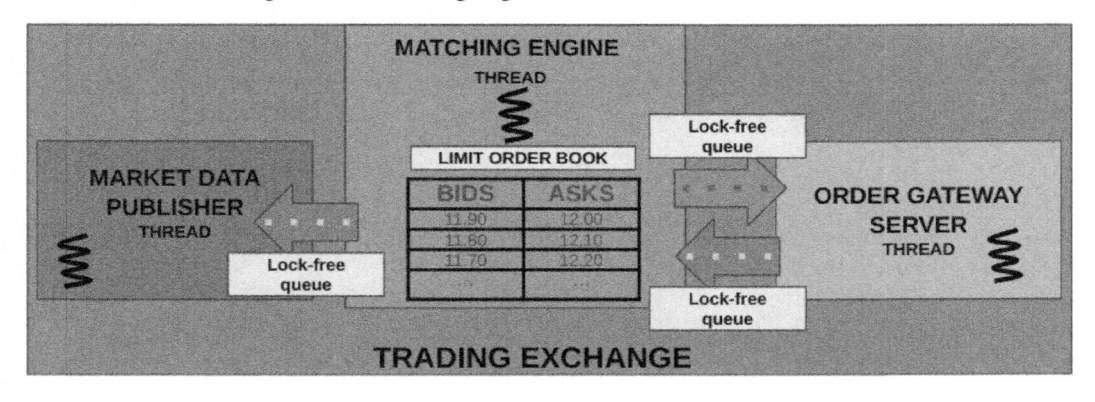

Figure 5.2 – Design of our matching engine component

We present a few more details in this diagram compared to *Figure 5.1* by discussing the major design choices for the matching engine next.

Threading model

In our system, the matching engine, the market data publisher, and the order gateway server will be independent threads. This is intentional so that each one of these components can operate independently, and during periods of bursts in market activity, the entire system can achieve maximum throughput. Also, there are other tasks that each component needs to perform – for example, the order gateway server must maintain connectivity with all market participants, even when the matching engine is busy. Similarly, let us assume the market data publisher is busy sending out market data on the network; we do not want the matching engine or the order gateway server to slow down. We already saw how to create threads, set affinity on them, and assign tasks for them to do in the previous chapter, *Building the C++ Building Blocks for Low-Latency Applications*, in the *C++ threading for multi-threaded low-latency applications* section.

Communication between threads

Another important thing to discuss here is the communication between the matching engine and the order gateway server infrastructure. The order gateway server serializes the order requests coming in from the market participants and forwards them to the matching engine for processing. The matching engine needs to generate a response for order requests and send them back to the order gateway server. Additionally, it also needs to inform the order gateway server about executions that happen on the participant's orders so that they can be informed about the trades. So, it needs a bi-directional queue, or one queue from the order gateway server to the matching engine and another queue from the matching engine to the order gateway server.

Another communication channel is when the matching engine generates and sends market data updates to reflect the updated state of the limit order book for the public market data publisher component.

Finally, since the matching engine, the order gateway server, and the market data publisher are all different threads, here we find a perfect case for a lock-free queue. We will use the lock-free FIFO queue we created in the previous chapter in the *Transferring data using lock-free queues* section.

Limit order book

Finally, for the limit order book, we will use a couple of different data structures to implement it efficiently. Without diving into specific implementation details (which we will look at in the next chapter), we need to maintain the bids and asks in the correct sorted order on both sides to facilitate efficient matching when aggressive orders come in. We need to be able to efficiently insert and remove orders from the price levels to support operations such as adding, modifying, and deleting orders based on client requests. One other particularly important consideration here is that the data structures we use and the order objects themselves must avoid dynamic memory allocations and copy as little data around as possible. We will make heavy use of the memory pool we created in the previous chapter in the *Designing C++ memory pools to avoid dynamic memory allocations* section.

Understanding how an exchange publishes information to participants

The previous section was dedicated to discussing the details of the matching engine, and in that discussion, we assumed that the matching engine receives market participants' order requests from the order gateway server infrastructure. We also implicitly assumed that the matching engine would communicate changes to the limit order book it maintains to all the market participants listening to the market data feed. In this section, we will discuss the market data publisher and the order gateway server components that the matching engine relies on to communicate with the market participants.

Communicating market events through markets data

Let us discuss the market data publisher component first. This component is responsible for converting the updates to the limit order book maintained by the matching engine. We mentioned before that the market data network level protocol can be TCP or UDP but generally, the preferred protocol in practice is UDP, and that is the protocol we will be using in our market data publisher as well.

In simple terms, the market data protocol represents the format of the messages that the market data publisher publishes over the UDP (or in some cases TCP) protocol. **FIX Adapted for STreaming (FAST)** is the most well-known and popular messaging format for market data that is currently used by a lot of electronic trading exchanges. There are other protocols, such as **ITCH**, **PITCH**, **Enhanced Order Book Interface** (**EOBI**), **Simple Binary Encoding** (**SBE**), and many others, but for the purposes of this book, we will create a simple custom binary protocol such as EOBI or SBE that we will use.

Since FIX is the most common protocol used in financial applications, we will present a few details here. FIX data is organized as a set of TAG=VALUE style fields. It will be easier to understand this with a simple example, so for a hypothetical market data update, you might receive the following collection of fields to convey all the data for that update. This hypothetical market data update corresponds to a new buy order of a quantity of 1,000 being added for the Apple company stock (stock symbol AAPL and numeric security ID 68475) at a price of 175.16.

TAG	FIX NAME	VALUE	DESCRIPTION
268	NoMDEntries	1	Number of market data updates
279	MDUpdateAction	0 (New)	Type of market data update
269	MDEntryType	0 (Bid)	Type of market data entry
48	SecurityID	68475 (AAPL)	Integer identifier for the trading product
270	MDEntryPx	175.16	Price of this market data update
271	MDEntrySize	1000	Quantity of this market data update
...	...	...	...

Table 5.8 – An example of a FIX message corresponding to a hypothetical market data update

The different kinds of messages that make up the market data protocol are roughly categorized into the following categories:

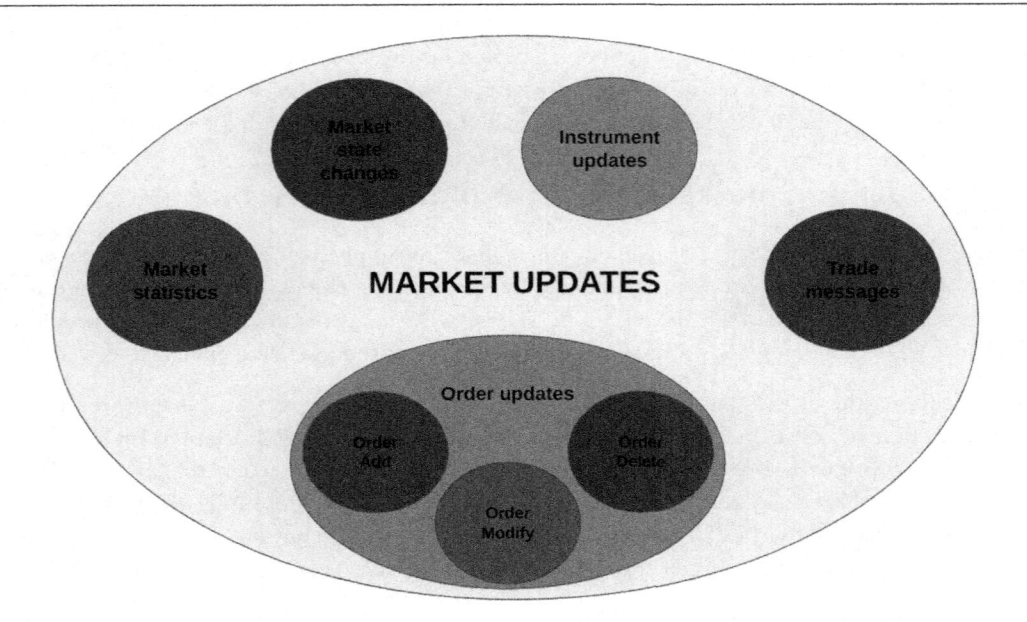

Figure 5.3 – Different market updates that an exchange sends out

Let us discuss these next.

Market state changes

These messages notify the market participants about changes in the market and/or matching engine state. Typically, markets go through states such as **Closed** for trading, **Pre-open** (market state before regular trading sessions), **Opening** (when markets transition from the Pre-open to Trading states), and **Trading** (regular trading session).

Instrument updates

The exchange uses instrument update messages to inform market participants about the different instruments available for trading. Some exchanges support special types of instruments that the market participants can create on the fly, and these messages are used to inform participants about changes to such instruments. Usually, these messages are used to inform participants about instrument metadata such as minimum price increments, tick size value, and more. The **minimum price increment** is the minimum price difference in order prices. In the examples we have seen so far, we assumed the minimum price increment to be 0.10 (i.e., valid prices are multiples of 0.10). The **tick size value** is the amount of money made or lost when we buy and sell at prices that are apart by a single minimum price increment. Very often, for products such as stocks, **Exchange Traded Fund** (ETFs), and so on, the tick size multiplier is just 1, meaning the profit or loss is simply the sell price minus the buy price for a pair of trades. ETFs are securities that trade at the exchange and are an investment option which consists of a basket of securities, i.e., by investing in an ETF, you invest in a bunch of assets that make up that ETF. But for some leveraged products such as futures, options, and so on, this tick size multiplier can be something other than 1, and the final profit or loss is computed as follows:

`((sell-price - buy-price) / min-price-increment) * trade-qty * tick-size.`

Order updates

The market data publisher uses order update messages to communicate changes to the orders in the limit order book maintained by the matching engine – specifically, updates to the order book similar to what we discussed in the *Understanding the exchange order book* subsection in the *Designing the C++ matching engine in a trading exchange* section. Generally, the different kinds of order updates messages are the following:

- **Order Add** – This is used by the exchange to notify the participants that a new passive order was added to the limit order book. Typical attributes here are `instrument-id`, `order-id`, `price`, `side`, `quantity`, and `priority`. The `priority` field here is used to specify the position of the order in the FIFO queue of orders at that price.

- **Order Modify** – This is used by the exchange to let the participants know that a passive order was modified in price or quantity or both. This message has similar fields as an Order Add message. As mentioned before, in most cases (except when the order quantity is reduced), a new order priority value will be assigned for Order Modify events.

- **Order Delete** – This message is used to notify the market participants that a passive order was deleted from the order book. The important attributes here are `instrument-id` and `order-id` to specify the order being deleted from the order book.

Trade messages

Trade messages are used by the exchange to notify the market participants that a match happened in the market. Generally, the attributes here are `instrument-id`, side of the aggressive order, execution price of the trade, and the traded quantity. Generally, when trades happen, the exchange also publishes as many Order Delete, Order Modify, and Order Add messages as needed to communicate information about which orders were fully and/or partially executed and need to be removed from the book or modified to reflect the new state of the order book.

Market statistics

These are optional messages that some exchanges publish to communicate different types of statistics about trading instruments. These statistics can be information about traded volume for an instrument, open interest for the instrument, the highest, lowest, opening, and closing prices for the instrument, and so on.

We covered a lot of details about the market data messaging types and the information they try to convey. Now we are ready to design the market data publisher we will build in our electronic trading exchange next.

Designing the market data publisher

Let us discuss a few design details for the market data publisher we will implement in our electronic exchange. We present only the market data publisher from *Figure 5.1* here so we can discuss the design in greater detail.

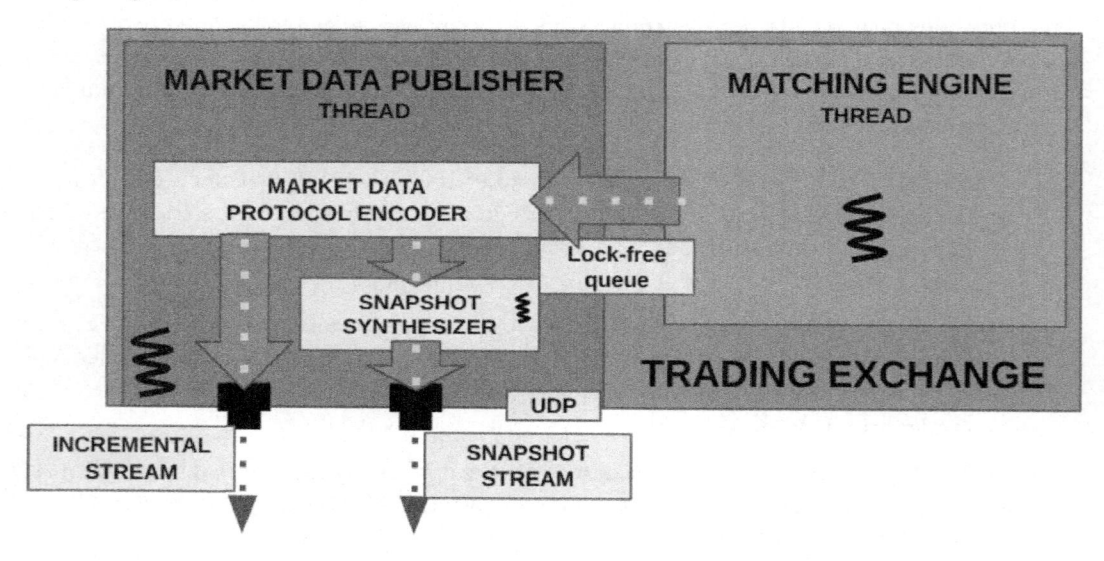

Figure 5.4 – Design of our market data publisher infrastructure

There are two main components of the market data publisher infrastructure. Both use the socket utilities we built in the previous chapter in the *C++ network programming using sockets* section to put the market data on the wire. This is in addition to the threading library we built, which will be used to create, launch, and run the market data publisher thread.

Market data protocol encoder

The market data protocol encoder component inside the market data publisher infrastructure is responsible for encoding the market data updates published by the matching engine. The market data encoder consumes market data updates that reflect changes to the order book and converts them into the public market data messaging format with some additional information. This component also publishes the incremental market data updates to the UDP multicast stream configured for incremental streams. Remember that the incremental stream only contains market updates that can be used to update the order book, assuming the participant had an accurate view of the limit order book prior to the incremental update. The encoded market data updates are also published to the snapshot synthesizer component, which we will discuss in more detail in the next section.

The market data stream is generally very high volume in terms of network traffic and experiences large bursts in activity, especially during periods of high volatility in the market. Since the TCP protocol adds extra bandwidth due to acknowledgments of message receipts and retransmissions of lost data, typically, UDP is the network protocol of choice for market data. Multicast streaming over UDP is also preferred since the market data can be disseminated on the multicast streams once and all interested subscribers can subscribe to that stream instead of having a one-to-one connection with each market data consumer over TCP. This design is not without some drawbacks, namely the possibility of market data consumers dropping UDP packets due to network congestion, slow hardware or software, and so on. When that happens, the order book that the trading client is maintaining is incorrect since they might have lost an update corresponding to a new order being added, an order being modified or canceled, and so on. This is the problem that the snapshot multicast streams solve, which we will explore with examples in subsequent chapters as we implement our market data consumers, but we will briefly introduce the snapshot synthesizer component in the next section.

Snapshot synthesizer

The snapshot synthesizer consumes the encoded market date updates published by the market data protocol encoder, synthesizes the latest snapshot of the limit order book, and publishes the snapshot periodically to the snapshot multicast stream. The important point here is that the snapshot synthesis does not interfere with the incremental stream publishing so that incremental updates to the order book can be published as quickly as possible. It is a separate thread of execution, and the sole responsibility here is to generate an accurate snapshot of the order book based on the incremental updates. This component also adds the correct sequence information on the snapshot updates to facilitate synchronization at the client's end before publishing it on the snapshot UDP multicast stream. What this means is that in the snapshot messages it sends out, it will provide the last sequence number from the incremental stream that was used to synthesize this snapshot message. This is important because the downstream market data consumer clients can use this sequence number of the last update in the incremental stream to perform successful synchronization/catch-up. This will become very clear when we build our market data publisher and market data consumer components because we will cover all the details with examples then. Another thing to understand is that the low-latency criteria that apply to the other components in our system do not apply here since this is a delayed and sub-sampled stream of information anyway. Additionally, packet drops are expected to be extremely rare on the client's end and the snapshot synchronization process is slow on the client's end, so trying to make this component super low latency is unnecessary. For our snapshot synthesizer component, we will also use the UDP protocol to keep it simple, but in practice, this is often a combination of TCP and UDP protocols. For low-latency market participants, packet drops on the UDP stream are expected to be rare because typically, the network connection to the exchange and switches along the way have a large bandwidth capacity and low switching latencies. Additionally, the participants invest resources into procuring and installing super-fast servers, building low-latency market data consumer software, and using special **Network Interface Cards** (**NICs**) to handle large volumes of market data.

This concludes our high-level design of the market data publisher infrastructure we will build in this book. Next, we need to discuss the other channel that the exchange uses to notify market participants about responses to their order requests as well as when their orders get executed – the order gateway interface.

Notifying market participants through the order gateway interfaces

We discussed that the market data consumer is used by the electronic trading exchange to disseminate public information about changes to the order book and matches happening for the different trading instruments available at the exchange. The point here is that this is public market data that is available to everyone that has access to and is subscribed to the market data stream. This section will discuss the other interface that the exchange uses to communicate with market participants about updates for their orders – the order gateway interface.

There are a few key differences between the information provided by the public market data feed and the information provided by the order gateway infrastructure.

Understanding the difference in network protocols

We mentioned this before but we will reiterate here that typically, market data publishers use the UDP protocol at the network level, and the order gateway infrastructure uses the TCP protocol at the network level in their connections with market participants. This is because the data published by market data publishers is very voluminous and needs to be published as quickly as possible, hence the choice of UDP over TCP. There are generally additional synchronization mechanisms available on the market data publisher to deal with rare packet drops over UDP. The order gateway infrastructure relies on TCP because it needs a reliable method of communicating with the clients, and packet drops here are difficult to handle gracefully without TCP. Intuitively, it should be clear that it would be a major headache if clients were not sure that their orders reached the exchange or if clients weren't sure they received immediate notifications when their orders are updated or matched.

Differentiating between public and private information

Perhaps the biggest difference between the market data publisher and the order gateway infrastructure is that the market data publisher publishes public information while hiding some sensitive information, such as which client an order belongs to or which clients participated in a matching transaction. This information is also published for all market participants and is meant to be used to construct the limit order book to reflect the state of a trading instrument. The order gateway server, on the other hand, only publishes order update notifications to the clients who own the orders that are being updated. Another way to think about this is that to receive and process public market data, a participant does not need to have any orders in the order book. But to receive private order gateway notifications the participant must have orders in the book, otherwise, there is nothing for the exchange to notify the client privately about.

Sending order requests for participants' orders

Another major difference that should be obvious by now is that the order gateway component sending facilitates a bi-directional communication channel. What this means is that clients can send order requests to the exchange such as new orders, modify orders, cancel orders, and so on. On the other hand, as we discussed, the exchange uses the order gateway infrastructure to send private notifications for market participants' orders. The market data publisher infrastructure does not generally service any client requests (i.e., the communication path is from the exchange to market data subscribers only).

The final sending component we need to design on the side of the electronic trading exchange is the order gateway infrastructure we just discussed; let us do that in the next section.

Designing the order gateway server

Let us discuss a few design details for the order gateway server we will implement in our electronic exchange. We present only the order gateway server infrastructure from *Figure 5.1* here so we can discuss the design of our order gateway server in a little more detail.

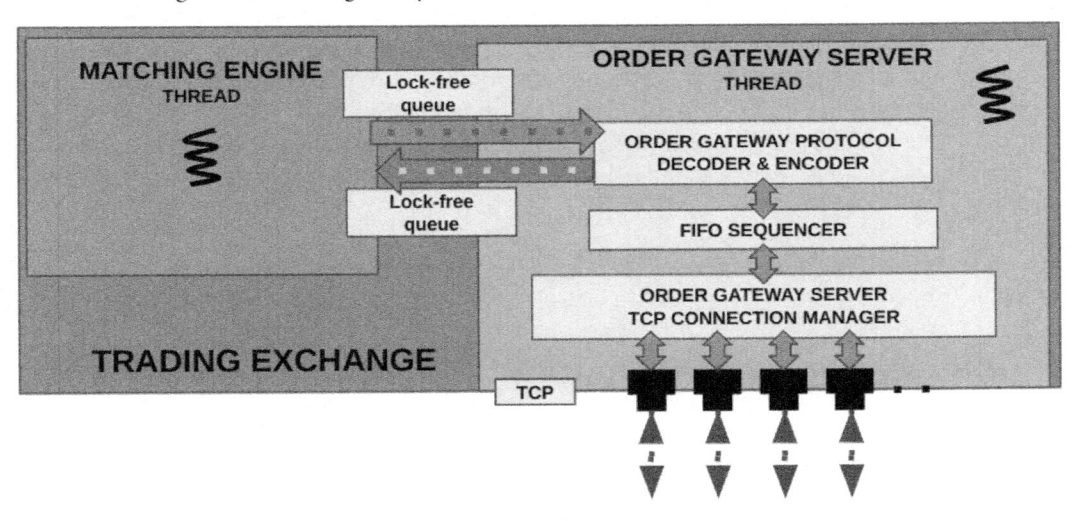

Figure 5.5 – Design of our order gateway server infrastructure

We present a few more details in this diagram compared to *Figure 5.1* and break down some details about the subcomponents for the order gateway server infrastructure.

TCP connection server/manager

The first component inside the order gateway infrastructure is the TCP connection manager. This component is responsible for setting up a TCP server that listens to and accepts incoming TCP connections from market participants' order gateway clients. It is also responsible for detecting clients who disconnect and removing them from the list of active connections. Finally, this component needs to forward order responses from the matching engine to the correct client for which the response is meant. We will use the socket utilities, TCP socket, and TCP server functionality we implemented in the *C++ network programming using sockets* section in the previous chapter, *Building the C++ Building Blocks for Low-Latency Applications*.

FIFO sequencer

Another important task this component needs to do is maintain fairness when processing requests from market participants. As mentioned previously, to maintain fairness, client responses must be processed in the exact order they were received at the exchange infrastructure. So, the FIFO sequencer must ensure that it forwards client requests to the matching engine across the different client connections that the TCP connection manager maintains in the order in which they are received.

Exchange messaging protocol decoder and encoder

The encoder-decoder component is responsible for translating between the exchange messaging protocol and whatever internal structures the matching engine expects client requests in and publishes client responses in. Depending on the complexity of the exchange protocol, this can be as straightforward as packaging and extracting the correct fields into and from a packed binary structure. If the exchange messaging format is more complicated, then there will be additional encoding and decoding steps involved. For this book's purposes, we will have a simple exchange order messaging protocol that uses packed binary structures and has additional information on top of the format the exchange matching engine uses.

This concludes our discussion of the electronic trading exchange, and now we can move on to building the client-side infrastructure for a market participant that wishes to trade on this exchange.

Building a market participant's interface to the exchange

We will now discuss the purpose and design of the components in the market participants' systems. Specifically, we will start by discussing the market data consumer in the client's trading system, which subscribes to, consumes, and decodes the public market data published by the exchange. We will also discuss the order gateway client infrastructure in the client's trading system, which connects to the exchange order gateway server. The order gateway client is also responsible for sending order requests to the exchange and receiving and decoding responses for the client's orders.

Understanding the market data consumer infrastructure

The market data consumer component in a market participant's trading system is the direct complement of the market data publisher component in the electronic trading exchange. It is responsible for subscribing to and consuming the multicast network traffic that the exchange publishes, decoding and normalizing the market data it reads from the exchange protocol to an internal format, and implementing packet drop-related synchronization mechanisms.

Subscribing to and consuming UDP multicast traffic

The first and most obvious task is to subscribe to the multicast stream that the exchange is publishing market data on. Typically, in the interest of load balancing, the exchange groups different trading instruments on different multicast stream addresses. This lets clients choose a subset of all the data that the exchange is publishing, depending on the trading instrument and products that the client is interested in. Typically, this involves the clients joining the correct multicast streams, the addresses of which are public information available from the exchange.

Decoding and normalizing from exchange protocol

The next thing the market data consumer needs to do is convert from the exchange market data protocol into an internal format that the rest of the components in the participant's system use. Depending on the exchange market data protocol, this part of the component can vary in complexity and performance latencies. The fastest protocols are the ones where minimal decoding is required, such as EOBI and SBE, which are just binary-packed structures. What this means is that the market data format is such that decoding the stream just involves reinterpreting the byte stream as the binary-packed structure we expect to find in the stream and is as fast as it gets. More complicated protocols such as FAST generally take longer to decode and normalize.

Synchronizing on startup and packet drops

Remember that we discussed that usually exchanges prefer UDP to be the network protocol to deliver market data to the participants. While this speeds up the delivery of data to clients and achieves higher throughput, this also leaves us open to packet drops and out-of-order delivery due to the unreliable nature of UDP. To make sure that market participants see market data packets in the correct order, as well as detect packet drops when they occur, typically, there are packet-level and instrument-level sequence numbers that the participants should check.

Another thing that needs to be designed, both on the exchange market data publisher and the participants' market data consumers, is a mechanism to recover from such packet drops. This same mechanism is also used by participants who join the market data stream after the markets are already open or if the participants need to restart their market data consumer components for any reason. In all such cases, the market data consumers in the client's trading system needs to perform some synchronization to get the current and complete state of the limit order book.

The commonly used design to achieve this synchronization is explained in this section. Usually, the exchange market data streams are broken down into two major groups – **snapshot streams** and **incremental streams**. We will explain the reason for having these two streams and how they help market participants handle cases of packet drops next.

Incremental market data streams

The incremental market data stream assumes that the market participant already has the correct view of the limit order book maintained by the matching engine, and this stream only publishes incremental updates to the previous state of the order book. This means that this stream is much lower in bandwidth requirements since it publishes only incremental updates to the book. Typically, under normal operating conditions, it is expected that market participants only be subscribed to the incremental streams to maintain the correct state of the order book.

If the client drops a packet from this stream, then the state of the order book that they maintain might be inconsistent with what the matching engine has. The mechanism to handle this failure is to clear or reset the order book that the participant maintains. Then it needs to subscribe to the snapshot stream, which contains data for the full state of the entire order book (instead of only incremental updates) to synchronize to the correct state of the book once again. The protocol here is to clear the book, start queuing up incremental updates received from the incremental stream and wait to build the full state of the order book, and then apply the incremental updates to that full order book to finish the synchronization. Now, let us understand a few more details of what is published by the exchange on the snapshot market data streams.

Snapshot market data streams

As we mentioned before, the snapshot market data stream contains data that can be used to build the full order book from a completely empty state. Usually, this stream just contains a thorough list of *Order Add* messages corresponding to every single passive order that exists in the order book. The exchange usually throttles how often this list is updated and published, meaning it might only send out a stream of snapshot messages every couple of seconds or so. This is because, since this stream contains information about all the orders in the order book for every single trading instrument, it can become quite bandwidth-heavy. Additionally, since packet drops are an exceedingly rare occurrence and participants do not mind waiting a few seconds when they first start up to grab the correct state of the order book, the throttling does not usually have a large negative impact.

This concludes the discussion of the market data protocols and the synchronization process, so now we can design the market data consumer that we will implement.

Designing the market data consumer

Let us discuss a few design details for the market data consumer we will implement in our market participant's trading system. We present only the market data consumer from *Figure 5.1* here so we can discuss the design in greater detail.

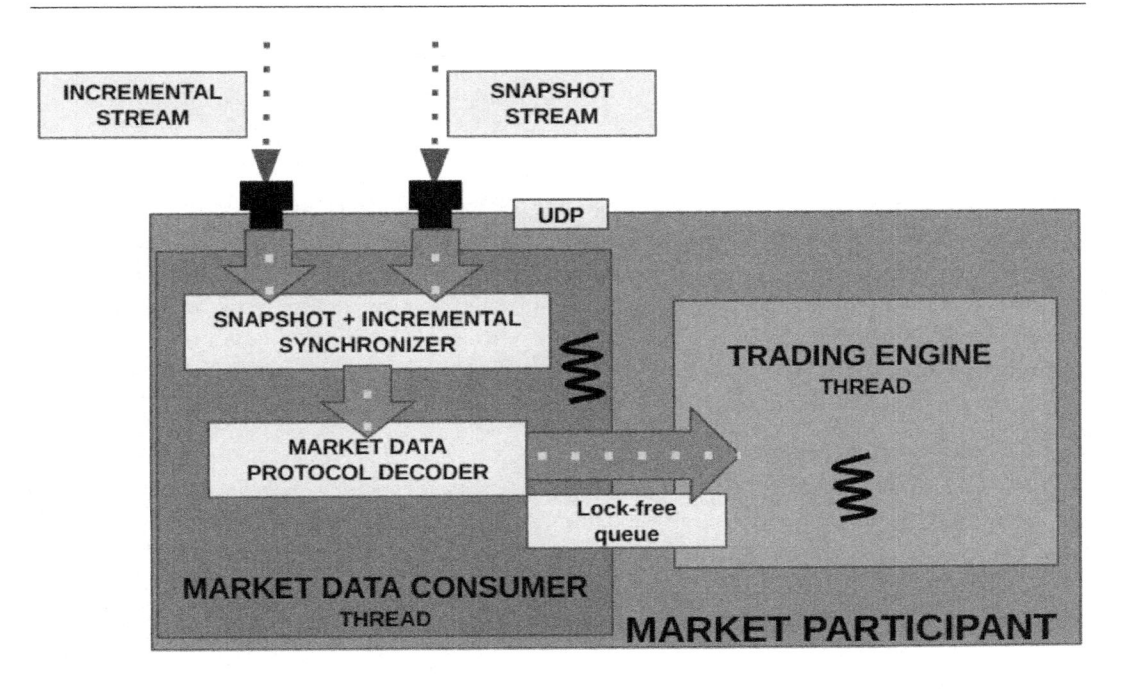

Figure 5.6 – Design of our market data consumer infrastructure

Let us discuss the two primary subcomponents when it comes to the design of the market data consumer infrastructure in a market participant's trading system. Both use the socket utilities we built in the previous chapter in the *C++ network programming using sockets* section to subscribe to and consume the market data from the network.

Snapshot and incremental stream synchronizer

The market data consumer needs to have a subcomponent that can be used to subscribe to the snapshot stream in addition to being subscribed to the incremental stream. Remember that we explained that when a market participant's system first starts up or needs to restart in the middle of the day or drops a market data packet from the incremental stream, it does not have the correct view of the limit order book. In such a scenario, the correct recovery/synchronization procedure is to clear the limit order book, subscribe to the snapshot stream, and wait till a full snapshot of the order book is received. Additionally, the updates that continue to come in over the incremental market data stream need to be queued up. Once the full snapshot is received and all incremental updates starting from the sequence number of the last update in the snapshot are also queued up and available, we are done. At this point, the limit order book is reconstructed from the snapshot stream, and all queued-up incremental updates are applied to this book to synchronize/catch up with the exchange. At this point, the consumer can stop consuming data from the snapshot stream and leave the snapshot stream, and only consume data from the incremental stream. The component in the market data consumer infrastructure responsible for this synchronization mechanism is what we will refer to as the snapshot and incremental stream synchronization subcomponent.

Market data protocol decoder

The other subcomponent is responsible for decoding the stream of data coming in from the snapshot and/or the incremental market data streams. This component translates the data from the exchange feed format to the internal format of the trading strategy framework. This is usually a subset of the fields that the exchange provides and is often normalized across different trading exchanges to make the trading strategy framework independent of exchange-specific details. For our market data consumer infrastructure, we will keep this component quite simple since we will be using a packed binary structure, but as mentioned before, in practice, this can be a much more complicated format such as FAST.

We discussed the details and design of how a market participant's system consumes the public market data feed from the exchange. We can move on to the order gateway client infrastructure, which the participant uses to send order requests and receive responses and execution notifications.

Understanding the order gateway client infrastructure

The order gateway client infrastructure in the market participant's trading system is a TCP client that connects to the exchange's order gateway server. The other task that this component performs is receiving updates from the exchange on this TCP connection, decoding the messages received from the exchange order messaging protocol into a normalized internal format for use by the rest of the system. Finally, the order gateway client component is also responsible for taking the order actions requested by the trading framework and encoding them in the order messaging format that the exchange understands and sending it through to the exchange.

The important thing to remember here is that the order gateway client must always maintain a reliable TCP connection to the exchange. This is to make sure that the exchange does not miss any order request from the client and that the client does not miss any updates to its orders from the exchange. In addition to the reliability mechanisms implemented by the TCP networking protocol itself, there usually exists an application-level reliability mechanism implemented by the exchange and the participants. This application-level reliability mechanism usually consists of strictly incrementing sequence numbers on the messages sent from exchange to client and from client to exchange. Additionally, there can be heart-beating mechanisms in place, which are simply messages sent from exchange to client and client to exchange to check whether a connection is still active during periods of low activity.

Additionally, there are mechanisms to authenticate and identify clients when they first connect, and this is usually implemented as a handshake mechanism with user identification and password, and so on. There can be additional administrative messages, such as the logon authentication message, and it depends on the exchange and can have a wide range of purposes. For this book's purposes, we will limit the scope to not focus on these administrative messages since they do not matter to our low latency goals.

Next, let us design our order gateway client infrastructure.

Designing the order gateway client infrastructure

Let us discuss a few design details for the market data publisher we will implement in our market participant's trading system. We present only the order gateway client from *Figure 5.1* here so we can discuss the design in greater detail.

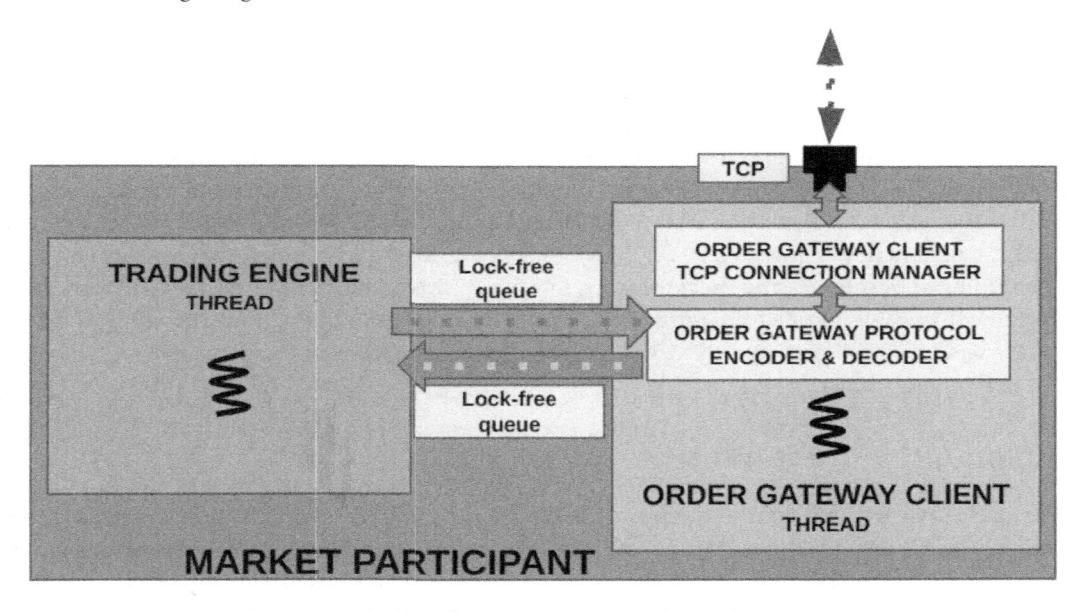

Figure 5.7 – Design of our order gateway client infrastructure

There are two simple components that make up the order gateway client inside the market participant's trading system.

TCP connection manager

The order gateway client in a market participant's trading system oversees connecting to the exchange order gateway server and managing that connection. In practice, a single participant will have multiple connections to the exchange for load balancing, redundancy, and latency reasons. But in the electronic trading ecosystem that we will be building, we will design it such that an order gateway client creates a single connection to the exchange order gateway server. We will use the TCP socket client library we built in the previous chapter under the *C++ network programming using sockets* section.

Order gateway protocol encoder and decoder

The order messaging format encoder and decoder translate order requests from the internal format that the trading strategy uses to the exchange format and translate order responses and execution notifications from the exchange to an internal format for the strategy framework. This component can vary in complexity depending on the exchange format, but for our trading system, we will keep the encoding and decoding complexity low by using a binary-packed structure.

Next, we move away from our discussion of the order gateway infrastructure and on to the most complex (and most interesting) component of the participant's system – the trading strategy framework.

Designing a framework for low-latency C++ trading algorithms

Now that we have discussed the market data consumer and order gateway client components on the market participants' trading systems, the last component we need to discuss is the framework that makes trading decisions. This component is one of the most important components in a trading system since this is where intelligence lies. By intelligence, we mean the system that processes normalized market data updates, builds a view into the market conditions, and computes trading analytics to find trading opportunities and execute trades. Obviously, this component relies on the market data consumer to receive decoded and normalized market data updates and uses the order gateway client component to send order requests to and receive order responses from the exchange in a decoded and normalized format.

Building the order book

The market participant needs to construct the limit order book based on the market data that the exchange publishes. Note that it is not strictly necessary that the client must build the entire order book, especially if the trading strategies do not require information that is that granular. For this book's purposes, we will build a full order book in our trading framework, but we just wanted to point out that it is not strictly necessary in all cases. A simple example of such a case would be strategies that only care about knowing the prices and/or quantity of the most aggressively priced orders – that is, the highest bid price and lowest offer price (known as **Top Of Book** (**TOB**) or **Best Bid and Offer** (**BBO**)). Another example would be strategies that only rely on trade prices to make decisions and do not require a view into the full order book.

One thing to reiterate here is that the order book that the client builds is slightly different from the one that the exchange maintains because the client does not usually know which order belongs to which market participant. Additionally, depending on the exchange, a few more pieces of information might be hidden from the market participants, such as which orders are icebergs, which new orders are stop orders, self-match-prevention considerations, and so on. **Iceberg orders** are orders that have a larger hidden quantity than what is displayed in the public market data. **Stop orders** are orders that lie dormant and then become active when a specific price trades. **Self-match prevention** (**SMP**) is a constraint that prevents a client from trading against themselves, which some exchanges choose to enforce in the matching engine. For the purposes of this book, we will ignore and not implement such special functionality. Another thing to understand is that the book that the trading participants have is a slightly delayed version of the order book that the matching engine has. This is because there is some latency between the matching engine updating its order book to the trading client getting the market updates corresponding to the changes and updating their book.

Building a feature engine

Sophisticated trading strategies need to build additional intelligence over just the order book. These trading strategies need to implement various trading signals and intelligence on top of the prices, liquidity, trade transactions, and order book published by the exchange. The idea here is to build intelligence, which can be a combination of technical analysis style indicators, statistical predictive signals and models, and market microstructure-related statistical edges. A detailed discussion of various kinds of trading signals and predictive analysis is outside the scope of this book, but there are plenty of texts dedicated to this topic. There are many different terms used in practice for such predictive edges – trading signals, indicators, features, and so on. The component inside the trading system that constructs and wires together a collection of such predictive signals is often referred to as a feature/signal/indicator engine. In this book, we will build a minimal feature engine for our trading strategies, but we reiterate here that feature engines can get quite sophisticated and complicated depending on the strategy's complexity.

Developing the execution logic

After building the order book and deriving some trading signals from the current state of the market, if the trading strategies find an opportunity, they still need to execute their orders at the exchange. This is achieved by sending new orders, modifying existing orders to either move them to a more aggressive or less aggressive price, and/or canceling existing orders to avoid getting filled on them. The subcomponent in the trading infrastructure responsible for sending, modifying, and canceling orders – basically, managing a strategy's orders at the exchange – is called the execution system. For the execution systems, the ability to react quickly to market data and order responses coming from the exchange and send out order requests as quickly as possible is extremely important. A large part of a high-frequency trading system's profitability and sustainability depends on achieving the lowest possible latencies in the execution systems.

Understanding the risk management systems

The risk management system is an important piece of the trading strategy infrastructure. Technically speaking, in practice, there are multiple layers of risk management systems in a modern electronic trading ecosystem. In practice, there are risk management systems in the client's trading strategy framework, order gateway clients in the market participant's system, and backend systems at the clearing broker's end. For this book's purposes, we will only implement a minimal risk management system in the trading strategy framework. Risk management systems try to manage the different forms of risk, as depicted in the following diagram:

```
┌─────────────────────────────────────────────────────────────────┐
│                        Maximum order quantity.                  │
│                                                                 │
│                   Maximum position for a desk / firm.           │
│                                                                 │
│                  Worst case position for a desk / firm.         │
│   RISK                                                          │
│   MANAGEMENT      Maximum realized and unrealized losses.       │
│                                                                 │
│                 Maximum traded volumes for an algorithm.        │
│                                                                 │
│                     Rate-based risk measures.                   │
│                        - Number of orders sent.                 │
│                        - Number of trades executed.             │
│                        - Realized losses in a time period.      │
└─────────────────────────────────────────────────────────────────┘
```

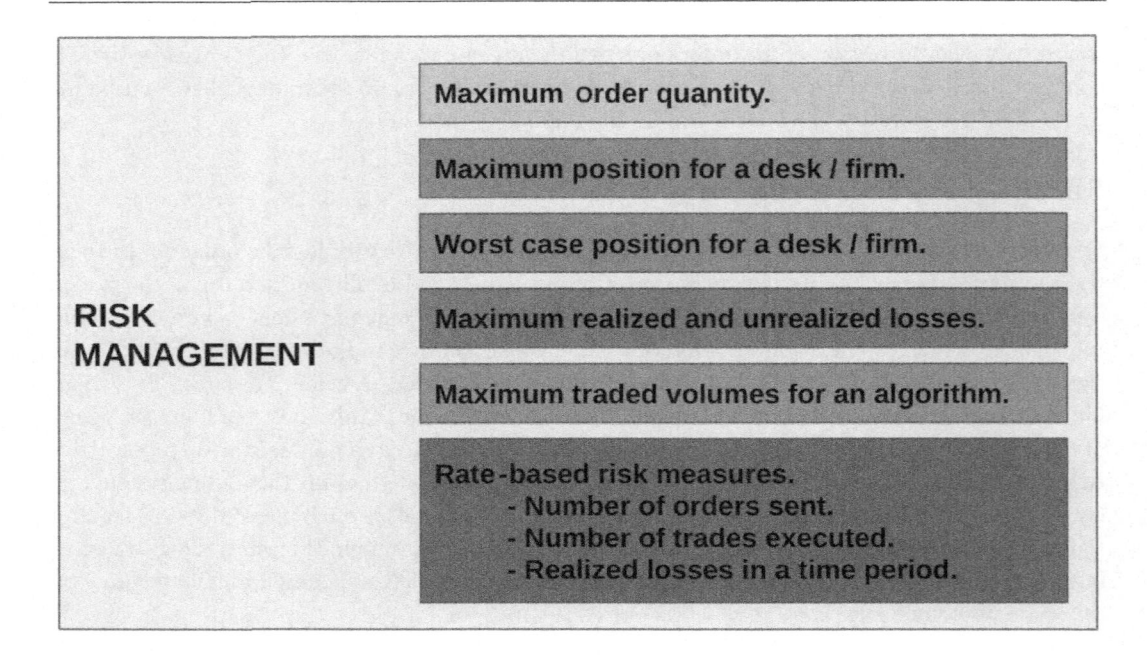

Figure 5.8 – Different risk metrics in an automated risk management system

Let us discuss these risk measures in more detail next.

Risk based on order quantities

One measure that a lot of trading systems care about is the maximum possible quantity that the algorithm is allowed to send for a single order. This is mostly to prevent bugs and user errors in the system where the algorithm ends up accidentally sending an order much larger than expected. These types of errors in practice are referred to as **Fat Finger** errors, to refer to what would happen if a user accidentally pressed more keys than intended.

Risk based on firm positions

An obvious measure of risk is the position that a strategy has in a certain trading instrument. The size of the position directly dictates how much money is lost if the market prices change a certain amount. This is why the realized position that a strategy or a firm has in a certain trading instrument is an extremely important one and is closely monitored to make sure it falls within agreed-upon limits. Note that realized position is the position that the strategy currently holds, and this ignores additional orders that the strategy might have, which might increase or decrease the position on execution.

Risk based on worst-case position

Note that in the last section, we mentioned that realized position metrics ignore how many additional live orders exist in the market. The worst-case scenario position metric tracks what the position would be considering the live orders on the side that would increase the realized position along with the actual realized position. This means if the strategy or firm is long (position from buying an instrument), then it will also check how much additional unexecuted buy quantity the strategy has in the market to compute the absolute worst-case position. This is important because some strategies might never build up to large positions but might always have a lot of active orders in the market. The perfect example of such a strategy is a market-making strategy, which we will see later in this book, but the point here is that it is important to think about worst-case scenarios when it comes to risk management.

Risk to manage realized and unrealized loss

This is what most people think of when they think of risk in the context of electronic trading. This risk metric tracks and imposes limits on how much money a strategy or firm has lost. If that value crosses a certain threshold, then depending on how much the firm has in its brokerage account, how much collateral they have, and so on, there can be consequences for the firm. Not only is it important to track the realized losses for a strategy when the strategy opens and closes positions but it is also important to track the open positions against the market prices.

To understand this, let us explain the following scenario: a strategy buys a certain quantity of an instrument and then sells the same amount of quantity back at a lower price where the strategy has a realized loss and no open position. Now, let us say the strategy buys some amount of the trading instrument, and then after the purchase where the strategy has a long position, the price of the instrument in the market moves lower. Here, this strategy not only has the realized loss it is carrying from the previous set of trades but now it also has an unrealized loss on this most recently opened long position. The risk management system needs to compute realized and unrealized losses in near real time to get an accurate view of the actual risk.

Risk based on traded volumes

This measure is not necessarily a risk; a strategy that trades a lot of volume on a certain day or in general is not a problem in itself. This risk metric seeks mostly to prevent runaway algorithms from overtrading in the market in cases of software or configuration bugs or just unexpected market conditions. This can be implemented in many ways, but the simplest implementation would be to have a cap on how much volume a strategy is allowed to trade for a trading instrument before it automatically stops sending any new orders or trading further. Usually, at this point, an external human operator needs to make sure that the algorithm behavior is as expected and then resume the trading strategy or stop it.

Risk to manage rate of orders, trades, and losses

The risk metrics we will discuss in this subsection fall into the **rate-based** risk management category. What we mean by rate-based is that the risk is computed for sliding windows of time to make sure that the strategy does not send too many orders in each window, does not trade too much in each time window, does not lose too much money in each window, and so on. Again, these metrics are to prevent trading strategy behavior that is unexpected or resembles an out-of-control or runaway algorithm. These are implemented by either resetting the counters for the underlying metric (number of orders or number of trades or traded volume or loss) at the end of the time-period window or using a rolling counter of these metrics. These risk metrics also implicitly prevent the trading strategy from behaving unexpectedly during periods of super-heightened volatility or flash crash-style scenarios.

Finally, we will design the last major component in our electronic trading ecosystem.

Designing our trading strategy framework

Let us discuss a few design details for the trading strategy framework we will implement in our participant's trading system. We present only the trading strategy framework from *Figure 5.1* here so we can discuss the design in greater detail.

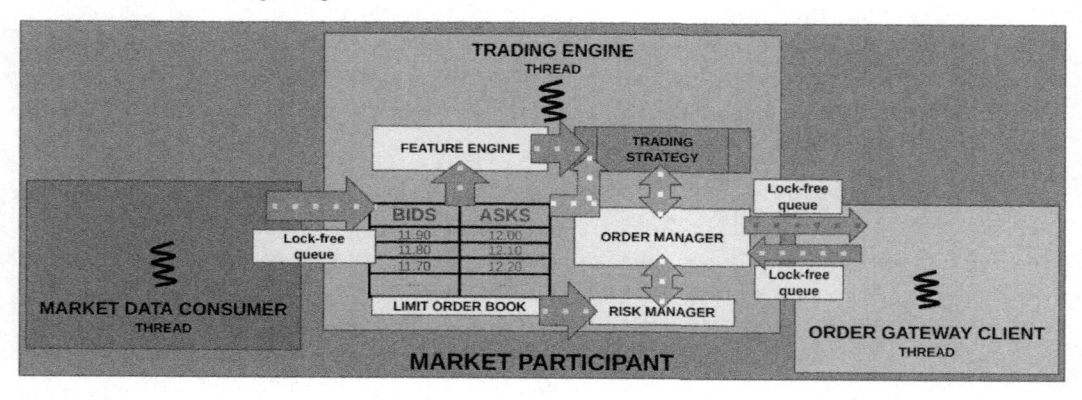

Figure 5.9 – Design of our trading strategy framework

Now we will discuss the design of the major subcomponents in the trading strategy framework we will build in this book. Note that we use the terms **trading strategy framework** and **trading engine** interchangeably and they mean the same thing in the context of this book – a collection of components to house and run automated trading algorithms.

Limit order book

The limit order book in the trading strategy framework is similar to the one that the exchange matching engine builds. Obviously, the goal here is not to perform matching between orders but instead to build, maintain, and update the limit order book from the market data updates consumed by the market data consumer via the lock-free queue. The requirement to support efficient insertion, modification, and deletion of orders into this book still applies here. The other goal here is to also make this order book accessible for use cases that the feature engine and trading strategy components require. There can be various use cases; one example is being able to synthesize a BBO or TOB quickly and efficiently for components that only need the best prices and quantities. Another example would be the ability to track the strategy's own orders in the limit order book to find where they are in the FIFO queue at a price level. Yet another example would be the ability to detect executions on a strategy's orders from the public market data feed, which can be a big boost during times when the private order feed is lagging behind the public market data feed. Implementing these details in the trading strategies we build in this book is out of the scope of what we can cover. But in practice, these details are extremely important since the advantage one gains from detecting executions from both the order responses and market data can be tens, hundreds, or even thousands of microseconds in latency. Here, we will use the lock-free queue that we built in the *Transferring data using lock-free queues* section and the memory pool we built in the *Designing C++ memory pools to avoid dynamic memory allocations* section in the previous chapter, *Building the C++ Building Blocks for Low-Latency Applications*.

Feature engine

We mentioned before that we will be building a minimal feature engine in this book. Our feature engine will only support a single feature computed from the data available from our order book, and this single feature will be used to drive our trading strategies. This feature will be updated when there are substantial changes to the order book in terms of price or liquidity and as trades occur in the market. When the feature is updated, the trading strategy can use the new feature value to re-evaluate its position, live orders, and so on to make a trading decision.

Trading strategy

The trading strategy is the component that finally makes the trading decisions based on a multitude of factors. The trading decisions depend on the trading algorithm itself, the feature values from the feature engine, the state of the order book, the prices and FIFO position of the strategy's orders in the order book, risk evaluations from the risk manager, the state of the live orders from the order manager, and so on. This is where most of the complexity of the trading strategy framework resides because it needs to handle a lot of different conditions and execute the orders safely and profitably. In this book, we will build two distinct kinds of basic trading algorithms – **market-making**, also known as **liquidity-providing strategies**, and **taking strategies**, also known as **liquidity-removing strategies**. Market-making strategies have passive orders in the book and rely on other market participants crossing the spread to trade against us. Liquidity-taking strategies are the strategies that cross the spread and send aggressive orders to take out passive liquidity.

Order manager

The order manager component is an abstraction that hides the lower-level details of sending order requests, managing the states of active orders, handling **in-flight conditions** (we will explain this shortly) for these orders, handling responses from the exchange, handling scenarios around partial and full executions of orders, and managing positions. The order manager also builds and maintains a couple of different data structures to track the state of the strategy's orders. In some sense, the order manager is like the limit order book, except it manages a tiny subset of the orders that belong to the strategy.

On the other hand, there is some additional complexity in the order management since there are some cases where order requests are in-flight from the market participant to the exchange and some events happen in the exchange matching engine at the same time. An example of an in-flight condition would be the scenario where the client tries to cancel an active order and sends a cancel request to the exchange. But while this cancel request is in-flight to the exchange, the matching engine at the exchange executes the order because an aggressor that would match this order shows up. Then, by the time the cancel request finally reaches the matching engine, the order is already executed and removed from the limit order book at the exchange, resulting in a cancel reject for this request. The order manager needs to be able to handle all different scenarios like this one accurately and efficiently.

In this book, we will build an order manager that can be used to manage passive and aggressive orders and can handle all these different conditions.

Risk manager

The risk manager tracks the different risk metrics we described in the previous section, *Understanding the risk management systems*. Additionally, the risk manager needs to notify the trading strategy about events where risk limits are breached so that the trading strategy can reduce risk and/or shut down safely. In our trading infrastructure, we will implement a few basic risk metrics, such as position, total loss, and messaging rates for order requests.

Summary

This concludes our discussion of the details and design of the major components in our electronic trading ecosystem. Let us summarize the concepts, components, and interactions we discussed, as well as the design of the components that build the electronic trading ecosystem we will build.

We started off by presenting the topology of the electronic trading ecosystem. This consists of the electronic trading exchange and many market participants that want to trade on that exchange. The electronic trading exchange infrastructure itself consists of three major components at a high level – the matching engine, the market data publisher, and the order gateway server infrastructure. From a market participant's perspective, the major components are the market data subscriber and consumer, the trading strategy framework with all its subcomponents, and the order gateway client infrastructure.

Next, we performed a deep dive into the exchange matching engine details. We explained the responsibilities of this component and how it builds, maintains, and updates the limit order book and matches participant orders that cross against each other. We concluded that section by designing our simplified matching engine component and its subcomponents, which we will implement in the next chapter.

The next topics of discussion were the market data publisher and the order gateway server infrastructure at the exchange. We described in great detail the different messages that the market data feed is composed of, the market data feed protocol, as well as designing the components inside the market data publisher. We also discussed the order gateway server, which the exchange hosts as an endpoint for the market participants to connect to, forward order requests, and receive order responses and notifications for their orders getting executed by the matching engine. We presented the design of the order gateway server with all its subcomponents, which we will implement in later chapters of this book.

The section following that took a look at the market participants' trading systems. First, we discussed the details for the market data consumer and the order gateway client infrastructure, which the participants use to consume the public market data feed from the exchange and connect to and communicate with the exchange. We also presented and discussed the design of the market data consumer we will build, as well as how it synchronizes and decodes the exchange market data feed. Finally, we designed the order gateway client infrastructure, which the trading system will use to connect to and communicate with the exchange's order gateway server infrastructure.

The final section of this chapter was dedicated to describing and designing the framework for trading strategies. We described the major components we will need to build this framework – the order book, the feature engine, the execution logic framework, and the risk management subcomponent. Finally, we laid out the design of the trading infrastructure we will build so that you can understand the higher-level design of this component before we dive into the lower-level details in subsequent chapters.

The next chapter jumps into the implementation details of the matching engine framework we designed in this chapter. Note that we will reuse a lot of the basic building blocks we built in the previous chapter moving forward as we implement our electronic trading ecosystem. The motivation for building the basic building blocks will become clearer as we implement the rest of the system, starting in the next chapter.

6
Building the C++ Matching Engine

We spent the last chapter discussing the design of the electronic trading ecosystem we will build in this book. The first component we will start with is the matching engine at the exchange. In this chapter, we will focus on the task of building the order book of the exchange matching engine, based on orders that clients enter. We will implement the various data structures and algorithms needed to track these orders, perform matching when orders *cross* each other, and update the order book. *Crossing* means when a buy order has a price equal to or greater than a sell order and then can execute against each other, but we will discuss this in greater detail in this chapter. We will focus on achieving the lowest latencies possible in these operations, since the exchanges with the best infrastructure are likely to do the most business and be preferred by participants. For now, we will not worry about the details of the market data publisher and order gateway server components at the trading exchange.

In this chapter, we will cover the following topics:

- Defining the operations and interactions in our matching engine
- Building the matching engine and exchanging external data
- Building the order book and matching orders

We will kick off this chapter by first clarifying some assumptions we will make to simplify the matching engine and limit the scope of what we can cover in this book. We will also define some types, constants, and basic structures in the first section.

Technical requirements

All the code for this book can be found in the GitHub repository for this book at `https://github.com/PacktPublishing/Building-Low-Latency-Applications-with-CPP`. The source code for this chapter is in the `Chapter6` directory in the repository.

It is important that you have read and understand the design of the electronic trading ecosystem presented in the *Designing Our Trading Ecosystem* chapter. Note that in this chapter, we will also use the code we built in *Chapter 4, Building the C++ Building Blocks for Low Latency Applications*, which can be found in the `Chapter6/common/` directory in the GitHub repository for this book.

The specifications of the environment in which the source code for this book was developed are shown as follows. We present the details of this environment because all the C++ code presented in this book is not necessarily portable and might require some minor changes to work in your environment:

- OS: `Linux 5.19.0-41-generic #42~22.04.1-Ubuntu SMP PREEMPT_DYNAMIC Tue Apr 18 17:40:00 UTC 2 x86_64 x86_64 x86_64 GNU/Linux`.
- GCC: `g++ (Ubuntu 11.3.0-1ubuntu1~22.04.1) 11.3.0`
- CMake: `cmake version 3.23.2`
- Ninja: `1.10.2`

Defining the operations and interactions in our matching engine

Here, we will declare and define the types, constants, and structures we will need as we build the matching engine in this chapter.

Defining some types and constants

Let us define a few common typedefs to document the types we will use in the rest of this book. We will also define some constants to represent some assumptions that exist, purely for the purpose of simplifying the design of our matching engine. Note that you don't need these limits/constants, and we leave this enhancement up to the interested among you. All the code for this subsection can be found in the `Chapter6/common/types.h` file in the GitHub repository for this book.

Defining a few basic types

We will define some types to hold different attributes in our electronic trading system, such as the following:

- `OrderId` to identify orders
- `TickerId` to identify trading instruments
- `ClientId` for the exchange to identify different clients
- `Price` to hold prices for instruments
- `Qty` to hold quantity values for orders

- `Priority` to capture the position of an order in the **First In First Out** (**FIFO**) queue at a price level, as discussed in the *Designing Our Trading Ecosystem* chapter.
- `Side` to signify the side (buy/sell) of an order

We will also provide basic methods to convert these to strings purely for logging purposes. Let us look at each one of these code blocks to understand the declarations next:

```cpp
#pragma once

#include <cstdint>
#include <limits>
#include "common/macros.h"
```

First, we define the `OrderId` type to identify orders, which is simply `uint64_t`, and a corresponding `orderIdToString()` method to log it. We also add a `OrderId_INVALID` sentinel method to signify invalid values:

```cpp
namespace Common {
  typedef uint64_t OrderId;
  constexpr auto OrderId_INVALID =
    std::numeric_limits<OrderId>::max();

  inline auto orderIdToString(OrderId order_id) ->
    std::string {
    if (UNLIKELY(order_id == OrderId_INVALID)) {
      return "INVALID";
    }

    return std::to_string(order_id);
  }
```

We define the `TickerId` type to identify trading instruments, which is simply a `uint32_t` type, and add a corresponding `tickerIdToString()` method for it. We have a `TickerId_INVALID` sentinel value for invalid instruments:

```cpp
  typedef uint32_t TickerId;
  constexpr auto TickerId_INVALID =
    std::numeric_limits<TickerId>::max();

  inline auto tickerIdToString(TickerId ticker_id) ->
    std::string {
    if (UNLIKELY(ticker_id == TickerId_INVALID)) {
      return "INVALID";
```

```
  }

  return std::to_string(ticker_id);
}
```

The `ClientId` type is used to differentiate between different trading participants. The `ClientId_INVALID` value represents an invalid sentinel. The `clientIdToString()` method is used for logging purposes:

```
typedef uint32_t ClientId;
constexpr auto ClientId_INVALID =
  std::numeric_limits<ClientId>::max();

inline auto clientIdToString(ClientId client_id) ->
  std::string {
  if (UNLIKELY(client_id == ClientId_INVALID)) {
    return "INVALID";
  }

  return std::to_string(client_id);
}
```

The next type is `Price`, which is used to capture prices on orders. We also add a `Price_INVALID` constant to represent invalid prices. Finally, a `priceToString()` method to *stringify* these values:

```
typedef int64_t Price;
constexpr auto Price_INVALID =
  std::numeric_limits<Price>::max();

inline auto priceToString(Price price) -> std::string {
  if (UNLIKELY(price == Price_INVALID)) {
    return "INVALID";
  }

  return std::to_string(price);
}
```

The `Qty` type is `typedef` for `uint32_t` and represents order quantities. We also provide the usual `Qty_INVALID` sentinel and the `qtyToString()` method to convert them to strings:

```
typedef uint32_t Qty;
constexpr auto Qty_INVALID =
  std::numeric_limits<Qty>::max();

inline auto qtyToString(Qty qty) -> std::string {
```

```
      if (UNLIKELY(qty == Qty_INVALID)) {
        return "INVALID";
      }

      return std::to_string(qty);
    }
```

The `Priority` type is just a position in the queue of type `uint64_t`. We assign the `Priority_INVALID` sentinel value and the `priorityToString()` method:

```
    typedef uint64_t Priority;
    constexpr auto Priority_INVALID =
      std::numeric_limits<Priority>::max();

    inline auto priorityToString(Priority priority) ->
      std::string {
      if (UNLIKELY(priority == Priority_INVALID)) {
        return "INVALID";
      }

      return std::to_string(priority);
    }
```

The `Side` type is an enumeration and contains two valid values, as shown in the following code block. We also define a `sideToString()` method, as we did for the other types previously:

```
    enum class Side : int8_t {
      INVALID = 0,
      BUY = 1,
      SELL = -1
    };

    inline auto sideToString(Side side) -> std::string {
      switch (side) {
        case Side::BUY:
          return "BUY";
        case Side::SELL:
          return "SELL";
        case Side::INVALID:
          return "INVALID";
      }

      return "UNKNOWN";
    }
```

Those are all the basic types we need for this chapter. Next, we will define some limits to simplify the design of our system.

Defining some limits and constraints

We will define the following constant limits:

- `LOG_QUEUE_SIZE` represents the size of the lock-free queue used by the logger. This holds the maximum number of characters that can be held in memory without the logger queue being full.
- `ME_MAX_TICKERS` represents the number of trading instruments the exchange supports.
- `ME_MAX_CLIENT_UPDATES` holds the maximum number of unprocessed order requests from all clients that the matching engine has not processed yet. This also represents the maximum number of order responses from the matching engine that the order server has not published yet.
- `ME_MAX_MARKET_UPDATES` represents the maximum number of market updates generated by the matching engine that have not yet been published by the market data publisher.
- `ME_MAX_NUM_CLIENTS` holds how many maximum simultaneous market participants can exist in our trading ecosystem.
- `ME_MAX_ORDER_IDS` is the maximum number of orders possible for a single trading instrument.
- `ME_MAX_PRICE_LEVELS` represents the maximum depth of price levels for the limit order book that the matching engine maintains.

Note that these values have been chosen arbitrarily here; these can be increased or decreased, depending on the capacity of the system on which we run the electronic trading ecosystem. We chose powers of two to enable the possibility of using shifts over multiplies when trying to compute addresses; however, the effect is negligible on modern processors, and we would not recommend worrying about this too much. The source for the constants we described previously is presented here:

```
namespace Common {
  constexpr size_t LOG_QUEUE_SIZE = 8 * 1024 * 1024;

  constexpr size_t ME_MAX_TICKERS = 8;

  constexpr size_t ME_MAX_CLIENT_UPDATES = 256 * 1024;
  constexpr size_t ME_MAX_MARKET_UPDATES = 256 * 1024;

  constexpr size_t ME_MAX_NUM_CLIENTS = 256;
  constexpr size_t ME_MAX_ORDER_IDS = 1024 * 1024;
  constexpr size_t ME_MAX_PRICE_LEVELS = 256;
}
```

These are all the constants we require for now. Now, we can shift our attention to more complex structures that we will need inside the matching engine.

Designing the matching engine

We will need a few structures for our matching engine to communicate with the market data publisher and order server components.

Defining the MEClientRequest and ClientRequestLFQueue types

The `MEClientRequest` structure is used by the order server to forward order requests from the clients to the matching engine. Remember that the communication from the order server to the matching engine is established through the lock-free queue component we built earlier. `ClientRequestLFQueue` is a typedef for a lock-free queue of `MEClientRequest` objects. The code for this structure can be found in the `Chapter6/order_server/client_request.h` file in the GitHub repository:

```
#pragma once

#include <sstream>

#include "common/types.h"
#include "common/lf_queue.h"

using namespace Common;

namespace Exchange {
```

Note two things here – we use the `#pragma pack()` directive to make sure these structures are packed and do not contain any extra padding. This is important because these will be sent and received over a network as flat binary structures in later chapters. We also define a `ClientRequestType` enumeration to define what type of order request it is – whether it is a new order or a cancel request for an existing order. We also define an `INVALID` sentinel value and a `clientRequestTypeToString()` method to convert this enumeration into human-readable strings:

```
#pragma pack(push, 1)
  enum class ClientRequestType : uint8_t {
    INVALID = 0,
    NEW = 1,
    CANCEL = 2
  };

  inline std::string
    clientRequestTypeToString(ClientRequestType type) {
    switch (type) {
```

```cpp
    case ClientRequestType::NEW:
      return "NEW";
    case ClientRequestType::CANCEL:
      return "CANCEL";
    case ClientRequestType::INVALID:
      return "INVALID";
  }
  return "UNKNOWN";
}
```

Now, we can define the `MEClientRequest` structure, which will contain information for a single order request from the trading participant to the exchange. Note that this is the internal representation that the matching engine uses, not necessarily the exact format that the client sends. We will look at that in the next chapter, *Communicating with Market Participants*. The important members of this struct are the following:

- A `type_` variable of type `ClientRequestType`
- The `client_id_` variable of type `ClientId` of the trading client that sent this request
- A `ticker_id_` variable of type `TickerId` of the instrument for which this request is meant
- `OrderId` (`order_id_`) of the order for which this request is made, which can be a new order or reference an existing order
- `Side` of the order in the `side_` variable
- `Price` of the order in the `price_` variable
- `Qty` of the order saved in the `qty_` variable

Additionally, we will also add a simple `toString()` method to help us later on with logging, as shown here:

```cpp
  struct MEClientRequest {
    ClientRequestType type_ = ClientRequestType::INVALID;

    ClientId client_id_ = ClientId_INVALID;
    TickerId ticker_id_ = TickerId_INVALID;
    OrderId order_id_ = OrderId_INVALID;
    Side side_ = Side::INVALID;
    Price price_ = Price_INVALID;
    Qty qty_ = Qty_INVALID;

    auto toString() const {
      std::stringstream ss;
      ss << "MEClientRequest"
```

```
            << " ["
            << "type:" << clientRequestTypeToString(type_)
            << " client:" << clientIdToString(client_id_)
            << " ticker:" << tickerIdToString(ticker_id_)
            << " oid:" << orderIdToString(order_id_)
            << " side:" << sideToString(side_)
            << " qty:" << qtyToString(qty_)
            << " price:" << priceToString(price_)
            << "]";
      return ss.str();
    }
  };
```

As discussed previously, we also define the `ClientRequestLFQueue` typedef to represent the lock-free queue of these structures, as shown in the following code snippet. The `#pragma pack(pop)` simply restores the alignment setting to the default – that is, not tightly packed (which we had set by specifying the `#pragma pack(push, 1)` directive). This is because we only want to tightly pack the structures that will be sent over a network and no others:

```
#pragma pack(pop)

  typedef LFQueue<MEClientRequest> ClientRequestLFQueue;
}
```

We will define a similar structure used by the matching engine that sends order responses to the order server component. Let us look at that in the next subsection.

Defining the MEClientResponse and ClientResponseLFQueue types

Let us present the implementation of the structure used by the matching engine that sends order responses for the order server component to dispatch to clients. Similar to the last section, we will also define `ClientResponseLFQueue`, which is a lock-free queue of the `MEClientResponse` objects. The code for this structure is available in the `Chapter6/order_server/client_response.h` source file in the GitHub repository:

```
#pragma once

#include <sstream>

#include "common/types.h"
#include "common/lf_queue.h"

using namespace Common;
```

```
namespace Exchange {
```

First, we will define a `ClientResponseType` enumeration to represent the type of response for client orders. In addition to the `INVALID` sentinel value, it contains values that represent when a request for a new order is accepted, an order is canceled, an order is executed, or a cancel request is rejected by the matching engine. We also add the `clientResponseTypeToString()` method to convert the `ClientResponseType` values to strings:

```
#pragma pack(push, 1)
  enum class ClientResponseType : uint8_t {
    INVALID = 0,
    ACCEPTED = 1,
    CANCELED = 2,
    FILLED = 3,
    CANCEL_REJECTED = 4
  };

  inline std::string
    clientResponseTypeToString(ClientResponseType type) {
    switch (type) {
      case ClientResponseType::ACCEPTED:
        return "ACCEPTED";
      case ClientResponseType::CANCELED:
        return "CANCELED";
      case ClientResponseType::FILLED:
        return "FILLED";
      case ClientResponseType::CANCEL_REJECTED:
        return "CANCEL_REJECTED";
      case ClientResponseType::INVALID:
        return "INVALID";
    }
    return "UNKNOWN";
  }
```

Finally, we define the `MEClientResponse` message used internally by the matching engine to communicate order response messages for the trading clients when there are updates to the client's orders. Before we look at the source code, the important data members in this struct are listed as follows:

- A `ClientResponseType type_` variable to represent the type of the client response.
- A `client_id_` variable of type `ClientId` to represent which market participant the response message is meant for.
- The `ticker_id_` variable of type `TickerId` to represent the trading instrument of this response.

- A `client_order_id_` variable that identifies `OrderId` of the order this response message affects. This `OrderId` is the one that the client sent in the original `MEClientRequest` message for the order.
- A `market_order_id_` variable, also of type `OrderId`, but this one identifies this order in the public market data stream. This `OrderId` is unique across all market participants, since it is possible for different market participants to send orders with the same `client_order_id_` value. Even in those cases, two orders with the same `client_order_id_` will have different `market_order_id_` values in their responses. This `market_order_id_` value is also used when generating market updates for this order.
- A `side_` variable of type `Side` to represent the side of this order response.
- `Price` of this client response update and whether it is accepted, canceled or executed.
- An `exec_qty_` variable of type `Qty`, which is only used in the event of an order execution. This variable is used to hold how much quantity was executed in this `MEClientResponse` message. This value is not cumulative, meaning that when an order gets partially executed multiple times, a `MEClientResponse` message is generated for each individual execution and only contains the quantity executed in that particular execution, not across all of them.
- A `leaves_qty_` variable, also of type `Qty`, which represents how much of the original order's quantity is still live in the matching engine's order book. This is used to communicate the size of this specific order in the book, which is still active for further possible executions.

Finally, we also have our usual `toString()` method for easy logging purposes. The definition of the `MEClientResponse` structure, as discussed previously, is presented next:

```cpp
struct MEClientResponse {
  ClientResponseType type_ = ClientResponseType::INVALID;
  ClientId client_id_ = ClientId_INVALID;
  TickerId ticker_id_ = TickerId_INVALID;
  OrderId client_order_id_ = OrderId_INVALID;
  OrderId market_order_id_ = OrderId_INVALID;
  Side side_ = Side::INVALID;
  Price price_ = Price_INVALID;
  Qty exec_qty_ = Qty_INVALID;
  Qty leaves_qty_ = Qty_INVALID;

  auto toString() const {
    std::stringstream ss;
    ss << "MEClientResponse"
       << " ["
       << "type:" << clientResponseTypeToString(type_)
       << " client:" << clientIdToString(client_id_)
       << " ticker:" << tickerIdToString(ticker_id_)
```

```
                << " coid:" << orderIdToString(client_order_id_)
                << " moid:" << orderIdToString(market_order_id_)
                << " side:" << sideToString(side_)
                << " exec_qty:" << qtyToString(exec_qty_)
                << " leaves_qty:" << qtyToString(leaves_qty_)
                << " price:" << priceToString(price_)
                << "]";
        return ss.str();
      }
    };

#pragma pack(pop)
```

The `ClientResponseLFQueue` type definition is presented as follows, which represents a lock-free queue of the structures we discussed previously:

```
    typedef LFQueue<MEClientResponse> ClientResponseLFQueue;
}
```

That concludes the discussion of the structures we need to represent client requests and responses to and from the matching engine. Let us move on to the market update structure in the next subsection.

Defining the MEMarketUpdate and MEMarketUpdateLFQueue types

The market update structure is used by the matching engine to provide market data updates to the market data publishing component. We also have a `MEMarketUpdateLFQueue` type to represent a lock-free queue of the `MEMarketUpdate` objects. The code for this can be found in the `Chapter6/exchange/market_data/market_update.h` source file:

```
#pragma once

#include <sstream>

#include "common/types.h"

using namespace Common;

namespace Exchange {
```

The `MEMarketUpdate` struct also needs to be a packed structure, since it will be part of the message that is sent and received over the network; hence, we use the `#pragma pack()` directive again. Before we define the struct, we need to define the `MarketUpdateType` enumeration that represents the update action in the market update for an order. In addition to taking on an `INVALID` sentinel value, it can also be used to represent events such as an order being added, modified, or canceled in the order book, as well as trade events in the market:

```
#pragma pack(push, 1)
  enum class MarketUpdateType : uint8_t {
    INVALID = 0,
    ADD = 1,
    MODIFY = 2,
    CANCEL = 3,
    TRADE = 4
  };

  inline std::string
    marketUpdateTypeToString(MarketUpdateType type) {
    switch (type) {
      case MarketUpdateType::ADD:
        return "ADD";
      case MarketUpdateType::MODIFY:
        return "MODIFY";
      case MarketUpdateType::CANCEL:
        return "CANCEL";
      case MarketUpdateType::TRADE:
        return "TRADE";
      case MarketUpdateType::INVALID:
        return "INVALID";
    }
    return "UNKNOWN";
  }
```

Finally, we define the `MEMarketUpdate` struct, which contains the following important data members:

- The `type_` variable of `MarketUpdateType` to represent the type of the market update.
- An `order_id_` variable of type `OrderId` to represent the specific order in the limit order book for which this order update is applicable.
- A `ticker_id_` variable of type `TickerId` to represent the trading instrument that this update applies to.
- A `Side` variable to represent the side of this order.
- A `Price` variable for the exact price of the order in this market order update.

- A `priority_` field of type `Priority`, which, as we discussed before, will be used to specify the exact position of this order in the FIFO queue. We build a FIFO queue of all orders at the same price. This field specifies the position/location of this order in that queue.

The complete `MEMarketUpdate` struct is shown in the following code block, along with the `MEMarketUpdateLFQueue` typedef, which captures a lock-free queue of `MEMarketUpdate` struct messages:

```
struct MEMarketUpdate {
  MarketUpdateType type_ = MarketUpdateType::INVALID;

  OrderId order_id_ = OrderId_INVALID;
  TickerId ticker_id_ = TickerId_INVALID;
  Side side_ = Side::INVALID;
  Price price_ = Price_INVALID;
  Qty qty_ = Qty_INVALID;
  Priority priority_ = Priority_INVALID;

  auto toString() const {
    std::stringstream ss;
    ss << "MEMarketUpdate"
       << " ["
       << " type:" << marketUpdateTypeToString(type_)
       << " ticker:" << tickerIdToString(ticker_id_)
       << " oid:" << orderIdToString(order_id_)
       << " side:" << sideToString(side_)
       << " qty:" << qtyToString(qty_)
       << " price:" << priceToString(price_)
       << " priority:" << priorityToString(priority_)
       << "]";
    return ss.str();
  }
};

#pragma pack(pop)

  typedef Common::LFQueue<Exchange::MEMarketUpdate>
    MEMarketUpdateLFQueue;
}
```

This concludes the structures we will need to represent and publish market data updates from the matching engine. In the next subsection, we will build some structures and define some types that we will use to build the limit order book.

Designing the exchange order book

In this section, we will define some building blocks that will be used to build, maintain, and update the limit order book in an efficient manner. Before we discuss each of the structures and objects we will need, we will present a diagram for you to build a visual understanding of the limit order book implementation.

The limit order book is organized as a collection of buy orders (referred to as bids) and sell orders (referred to as asks). Orders that are entered at the same price are organized in the **First In First Out** (**FIFO**) order in our matching engine. We discussed these details in the *Designing Our Trading Ecosystem* chapter, in the *Designing the C++ matching engine in a trading exchange* section.

For the order book we build inside the matching engine, we have a list of bid prices and ask prices that have active orders. Each price level is represented by the MEOrdersAtPrice struct, as shown in the following diagram. The bids are sorted from highest to lowest price level, and the asks are sorted from lowest to highest price level. Each MEOrdersAtPrice stores the individual orders from highest to lowest priority in a doubly linked list. Information for each individual order is contained in the MEOrder structs. We will track each price level in a hash map of type OrdersAtPriceHashMap, which is indexed by the price of that level. We will also track each MEOrder object by their market_order_id_ value in a hash map of type OrderHashMap. The diagram representing this design of our matching engine order book is presented as follows.

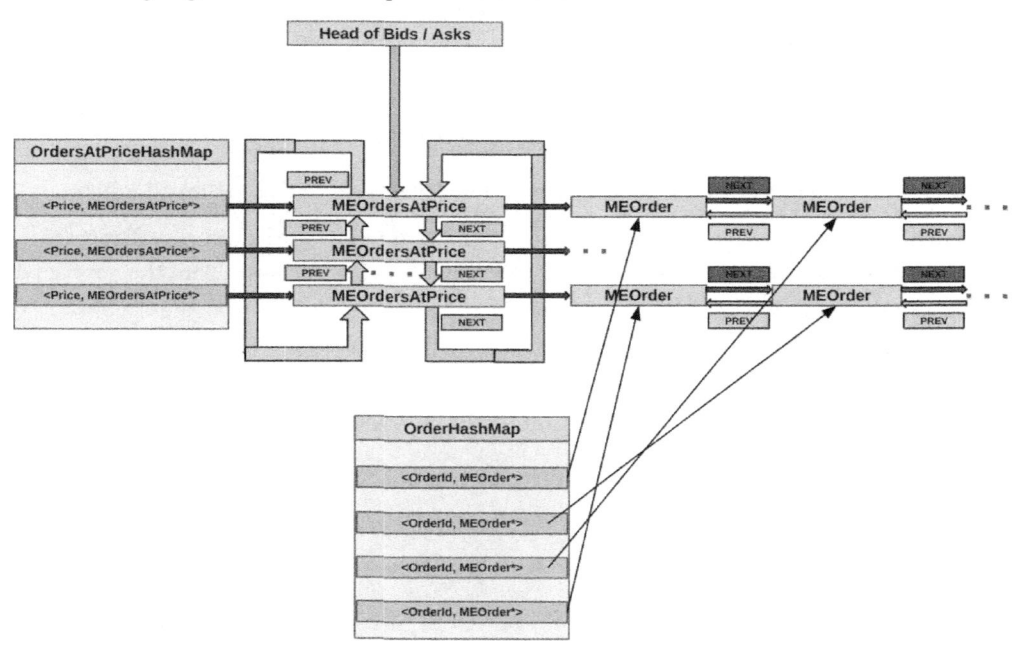

Figure 6.1 – The design of the limit order book inside the matching engine

Now that we have discussed the overall design of the limit order book data structure and the components that make it up, we can start defining the basic structs we need to implement that design. In the next subsection, we will first design the basic blocks – the `MEOrder` structure to hold information for a single order.

Defining the MEOrder, OrderHashMap, and ClientOrderHashMap types

The first structure is used to hold information inside the book for a single limit order, which we will call `MEOrder`. This is shown in the following code blocks, and the code can be found in the `Chapter6/matcher/me_order.h` and `Chapter6/matcher/me_order.cpp` source files in the GitHub repository.

The `MEOrder` struct has the following important data members in it to save the attributes required to represent a single order in the limit order book:

- A `ticker_id_` variable of type `TickerId` to represent the instrument that this order corresponds to.
- A `client_id_` variable of type `ClientId` that captures the market participant who owns this order.
- Two `OrderId` sets, as we discussed before – `client_order_id_`, which is what the client sent on its order request, and `market_order_id_`, which is generated by the matching engine and is unique across all clients.
- `Side side_` to represent whether the order is a buy or sell order.
- A `price_` variable of type `Price` to represent the price of the order.
- `Qty qty_` to represent the quantity of the order that is still active in the order book.
- A `priority_` variable of type `Priority`, which, as we discussed before, will represent the exact position of this order in the queue of other `MEOrder` instances with the same `side_` and `price_` values.
- The `MEOrder` structure also has two pointers to other `MEOrder` objects. This is because the `MEOrder` objects are also maintained as a doubly linked list of orders arranged at a price level in the `MEOrdersAtPrice` structure, as we discussed in the previous section:

```
#pragma once

#include <array>
#include <sstream>
#include "common/types.h"

using namespace Common;

namespace Exchange {
```

```cpp
struct MEOrder {
  TickerId ticker_id_ = TickerId_INVALID;
  ClientId client_id_ = ClientId_INVALID;
  OrderId client_order_id_ = OrderId_INVALID;
  OrderId market_order_id_ = OrderId_INVALID;
  Side side_ = Side::INVALID;
  Price price_ = Price_INVALID;
  Qty qty_ = Qty_INVALID;
  Priority priority_ = Priority_INVALID;

  MEOrder *prev_order_ = nullptr;
  MEOrder *next_order_ = nullptr;

  // only needed for use with MemPool.
  MEOrder() = default;

  MEOrder(TickerId ticker_id, ClientId client_id, OrderId
    client_order_id, OrderId market_order_id, Side side,
    Price price,Qty qty, Priority priority, MEOrder
    *prev_order, MEOrder *next_order) noexcept
      :       ticker_id_(ticker_id),
              client_id_(client_id),
              client_order_id_(client_order_id),
              market_order_id_(market_order_id),
              side_(side),
              price_(price),
              qty_(qty),
              priority_(priority),
              prev_order_(prev_order),
              next_order_(next_order) {}

  auto toString() const -> std::string;
};
```

Additionally, the `OrderHashMap` type is used to represent a hash map, implemented using `std::array`, where `OrderId` is the key and `MEOrder` is the value. We will also define another type, `ClientOrderHashMap`, which is a hash map, implemented using `std::array` to represent a mapping from `ClientId` to the `OrderHashMap` objects:

```cpp
  typedef std::array<MEOrder *, ME_MAX_ORDER_IDS>
    OrderHashMap;
  Typedef std::array<OrderHashMap, ME_MAX_NUM_CLIENTS>
    ClientOrderHashMap;
}
```

We present the `toString()` method for the `MEOrder` structure, which is very simple and available in the `Chapter6/exchange/matcher/me_order.cpp` file:

```cpp
#include "me_order.h"

namespace Exchange {
  auto MEOrder::toString() const -> std::string {
    std::stringstream ss;
    ss << "MEOrder" << "["
       << "ticker:" << tickerIdToString(ticker_id_) << " "
       << "cid:" << clientIdToString(client_id_) << " "
       << "oid:" << orderIdToString(client_order_id_) << " "
       << "moid:" << orderIdToString(market_order_id_) << " "
       << "side:" << sideToString(side_) << " "
       << "price:" << priceToString(price_) << " "
       << "qty:" << qtyToString(qty_) << " "
       << "prio:" << priorityToString(priority_) << " "
       << "prev:" << orderIdToString(prev_order_ ?
         prev_order_->market_order_id_ :
         OrderId_INVALID) << " "
       << "next:" << orderIdToString(next_order_ ?
         next_order_->market_order_id_ :
         OrderId_INVALID) << "]";

    return ss.str();
  }
}
```

Next, we will build some additional structures that contain and manage order objects.

Defining the MEOrdersAtPrice and OrdersAtPriceHashMap types

As discussed in *Figure 6.1*, we define another structure that maintains a list of `MEOrder` objects, and we call it `MEOrdersAtPrice`. This structure, presented in the following code block, will be used to hold all the orders entered at the same price, arranged in the FIFO priority order. This is achieved by creating a singly linked list of `MEOrder` objects, arranged in order of highest to lowest priority. For that, we create a `first_me_order_` variable of the `MEOrder` type pointer, which will represent the first order at this price level, and the other orders following it are chained together in the FIFO order.

The `MEOrdersAtPrice` structure also has two pointers to the `MEOrdersAtPrice` objects, one for the previous (`prev_entry_`) and one for the next (`next_entry_`). This is because the structure itself is a node in a doubly linked list of `MEOrdersAtPrice` objects. The doubly linked list of `MEOrdersAtPrice` is arranged from the most aggressive to the least aggressive prices on the buy and sell sides.

The two other variables this struct contains are a `side_` variable of type `Side` and a `price_` variable of type `Price`, respectively representing the side and price of this price level:

```
namespace Exchange {
  struct MEOrdersAtPrice {
    Side side_ = Side::INVALID;
    Price price_ = Price_INVALID;

    MEOrder *first_me_order_ = nullptr;

    MEOrdersAtPrice *prev_entry_ = nullptr;
    MEOrdersAtPrice *next_entry_ = nullptr;
```

We add a default constructor and a trivial custom container to initialize objects of this structure:

```
    MEOrdersAtPrice() = default;

    MEOrdersAtPrice(Side side, Price price, MEOrder
      *first_me_order, MEOrdersAtPrice *prev_entry,
      MEOrdersAtPrice *next_entry)
        : side_(side), price_(price),
        first_me_order_(first_me_order),
        prev_entry_(prev_entry), next_entry_(next_entry) {}
```

We also add a simple `toString()` method for logging purposes, as shown here:

```
    auto toString() const {
      std::stringstream ss;
      ss << "MEOrdersAtPrice["
         << "side:" << sideToString(side_) << " "
         << "price:" << priceToString(price_) << " "
         << "first_me_order:" << (first_me_order_ ?
            first_me_order_->toString() : "null") << " "
         << "prev:" << priceToString(prev_entry_ ?
            prev_entry_->price_ : Price_INVALID) << " "
         << "next:" << priceToString(next_entry_ ?
            next_entry_->price_ : Price_INVALID) << "]";

      return ss.str();
    }
  };
```

The `OrdersAtPriceHashMap` type represents a hash map, implemented through a `std::array` to represent a mapping from Price to `MEOrdersAtPrice`:

```
  typedef std::array<MEOrdersAtPrice *,
    ME_MAX_PRICE_LEVELS> OrdersAtPriceHashMap;
}
```

This concludes this section on setting up the initial types, definitions, and basic structures for the matching engine and limit order book. Next, we can look at how the matching engine framework is built.

Building the matching engine and exchanging external data

In this section, we will build various parts of the matching engine class. A lot of the heavy lifting of handling client requests, building and updating the limit order book, and generating order responses and market updates will be offloaded to the order book class, which we will discuss in the next section. Please reread the *Designing the C++ matching engine in a trading exchange* section in the previous chapter, *Designing Our Trading Ecosystem*, for a refresher on the components we will build in this section and the design principles behind them. We present the diagram from that chapter here for easy reference, showing the design of the matching engine.

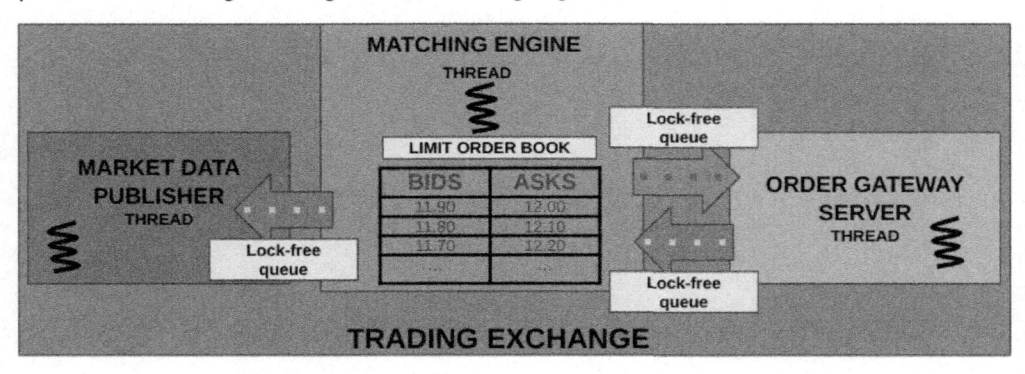

Figure 6.2 – The design of our matching engine component

The matching engine is an independent thread of execution that consumes order requests from `ClientRequestLFQueue`, publishes order responses to `ClientResponseLFQueue`, and publishes market updates to `MEMarketUpdateLFQueue`. Let us first declare and define some code for the construction, destruction, thread management, and boilerplate functionality for the matching engine.

Building the matching engine

The `MatchingEngine` class contains a couple of important data members – first, an `OrderBookHashMap` object to track the limit order book for each of the trading instruments. The class also contains pointers to the following objects – `ClientRequestLFQueue`, `ClientResponseLFQueue`, and `MEMarketUpdateLFQueue`, all of which will be passed to it in the constructor. Let us first declare and define some code for the construction, destruction, thread management, and boilerplate functionality for the matching engine. We will also have a Boolean, `run_`, to track the thread state, a `time_str_` string, and a `Logger` object to output some logs. The code for the next sub-sections is available in the `Chapter6/exchange/matcher/matching_engine.h` source file in the GitHub repository for this book.

First, the header files we need to include to build our matching engine are presented here:

```
#pragma once

#include "common/thread_utils.h"
#include "common/lf_queue.h"
#include "common/macros.h"

#include "order_server/client_request.h"
#include "order_server/client_response.h"
#include "market_data/market_update.h"

#include "me_order_book.h"
```

We declare the constructor and destructor methods next, and we add the `start()` and `stop()` methods to respectively start and stop the execution of the main matching engine loop, which we will build shortly:

```
namespace Exchange {
  class MatchingEngine final {
  public:
    MatchingEngine(ClientRequestLFQueue *client_requests,
                   ClientResponseLFQueue *client_responses,
                   MEMarketUpdateLFQueue *market_updates);

    ~MatchingEngine();

    auto start() -> void;

    auto stop() -> void;
```

We add our usual boilerplate code for the constructors and assignment operators to prevent accidental copies:

```cpp
// Deleted default, copy & move constructors and
// assignment-operators.
MatchingEngine() = delete;

MatchingEngine(const MatchingEngine &) = delete;

MatchingEngine(const MatchingEngine &&) = delete;

MatchingEngine &operator=(const MatchingEngine &) =
  delete;

MatchingEngine &operator=(const MatchingEngine &&) =
  delete;
```

Finally, we add the data members for this `MatchingEngine` class, as discussed before. The `ticker_order_book_` variable of type `OrderBookHashMap` is used to store `MEOrderBook` for each instrument. We store the `incoming_requests_`, `outgoing_ogw_responses_`, and `outgoing_md_updates_` pointers of the `ClientRequestLFQueue`, `ClientResponseLFQueue`, and `MEMarketUpdateLFQueue` types respectively to communicate with the other threads. Then, we have the `run_` Boolean variable, which we mark `volatile`, since it will be accessed from different threads:

```cpp
  private:
    OrderBookHashMap ticker_order_book_;

    ClientRequestLFQueue *incoming_requests_ = nullptr;
    ClientResponseLFQueue *outgoing_ogw_responses_ =
      nullptr;
    MEMarketUpdateLFQueue *outgoing_md_updates_ = nullptr;

    volatile bool run_ = false;

    std::string time_str_;
    Logger logger_;
  };
}
```

Let us look at the implementation of the constructor, the destructor, and the `start()` method that creates and launches a thread to execute the `run()` method (which we will look at shortly). This code is in the `Chapter6/exchange/matcher/matching_engine.cpp` source file.

The constructor itself is straightforward – it initializes the internal data members and creates an `MEOrderBook` instance for each one of the supported trading instruments:

```
#include "matching_engine.h"

namespace Exchange {
  MatchingEngine::MatchingEngine(ClientRequestLFQueue
    *client_requests, ClientResponseLFQueue
    *client_responses, MEMarketUpdateLFQueue
    *market_updates)
      : incoming_requests_(client_requests),
        outgoing_ogw_responses_(client_responses),
        outgoing_md_updates_(market_updates),
        logger_("exchange_matching_engine.log") {
    for(size_t i = 0; i < ticker_order_book_.size(); ++i) {
      ticker_order_book_[i] = new MEOrderBook(i, &logger_,
        this);
    }
  }
}
```

The destructor does the opposite of the constructor and resets the internal data member variables. It also deletes the `MEOrderBook` objects it created in the constructor:

```
MatchingEngine::~MatchingEngine() {
  run_ = false;

  using namespace std::literals::chrono_literals;
  std::this_thread::sleep_for(1s);

  incoming_requests_ = nullptr;
  outgoing_ogw_responses_ = nullptr;
  outgoing_md_updates_ = nullptr;

  for(auto& order_book : ticker_order_book_) {
    delete order_book;
    order_book = nullptr;
  }
}
```

The `start()` method creates and launches a new thread, assigning it the `MatchingEngine::run()` method. Before it does that, it enables `run_` flag, since it controls the execution of the `run()` method:

```
auto MatchingEngine::start() -> void {
  run_ = true;
```

```
    ASSERT(Common::createAndStartThread(-1,
      "Exchange/MatchingEngine", [this]() { run(); }) !=
      nullptr, "Failed to start MatchingEngine thread.");
}
```

The `stop()` method simply sets the `run_` flag to be `false`, and that in turn causes the `run()` method to exit out of its main loop, but this will become clear shortly:

```
  auto MatchingEngine::stop() -> void {
    run_ = false;
  }
}
```

Next, we will investigate the source code that handles how the matching engine consumes the order requests and publishes order responses and market updates. But first, let us present the main `run()` loop that the matching engine thread executes. This code is very simple – it simply consumes `MEClientRequest` objects from the `incoming_requests_` lock-free queue and forwards them to the `processClientRequest()` method. To achieve this, it simply checks the `LFQueue::getNextToRead()` method to see whether there is a valid entry to be read, and if so, forwards the object at that entry to be processed, and updates the read index in the lock-free queue using the `LFQueue::updateReadIndex()` method. This code is in the `Chapter6/exchange/matcher/matching_engine.h` source file:

```
  auto run() noexcept {
    logger_.log("%:% %() %\n", __FILE__, __LINE__,
      __FUNCTION__, Common::getCurrentTimeStr(&time_str_));
    while (run_) {
      const auto me_client_request =
        incoming_requests_->getNextToRead();
      if (LIKELY(me_client_request)) {
        logger_.log("%:% %() % Processing %\n", __FILE__,
          __LINE__, __FUNCTION__,
          Common::getCurrentTimeStr(&time_str_),
          me_client_request->toString());
        processClientRequest(me_client_request);
        incoming_requests_->updateReadIndex();
      }
    }
  }
```

Now, let us look at the source code to handle client requests.

Consuming from and publishing to the order gateway queue

First, we will start with the implementation of `processClientRequest()` in the `MatchingEngine` class in the `matching_engine.h` header file. This implementation simply checks for the type of the `MEClientRequest` and forwards it to the limit order book for the corresponding instrument. It finds the correct order book instance that this `MEClientRequest` is meant for by accessing the `ticker_order_book_` container, using the `ticker_id_` field in `MEClientRequest`:

```
auto processClientRequest(const MEClientRequest *client_request)
noexcept {
  auto order_book = ticker_order_book_[client_request
    ->ticker_id_];
```

For client requests that try to add a new order (`ClientRequestType::NEW`), we call the `MEOrderBook::add()` method and let it service that request:

```
  switch (client_request->type_) {
    case ClientRequestType::NEW: {
      order_book->add(client_request->client_id_,
        client_request->order_id_,
        client_request->ticker_id_,
        client_request->side_, client_request->price_,
        client_request->qty_);
    }
      break;
```

Similarly, client requests that try to cancel an existing order (`ClientRequestType::CANCEL`) are forwarded to the `MEOrderBook::cancel()` method:

```
    case ClientRequestType::CANCEL: {
      order_book->cancel(client_request->client_id_,
        client_request->order_id_,
        client_request->ticker_id_);
    }
      break;

    default: {
      FATAL("Received invalid client-request-type:" +
        clientRequestTypeToString(client_request->type_));
    }
      break;
  }
}
```

We will also define a method in the same class that the limit order book will use to publish order responses through `MEClientResponse` messages. This simply writes the response to the `outgoing_ogw_responses_` lock-free queue and advances the writer index. It does that by finding the next valid index to write the `MEClientResponse` message to by calling the `LFQueue::getNextToWriteTo()` method, moving the data into that slot, and updating the next write index by calling the `LFQueue::updateWriteIndex()` method:

```cpp
auto sendClientResponse(const MEClientResponse *client_response)
  noexcept {
  logger_.log("%:% %() % Sending %\n", __FILE__, __LINE__,
    __FUNCTION__, Common::getCurrentTimeStr(&time_str_),
    client_response->toString());
  auto next_write = outgoing_ogw_responses_
    ->getNextToWriteTo();
  *next_write = std::move(*client_response);
  outgoing_ogw_responses_->updateWriteIndex();
}
```

Now, we will look at some code that is similar to what we just saw, except it is used to publish market data updates.

Publishing to the market data publisher queue

The `sendMarketUpdate()` method in `Chapter6/exchange/matcher/matching_engine.h` is used by the limit order book to publish market data updates through the `MEMarketUpdate` structure. It simply writes to the `outgoing_md_updates_` lock-free queue and advances the writer. It does this exactly the same way we saw before – by calling the `getNextToWriteTo()` method, writing the `MEMarketUpdate` message to that slot, and updating the next write index using `updateWriteIndex()`:

```cpp
auto sendMarketUpdate(const MEMarketUpdate *market_update) noexcept {
  logger_.log("%:% %() % Sending %\n", __FILE__, __LINE__,
    __FUNCTION__, Common::getCurrentTimeStr(&time_str_),
    market_update->toString());
  auto next_write = outgoing_md_updates_
    ->getNextToWriteTo();
  *next_write = *market_update;
  outgoing_md_updates_->updateWriteIndex();
}
```

That concludes this section, and we now have the finished implementation of the matching engine. In the next subsection, we will tie all these pieces together into the trading exchange binary, all except the limit order book implementation, which is the last section we will discuss in this chapter.

Building the exchange application binary

We can now build the trading exchange binary. We will instantiate the three lock-free queues for order requests, order responses, and market updates that the matching engine object needs. We will also create the `MatchingEngine` object and launch the thread, and then the binary simply sleeps forever. Since the application goes into an infinite loop, we will also install a signal handler for this application to trap external signals and exit gracefully. Note that this code will be extended in later chapters in this book as we build the order server and market data publisher components on the trading exchange side that need to be added here. The code for this application is in `Chapter6/exchange/exchange_main.cpp` in the GitHub repository for this book. Let us break down the source file and understand each of the code blocks.

First, we add some variables that will be pointers for the `Logger` object and the `MatchingEngine` object. We will also add a `signal_handler()` method to be invoked when killing the exchange application. The signal handler simply deletes these objects and exits:

```
#include <csignal>

#include "matcher/matching_engine.h"

Common::Logger* logger = nullptr;
Exchange::MatchingEngine* matching_engine = nullptr;

void signal_handler(int) {
  using namespace std::literals::chrono_literals;
  std::this_thread::sleep_for(10s);

  delete logger; logger = nullptr;
  delete matching_engine; matching_engine = nullptr;

  std::this_thread::sleep_for(10s);

  exit(EXIT_SUCCESS);
}
```

The `main()` method is pretty simple for now till we add other components in the next chapter. It installs the `signal_handler()` method using the `std::signal()` routine to trap external SIGINT signals. The SIGINT signal is the signal value 2, which is sent to a running process when either *Ctrl* + *C* is pressed in Linux or `kill -2 PID` is sent to that **Process ID** (**PID**). This is the common way to terminate processes gracefully. It then initializes the `ClientRequestLFQueue` variable, `client_requests`, and the `ClientResponseLFQueue` variable, `client_responses`, to be of the ME_MAX_CLIENT_UPDATES size. We also initialize the lock-free queue variable, `market_updates`, of type `MEMarketUpdateLFQueue` to be of ME_MAX_MARKET_UPDATES capacity. The `main()` method also initializes the `logger` variable with an instance of the `Logger` class:

```cpp
int main(int, char **) {
  logger = new Common::Logger("exchange_main.log");

  std::signal(SIGINT, signal_handler);

  const int sleep_time = 100 * 1000;

  Exchange::ClientRequestLFQueue
    client_requests(ME_MAX_CLIENT_UPDATES);
  Exchange::ClientResponseLFQueue
    client_responses(ME_MAX_CLIENT_UPDATES);
  Exchange::MEMarketUpdateLFQueue
    market_updates(ME_MAX_MARKET_UPDATES);
```

Finally, the `main()` method initializes the `matching_engine` variable with an instance of the `MatchingEngine` class we created and passes it the three lock-free queues it needs from the preceding code block. It then calls the `start()` method so that the main matching engine thread can start executing. At this point, the `main()` method is done, so it enters into an infinite loop, where it sleeps most of the time and waits for an external signal that will kill this process:

```cpp
  std::string time_str;

  logger->log("%:% %() % Starting Matching Engine...\n",
    __FILE__, __LINE__, __FUNCTION__,
    Common::getCurrentTimeStr(&time_str));
  matching_engine = new
    Exchange::MatchingEngine(&client_requests,
    &client_responses, &market_updates);
  matching_engine->start();

  while (true) {
    logger->log("%:% %() % Sleeping for a few
    milliseconds..\n", __FILE__, __LINE__, __FUNCTION__,
    Common::getCurrentTimeStr(&time_str));
    usleep(sleep_time * 1000);
  }
}
```

To make it easy to build the main binary, we have provided a script, `Chapter6/build.sh`, which uses CMake and Ninja to build this binary. You will have to update this script to point to the correct binaries on your system, or use a different build system if you prefer. The next section will provide some information on how to run this `exchange_main` application.

Running the exchange application binary

Running the `exchange_main` application is achieved at this point simply by calling the `exchange_main` binary, as shown in the following code block. We also show the output you should be able to see on the terminal:

```
sghosh@sghosh-ThinkPad-X1-Carbon-3rd:~/Building-Low-Latency-
Applications-with-CPP/Chapter6$ ./cmake-build-release/exchange_main
Set core affinity for Common/Logger exchange_main.log 139685103920704
to -1
Set core affinity for Common/Logger exchange_matching_engine.log
139684933506624 to -1
Set core affinity for Exchange/MatchingEngine 139684925113920 to -1
```

This process can be stopped by sending it the `SIGINT` signal, as we mentioned before. At this point, it will generate three log files, similar to the ones shown in the following snippet. However, note at this point that there is nothing interesting in the log files, since we have only built the matching engine component out of all the components we need to build the full trading ecosystem. At the end of the next chapter, *Communicating with Market Participants*, we will run this application again with additional components and have slightly more interesting output:

```
exchange_main.log exchange_matching_engine.log
```

The next section will look at the internal workings of the order book and how it handles client order requests and generates order responses and market updates.

Building the order book and matching orders

This final section implements the order book functionality. Remember that the order book handles client order requests forwarded from the matching engine. It checks the order request type, updates the order book, generates order responses for the client, and generates market data updates for the public market data feed. All the code for the limit order book in the matching engine is in the `me_order_book.h` and `me_order_book.cpp` source files, saved in the `Chapter6/exchange/matcher/` directory in the GitHub repository for this book.

Building the internal data structures

First, we will declare the data members for the limit order book. We presented a diagram depicting the data structures that make up the limit order book previously, in Figure 6.1. The limit order book contains the following important data members:

- A `matching_engine_` pointer variable to the `MatchingEngine` parent for the order book to publish order responses and market data updates to.
- The `ClientOrderHashMap` variable, `cid_oid_to_order_`, to track the `OrderHashMap` objects by their `ClientId` key. As a reminder, `OrderHashMap` tracks the `MEOrder` objects by their `OrderId` keys.
- The `orders_at_price_pool_` memory pool variable of the `MEOrdersAtPrice` objects to create new objects from and return dead objects back to.
- The head of the doubly linked list of bids (`bids_by_price_`) and asks (`asks_by_price_`), since we track orders at the price level as a list of `MEOrdersAtPrice` objects.
- A hash map, `OrdersAtPriceHashMap`, to track the `MEOrdersAtPrice` objects for the price levels, using the price of the level as a key into the map.
- A memory pool of the `MEOrder` objects, called `order_pool_`, where `MEOrder` objects are created from and returned to without incurring dynamic memory allocations.
- Some minor members, such as `TickerId` for the instrument for this order book, `OrderId` to track the next market data order ID, an `MEClientResponse` variable (`client_response_`), an `MEMarketUpdate` object (`market_update_`), a string to log time, and the `Logger` object for logging purposes.

First, we include some dependent header files and also forward-declare the `MatchingEngine` class because we will reference that type without fully defining it yet:

```
#pragma once

#include "common/types.h"
#include "common/mem_pool.h"
#include "common/logging.h"
#include "order_server/client_response.h"
#include "market_data/market_update.h"

#include "me_order.h"

using namespace Common;

namespace Exchange {
```

```
      class MatchingEngine;

      class MEOrderBook final {
```

Now, we will define the data member variables, as discussed previously:

```
    private:
      TickerId ticker_id_ = TickerId_INVALID;

      MatchingEngine *matching_engine_ = nullptr;

      ClientOrderHashMap cid_oid_to_order_;

      MemPool<MEOrdersAtPrice> orders_at_price_pool_;
      MEOrdersAtPrice *bids_by_price_ = nullptr;
      MEOrdersAtPrice *asks_by_price_ = nullptr;

      OrdersAtPriceHashMap price_orders_at_price_;

      MemPool<MEOrder> order_pool_;

      MEClientResponse client_response_;
      MEMarketUpdate market_update_;

      OrderId next_market_order_id_ = 1;

      std::string time_str_;
      Logger *logger_ = nullptr;
```

At this point, we will also define the `OrderBookHashMap` type, which we referenced before and is `std::array` of the `MEOrderBook` objects indexed by `TickerId`:

```
      typedef std::array<MEOrderBook *, ME_MAX_TICKERS> OrderBookHashMap;
      };
    }
```

Next, let us present the straightforward implementation of the constructor and the destructor, as well as the boilerplate code for the default constructor and assignment operators:

```
#include "me_order_book.h"

#include "matcher/matching_engine.h"
MEOrderBook::MEOrderBook(TickerId ticker_id, Logger *logger,
```

```
                    MatchingEngine *matching_engine)
        : ticker_id_(ticker_id),
          matching_engine_(matching_engine),
          orders_at_price_pool_(ME_MAX_PRICE_LEVELS),
          order_pool_(ME_MAX_ORDER_IDS), logger_(logger) {
  }

  MEOrderBook::~MEOrderBook() {
    logger_->log("%:% %() % OrderBook\n%\n", __FILE__,
      __LINE__, __FUNCTION__,
      Common::getCurrentTimeStr(&time_str_),
              toString(false, true));

    matching_engine_ = nullptr;
    bids_by_price_ = asks_by_price_ = nullptr;
    for (auto &itr: cid_oid_to_order_) {
      itr.fill(nullptr);
    }
  }
```

Then, we add the boilerplate code to most of our classes to prevent accidental copies and assignments of the `MEOrderBook` objects:

```
// Deleted default, copy & move constructors and
// assignment-operators.
MEOrderBook() = delete;

MEOrderBook(const MEOrderBook &) = delete;

MEOrderBook(const MEOrderBook &&) = delete;

MEOrderBook &operator=(const MEOrderBook &) = delete;

MEOrderBook &operator=(const MEOrderBook &&) = delete;
```

Before we move on to the implementation of the different operations that will be performed on the order book, let us present a few simple methods to generate new market order IDs, convert `Price` to an index in `OrdersAtPriceHashMap`, and access the `OrdersAtPriceHashMap price_orders_at_price_` map when given `Price`:

```
namespace Exchange {
  class MatchingEngine;

  class MEOrderBook final {
  private:
```

The `generateNewMarketOrderId()` method is basic; it returns the `next_market_order_id_` value and increments it the next time this method is called:

```
auto generateNewMarketOrderId() noexcept -> OrderId {
  return next_market_order_id_++;
}
```

The `priceToIndex()` method converts a `Price` argument into an index that ranges between 0 and `ME_MAX_PRICE_LEVELS-1`, which is then used to index the price levels `std::array`:

```
auto priceToIndex(Price price) const noexcept {
  return (price % ME_MAX_PRICE_LEVELS);
}
```

Finally, the `getOrdersAtPrice()` utility method indexes `std::array` of `price_orders_at_price_` by converting `Price` it is provided into an index, using the `priceToIndex()` method, which returns the `MEOrdersAtPrice` object:

```
auto getOrdersAtPrice(Price price) const noexcept ->
  MEOrdersAtPrice * {
    return price_orders_at_price_.at(priceToIndex(price));
  }
  };
}
```

The next few subsections will detail the important operations of handling new order requests and cancellation requests for existing orders, and matching aggressive orders that cross existing passive orders on the other side of the order book. We will also generate and publish order responses and market data updates back to the matching engine.

Handling new passive orders

The first important task we need to perform in the order book is handling client order requests that want to enter new orders in the market. We will implement the `MEOrderBook::add()` method, which the matching engine calls first. It generates and sends `MEClientResponse`, accepting the new order, and sends it to the matching engine (to be sent to the client who sent the new order). It then also checks to see whether this new order crosses an existing passive order on the other side and whether it matches either fully or partially, by calling the `checkForMatch()` method. If the new order either does not match at all or is partially filled and leaves some quantity in the book, `MEOrder` is added to the order book. In this case, it also generates `MEMarketUpdate` for the public market data feed and sends it back to the matching engine (to be published by the market data publisher component).

We will discuss the `getNextPriority()`, `checkForMatch()`, and `addOrder()` methods shortly in this section, but let us first explore the `MEOrderBook::add()` method:

```cpp
auto MEOrderBook::add(ClientId client_id, OrderId client_order_id,
  TickerId ticker_id, Side side, Price price, Qty qty) noexcept -> void
{
```

The first thing it does is generate `new_market_order_id_` to be used for `MEClientResponse` and `MEMarketUpdate`. It updates the `client_response_` data member with the attributes from this request and calls the `MatchingEngine::sendClientResponse()` method to publish that response back to the matching engine:

```cpp
const auto new_market_order_id =
  generateNewMarketOrderId();
client_response_ = {ClientResponseType::ACCEPTED,
  client_id, ticker_id, client_order_id,
  new_market_order_id, side, price, 0, qty};
matching_engine_->sendClientResponse(&client_response_);
```

Next, the `MEOrderBook::add()` method calls the `MEOrderBook::checkForMatch()` method, which checks the current state of the order book against the new client request that just came in. It checks whether a partial or complete match can be made. The `checkForMatch()` method (which we will build shortly) returns the quantity of the order left over (if any) after the matching event. For orders that do not execute at all, `leaves_qty` returned is the same as the original quantity on the order. For orders that partially execute, it is whatever is left after matching. For orders that fully execute, this method will return a 0 value and that will be assigned to `leaves_qty`. We will see the complete implementation of `checkForMatch()` shortly, but for now, let us use it:

```cpp
const auto leaves_qty = checkForMatch(client_id,
  client_order_id, ticker_id, side, price, qty,
  new_market_order_id);
```

In the event that there is a quantity left over after the matching event, we need to generate a market data update corresponding to this new order that will join the book. To do that, the `MEOrderBook::add()` method finds out the correct priority value for this order by calling the `MEOrderBook::getNextPriority()` method. It allocates a new `MEOrder` object from the `order_pool_` memory pool and assigns it the attributes for this order. It then calls the `MEOrderBook::addOrder()` method to actually add it at the correct price level and priority in the `MEOrdersAtPrice` data structures. Finally, it fills in the `market_update_` object with the values for the market update and calls the `MatchingEngine::sendMarketUpdate()` method to publish it to the matching engine:

```cpp
if (LIKELY(leaves_qty)) {
  const auto priority = getNextPriority(ticker_id,
    price);
```

```
    auto order = order_pool_.allocate(ticker_id, client_id,
      client_order_id, new_market_order_id, side, price,
      leaves_qty, priority, nullptr, nullptr);
    addOrder(order);

    market_update_ = {MarketUpdateType::ADD,
      new_market_order_id, ticker_id, side, price,
      leaves_qty, priority};
    matching_engine_->sendMarketUpdate(&market_update_);
  }
}
```

The getNextPriority() method is quite straightforward. If a price level already exists at a certain price, then it just returns a priority value one higher than the last order at that price. If a price level does not already exist, then it returns 1 for the first order at that price level:

```
auto getNextPriority(Price price) noexcept {
  const auto orders_at_price = getOrdersAtPrice(price);
  if (!orders_at_price)
    return 1lu;

  return orders_at_price->first_me_order_->prev_order_
    ->priority_ + 1;
}
```

Next, we will lay out the details of adding a new order to the limit order book. The method appends the MEOrder object passed to it at the end of the MEOrdersAtPrice entry at the price for this order. If an MEOrdersAtPrice entry does not already exist (new price level), it first allocates a new entry, adds the new level into the book using the addOrdersAtPrice() method, and then appends the order. Additionally, it tracks the MEOrder object in the ClientOrderHashMap id_oid_to_order_ map, mapping from ClientId and OrderId to the MEOrder objects:

```
auto addOrder(MEOrder *order) noexcept {
```

First, we try to check and fetch MEOrdersAtPrice if one exists by calling the getOrdersAtPrice() method and saving it in the orders_at_price variable. Then, we check whether a valid MEOrdersAtPrice exists, meaning a price level with the price and side of this order already exists. If such a price level does not exist and this is the first order that forms that level, we create a new MEOrdersAtPrice from orders_at_price_pool_, initialize it, and call the addOrdersAtPrice() method on it:

```
  const auto orders_at_price = getOrdersAtPrice(order
    ->price_);
```

```cpp
if (!orders_at_price) {
  order->next_order_ = order->prev_order_ = order;

  auto new_orders_at_price =
    orders_at_price_pool_.allocate(order->side_,
    order->price_, order, nullptr, nullptr);
  addOrdersAtPrice(new_orders_at_price);
}
```

If a valid price level exists, we append the new order at the very end of the doubly linked list of `MEOrder` objects, reachable from the `first_me_order_` member of `MEOrdersAtPrice`. We then update the `prev_order_` and `next_order_` pointers on `MEOrder` being added as well as the last element on the list, after which the `MEOrder` object is appended:

```cpp
else {
  auto first_order = (orders_at_price ?
    orders_at_price->first_me_order_ : nullptr);

  first_order->prev_order_->next_order_ = order;
  order->prev_order_ = first_order->prev_order_;
  order->next_order_ = first_order;
  first_order->prev_order_ = order;
}
```

Finally, we add this `MEOrder` pointer to the `cid_oid_to_order_` container, which is `std::array` of `std::array` instances, indexed first by `client_id_` of the order and then by `client_order_id_` of the order:

```cpp
  cid_oid_to_order_.at(order->client_id_)
    .at(order->client_order_id_) = order;
}
```

Finally, to finish the discussion of adding new orders to the book, we need to implement the `addOrdersAtPrice()` method to add new price levels to the book. This method first adds the new `MEOrdersAtPrice` entry into `OrdersAtPriceHashMap price_orders_at_price_`. Then, it walks through the bid or ask price levels, from the most aggressive to the least aggressive price, to find the correct spot for the new price level. Note that this implementation iterates through the doubly linked list of `MEOrdersAtPrice` objects on the side. It is possible to have an alternative implementation that walks through the `price_orders_at_price_` hash map to find the right spot. Both implementations are viable and perform differently, depending on the number of price levels and the distance between consecutive prices. We will revisit this topic at the end of the book, in the *Optimizing the Performance of Our C++ System* chapter.

The first task for the `addOrdersAtPrice()` method is to insert the new `MEOrdersAtPrice` in the `price_orders_at_price_` hash map, mapping from `Price` to `MEOrdersAtPrice`:

```
auto addOrdersAtPrice(MEOrdersAtPrice *new_orders_at_price) noexcept {
  price_orders_at_price_.at(priceToIndex(
    new_orders_at_price->price_)) = new_orders_at_price;
```

Then, we need to insert it in its correct location for the bids/asks arranged by price. We do this by first assigning a `best_orders_by_price` variable to the beginning of the bids or asks, sorted by price:

```
const auto best_orders_by_price = (new_orders_at_price->
  side_ == Side::BUY ? bids_by_price_ : asks_by_price_);
```

We need to handle an edge case where there are no bids or no asks – that is, a side of the order book is empty. In such a case, we set the `bids_by_price_` or `asks_by_price_` members, which point to the head of the sorted list for that side:

```
if (UNLIKELY(!best_orders_by_price)) {
  (new_orders_at_price->side_ == Side::BUY ?
    bids_by_price_ : asks_by_price_) =
    new_orders_at_price;
  new_orders_at_price->prev_entry_ =
    new_orders_at_price->next_entry_ =
    new_orders_at_price;
}
```

Otherwise, we need to find the correct entry in the doubly linked list of price levels. We do this by walking through the bids or the asks till we find the correct price level, before or after which we insert the new price level. We track the price level before or after the new one in the following `target` variable, and we track whether we need to insert after or before the target variable using the `add_after` Boolean flag:

```
  else {
    auto target = best_orders_by_price;
    bool add_after = ((new_orders_at_price->side_ ==
      Side::SELL && new_orders_at_price->price_ >
      target->price_) || (new_orders_at_price->side_ ==
      Side::BUY && new_orders_at_price->price_ <
      target->price_));
    if (add_after) {
      target = target->next_entry_;
      add_after = ((new_orders_at_price->side_ ==
        Side::SELL && new_orders_at_price->price_ >
        target->price_) || (new_orders_at_price->side_ ==
        Side::BUY && new_orders_at_price->price_ <
```

```
          target->price_));
    }
    while (add_after && target != best_orders_by_price) {
      add_after = ((new_orders_at_price->side_ ==
      Side::SELL && new_orders_at_price->price_ >
      target->price_) || (new_orders_at_price->side_ ==
      Side::BUY && new_orders_at_price->price_ <
      target->price_));
      if (add_after)
        target = target->next_entry_;
    }
```

Once we find the correct location for the new `MEOrdersAtPrice` entry, we append the new price level by updating the `prev_entry_` or `next_entry_` variables in the `target MEOrdersAtPrice` structure, as well as the new `MEOrdersAtPrice` being appended, as shown here:

```
  if (add_after) { // add new_orders_at_price after
                   // target.
    if (target == best_orders_by_price) {
      target = best_orders_by_price->prev_entry_;
    }
    new_orders_at_price->prev_entry_ = target;
    target->next_entry_->prev_entry_ =
      new_orders_at_price;
    new_orders_at_price->next_entry_ =
      target->next_entry_;
    target->next_entry_ = new_orders_at_price;
  } else { // add new_orders_at_price before target.
    new_orders_at_price->prev_entry_ =
      target->prev_entry_;
    new_orders_at_price->next_entry_ = target;
    target->prev_entry_->next_entry_ =
      new_orders_at_price;
    target->prev_entry_ = new_orders_at_price;
```

Finally, if we add the new price level before an existing price level, we need to check whether prepending this price level changes the `bids_by_price_` or `asks_by_price_` variable. Remember that these variables track the start of the bids or asks, respectively – that is, the highest bid price and the lowest ask price. If we have a new best bid/ask price level, we update the `bids_by_price_` or `asks_by_price_` variable, respectively:

```
    if ((new_orders_at_price->side_ == Side::BUY &&
      new_orders_at_price->price_ > best_orders_by_price
      ->price_) || new_orders_at_price->side_ ==
```

```
          Side::SELL && new_orders_at_price->price_ <
          best_orders_by_price->price_)) {
          target->next_entry_ = (target->next_entry_ ==
          best_orders_by_price ? new_orders_at_price :
          target->next_entry_);
          (new_orders_at_price->side_ == Side::BUY ?
            bids_by_price_ : asks_by_price_) =
            new_orders_at_price;
        }
      }
    }
  }
```

Next, we will discuss the source code that handles order cancellation requests.

Handling order cancellation requests

The code to handle order cancellation requests is forwarded from the matching engine. First, it checks to see whether the cancel request is valid, meaning that `ClientId` is valid and `OrderId` on the cancellation request corresponds to an active order in the order book. If the order is not cancellable, it generates and publishes an `MEClientResponse` message to signify a rejected cancel request back to the matching engine. If the order can be canceled, it generates `MEClientResponse` to signify the successful cancel attempt and calls the `removeOrder()` method to remove the order from the limit order book. We will discuss the details of `removeOrder()` right after this next method.

We will track an `is_cancelable` Boolean variable that determines whether we were able to successfully find and cancel the client's order or not. If `client_id` is larger than the maximum possible client ID value, then we cannot cancel the order. If the client ID is valid, then we check the container from `cid_oid_to_order_` for the provided `client_id` and the `order_id` value. If a valid order does not exist, then we confirm that the order is not cancelable:

```
auto MEOrderBook::cancel(ClientId client_id, OrderId order_id,
TickerId ticker_id) noexcept -> void {
  auto is_cancelable = (client_id <
    cid_oid_to_order_.size());
  MEOrder *exchange_order = nullptr;
  if (LIKELY(is_cancelable)) {
    auto &co_itr = cid_oid_to_order_.at(client_id);
    exchange_order = co_itr.at(order_id);
    is_cancelable = (exchange_order != nullptr);
  }
```

If we determine that the order cannot be cancelled, we generate an `MEClientResponse` message of type `ClientResponseType::CANCEL_REJECTED` to notify the matching engine:

```cpp
if (UNLIKELY(!is_cancelable)) {
  client_response_ =
    {ClientResponseType::CANCEL_REJECTED, client_id,
    ticker_id, order_id, OrderId_INVALID,
    Side::INVALID, Price_INVALID, Qty_INVALID,
    Qty_INVALID};
}
```

If we can successfully cancel the order, we update the attributes in the `client_response_` member variable and the `market_update_` member variable. Then, we call the `removeOrder()` method to update our order book and delete this order from it. Finally, we send the market update to the matching engine, using the `sendMarketUpdate()` method, and we send the client response to the matching engine, using the `sendClientResponse()` method:

```cpp
else {
  client_response_ = {ClientResponseType::CANCELED,
    client_id, ticker_id, order_id,
    exchange_order->market_order_id_,
    exchange_order->side_, exchange_order->price_,
    Qty_INVALID, exchange_order->qty_};
  market_update_ = {MarketUpdateType::CANCEL,
    exchange_order->market_order_id_, ticker_id,
    exchange_order->side_, exchange_order->price_, 0,
    exchange_order->priority_};

  removeOrder(exchange_order);

  matching_engine_->sendMarketUpdate(&market_update_);
}

  matching_engine_->sendClientResponse(&client_response_);
}
```

Next, let us implement the `removeOrder()` method. It first finds `MEOrdersAtPrice` that the order being removed belongs to and then finds and removes `MEOrder` from the list of orders contained in `MEOrdersAtPrice`. If the order being removed is the only order at the price level, the method also calls `removeOrdersAtPrice()` to remove the entire price level, since after this deletion, that no longer exists. Finally, it removes the entry for that `MEOrder` from the `cid_oid_to_order_` hash map and returns the deallocated `MEOrder` object to the `order_pool_` memory pool:

```
auto removeOrder(MEOrder *order) noexcept {
  auto orders_at_price = getOrdersAtPrice(order->price_);

  if (order->prev_order_ == order) { // only one element.
    removeOrdersAtPrice(order->side_, order->price_);
  } else { // remove the link.
    const auto order_before = order->prev_order_;
    const auto order_after = order->next_order_;
    order_before->next_order_ = order_after;
    order_after->prev_order_ = order_before;

    if (orders_at_price->first_me_order_ == order) {
      orders_at_price->first_me_order_ = order_after;
    }

    order->prev_order_ = order->next_order_ = nullptr;
  }

  cid_oid_to_order_.at(order->client_id_).at(order
    ->client_order_id_) = nullptr;
  order_pool_.deallocate(order);
}
```

To conclude our discussion of tasks involved in handling order cancellation requests, we will implement the `removeOrdersAtPrice()` method. It finds and removes `MEOrdersAtPrice` from the doubly linked list of `MEOrdersAtPrice` for the bid or ask side. If this price entry being removed happens to be the only `MEOrdersAtPrice` entry on that side of the book, it sets the head of the doubly linked list to be `nullptr`, representing an empty side of the book. Finally, the method removes the entry from the `price_orders_at_price_` hash map for that price and returns the deallocated `MEOrdersAtPrice` to the `orders_at_price_pool_` memory pool:

```
auto removeOrdersAtPrice(Side side, Price price) noexcept {
  const auto best_orders_by_price = (side == Side::BUY ?
    bids_by_price_ : asks_by_price_);
  auto orders_at_price = getOrdersAtPrice(price);

  if (UNLIKELY(orders_at_price->next_entry_ ==
    orders_at_price)) { // empty side of book.
    (side == Side::BUY ? bids_by_price_ : asks_by_price_) =
      nullptr;
  } else {
    orders_at_price->prev_entry_->next_entry_ =
      orders_at_price->next_entry_;
    orders_at_price->next_entry_->prev_entry_ =
```

```
        orders_at_price->prev_entry_;

    if (orders_at_price == best_orders_by_price) {
      (side == Side::BUY ? bids_by_price_ : asks_by_price_)
        = orders_at_price->next_entry_;
    }

    Orders_at_price->prev_entry_ = orders_at_price
      ->next_entry_ = nullptr;
  }

  price_orders_at_price_.at(priceToIndex(price)) = nullptr;

  orders_at_price_pool_.deallocate(orders_at_price);
}
```

The last operation we need to tackle is an important one – matching aggressive orders against passive orders on the other side of the order book. We will look at the implementation of that operation next.

Matching aggressive orders and updating the order book

In this subsection, we will implement the matching functionality in the limit order book by presenting the `MEOrderBook::checkForMatch()` method we encountered earlier. The diagram presented in *Figure 6.3* shows what would happen in a hypothetical state of the limit order book. Here, the state of the ask side is shown, and the passive sell prices represented by `MEOrdersAtPrice` are **117**, **118**, **119**, and so on, in that order. At the best ask price, **117**, the first two `MEOrder` objects are shown, the first one with a priority of **11**, a market order ID of **1200**, and a quantity of **20**. `MEOrder` following that in the FIFO queue has a priority of **13**, a market order ID of **1400**, and a quantity of **10**. In this case, a new buy order with a quantity of **25** and a price of **117** (represented in blue) will match the first order with a market order ID of **1200** (represented in yellow) and execute it fully. It will then partially execute the remaining quantity of **5** against the order with a market order ID of **1400** (represented in magenta), and the matching event is finished. These steps are presented in the algorithm right after the following diagram.

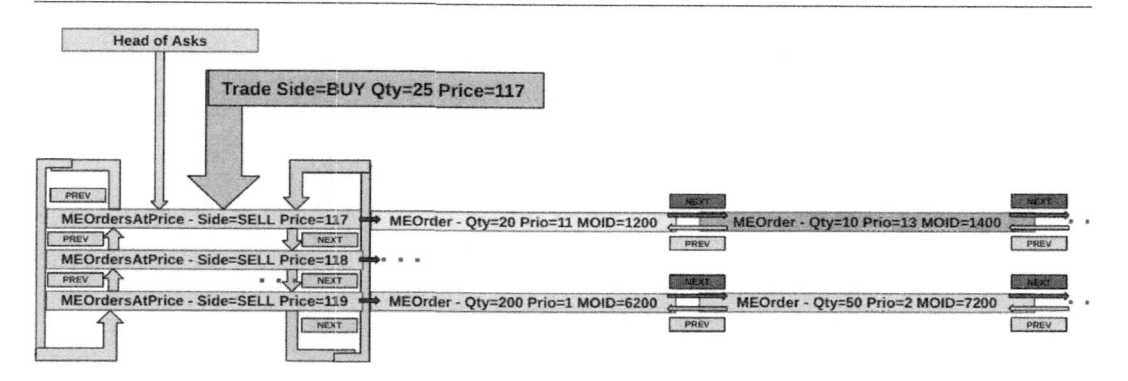

Figure 6.3 – An example of a matching event in the limit order book

This method iterates through the `MEOrdersAtPrice` objects on the side of the book opposite to the new (and possibly aggressive) order. It iterates through the price levels from the most aggressive to least aggressive price and, for each price level, matches the `MEOrder` objects contained at that price level from the first to last, in the FIFO order. It continues matching the new order against the passive orders on the other side, from the most aggressive to the least aggressive price and in the first to last order at a price level, by calling the `match()` method. It stops and returns when either the new aggressive order has no more unmatched quantity left to match, the remaining price levels on the other side no longer cross the new order's price, or the side of the book is empty. At that point, it returns the remaining unmatched quantity on the new order to the caller:

```
auto MEOrderBook::checkForMatch(ClientId client_id, OrderId client_
  order_id, TickerId ticker_id, Side side, Price price, Qty qty, Qty
  new_market_order_id) noexcept {
  auto leaves_qty = qty;
```

We keep iterating through all the ask price levels, arranged from the lowest to the highest prices, starting from the `asks_by_price_` level. For the `asks_by_price_` level, we start from the `first_me_order_` object of the `MEOrder` type pointer and iterate in the FIFO order, from the lowest to the highest priority. For each order that can match against the new aggressive order, we call the `MEOrder::match()` method to perform the actual match. We continue doing this till either there is no more `leaves_qty` left, the `asks_by_price_` variable is `nullptr` to signify an empty book side, or the remaining price levels cannot be used to match the new order:

```
    if (side == Side::BUY) {
      while (leaves_qty && asks_by_price_) {
        const auto ask_itr = asks_by_price_->first_me_order_;
        if (LIKELY(price < ask_itr->price_)) {
          break;
        }

        match(ticker_id, client_id, side, client_order_id,
```

```
          new_market_order_id, ask_itr, &leaves_qty);
    }
}
```

If the new order has a side of sell, we perform the same logic as described previously, except we iterate through the `bids_by_price_` price levels, which are arranged from the highest buy price to the lowest buy price, as shown here:

```
if (side == Side::SELL) {
  while (leaves_qty && bids_by_price_) {
    const auto bid_itr = bids_by_price_->first_me_order_;
    if (LIKELY(price > bid_itr->price_)) {
      break;
    }

    match(ticker_id, client_id, side, client_order_id,
      new_market_order_id, bid_itr, &leaves_qty);
  }
}

return leaves_qty;
}
```

The `match()` method is called when a new aggressive order matches an existing passive order on the other side of the book. It computes the executed quantity, which is the minimum of the quantity of the new order and the existing passive order it would match against. It subtracts this executed quantity from the remaining quantity of the aggressive order, as well as the passive order it matched against. It generates two execution order responses and sends them to the matching engine – one for the client who sent the aggressive order and another one for the client whose passive order got executed against the new order. It also creates and publishes a market update of type `MarketUpdateType::TRADE` to notify participants about the execution on the public market data feed. Finally, it checks whether this trade transaction fully executes the passive order or not, and if there is a full execution, it generates another market update of type `MarketUpdateType::CANCEL` to notify participants that the passive order has been removed. If the passive order is only partially matched, it instead generates a market update of type `MarketUpdateType::MODIFY` with the new remaining quantity of the passive limit order.

What this means is that participants who choose to ignore trade messages from the market data stream can still accurately build and maintain the limit order book. We could theoretically eliminate the extra cancel or modify market update, but that would require downstream market data consumers to apply trade messages to their order books and update them.

The `MEOrderBook::match()` method takes a few arguments to identify the client information, but the key arguments are the `MEOrder` pointer, `itr`, and the `Qty` pointer, `leaves_qty`. The `MEOrder` pointer represents the order in the book that the new order is being matched against, and `Qty` represents the remaining quantity on the new order. These arguments are passed by pointer because we will modify them directly in this method and expect the changes to be reflected in the calling method:

```cpp
auto MEOrderBook::match(TickerId ticker_id, ClientId client_id, Side
  side, OrderId client_order_id, OrderId new_market_order_id, MEOrder*
  itr, Qty* leaves_qty) noexcept {
```

We compute the `fill_qty` variable to be the minimum of the quantity on the passive order that exists in the book and the new order's quantity. We then use `fill_qty` to decrease both `leaves_qty` and the `qty_` member on the `MEOrder` object:

```cpp
const auto order = itr;
const auto order_qty = order->qty_;
const auto fill_qty = std::min(*leaves_qty, order_qty);

*leaves_qty -= fill_qty;
order->qty_  -= fill_qty;
```

We generate a client response message of type `ClientResponseType::FILLED`, meant for the client who sent the new order, and dispatch it to the matching engine using the `sendClientResponse()` method:

```cpp
client_response_ = {ClientResponseType::FILLED,
    client_id, ticker_id, client_order_id,
    new_market_order_id, side, itr->price_, fill_qty,
    *leaves_qty};
matching_engine_->sendClientResponse(&client_response_);
```

We also generate a second client response message of `type_ ClientResponseType::FILLED`; this one is meant for the client whose order was in the order book and got matched:

```cpp
client_response_ = {ClientResponseType::FILLED, order
    ->client_id_, ticker_id, order->client_order_id_,
    order->market_order_id_, order->side_, itr->price_,
    fill_qty, order->qty_};
matching_engine_->sendClientResponse(&client_response_);
```

We will also generate a market update of type `MarketUpdateType::TRADE` and publish it using `sendMarketUpdate()`, notifying the participants about the trade transaction that occurred and providing them with `fill_qty`:

```cpp
market_update_ = {MarketUpdateType::TRADE,
  OrderId_INVALID, ticker_id, side, itr->price_,
  fill_qty, Priority_INVALID};
matching_engine_->sendMarketUpdate(&market_update_);
```

Finally, we will generate a market update for the passive client order that existed in the book. If there is some quantity remaining on this MEOrder, then we generate a `MarketUpdateType::MODIFY` message and pass the remaining quantity left on that order. If the order is fully executed, then we generate a `MarketUpdateType::CANCEL` update, publish it, and also call the `MEOrderBook::removeOrder()` method to remove this MEOrder from the order book:

```cpp
if (!order->qty_) {
  market_update_ = {MarketUpdateType::CANCEL,
    order->market_order_id_, ticker_id, order->side_,
    order->price_, order_qty, Priority_INVALID};
  matching_engine_->sendMarketUpdate(&market_update_);

  removeOrder(order);
} else {
  market_update_ = {MarketUpdateType::MODIFY,
    order->market_order_id_, ticker_id, order->side_,
    order->price_, order->qty_, order->priority_};
  matching_engine_->sendMarketUpdate(&market_update_);
}
}
```

This concludes our discussion of the operations involved in handling client order requests, updating the limit order book inside the matching engine, and generating and publishing order responses and market updates.

Summary

We started the C++ implementation of our electronic trading ecosystem in this chapter. The first component we built was the exchange matching engine in charge of accepting and answering order requests from the order server component in the exchange infrastructure. This component is also responsible for generating and publishing market data updates to the market data publisher component in the exchange's infrastructure.

First, we declared some assumptions in our matching engine and limit order books. We also defined a couple of basic **Plain Old Data** (**POD**)-style structures to encapsulate information for a single order in the limit order book, a single order request sent from the order server, an order response sent back to the order server, and a single market data update. We showed how to use the lock-free queue to facilitate communication between the matching engine and order server and market data publisher for order requests, order responses, and market data updates. To build the limit order book, we also defined some hash maps to track orders by `OrderId` and chain together orders at the same price inside the `MEOrdersAtPrice` structure. Reiterating what we already covered, these price levels themselves are maintained in a doubly linked list and a hash map indexed by price.

Then, we built the matching engine component, which is an independent thread of execution that consumes updates from the order server and publishes responses and market data updates back to the order server and the market data publisher. We also built the main application binary for the electronic trading exchange, which we will enhance in the next chapter.

Finally, we laid out the details of the mechanism involved in building and updating the data structures for the limit order book. We discussed the tasks involved in handling new order requests and order cancelation requests. We also implemented the functionality of the matching engine to perform the actual matching between new aggressive orders against existing passive orders that cross in price. Match events generate private execution messages for the market participants involved in a match event. Additionally, the event also generates trade messages and order deletion or modification on the public market data feed.

In the next chapter, we will build the market data publisher component, which is the component that consumes the market data updates generated from the matching engine and puts them on the wire for participants to consume. Additionally, we will also build the order server component that resides in the electronic trading exchange and manages the communication with the different market participant order gateways, forwarding requests and responses to and from the matching engine.

7
Communicating with Market Participants

In this chapter, we will build the order gateway component at the electronic trading exchange that is responsible for accepting client connections, handling requests, and publishing responses to clients about their orders when there are updates. Fairness, low latency, and low jitter (latency variance) are important requirements here to facilitate high-frequency trading participants. We will also build the component that publishes market data from the trading exchange. These market data updates are designed to allow clients to construct the order book of all client orders that the electronic trading exchange holds. These market updates need to be sent out as soon as possible when there are order updates and when matches occur, so the focus will be on super-low-latency performance. Additionally, the exchange needs to periodically provide snapshots of the order book for participants that drop packets or start after the market is already open.

In this chapter, we will cover the following topics:

- Defining the market data protocol and order data protocol
- Building the order gateway server
- Building the market data publisher
- Building the main exchange application

Technical requirements

All the code for this book can be found in the GitHub repository for this book at https://github.com/PacktPublishing/Building-Low-Latency-Applications-with-CPP. The source code for this chapter can be found in the Chapter7 directory in the repository.

It is important that you have read and understood the design of the electronic trading ecosystem presented in the *Designing Our Trading Ecosystem* chapter. The components we build in this chapter will interact with the matching engine we built in the *Building the C++ Matching Engine* chapter, so we assume you are familiar with that. As before, we will use the building blocks we built in the *Building the C++ Building Blocks for Low-Latency Applications* chapter.

Defining the market data protocol and order data protocol

Before we build the components inside the trading exchange that publish market data updates and receive and respond to client requests, we need to finalize the protocol. The protocol needs to be publicly available so that market participants who want to connect to the exchange, process updates, and send order requests can build their software. The protocol is the *language* that the exchange and market participants will use to communicate. We will have two protocols – one for the format of the market data updates and one for the format to send order requests and receive order responses in.

Designing the market data protocol

For the market data protocol, we will define an internal format that the matching engine uses, and a public format meant for the market participants. We saw the internal matching format, that is, the `MEMarketUpdate` struct, in the *Building the Matching Engine* chapter, in the *Defining the operations and interactions in our matching engine* section. In this section, we will define the public market data format, which will be encapsulated in the `MDPMarketUpdate` struct. Remember that we mentioned that market data formats can be of several types and different complexity, for example, the FAST protocol or the SBE protocol. For our market data format, we will use the **Simple Binary Encoding** (**SBE**) format, which is simply a binary data format. The code we discuss in this subsection can be found in the `Chapter7/exchange/market_data/market_update.h` source file.

Before we look at the market data protocol, a reminder that we first explained what a snapshot of market data is, why it is needed, and how it is synthesized using incremental market data updates in the *Designing Our Trading Ecosystem* chapter in the *Understanding how an exchange publishes information to participants* section, in the *Designing the market data publisher* subsection. Additionally, we discussed additional details about the snapshot data stream in the same chapter, in the *Building a market participant's interface to the exchange* section. So, it would be worthwhile to revisit those sections if a refresher of those concepts is required. But just to re-introduce snapshot messages, these are messages that contain full information about the state of the limit order book at any given time and can be used by market participants if they need to re-construct the full limit order book.

Before we look at the `MDPMarketUpdate` struct, let us first revisit the `MarketUpdateType` enumeration we created in the previous chapter. In this chapter, we will add a few new enumeration types here – `CLEAR`, `SNAPSHOT_START`, and `SNAPSHOT_END` – which will be needed later. The `CLEAR` message is used to notify clients that they should clear/empty the order book on their end, `SNAPSHOT_START` signifies that a snapshot message is starting, and `SNAPSHOT_END` signifies that all updates in the snapshot update have been delivered.

The updated enumeration list is shown as follows:

```
#pragma once

#include <sstream>
#include "common/types.h"

using namespace Common;

namespace Exchange {
  enum class MarketUpdateType : uint8_t {
    INVALID = 0,
    CLEAR = 1,
    ADD = 2,
    MODIFY = 3,
    CANCEL = 4,
    TRADE = 5,
    SNAPSHOT_START = 6,
    SNAPSHOT_END = 7
  };
}
```

Our `MDPMarketUpdate` structure contains an important addition over the `MEMarketUpdate` structure, which is a sequence number field. This `size_t seq_num_` field is an increasing sequence number value for every market update published by the exchange. For every new market update, the sequence number is exactly 1 greater than the previous market update. This sequence number field will be used by the market data consumers in the market participants' trading systems to detect gaps in market updates. Remember that for our market data publisher, we will publish the market data in UDP format, which is an unreliable protocol. So, when there are drops in packets at the network level, or if a participant's system drops a packet, they can use the sequence number field to detect that. We present the internal `MEMarketUpdate` format again, and the new public `MDPMarketUpdate` format as follows:

```
#pragma pack(push, 1)

  struct MEMarketUpdate {
    MarketUpdateType type_ = MarketUpdateType::INVALID;

    OrderId order_id_ = OrderId_INVALID;
    TickerId ticker_id_ = TickerId_INVALID;
    Side side_ = Side::INVALID;
    Price price_ = Price_INVALID;
    Qty qty_ = Qty_INVALID;
    Priority priority_ = Priority_INVALID;
```

```cpp
    auto toString() const {
      std::stringstream ss;
      ss << "MEMarketUpdate"
          << " ["
          << " type:" << marketUpdateTypeToString(type_)
          << " ticker:" << tickerIdToString(ticker_id_)
          << " oid:" << orderIdToString(order_id_)
          << " side:" << sideToString(side_)
          << " qty:" << qtyToString(qty_)
          << " price:" << priceToString(price_)
          << " priority:" << priorityToString(priority_)
          << "]";
      return ss.str();
    }
  };

  struct MDPMarketUpdate {
    size_t seq_num_ = 0;
    MEMarketUpdate me_market_update_;

    auto toString() const {
      std::stringstream ss;
      ss << "MDPMarketUpdate"
          << " ["
          << " seq:" << seq_num_
          << " " << me_market_update_.toString()
          << "]";
      return ss.str();
    }
  };

#pragma pack(pop)
```

Hence, `MDPMarketUpdate` is simply `MEMarketUpdate` with a leading `seq_num_` field. Before we finish this subsection, we will define two simple typedefs that we will need later in this chapter. We saw the first one, `MEMarketUpdateLFQueue`, in the previous chapter; the new `MDPMarketUpdateLFQueue` is similar and represents a lock-free queue of `MDPMarketUpdate` structures:

```cpp
  typedef Common::LFQueue<Exchange::MEMarketUpdate>
    MEMarketUpdateLFQueue;
  typedef Common::LFQueue<Exchange::MDPMarketUpdate>
    MDPMarketUpdateLFQueue;
```

Designing the order data protocol

In this subsection, we will design the public order data protocol the clients will use to send order requests to the exchange and receive order responses from it, specifically the order gateway server.

First, we will see the format of messages sent from the market participant's order gateway to the exchange's order gateway server. We already discussed the `ClientRequestType` enumeration, the `MEClientRequest` struct, and the `ClientRequestLFQueue` typedef used by the matching engine in the *Building the C++ Matching Engine* chapter, in the *Defining the operations and interactions in our matching engine* section. `MEClientRequest` is the internal format used by the matching engine, but `OMClientRequest` is the format that the market participants need to use when sending order requests to the exchange order gateway server. Like the market data format, `OMClientRequest` has a sequence number field, `seq_num_`, and then the `MEClientRequest` struct after that. The sequence number field here serves a similar purpose as before, to make sure that the exchange and client's order gateway components are in sync with each other. The code for this structure is in the `Chapter7/exchange/order_server/client_request.h` file:

```
#pragma once

#include <sstream>
#include "common/types.h"
#include "common/lf_queue.h"

using namespace Common;

namespace Exchange {
#pragma pack(push, 1)

  struct OMClientRequest {
    size_t seq_num_ = 0;
    MEClientRequest me_client_request_;

    auto toString() const {
      std::stringstream ss;
      ss << "OMClientRequest"
         << " ["
         << "seq:" << seq_num_
         << " " << me_client_request_.toString()
         << "]";
      return ss.str();
    }
  }
```

```
    };

#pragma pack(pop)
}
```

We have a symmetrical design of the responses sent from the exchange's order gateway server to the client's order gateway component. We saw the `MEClientResponse` structure in the previous chapter, which is used internally between the matching engine and the order gateway server component inside the trading exchange infrastructure. The `OMClientResponse` structure is the public format that the market participants will use to receive and process order responses in. Like the other structures we saw before, there is a sequence number field for synchronization purposes and the remaining payload for this structure is the `MEClientResponse` structure. This structure can be found in the `Chapter7/exchange/order_server/client_response.h` file:

```cpp
#pragma once

#include <sstream>
#include "common/types.h"
#include "common/lf_queue.h"

using namespace Common;

namespace Exchange {
#pragma pack(push, 1)

  struct OMClientResponse {
    size_t seq_num_ = 0;
    MEClientResponse me_client_response_;

    auto toString() const {
      std::stringstream ss;
      ss << "OMClientResponse"
         << " ["
         << "seq:" << seq_num_
         << " " << me_client_response_.toString()
         << "]";
      return ss.str();
    }
  };

#pragma pack(pop)
}
```

This concludes the design of the new structures we will need in this chapter. Next, we will start discussing the implementation of the order gateway server, starting with how it handles incoming client requests from market participants.

Building the order gateway server

In this section, we will start building the order gateway server infrastructure, which is responsible for setting up a TCP server for clients to connect to. The order gateway server also needs to process incoming client requests from different clients in the order in which they arrive and forward those to the matching engine. Finally, it also needs to receive the order responses from the matching engine and forward them to the correct TCP connection for the corresponding market participant. We will revisit the design of the order gateway server and how it interacts with the matching engine and the market participants, as follows.

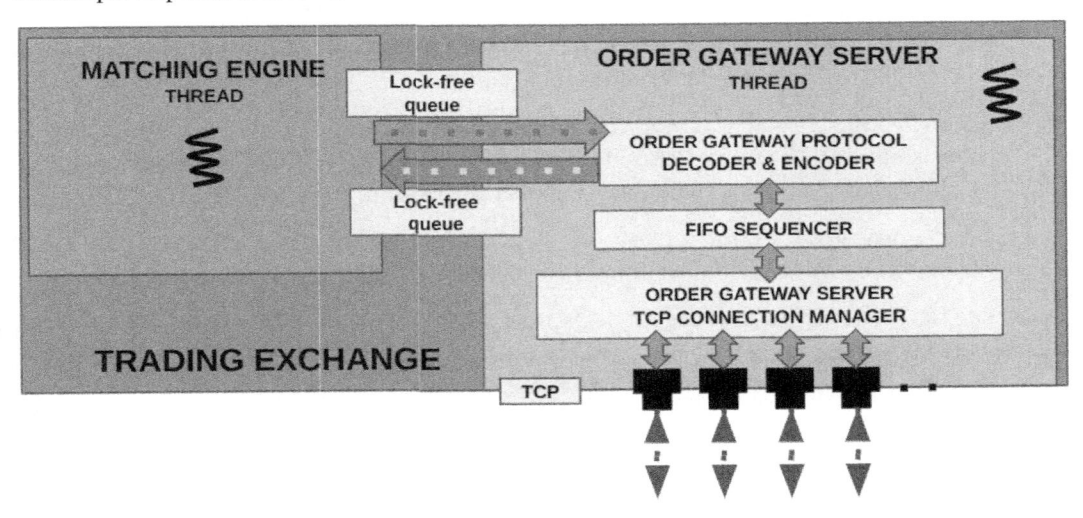

Figure 7.1 – Order gateway server and its subcomponents

To refresh your memory, the order gateway server receives new TCP connections or client requests on established TCP connections. Then, those requests go through a FIFO sequencer stage to make sure that requests are processed in the exact order in which they arrived at the exchange's infrastructure. There is a transformation between the internal matching engine format and the public order data format we described in the previous section. In the previous chapter on *Building the Matching Engine*, we already built the communication path to and from the matching engine, which is through lock-free queues. All the details behind the design of this component as well as what purpose it serves in our electronic trading ecosystem were discussed in the *Designing Our Trading Ecosystem* chapter, specifically in the *Understanding the layout of the electronic trading ecosystem* and *Understanding how an exchange publishes information to participants* sections. So, we would strongly recommend revisiting that chapter as you build the order gateway server at the exchange.

First, we will build the `OrderServer` class, which represents the order gateway server component in the preceding diagram. The code for `OrderServer` resides in the `Chapter7/exchange/order_server/order_server.h` and `Chapter7/exchange/order_server/order_server.cpp` files.

Defining the data members in the order gateway server

The `OrderServer` class has a few important data members:

- A `tcp_server_` variable, which is an instance of the `Common::TCPServer` class, which will be used to host a TCP server to poll for, accept incoming connections from market participants, and poll the established TCP connections to see whether there is data to be read from any of the connections.

- A `fifo_sequencer_` variable, which is an instance of the `FIFOSequencer` class and is responsible for making sure that client requests that come in on different TCP connections are processed in the correct order in which they came.

- A lock-free queue variable, `outgoing_responses_`, of the `ClientResponseLFQueue` type, using which it receives `MEClientResponse` messages from the matching engine, which need to be sent out to the correct market participant.

- A `std::array cid_tcp_socket_` of `TCPSocket` objects of size `ME_MAX_NUM_CLIENTS`, which will be used as a hash map from client-id to the `TCPSocket` connection for that client.

- Two `std::arrays` also of size `ME_MAX_NUM_CLIENTS` to track the exchange-to-client and client-to-exchange sequence numbers on the `OMClientResponse` and `OMClientRequest` messages. These are the `cid_next_outgoing_seq_num_` and `cid_next_exp_seq_num_` variables.

- A Boolean `run_` variable, which will be used to start and stop the `OrderServer` thread. Note that it is marked `volatile` since it will be accessed from different threads, and we want to prevent compiler optimizations here for correct functionality in a multi-threaded environment:

```
#pragma once

#include <functional>

#include "common/thread_utils.h"
#include "common/macros.h"
#include "common/tcp_server.h"

#include "order_server/client_request.h"
#include "order_server/client_response.h"
#include "order_server/fifo_sequencer.h"
```

```cpp
namespace Exchange {
  class OrderServer {
  private:
    const std::string iface_;
    const int port_ = 0;

    ClientResponseLFQueue *outgoing_responses_ = nullptr;

    volatile bool run_ = false;

    std::string time_str_;
    Logger logger_;

    std::array<size_t, ME_MAX_NUM_CLIENTS> cid_next_outgoing_seq_num_;
    std::array<size_t, ME_MAX_NUM_CLIENTS> cid_next_exp_seq_num_;
    std::array<Common::TCPSocket *, ME_MAX_NUM_CLIENTS> cid_tcp_socket_;

    Common::TCPServer tcp_server_;

    FIFOSequencer fifo_sequencer_;
  };
}
```

One more minor declaration before we move on to the next subsection is that the `OrderServer` class has the following method declarations, which we will define in the subsequent subsections. These are methods corresponding to the constructor, the destructor, a `start()` method, and a `stop()` method, but for now, do not worry about the details of these; we will be defining them very soon:

```cpp
OrderServer(ClientRequestLFQueue *client_requests,
ClientResponseLFQueue *client_responses, const std::string &iface,
int port);
~OrderServer();
auto start() -> void;
auto stop() -> void;
```

In the next subsection, we will initialize and de-initialize the `OrderServer` class and its member variables.

Initializing the order gateway server

The constructor for this class is straightforward. We initialize the three arrays with some basic values: sequence numbers set to 1 and `TCPSockets` set to `nullptr`. We will also set the two callback members, `recv_callback_` and `recv_finished_callback_`, to point to the `recvCallback()` and `recvFinishedCallback()` member functions. We will discuss these callback handling methods in the next few subsections. The constructor for `OrderServer` accepts pointers to two lock-free queue objects: one to forward `MEClientRequest`s to the matching engine and one to receive `MEClientResponse`s from the matching engine. It also accepts a network interface and port to use that the order gateway server will listen to and accept client connections on:

```cpp
#include "order_server.h"

namespace Exchange {
  OrderServer::OrderServer(ClientRequestLFQueue *client_requests,
    ClientResponseLFQueue *client_responses, const std::string &iface,
    int port)
      : iface_(iface), port_(port), outgoing_responses_(client_
    responses), logger_("exchange_order_server.log"),
        tcp_server_(logger_), fifo_sequencer_(client_requests,
    &logger_) {
    cid_next_outgoing_seq_num_.fill(1);
    cid_next_exp_seq_num_.fill(1);
    cid_tcp_socket_.fill(nullptr);

    tcp_server_.recv_callback_ = [this](auto socket, auto rx_time) {
    recvCallback(socket, rx_time); };
    tcp_server_.recv_finished_callback_ = [this]() {
    recvFinishedCallback(); };
  }
}
```

We will also define a `start()` method, which will set the bool `run_` to be true. This is the flag that controls how long the main thread will run. We also initialize the `TCPServer` member object to start listening on the interface and port that `OrderServer` was provided in the constructor. Finally, it creates and launches a thread that will execute the `run()` method, which we will also see in the next few subsections. For now, we will not set affinity on any threads we create in this application, but we will discuss optimization possibilities at the end of this book:

```cpp
auto OrderServer::start() -> void {
    run_ = true;
    tcp_server_.listen(iface_, port_);

    ASSERT(Common::createAndStartThread(-1, "Exchange/OrderServer",
    [this]() { run(); }) != nullptr, "Failed to start OrderServer
    thread.");
}
```

We define a complementary `stop()` method, which simply sets the `run_` flag to false, which will cause the `run()` method to finish execution (more on this shortly):

```
auto OrderServer::stop() -> void {
  run_ = false;
}
```

The destructor for the `OrderServer` class is also quite simple. It calls the `stop()` method to instruct the main thread to stop execution and then waits a brief period of time for the thread to finish any pending tasks:

```
OrderServer::~OrderServer() {
  stop();

  using namespace std::literals::chrono_literals;
  std::this_thread::sleep_for(1s);
}
```

This concludes the subsection on the initialization of this class. Next, we will investigate the functionality needed for `OrderServer` to handle incoming client requests over TCP connections.

Handling incoming client requests

In this subsection, we will discuss the code we need to handle incoming client requests. These client requests are received over TCP connections, and these are dispatched to the `recvCallback()` and `recvFinishedCallback()` methods through the `TCPServer` like we set up in the constructor. We will break down the implementation of this method into different blocks so we can understand it better here.

The first code block in this method checks whether the size of the available data is at least as large as a complete `OMClientRequest` struct. Then it breaks up the available data into blocks of size equal to the size of an `OMClientRequest` object, and iterates through the available data. It reinterprets `rcv_buffer_` in `TCPSocket` as an `OMClientRequest` struct and saves it in the request variable, which is of the `OMClientRequest` pointer type:

```
auto recvCallback(TCPSocket *socket, Nanos rx_time) noexcept {
  logger_.log("%:% %() % Received socket:% len:% rx:%\n", __FILE__,
    __LINE__, __FUNCTION__, Common::getCurrentTimeStr(&time_str_),
         socket->fd_, socket->next_rcv_valid_index_, rx_
time);

  if (socket->next_rcv_valid_index_ >= sizeof(OMClientRequest)) {
    size_t i = 0;
    for (; i + sizeof(OMClientRequest) <= socket->next_rcv_valid_
```

```
  index_; i += sizeof(OMClientRequest)) {
auto request = reinterpret_cast<const OMClientRequest
*>(socket->rcv_buffer_ + i);
  logger_.log("%:% %() % Received %\n", __FILE__, __LINE__,
  __FUNCTION__, Common::getCurrentTimeStr(&time_str_),
request->toString());
```

Once it has the `OMClientRequest` it needs to process, it checks whether this is the first request from this client. If that is the case, then it tracks the `TCPSocket` instance for this client by adding it to the `cid_tcp_socket_` `std::array`, which we are using as a hash map:

```
  if (UNLIKELY(cid_tcp_socket_[request->me_client_request_.
  client_id_] == nullptr)) {
    cid_tcp_socket_[request->me_client_request_.client_id_] =
    socket;
  }
```

If a `TCPSocket` entry for this client-id already existed in the `cid_tcp_socket_` container, then we would make sure that the previously tracked `TCPSocket` for this client-id matches the `TCPSocket` for the current request. If they do not match, we log an error and skip processing this request:

```
  if (cid_tcp_socket_[request->me_client_request_.client_id_]
  != socket) {
    logger_.log("%:% %() % Received ClientRequest from
    ClientId:% on different socket:% expected:%\n", __FILE__,
    __LINE__, __FUNCTION__,
              Common::getCurrentTimeStr(&time_str_),
              request->me_client_request_.client_id_,
              socket->fd_,
              cid_tcp_socket_[request->me_client_request_.
              client_id_]->fd_);
    continue;
  }
```

Next, we will perform a sequence number check to make sure that the sequence number on this `OMClientRequest` is exactly what we expect it to be based on the last message we have seen. If there is a mismatch between the expected and received sequence numbers, then we log an error and ignore this request:

```
  auto &next_exp_seq_num = cid_next_exp_seq_num_[request->me_
  client_request_.client_id_];
  if (request->seq_num_ != next_exp_seq_num) {
    logger_.log("%:% %() % Incorrect sequence number.
    ClientId:% SeqNum expected:% received:%\n", __FILE__,
    __LINE__, __FUNCTION__,
```

```
                         Common::getCurrentTimeStr(&time_str_),
                         request->me_client_request_.client_id_, next_
                         exp_seq_num, request->seq_num_);
      continue;
    }
```

One note here is that in a realistic setup, the exchange will send a reject back to the client if it receives a request on an incorrect socket or if there is a sequence number mismatch, to notify them of the error. We have omitted that here for simplicity's sake, but it is not difficult to add if needed. If we have made it this far in the execution of this loop, then we increment the next expected sequence number on the next `OMClientRequest` for this client and forward this request to the FIFO sequencer data member. One important thing to note here is that we also forward `rx_time`, which is the software receive time of this TCP packet, to the FIFO sequencer since it will need that information to sequence the requests correctly. We will discuss the details of how the FIFO sequencer achieves this in the next subsection:

```
      ++next_exp_seq_num;

      fifo_sequencer_.addClientRequest(rx_time, request->me_
      client_request_);
    }
    memcpy(socket->rcv_buffer_, socket->rcv_buffer_ + i, socket-
    >next_rcv_valid_index_ - i);
    socket->next_rcv_valid_index_ -= i;
  }
}
```

Remember that the `recvFinishedCallback()` method is called when all the `recvCallback()` methods have been dispatched from the current call to `TCPServer::sendAndRecv()`. The `recvFinishedCallback()` method instructs `FIFOSequencer` to correctly order the `MEClientRequests` that it has queued up and push them to the matching engine. This mechanism will become clear when we discuss the design and implementation of the `FIFOSequencer` in the next subsection:

```
    auto recvFinishedCallback() noexcept {
      fifo_sequencer_.sequenceAndPublish();
    }
```

Next, we will discuss the FIFO sequencer component, which is responsible for maintaining fairness from the perspective of processing client requests. It does this by making sure that requests received across different TCP connections are processed in the exact order in which they were received in the order gateway server.

Processing requests fairly using the FIFO sequencer

The FIFO sequencer subcomponent in the order gateway server is responsible for making sure that client requests are processed in the order of their arrival time. This is necessary because the order gateway server reads and dispatches client requests from different TCP connections, which arrive at different times. Let us get started by first defining the data members inside this class. The code for the FIFO sequencer is in the Chapter7/exchange/order_server/fifo_sequencer.h source file.

Defining the data members in the FIFO sequencer

First, we define a constant, ME_MAX_PENDING_REQUESTS, which represents the maximum number of simultaneously pending requests available at the network socket across all TCP connections. If the order gateway server is busy with other tasks and has not polled the TCP connections for a very short period of time, it is possible client requests arrived during that time and are queued at the network socket level.

The FIFO sequencer uses this constant to create a std::array of that size of RecvTimeClientRequest structures. This member variable is named pending_client_requests_ in this FIFOSequencer class. To count the number of actual pending request entries in this pending_client_requests_ array, we will maintain a pending_size_ variable of the size_t type.

The RecvTimeClientRequest struct has two members – recv_time_, of the Nanos type, and a request_ variable of the MEClientRequest type. This structure captures the client request as well as the time of its arrival at the order gateway server. We will sort these by time and then process them in order of arrival. To make sorting easy, we will define a < operator, which returns true if the client request on the **left-hand side** (**LHS**) was received before the client request on the **right-hand side** (**RHS**) of that operator.

Finally, the last important member of this class is the incoming_requests_ variable, which is of the ClientRequestLFQueue type, which is the lock-free queue that the FIFO sequencer uses to send MEClientRequests to the matching engine:

```
#pragma once

#include "common/thread_utils.h"
#include "common/macros.h"

#include "order_server/client_request.h"

namespace Exchange {
  constexpr size_t ME_MAX_PENDING_REQUESTS = 1024;
  class FIFOSequencer {
  private:
    ClientRequestLFQueue *incoming_requests_ = nullptr;
```

```
    std::string time_str_;
    Logger *logger_ = nullptr;

    struct RecvTimeClientRequest {
      Nanos recv_time_ = 0;
      MEClientRequest request_;

      auto operator<(const RecvTimeClientRequest &rhs) const {
        return (recv_time_ < rhs.recv_time_);
      }
    };

    std::array<RecvTimeClientRequest, ME_MAX_PENDING_REQUESTS>
    pending_client_requests_;
    size_t pending_size_ = 0;
  };
}
```

Now, let us look at the source code to initialize the FIFO sequencer.

Initializing the FIFO sequencer

The constructor for the `FIFOSequencer` class is straightforward and self-explanatory. It is presented as follows and initializes `incoming_requests_ ClientRequestLFQueue` and `logger_`, which are both passed to it in the constructor for this class:

```
class FIFOSequencer {
public:
  FIFOSequencer(ClientRequestLFQueue *client_requests, Logger
  *logger)
      : incoming_requests_(client_requests), logger_(logger) {
  }
```

Now, we will look at the most important functionality inside the FIFO sequencer – queueing up client requests and publishing them in order of their receive time.

Publishing client requests in order

We used the `FIFOSequencer::addClientRequest()` method in a previous subsection, *Handling incoming client requests*. Here, we present the implementation, which is quite simple and involves simply adding it to the end of `pending_client_requests_` and incrementing the `pending_size_` variable to signify that there is an additional entry that was added. Note here that we only ever expect a maximum of `ME_MAX_PENDING_REQUESTS` at a time since we set it to a high value. If this limit is not enough, we have the option of increasing the array size and possibly switching to using a `MemPool` of `RecvTimeClientRequest` objects:

```
auto addClientRequest(Nanos rx_time, const MEClientRequest
&request) {
  if (pending_size_ >= pending_client_requests_.size()) {
    FATAL("Too many pending requests");
  }
  pending_client_requests_.at(pending_size_++) =
    std::move(RecvTimeClientRequest{rx_time, request});
}
```

We also used the `FIFOSequencer::sequenceAndPublish()` method in a previous subsection, *Handling incoming client requests*. This is the most important method in the `FIFOSequencer` class and performs the following tasks:

- First, it sorts all the `RecvTimeClientRequest` entries in the `pending_client_requests_` container in ascending order of their arrival times. It achieves this by using the `std::sort()` algorithm, which in turn uses the `<` operator we built for `RecvTimeClientRequest` objects to sort the container. One word here: sorting can become time consuming if the number of elements is very large, but we rarely expect that to be the case here, since the number of simultaneously pending requests is expected to be quite low. This would be another optimization area, but we need to measure the load and performance of our system in practice before deciding how to improve this.

- After the sorting step, it writes each of the `MEClientRequest` entries to the `incoming_requests_` LFQueue, which goes to the matching engine.

- Finally, it resets the `pending_size_` variable to mark the end of processing and returns from the method:

```
auto sequenceAndPublish() {
  if (UNLIKELY(!pending_size_))
    return;

  logger_->log("%:% %() % Processing % requests.\n", __
  FILE__, __LINE__, __FUNCTION__, Common::getCurrentTimeStr
  (&time_str_), pending_size_);

  std::sort(pending_client_requests_.begin(), pending_
  client_requests_.begin() + pending_size_);

  for (size_t i = 0; i < pending_size_; ++i) {
    const auto &client_request = pending_client_requests_.
    at(i);
```

```
        logger_->log("%:% %() % Writing RX:% Req:%
        to FIFO.\n", __FILE__, __LINE__, __FUNCTION__,
        Common::getCurrentTimeStr(&time_str_),
                client_request.recv_time_, client_request.
                request_.toString());

        auto next_write = incoming_requests_->getNextToWriteTo();
        *next_write = std::move(client_request.request_);
        incoming_requests_->updateWriteIndex();
    }

    pending_size_ = 0;
}
```

This concludes the design and implementation of the `FIFOSequencer` subcomponent inside our order gateway server. Now, we can go back to our design of the `OrderServer` class by adding functionality to send client responses back out to the clients over TCP.

Sending client responses

In this subsection, we will look at how `OrderServer` performs two important tasks in the `run()` method. Remember that this `run()` method is the main loop for this class, which is run on the thread we created and launched in the *Initializing the order gateway server* subsection, specifically in the `start()` method. The `run()` method performs the following two main tasks:

- It calls the `poll()` method on the `TCPServer` object it holds. Remember that the `poll()` method checks for and accepts new connections, removes dead connections, and checks whether there is data available on any of the established TCP connections, that is, client requests.

- It also calls the `sendAndRecv()` method on the `TCPServer` object it holds. The `sendAndRecv()` method reads the data from each of the TCP connections and dispatches the callbacks for them. The `sendAndRecv()` call also sends out any outgoing data on the TCP connections, that is, client responses. This code block is shown as follows and should be quite easy to understand:

```
        auto run() noexcept {
          logger_.log("%:% %() %\n", __FILE__, __LINE__, __
        FUNCTION__, Common::getCurrentTimeStr(&time_str_));
          while (run_) {
            tcp_server_.poll();
            tcp_server_.sendAndRecv();
```

- The `run()` loop also drains the `outgoing_responses_` lock-free queue, which the matching engine uses to send out `MEClientResponse` messages that need to be dispatched to the correct clients.
- It iterates through the available data in the `outgoing_responses_` queue and then for each `MEClientResponse` it reads, it first finds out what the correct outgoing sequence number is. This is the sequence number on the `OMClientResponse` message to be sent to that client ID. It does this by looking up that answer in the `cid_next_outgoing_seq_num_` array, which we are really using as a hash map from the client ID to the sequence number:

```
for (auto client_response = outgoing_responses_-
>getNextToRead(); outgoing_responses_->size() &&
client_response; client_response = outgoing_responses_-
>getNextToRead()) {
  auto &next_outgoing_seq_num = cid_next_outgoing_seq_
  num_[client_response->client_id_];
  logger_.log("%:% %() % Processing cid:% seq:% %\n", __
  FILE__, __LINE__, __FUNCTION__,
  Common::getCurrentTimeStr(&time_str_),
  client_response->client_id_, next_
  outgoing_seq_num, client_response-
  >toString());
```

- It also checks that it has a valid `TCPSocket` for the client ID that this response is meant for. It looks up that information in the `cid_tcp_socket_` array, which is a hash map from the client ID to `TCPSocket` objects.
- It then sends an `OMClientResponse` message on `TCPSocket` for this client ID by calling the `TCPSocket::send()` method. It achieves this by first sending the `next_outgoing_seq_num_` value and then the `MEClientResponse` message that the matching engine generated. It might not be immediately clear, but this is actually sending an `OMClientResponse` message because the `OMClientResponse` message is actually just a sequence number field followed by a `MEClientResponse` message, which is what we just did.
- Finally, it updates the read index and the sequence number of the next outgoing message and continues with the loop:

```
ASSERT(cid_tcp_socket_[client_response->client_id_] !=
nullptr,
     "Dont have a TCPSocket for ClientId:" +
     std::to_string(client_response->client_id_));
cid_tcp_socket_[client_response->client_id_]-
>send(&next_outgoing_seq_num, sizeof(next_outgoing_
seq_num));
cid_tcp_socket_[client_response->client_id_]-
>send(client_response, sizeof(MEClientResponse));
```

```
            outgoing_responses_->updateReadIndex();

            ++next_outgoing_seq_num;
        }
    }
}
```

This concludes the full design and implementation of the order gateway server component in our electronic trading infrastructure. Next, we will look at the component that publishes the public market data to the participants.

Building the market data publisher

The last component in the electronic trading exchange we need to build is the market data publisher, which is how the exchange publishes public market data updates to any market participants that need it. Revisiting the design of the market data publisher, we present a diagram of how this component communicates with the matching engine and publishes to the market data participants over UDP, as follows.

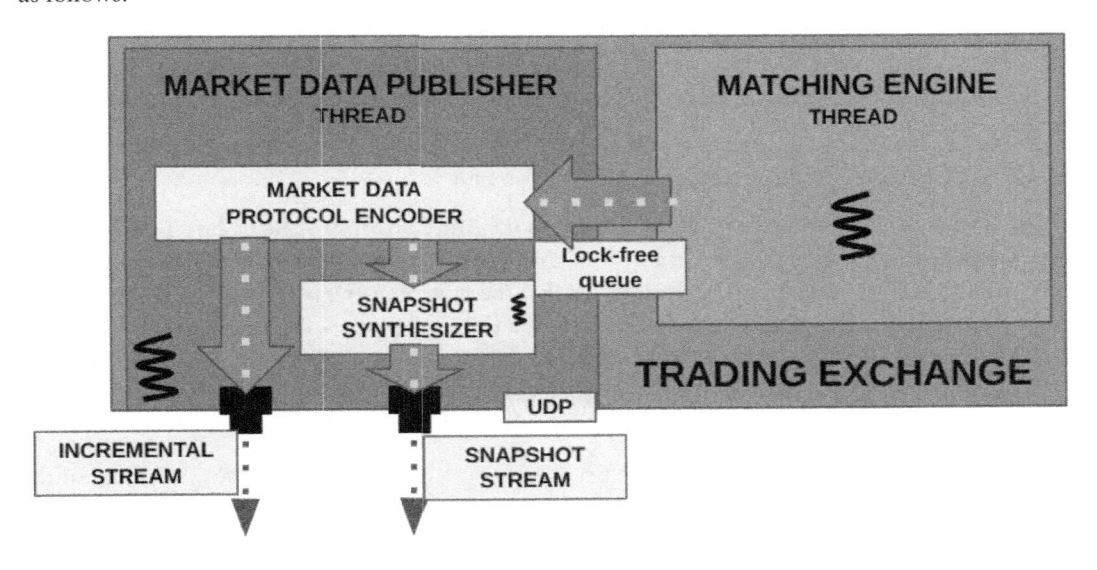

Figure 7.2 – Market data publisher and its subcomponents

We would like to remind you that the purpose and design of the market data publisher were discussed in detail in the *Designing Our Trading Ecosystem* chapter, specifically in the *Understanding the layout of the electronic trading ecosystem* and *Understanding how an exchange publishes information to participants* sections. We would strongly encourage you to revisit those sections to follow along as we build our market data publisher component.

Let us get started by first understanding how updates are consumed from the matching engine and published by jumping into the `MarketDataPublisher` class. All the source code for the `MarketDataPublisher` class is in the `Chapter7/exchange/market_data/market_data_publisher.h` and `Chapter7/exchange/market_data/market_data_publisher.cpp` source files.

Defining the data members in the market data publisher

The `MarketDataPublisher` class has the following important members:

- A `next_inc_seq_num_` variable of the `size_t` type, which represents the sequence number to set on the next outgoing incremental market data message. We discussed the concepts of incremental and snapshot market data updates in the *Designing Our Trading Ecosystem* chapter, in the *Understanding how an exchange publishes information to participants* and *Building a market participant's interface to the exchange* sections.

- An `outgoing_md_updates_` variable of the `MEMarketUpdateLFQueue` type, which is a lock-free queue of `MEMarketUpdate` messages. We discussed the `MEMarketUpdate` structure in the *Building the C++ Matching Engine* chapter, in the *Defining the operations and interactions in our matching engine* section. This `LFQueue` is how the matching engine sends the `MEMarketUpdate` messages that the market data publisher then publishes over UDP.

- An `incremental_socket_` member, which is an `McastSocket` to be used to publish UDP messages on the incremental multicast stream.

- A `snapshot_synthesizer_` variable of the `SnapshotSynthesizer` type, which we will discuss in the next subsection. This object will be responsible for generating a snapshot of the limit order book from the updates that the matching engine provides and periodically publishing a snapshot of the full order book on the snapshot multicast stream. This was discussed in the *Designing Our Trading Ecosystem* chapter, in the *Understanding how an exchange publishes information to participants* section, specifically in the *Designing the market data publisher* subsection.

- A lock-free queue instance called `snapshot_md_updates_`, which will be of the `MDPMarketUpdateLFQueue` type, which is a lock-free queue containing `MDPMarketUpdate` messages. This queue is used by the market data publisher thread to publish `MDPMarketUpdate` messages that it sends on the incremental stream to the `SnapshotSynthesizer` component. This `LFQueue` is necessary since `SnapshotSynthesizer` runs on a different thread than `MarketDataPublisher`, which is primarily so that the snapshot synthesis and publishing process do not slow down the latency-sensitive `MarketDataPublisher` component.

- The last important member of the `MarketDataPublisher` class is the `run_` Boolean variable, which is just used to control when the `MarketDataPublisher` thread is started and stopped. Since it is accessed from different threads, like the `run_` variable in the `OrderServer` class, it is also marked as `volatile`:

```
#pragma once

#include <functional>

#include "market_data/snapshot_synthesizer.h"

namespace Exchange {
  class MarketDataPublisher {
  private:
    size_t next_inc_seq_num_ = 1;
    MEMarketUpdateLFQueue *outgoing_md_updates_ = nullptr;

    MDPMarketUpdateLFQueue snapshot_md_updates_;

    volatile bool run_ = false;

    std::string time_str_;
    Logger logger_;

    Common::McastSocket incremental_socket_;

    SnapshotSynthesizer *snapshot_synthesizer_ = nullptr;
  };
}
```

In the next section, we will see how these data members are initialized.

Initializing the market data publisher

In this subsection, we will look at how to initialize `MarketDataPublisher`, and how to start and stop the `MarketDataPublisher` component. First, we will look at the constructor, which is presented as follows. The `market_updates` argument passed to it is the `MEMarketUpdateLFQueue` object, which the matching engine will publish market updates on. The constructor also receives the network interface and two sets of IPs and ports – one for the incremental market data stream and one for the snapshot market data stream. In the constructor, it initializes the `outgoing_md_updates_` member with the argument passed in the constructor and the `snapshot_md_updates_` LFQueue to be of the size `ME_MAX_MARKET_UPDATES`, which we first defined back in the *Designing the C++ matching engine* chapter, in the *Defining the operations and interactions in our matching engine section*, and is available in the `common/types.h` source file. It also initializes the `logger_` object with a log file for this class and initializes the `incremental_socket_` variable with the incremental IP and port provided in the constructor. Finally, it creates a `SnapshotSynthesizer` object and passes the `snapshot_md_updates_` LFQueue and the snapshot multicast stream information:

```cpp
#include "market_data_publisher.h"

namespace Exchange
{   MarketDataPublisher::MarketDataPublisher(MEMarketUpdateLFQueue
    *market_updates, const std::string &iface,
                                            const std::string
                                            &snapshot_ip, int snapshot_
                                            port,
                                            const std::string
                                            &incremental_ip, int
                                            incremental_port)
      : outgoing_md_updates_(market_updates), snapshot_md_updates_(ME_
    MAX_MARKET_UPDATES),
        run_(false), logger_("exchange_market_data_publisher.log"),
        incremental_socket_(logger_) {
    ASSERT(incremental_socket_.init(incremental_ip, iface,
    incremental_port, /*is_listening*/ false) >= 0,
           "Unable to create incremental mcast socket. error:" +
           std::string(std::strerror(errno)));
    snapshot_synthesizer_ = new SnapshotSynthesizer(&snapshot_md_
    updates_, iface, snapshot_ip, snapshot_port);
  }
```

We also present a `start()` method, shown as follows, which is similar in functionality to the `start()` method we saw for the `OrderServer` class. First, it sets the `run_` flag to `true`, then creates and launches a new thread and assigns the `run()` method to that thread, which will be our main run loop for the `MarketDataPublisher` component. It also calls the `start()` method on the `SnapshotSynthesizer` object so that the `SnapshotSynthesizer` thread can also be launched:

```cpp
    auto start() {
      run_ = true;

      ASSERT(Common::createAndStartThread(-1, "Exchange/
      MarketDataPublisher", [this]() { run(); }) != nullptr, "Failed
      to start MarketData thread.");

      snapshot_synthesizer_->start();
    }
```

The destructor is quite self-explanatory; it calls the `stop()` method to stop the running `MarketDataPublisher` thread, then waits a short amount of time to let the thread finish any pending tasks and deletes the `SnapshotSynthesizer` object. We will see the implementation of the `stop()` method right after the destructor, but it should not be too difficult to guess what that method looks like:

```
~MarketDataPublisher() {
  stop();

  using namespace std::literals::chrono_literals;
  std::this_thread::sleep_for(5s);

  delete snapshot_synthesizer_;
  snapshot_synthesizer_ = nullptr;
}
```

Finally, as mentioned before, we present the `stop()` method. This method simply sets the `run_` flag to `false` and instructs the `SnapshotSynthesizer` thread to stop as well:

```
auto stop() -> void {
  run_ = false;

  snapshot_synthesizer_->stop();
}
```

Now that we have seen how to initialize this class, we will look at how `MarketDataPublisher` will publish order book updates, first the updates on the incremental updatesmarket data channel first and then the market updates on the snapshot updates secondmarket data channel.

Publishing order book updates

The main `run()` loop in `MarketDataPublisher` does a couple of important things, which we will discuss here. First, it drains the `outgoing_md_updates_` queue by reading any new `MEMarketDataUpdates` published by the matching engine. This part of the code block is shown as follows:

```
auto MarketDataPublisher::run() noexcept -> void {
  logger_.log("%:% %() %\n", __FILE__, __LINE__, __FUNCTION__,
    Common::getCurrentTimeStr(&time_str_));
  while (run_) {
    for (auto market_update = outgoing_md_updates_->getNextToRead();
         outgoing_md_updates_->size() && market_update; market_
         update = outgoing_md_updates_->getNextToRead()) {
      logger_.log("%:% %() % Sending seq:% %\n", __FILE__, __LINE__,
```

```
            __FUNCTION__, Common::getCurrentTimeStr(&time_str_), next_inc_
seq_num_,
            market_update->toString().c_str());
```

Once it has a `MEMarketUpdate` message from the matching engine, it will proceed to write it to the `incremental_socket_` UDP socket. But it needs to write out the message in the `MDPMarketUpdate` format, which is just a sequence number followed by a `MEMarketUpdate` message. As we saw with `OrderServer`, it will achieve this here by first writing `next_inc_seq_num_`, which is the next incremental sequence number to be sent out on the incremental stream, and then write `MEMarketUpdate`, which it received from the matching engine. This logic is shown in the following code block, along with the line to increment the read index in the `LFQueue` that it just read from:

```
        incremental_socket_.send(&next_inc_seq_num_, sizeof(next_inc_
seq_num_));
        incremental_socket_.send(market_update,
sizeof(MEMarketUpdate));
        outgoing_md_updates_->updateReadIndex();
```

It needs to do one additional step here, which is to write the same incremental update it wrote to the socket to the `snapshot_md_updates_` LFQueue to inform the `SnapshotSynthesizer` component about the new incremental update from the matching engine that was sent to the clients. That code block is shown as follows:

```
        auto next_write = snapshot_md_updates_.getNextToWriteTo();
        next_write->seq_num_ = next_inc_seq_num_;
        next_write->me_market_update_ = *market_update;
        snapshot_md_updates_.updateWriteIndex();
```

Finally, it increments the incremental stream sequence number tracker for the next message that will be sent out and calls `sendAndRecv()` on `incremental_socket_` so that the messages get put on the wire:

```
        ++next_inc_seq_num_;
      }

      incremental_socket_.sendAndRecv();
    }
  }
}
```

That concludes all the tasks we need to perform to consume updates from the matching engine and generate the incremental market update multicast stream. In the next subsection, we will take care of the final key step in the market data publisher, which is synthesizing order book snapshots and publishing them periodically on the snapshot multicast stream.

Synthesizing and publishing snapshots

This section will be dedicated to the design and implementation of the `SnapshotSynthesizer` class, which consumes incremental `MDPMarketDataUpdates` from the `MarketDataPublisher` thread, synthesizes a full snapshot of the order book, and periodically publishes the full book snapshot on the snapshot multicast stream. All the source code for `SnapshotSynthesizer` can be found in the `Chapter7/exchange/market_data/snapshot_synthesizer.h` and `Chapter7/exchange/market_data/snapshot_synthesizer.cpp` source files.

Defining the data members in the snapshot synthesizer

Let us first define the data members in the `SnapshotSynthesizer` class. The important ones are described as follows:

- First, `snapshot_md_updates_` of the `MDPMarketUpdateLFQueue` type, which is what `MarketDataPublisher` uses to publish incremental `MDPMarketUpdates` to this component, which we saw in the previous section.

- It also has a `snapshot_socket_` variable, which is an `McastSocket` to be used to publish snapshot market data updates to the snapshot multicast stream.

- One of the most important data members is the `ticker_orders_` variable, which is a `std::array` of size `ME_MAX_TICKERS` to represent the snapshot of the book for each trading instrument. Each element of this array is a `std::array` of `MEMarketUpdate` pointers and a maximum size of `ME_MAX_ORDER_IDS` to represent a hash map from `OrderId` to the order corresponding to that `OrderId`. As we have done before, we use the first `std::array` as a hash map from `TickerId` to the snapshot of the limit order book. The second `std::array` is also a hash map from `OrderId` to the order information. We will also have an `order_pool_` data member of the `MemPool` type of `MEMarketUpdate` objects. This memory pool is what we will use to allocate and deallocate `MEMarketUpdate` objects from as we update the order book snapshot in the `ticker_orders_` container.

- We have two variables to track information about the last incremental market data update that `SnapshotSynthesizer` has processed. The first one is the `last_inc_seq_num_` variable to track the sequence number on the last incremental `MDPMarketUpdate` it has received. The second one is the `last_snapshot_time_` variable used to track when the last snapshot was published over UDP since this component will only periodically publish the full snapshot of all the books.

- There is also a Boolean `run_` variable, which serves a similar purpose as the `run_` variables in the `OrderServer` and `MarketDataPublisher` components we built before. This will be used to start and stop the `SnapshotSynthesizer` thread and will be marked `volatile` since it will be accessed from multiple threads:

```cpp
#pragma once

#include "common/types.h"
#include "common/thread_utils.h"
#include "common/lf_queue.h"
#include "common/macros.h"
#include "common/mcast_socket.h"
#include "common/mem_pool.h"
#include "common/logging.h"

#include "market_data/market_update.h"
#include "matcher/me_order.h"

using namespace Common;

namespace Exchange {
  class SnapshotSynthesizer {
  private:
    MDPMarketUpdateLFQueue *snapshot_md_updates_ = nullptr;

    Logger logger_;

    volatile bool run_ = false;

    std::string time_str_;

    McastSocket snapshot_socket_;

    std::array<std::array<MEMarketUpdate *, ME_MAX_ORDER_IDS>,
    ME_MAX_TICKERS> ticker_orders_;
    size_t last_inc_seq_num_ = 0;
    Nanos last_snapshot_time_ = 0;

    MemPool<MEMarketUpdate> order_pool_;
  };
}
```

In the next subsection, we will see how these variables are initialized as we look at the initialization of the `SnapshotSynthesizer` class.

Initializing the snapshot synthesizer

The `SnapshotSynthesizer` constructor takes an argument of the `MDPMarketUpdateLFQueue` type passed to it from the `MarketDataPublisher` component. It also receives the network interface name and the snapshot IP and port to represent the multicast stream. The constructor initializes the `snapshot_md_updates_` data member from the argument passed to it and initializes `logger_` with a new filename. It initializes `MEMarketUpdate MemPool` to be of the size `ME_MAX_ORDER_IDS`. It also initializes `snapshot_socket_` and configures it to publish messages on the snapshot multicast IP and port on the provided network interface:

```cpp
#include "snapshot_synthesizer.h"

namespace Exchange {
  SnapshotSynthesizer::SnapshotSynthesizer(MDPMarketUpdateLFQueue
  *market_updates, const std::string &iface,
                                           const std::string &snapshot_
                                           ip, int snapshot_port)
    : snapshot_md_updates_(market_updates), logger_("exchange_
    snapshot_synthesizer.log"), snapshot_socket_(logger_), order_
    pool_(ME_MAX_ORDER_IDS) {
    ASSERT(snapshot_socket_.init(snapshot_ip, iface, snapshot_port,
    /*is_listening*/ false) >= 0,
          "Unable to create snapshot mcast socket. error:" +
          std::string(std::strerror(errno)));
  }
```

We also add a `start()` method here in the same way as we did with our other classes before. This `start()` method sets the `run_` flag to true, creates and launches a thread, and assigns the `run()` method to the thread:

```cpp
void SnapshotSynthesizer::start() {
  run_ = true;
  ASSERT(Common::createAndStartThread(-1, "Exchange/
  SnapshotSynthesizer", [this]() { run(); }) != nullptr,
        "Failed to start SnapshotSynthesizer thread.");
}
```

The destructor for this class is extremely simple; it just calls the `stop()` method. The `stop()` method is also extremely simple and just sets the `run_` flag to false so that the `run()` method exits:

```cpp
SnapshotSynthesizer::~SnapshotSynthesizer() {
  stop();
}
void SnapshotSynthesizer::stop() {
  run_ = false;
}
```

Next, we will look at the important pieces of `SnapshotSynthesizer`, which will synthesize the order book snapshots and publish the snapshots periodically.

Synthesizing the snapshot of the order book

The process of synthesizing the snapshot of the order books for the different trading instruments is like building `OrderBook`. However, the difference here is that the snapshot synthesis process only needs to maintain the last state of the live orders, so it is a simpler container. The `addToSnapshot()` method we will build next receives an `MDPMarketUpdate` message every time there is a new incremental market data update provided to `SnapshotSynthesizer`. We will break this method up into several code blocks so that it is easier to follow.

In the first code block, we extract the `MEMarketUpdate` piece of the `MDPMarketUpdate` message and store it in the `me_market_update` variable. It also finds the `std::array` of `MEMarketUpdate` messages for the correct `TickerId` for this instrument from the `ticker_orders_` `std::array` hash map. We then have a switch case on the type of `MarketUpdateType` and then handle each of those cases individually. Before we look at each of the cases under the switch case, let us present the initial code block in the `addToSnapshot()` method we described:

```
auto SnapshotSynthesizer::addToSnapshot(const MDPMarketUpdate
*market_update) {
  const auto &me_market_update = market_update->me_market_update_;
  auto *orders = &ticker_orders_.at(me_market_update.ticker_id_);
  switch (me_market_update.type_) {
```

Now, we will show the implementation of the `MarketUpdateType::ADD` case in the switch case. To handle a `MarketUpdateType::ADD` message, we simply insert it into the `MEMarketUpdate` `std::array` at the correct `OrderId` location. We create a `MEMarketUpdate` message by allocating it from the `order_pool_` memory pool using the `allocate()` call and passing it the `MEMarketUpdate` object to copy the fields from:

```
    case MarketUpdateType::ADD: {
      auto order = orders->at(me_market_update.order_id_);
      ASSERT(order == nullptr, "Received:" + me_market_update.
toString() + " but order already exists:" + (order ? order-
>toString() : ""));
      orders->at(me_market_update.order_id_) = order_pool_.
allocate(me_market_update);
    }
      break;
```

`MarketUpdateType::MODIFY` is handled similarly to `MarketUpdateType::ADD`. The minor difference here is that we just update the `qty_` and `price_` fields and leave the `type_` field on the entry as is:

```cpp
    case MarketUpdateType::MODIFY: {
      auto order = orders->at(me_market_update.order_id_);
      ASSERT(order != nullptr, "Received:" + me_market_update.
        toString() + " but order does not exist.");
      ASSERT(order->order_id_ == me_market_update.order_id_,
        "Expecting existing order to match new one.");
      ASSERT(order->side_ == me_market_update.side_, "Expecting
        existing order to match new one.");

      order->qty_ = me_market_update.qty_;
      order->price_ = me_market_update.price_;
    }
      break;
```

The `MarketUpdateType::CANCEL` type does the opposite of what `MarketUpdateType::ADD` did. Here, we find `MEMarketUpdate` in the hash map and call `deallocate()` on it. We also set the entry in the hash map style `std::array` to `nullptr` to mark it as canceled or a dead order:

```cpp
    case MarketUpdateType::CANCEL: {
      auto order = orders->at(me_market_update.order_id_);
      ASSERT(order != nullptr, "Received:" + me_market_update.
        toString() + " but order does not exist.");
      ASSERT(order->order_id_ == me_market_update.order_id_,
        "Expecting existing order to match new one.");
      ASSERT(order->side_ == me_market_update.side_, "Expecting
        existing order to match new one.");

      order_pool_.deallocate(order);
      orders->at(me_market_update.order_id_) = nullptr;
    }
      break;
```

We do not need to do anything with the other enumeration values, so we ignore them. We just update the last sequence number we have seen on the incremental market data stream, which is stored in the `last_inc_seq_num_` data members:

```cpp
    case MarketUpdateType::SNAPSHOT_START:
    case MarketUpdateType::CLEAR:
    case MarketUpdateType::SNAPSHOT_END:
    case MarketUpdateType::TRADE:
    case MarketUpdateType::INVALID:
      break;
  }
```

```
            ASSERT(market_update->seq_num_ == last_inc_seq_num_ + 1, "Expected
        incremental seq_nums to increase.");
        last_inc_seq_num_ = market_update->seq_num_;
    }
```

This concludes the code to synthesize and update the order book snapshot from the incremental `MEMarketUpdate` messages. Next, we will look at how the full snapshot stream is generated and published.

Publishing the snapshots

The next method – `publishSnapshot()` – is called whenever we want to publish a complete snapshot of the current state of the order book. Before we look at the code to publish the snapshot messages, let us first try to understand the format and content of a snapshot message containing the full state of the book for multiple instruments. The format of a full snapshot message looks like the following:

1. The first `MDPMarketUpdate` message is of the `MarketUpdateType::SNAPSHOT_START` type with `seq_num_` = 0 to mark the beginning of the snapshot messages.

2. Then, for each instrument, we publish the following:

    I. A `MDPMarketUpdate` message of the `MarketUpdateType::CLEAR` type to instruct the client to clear their order book before applying the messages that follow

    II. For each order that exists in the snapshot for this instrument, we publish a `MDPMarketUpdate` message with `MarketUpdateType::ADD` till we have published the information for all the orders

3. Finally, we publish a `MDPMarketUpdate` message of the `MarketUpdateType::SNAPSHOT_END` type to mark the end of the snapshot messages. One thing to note is that for the `SNAPSHOT_START` and `SNAPSHOT_END` messages, we set the `OrderId` value to be the last incremental sequence number that was used to construct this snapshot. The market participants will use this sequence number to synchronize the snapshot market data stream with the incremental market data stream.

This design is represented in the following diagram, with a snapshot containing data for three instruments.

Building the market data publisher 265

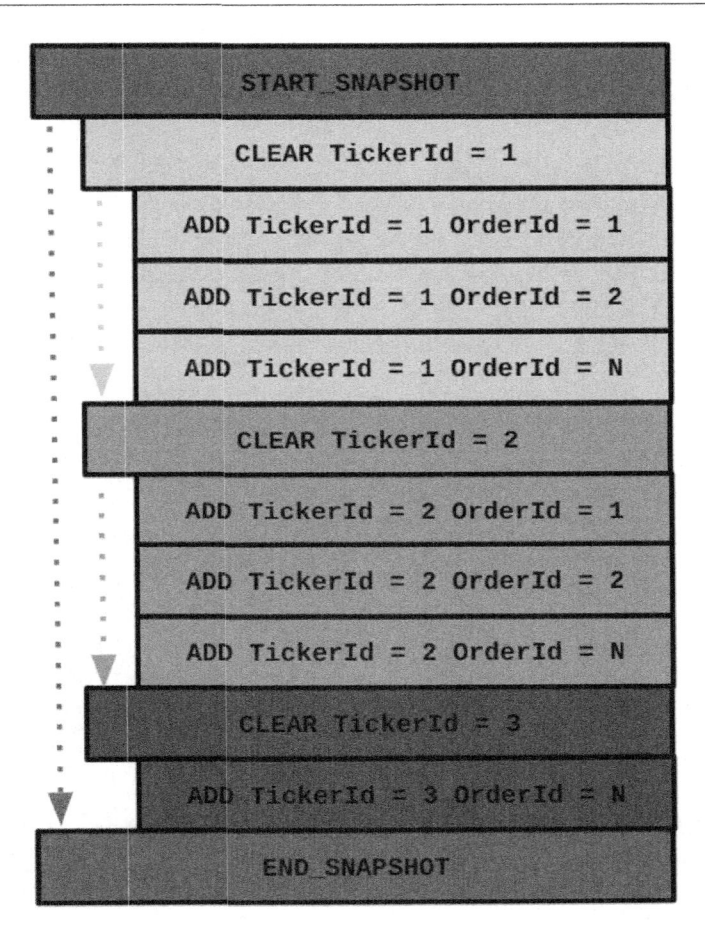

```
                    START_SNAPSHOT

                    CLEAR TickerId = 1

                ADD TickerId = 1 OrderId = 1

                ADD TickerId = 1 OrderId = 2

                ADD TickerId = 1 OrderId = N

                    CLEAR TickerId = 2

                ADD TickerId = 2 OrderId = 1

                ADD TickerId = 2 OrderId = 2

                ADD TickerId = 2 OrderId = N

                    CLEAR TickerId = 3

                ADD TickerId = 3 OrderId = N

                      END_SNAPSHOT
```

Figure 7.3 – Diagram describing the layout of our market data snapshot messages

With that format in mind, let us look at the code to synthesize and publish the snapshot message format we described previously. First, we publish the `MarketUpdateType::SNAPSHOT_START` message, as follows:

```
auto SnapshotSynthesizer::publishSnapshot() {
  size_t snapshot_size = 0;

  const MDPMarketUpdate start_market_update{snapshot_size++,
    {MarketUpdateType::SNAPSHOT_START, last_inc_seq_num_}};
  logger_.log("%:% %() % %\n", __FILE__, __LINE__, __FUNCTION__,
    getCurrentTimeStr(&time_str_), start_market_update.toString());
  snapshot_socket_.send(&start_market_update,
    sizeof(MDPMarketUpdate));
```

Then, we iterate through all the instruments that we will publish the snapshots for. The first thing we do is publish the `MDPMarketUpdate` message of the `MarketUpdateType::CLEAR` type for that instrument:

```cpp
for (size_t ticker_id = 0; ticker_id < ticker_orders_.size();
 ++ticker_id) {
  const auto &orders = ticker_orders_.at(ticker_id);

  MEMarketUpdate me_market_update;
  me_market_update.type_ = MarketUpdateType::CLEAR;
  me_market_update.ticker_id_ = ticker_id;

  const MDPMarketUpdate clear_market_update{snapshot_size++, me_market_update};
  logger_.log("%:% %() % %\n", __FILE__, __LINE__, __FUNCTION__,
              getCurrentTimeStr(&time_str_), clear_market_update.toString());
  snapshot_socket_.send(&clear_market_update,
                        sizeof(MDPMarketUpdate));
```

Then, we iterate through all the orders for this trading instrument and check for live orders – entries that do not have `nullptr` values. For each valid order, we publish the `MDPMarketUpdate` message for that `OrderId` with `MarketUpdateType::ADD`:

```cpp
  for (const auto order: orders) {
    if (order) {
      const MDPMarketUpdate market_update{snapshot_size++, *order};
      logger_.log("%:% %() % %\n", __FILE__, __LINE__, __
FUNCTION__, getCurrentTimeStr(&time_str_), market_update.
toString());
      snapshot_socket_.send(&market_update, sizeof(MDPMarketUpdate));
      snapshot_socket_.sendAndRecv();
    }
  }
}
```

Finally, we publish the `MDPMarketUpdate` message with the `MarketUpdateType::SNAPSHOT_END` type to signify the end of the snapshot messages this round:

```cpp
const MDPMarketUpdate end_market_update{snapshot_size++,
  {MarketUpdateType::SNAPSHOT_END, last_inc_seq_num_}};
  logger_.log("%:% %() % %\n", __FILE__, __LINE__, __FUNCTION__,
              getCurrentTimeStr(&time_str_), end_market_update.toString());
  snapshot_socket_.send(&end_market_update,
                        sizeof(MDPMarketUpdate));
  snapshot_socket_.sendAndRecv();
```

```
      logger_.log("%:% %() % Published snapshot of % orders.\n",
                  __FILE__, __LINE__, __FUNCTION__, getCurrentTimeStr(&time_str_),
                  snapshot_size - 1);
    }
```

That concludes the design of the snapshot stream and the code to publish it in the `publishSnapshot()` method. In the next subsection, we will finish our discussion of the `SnapshotSynthesizer` component in the market data publisher infrastructure by implementing the main `run()` loop that ties everything together.

Running the main loop

Remember that `SnapshotSynthesizer` runs on its own thread separate from the `MarketDataPublisher` thread to not cause latencies on the component that publishes the incremental market data stream. The `run()` method is the method assigned to the `SnapshotSynthesizer` thread. The only task it performs is checking the `snapshot_md_updates_` lock-free queue for new entries, which the `MarketDataPublisher` sends incremental `MDPMarketUpdate` messages on. For each incremental `MDPMarketUpdate` message it reads, it calls the `addToSnapshot()` method we built earlier. Additionally, it checks the `last_snapshot_time_` variable against the current time obtained from `getCurrentTime()` to see whether a minute has elapsed. If at least a minute has elapsed since the last time a snapshot was published, it calls the `publishSnapshot()` method to publish a new snapshot. It also remembers the current time as the last time a full snapshot was published:

```
    void SnapshotSynthesizer::run() {
      logger_.log("%:% %() %\n", __FILE__, __LINE__, __FUNCTION__,
                  getCurrentTimeStr(&time_str_));
      while (run_) {
        for (auto market_update = snapshot_md_updates_->getNextToRead();
             snapshot_md_updates_->size() && market_update; market_update =
             snapshot_md_updates_->getNextToRead()) {
          logger_.log("%:% %() % Processing %\n", __FILE__, __LINE__,
                      __FUNCTION__, getCurrentTimeStr(&time_str_),
                      market_update->toString().c_str());

          addToSnapshot(market_update);

          snapshot_md_updates_->updateReadIndex();
        }

        if (getCurrentNanos() - last_snapshot_time_ > 60 * NANOS_TO_
      SECS) {
          last_snapshot_time_ = getCurrentNanos();
```

```
            publishSnapshot();
        }
      }
    }
  }
}
```

This concludes the design and implementation of `SnapshotSynthesizer` as well as the `MarketDataPublisher` component and our complete electronic trading exchange infrastructure. In the next section, we will build the main electronic exchange application, which will tie together all the components we have built so far on the side of the electronic exchange.

Building the main exchange application

In this final section of the chapter, as well as the final section of the electronic trading exchange discussion, we will build the main exchange application. This will be a standalone binary application that will run an order gateway server, the matching engine, and the market data publisher and perform the following tasks:

- The order gateway server accepts client connections and client requests.
- The matching engine builds the limit order book.
- The matching engine also performs matching between client orders.
- The matching engine and the order gateway server publish client responses.
- The matching engine and the market data publisher publish incremental market data updates in response to client requests.
- The market data publisher also synthesizes and periodically publishes a full snapshot of the order book.

The complete design is presented in the following diagram.

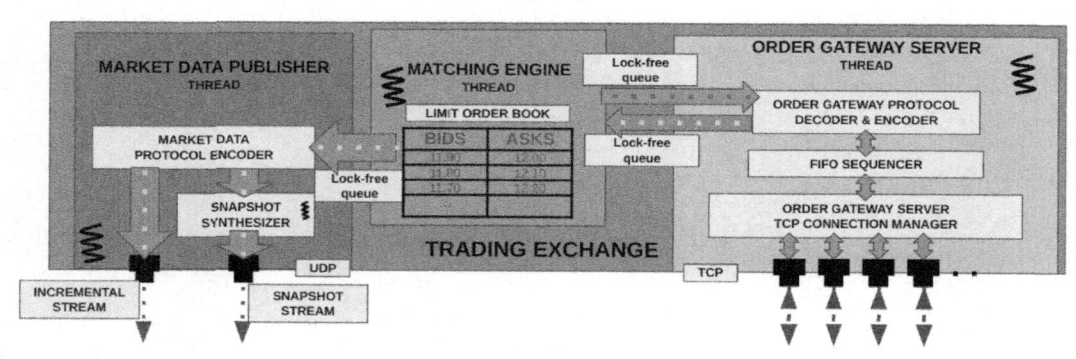

Figure 7.4 – The final trading exchange application and all its components

Building the main exchange application

The code for this exchange application is available in the `Chapter7/exchange/exchange_main.cpp` source file.

We will create a `Logger`, `MatchingEngine`, `MarketDataPublisher`, and `OrderServer` instance in the global scope. We will also create a signal handling function since this application will be killed when a UNIX signal is sent to it. The signal handler cleans up the components and exits:

```
#include <csignal>

#include "matcher/matching_engine.h"
#include "market_data/market_data_publisher.h"
#include "order_server/order_server.h"

Common::Logger *logger = nullptr;
Exchange::MatchingEngine *matching_engine = nullptr;
Exchange::MarketDataPublisher *market_data_publisher = nullptr;
Exchange::OrderServer *order_server = nullptr;

void signal_handler(int) {
  using namespace std::literals::chrono_literals;
  std::this_thread::sleep_for(10s);

  delete logger;
  logger = nullptr;
  delete matching_engine;
  matching_engine = nullptr;
  delete market_data_publisher;
  market_data_publisher = nullptr;
  delete order_server;
  order_server = nullptr;

  std::this_thread::sleep_for(10s);

  exit(EXIT_SUCCESS);
}
```

The `main()` function initializes the logger object, installs the signal handler, and sets up three lock-free queues – `client_requests`, of the `ClientRequestLFQueue` type, `client_responses`, of the `ClientResponseLFQueue` type, and `market_updates`, of the `MEMarketUpdateLFQueue` type – to facilitate communication between the three major components:

```
int main(int, char **) {
  logger = new Common::Logger("exchange_main.log");
```

```
std::signal(SIGINT, signal_handler);

const int sleep_time = 100 * 1000;

Exchange::ClientRequestLFQueue client_requests(ME_MAX_CLIENT_
UPDATES);
Exchange::ClientResponseLFQueue client_responses(ME_MAX_CLIENT_
UPDATES);
Exchange::MEMarketUpdateLFQueue market_updates(ME_MAX_MARKET_
UPDATES);
```

Then, we create and start the instance of the `MatchingEngine` component and pass the three LFQueue objects:

```
std::string time_str;

logger->log("%:% %() % Starting Matching Engine...\n", __FILE__, __
LINE__, __FUNCTION__, Common::getCurrentTimeStr(&time_str));
matching_engine = new Exchange::MatchingEngine(&client_requests,
&client_responses, &market_updates);
matching_engine->start();
```

We will also create and start the instance of `MarketDataPublisher` and provide it with the snapshot and incremental stream information and the `market_updates LFQueue` object.

One note about the interfaces and the IPs and ports specified in this chapter as well as the subsequent ones is that we chose these arbitrarily; feel free to change them if needed. The important thing here is that the market data stream IP:port information used by the electronic exchange and trading clients should match, and similarly, the order server IP:port information used by the electronic exchange and trading clients match:

```
const std::string mkt_pub_iface = "lo";
const std::string snap_pub_ip = "233.252.14.1", inc_pub_ip =
"233.252.14.3";
const int snap_pub_port = 20000, inc_pub_port = 20001;

logger->log("%:% %() % Starting Market Data Publisher...\n", __
FILE__, __LINE__, __FUNCTION__, Common::getCurrentTimeStr(&time_
str));
market_data_publisher = new Exchange::MarketDataPublisher(&market_
updates, mkt_pub_iface, snap_pub_ip, snap_pub_port, inc_pub_ip, inc_
pub_port);
market_data_publisher->start();
```

We perform similar tasks with the `order_server` object – create `OrderServer` and start it after providing it with the order gateway server configuration information:

```
const std::string order_gw_iface = "lo";
const int order_gw_port = 12345;

logger->log("%:% %() % Starting Order Server...\n", __FILE__, __
  LINE__, __FUNCTION__, Common::getCurrentTimeStr(&time_str));
order_server = new Exchange::OrderServer(&client_requests, &client_
  responses, order_gw_iface, order_gw_port);
order_server->start();
```

Finally, the `main()` thread just sleeps infinitely since the threads within the three components will run the exchange from this point on:

```
  while (true) {
    logger->log("%:% %() % Sleeping for a few milliseconds..\n", __
      FILE__, __LINE__, __FUNCTION__, Common::getCurrentTimeStr(&time_
      str));
    usleep(sleep_time * 1000);
  }
}
```

Running the application as follows will produce some minimal output to the screen, but most of the output goes to the log files we create from the three components and their subcomponents:

```
(base) sghosh@sghosh-ThinkPad-X1-Carbon-3rd:~/Building-Low-Latency-
Applications-with-CPP/Chapter7$ ./cmake-build-release/exchange_main
Set core affinity for Common/Logger exchange_main.log 140329423955712
to -1
Set core affinity for Common/Logger exchange_matching_engine.log
140329253541632 to -1
Set core affinity for Exchange/MatchingEngine 140329245148928 to -1
...
Sun Mar 26 13:58:04 2023 Flushing and closing Logger for exchange_
order_server.log
Sun Mar 26 13:58:04 2023 Logger for exchange_order_server.log exiting.
```

The `exchange_main` application was killed by sending it the `SIGINT` signal using the `kill -2 PID` command. We can inspect the log files to see what the different components did. Note, however, that the output right now is not super interesting. It simply logs that the components were created and started. This output will have a lot more information once we add clients for this trading exchange that connect and send client requests to it:

```
(base) sghosh@sghosh-ThinkPad-X1-Carbon-3rd:~/Building-Low-Latency-
Applications-with-CPP/Chapter7$ tail -n 10 *.log
```

The `exchange_main.log` file contains information about the creation of the different components, as shown:

```
==> exchange_main.log <==
/home/sghosh/Building-Low-Latency-Applications-with-CPP/Chapter7/exchange/exchange_main.cpp:43 main() Sun Mar 26 09:13:49 2023 Starting Matching Engine...
/home/sghosh/Building-Low-Latency-Applications-with-CPP/Chapter7/exchange/exchange_main.cpp:51 main() Sun Mar 26 09:13:51 2023 Starting Market Data Publisher...
/home/sghosh/Building-Low-Latency-Applications-with-CPP/Chapter7/exchange/exchange_main.cpp:58 main() Sun Mar 26 09:13:56 2023 Starting Order Server...
/home/sghosh/Building-Low-Latency-Applications-with-CPP/Chapter7/exchange/exchange_main.cpp:63 main() Sun Mar 26 09:13:58 2023 Sleeping for a few milliseconds..
```

The `exchange_market_data_publisher.log` file creates the UDP sockets and calls the `run()` method as shown:

```
==> exchange_market_data_publisher.log <==
/home/sghosh/Building-Low-Latency-Applications-with-CPP/Chapter7/common/socket_utils.cpp:68 createSocket() Sun Mar 26 09:13:52 2023 ip:233.252.14.3 iface:lo port:20001 is_udp:1 is_blocking:0 is_listening:0 ttl:32 SO_time:0
/home/sghosh/Building-Low-Latency-Applications-with-CPP/Chapter7/exchange/market_data/market_data_publisher.cpp:15 run() Sun Mar 26 09:13:54 2023
```

The `exchange_matching_engine.log` file does not have much meaningful output yet since no matching was performed and no order book was built:

```
==> exchange_matching_engine.log <==

                                X



/home/sghosh/Building-Low-Latency-Applications-with-CPP/Chapter7/exchange/matcher/me_order_book.cpp:12 ~MEOrderBook() Sun Mar 26 09:15:00 2023 OrderBook
Ticker:7

                                X


```

The `exchange_order_server.log` file also contains some information about the creation of `TCPServer` and the `run()` method for the main thread:

```
==> exchange_order_server.log <==
/home/sghosh/Building-Low-Latency-Applications-with-CPP/Chapter7/
common/socket_utils.cpp:68 createSocket() Sun Mar 26 09:13:57 2023
ip:127.0.0.1 iface:lo port:12345 is_udp:0 is_blocking:0 is_listening:1
ttl:0 SO_time:1
/home/sghosh/Building-Low-Latency-Applications-with-CPP/Chapter7/
exchange/order_server/order_server.h:25 run() Sun Mar 26 09:13:57 2023
```

Finally, the `exchange_snapshot_synthesizer.log` file outputs the messages in an empty snapshot for the different trading instruments, since there are no orders in the order book yet:

```
==> exchange_snapshot_synthesizer.log <==
/home/sghosh/Building-Low-Latency-Applications-with-CPP/Chapter7/
exchange/market_data/snapshot_synthesizer.cpp:82 publishSnapshot()
Sun Mar 26 09:14:55 2023 MDPMarketUpdate [ seq:2 MEMarketUpdate [
type:CLEAR ticker:1 oid:INVALID side:INVALID qty:INVALID price:INVALID
priority:INVALID]]
/home/sghosh/Building-Low-Latency-Applications-with-CPP/Chapter7/
exchange/market_data/snapshot_synthesizer.cpp:82 publishSnapshot()
Sun Mar 26 09:14:55 2023 MDPMarketUpdate [ seq:3 MEMarketUpdate [
type:CLEAR ticker:2 oid:INVALID side:INVALID qty:INVALID price:INVALID
priority:INVALID]]
...
/home/sghosh/Building-Low-Latency-Applications-with-CPP/Chapter7/
exchange/market_data/snapshot_synthesizer.cpp:96 publishSnapshot()
Sun Mar 26 09:14:55 2023 MDPMarketUpdate [ seq:9 MEMarketUpdate [
type:SNAPSHOT_END ticker:INVALID oid:0 side:INVALID qty:INVALID
price:INVALID priority:INVALID]]
/home/sghosh/Building-Low-Latency-Applications-with-CPP/Chapter7/
exchange/market_data/snapshot_synthesizer.cpp:100 publishSnapshot()
Sun Mar 26 09:14:55 2023 Published snapshot of 9 orders.
```

This concludes our discussion, design, and implementation of the electronic trading exchange. In the next chapter, we will build the trading system on the client's end.

Summary

This chapter was dedicated to building the order gateway server and the market data publisher components. We also combined the matching engine component we built in the previous chapter with the order gateway server and market data publisher components we built in this chapter to build the final trading exchange main application.

First, we defined the public market data protocol that will be used by the exchange to publish data on the wire and used by the clients to write market data consumer applications. We performed a similar task with the order gateway protocol so that client applications can understand the format of the client requests that they send to the exchange's order gateway server and receive responses from.

We built the order gateway server, whose design we established in the *Designing Our Trading Ecosystem* chapter. We built the `OrderServer` class, which builds and runs `TCPServer`, to accept and manage TCP client connections. We added functionality to handle incoming client requests and send client responses. We also built the `FIFOSequencer` component, which is responsible for sequencing/ordering the incoming TCP client requests in the order in which they were received to maintain fairness in the market.

The next component we built was designed in the same chapter, *Designing Our Trading Ecosystem*, which is the market data publisher. We built `MarketDataPublisher`, which consumes market data updates from the matching engine and generates a multicast stream of incremental market data updates. We also added the `SnapshotSynthesizer` component, which runs on a different thread and is responsible for consuming market data updates from `MarketDataPublisher` and synthesizing the snapshot of the full order book. This full snapshot is periodically published by `SnapshotSynthesizer` on the snapshot multicast stream.

Finally, we built the main electronic trading exchange application, which ties together all the exchange side components we have built so far. This will serve as the central electronic trading exchange that supports multiple clients and different trading instruments for clients to connect and trade as well as receive market data updates for.

In the next chapter, we switch our focus from the exchange-side infrastructure to the market participants' infrastructure. The next chapter will focus on the functionality to connect to the order gateway server and communicate with it, as well as receiving and processing the market data updates published by the electronic exchange.

Part 3: Building Real-Time C++ Algorithmic Trading Systems

In this part, we will start building the trading client-side C++ algorithmic trading system. We will be building components that interface with the trading exchange to process market data and connect to and communicate with the exchange order gateway. We will also build the C++ framework on which we will build market-making and liquidity-taking trading algorithms. In the HFT space, this is where participants spend a lot of time and effort trying to reduce latencies and maximize performance (and profits). Finally, we will implement the market-making and liquidity-taking trading algorithms in this framework, run the entire trading ecosystem, and understand the interactions between all the components.

This part contains the following chapters:

- *Chapter 8, Processing Market Data and Sending Orders to the Exchange in C++*
- *Chapter 9, Building the C++ Trading Algorithm Building Blocks*
- *Chapter 10, Building the C++ Market-Making and Liquidity-Taking Algorithms*

8

Processing Market Data and Sending Orders to the Exchange in C++

In this chapter, we will build the client's C++ system that receives and processes market data updates from the trading exchange. We will also have to deal with creating and reading from UDP sockets, dealing with packet losses, etc. We will discuss the design of an order book on the client side to track the order book maintained at the trading exchange. We will also implement the C++ components needed to establish and maintain TCP connections to the trading exchange. We will also implement functionality to send orders to the exchange from the strategies and receive and process order responses.

In this chapter, we will cover the following topics:

- Subscribing to market data and decoding the market data protocol
- Building order books from market data
- Connecting to the exchange, sending order requests, and receiving responses

Technical requirements

All the code for this book can be found in the GitHub repository for this book at https://github.com/PacktPublishing/Building-Low-Latency-Applications-with-CPP. The source for this chapter is in the `Chapter 8` directory in the repository.

You must read and understand the design of the electronic trading ecosystem presented in the chapter *Designing Our Trading Ecosystem*. The components we build in this chapter will interact with the electronic trading exchange application we built in the chapter *Communicating With Market Participants*, so we assume you are familiar with that. The limit order book we will build in the client application's trade engine component is almost identical to the order book we built inside the matching engine in the chapter *Building the C++ Matching Engine* within the *Building the order book and matching orders* section. So, we assume the reader is very familiar with that chapter and the code we discussed there as we will make references to that in this chapter. As before, we will use the building blocks we built in the *Building the C++ Building Blocks for Low Latency Applications* chapter.

The specifications of the environment in which the source code for this book was developed are shown in the following bullet list. We present the details of this environment since all the C++ code presented in this book is not necessarily portable and might require some minor changes to work in your environment:

- OS – `Linux 5.19.0-41-generic #42~22.04.1-Ubuntu SMP PREEMPT_DYNAMIC Tue Apr 18 17:40:00 UTC 2 x86_64 x86_64 x86_64 GNU/Linux`
- GCC – `g++ (Ubuntu 11.3.0-1ubuntu1~22.04.1) 11.3.0`
- CMAKE – `cmake version 3.23.2`
- NINJA – `1.10.2`

Subscribing to market data and decoding the market data protocol

The first component we need to build inside the market participants' trading system is the market data consumer. This component is responsible for subscribing to the multicast stream of public market data updates published by the trading exchange. It needs to decode the market data stream generated by the exchange from the public `MDPMarketUpdate` format we discussed earlier. Because of the choice of the **Simple Binary Encoding** (**SBE**) protocol, the decoding step is straightforward in our application and does not involve any complicated stream decoding logic. Another important responsibility of this component is detecting packet drops on the incremental market data stream and providing mechanisms to recover and synchronize with the market data stream again. This mechanism is also required for trading systems that subscribe to the market data stream after there is a non-empty order book, i.e. after the trading exchange is already open and accepting client orders. Also, this will be required if the trading application needs to be restarted in the middle of the day.

We present a detailed diagram of the market data consumer component we have seen before. As shown in *Figure 8.1*, it consumes multicast data containing market data updates from the incremental and optionally the snapshot stream. After checking for sequence numbers on the market data updates and potentially needing to synchronize between the snapshot and the incremental streams, it decodes the market data updates. It then generates a stream of decoded and in-order market data updates for the trading engine to consume and publishes them over a lock-free queue:

Subscribing to market data and decoding the market data protocol | 279

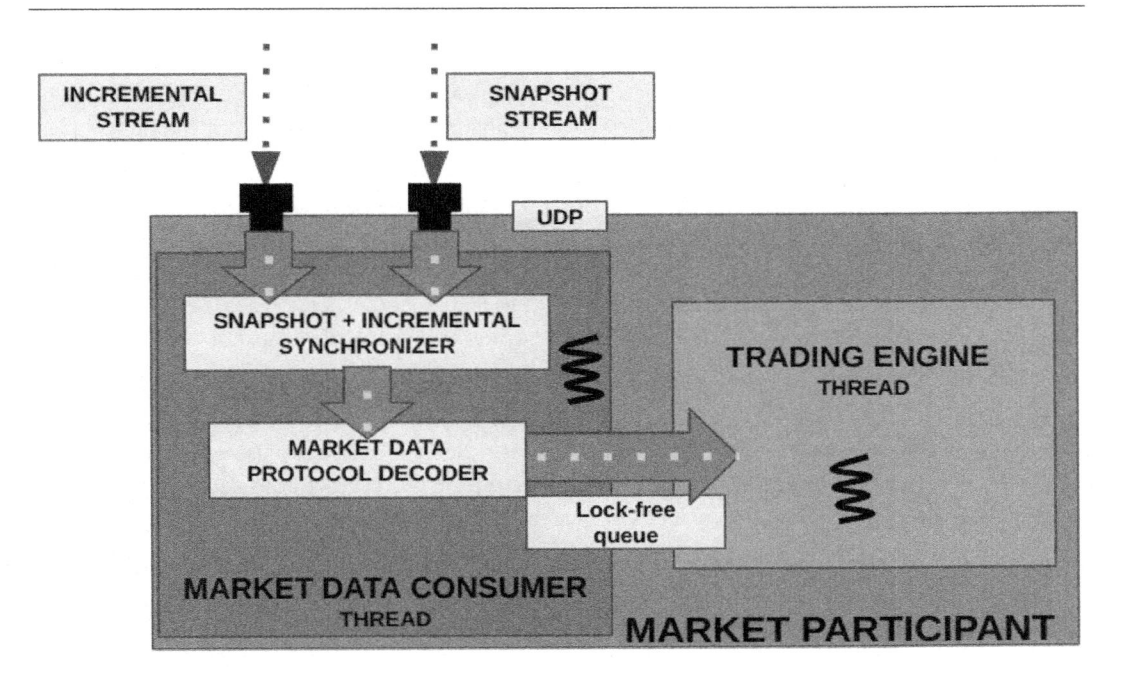

Figure 8.1 – An overview of the market data consumer component and its sub-components

Before we jump into the design and implementation of the market data consumer component, we would like to mention that the source code for this component can be found in the `Chapter8/trading/market_data/market_data_consumer.h` source file and the `Chapter8/trading/market_data/market_data_consumer.cpp` source file. Next, let us get started by first defining the internal data members that the market data consumer component will need.

Defining the data members in the market data consumer

The `MarketDataConsumer` class we are going to build will need a couple of important data members as shown in the following bullet list:

- First, it needs a lock-free `incoming_md_updates_` queue instance of the `Exchange::MEMarketUpdateLFQueue` type, which we defined before. This is meant to be used by `MarketDataConsumer` to publish the `MEMarketUpdate` messages to the trading engine component.

- We will maintain a `next_exp_inc_seq_num_` variable of the `size_t` type, which will be used to make sure that we process updates from the incremental market data stream in the correct order and detect packet drops on the incremental market data stream.

- We will have two multicast subscriber sockets – `incremental_mcast_socket_` and `snapshot_mcast_socket_` of the `Common::McastSocket` types. These correspond to the sockets we will use to subscribe to and consume multicast data from the incremental and the snapshot multicast streams, respectively.

To perform the recovery/synchronization from the snapshot market data stream when needed, we will need to maintain a couple of extra data members, as shown in the following bullet list:

- First, we will store an `in_recovery_` boolean flag to signify if `MarketDataConsumer` detected a packet drop and is currently trying to recover using the snapshot and incremental market data streams.
- Since we will join and leave the snapshot multicast stream as needed, we will have the multicast stream and network interface information in the `iface_` variable, the `snapshot_ip_variable`, and the `snapshot_port_` variable. These represent the network interface to use, the IP address, and the port of the snapshot multicast stream.
- Finally, we define a type to queue up messages and order them by their corresponding sequence number. We will use the **Standard Template Library** (**STL**) `std::map` type here and paramaterize it to use keys of the `size_t` type (to represent the sequence number of the update), hold objects of `Exchange::MEMarketUpdate`, and call this type `QueuedMarketUpdates` using `typedef`. We chose the `std::map` type here since it is easier to iterate over sorted keys compared to, say, `std::unordered_map`. Note that `std::map` is not efficient for a wide range of reasons – the internal data structure is **Red Black Tree**, which has an asymptotic insertion performance of `O(log(N))` and causes dynamic memory allocations, etc. However, we make an exception in this case because snapshot recovery is expected to be extremely rare, and when the `MarketDataConsumer` class is recovering from the snapshot stream, trading is generally paused inside the client's trading application since it does not have an accurate view of the state of the order book. Additionally, the snapshot stream is delayed and throttled from the exchange's side, so the snapshot synchronization process itself is not required to be low latency.
- We create two instances of this `QueuedMarketUpdates` type – `snapshot_queued_msgs_` and `incremental_queued_msgs_`, one to queue up `MEMarketUpdate` messages from the snapshot stream and one to queue up `MEMarketUpdate` messages from the incremental stream.
- The `MarketDataConsumer` class is also a different thread of execution, so similar to the classes we have seen before, it has a `run_` boolean flag to control the execution of the thread and it is marked `volatile` since it is accessed from different threads:

```
#pragma once

#include <functional>
#include <map>
```

```cpp
#include "common/thread_utils.h"
#include "common/lf_queue.h"
#include "common/macros.h"
#include "common/mcast_socket.h"

#include "exchange/market_data/market_update.h"

namespace Trading {
  class MarketDataConsumer {
  private:
      size_t next_exp_inc_seq_num_ = 1;
      Exchange::MEMarketUpdateLFQueue *incoming_md_updates_ =
        nullptr;

      volatile bool run_ = false;

      std::string time_str_;
      Logger logger_;
      Common::McastSocket incremental_mcast_socket_,
        snapshot_mcast_socket_;

      bool in_recovery_ = false;
      const std::string iface_, snapshot_ip_;
      const int snapshot_port_;
      typedef std::map<size_t, Exchange::MEMarketUpdate>
        QueuedMarketUpdates;
      QueuedMarketUpdates snapshot_queued_msgs_,
        incremental_queued_msgs_;
  };
}
```

We will initialize the `MarketDataConsumer` class and these data members in the next section.

Initializing the market data consumer

The constructor for the `MarketDataConsumer` class accepts the following arguments:

- A `client_id` argument of the `Common::ClientId` type, which in this case is used purely to create a unique log filename to be used to initialize the `Logger logger_` component in this class.
- It also expects a pointer to a `MEMarketUpdateLFQueue` lock-free queue object called `market_updates`, where it will publish decoded and in-order market updates.

- It expects the network interface name in the `iface` argument and the addresses of the snapshot and incremental market data streams. These will be passed in the `snapshot_ip` argument, the `snapshot_port` argument, the `incremental_ip` argument, and the `incremental_port` argument:

```
#include "market_data_consumer.h"

namespace Trading {
  MarketDataConsumer::MarketDataConsumer(Common::ClientId
    client_id, Exchange::MEMarketUpdateLFQueue
      *market_updates,
const std::string &iface,
const std::string &snapshot_ip, int snapshot_port,
const std::string &incremental_ip, int incremental_port)
      : incoming_md_updates_(market_updates), run_(false),
        logger_("trading_market_data_consumer_" + std::
          to_string(client_id) + ".log"),
        incremental_mcast_socket_(logger_),
        snapshot_mcast_sccket_(logger_),
        iface_(iface), snapshot_ip_(snapshot_ip),
        snapshot_port_(snapshot_port) {
```

The constructor performs the following tasks:

- As we mentioned, the constructor creates a `Logger` instance for this class and uses that `logger_` object to initialize the `incremental_mcast_socket_` variable and the `snapshot_mcast_socket_` variable. It also initializes the `iface_`, `snapshot_ip_`, and `snapshot_port_` members from the arguments passed to it.

- Using the `recv_callback()` lambda method, it initializes the `recv_callback_` variable in the `incremental_mcast_socket_` variable and the `snapshot_mcast_socket_` variable. The lambda just forwards the callbacks to the `recvCallback()` member method in the `MarketDataConsumer` class, which we will see later. The key point here is that we expect the `MarketDataConsumer::recvCallback()` method to be called when there is data available on the incremental or the snapshot multicast sockets.

- The last thing the constructor does is fully initialize `incremental_mcast_socket_` by calling the `McastSocket::init()` method, which creates the actual socket internally. It also calls the `McastSocket::join()` method to subscribe to the multicast stream for this socket. Note that we do not do the same for `snapshot_mcast_socket_` yet. That is done on demand as packet drops or sequence gaps are detected:

```
auto recv_callback = [this](auto socket) {
  recvCallback(socket);
};
```

```
    incremental_mcast_socket_.recv_callback_ =
      recv_callback;
    ASSERT(incremental_mcast_socket_.init(incremental_ip,
      iface, incremental_port, /*is_listening*/ true) >= 0,
        "Unable to create incremental mcast socket.
          error:" + std::string(std::strerror(errno)));

    ASSERT(incremental_mcast_socket_.join(incremental_ip,
      iface, incremental_port),
        "Join failed on:" + std::to_string
          (incremental_mcast_socket_.fd_) + " error:" +
            std::string(std::strerror(errno)));

    snapshot_mcast_socket_.recv_callback_ = recv_callback;
  }
```

We add a `start()` method like what we have seen for our other components on the side of the trading exchange. This sets the `run_` variable to be `true` and creates and launches a thread to execute the `MarketDataConsumer::run()` method, which we will build later:

```
  auto start() {
    run_ = true;
    ASSERT(Common::createAndStartThread(-1,
      "Trading/MarketDataConsumer", [this]() { run(); })
        != nullptr, "Failed to start MarketData
          thread.");
  }
```

The destructor for this class is straightforward and calls the `stop()` method, which simply sets the `run_` flag to `false` to end the execution of the `run()` method:

```
  ~MarketDataConsumer() {
    stop();

    using namespace std::literals::chrono_literals;
    std::this_thread::sleep_for(5s);
  }
  auto stop() -> void {
    run_ = false;
  }
```

Now that we have initialized the `MarketDataConsumer` class, we will first look at the main `run()` loop, which executes a loop of consuming multicast traffic from the exchange.

Running the market data consumer main loop

The `run()` method is simple for our market data consumer component. It simply calls the `sendAndRecv()` method on the `incremental_mcast_socket_` socket and the `snapshot_mcast_socket_` object, which in our case, consumes any additional data received on the incremental or snapshot channels and dispatches the callbacks:

```
auto MarketDataConsumer::run() noexcept -> void {
  logger_.log("%:% %() %\n", __FILE__, __LINE__,
    __FUNCTION__, Common::getCurrentTimeStr(&time_str_));
  while (run_) {
    incremental_mcast_socket_.sendAndRecv();
    snapshot_mcast_socket_.sendAndRecv();
  }
}
```

The next section deals with the data available on the network sockets within the `recvCallback()` method that get dispatched from the previous logic.

Processing market data updates and handling packet drops

This section implements important functionality responsible for processing market data updates received on the incremental and the snapshot streams. Market updates on the incremental stream are received during the entire runtime of the `MarketDataConsumer` component. However, data is received and processed from the snapshot stream only when a sequence number gap is detected on the incremental stream, which causes `MarketDataConsumer` to initialize `snapshot_mcast_socket_` and subscribe to the snapshot multicast stream. Remember that in the constructor of `MarketDataConsumer`, we intentionally did not fully initialize `snapshot_mcast_socket_` as we did with the `incremental_mcast_socket_`. The important thing to understand here is that data on the snapshot socket is only received when we are in recovery mode and not otherwise.

The first code block in the `recvCallback()` method determines if the data we are processing came from the incremental or snapshot stream by comparing the file descriptor of the socket on which it was received. In the extremely unlikely edge case that we received data on the snapshot socket but we are not in recovery, we simply log a warning, reset the socket receive buffer index, and return:

```
auto MarketDataConsumer::recvCallback(McastSocket
  *socket) noexcept -> void {
  const auto is_snapshot = (socket->fd_ ==
    snapshot_mcast_socket_.fd_);
  if (UNLIKELY(is_snapshot && !in_recovery_)) {
    socket->next_rcv_valid_index_ = 0;

    logger_.log("%:% %() % WARN Not expecting snapshot
```

```
        messages.\n",
                __FILE__, __LINE__, __FUNCTION__,
                Common::getCurrentTimeStr(&time_str_));

    return;
}
```

Otherwise, we proceed further and read `Exchange::MDPMarketUpdate` messages from the socket buffer using the same code that we have seen before. We go through the data contained in the `socket->rcv_buffer_` buffer and read it in chunks of size equal to the size of `Exchange::MDPMarketUpdate`. The goal here is to read as many full `MDPMarketUpdate` messages as possible until we have read them all from the buffer. We use `reinterpret_cast` to convert the data in the buffer to an object of the `Exchange::MDPMarketUpdate` type:

```
      if (socket->next_rcv_valid_index_ >= sizeof
        (Exchange::MDPMarketUpdate)) {
        size_t i = 0;
        for (; i + sizeof(Exchange::MDPMarketUpdate) <=
          socket->next_rcv_valid_index_; i +=
            sizeof(Exchange::MDPMarketUpdate)) {
          auto request = reinterpret_cast<const
            Exchange::MDPMarketUpdate *>(socket->rcv_buffer_
              + i);
          logger_.log("%:% %() % Received % socket len:%
            %\n", __FILE__, __LINE__, __FUNCTION__,
                    Common::getCurrentTimeStr(&time_str_),
                    (is_snapshot ? "snapshot" :
                      "incremental"), sizeof
                        (Exchange::MDPMarketUpdate),
                          request->toString());
```

For each `MDPMarketUpdate` message, we check the sequence number on the message we just read to see if there is a sequence number gap or not. We set the `in_recovery_` member flag to be `true` if we detect a sequence number gap or if we were already in recovery:

```
          const bool already_in_recovery = in_recovery_;
          in_recovery_ = (already_in_recovery || request->
            seq_num_ != next_exp_inc_seq_num_);
```

First, we will see the handling of the message if we are in recovery mode. In the next code block, we first check the `already_in_recovery_` flag to see if we were previously not in recovery and just started recovery due to this message or not. If we were previously not in recovery and started recovery because we saw a sequence number gap, we call the `startSnapshotSync()` method, which we will see shortly. Just to provide a brief introduction here, the `startSnapshotSync()` method will initialize the `snapshot_mcast_socket_` object and subscribe to the snapshot multicast stream, but more on that later. When in recovery, we call the `queueMessage()` method to store the `MDPMarketUpdate` message we just received. We stay in recovery mode and queue up market data updates on both the snapshot and incremental streams. We will do this until we have a complete snapshot of the book from the snapshot stream and all the incremental messages after the snapshot message to catch up with the incremental stream. We will cover more details on that shortly when we present the actual implementation of the `checkSnapshotSync()` method:

```cpp
if (UNLIKELY(in_recovery_)) {
  if (UNLIKELY(!already_in_recovery)) {
    logger_.log("%:% %() % Packet drops on %
      socket. SeqNum expected:% received:%\n",
        __FILE__, __LINE__, __FUNCTION__,
            Common::getCurrentTimeStr
                (&time_str_), (is_snapshot ?
                  "snapshot" : "incremental"),
                next_exp_inc_seq_num_,
                    request->seq_num_);
    startSnapshotSync();
  }

  queueMessage(is_snapshot, request);
}
```

For the branch where we are not in recovery and the message we received is from the incremental market data stream, we simply update `next_exp_inc_seq_num_`. This a reminder that the `next_exp_inc_seq_num_` variable tracks the next sequence number we expect on the next incremental market data update. We then write the `MEMarketUpdate` message to the `incoming_md_updates_` lock-free queue, which will be consumed by the trading engine component on the other end:

```cpp
else if (!is_snapshot) {
logger_.log("%:% %() % %\n", __FILE__, __LINE__,
  __FUNCTION__,
      Common::getCurrentTimeStr
        (&time_str_), request->toString());

++next_exp_inc_seq_num_;

auto next_write = incoming_md_updates_->
  getNextToWriteTo();
*next_write = std::move(request->
  me_market_update_);
incoming_md_updates_->updateWriteIndex();
```

```
      }
    }
```

Finally, we shift the remaining partial data left in the socket's `rcv_buffer_` buffer and update the next valid receive index for the next read:

```
      memcpy(socket->rcv_buffer_, socket->rcv_buffer_ + i,
        socket->next_rcv_valid_index_ - i);
      socket->next_rcv_valid_index_ -= i;
    }
  }
```

That concludes the implementation of the `recvCallback()` method and we will now look at the methods that handle snapshot subscription and synchronization logic. First, we investigate the `startSnapshotSync()` method, which, as we mentioned before, prepares the `MarketDataConsumer` class to start the snapshot synchronization mechanism on sequence number gaps. The first thing we do for this task is clear the two `std::map` containers – `snapshot_queued_msgs_` and `incremental_queued_msgs_`, which we use to queue up market update messages from the snapshot and incremental streams. Then we initialize the `snapshot_mcast_socket_` object using the `McastSocket::init()` method so that the socket gets created for the `snapshot_ip_` and `snapshot_port_` address. Then we call the `McastSocket::join()` method to start the multicast subscription for the snapshot market data stream. Remember that for multicast sockets, we need to make sure that not only do we have a socket that is reading market data, but we also have to issue the IGMP join membership network-level message so that messages can flow to the application, which is achieved by the call to `snapshot_mcast_socket_.join()`:

```
  auto MarketDataConsumer::startSnapshotSync() -> void {
    snapshot_queued_msgs_.clear();
    incremental_queued_msgs_.clear();

    ASSERT(snapshot_mcast_socket_.init(snapshot_ip_,
      iface_, snapshot_port_, /*is_listening*/ true) >= 0,
         "Unable to create snapshot mcast socket. error:"
           + std::string(std::strerror(errno)));
    ASSERT(snapshot_mcast_socket_.join(snapshot_ip_,
      iface_, snapshot_port_),
         "Join failed on:" + std::to_string
           (snapshot_mcast_socket_.fd_) + " error:" +
             std::string(std::strerror(errno)));
  }
```

The next section handles a very important responsibility of the `MarketDataConsumer` component, which is queueing up market data updates from the snapshot and incremental stream and synchronizing when needed.

Synchronizing with the snapshot stream

The first method we need to implement is the `MarketDataConsumer::queueMessage()` method, which we invoked earlier. This method receives an `MDPMarketUpdate` message and a flag that captures whether it was received from the snapshot stream or the incremental stream.

If the message came over the incremental market data stream, then it adds it to `incremental_queued_msgs_ std::map`. If it is received over the snapshot stream, then first, it checks to see if a market update for that sequence number already exists in the `snapshot_queued_msgs_` container. If the entry for that sequence number already exists in the container, then that means that we are receiving a new snapshot messages cycle and we were not able to successfully recover from the previous snapshot messages cycle. In this case, it clears the `snapshot_queued_msgs_` container since we will have to restart the snapshot recovery process from the beginning. Finally, the `MEMarketUpdate` message is added to the `snapshot_queued_msgs_` container:

```cpp
auto MarketDataConsumer::queueMessage(bool is_snapshot,
                                      const Exchange::
                                      MDPMarketUpdate
                                      *request) {
  if (is_snapshot) {
    if (snapshot_queued_msgs_.find(request->seq_num_) !=
      snapshot_queued_msgs_.end()) {
      logger_.log("%:% %() % Packet drops on snapshot
        socket. Received for a 2nd time:%\n", __FILE__,
          __LINE__, __FUNCTION__,
            Common::getCurrentTimeStr(&time_str_),
              request->toString());
      snapshot_queued_msgs_.clear();
    }
    snapshot_queued_msgs_[request->seq_num_] = request->
      me_market_update_;
  } else {
    incremental_queued_msgs_[request->seq_num_] =
      request->me_market_update_;
  }
```

After the new message is queued in the correct container, we call the `checkSnapshotSync()` method to see if we can successfully recover from the snapshot and the incremental messages we have queued up so far:

```
    logger_.log("%:% %() % size snapshot:% incremental:% %
      => %\n", __FILE__, __LINE__, __FUNCTION__,
            Common::getCurrentTimeStr(&time_str_),
            snapshot_queued_msgs_.size(),
            incremental_queued_msgs_.size(),
            request->seq_num_, request->
            toString());

    checkSnapshotSync();
}
```

Now, we will implement the last and most important method in the `MarketDataConsumer` class – `checkSnapshotSync()`, which inspects the queued `MEMarketUpdate` messages in the snapshot and incremental containers to see if we can successfully recover or synchronize with the snapshot and incremental streams and *catch up*:

1. The logic is to queue up messages received on the snapshot and incremental market data streams.
2. Then, when we receive `MarketUpdateType::SNAPSHOT_END`, we make sure that no messages were dropped on the snapshot market data stream by checking that there is no gap in the sequence number field on the snapshot messages.
3. Then, we inspect the queued market updates from the incremental data stream and check to see if we have messages following the last message that was used to synthesize this round of snapshot messages. We do this by checking if we have market updates in the incremental queue starting with a sequence number equal to the `OrderId + 1` value from the `SNAPSHOT_END` message in the snapshot queue.
4. Finally, we check to make sure that from that point on in the incremental queued messages, we do not have another gap.

To better understand how the snapshot recovery logic works, we present *Figure 8.2*, a concrete example of when recovery is possible:

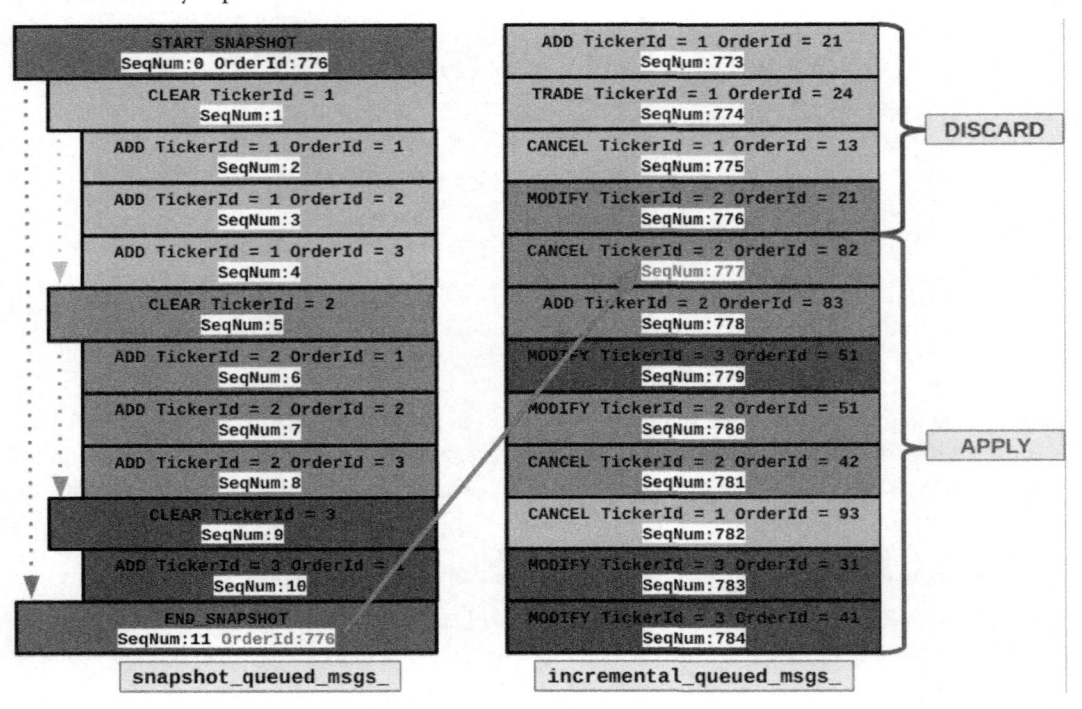

snapshot_queued_msgs_	incremental_queued_msgs_	
START_SNAPSHOT SeqNum:0 OrderId:776	ADD TickerId = 1 OrderId = 21 SeqNum:773	
CLEAR TickerId = 1 SeqNum:1	TRADE TickerId = 1 OrderId = 24 SeqNum:774	DISCARD
ADD TickerId = 1 OrderId = 1 SeqNum:2	CANCEL TickerId = 1 OrderId = 13 SeqNum:775	
ADD TickerId = 1 OrderId = 2 SeqNum:3	MODIFY TickerId = 2 OrderId = 21 SeqNum:776	
ADD TickerId = 1 OrderId = 3 SeqNum:4	CANCEL TickerId = 2 OrderId = 82 SeqNum:777	
CLEAR TickerId = 2 SeqNum:5	ADD TickerId = 2 OrderId = 83 SeqNum:778	
ADD TickerId = 2 OrderId = 1 SeqNum:6	MODIFY TickerId = 3 OrderId = 51 SeqNum:779	
ADD TickerId = 2 OrderId = 2 SeqNum:7	MODIFY TickerId = 2 OrderId = 51 SeqNum:780	APPLY
ADD TickerId = 2 OrderId = 3 SeqNum:8	CANCEL TickerId = 2 OrderId = 42 SeqNum:781	
CLEAR TickerId = 3 SeqNum:9	CANCEL TickerId = 1 OrderId = 93 SeqNum:782	
ADD TickerId = 3 OrderId = SeqNum:10	MODIFY TickerId = 3 OrderId = 31 SeqNum:783	
END_SNAPSHOT SeqNum:11 OrderId:776	MODIFY TickerId = 3 OrderId = 41 SeqNum:784	

Figure 8.2 – Example state of snapshot and incremental queues when recovery is possible

Applying the logic we just presented in *Figure 8.2*, we first check the `snapshot_queued_msgs_` container to make sure we have a `SNAPSHOT_START` message and a `SNAPSHOT_END` message. We also make sure that we do not have any gaps in the snapshot messages by checking the sequence numbers, which start from zero and increment by one for each message. We find the last sequence number, which was used to synthesize this snapshot from the `SNAPSHOT_END` message and use the order ID field in that message, which in this case, is set to **776**.

Once we determine that we have a complete sequence of snapshot messages, we check the queue of incremental market data updates. All queued-up incremental messages with a sequence number less than or equal to **776** will be discarded since the snapshot messages incorporate that information. Then we process/apply all the queued-up incremental updates starting with sequence number **777** and making sure that we do not have a gap in the incremental queued-up messages. We achieve that by checking the sequence number field on those messages and making sure there is no gap in it. Once we have processed all the queued-up incremental market data updates, we are done. At this point, we have finished the recovery/synchronization process and are *caught up*. Now that we understand how the logic is supposed to work, let us look at the C++ implementation of the `checkSnapshotSync()` method.

First, we check if the `snapshot_queued_msgs_` container is empty. Obviously, we cannot recover since we need a full snapshot messages cycle and all the incremental messages from that point on to catch up with the incremental stream:

```
auto MarketDataConsumer::checkSnapshotSync() -> void {
  if (snapshot_queued_msgs_.empty()) {
    return;
  }
```

The next thing we need to check is if we have `MEMarketUpdate` of the `MarketUpdateType::SNAPSHOT_START` type. Otherwise, we clear the queue and wait for the next round of snapshot messages:

```
    const auto &first_snapshot_msg =
      snapshot_queued_msgs_.begin()->second;
    if (first_snapshot_msg.type_ != Exchange::
      MarketUpdateType::SNAPSHOT_START) {
      logger_.log("%:% %() % Returning because have not
        seen a SNAPSHOT_START yet.\n",
                __FILE__, __LINE__, __FUNCTION__,
                  Common::getCurrentTimeStr(&time_str_));
      snapshot_queued_msgs_.clear();
      return;
    }
```

Next, we will iterate through the queued snapshot messages and make sure that there is no gap in the snapshot messages we queued up by checking the sequence numbers. Remember that the key in the `snapshot_queued_msgs_` container is actually the `seq_num_` field from the `MDPMarketUpdate` messages. If we detect a gap in the snapshot messages, we set the `have_complete_snapshot` flag to `false` and exit out of the loop. We collect each message from the snapshot queue into the `final_events` container of type `std::vector` of `MEMarketUpdate` messages, which will be the container of all the events we will process if we successfully recover from this snapshot:

```
    std::vector<Exchange::MEMarketUpdate> final_events;

    auto have_complete_snapshot = true;
    size_t next_snapshot_seq = 0;
    for (auto &snapshot_itr: snapshot_queued_msgs_) {
      logger_.log("%:% %() % % => %\n", __FILE__, __LINE__,
        __FUNCTION__,
                Common::getCurrentTimeStr(&time_str_),
                  snapshot_itr.first,
                    snapshot_itr.second.toString());
      if (snapshot_itr.first != next_snapshot_seq) {
```

```cpp
            have_complete_snapshot = false;
            logger_.log("%:% %() % Detected gap in snapshot 
              stream expected:% found:% %.\n", __FILE__, 
                __LINE__, __FUNCTION__, 
                    Common::getCurrentTimeStr(&time_str_), 
                        next_snapshot_seq, 
                            snapshot_itr.first, snapshot_itr.
                                second.toString()); 
          break;
        }

        if (snapshot_itr.second.type_ != 
          Exchange::MarketUpdateType::SNAPSHOT_START && 
            snapshot_itr.second.type_ != 
              Exchange::MarketUpdateType::SNAPSHOT_END) 
          final_events.push_back(snapshot_itr.second);

        ++next_snapshot_seq;
      }
```

Once we finish the loop, we check the `have_complete_snapshot` flag to see if we found a gap in the snapshot messages or not. If the flag is set to `false`, meaning we found a gap, we clear the `snapshot_queued_msgs_` container and return, since we cannot recover and must wait for the next round of snapshot messages:

```cpp
      if (!have_complete_snapshot) {
        logger_.log("%:% %() % Returning because found gaps 
          in snapshot stream.\n", 
                __FILE__, __LINE__, __FUNCTION__, 
                    Common::getCurrentTimeStr(&time_str_)); 
        snapshot_queued_msgs_.clear();
        return;
      }
```

Assuming we made it this far, we extract the last message in the queue of snapshot messages and make sure that it is of the `MarketUpdateType::SNAPSHOT_END` type since we will need to use the `order_id_` field in this message to process the incremental queue of messages:

```cpp
      const auto &last_snapshot_msg = snapshot_queued_msgs_
        .rbegin()->second;
      if (last_snapshot_msg.type_ != Exchange::
        MarketUpdateType::SNAPSHOT_END) { 
        logger_.log("%:% %() % Returning because have not 
          seen a SNAPSHOT_END yet.\n",
```

```
                    __FILE__, __LINE__, __FUNCTION__,
                    Common::getCurrentTimeStr(&time_str_));
    return;
  }
```

Now, we move on to inspecting the queued incremental messages to see if we can synchronize successfully. We define a `have_complete_incremental` boolean flag, which will represent if we have all the messages from the incremental stream without any gaps. We also set the `next_exp_inc_seq_num_` member variable to be `last_snapshot_msg.order_id_ + 1` from the SNAPSHOT_END message:

```
auto have_complete_incremental = true;
size_t num_incrementals = 0;
next_exp_inc_seq_num_ = last_snapshot_msg.order_id_ + 1;
```

Now we iterate through all the messages in our `incremental_queued_msgs_` container. We discard the messages that have sequence numbers less than the `next_exp_inc_seq_num_` variable we just assigned. Otherwise, we make sure that there are no gaps in the queue of incremental messages by making sure that the sequence number on the next message is equal to `next_exp_inc_seq_num_` and setting the `have_complete_incremental` flag to `false` if we detect a gap:

```
for (auto inc_itr = incremental_queued_msgs_.begin();
  inc_itr != incremental_queued_msgs_.end(); ++inc_itr) {
  logger_.log("%:% %() % Checking next_exp:% vs. seq:%
    %.\n", __FILE__, __LINE__, __FUNCTION__,
          Common::getCurrentTimeStr(&time_str_),
            next_exp_inc_seq_num_, inc_itr->first,
              inc_itr->second.toString());

  if (inc_itr->first < next_exp_inc_seq_num_)
    continue;

  if (inc_itr->first != next_exp_inc_seq_num_) {
    logger_.log("%:% %() % Detected gap in incremental
      stream expected:% found:% %.\n", __FILE__,
        __LINE__, __FUNCTION__,
          Common::getCurrentTimeStr(&time_str_),
            next_exp_inc_seq_num_, inc_itr->
              first, inc_itr->second.toString());
    have_complete_incremental = false;
    break;
  }
```

If we do not detect a gap in the market update message from the incremental queue, we add it to the `final_events` container as we did before. We also increment the `next_exp_inc_seq_num_` variable, since that is the next sequence number we expect if there are no gaps:

```cpp
      logger_.log("%:% %() % % => %\n", __FILE__, __LINE__,
        __FUNCTION__,
                  Common::getCurrentTimeStr(&time_str_),
                    inc_itr->first, inc_itr->second
                      .toString());

      if (inc_itr->second.type_ != Exchange::
        MarketUpdateType::SNAPSHOT_START &&
          inc_itr->second.type_ != Exchange::
            MarketUpdateType::SNAPSHOT_END)
        final_events.push_back(inc_itr->second);

      ++next_exp_inc_seq_num_;
      ++num_incrementals;
    }
```

After exiting the loop, we check the `have_complete_incremental` flag to make sure there was no gap in the queue of incremental updates. If we did find a gap, we clear the `snapshot_queued_msgs_` container and return, since we cannot successfully synchronize:

```cpp
    if (!have_complete_incremental) {
      logger_.log("%:% %() % Returning because have gaps in
        queued incrementals.\n",
                  __FILE__, __LINE__, __FUNCTION__,
                    Common::getCurrentTimeStr(&time_str_));
      snapshot_queued_msgs_.clear();
      return;
    }
```

At this point, we have successfully recovered, so we iterate through all the `MEMarketUpdate` messages in the `final_events` container and write them to the `incoming_md_updates_` lock-free queue to be sent to the trading engine component:

```cpp
    for (const auto &itr: final_events) {
      auto next_write = incoming_md_updates_->
        getNextToWriteTo();
      *next_write = itr;
      incoming_md_updates_->updateWriteIndex();
    }
```

Finally, we clear the `snapshot_queued_msgs_` container and the `incremental_queued_msgs_` container and set the `in_recovery_` flag to `false` since we are no longer in recovery mode. Finally, we call the `McastSocket::leave()` method on `snapshot_mcast_socket_`, since we no longer need to be subscribed to the snapshot stream or receive or process the snapshot messages:

```
    logger_.log("%:% %() % Recovered % snapshot and %
      incremental orders.\n", __FILE__, __LINE__,
        __FUNCTION__,
             Common::getCurrentTimeStr(&time_str_),
               snapshot_queued_msgs_.size() - 2,
                 num_incrementals);

  snapshot_queued_msgs_.clear();
  incremental_queued_msgs_.clear();
  in_recovery_ = false;

  snapshot_mcast_socket_.leave(snapshot_ip_,
    snapshot_port_);;
}
```

With this method, we have concluded the design and implementation of our `MarketDataConsumer` component. Next, we will move on to the topic of constructing the limit order book inside the trading engine from these market data update messages.

Building order books from market data

In the previous section, we built the market data consumer component, which subscribes to the market data stream, synchronizes between the snapshot and incremental streams, and decodes the market data updates and publishes them to the trading engine component. The trading engine component then needs to process these market data updates and build a limited order book like the one that the matching engine builds, except this is a much more limited version of the matching engine's order book. As a reminder, we discussed this in the chapter *Designing Our Trading Ecosystem* in the *Designing a framework for low latency C++ trading algorithms* section. One last thing to note is that we will re-use the design and code of the order book in the matching engine to create the order book in the client's system. We will re-use the source code we built in the chapter *Building the C++ Matching Engine* in the *Building the order book and matching orders* section. Now, let us get started with the implementation of the order book, which we will call `MarketOrderBook`, to easily differentiate it from the order book inside the matching engine, which was called `MEOrderBook`.

Defining the structures for the market order book

First, we will define the structures and types that make up the `MarketOrderBook` data structure. We use an identical design here as we did for the `MEOrderBook` class, and that design is presented in *Figure 8.3*. We recommend revisiting the design of the order book and the motivation behind the different choices presented in the *Building the C++ Matching Engine* chapter in the *Designing the exchange order book* section.

Each order is represented in a `MarketOrder` struct, which is a subset of the `MEOrder` struct we built for the matching engine. We will also have an `OrderHashMap` type, as we did in the matching engine, which will be a hash map from `OrderId` to these `MarketOrder` objects. Orders at the same price are held in a `MarketOrdersAtPrice` struct as we did in the matching engine, which will be a doubly linked list of `MarketOrder` objects. Remember that we need this structure to maintain all the orders with the same price and side attribute and arrange them in FIFO order. We will also build an `OrdersAtPriceHashMap` map, as we did in the matching engine to be a hash map from `Price` to these `MarketOrdersAtPrice` objects. The design is represented in *Figure 8.3*, which is similar to the diagram we presented for the order book in the matching engine, except with different structures in this case:

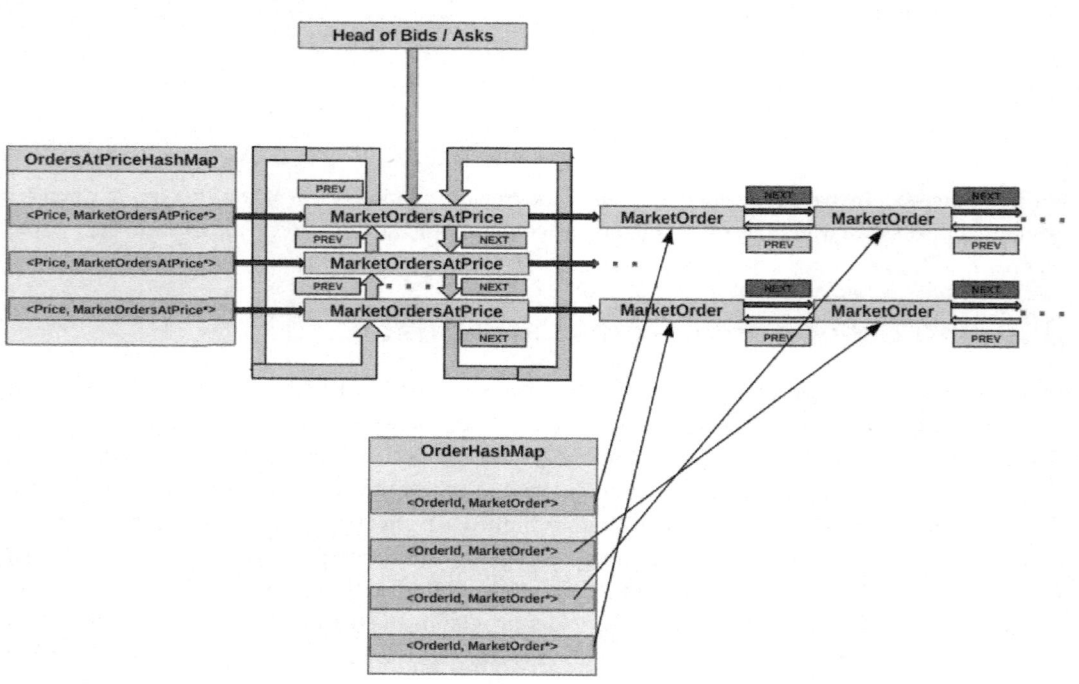

Figure 8.3 – Architecture of the limit order book in the market participant's trading engine

All the source code for the structures and types we define in the next two sub-sections can be found in the `Chapter8/trading/strategy/market_order.h` source file and the `Chapter8/trading/strategy/market_order.cpp` source file. Let us get started with the `MarketOrderBook` implementation by first defining the data structures and types we will need.

Defining the MarketOrder structure and OrderHashMap type

First, we will define the `MarketOrder` structure, which represents a single order in the market data stream. This structure contains the `OrderId`, `Side`, `Price`, `Qty`, and `Priority` attributes. It also contains a `prev_order_` and a `next_order_` member of type `MarketOrder` pointer since we will chain these objects in a doubly linked list:

```cpp
#pragma once

#include <array>
#include <sstream>
#include "common/types.h"

using namespace Common;

namespace Trading {
  struct MarketOrder {
    OrderId order_id_ = OrderId_INVALID;
    Side side_ = Side::INVALID;
    Price price_ = Price_INVALID;
    Qty qty_ = Qty_INVALID;
    Priority priority_ = Priority_INVALID;

    MarketOrder *prev_order_ = nullptr;
    MarketOrder *next_order_ = nullptr;
```

The constructor is straightforward; it simply initializes the fields it is provided in the constructor:

```cpp
    // only needed for use with MemPool.
    MarketOrder() = default;

    MarketOrder(OrderId order_id, Side side, Price price,
      Qty qty, Priority priority, MarketOrder *prev_order,
        MarketOrder *next_order) noexcept
        : order_id_(order_id), side_(side), price_(price),
          qty_(qty), priority_(priority),
            prev_order_(prev_order),
              next_order_(next_order) {}

    auto toString() const -> std::string;
  };
```

We also define the `OrderHashMap` type, which is an `std::array` array of `MarketOrder` pointer objects and of size `ME_MAX_ORDER_IDS`, in the same way as we did in the matching engine order book:

```cpp
  typedef std::array<MarketOrder *, ME_MAX_ORDER_IDS> OrderHashMap;
```

The `toString()` method we will use for logging purposes is self-explanatory:

```
auto MarketOrder::toString() const -> std::string {
  std::stringstream ss;
  ss << "MarketOrder" << "["
     << "oid:" << orderIdToString(order_id_) << " "
     << "side:" << sideToString(side_) << " "
     << "price:" << priceToString(price_) << " "
     << "qty:" << qtyToString(qty_) << " "
     << "prio:" << priorityToString(priority_) << " "
     << "prev:" << orderIdToString(prev_order_ ?
          prev_order_->order_id_ : OrderId_INVALID) << " "
     << "next:" << orderIdToString(next_order_ ?
        next_order_->order_id_ : OrderId_INVALID) << "]";

  return ss.str();
}
```

Next, we will define the `MarketOrdersAtPrice` structure, which holds a linked list of `MarketOrder` objects.

Defining the MarketOrdersAtPrice structure and OrdersAtPriceHashMap type

The `MarketOrdersAtPrice` struct is identical to the `MEOrdersAtPrice` struct we built for the matching `MEOrderBook` engine. It contains `Side`, `Price`, and a `MarketOrder first_mkt_order_` pointer to represent the beginning of the `MarketOrder`-linked list at this price. It also contains two `MarketOrdersAtPrice` pointers, `prev_entry_` and `next_entry_`, since we will create a doubly linked list of `MarketOrdersAtPrice` objects to represent the price levels:

```
struct MarketOrdersAtPrice {
  Side side_ = Side::INVALID;
  Price price_ = Price_INVALID;

  MarketOrder *first_mkt_order_ = nullptr;

  MarketOrdersAtPrice *prev_entry_ = nullptr;
  MarketOrdersAtPrice *next_entry_ = nullptr;
```

The constructors for this class are self-explanatory. It simply initializes the data members with the arguments provided:

```
MarketOrdersAtPrice() = default;

MarketOrdersAtPrice(Side side, Price price, MarketOrder
  *first_mkt_order, MarketOrdersAtPrice *prev_entry,
```

```
                    MarketOrdersAtPrice *next_entry)
        : side_(side), price_(price),
          first_mkt_order_(first_mkt_order),
            prev_entry_(prev_entry),
              next_entry_(next_entry) { }
```

The `toString()` method is identical to the one in the matching engine, so we will skip repeating it here:

```
    auto toString() const;
};
```

Finally, `OrdersAtPriceHashMap` is identical to the one we built for the matching engine. It represents a hash map from `Price` to `MarketOrdersAtPrice` pointers:

```
typedef std::array<MarketOrdersAtPrice *,
  ME_MAX_PRICE_LEVELS> OrdersAtPriceHashMap;
```

Now, we can finally implement the `MarketOrderBook` class in the next section, but before that, we need to define one more structure that will be used by various components to build a view of the **Best Bid Offer** (**BBO**).

Defining the BBO structure

Finally, we need to define another structure that will represent the total quantity available at the best bid and ask prices. This will represent the best (most aggressive) buy and sell prices available in the market as well as the sum of the quantities of all the orders at those prices. This structure, called **BBO**, only has four members – `bid_price_` and `ask_price_` (both `Price` types to represent the best prices), and `bid_qty_` and `ask_qty_` to represent the total quantity of all orders at these prices.

The BBO abstraction is used by many different components inside the trade engine. Typically, this is used by components that need a summary of the best market prices and liquidity, instead of the full depth of the book and all the details about each order in the book. For example, a component such as the `RiskManager` component, which only needs to compute the open **Profit and Loss** (**PnL**) for an open position when the top-of-book prices change, does not need access to the full order book and instead can be simplified using a BBO abstraction. Other components, such as `FeatureEngine`, `PositionKeeper`, `LiquidityTaker`, and `MarketMaker`, also use the BBO abstraction where the full order book is not needed.

To make it easy to log such objects, we will also add a `toString()` method:

```
struct BBO {
  Price bid_price_ = Price_INVALID, ask_price_ =
    Price_INVALID;
  Qty bid_qty_ = Qty_INVALID, ask_qty_ = Qty_INVALID;
```

```cpp
    auto toString() const {
      std::stringstream ss;
      ss << "BBO{"
         << qtyToString(bid_qty_) << "@" <<
           priceToString(bid_price_)
         << "X"
         << priceToString(ask_price_) << "@" <<
           qtyToString(ask_qty_)
         << "}";

      return ss.str();
    };
  };
```

Now, we can finally move on to our implementation of the `MarketOrderBook` class.

Defining the data members in the order book

To build the `MarketOrderBook` class, we first need to define the data members in this class. All the source code for this class can be found in the `Chapter8/trading/strategy/market_order_book.h` source file and the `Chapter8/trading/strategy/market_order_book.cpp` source file.

The important data members in this class are the following:

- A `trade_engine_` variable of the `TradeEngine` pointer type. We have not defined this class yet, but we will in this chapter. For now, it represents the class that is the trading engine framework. We will communicate changes to the order book using this variable.

- Two memory pools, `order_pool_` for `MarketOrder` objects and `orders_at_price_pool_` for `MarketOrdersAtPrice` objects, are to be used to allocate and deallocate these objects as needed. The first pool, `order_pool_`, is used to allocate and deallocate `MarketOrder` objects. The second pool, `orders_at_price_pool_`, is used to allocate and deallocate `MarketOrdersAtPrice` objects. Remember that a single `MemPool` instance is tied to a specific object type provided to it as a template parameter.

- A `bbo_` variable of the `BBO` type, which will be used to compute and maintain a BBO-view of the order book when there are updates and provided to any components that require it.

- An `oid_to_order_` variable of the `OrderHashMap` type will be used to track `MarketOrder` objects by `OrderId`.

- A `price_orders_at_price_` variable of the `OrdersAtPriceHashMap` type to track `OrdersAtPrice` objects by `Price`.

- Two pointers to `MarketOrdersAtPrice` – `bids_by_price_` to represent the doubly linked list of bids sorted by price and `asks_by_price_` to represent the doubly linked list of asks sorted by price.
- Finally, some variables that are not so important, such as `ticker_id_`, `time_str_`, and `logger_` for logging purposes:

```
#pragma once

#include "common/types.h"
#include "common/mem_pool.h"
#include "common/logging.h"

#include "market_order.h"
#include "exchange/market_data/market_update.h"

namespace Trading {
  class TradeEngine;

  class MarketOrderBook final {
  private:
    const TickerId ticker_id_;

    TradeEngine *trade_engine_ = nullptr;

    OrderHashMap oid_to_order_;

    MemPool<MarketOrdersAtPrice> orders_at_price_pool_;
    MarketOrdersAtPrice *bids_by_price_ = nullptr;
    MarketOrdersAtPrice *asks_by_price_ = nullptr;

    OrdersAtPriceHashMap price_orders_at_price_;

    MemPool<MarketOrder> order_pool_;

    BBO bbo_;

    std::string time_str_;
    Logger *logger_ = nullptr;
  };
```

We will also define a `MarketOrderBookHashMap` type, which is just a hash map from `TickerId` to `MarketOrderBook` objects of the `ME_MAX_TICKERS` size. This constant, as well as the others we will encounter in the next code snippet, were defined in the *Building the C++ Matching Engine* chapter in the *Defining the operations and interactions in our matching engine* section, within the *Defining some types and constants* sub-section:

```
typedef std::array<MarketOrderBook *, ME_MAX_TICKERS>
  MarketOrderBookHashMap;
}
```

Next, we will see how to initialize the `MarketOrderBook` class and its member variables.

Initializing the order book

In this sub-section, we will implement the code to initialize the `MarketOrderBook` class as well as its internal data members. The constructor is straightforward and accepts the `TickerId` and `Logger` instances it will use to log. It initializes `orders_at_price_pool_` of `MarketOrdersAtPrice` objects to be of the `ME_MAX_PRICE_LEVELS` size and `order_pool_` of the `MarketOrder` objects to be of the `ME_MAX_ORDER_IDS` size:

```cpp
#include "market_order_book.h"

#include "trade_engine.h"

namespace Trading {
  MarketOrderBook::MarketOrderBook(TickerId ticker_id,
    Logger *logger)
      : ticker_id_(ticker_id),
        orders_at_price_pool_(ME_MAX_PRICE_LEVELS),
          order_pool_(ME_MAX_ORDER_IDS), logger_(logger) {
  }
```

The destructor for this class just resets the internal data members:

```cpp
MarketOrderBook::~MarketOrderBook() {
  logger_->log("%:% %() % OrderBook\n%\n", __FILE__,
    __LINE__, __FUNCTION__,
            Common::getCurrentTimeStr(&time_str_),
              toString(false, true));

  trade_engine_ = nullptr;
  bids_by_price_ = asks_by_price_ = nullptr;
  oid_to_order_.fill(nullptr);
}
```

There is an additional utility method called `setTradeEngine()`, which is a better method to set the `trade_engine_` variable with an instance of a `TradeEngine` object:

```
  auto setTradeEngine(TradeEngine *trade_engine) {
    trade_engine_ = trade_engine;
  }
```

Now that we have seen how to initialize our `MarketOrderBook` class, we will discuss the most important functionality for this class, which is updating the order book from `MEMarketUpdate` messages that it will receive from the `TradeEngine` engine.

Processing market updates and updating the order book

The `onMarketUpdate()` method is called along with the `MEMarketUpdate` message that needs to be processed. This method updates the order book from the market update, which is passed as an argument. We will understand the source code to handle these messages, but we will go code block by code block for each case of `MarketUpdateType`.

Before we get into the handling of the actual messages, we will first initialize a `bid_updated` boolean flag and an `ask_updated` boolean flag, which will represent if BBO will need to be updated because of this market update. We figure that out by checking if the market update we received corresponds to `side_ == Side::BUY` and `price_` of `market_update` is equal to or greater than `price_` of the current best bid, which we fetch from the `bids_by_price_->price_` variable. We do the same thing for the ask side by checking for `Side::SELL` on `market_update_->side_` and checking if `price_` of `market_update` is less than or equal to the price of the best ask (`asks_by_price_->price_`):

```
  auto MarketOrderBook::onMarketUpdate(const
    Exchange::MEMarketUpdate *market_update) noexcept -> void {
    const auto bid_updated = (bids_by_price_ &&
      market_update->side_ == Side::BUY && market_update->
        price_ >= bids_by_price_->price_);
    const auto ask_updated = (asks_by_price_ &&
      market_update->side_ == Side::SELL && market_update->
        price_ <= asks_by_price_->price_);
```

First, we see the handling for `MarketUpdateType::ADD`. We will allocate a new `MarketOrder` object and call the `addOrder()` method on it. This `addOrder()` method is identical to the `addOrder()` method we built for the matching engine except it operates on `MarketOrder` and `MarketOrdersAtPrice` objects. We will discuss this `addOrder()` method briefly in the next sub-section, but we will not be fully re-implementing it since we have seen all the details in the *Building the C++ Matching Engine* chapter:

```
    switch (market_update->type_) {
      case Exchange::MarketUpdateType::ADD: {
        auto order = order_pool_.allocate(market_update->
          order_id_, market_update->side_, market_update->
```

```
        price_,
        market_update->qty_, market_update->priority_,
          nullptr, nullptr);
    addOrder(order);
  }
    break;
```

The handling for the `MarketUpdateType::MODIFY` case finds the `MarketOrder` structure for which the modified message is targeted. It then updates the `qty_` attribute on that order:

```
    case Exchange::MarketUpdateType::MODIFY: {
      auto order = oid_to_order_.at(market_update->
        order_id_);
      order->qty_ = market_update->qty_;
    }
      break;
```

The handling for `MarketUpdateType::CANCEL` is straightforward, and it finds `MarketOrder`, for which the cancel message is, and then calls the `removeOrder()` method on it. The `removeOrder()` method is also identical to the `removeOrder()` method we built for the matching engine order book in the *Building the C++ Matching Engine* chapter, except it operates on `MarketOrder` and `MarketOrdersAtPrice` objects. Again, we will not fully re-implement these methods since they are identical to what we have seen, and the details can be found in that chapter and the source files:

```
    case Exchange::MarketUpdateType::CANCEL: {
      auto order = oid_to_order_.at(market_update->
        order_id_);
      removeOrder(order);
    }
      break;
```

The `MarketUpdateType::TRADE` messages do not change the order book, so here, we simply forward that trade message back to the `TradeEngine` engine using the `onTradeUpdate()` method. One thing to note here is that in the case of `MarketUpdateType::TRADE`, we simply return after calling the `TradeEngine::onTradeUpdate()` method. This is because the trade messages do not update the order book in our market data protocol, so the subsequent code after this `switch case` does not need to be executed:

```
    case Exchange::MarketUpdateType::TRADE: {
      trade_engine_->onTradeUpdate(market_update, this);
      return;
    }
      break;
```

The `MarketOrderBook` class needs to handle the `MarketUpdateType::CLEAR` messages. It receives these messages when the book needs to be cleared because we dropped a packet and are recovering from the snapshot stream. All it does here is deallocate all the valid `MarketOrder` objects in the book and clear the `oid_to_order_` container by setting each entry to `nullptr`. It then iterates through the double-linked list starting with the `bids_by_price_` pointer and deallocates each `MarketOrdersAtPrice` object back to the `orders_at_price_pool_` memory pool. It does the same thing with the `asks_by_price_` linked list and, finally, sets both `bids_by_price_` and `asks_by_price_` to be `nullptr` to represent an empty book:

```cpp
case Exchange::MarketUpdateType::CLEAR: {
  for (auto &order: oid_to_order_) {
    if (order)
      order_pool_.deallocate(order);
  }
  oid_to_order_.fill(nullptr);

  if(bids_by_price_) {
    for(auto bid = bids_by_price_->next_entry_; bid
      != bids_by_price_; bid = bid->next_entry_)
      orders_at_price_pool_.deallocate(bid);
    orders_at_price_pool_.deallocate(bids_by_price_);
  }

  if(asks_by_price_) {
    for(auto ask = asks_by_price_->next_entry_; ask
      != asks_by_price_; ask = ask->next_entry_)
      orders_at_price_pool_.deallocate(ask);
    orders_at_price_pool_.deallocate(asks_by_price_);
  }

  bids_by_price_ = asks_by_price_ = nullptr;
}
  break;
```

The `MarketOrderBook` class does not need to handle `INVALID`, `SNAPSHOT_START`, and `SNAPSHOT_END` `MarketUpdateType`s, so it does nothing with those messages:

```cpp
case Exchange::MarketUpdateType::INVALID:
case Exchange::MarketUpdateType::SNAPSHOT_START:
case Exchange::MarketUpdateType::SNAPSHOT_END:
  break;
}
```

At this point, we will call the `updateBBO()` method and pass it to the two boolean flags we computed: `bid_updated` and `ask_updated`. We will look at the implementation of this method shortly, but for now, you should understand that it will use the two boolean flags passed to it to decide if it needs to update the bid side or the ask side BBO values:

```
updateBBO(bid_updated, ask_updated);
```

Finally, it notifies the `TradeEngine` engine that the order book was updated using the `onOrderBookUpdate()` method, which we will discuss later in this chapter and enrich further in the next chapter:

```
    trade_engine_->onOrderBookUpdate(market_update->
      ticker_id_, market_update->price_, market_update->
        side_);

    logger_->log("%:% %() % OrderBook\n%\n", __FILE__,
      __LINE__, __FUNCTION__,
                Common::getCurrentTimeStr(&time_str_),
                toString(false, true));
  }
```

Before we conclude this section, let us look at the implementation of the `updateBBO()` method we referred to before. The implementation itself is relatively straightforward, so let us look at the handling for the bid side first. Once we understand how we handle the bid side, understanding the ask side will be very simple since it is exactly the same. The first thing we do is check if the `update_bid` parameter passed to it is `true`. Only then do we have to update the bid side of the BBO object. Next, we check if the `bids_by_price_` member is not `nullptr`. If it is not valid, then we set the `bid_price_` variable and the `bid_qty_` variable to be invalid (`Price_INVALID` and `Qty_INVALID` respectively) since the side is empty. The more interesting handling is in the case where the `bids_by_price_` member is valid.

In that case, we set the bid_price_ member variable in the `bbo_` object to be the price of the best bid: `bids_by_price_->price_`. To compute `bid_qty_` in the `bbo_` object, we first assign it `qty_` of the first order at that price level, which we access using the `bids_by_price_->first_mkt_order_->qty_` value. Then, we linearly iterate over all the orders at that price level by following the `next_order_` pointers until we wrap around, i.e. the `next_order_` points to the `first_mkt_order_` object. For each order we iterate over, we accumulate the `qty_` value of that order into the `bid_qty_` member in our `bbo_` object. At this point, we are done updating the bid side of the BBO object. Note here that the linear iteration is slightly inefficient and can be improved for example by tracking and updating these values during the processing of the `MEMarketUpdate` messages itself, but we leave that (simple) exercise up to the interested reader:

```
    auto updateBBO(bool update_bid, bool update_ask)
      noexcept {
```

```cpp
      if(update_bid) {
        if(bids_by_price_) {
          bbo_.bid_price_ = bids_by_price_->price_;
          bbo_.bid_qty_ = bids_by_price_->first_mkt_order_-
            >qty_;
          for(auto order = bids_by_price_->
            first_mkt_order_->next_order_; order !=
              bids_by_price_->first_mkt_order_; order =
              order->next_order_)
            bbo_.bid_qty_ += order->qty_;
        }
        else {
          bbo_.bid_price_ = Price_INVALID;
          bbo_.bid_qty_ = Qty_INVALID;
        }
      }
```

The handling for the ask side of the BBO is identical to the handling for the bid side we just discussed. We will not repeat ourselves, but here is that handling:

```cpp
      if(update_ask) {
        if(asks_by_price_) {
          bbo_.ask_price_ = asks_by_price_->price_;
          bbo_.ask_qty_ = asks_by_price_->first_mkt_order_-
            >qty_;
          for(auto order = asks_by_price_->
            first_mkt_order_->next_order_; order !=
              asks_by_price_->first_mkt_order_; order =
              order->next_order_)
            bbo_.ask_qty_ += order->qty_;
        }
        else {
          bbo_.ask_price_ = Price_INVALID;
          bbo_.ask_qty_ = Qty_INVALID;
        }
      }
    }
```

That concludes most of the functionality we need in our `MarketOrderBook` class. In the next sub-section, we will quickly recap a couple of the utility methods we built for the order book in the matching engine, and we will replicate them for the trading engine's order book.

Revisiting the generic utility methods for order book management

In the *Building the C++ Matching Engine* chapter, we built `MEOrderBook` in the matching engine in the *Building the order book and matching orders* section.

We explained and implemented the `priceToIndex()` method and the `getOrdersAtPrice()` method in the *Building the internal data structures* sub-section. We have identical methods in our `MarketOrderBook` class, except they operate on `MarketOrdersAtPrice` instead of `MEOrdersAtPrice`. We will not discuss them again or re-implement them here, but we provide the signatures for those two methods:

```
auto priceToIndex(Price price) const noexcept;
auto getOrdersAtPrice(Price price) const noexcept ->
  MarketOrdersAtPrice;
```

In the *Handling new passive orders* sub-section in that chapter, we explained the logic and implemented the methods `addOrder()` and `addOrdersAtPrice()`. Again, for the `MarketOrderBook` class, the logic is identical except it operates on `MarketOrder` instead of the `MEOrder` structure and `MarketOrdersAtPrice` objects instead of `MEOrdersAtPrice` objects. The signatures for those two methods in the `MarketOrderBook` class are presented here, but we will skip repeating the explanation and source code here since it is identical:

```
auto addOrder(MarketOrder *order) noexcept -> void;
auto addOrdersAtPrice(MarketOrdersAtPrice
  *new_orders_at_price) noexcept;
```

Similarly, in the *Handling order cancellation requests* sub-section, we covered the details behind the `removeOrder()` and `removeOrdersAtPrice()` methods. Again, for our `MarketOrderBook` class, these methods work exactly the same except they operate on the `MarketOrder` and `MarketOrdersAtPrice` structures:

```
Auto removeOrdersAtPrice(Side side, Price price)
  noexcept;
auto removeOrder(MarketOrder *order) noexcept -> void;
```

This concludes the design and implementation of the order book inside the trading engine framework. Next, we need to discuss the order gateway infrastructure component, which is what the `TradeEngine` component will use to communicate with the electronic trading exchange.

Connecting to the exchange and sending and receiving order flow

The order gateway client component in the market participant's trading infrastructure receives order requests from the trading engine through a lock-free queue and sends order responses back to the trading engine through another lock-free queue. It also establishes a TCP connection to the order gateway server in the exchange side infrastructure. It encodes order requests in the exchange's order format and sends them over the TCP connection. It also consumes order responses sent by the exchange over that TCP connection and decodes them from the order data format. We present the order gateway client diagram again to refresh your memory on that component's design.

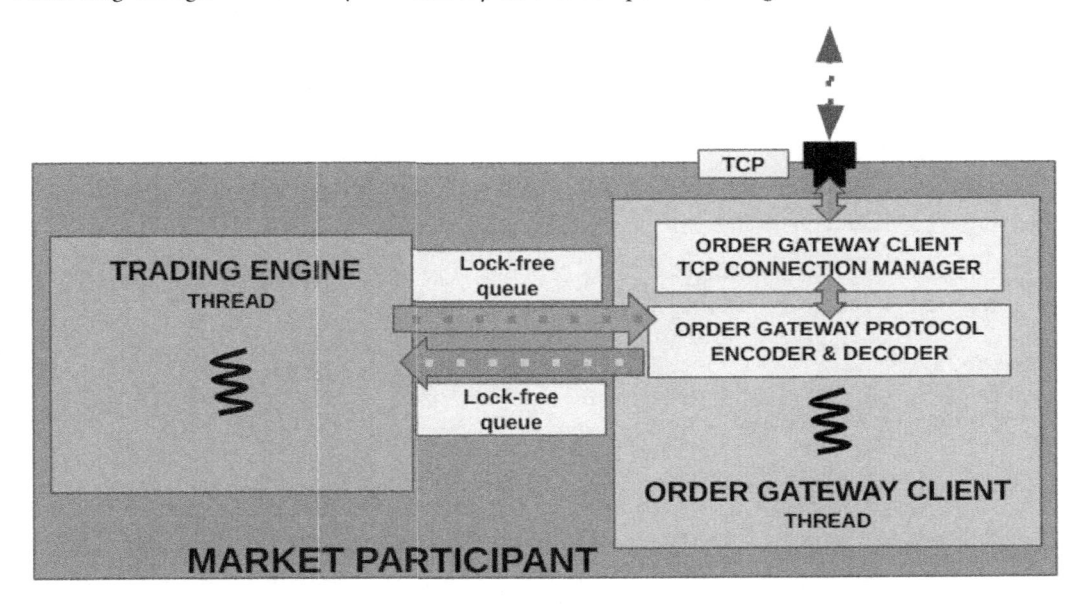

Figure 8.4 – Diagram presenting the order gateway client component inside the client's trading infrastructure

We will start the implementation of this order gateway client component by defining the internal data members of that class first. All the source code for the order gateway client component is in the Chapter8/trading/order_gw/order_gateway.h source file and the Chapter8/trading/order_gw/order_gateway.cpp source files.

Defining the data members in the order gateway client

The important data members in the OrderGateway class are described here:

- Two lock-free queue pointers. The first one is named outgoing_requests_ of the ClientRequestLFQueue type, which we defined before as an LFQueue instance of

`MEClientRequest` structures. The other member is called `incoming_responses_`, which is of the `ClientResponseLFQueue` type, which we also defined earlier as an `LFQueue` instance of the `MEClientResponse` structures. These will be used by `OrderGateway` to receive order requests and send order responses to `TradeEngine`.

- It also contains a `tcp_socket_` member variable of the `TCPSocket` type, which is the TCP socket client to be used to connect to the exchange order gateway server and to send and receive messages.

- Two `size_t` variables to represent sequence numbers. The first one, `next_outgoing_seq_num_`, tracks the sequence number that will be sent on the next outgoing `OMClientRequest` message sent to the exchange. The second one, `next_exp_seq_num_`, is used to check and validate that the `OMClientResponse` messages received from the exchange are in sequence.

- A boolean `run_` flag, which serves a similar purpose as it did in all the other components we saw before. It will be used to start and stop the execution of the `OrderGateway` thread and is marked `volatile` since it is accessed from different threads.

- It also saves the network interface in the `iface_` variable and the IP and port of the exchange's order gateway server in the `ip_` and `port_` member variables.

- Finally, it stores the `client_id_` variable of the `ClientId` type to make sure that responses received on the TCP socket are meant for the correct client:

```
#pragma once

#include <functional>

#include "common/thread_utils.h"
#include "common/macros.h"
#include "common/tcp_server.h"

#include "exchange/order_server/client_request.h"
#include "exchange/order_server/client_response.h"

namespace Trading {
  class OrderGateway {
  private:
    const ClientId client_id_;

    std::string ip_;
    const std::string iface_;
    const int port_ = 0;

    Exchange::ClientRequestLFQueue *outgoing_requests_ =
      nullptr;
```

```
    Exchange::ClientResponseLFQueue *incoming_responses_ =
      nullptr;

    volatile bool run_ = false;

    std::string time_str_;
    Logger logger_;

    size_t next_outgoing_seq_num_ = 1;
    size_t next_exp_seq_num_ = 1;
    Common::TCPSocket tcp_socket_;
  };
}
```

In the next section, we will initialize these data members as well as the `OrderGateway` class itself.

Initializing the order gateway client

The constructor accepts the `client_id` ID of the trading client, a pointer to a `ClientRequestsLFQueue` object (`client_requests`), a pointer to a `ClientResponseLFQueue` object (`client_responses`), and the `ip`, `port`, and interface information (`iface`) for the TCP connection. It initializes its own internal variables with these arguments and initializes the `Logger` data member (`logger_`) with a filename for the order gateway logs for this client. It updates the `recv_callback_` member inside the `tcp_socket_` variable of the `TCPSocket` type so that callbacks dispatched on data reads will go to the `OrderGateway::recvCallback()` method. We will see the implementation of that method briefly:

```
#include "order_gateway.h"

namespace Trading {
  OrderGateway::OrderGateway(ClientId client_id,

      Exchange::ClientRequestLFQueue *client_requests,
  Exchange::ClientResponseLFQueue *client_responses,
    std::string ip, const std::string &iface, int port)
      : client_id_(client_id), ip_(ip), iface_(iface),
        port_(port), outgoing_requests_(client_requests),
          incoming_responses_(client_responses),
      logger_("trading_order_gateway_" + std::::
        to_string(client_id) + ".log"),
          tcp_socket_(logger_) {
    tcp_socket_.recv_callback_ = [this](auto socket, auto
      rx_time) { recvCallback(socket, rx_time); };
```

Like the design of our other components, we will add a `start()` method, which will enable the `run_` flag and create and launch a thread to execute the `run()` method. We will also initialize our `tcp_socket_` member variable and have it connect to the `ip_` and `port_` interface information of the order gateway server at the exchange:

```cpp
auto start() {
  run_ = true;
  ASSERT(tcp_socket_.connect(ip_, iface_, port_, false)
    >= 0,
      "Unable to connect to ip:" + ip_ + " port:" +
        std::to_string(port_) + " on iface:" +
          iface_ + " error:" +
            std::string(std::strerror(errno)));
  ASSERT(Common::createAndStartThread(-1,
    "Trading/OrderGateway", [this]() { run(); }) !=
      nullptr, "Failed to start OrderGateway
        thread.");
}
```

The destructor for the `OrderGateway` class calls the `stop()` method to stop the execution of the `run()` method and waits for a little bit before returning:

```cpp
~OrderGateway() {
  stop();

  using namespace std::literals::chrono_literals;
  std::this_thread::sleep_for(5s);
}
```

The `stop()` method simply sets the `run_` flag to be `false` to stop the execution of the `run()` loop:

```cpp
auto stop() -> void {
  run_ = false;
}
```

Now we can move on to the two remaining important tasks: sending order requests to the exchange and receiving order responses from the exchange.

Sending order requests to the exchange

In this sub-section, we will implement the `run()` method, which is the main loop for the `OrderGateway` class. The goal of this method is to send out any client requests that are ready to be sent out on the TCP socket to read any data available on the socket and dispatch the `recv_callback_()` method.

First, it calls the `TCPSocket::sendAndRecv()` method to send and receive data on the established TCP connection:

```
auto OrderGateway::run() noexcept -> void {
  logger_.log("%:% %() %\n", __FILE__, __LINE__,
    __FUNCTION__, Common::getCurrentTimeStr(&time_str_));
  while (run_) {
    tcp_socket_.sendAndRecv();
```

It also reads any `MEClientRequest` messages available on the `outgoing_requests_` `LFQueue` sent by the `TradeEngine` engine and writes them to the `tcp_socket_` send buffer using the `TCPSocket::send()` method. Note that it needs to write out `OMClientRequest` messages, which it achieves by first writing the `next_outgoing_seq_num_` field and then the `MEClientRequest` object that the `TradeEngine` sent. This works because we designed the `OMClientRequest` object to be a struct that contains a `size_t seq_num_` field followed by a `MEClientRequest` object. We also increment the `next_outgoing_seq_num_` instance for the next outgoing socket message:

```
      for(auto client_request = outgoing_requests_->
        getNextToRead(); client_request; client_request =
          outgoing_requests_->getNextToRead()) {
        logger_.log("%:% %() % Sending cid:% seq:% %\n",
          __FILE__, __LINE__, __FUNCTION__,
                Common::getCurrentTimeStr(&time_str_),
                    client_id_, next_outgoing_seq_num_,
                      client_request->toString());
        tcp_socket_.send(&next_outgoing_seq_num_,
          sizeof(next_outgoing_seq_num_));
        tcp_socket_.send(client_request,
          sizeof(Exchange::MEClientRequest));
        outgoing_requests_->updateReadIndex();

        next_outgoing_seq_num_++;
      }
    }
  }
```

We will deal with the task of receiving and processing order responses that the exchange sends to the TCP connection `OrderGateway` establishes.

Processing order responses from the exchange

The `recvCallback()` method is called when there is data available on the `tcp_socket_` and the `TCPSocket::sendAndRecv()` method is called from the `run()` method in the previous section. We go through the `rcv_buffer_` buffer on `TCPSocket` and re-interpret the data as `OMClientResponse` messages:

```cpp
auto OrderGateway::recvCallback(TCPSocket *socket, Nanos
  rx_time) noexcept -> void {
  logger_.log("%:% %() % Received socket:% len:% %\n",
    __FILE__, __LINE__, __FUNCTION__,
      Common::getCurrentTimeStr(&time_str_), socket->fd_,
      socket->next_rcv_valid_index_, rx_time);

  if (socket->next_rcv_valid_index_ >=
    sizeof(Exchange::OMClientResponse)) {
    size_t i = 0;
    for (; i + sizeof(Exchange::OMClientResponse) <=
      socket->next_rcv_valid_index_; i +=
        sizeof(Exchange::OMClientResponse)) {
      auto response = reinterpret_cast<const
        Exchange::OMClientResponse *>(socket->rcv_buffer_
          + i);
      logger_.log("%:% %() % Received %\n", __FILE__,
        __LINE__, __FUNCTION__,
          Common::getCurrentTimeStr(&time_str_), response-
            >toString());
```

For the `OMClientResponse` message we just read into the response variable, we check to make sure the client ID on the response matches the `OrderGateway`'s client ID and ignore the response if it does not match:

```cpp
if(response->me_client_response_.client_id_ !=
  client_id_) {
  logger_.log("%:% %() % ERROR Incorrect client id.
    ClientId expected:% received:%.\n", __FILE__,
      __LINE__, __FUNCTION__,
        Common::getCurrentTimeStr(&time_str_)
          , client_id_, response->
            me_client_response_.client_id_);
  continue;
}
```

We also check to make sure that the sequence number on `OMClientResponse` matches what we expect it to be. If there is a mismatch, we log an error and ignore the response. There is an opportunity to improve the error handling here, but for the sake of simplicity, we just log an error and continue:

```cpp
if(response->seq_num_ != next_exp_seq_num_) {
  logger_.log("%:% %() % ERROR Incorrect sequence
```

```
                    number. ClientId:%. SeqNum expected:%
                received:%.\n", __FILE__, __LINE__,
                    __FUNCTION__,
                        Common::getCurrentTimeStr(&time_str_)
                        , client_id_, next_exp_seq_num_,
                            response->seq_num_);
        continue;
      }
```

Finally, we increment the expected sequence number on the next `OMClientResponse` and write the response we just read to the `incoming_responses_` `LFQueue` for the `TradeEngine` to read. It also updates the `rcv_buffer_` buffer and the next receive index into the `TCPSocket` buffer we just consumed some messages from:

```
        ++next_exp_seq_num_;

        auto next_write = incoming_responses_->
          getNextToWriteTo();
        *next_write = std::move(response->
          me_client_response_);
        incoming_responses_->updateWriteIndex();
      }
      memcpy(socket->rcv_buffer_, socket->rcv_buffer_ + i,
        socket->next_rcv_valid_index_ - i);
      socket->next_rcv_valid_index_ -= i;
    }
  }
```

With this method implementation, we have finished the design and implementation of the `OrderGateway` component. That will be all the core infrastructure components we build in this chapter, and we will summarize everything we worked on in the next chapter.

One important note is that we will need to build all the components presented in this chapter as well as the *Building the C++ Trading Algorithm Building Blocks* and *Building the C++ Market Making and Liquidity Taking Algorithms* chapters before we can build and run a meaningful trading client. Since our ecosystem consists of a server (trading exchange) and client (trading client) infrastructure, we will need to wait until the *Building and running the main trading application* section in the *Building the C++ Market Making and Liquidity Taking Algorithms* chapter before we can run the full ecosystem.

Summary

This chapter was dedicated to building the important core infrastructure components inside the market participant's trading system. First, we build the market data consumer component, which is responsible for subscribing to the multicast market data stream generated by the exchange. It needs to detect gaps in market data updates on the incremental market data stream and initiate snapshot recovery and synchronization mechanisms to re-synchronize with the incremental market data stream. It decodes the market data updates from the format that the exchange publishes to a simpler internal market data format.

The order book sub-component inside the trading engine component processes the market data updates it receives from the market data consumer. It builds and updates an order book data structure from these updates for the trading engine to get an accurate view of the market.

The order gateway component inside the trading system establishes and maintains a bi-directional TCP connection with the electronic trading exchange. It receives order action requests from the trading engine and sends them out to the exchange in the exchange's order data format. It also receives order responses that the exchange sends to the trading client, decodes them, and forwards them to the trading engine.

Note that we do not have everything we need in the trading client's trading system, that is, we are missing the components we need to build and run trading strategies and associated components. The next chapter will build the additional components we need in the trading strategy framework. The chapter after that will tie all the components together and finish the final trading application and the full trading ecosystem.

9

Building the C++ Trading Algorithm's Building Blocks

In this chapter, we will build components that make up the intelligence in our trading applications. These are the components that the trading strategies will rely on very heavily to make decisions, send and manage orders, track and manage positions, **profits and losses** (**PnLs**), and manage risk. Not only do the trading strategies need to track the trading PnLs since the goal is to make money, but these components also need to track the PnLs to decide when to stop trading if needed. We will learn how to compute complex features from market data updates, track trading performance based on order executions and market updates, send and manage live strategy orders in the market, and manage market risk. In this chapter, we will cover the following topics:

- Reacting to executions and managing positions, PnLs, and risk
- Building the feature engine and computing complex features
- Using executions and updating positions and PnLs
- Sending and managing orders
- Computing and managing risk

Technical requirements

All the code for this book can be found in this book's GitHub repository at https://github.com/PacktPublishing/Building-Low-Latency-Applications-with-CPP. The source for this chapter is in the Chapter9 directory in this repository.

You must have read and understood the design of the electronic trading ecosystem that was presented in *Chapter, Designing Our Trading Ecosystem*, especially the *Designing a framework for low-latency C++ trading algorithms* section. As before, we will use the building blocks we built in *Chapter, Building the C++ Building Blocks for Low-Latency Applications*.

The specifications of the environment in which the source code for this book was developed are shown here. We have provided the details of this environment since all the C++ code presented in this book is not necessarily portable and might require some minor changes for it to work in your environment:

- **OS**: `Linux 5.19.0-41-generic #42~22.04.1-Ubuntu SMP PREEMPT_DYNAMIC Tue Apr 18 17:40:00 UTC 2 x86_64 x86_64 x86_64 GNU/Linux`.
- **GCC**: `g++ (Ubuntu 11.3.0-1ubuntu1~22.04.1) 11.3.0`.
- **CMAKE**: `cmake version 3.23.2`.
- **NINJA**: `1.10.2`.

Reacting to executions and managing positions, PnLs, and risk

We need to build a few basic building blocks that will build and support our trading strategies. We discussed the need for these components in *Chapter, Designing Our Trading Ecosystem*, in the *Designing a framework for low-latency C++ trading algorithms* section. We have already implemented a major component – the limit order book – but in this section, we will build the remaining components we need, namely the following:

- A `FeatureEngine`, which will be used to compute simple and complex features/signals that drive the trading strategy decisions
- A `PositionKeeper`, which will receive executions and compute important measures such as position, PnLs, traded volumes, and more
- An `OrderManager`, which will be used by the strategies to send orders, manage them, and update these orders when there are updates
- A `RiskManager` to compute and check the market risk that a trading strategy is attempting to take on, as well as the risk it has realized

The following diagram shows the topology of all these components and how they interact with each other. If you need to refresh your memory on why these components exist, what purpose they serve, how they interact with each other, and how they are designed, please revisit *Chapter, Designing Our Trading Ecosystem*, and look at the subsections in the *Designing a framework for low-latency C++ trading algorithms* section:

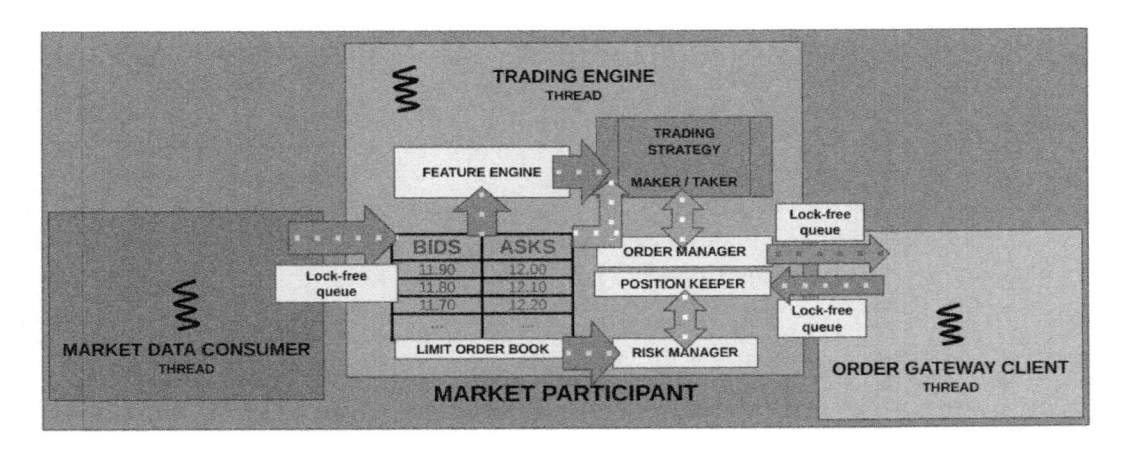

Figure 9.1 – The sub-components inside our trading engine

Now, let's kick off our effort of implementing these components, starting with the feature engine in the next sub-section. But before we do that, we need to add two additional methods for the `Side` enumeration, which will make a lot of our source code simpler down the road. Both of these can be found in the `Chapter9/common/types.h` header file.

The first method we will add is the `sideToIndex()` method, which converts a `Side` value into an index that can be used to index into an array. This will allow us to maintain arrays of different types of objects that are indexed by a `Side` value. The implementation is simple – we simply typecast the side to a `size_t` type and add a 1 to account for the fact that `Side::SELL` has a value of -1 and valid that indices start from 0:

```
inline constexpr auto sideToIndex(Side side) noexcept {
  return static_cast<size_t>(side) + 1;
}
```

We will also define a `sideToValue()` method, which converts a `Side` value into either a 1 for `Side::BUY` or a -1 for `Side::SELL`. This will help us when we compute positions and PnLs, which we will see shortly in this section:

```
inline constexpr auto sideToValue(Side side) noexcept {
  return static_cast<int>(side);
}
```

Now that we have that additional functionality out of the way, we can start computing the feature engine.

Building the feature and computing complex features

In this section, we will build a minimal version of a feature engine. We will only compute two simple features – one (market price) that computes fair market prices based on the top of book prices and quantity and another (aggressive trade qty ratio) that computes how big a trade is compared to the top of book quantities. We will use these feature values to drive our market-making and liquidity-taking trading algorithms later in this chapter. The source code for the `FeatureEngine` class we will build here can be found in the `Chapter9/trading/strategy/feature_engine.h` file on GitHub. We discussed the details of this component in *Chapter, Designing Our Trading Ecosystem*, in the *Designing a framework for low-latency C++ trading algorithms* section.

Defining the data members in the feature engine

First, we need to declare the `FeatureEngine` class and define the data members inside this class. First, we will include the required header files and define a constant sentinel value to represent invalid or uninitialized feature values. This is called `Feature_INVALID`, as shown here:

```cpp
#pragma once

#include "common/macros.h"
#include "common/logging.h"

using namespace Common;

namespace Trading {
  constexpr auto Feature_INVALID =
    std::numeric_limits<double>::quiet_NaN();
```

Our `FeatureEngine` class is basic and has two important data members of the `double` type – one to compute and store the fair market price value, `mkt_price_`, and another to compute and store the aggressive trade quantity ratio feature value, `agg_trade_qty_ratio_`. It also stores a pointer to a `Logger` object (`logger_`) for logging purposes:

```cpp
class FeatureEngine {
private:
  std::string time_str_;
  Common::Logger *logger_ = nullptr;

  double mkt_price_ = Feature_INVALID,
    agg_trade_qty_ratio_ = Feature_INVALID;
};
```

Next, we will look at how to initialize this class since we have already initialized the two feature variables with the `Feature_INVALID` value.

Initializing the feature engine

The constructor for this class accepts a `Logger` object and initializes the `logger_` data member – that's all:

```
FeatureEngine(Common::Logger *logger)
    : logger_(logger) {
}
```

Here, we will present two getter methods – `getMktPrice()` and `getAggTradeQtyRatio()` – to fetch the value of the two features that the `FeatureEngine` class is responsible for computing:

```
auto getMktPrice() const noexcept {
  return mkt_price_;
}
auto getAggTradeQtyRatio() const noexcept {
  return agg_trade_qty_ratio_;
}
```

In the next two subsections, we will see how this component handles order book updates and trade events and updates the feature values.

Computing the feature on order book changes

The `FeatureEngine` class expects the `onOrderBookUpdate()` method to be called when there is an update to the order book. First, it uses `MarketOrderBook::getBBO()` to extract the BBO. As a reminder, **BBO** stands for **Best Bid Offer** and is a summary view that represents the best bid and offer prices and quantities. It proceeds to check that the bid and ask prices are valid and then computes the `mkt_price_` value if they are valid. The fair market price is formulated as the book quantity weighted price, `(bid_price * ask_qty + ask_price * bid_qty) / (bid_qty + ask_qty)`. Note that this is just a single formulation for a fair market price; the important thing to remember with feature engineering is that there is no single correct formulation. You are encouraged to formulate a version of a fair market price or any other feature value you want to use in the future. The formulation we are using here tries to move the fair market price closer to the offer if there are more buy orders than sell orders and moves it closer to the bid if there are more sell orders than buy orders:

```
auto onOrderBookUpdate(TickerId ticker_id, Price price,
    Side side, MarketOrderBook* book) noexcept -> void {
  const auto bbo = book->getBBO();
  if(LIKELY(bbo->bid_price_ != Price_INVALID && bbo-
    >ask_price_ != Price_INVALID)) {
    mkt_price_ = (bbo->bid_price_ * bbo->ask_qty_ +
      bbo->ask_price_ * bbo->bid_qty_) /
```

```
            static_cast<double>(bbo->bid_qty_ + bbo->
              ask_qty_);
      }

      logger_->log("%:% %() % ticker:% price:% side:% mkt-
        price:% agg-trade-ratio:%\n", __FILE__, __LINE__,
          __FUNCTION__,
                Common::getCurrentTimeStr(&time_str_),
                    ticker_id, Common::priceToString
                      (price).c_str(),
                  Common::sideToString(side).c_str(),
                    mkt_price_, agg_trade_qty_ratio_);
    }
```

The next subsection will compute the other feature, which we will refer to as the Aggressive Trade Quantity Ratio, for computing the trade quantity as a fraction of the book price level quantity.

Computing the feature on trade events

FeatureEngine expects the onTradeUpdate() method to be called when there is a trade event in the market data stream. As we saw previously, it fetches the BBO and checks if the prices are valid and then computes the agg_trade_qty_ratio_ feature to be a ratio of the trade quantity and the quantity of the BBO that the trade aggresses on. As we mentioned with the previous feature, there is no single correct formulation of a feature – this is just the formulation we are using for now; hopefully, you will add your own formulations in the future. This formulation tries to measure how big a trade aggressor was compared to how much liquidity was available on the BBO side the aggressor trades against. We are simply trying to quantify the trade pressure with this feature that we are computing. As we mentioned previously, there are many other possible formulations:

```
      auto onTradeUpdate(const Exchange::MEMarketUpdate
        *market_update, MarketOrderBook* book) noexcept -> void {
        const auto bbo = book->getBBO();
        if(LIKELY(bbo->bid_price_ != Price_INVALID && bbo->
          ask_price_ != Price_INVALID)) {
          agg_trade_qty_ratio_ = static_cast<double>
            (market_update->qty_) / (market_update->side_ ==
              Side::BUY ? bbo->ask_qty_ : bbo->bid_qty_);
        }

        logger_->log("%:% %() % % mkt-price:% agg-trade-ratio
          :%\n", __FILE__, __LINE__, __FUNCTION__,
                Common::getCurrentTimeStr(&time_str_),
                  market_update->toString().c_str(),
```

```
                        mkt_price_, agg_trade_qty_ratio_);
  }
```

That is the entire implementation of our `FeatureEngine` for this book. In the next section, we will learn how to handle executions and use that to update positions and PnLs.

Using executions to update positions and PnLs

Now, we will build a `PositionKeeper` class that will be responsible for processing executions on a strategy's orders and computing and tracking positions and PnLs. This component is used by the strategy as well as the risk manager to compute positions and PnLs for different purposes. All the source code for the `PositionKeeper` class is in the `Chapter9/trading/strategy/position_keeper.h` file on GitHub. Before we build the `PositionKeeper` class, which manages positions for all trading instruments, we will need to build a `PositionInfo` struct, which is also present in the same source file. The `PositionInfo` struct is the lower-level struct for managing the positions and PnLs for a single trading instrument; we will cover it in more detail in the next few subsections. We discussed the details of this component in *Chapter, Designing Our Trading Ecosystem*, in the *Designing a framework for low-latency C++ trading algorithms* section.

Declaring the data members in PositionInfo

First, we must specify the `include` files that will be needed for the `position_keeper.h` file, as shown here:

```
#pragma once

#include "common/macros.h"
#include "common/types.h"
#include "common/logging.h"

#include "exchange/order_server/client_response.h"

#include "market_order_book.h"

using namespace Common;
```

The data members inside the `PositionInfo` struct are presented in the source code. The important data members are as follows:

- A `position_` variable of the `int32_t` type to represent the current position. This can be positive, negative, or 0.
- Three `double` values – `real_pnl_`, `unreal_pnl_`, and `total_pnl_` – to track the realized or closed PnL for positions that have been closed (`real_pnl_`), the unrealized or

open PnL for the currently open position (`unreal_pnl_`), and the total PnL, which is a summation of the two values (`total_pnl_`), respectively. The realized PnL only changes when additional order executions occur; the unrealized PnL can change even without order executions if there is a non-zero position and market prices change.

- A `std::array` of `double` of a size large enough to accommodate entries for the buy side and sell side. This array will be indexed using the `sideToIndex(Side::BUY)` and `sideToIndex(Side::SELL)` values. This `open_vwap_` `std::array` variable tracks the product of price and execution quantity on each side when there is an open long (positive) or short (negative) position. We will need this to compute the unrealized PnL by comparing the **volume-weighted average price** (**VWAP**) of the open long or short position against the current market price.
- A `volume_` variable of the `Qty` type to track the total quantity that has been executed.
- A `const` pointer variable to a BBO object called `bbo_`, which will be used on market updates to fetch the updated top-of-book prices:

```
namespace Trading {
  struct PositionInfo {
    int32_t position_ = 0;
    double real_pnl_ = 0, unreal_pnl_ = 0, total_pnl_ = 0;
    std::array<double, sideToIndex(Side::MAX) + 1>
      open_vwap_;
    Qty volume_ = 0;
    const BBO *bbo_ = nullptr;
```

We will also add a simple `toString()` method to this struct to *stringify* instances of this structure:

```
    auto toString() const {
      std::stringstream ss;
      ss << "Position{"
         << "pos:" << position_
         << " u-pnl:" << unreal_pnl_
         << " r-pnl:" << real_pnl_
         << " t-pnl:" << total_pnl_
         << " vol:" << qtyToString(volume_)
         << " vwaps:[" << (position_ ? open_vwap_
            .at(sideToIndex(Side::BUY)) / std::abs
              (position_) : 0)
         << "X" << (position_ ? open_vwap_
            .at(sideToIndex(Side::SELL)) / std::abs
              (position_) : 0)
         << "] "
         << (bbo_ ? bbo_->toString() : "") << "}";
```

```
        return ss.str();
    }
```

Next, we need to process order executions and update the positions and PnLs based on those executions.

Handling order executions in PositionInfo

When a trading strategy's orders are executed, `PositionKeeper` needs to update the positions and PnLs that have been tracked for the trading instrument of the execution. It does this by providing the `MEClientResponse` message corresponding to order executions to the `PositionInfo::addFIll()` method. We will build this in this subsection.

Before we look at the source code for our implementation of the `PositionInfo::addFill()` method, we will look at an example of how the algorithm to update the realized and unrealized PnLs works. This will help you easily understand the source code for the implementation. We will track the evolution of the different variables as we work our way through a few hypothetical executions for a hypothetical trading instrument. We will display the following variables as columns in our tables:

- **position – old**: This is the position before the current execution message is processed
- **position – new**: This will be the new position after processing the current execution message
- **open_vwap – BUY**: This is the sum of the products of execution price and execution quantity for buy executions only
- **open_vwap – SELL**: This is the sum of the products of execution price and execution quantity for sell executions only
- **VWAP – BUY**: This is the actual VWAP of the current long/positive position, represented in units of price and not price x quantity
- **VWAP – SELL**: This is the actual VWAP of the current short/negative position, represented in units of price and not price x quantity
- **PnL – real**: This is the realized PnL after processing this execution
- **PnL – unreal**: This is the unrealized PnL for the open position after processing this execution

Assuming we get an execution for buying 10 at 100.0, we must update `open_vwap`, VWAP on the BUY side, and the new position, as shown here. No changes need to be made to the unreal PnL yet:

position		open_vwap		VWAP		PnL	
Old	new	BUY	SELL	BUY	SELL	real	unreal
0	10	1000.0	0.0	100.0	0.0	0.0	0.0

Assuming we get another execution for buying 10 at 90.0, our old position was 10 and the new position will be 20. The `open_vwap` property for BUY now gets 10 * 90 added to the previous

1,000 and becomes 1,900. The VWAP column for the open long/positive position is 95, which can be computed by dividing 1,900 (BUY open_vwap) by 20 (new position). We compute the unreal PnL by using a VWAP of 95 and the latest execution price of 90 and multiplying the difference of -5 by the position of 20 to get -100. We have a negative unrealized PnL because our long/positive position's VWAP is higher than current market prices (represented by the latest execution price):

position		open_vwap		VWAP		PnL	
old	new	BUY	SELL	BUY	SELL	real	unreal
10	20	1900.0	0.0	95.0	0.0	0.0	-100.0

Now, let's assume we get a sell execution for selling 10 at 92. Our old position of 20 will be reduced to 10. Our open_vwap and VWAP on the BUY side do not change since this was a sell execution. Since we closed 10 out of our long/positive 20 positions, we will have some realized PnL and the remaining 10 long/positive positions will have some unrealized PnL based on the execution price of this latest execution. The realized PnL is computed using the sell execution price of 92, the VWAP property of the long/positive position, which is 95, and the execution quantity of 10 to yield a realized PnL of (92 - 95) * 10 = -30. In this case, the unrealized PnL is also the same since there is a long/positive 10 position left:

position		open_vwap		VWAP		PnL	
Old	new	BUY	SELL	BUY	SELL	real	unreal
20	10	1900.0	0.0	95.0	0.0	-30.0	-30.0

Now, let's assume we receive another sell execution for selling 20 at 97. This will cause our position to flip from 10 to –10 (note that we set open_vwap and VWAP for the BUY side to 0). The open_vwap property for the SELL side becomes 970 because of the -10 position and the execution price of 97. We close the previous position of 10, which had a VWAP of 95 with this sell at 97. Since we sold higher than the VWAP property of our long/positive position, we make a profit of (97 - 95) * 10 = 20, which when added to the previous realized PnL of -30, yields the final realized PnL of -10. The unrealized PnL here is 0 since a VWAP of 97 is the same as the current execution price of 97:

position		open_vwap		VWAP		PnL	
Old	new	BUY	SELL	BUY	SELL	real	unreal
10	-10	0.0	970.0	0.0	97.0	-10.0	0.0

Let's assume that we get another sell execution of selling 20 and 94. Here, the short/negative position increases from -10 to -30. The open_vwap property on the SELL side is updated by adding (20 * 94) to the previous value of 970 to yield 2,850. The VWAP property of our short position is updated to 95 by dividing the open_vwap property of 2,850 by the position of 30 to yield 95. The realized PnL does not change since the position was increased and nothing was reduced or closed. The unreal PnL uses the execution price of 94 on this new execution, compares it to the VWAP property of 95, and uses the new position of -30 to yield (95 - 94) * 30 = 30:

position		open_vwap		VWAP		PnL	
Old	new	BUY	SELL	BUY	SELL	real	unreal
-10	-30	0.0	2850.0	0.0	95.0	-10.0	30.0

Let's assume that there is yet another sell execution of selling 10 at 90. The short/negative position increases from -30 to -40. We add the new execution's price and quantity product (10 * 90) to the previous `open_vwap` property's `SELL` of 2,850 to yield 3,750. The actual `VWAP` of the short position changes from 95 to 93.75 and was obtained by dividing this 3,750 value by the new position of 40. The realized PnL does not change since the position was increased, but the unrealized PnL is updated using (93.75 - 90) * 40 = 150:

position		open_vwap		VWAP		PnL	
Old	new	BUY	SELL	BUY	SELL	real	unreal
-30	-40	0.0	3750.0	0.0	93.75	-10.0	150.0

Finally, let's assume that we receive a buy execution for buying 40 at 88. This execution will flatten our short/negative position of -40, so the new position will be 0. The unrealized PnL will be 0 and the `open_vwap` and `VWAP` properties will be 0 for both sides since there is no open position anymore. The realized PnL is updated using the previous `VWAP` property, the execution price, and the position of 40, so (93.75 - 88) * 40 = 230. This is added to the previously realized PnL of –10 to yield the final realized PnL of 220:

position		open_vwap		VWAP		PnL	
Old	new	BUY	SELL	BUY	SELL	real	unreal
-40	0	0.0	0.0	0.0	0.0	220.0	0.0

Now, we can move on and discuss the implementation details of this algorithm.

The first thing we must do is initialize a few local variables. Here, the `old_position` variable saves the `current position_` value before updating it. `side_index` and `opp_side_index` use the `sideToIndex()` method to find the indices in the `open_vwap_` array that correspond to the side of the execution and the side opposite to the side of execution, respectively. We must also initialize a `side_value` variable, which will be +1 for a buy execution and -1 for a sell execution:

```
auto addFill(const Exchange::MEClientResponse
  *client_response, Logger *logger) noexcept {
  const auto old_position = position_;
  const auto side_index = sideToIndex(client_response->
    side_);
  const auto opp_side_index = sideToIndex
    (client_response->side_ == Side::BUY ? Side::SELL :
      Side::BUY);
  const auto side_value = sideToValue(client_response->
    side_);
```

Now, we must update the `position_` variable using the quantity executed (`exec_qty_`) in this response and the `side_value` variable we initialized. We must also update the `volume_` member by adding the new execution quantity to it. When we receive an execution on a buy order, our position increases; conversely, when we receive an execution on a sell order, our position decreases. When our position is positive, also known as a *long position*, we profit when prices increase and make a loss when prices decrease. When our position is negative, also known as a *short position*, we profit when prices decrease and make a loss when prices increase:

```
position_ += client_response->exec_qty_ * side_value;
volume_   += client_response->exec_qty_;
```

The next important step for us is to update the `open_vwap_` entry's `std::array` variable. We will check if we were flat (position 0) before this execution and open a new position with this execution or if we already had an open position and we got an execution that increases that position. In this case, we will simply update the `open_vwap_` variable using `side_index` to index the correct side. Since `open_vwap_` tracks the product of execution prices and executed quantities at those prices, we can simply multiply `price_` and `exec_qty_` on this execution and add it to the existing sum, as shown here:

```
if (old_position * sideToValue(client_response->
  side_) >= 0) { // opened / increased position.
  open_vwap_[side_index] += (client_response->price_
    * client_response->exec_qty_);
}
```

Now, we need to handle the case where we had a pre-existing open position. This most recent execution reduces or flattens the position. In this case, we will need to update the realized PnL (`real_pnl_`) using the `open_vwap_` entry for the side opposite to the side of execution. One thing to understand is that the realized PnL is only updated when an open position is reduced or closed because, in this case, we have bought and sold a certain quantity. Another way to think about this is that we can match some of the buy quantity with some of the sell quantity and create a pair of buy and sell trades. In this case, we have closed at least part of our position. In the previous case, where we either opened a new position or increased an already open position, we did not have a pair of buy and sell trades to match up, so we did not need to update the realized PnL.

First, we will compute an `opp_side_vwap` value, which is the average price of all the executions on the other side, using the `open_vwap_` entry for `opp_side_index` and normalize it using the absolute value of `old_position` before this execution. Remember that the `open_vwap_` variable is named poorly; it tracks the product of execution price and quantity, not just the price, so dividing it by the quantity represented by `old_position` yields the actual VWAP. Then, we will update the `open_vwap_` entry for `opp_side_index` using the product of the VWAP we computed in `opp_side_vwap` and the absolute value of the new `position_` value.

We can update the `real_pnl_` value by finding the minimum quantity value of the execution quantity (`exec_qty_`) and the absolute value of `old_position`. We must multiply that by the difference between the current execution message's price (`price_`) and `opp_side_vwap`. Finally, we need to multiply this product by `opp_side_value` to account for whether a profit was made (bought at a lower price than the sell VWAP or sold at a higher price than the buy VWAP) or a loss was made (bought at a higher price than the sell VWAP or sold at a lower price than the buy VWAP):

```
else { // decreased position.
  const auto opp_side_vwap = open_vwap_
    [opp_side_index] / std::abs(old_position);
  open_vwap_[opp_side_index] = opp_side_vwap * std::
    abs(position_);
  real_pnl_ += std::min
    (static_cast<int32_t>(client_response->
      exec_qty_), std::abs(old_position)) *
            (opp_side_vwap - client_response->
              price_) * sideToValue
                (client_response->side_);
```

We need to handle an edge case if this execution causes the position to flip, meaning it goes from a long position to a short position or vice versa. This position flip can happen, for instance, when we have a long/positive position of a certain amount and we receive a sell execution of a quantity larger than that position. Conversely, this can happen if we have a short/negative position of a certain amount and we receive a buy execution of a quantity larger than that position. In each of these cases, we go from having a positive/long position to a negative/short position or go from having a negative/short position to a positive/long position. In this case, we can simply reset the `open_vwap_` value corresponding to the opposite side to 0 and reset the `open_vwap_` value for the side of execution (and thus the side of the new position) so that it's the product of the latest execution price and the absolute value of our current `position_`:

```
    if (position_ * old_position < 0) { // flipped
      position to opposite sign.
      open_vwap_[side_index] = (client_response->price_
        * std::abs(position_));
      open_vwap_[opp_side_index] = 0;
    }
  }
```

Finally, we will wrap up the `PositionInfo::addFill()` method by updating the unrealized PnL (`unreal_pnl_`) value. The case where we are now flat (`position_ == 0`) is straightforward – we reset the `open_vwap_` variable for both sides and set `unreal_pnl_` to 0 since no open position implies no `unreal_pnl_`:

```
    if (!position_) { // flat
      open_vwap_[sideToIndex(Side::BUY)] = open_vwap_
```

```
            [sideToIndex(Side::SELL)] = 0;
    unreal_pnl_ = 0;
}
```

If we still have an open `position_` after this execution, then we can compute the `unreal_pnl_` value that was obtained by multiplying the absolute value of `position_` with the difference between the execution price from the current execution and the VWAP computed from the `open_vwap_` entry for the `position_` side:

```
else {
if (position_ > 0)
  unreal_pnl_ =
      (client_response->price_ - open_vwap_
        [sideToIndex(Side::BUY)] / std::abs
          (position_)) *
      std::abs(position_);
else
  unreal_pnl_ =
      (open_vwap_[sideToIndex(Side::SELL)] / std::
        abs(position_) - client_response->price_) *
      std::abs(position_);
}
```

Finally, `total_pnl_` is just the summation of `real_pnl_` and `unreal_pnl_`, as explained previously:

```
    total_pnl_ = unreal_pnl_ + real_pnl_;

    std::string time_str;
    logger->log("%:% %() % % %\n", __FILE__, __LINE__,
        __FUNCTION__, Common::getCurrentTimeStr(&time_str),
            toString(), client_response->
              toString().c_str());
}
```

The final piece of functionality we need to add to `PositionInfo` is for handling changes in market prices and updating the unrealized PnL for any open position. We will investigate this functionality in the next subsection.

Handling order book changes in PositionInfo

When there are market updates that cause changes in the order book we build, we need to update the unrealized and total PnL values. The `PositionInfo::updateBBO()` method is called by the `PositionKeeper` class for the trading instrument, which receives a market update. This, in turn, leads to an order book change. We provide the BBO object that corresponds to the trading instrument that was updated in the `updateBBO()` method. We save the `bbo` argument provided in this method in the `bbo_` data member in our `PositionInfo` struct. This method only has anything to do if `position_` is non-zero and the bid and ask price values on the BBO provided are valid. This is the first thing we will check for:

```
auto updateBBO(const BBO *bbo, Logger *logger) noexcept {
  std::string time_str;
  bbo_ = bbo;

  if (position_ && bbo->bid_price_ != Price_INVALID &&
    bbo->ask_price_ != Price_INVALID) {
```

If we need to update the unrealized PnL, we can use the mid-price of the BBO prices, which we can compute and save in the `mid_price` variable, as shown here:

```
const auto mid_price = (bbo->bid_price_ + bbo->
  ask_price_) * 0.5;
```

After that, we can update `unreal_pnl_` using the same logic that we saw in the previous subsection, except that we use the `mid_price` value instead of an execution price. Let's explain why we update the unrealized PnL even though we do not have additional executions. Let's say we have a long position from an execution at a hypothetical price of 100. At this point, the initial unrealized PnL is 0. Let's also assume that, in the future, the market prices (represented by our `mid_price` variable) go up to 110. In that case, our realized PnL has not changed because we have not executed any sell orders. However, our unrealized PnL increases because if we decide to liquidate our long position, we would get executions at a price roughly equal to `mid_price`. This is why we update the unrealized PnL when market prices change, even though no additional orders have been executed. Also, note that the realized PnL captures the PnL of pairs of buy and sell executions, so that does not need to be updated here since there were no additional executions:

```
if (position_ > 0)
  unreal_pnl_ =
      (mid_price - open_vwap_
        [sideToIndex(Side::BUY)] / std::
          abs(position_)) *
      std::abs(position_);
else
  unreal_pnl_ =
      (open_vwap_[sideToIndex(Side::SELL)] / std::
        abs(position_) - mid_price) *
      std::abs(position_);
```

Finally, we must update the `total_pnl_` data member and log it if it has changed since the last time:

```
const auto old_total_pnl = total_pnl_;
total_pnl_ = unreal_pnl_ + real_pnl_;
```

```cpp
            if (total_pnl_ != cld_total_pnl)
                logger->log("%:% %() % % %\n", __FILE__, __LINE__
                    , __FUNCTION__, Common::
                        getCurrentTimeStr(&time_str),
                            toString(), bbo_->toString());
        }
    }
```

This concludes all the functionality we need for the `PositionInfo` struct. We will now shift our discussion to the `PositionKeeper` class, which we will use to manage the position and PnL for the entire trading engine across all trading instruments.

Designing PositionKeeper

The `PositionKeeper` class manages the position and PnL across all trading instruments in the trading engine. The `PositionKeeper` class contains a `std::array` of `PositionInfo` objects and is large enough to accommodate `ME_MAX_TICKERS` number of objects:

```cpp
class PositionKeeper {
private:
    std::string time_str_;
    Common::Logger *logger_ = nullptr;

    std::array<PositionInfo, ME_MAX_TICKERS>
        ticker_position_;
};
```

We will add a getter method to fetch and return the `PositionInfo` instance for a provided `TickerId` called `getPositionInfo()`:

```cpp
auto getPositionInfo(TickerId ticker_id) const noexcept {
    return &(ticker_position_.at(ticker_id));
}
```

We will also add a simple `toString()` method, which we will use for logging purposes later:

```cpp
auto toString() const {
    double total_pnl = 0;
    Qty total_vol = 0;

    std::stringstream ss;
    for(TickerId i = 0; i < ticker_position_.size(); ++i) {
        ss << "TickerId:" << tickerIdToString(i) << " " <<
            ticker_position_.at(i).toString() << "\n";
```

```
            total_pnl += ticker_position_.at(i).total_pnl_;
            total_vol += ticker_position_.at(i).volume_;
        }
        ss << "Total PnL:" << total_pnl << " Vol:" <<
            total_vol << "\n";

        return ss.str();
    }
```

Initializing an object of this class is straightforward and something we will discuss next.

Initializing PositionKeeper

The `PositionKeeper` constructor accepts a `Logger` object and initializes the `logger_` data member with that argument, as shown here:

```
    PositionKeeper(Common::Logger *logger)
        : logger_(logger) {
    }
```

Next, we will see how order executions and changes to BBO are handled in the `PositionKeeper` class and forwarded to the correct `PositionInfo` object.

Handling order executions and market updates in PositionKeeper

The `PositionKeeper::addFill()` method handles order executions and its implementation is straightforward. It simply calls the `PositionInfo::addFill()` method on the correct `PositionInfo` object for that `TickerId`, as shown here:

```
    auto addFill(const Exchange::MEClientResponse
      *client_response) noexcept {
        ticker_position_.at(client_response->
          ticker_id_).addFill(client_response, logger_);
    }
```

The `PositionKeeper::updateBBO()` method handles changes in BBO due to market updates and corresponding changes in the order book. It also simply calls the `PositionInfo::updateBBO()` method on the correct `PositionInfo` object for `TickerId`, as shown here:

```
    auto updateBBO(TickerId ticker_id, const BBO *bbo)
      noexcept {
        ticker_position_.at(ticker_id).updateBBO(bbo,
          logger_);
    }
```

That concludes the design and implementation of everything we need in our `PositionKeeper` class. In the next section, we will build an order manager class, which will be used by the trading strategies to manage their orders at a higher level.

Sending and managing orders

In *Chapter, Designing Our Trading Ecosystem*, we discussed the purpose of the trading system's order manager component (the *Designing a framework for low-latency C++ trading algorithms* section). In this section, we will implement an `OrderManager` class to encapsulate the order management logic inside this class and thus make it easy for trading strategies to manage their orders. Before we build the `OrderManager` class itself, we will need to define a basic building block called the `OMOrder` structure.

Defining the OMOrder struct and its related types

In this first subsection, we will define some enumerations and types to be used in the `OrderManager` class and its sub-components. All the source code for this subsection is in the `Chapter9/trading/strategy/om_order.h` source file on GitHub.

First, we must provide the `include` files that the `om_order.h` file needs:

```
#pragma once

#include <array>
#include <sstream>
#include "common/types.h"

using namespace Common;

namespace Trading {
```

Now, we must declare an `OMOrderState` enumeration, which will be used to track the state of a strategy order (`OMOrder`) in the order manager. These states represent the state of an `OMOrder`, as described here:

- The `INVALID` state represents an invalid order state
- The `PENDING_NEW` state signifies that a new order has been sent out by `OrderManager` but it has not been accepted by the electronic trading exchange yet
- When we receive a response from the exchange to signify acceptance, the order goes from `PENDING_NEW` to `LIVE`

- Like `PENDING_NEW`, the `PENDING_CANCEL` state represents the state of an order when a cancellation for an order has been sent to the exchange but has not been processed by the exchange or the response has not been received back
- The `DEAD` state represents an order that does not exist – it has either not been sent yet or fully executed or successfully cancelled:

```
enum class OMOrderState : int8_t {
  INVALID = 0,
  PENDING_NEW = 1,
  LIVE = 2,
  PENDING_CANCEL = 3,
  DEAD = 4
};
```

We must also add a method for converting `OMOrderState` enumerations into strings for logging purposes, as shown here:

```
inline auto OMOrderStateToString(OMOrderState side) ->
  std::string {
  switch (side) {
    case OMOrderState::PENDING_NEW:
      return "PENDING_NEW";
    case OMOrderState::LIVE:
      return "LIVE";
    case OMOrderState::PENDING_CANCEL:
      return "PENDING_CANCEL";
    case OMOrderState::DEAD:
      return "DEAD";
    case OMOrderState::INVALID:
      return "INVALID";
  }

  return "UNKNOWN";
}
```

Now, we can define the `OMOrder` structure, which has the following key fields:

- A `ticker_id_` variable of the `TickerId` type to represent which trading instrument this order is for
- An `order_id_` variable of the `OrderId` type, which is the unique order ID that's been assigned to this order object
- A `side_` variable to hold the `Side` property of this order

- The order's `Price` is held in the `price_` data member
- The live or requested `Qty` for this order is saved in the `qty_` variable
- An `order_state_` variable of the `OMOrderState` type, which we defined previously, to represent the current state of `OMOrder`:

```
struct OMOrder {
  TickerId ticker_id_ = TickerId_INVALID;
  OrderId order_id_ = OrderId_INVALID;
  Side side_ = Side::INVALID;
  Price price_ = Price_INVALID;
  Qty qty_ = Qty_INVALID;
  OMOrderState order_state_ = OMOrderState::INVALID;
```

We must also add a `toString()` method to stringify `OMOrder` objects for logging purposes:

```
  auto toString() const {
    std::stringstream ss;
    ss << "OMOrder" << "["
       << "tid:" << tickerIdToString(ticker_id_) << " "
       << "oid:" << orderIdToString(order_id_) << " "
       << "side:" << sideToString(side_) << " "
       << "price:" << priceToString(price_) << " "
       << "qty:" << qtyToString(qty_) << " "
       << "state:" << OMOrderStateToString(order_state_)
       << "]";

    return ss.str();
  }
};
```

Here, we define an `OMOrderSideHashMap` typedef to represent a `std::array` of `OMOrder` objects and indicate that the capacity of this array is large enough to hold an entry for the buy side and another for the sell side. Objects of the `OMOrderSideHashMap` type will be indexed by the `sideToIndex(Side::BUY)` and `sideToIndex(Side::SELL)` indices:

```
typedef std::array<OMOrder, sideToIndex(Side::MAX) + 1>
  OMOrderSideHashMap;
```

We must also define an `OMOrderTickerSideHashMap`, which is just another `std::array` of this `OMOrderSideHashMap` object that's large enough to hold all trading instruments – that is, of `ME_MAX_TICKERS` size:

```
typedef std::array<OMOrderSideHashMap, ME_MAX_TICKERS>
  OMOrderTickerSideHashMap;
```

Now, we can build the order manager class, which is used to manage `OMOrder` objects for trading strategies.

Designing the OrderManager class

Our simplified order manager will manage `OMOrder` objects on the trading strategy's behalf. To keep things simple, our `OrderManager` class will allow, at most, a single order on the buy side and a single order on the sell side. We will look at the details of this implementation in this section. All the code for the `OrderManager` class can be found in the `Chapter9/trading/strategy/order_manager.h` and `Chapter9/trading/strategy/order_manager.cpp` source files.

Defining the data members in OrderManager

We need to define the data members that belong within our `OrderManager` class. But before we do that, in the following code block, we have provided the header files we will need to include in the `order_manager.h` source file. We must also forward declare the `TradeEngine` class since we will refer to it in this class but want to avoid circular dependency issues:

```
#pragma once

#include "common/macros.h"
#include "common/logging.h"

#include "exchange/order_server/client_response.h"

#include "om_order.h"
#include "risk_manager.h"

using namespace Common;

namespace Trading {
  class TradeEngine;
```

Now, we can design the internal data members in the `OrderManager` class. The key members are as follows:

- A `trade_engine_` variable. This is a pointer to a `TradeEngine` object. We will use this to store the parent `TradeEngine` instance that is using this order manager.
- A constant reference to a `RiskManager` object stored in the `risk_manager_` member variable. This will be used to perform *pre-trade* risk checks – that is, risk checks that are performed before new orders are sent out to the exchange.

- A `ticker_side_order_` variable of the `OMOrderTickerSideHashMap` type to hold a pair (a buy and a sell) of `OMOrder` objects for each trading instrument. This will be used as a hash map that's indexed first by the `TickerId` value of the instrument we want to send an order for and then indexed by the `sideToIndex(Side::BUY)` or `sideToIndex(Side::SELL)` values to manage the buy or sell order.
- New and unique order IDs starting from 1, which we will generate using a simple `next_order_id_` variable of the `OrderId` type:

```
class OrderManager {
private:
  TradeEngine *trade_engine_ = nullptr;
  const RiskManager& risk_manager_;

  std::string time_str_;
  Common::Logger *logger_ = nullptr;

  OMOrderTickerSideHashMap ticker_side_order_;
  OrderId next_order_id_ = 1;
};
}
```

That is all the data inside the `OrderManager` class. In the next subsection, we will learn how to initialize these members and the `OrderManager` class itself.

Initializing OrderManager

Initializing `OrderManager` is straightforward. In addition to what we initialized in the class definition itself, we must initialize the `trade_engine_`, `risk_manager_` and `logger_` data members, which we expect to be passed through the constructor arguments:

```
OrderManager(Common::Logger *logger, TradeEngine
  *trade_engine, RiskManager& risk_manager)
    : trade_engine_(trade_engine),
      risk_manager_(risk_manager), logger_(logger) {
}
```

As shown here, we must add a simple convenience function that we can use in our `OrderManager` implementation called `getOMOrderSideHashMap()`. This simply returns the `OMOrderSideHashMap` instance for the provided `TickerId`:

```
auto getOMOrderSideHashMap(TickerId ticker_id) const {
  return &(ticker_side_order_.at(ticker_id));
}
```

Next, we can move on to an important task in `OrderManager` – sending new orders.

Sending new orders from OrderManager

The `OrderManager::newOrder()` method is the lower-level method in our order manager class. It requires a pointer to an `OMOrder` object for which this new order is being sent. It also needs the `TickerId`, `Price`, `Side`, and `Qty` attributes to be set on the new order that's being sent out:

```
auto OrderManager::newOrder(OMOrder *order, TickerId
  ticker_id, Price price, Side side, Qty qty) noexcept -> void {
```

It creates a `MEClientRequest` structure of the `ClientRequestType::NEW` type and fills in the attributes that are passed through the arguments, sets `OrderId` to be `next_order_id_` and `ClientId` to be the client ID of `TradeEngine`, which can be obtained by calling the `clientId()` method. It also calls `TradeEngine::sendClientRequest()` and provides the `MEClientRequest` object (new_request) it just initialized:

```
const Exchange::MEClientRequest
  new_request{Exchange::ClientRequestType::NEW,
    trade_engine_->clientId(), ticker_id,
    next_order_id_, side, price, qty};
trade_engine_->sendClientRequest(&new_request);
```

Finally, it updates the `OMOrder` object pointer it was provided in the method parameters and assigns it the attributes that were just set on the new order that was sent out. Note that the state of this `OMOrder` is set to `OMOrderState::PENDING_NEW` since it will be sent out shortly but will not be active until the exchange accepts it and we receive that response. It also increments the `next_order_id_` variable to maintain uniqueness on any new orders that might be sent out later:

```
    *order = {ticker_id, next_order_id_, side, price, qty,
      OMOrderState::PENDING_NEW};
    ++next_order_id_;

    logger_->log("%:% %() % Sent new order % for %\n",
      __FILE__, __LINE__, __FUNCTION__,
        Common::getCurrentTimeStr(&time_str_),
          new_request.toString().c_str(), order->
            toString().c_str());
}
```

We will see where this `newOrder()` method gets called from shortly, but before that, let's look at the complementary task of cancelling orders.

Cancelling orders from OrderManager

`OrderManager::cancelOrder()` is the lower-level method in our order manager class and will be used to send a cancel request for live orders being managed by `OrderManager`. It only accepts a single parameter, which is the `OMOrder` object for which it is going to send the cancel request:

```
auto OrderManager::cancelOrder(OMOrder *order) noexcept
  -> void {
```

Like the `newOrder()` method, we must initialize an `MEClientRequest client_request` object of the `ClientRequestType::CANCEL` type and populate the attributes in it from the `OMOrder` object that was passed into the method. It calls the `TradeEngine::sendClientRequest()` method to send the cancel request out. One thing to understand is that the `next_order_id_` member variable is only used for generating new order IDs for new outgoing order requests. Cancelling an existing order does not change the `next_order_id_` variable, as shown in the following code block. In our design, `next_order_id_` keeps incrementing sequentially each time we send an `MEClientRequest` of the `ClientRequestType::NEW` type. Theoretically, we could reuse the `order_id_` value from the order we just cancelled on the next new order request, but that would require us to track the free order IDs, which is not too difficult either. This was just a design choice we made, but feel free to modify this scheme and track free order IDs if you wish:

```
const Exchange::MEClientRequest cancel_request
  {Exchange::ClientRequestType::CANCEL, trade_engine_->
    clientId(),
  order->ticker_id_, order->order_id_, order->side_,
    order->price_,
  order->qty_};
trade_engine_->sendClientRequest(&cancel_request);
```

Finally, we must update the `order_state_` value of the `OMOrder` object to `OMOrderState::PENDING_CANCEL` to represent the fact that a cancel request has been sent out:

```
  order->order_state_ = OMOrderState::PENDING_CANCEL;

  logger_->log("%:% %() % Sent cancel % for %\n",
    __FILE__, __LINE__, __FUNCTION__,
           Common::getCurrentTimeStr(&time_str_),
           cancel_request.toString().c_str(), order->
             toString().c_str());
}
```

Previously, we mentioned that `newOrder()` and `cancelOrder()` are lower-level methods in the `OrderManager` class. Trading strategies that use `OrderManager` will not call these methods directly; instead, they will have `OrderManager` manage the orders by calling the `OrderManager::moveOrders()` method. We will build this in the next subsection.

Adding methods to simplify order management

Before we build the `moveOrders()` method, we will build one more lower-level method that's used by `OrderManager`. This method, called `moveOrder()`, manages a single order and either sends a new order or cancels an existing order, depending on the arguments provided to it. The most important parameter for this method is a pointer to an `OMOrder` object. It also accepts the `TickerId`, `Price`, `Side`, and `Qty` parameters. The purpose of this method is to make sure that the `OMOrder` object that's passed to it is placed or replaced with the provided `price`, `side`, and `qty` arguments. This involves a combination of cancelling an existing order if it is not at the specified price and/or placing a new order with the `price` and `qty` parameters specified:

```
auto moveOrder(OMOrder *order, TickerId ticker_id,
    Price price, Side side, Qty qty) noexcept {
```

The action this method decides to take depends on the current `order_state_` of the `OMOrder` object passed to it. We will go through the different `OMOrderState` cases one by one, starting with `OMOrderState::LIVE`. If the `OMOrder` object is already live/active, it checks to make sure that the `price` parameter matches the order's `price_` attribute. If that is not the case, then it calls the `OrderManager::cancelOrder()` method to cancel this order and replaces it in the next iteration:

```
    switch (order->order_state_) {
      case OMOrderState::LIVE: {
        if(order->price_ != price || order->qty_ != qty)
          cancelOrder(order);
      }
        break;
```

For cases where the order is in an `INVALID` or `DEAD` state, which means not active in the market, we will place the order using the `OrderManager::newOrder()` method we built previously. But it needs to check with `RiskManager` whether this action is allowed by calling the `RiskManager::checkPreTradeRisk()` method and passing it the `TickerId`, `Side` and `Qty` attributes of the order we would like to send. At this point, it should be clear why this is called pre-trade risk – we check if we can perform the action/trade before we do it. We will discuss the design and implementation of `RiskManager`, as well as the `checkPreTradeRisk()` method, shortly. For now, all you need to know is that it returns a `RiskCheckResult` enumeration value of `RiskCheckResult::ALLOWED` if the risk checks pass and a different value if the risk checks fail – that is, the action/trade is not allowed. In the following code block, we only send the order by calling the `newOrder()` method if the `checkPreTradeRisk()` method returns `RiskCheckResult::ALLOWED`. As a final note, here, we log an error message if the risk check fails using the `riskCheckResultToString()` method. We will cover this shortly:

```
      case OMOrderState::INVALID:
      case OMOrderState::DEAD: {
        if(LIKELY(price != Price_INVALID)) {
```

```cpp
              const auto risk_result = risk_manager_
                .checkPreTradeRisk(ticker_id, side, qty);
              if(LIKELY(risk_result == RiskCheckResult
                ::ALLOWED))
                newOrder(order, ticker_id, price, side, qty);
              else
                logger_->log("%:% %() % Ticker:% Side:% Qty:%
                  RiskCheckResult:%\n", __FILE__, __LINE__,
                    __FUNCTION__,
                            Common::getCurrentTimeStr(&time_
                              str_),
                            tickerIdToString(ticker_id),
                            sideToString(side),
                             qtyToString(qty),
                            riskCheckResultToString
                              (risk_result));
            }
          }
        break;
```

For the cases where the `OMOrder` object's `order_state_` is `PENDING_NEW` or `PENDING_CANCEL`, we do nothing since we are waiting for a response from the electronic trading exchange before we can proceed:

```cpp
        case OMOrderState::PENDING_NEW:
        case OMOrderState::PENDING_CANCEL:
          break;
      }
    }
```

Now, we have all the pieces we need to build our `OrderManager::moveOrders()` method. This is the primary method that's used by trading strategies to generate and manage the orders it needs. It accepts a few parameters – the `TickerId` parameter of the instrument, the `Price` parameter's `bid_price` for the buy order, the `Price` parameter's `ask_price` for the sell order, and a `clip` parameter of the `Qty` type, which will be the quantity of the buy and sell orders. We will see where this `clip` parameter comes from in the *Defining the TradeEngineCfg structure* subsection, in the *Computing and managing risk* section. For now, note that the term `clip` comes from the term clip for ammunition for firearms, and in the context of our trading strategies, it means the size of each order that our trading strategy can send. We will see that this parameter gets used to set the size of outgoing new order requests. This is just the name of the variable we chose; it could also be `trade_size`, `order_size`, and so on.

One thing to note here is that passing a price value of `Price_INVALID` for `bid_price` or `ask_price` will cause the order to be cancelled – that is, it will only have an order on the buy side or the sell side instead of both. This is because the `moveOrder()` method cancels an order if the price on `OMOrder` does not match the price passed to the method. And because any `OMOrder` that is active in the market (`OMOrderState::LIVE`) will have a valid price other than `Price_INVALID`, that check evaluates to true and causes the order to be cancelled. One more thing to note here is that, currently, we support a single `clip` value for both the buy and sell orders, but it is easy to extend this so that we have different quantities for the buy order and the sell order. The implementation of this method is extremely simple – it fetches the buy order (`bid_order`) by indexing the `ticker_side_order_` container with the `ticker_id` value and indexing that with the `sideToIndex(Side::BUY)` value. It then calls the `OrderManager::moveOrder()` method on this `bid_order` and passes it the `bid_price` parameter for the price and passes it the `clip` parameter for the quantity. We do the same thing for the sell order (`ask_order`), except we use `sideToIndex(Side::SELL)` and `ask_price` for the sell side:

```
auto moveOrders(TickerId ticker_id, Price bid_price,
   Price ask_price, Qty clip) noexcept {
  auto bid_order =
    &(ticker_side_order_.at(ticker_id)
      .at(sideToIndex(Side::BUY)));
  moveOrder(bid_order, ticker_id, bid_price, Side::BUY,
    clip);

  auto ask_order = &(ticker_side_order_
    .at(ticker_id).at(sideToIndex(Side::SELL)));
  moveOrder(ask_order, ticker_id, ask_price, Side::
    SELL, clip);
}
```

We need to add one final functionality to our `OrderManager` class, which is handling incoming order responses. We will tackle this in the next subsection.

Handling order updates and updating orders

Before we can wrap up our discussion on the implementation of `OrderManager`, we need to add some code to handle incoming order responses in the form of `MEClientResponse` messages. The `OrderManager::onOrderUpdate()` method we will build here expects to be called and passed a `MEClientResponse` object:

```
auto onOrderUpdate(const Exchange::MEClientResponse
   *client_response) noexcept -> void {
  logger_->log("%:% %() % %\n", __FILE__, __LINE__,
    __FUNCTION__, Common::
      getCurrentTimeStr(&time_str_),
        client_response->toString().c_str());
```

First, we must fetch the `OMOrder` object that this `MEClientResponse` message is meant for. We can do that by accessing the `ticker_side_order_` container using the `ticker_id_` field in `client_response` and converting the `side_` field in the `client_response` message into an index using the `sideToIndex()` method. This is shown in the following code block:

```
auto order = &(ticker_side_order_.at(client_response
  ->ticker_id_).at(sideToIndex(client_response
  ->side_)));
logger_->log("%:% %() % %\n", __FILE__, __LINE__,
  __FUNCTION__, Common::
  getCurrentTimeStr(&time_str_),
       order->toString().c_str());
```

We will update the `OMOrder` object we fetched previously, but that depends on the type of `MEClientResponse` we received. In the case of `ClientResponseType::ACCEPTED`, all we need to do is set the `order_state_` member of this `OMOrder` object to `OMOrderState::LIVE` to mark it as accepted and active in the market:

```
switch (client_response->type_) {
case Exchange::ClientResponseType::ACCEPTED: {
  order->order_state_ = OMOrderState::LIVE;
}
  break;
```

If the type of the response is `ClientResponseType::CANCELED`, then we just update the `order_state_` variable of `OMOrder` to `OMOrderState::DEAD` since it is no longer active in the market:

```
case Exchange::ClientResponseType::CANCELED: {
  order->order_state_ = OMOrderState::DEAD;
}
  break;
```

If `MEClientResponse` is of the `ClientResponseType::FILLED` type, which is done to denote an execution, we update the `qty_` field on `OMOrder` to be the new `leaves_qty_`. This reflects the live quantity that still exists in the market. We also need to check that if the `qty_` field (and thus the `leaves_qty_` field on `client_response`) is 0, meaning the order was fully executed, the order is no longer active in the market. If so, we must set `order_state_` to `OMOrderState::DEAD`:

```
case Exchange::ClientResponseType::FILLED: {
  order->qty_ = client_response->leaves_qty_;
  if(!order->qty_)
    order->order_state_ = OMOrderState::DEAD;
}
  break;
```

We ignore the `CANCEL_REJECTED` and `INVALID` `ClientResponseType` enumeration values since there is no action that we need to take:

```
            case Exchange::ClientResponseType::CANCEL_REJECTED:
            case Exchange::ClientResponseType::INVALID: {
            }
                break;
        }
    }
```

This concludes the discussion, design, and implementation of our `OrderManager` component. However, we referenced and used `RiskManager` in the implementation of the `OrderManager` class without discussing all its details. We will do this in the next section.

Computing and managing risk

The final component we still need to build before we can build our trading strategies is `RiskManager`. The `RiskManager` component tracks the active order quantities that a trading strategy has in the market through the same `OrderManager` instance that a trading strategy uses. It also tracks the positions and realized and unrealized PnLs using the `PositionKeeper` instance, which tracks the trading strategy's positions and PnLs. It checks that the strategy stays within its assigned risk limits. If the trading strategy goes past its risk limits, such as if it loses more money than it's allowed, tries to send an order larger than it's allowed, or builds a position larger than it's allowed, it prevents it from trading. To keep our `RiskManager` simple, we will only implement risk checks on the maximum allowed order size, the maximum allowed position, and the maximum allowed loss for each trading instrument in the client's trading system. The source code for our `RiskManager` can be found in the `Chapter9/trading/strategy/risk_manager.h` and `Chapter9/trading/strategy/risk_manager.cpp` source files. First, we will declare an enumeration and a `RiskInfo` struct. We discussed the details of this component in *Chapter, Designing Our Trading Ecosystem*, in the *Designing a framework for low-latency C++ trading algorithms* section.

Defining the RiskCfg structure

First, we will define a structure that holds risk configurations. This is called the `RiskCfg` struct and is defined in the `Chapter9/common/types.h` header file. The risk configuration holds the following parameters:

- A `max_order_size_` member of the `Qty` type. It represents the maximum allowed order size that a strategy is allowed to send.
- A `max_position_` member variable of the `Qty` type. This represents the maximum position that a strategy is allowed to build.

- A `max_loss_` variable of the `double` type. This is the maximum allowed loss before the trading strategy is shut off from trading further.

We must also add a `toString()` method to the structure for logging purposes:

```
struct RiskCfg {
  Qty max_order_size_ = 0;
  Qty max_position_ = 0;
  double max_loss_ = 0;

  auto toString() const {
    std::stringstream ss;

    ss << "RiskCfg{"
       << "max-order-size:" <<
         qtyToString(max_order_size_) << " "
       << "max-position:" << qtyToString(max_position_)
       << " "
       << "max-loss:" << max_loss_
       << "}";

    return ss.str();
  }
};
```

We will define another configuration structure in the next section. This structure will be used to configure `TradeEngine`.

Defining the TradeEngineCfg structure

First, we must define a structure to encapsulate `TradeEngine` configurations. We will call it `TradeEngineCfg`. This is what we use as the higher-level `TradeEngine` configuration and is defined in the `Chapter9/common/types.h` header file. It has the following important data members:

- A `clip_` member of the `Qty` type. This is what the trading strategies will use as the quantity of the orders that they send out.
- A `threshold_` member of the `double` type. This will be used by the trading strategies and will be used against the feature values to decide if a trading decision needs to be made or not.
- The final member is a `risk_cfg_` variable of the `RiskCfg` type. We defined this previously so that it can hold the risk configuration.

As usual, we must also define a `toString()` method to convert these objects into strings for logging purposes. All the code described here can be seen in the following code block:

```
struct TradeEngineCfg {
  Qty clip_ = 0;
  double threshold_ = 0;
  RiskCfg risk_cfg_;

  auto toString() const {
    std::stringstream ss;
    ss << "TradeEngineCfg{"
        << "clip:" << qtyToString(clip_) << " "
        << "thresh:" << threshold_ << " "
        << "risk:" << risk_cfg_.toString()
        << "}";

    return ss.str();
  }
};
```

The `TradeEngineCfgHashMap` type we are defining here is a `std::array` of these `TradeEngineCfg` objects and is large enough to hold all possible `TickerId` values (ME_MAX_TICKERS):

```
typedef std::array<TradeEngineCfg, ME_MAX_TICKERS>
  TradeEngineCfgHashMap;
```

Now, we need to define a type to represent the outcome of risk checks – the `RiskCheckResult` enumeration.

Declaring the RiskCheckResult enumeration

First, we will formally declare the `RiskCheckResult` enumeration we encountered before. But before we do that, let's look at the `include` files we need in the `risk_manager.h` header file. We will also need to forward declare the `OrderManager` class we built before so that we can use it without running into circular header dependency issues:

```
#pragma once

#include "common/macros.h"
#include "common/logging.h"

#include "position_keeper.h"
#include "om_order.h"

using namespace Common;
```

```
namespace Trading {
  class OrderManager;
```

The `RiskCheckResult` enumeration is used to encapsulate information about the outcome of a risk check in `RiskManager`. Let's look at these values in more detail:

- `INVALID` represents an invalid sentinel value.
- `ORDER_TOO_LARGE` means that the risk check failed because the order quantity that we are attempting to send would exceed the maximum allowed order quantity limit.
- `POSITION_TOO_LARGE` means that the current position, plus the order quantity on the side we are attempting to send, would cause us to potentially exceed the maximum position limit that's been configured in `RiskManager`.
- The `LOSS_TOO_LARGE` enumeration represents the fact that the risk check failed because the trading strategy's total loss (realized plus unrealized loss) is above what is allowed in `RiskManager`.
- The `ALLOWED` enumeration is a value that represents that all risk checks passed successfully. As mentioned previously, this is the only value that allows the trading strategy to send additional orders to the exchange:

```
enum class RiskCheckResult : int8_t {
  INVALID = 0,
  ORDER_TOO_LARGE = 1,
  POSITION_TOO_LARGE = 2,
  LOSS_TOO_LARGE = 3,
  ALLOWED = 4
};
```

We will also add a `riskCheckResultToString()` method to convert these enumerations into strings for logging purposes:

```
inline auto riskCheckResultToString(RiskCheckResult
  result) {
  switch (result) {
    case RiskCheckResult::INVALID:
      return "INVALID";
    case RiskCheckResult::ORDER_TOO_LARGE:
      return "ORDER_TOO_LARGE";
    case RiskCheckResult::POSITION_TOO_LARGE:
      return "POSITION_TOO_LARGE";
    case RiskCheckResult::LOSS_TOO_LARGE:
      return "LOSS_TOO_LARGE";
    case RiskCheckResult::ALLOWED:
```

```
        return "ALLOWED";
    }

    return "";
}
```

In the next section, we will define the basic `RiskInfo` struct, which holds the information we need to perform risk checks for a single trading instrument.

Defining the RiskInfo structure

As mentioned previously, the `RiskInfo` struct holds the information needed to perform risk checks for a single trading instrument. The `RiskManager` class maintains and manages a container of `RiskInfo` objects. The `RiskInfo` struct needs the following important data members:

- A `const` pointer to `PositionInfo` called `position_info_`. This will be used to fetch the position and PnL information for the trading instrument.
- An object (`risk_cfg_`) of the `RiskCfg` type to hold the configured risk limits for this instrument. These are the limits that will be checked against:

```
struct RiskInfo {
  const PositionInfo *position_info_ = nullptr;

  RiskCfg risk_cfg_;
```

Let's add a `toString()` method to this class for logging purposes:

```
        auto toString() const {
          std::stringstream ss;
          ss << "RiskInfo" << "["
             << "pos:" << position_info_->toString() << " "
             << risk_cfg_.toString()
             << "]";

          return ss.str();
        }
```

Finally, we must define a `TickerRiskInfoHashMap` type, which is a `std::array` of `RiskInfo` objects of `ME_MAX_TICKERS` size. We will use this as a hash map of `TickerId` to `RiskInfo` objects:

```
    typedef std::array<RiskInfo, ME_MAX_TICKERS>
      TickerRiskInfoHashMap;
```

Next, we will look at the implementation of the `checkPreTradeRisk()` method, which performs the actual risk checks.

Performing risk checks in RiskInfo

The `checkPreTradeRisk()` method accepts a `Side` argument and a `Qty` argument and returns a `RiskCheckResult` enumeration value, depending on whether the risk check passes or fails for some reason:

```
auto checkPreTradeRisk(Side side, Qty qty) const
  noexcept {
```

First, it checks if the `qty` argument that's passed to the method is larger than the `max_order_size_` member in the `RiskCfg` object (`risk_cfg_`). If this is the case, the risk check fails, and it returns the `RiskCheckResult::ORDER_TOO_LARGE` enumeration:

```
if (UNLIKELY(qty > risk_cfg_.max_order_size_))
  return RiskCheckResult::ORDER_TOO_LARGE;
```

Then, it checks if the current `position_` (which it fetches from the `position_info_` data member), plus the additional `qty` we want to send, exceeds the maximum allowed `max_position_limit` in the `RiskCfg` object (`risk_cfg_`). Note that it uses the `sideToValue(side)` method here to correctly compute what the position could be if this new `qty` were to be executed and then uses the `std::abs()` method to correctly compare against the `max_position_` parameter. In the case of a failure, it signifies the error by returning the `RiskCheckResult::POSITION_TOO_LARGE` method:

```
if (UNLIKELY(std::abs(position_info_->position_ +
  sideToValue(side) * static_cast<int32_t>(qty)) >
    static_cast<int32_t>(risk_cfg_.max_position_)))
  return RiskCheckResult::POSITION_TOO_LARGE;
```

Finally, it checks the last risk metric in our `RiskManager`, which is the total loss. It checks `total_pnl_` from `position_info_` against the `max_loss_` parameter in the `risk_cfg_` configuration. If the loss exceeds the max loss allowed, it returns a `RiskCheckResult::LOSS_TOO_LARGE` enumeration value:

```
if (UNLIKELY(position_info_->total_pnl_ <
  risk_cfg_.max_loss_))
  return RiskCheckResult::LOSS_TOO_LARGE;
```

Finally, if all the risk checks pass successfully, it returns the `RiskCheckResult::ALLOWED` value:

```
  return RiskCheckResult::ALLOWED;
}
```

This important method concludes the design and implementation of the `RiskInfo` struct. Now, we can start building the `RiskManager` class, which is used by the other components we covered.

Designing the data members in RiskManager

Now, we will design our `RiskManager`, starting by defining the data members that make up this class. The key member is a `ticker_risk_` variable of the `TickerRiskInfoHashMap` type and holds `RiskInfo` objects. We defined this previously:

```
class RiskManager {
private:
  std::string time_str_;
  Common::Logger *logger_ = nullptr;

  TickerRiskInfoHashMap ticker_risk_;
};
```

Next, we will learn how to initialize the `RiskManager` class.

Initializing our RiskManager class

The `RiskManager` constructor expects a `Logger` object, a pointer to a `PositionKeeper` object, and a reference to an object of the `TradeEngineCfgHashMap` type (`ticker_cfg`) that holds the risk configurations. It initializes the `logger_` member variable and stores the `PositionInfo` objects from the `PositionKeeper` (`getPositionInfo()`) and `RiskCfg` objects from `TradeEngineCfgHashMap` (`risk_cfg_`) in the `TickerRiskInfoHashMap` data member (`ticker_risk_`):

```
RiskManager::RiskManager(Common::Logger *logger, const
  PositionKeeper *position_keeper, const
    TradeEngineCfgHashMap &ticker_cfg)
    : logger_(logger) {
  for (TickerId i = 0; i < ME_MAX_TICKERS; ++i) {
    ticker_risk_.at(i).position_info_ = position_keeper
      ->getPositionInfo(i);
    ticker_risk_.at(i).risk_cfg_ =
      ticker_cfg[i].risk_cfg_;
  }
}
```

Next, we will implement the final task that `RiskManager` needs to perform – performing risk checks.

Performing risk checks in RiskManager

Given a `TickerId` for an instrument, as well as a `Side` and `Qty` for the order we expect to send, performing risk checks for it in `RiskManager` is straightforward. It simply fetches the correct

`RiskInfo` object corresponding to the instrument, calls the `RiskInfo::checkPreTradeRisk()` method, and returns the return value from that method:

```
auto checkPreTradeRisk(TickerId ticker_id, Side side,
   Qty qty) const noexcept {
   return ticker_risk_.at(ticker_id)
      .checkPreTradeRisk(side, qty);
}
```

That concludes our design and implementation of the `RiskManager` component, as well as all the components we needed before we can start putting them together and building our trading strategies. We will start with that in the next chapter.

One important note is that we will need to build all the components presented in this chapter, as well as *Building the C++ Market-Making and Liquidity-Taking Algorithms* chapter before we can build and run a meaningful trading client. Since our ecosystem consists of a server (trading exchange) and client (trading client) infrastructure, we will need to wait until the *Building the C++ Market-Making and Liquidity-Taking Algorithms* chapter, the *Building and running the main trading application* section, before we can run the full ecosystem.

Summary

In this chapter, our primary focus was on adding intelligence and sophistication to the market participants' trading systems. First, we discussed our market-making and liquidity-taking trading strategies. We discussed the motivation behind these strategies, how they seek to profit in the markets, and the trading dynamics of these algorithms.

We implemented the important components that make up the intelligence around our trading strategies. The first one was the feature engine that's used to compute trading features/signals from the market data so that they can be used by the trading strategies to make informed trading decisions. The next one was the position keeper, which is in charge of tracking a trading strategy's positions and PnLs as the strategy's orders are executed in the market. After, we looked at the order manager component, which sends and manages live orders in the market to simplify the trading strategy's implementation. The risk manager was the final and possibly the most vital component that we looked at since it is in charge of tracking and regulating the risk that a trading algorithm has currently taken, as well as any additional risk it is trying to take.

Now that we have all the important components in one place, in the next chapter, we will build our market-making strategy to provide passive liquidity in the market. Then, we will build the liquidity-taking trading algorithm to send aggressive orders and initiate and manage positions in the market. Finally, we will build our trade engine framework, which will house all the necessary components and build and drive the trading algorithms we built. By doing this, we will complete our electronic trading ecosystem.

10
Building the C++ Market Making and Liquidity Taking Algorithms

In this chapter, we will implement a C++ market making algorithm on top of all the components we built in the previous chapters. This market making algorithm will connect to and send orders to the trading exchange we built previously. Additionally, we will implement a C++ liquidity taking algorithm in the same trading engine framework. This liquidity taking algorithm will also connect to and send orders to the trading exchange.

In this chapter, we will cover the following topics:

- Understanding the behavior of our trading algorithms
- Managing the passive liquidity provided in the order book
- Opening and closing positions aggressively
- Building the trade engine framework
- Building and running the main trading application

Technical requirements

All the code for this book can be found in its GitHub repository at https://github.com/PacktPublishing/Building-Low-Latency-Applications-with-CPP. The source for this chapter is in the Chapter10 directory in the repository.

It is important that you have read and understood the design of the electronic trading ecosystem presented in the *Designing Our Trading Ecosystem* chapter, especially the *Designing a framework for low latency C++ trading algorithms* section. It is also expected that you are quite familiar with the previous two chapters – *Processing Market Data and Sending Orders to the Exchange in C++* and *Building the C++ Trading Algorithm Building Blocks*, since we will be using every single component that we built in those two chapters in this chapter.

The specifications of the environment in which the source code for this book was developed are shown here. We present the details of this environment since all the C++ code presented in this book is not necessarily portable and might require some minor changes to work in your environment:

- OS: `Linux 5.19.0-41-generic #42~22.04.1-Ubuntu SMP PREEMPT_DYNAMIC Tue Apr 18 17:40:00 UTC 2 x86_64 x86_64 x86_64 GNU/Linux`
- GCC: `g++ (Ubuntu 11.3.0-1ubuntu1~22.04.1) 11.3.0`
- CMake: `cmake version 3.23.2`
- Ninja: `1.10.2`

Understanding the behavior of our trading algorithms

In this section, we will discuss some additional details about the behavior and motivation behind the two trading strategies we will build in this chapter – the market making trading strategy and the liquidity taking trading strategy. With the use of a hypothetical example for each strategy, we will also try to understand the strategy order flow mechanics and try to further our understanding when we implement these trading strategies in our C++ system, towards the end of this chapter.

Understanding the market making trading algorithm

The market making trading strategies seek to make profits by seeking to *capture the spread*, which just means buying at the best bid price in the market passively and quickly selling at the best ask price in the market passively (or selling first and buying after). The market making strategies, profitability depends on the spread of the trading instrument, how many buy and sell trades the strategy can execute over time, and how much market prices move between the buy and sell trades. It should be clear that the market making strategies will trade only against other strategies that *cross the spread* and send aggressive buy and sell orders, which is what we refer to as **liquidity taking trading strategies**. What this means is that market making trading strategies rarely expect to trade against other market making trading strategies, since all instances of such strategies seek to execute their orders passively. To achieve this, market making trading strategies send and manage passive limit orders in the order book and try to use intelligence to modify the prices on these orders, thereby improving their execution and the probability of successfully capturing the spread as often as possible. In the next subsection, we will discuss a hypothetical example of how a market making trading strategy would manage its orders.

Inspecting market making mechanics with an example

In this subsection, we will discuss the mechanics of how our market making trading strategy would behave under a hypothetical market condition. This will help strengthen your understanding of how the market making algorithm behaves. Before we do that, let us try to understand the following table.

The table presents a state of the market book known as the **price level-aggregated order book**. What this term means is that all the orders on the same side and same price are grouped/aggregated together into a single price level, so if there are 12 orders on the bid side, all at the same price (10.21), that add up to a total quantity of 2,500, they can be presented as a single entry. This is shown as follows, along with similar grouping on the next buy price level of 10.20 and ask levels of 10.22 and 10.23 prices.

Our MM strategy bid	Market bid order count	Market bid quantity	Market bid price	Market ask price	Market ask quantity	Market ask order count	Our MM strategy ask
	12	2500	10.21	10.22	4500	8	
	25	4700	10.20	10.23	5500	18	

Figure 10.1 – A snapshot of an order book, arranged as a price level-aggregated book

In the preceding diagram, the columns mean the following things (from left to right):

- **Our MM strategy bid**: This represents the quantity of the buy order that our **Market Making** (**MM**) strategy has at this price level, which in this case is none
- **Market bid order count**: This represents the number of buy orders in the market that make up this price level
- **Market bid quantity**: The sum of the quantities on all the buy orders at this price level
- **Market bid price**: This represents the price of this bid price level
- **Market ask price**: This represents the price of this ask price level
- **Market ask quantity**: The sum of the quantities of all the sell orders at this price level
- **Market ask order count**: This represents the number of sell orders in the market that make up this price level
- **Our MM strategy ask**: This represents the quantity of the sell order that our MM strategy has at this price level, which in this case is none

Now, let us suppose our MM strategy starts running at the time that the market is in the state we described here. Let us also assume that, for this example, our strategy will send a single passive bid order and a single passive ask order, and each has a quantity of 100 shares. Let us say that the strategy decides to join the best bid price level and the best ask price level at prices 10.21 and 10.22, respectively. It does this by sending a single buy order and a single sell order of a quantity of 100 at those prices.

The following diagram represents this event, and the blocks highlighted in gold represent the things that changed because of this action.

Our MM strategy bid	Market bid order count	Market bid quantity	Market bid price	Market ask price	Market ask quantity	Market ask order count	Our MM strategy ask
100	13	2600	10.21	10.22	4600	9	100
	25	4700	10.20	10.23	5500	18	

Figure 10.2 – An event where our MM order has joined the market on both sides

Finally, for one last scenario, let us assume that the orders on the best bid at 10.21 are either fully executed due to trade events and removed, or just canceled by the market participants that owned them. If the drop in quantity is large enough, let us assume that our MM trading strategy also decides to not be present at the price level. The state of the price aggregated order book looks like this right before our strategy decides to move its best bid order at a price one price level away from its current price, i.e., from price 10.21 to 10.20:

Our MM strategy bid	Market bid order count	Market bid quantity	Market bid price	Market ask price	Market ask quantity	Market ask order count	Our MM strategy ask
100	3	600	10.21	10.22	6500	11	100
	26	4800	10.20	10.23	5500	18	

Figure 10.3 – The state of the price level book when our MM order decides to move its bid

This decision can be due to a wide range of factors, depending on the strategy and its features. However, for this example, let us offer you a simple intuitive thought – a lot of people are less willing to buy at 10.21 (only 600 shares in total) compared to how many people are willing to sell at 10.22 (6,500 shares). You might conclude that perhaps it is no longer wise to try and buy at 10.21 or that the fair market price is perhaps at 10.21, and you want to try and buy at a price that is a little lower than that. The next diagram displays the state of the price level book when the MM strategy decides to cancel its buy order at 10.21 and repositions its buy order to 10.20.

Our MM strategy bid	Market bid order count	Market bid quantity	Market bid price	Market ask price	Market ask quantity	Market ask order count	Our MM strategy ask
	2	500	10.21	10.22	6500	11	100
100	26	4800	10.20	10.23	5500	18	

Figure 10.4 – An event where our MM strategy repositions its bid from a price of 10.21 to 10.20

The discussion in this subsection aimed to improve your understanding of the mechanics of a simple MM strategy, and in the next subsection, we will move on to the liquidity taking trading algorithm.

Understanding the liquidity taking trading algorithm

The liquidity taking trading algorithm in many ways is the opposite of the MM algorithm. Instead of sending passive orders to the book and waiting for them to be executed passively, it sends aggressive orders to execute trades when it needs them. In this sense, it *crosses the spread* (sends aggressive orders to execute) instead of trying to *capture the spread*, like the MM strategy. This strategy bets on getting the direction of the market correct – that is, it buys aggressively when it thinks that prices will increase further and sells aggressively when it thinks that prices will decrease further. The convenient fact about this trading algorithm is that order management is very easy since it does not always maintain live orders in the order book that it needs to manage. Another way to understand this is that when the strategy needs to execute a trade, it sends an order to the order book and gets executed almost immediately, and then it is done from an order management perspective. The inconvenient fact about this trading algorithm is that predicting market directions is extremely difficult, but we will not dive into that, since that is not the focus of this book. In the next subsection, we will understand the trading mechanics for this strategy as we did with the MM strategy.

Inspecting liquidity taking mechanics with an example

Once again, let us look at the price level-aggregated view of the order book, as discussed in the section on MM. The columns here mean the same thing, except they do not have the columns for the MM strategy orders, since the liquidity taking strategy will not rest orders passively in the order book. Let us assume the initial state of the price level book is as shown here, which was also the same initial state for the MM example.

Market bid order count	Market bid quantity	Market bid price	Market ask price	Market ask quantity	Market ask order count
12	2500	10.21	10.22	4500	8
25	4700	10.20	10.23	5500	18

Figure 10.5 – The state of the price level book at a given time for a hypothetical example

Let us assume that, for this example, our liquidity taking strategy has a feature that tries to follow in the same direction as very large trades. What this means is that if a very large trade event happens in the market, our liquidity taking algorithm decides to take the same direction as this trade event. So, if a very large buy trade happens, our liquidity taking algorithm will buy aggressively, and if a very sell trade happens, our liquidity taking algorithm will sell aggressively. As mentioned before, this is only an example feature; in practice, different liquidity taking algorithms will have many such features on which the decision to make a trade depends. For our simple liquidity taking algorithm example, we will use this feature of large aggressive trade in the market.

To understand what that looks like, let us assume that given the previous state of the price level book, a very large sell execution of a quantity of 2,200 hits the bid price level of 10.21, which had a total quantity of 2,500 prior to this. This event is shown in the following diagram, where the green arrow represents the trade aggressor in market data.

Market bid order count	Market bid quantity	Market bid price	Market ask price	Market ask quantity	Market ask order count
12	2500	10.21 ← Sell 2200@10.21	10.22	4500	8
25	4700	10.20	10.23	5500	18

Figure 10.6 – An event where a large sell aggressor causes a trade event

This trade event will cause the best bid quantity to reduce from 2,500 to 300 – that is, by the quantity of the trade aggressor. Additionally, let us assume that our liquidity taking strategy observes the large trade of a quantity of 2,200 and decides to send an aggressive sell order at the price of 10.21. Let us also assume that, like the MM strategy, our liquidity taking strategy also sends a sell order of a quantity of 100. This event is shown in the following diagram.

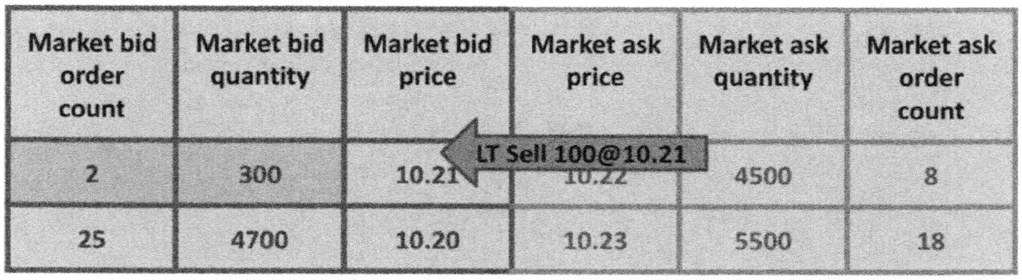

Market bid order count	Market bid quantity	Market bid price	Market ask price	Market ask quantity	Market ask order count
2	300	10.21	10.22	4500	8
25	4700	10.20	10.23	5500	18

LT Sell 100@10.21

Figure 10.7 – An event where our liquidity taking algorithm sends an aggressive sell order of a quantity of 100 at a price of 10.21

That concludes the theoretical discussion of the two trading strategies we seek to build as part of our trading system. We will get to their actual implementation inside our framework in a few sections' time, but first, we need to build some additional building blocks for these strategies, which we will do in the next section.

Adding an enumeration to define the type of algorithm

We will round up this discussion of our trading strategies by defining an `AlgoType` enumeration in the `Chapter10/common/types.h` header file. It has the following valid values – MAKER to represent MM, TAKER to represent liquidity taking, and RANDOM to represent the random trading strategy we built before. We also have INVALID and MAX values:

```
enum class AlgoType : int8_t {
  INVALID = 0,
  RANDOM = 1,
  MAKER = 2,
  TAKER = 3,
  MAX = 4
};
```

We will add a standard `algoTypeToString()` method used to stringify the `AlgoType` type, as shown here:

```
inline auto algoTypeToString(AlgoType type) -> std::string {
  switch (type) {
    case AlgoType::RANDOM:
      return "RANDOM";
    case AlgoType::MAKER:
      return "MAKER";
    case AlgoType::TAKER:
      return "TAKER";
    case AlgoType::INVALID:
      return "INVALID";
    case AlgoType::MAX:
```

```
      return "MAX";
  }

  return "UNKNOWN";
}
```

The `stringToAlgoType()` method, which we will build next, parses a string and converts it into an `AlgoType` enumeration value. It does this by iterating through all the possible `AlgoType` enumeration values and comparing the string argument against the output of `algoTypeToString()`, called on that `AlgoType` enumeration value. If the string representations match, then it returns the `algo_type` enumeration:

```
inline auto stringToAlgoType(const std::string &str) ->
  AlgoType {
  for (auto i = static_cast<int>(AlgoType::INVALID); i <=
    static_cast<int>(AlgoType::MAX); ++i) {
    const auto algo_type = static_cast<AlgoType>(i);
    if (algoTypeToString(algo_type) == str)
      return algo_type;
  }

  return AlgoType::INVALID;
}
```

Next, we will move on to building the different building blocks we need to support our trading strategies.

Managing the passive liquidity provided in the order book

At this point, we have all the sub-components we need to start building our trading strategies. The first strategy we will build will be the MM algorithm, which sends orders that are expected to rest passively in the order book. We discussed the details of this trading algorithm earlier in this chapter, so in this section, we will focus on the C++ implementation. All the source code for this `MarketMaker` trading algorithm can be found in the `Chapter10/trading/strategy/market_maker.h` and `Chapter10/trading/strategy/market_maker.cpp` source files.

Defining the data members in the MarketMaker algorithm

First, we need to define the data members that make up the `MarketMaker` class. The key members are the following:

- A pointer to a constant `FeatureEngine` object called `feature_engine_`, which we will use to fetch the fair market price, using the `FeatureEngine::getMktPrice()` method we saw earlier

- A pointer to an `OrderManager` object called `order_manager_`, which will be used to manage the passive orders that this strategy sends
- A `ticker_cfg_` variable of a constant `TradeEngineCfgHashMap` type to hold the trading parameters for the different trading instruments that this algorithm will trade

Let us inspect the class definition, starting with the `include` files needed in the `market_maker.h` header file:

```
#pragma once

#include "common/macros.h"
#include "common/logging.h"

#include "order_manager.h"
#include "feature_engine.h"

using namespace Common;
```

And now, in the next code block, we can define the `MarketMaker` class and the aforementioned data members:

```
namespace Trading {
  class MarketMaker {
  private:
    const FeatureEngine *feature_engine_ = nullptr;
    OrderManager *order_manager_ = nullptr;

    std::string time_str_;
    Common::Logger *logger_ = nullptr;

    const TradeEngineCfgHashMap ticker_cfg_;
  };
}
```

The next section will define the constructor to initialize an instance of this `MarketMaker` class.

Initializing the MarketMaker algorithm

The constructor implemented in the `market_maker.cpp` file is shown in the next code block. The constructor accepts a few arguments in the constructor:

- A `Logger` object, which will be saved in the `logger_` member variable and used for logging purposes.

- A pointer to a `TradeEngine` object, which will be used to bind the `algoOnOrderBookUpdate`, `algoOnTradeUpdate`, and `algoOnOrderUpdate` callbacks in the parent `TradeEngine` instance to the corresponding methods in the `MarketMaker` object. This is so that the `MarketMaker` trading strategy receives and processes the callbacks when `TradeEngine` receives them.
- A pointer to a constant `FeatureEngine` object, which will be stored in the `feature_engine_` data member and used to extract the feature values this algorithm needs, as described before.
- A pointer to an `OrderManager` object, which will be used to manage the orders for this strategy, and the constructor will simply be saved in the `order_manager_` data member.
- A reference to a constant `TradeEngineCfgHashMap`, which will be saved in the `ticker_cfg_` member and used to make trading decisions, since this contains the trading parameters:

```cpp
#include "market_maker.h"

#include "trade_engine.h"

namespace Trading {
  MarketMaker::MarketMaker(Common::Logger *logger,
    TradeEngine *trade_engine, const FeatureEngine
      *feature_engine,
OrderManager *order_manager, const
  TradeEngineCfgHashMap &ticker_cfg)
      : feature_engine_(feature_engine),
        order_manager_(order_manager),
          logger_(logger),
          ticker_cfg_(ticker_cfg) {
```

As mentioned before and as shown here, we will override the `TradeEngine::algoOnOrderBookUpdate()`, `TradeEngine::algoOnTradeUpdate()`, and `TradeEngine::algoOnOrderUpdate()` methods using lambda methods to forward them to the `MarketMaker::onOrderBookUpdate()`, `MarketMaker::onTradeUpdate()`, and `MarketMaker::onOrderUpdate()` methods, respectively:

```cpp
    trade_engine->algoOnOrderBookUpdate_ = [this](auto
      ticker_id, auto price, auto side, auto book) {
      onOrderBookUpdate(ticker_id, price, side, book);
    };
    trade_engine->algoOnTradeUpdate_ = [this](auto
      market_update, auto book) {
        onTradeUpdate(market_update, book); };
    trade_engine->algoOnOrderUpdate_ = [this](auto
      client_response) { onOrderUpdate(client_response); };
```

```
        }
    }
```

The next subsection tackles the most important task in the `MarketMaker` trading algorithm – handling order book updates and sending orders in reaction to them.

Handling order book updates and trade events

The `MarketMaker::onOrderBookUpdate()` method is called by `TradeEngine` through the `TradeEngine::algoOnOrderBookUpdate_ std::function` member variable. This is where the `MarketMaker` trading strategy makes trading decisions with regard to what prices it wants its bid and ask orders to be at:

```
      auto onOrderBookUpdate(TickerId ticker_id, Price price,
        Side side, const MarketOrderBook *book) noexcept -> void {
        logger_->log("%:% %() % ticker:% price:% side:%\n",
          __FILE__, __LINE__, __FUNCTION__,
               Common::getCurrentTimeStr(&time_str_),
                 ticker_id, Common::
                     priceToString(price).c_str(),
                Common::sideToString(side).c_str());
```

It fetches BBO from w using the `getBBO()` method and saves it in the `bbo` variable. We also fetch the market quantity-weighted BBO price and save it in the `fair_price` variable:

```
        const auto bbo = book->getBBO();
        const auto fair_price = feature_engine_->
          getMktPrice();
```

We perform a sanity check on the best `bid_price_` and `ask_price_` values from `bbo` and `fair_price` to make sure that the prices are not `Price_INVALID` and the feature value is not `Feature_INVALID`. Only if this is `true` will we take any action; otherwise, we risk acting on invalid features or sending orders at invalid prices:

```
        if (LIKELY(bbo->bid_price_ != Price_INVALID && bbo->
          ask_price_ != Price_INVALID && fair_price !=
            Feature_INVALID)) {
          logger_->log("%:% %() % % fair-price:%\n",
            __FILE__, __LINE__, __FUNCTION__,
                  Common::getCurrentTimeStr(&time_str_),
                  bbo->toString().c_str(), fair_price);
```

We fetch and save the `clip` quantity from the `ticker_cfg_` container, which will be the quantity on the passive orders we send to the exchange. We also extract and save the `threshold` value, which we will use to decide what prices to send the buy and sell orders at:

```
const auto clip = ticker_cfg_.at(ticker_id).clip_;
const auto threshold =
  ticker_cfg_.at(ticker_id).threshold_;
```

We initialize two price variables, `bid_price` and `ask_price`, to represent the prices on our buy and sell orders, respectively. We set `bid_price` to be the best bid price if the difference between `fair_price` we computed from the `FeatureEngine::getMktPrice()` method and the market bid price exceeds the `threshold` value. Otherwise, we set `bid_price` to be a price lower than the best market bid price. We compute `ask_price` using the same logic – use the best ask price if the difference from the fair price exceeds the threshold and a higher price otherwise. The motivation behind this is straightforward; when we think the fair price is higher than the best bid price, we are willing to buy at the best bid price, expecting the prices to go higher. When we think the fair price is lower than the best ask price, we are willing to sell at the best ask price, expecting the prices to go lower:

```
const auto bid_price = bbo->bid_price_ -
  (fair_price - bbo->bid_price_ >= threshold ? 0 :
    1);
const auto ask_price = bbo->ask_price_ + (bbo->
  ask_price_ - fair_price >= threshold ? 0 : 1);
```

We use the `bid_price` and `ask_price` variables we computed in the preceding code block a and pass them to the `OrderManager::moveOrders()` method to move the orders to the desired prices:

```
order_manager_->moveOrders(ticker_id, bid_price,
  ask_price, clip);
  }
}
```

The `MarketMaker` trading algorithm does not do anything when there are trade events and simply logs the trade message it receives, as shown here:

```
auto onTradeUpdate(const Exchange::MEMarketUpdate
  *market_update, MarketOrderBook * /* book */)
  noexcept -> void {
  logger_->log("%:% %() % %\n", __FILE__, __LINE__,
    __FUNCTION__, Common::
    getCurrentTimeStr(&time_str_),
           market_update->toString().c_str());
}
```

We have one more task to complete the `MarketMaker` trading strategy – handling order updates for its orders, which will be addressed in the next subsection.

Handling order updates in the MarketMaker algorithm

The handling of order updates for the `MarketMaker` trading algorithm's orders is simple; it simply forwards the `MEClientResponse` messages to the `order_manager_` member it uses to manage orders. This is achieved by calling the `OrderManager::onOrderUpdate()` method, which we implemented previously:

```
auto onOrderUpdate(const Exchange::MEClientResponse
  *client_response) noexcept -> void {
  logger_->log("%:% %() % %\n", __FILE__, __LINE__,
    __FUNCTION__, Common::
    getCurrentTimeStr(&time_str_),
            client_response->toString().c_str());
  order_manager_->onOrderUpdate(client_response);
}
```

That concludes our implementation of the MM trading algorithm. In the next section, we will tackle the other type of trading strategy we will build in this book – a liquidity taking algorithm.

Opening and closing positions aggressively

In this section, we will build a liquidity taking algorithm, whose behavior we covered in the first section of this chapter. This trading strategy does not send passive orders as the MM algorithm does; instead, it sends aggressive orders that trade against liquidity resting in the book. The source code for the `LiquidityTaker` algorithm is in the `Chapter10/trading/strategy/liquidity_taker.h` and `Chapter10/trading/strategy/liquidity_taker.cpp` source files. First, we will define the data members that make up the `LiquidityTaker` class in the next subsection.

Defining the data members in the LiquidityTaker algorithm

The `LiquidityTaker` trading strategy has the same data members as the `MarketMaker` algorithm we built in the previous section. Before we describe the data members themselves, we will present the header files we need to include in the `liquidity_taker.h` source file:

```
#pragma once

#include "common/macros.h"
#include "common/logging.h"

#include "order_manager.h"
```

```cpp
#include "feature_engine.h"

using namespace Common;
```

Now, we can define the data members, which are the same ones that the MM algorithm has. The `LiquidityTaker` class has a `feature_engine_` member, which is a constant pointer to a `FeatureEngine` object, an `order_manager_` pointer to an `OrderManager` object, and a constant `ticker_cfg_` member, which is of type `TradeEngineCfgHashMap`. These members serve the same purpose as they did in the `MarketMaker` class; `feature_engine_` is used to extract the ratio of aggressive trade to top-of-book quantity. The `order_manager_` object is used to send and manage the orders for this trading strategy. Finally, the `ticker_cfg_` object holds the trading parameters that will be used by this algorithm to make trading decisions and send orders to the exchange:

```cpp
namespace Trading {
  class LiquidityTaker {
  private:
    const FeatureEngine *feature_engine_ = nullptr;
    OrderManager *order_manager_ = nullptr;

    std::string time_str_;
    Common::Logger *logger_ = nullptr;

    const TradeEngineCfgHashMap ticker_cfg_;
  };
}
```

In the next section, we will see how to initialize a `LiquidityTaker` object.

Initializing the LiquidityTaker trading algorithm

The initialization for the `LiquidityTaker` class is identical to the initialization for the `MarketMaker` class. The constructor expects the following arguments – a `Logger` object, the `TradeEngine` object within which this algorithm runs, a `FeatureEngine` object to compute the feature, an `OrderManager` object used to manage orders for this trading strategy, and a `TradeEngineCfgHashMap` object containing the trading parameters for this strategy:

```cpp
#include "liquidity_taker.h"

#include "trade_engine.h"

namespace Trading {
  LiquidityTaker::LiquidityTaker(Common::Logger *logger,
    TradeEngine *trade_engine, FeatureEngine
```

```cpp
      *feature_engine,
  OrderManager *order_manager,
  const TradeEngineCfgHashMap &ticker_cfg):
    feature_engine_(feature_engine),
      order_manager_(order_manager), logger_(logger),
      ticker_cfg_(ticker_cfg) {
```

This constructor also overrides the callbacks in the `TradeEngine` object for order book updates, trade events, and updates to the algorithm's orders like the `MarketMaker` algorithm. The `std::function` members, `algoOnOrderBookUpdate_`, `algoOnTradeUpdate_`, and `algoOnOrderUpdate_`, in `TradeEngine` are bound, respectively, to the `onOrderBookUpdate`, `onTradeUpdate`, and `onOrderUpdate` methods within `LiquidityTaker` using lambda methods, as shown here (and as we saw before):

```cpp
    trade_engine->algoOnOrderBookUpdate_ = [this](auto
      ticker_id, auto price, auto side, auto book) {
      onOrderBookUpdate(ticker_id, price, side, book);
    };
    trade_engine->algoOnTradeUpdate_ = [this](auto
      market_update, auto book) {
      onTradeUpdate(market_update, book); };
    trade_engine->algoOnOrderUpdate_ = [this](auto
      client_response) { onOrderUpdate(client_response); };
  }
}
```

Next, we will discuss the code for handling trade events and order book updates due to events in the market data in this trading strategy.

Handling trade events and order book updates

For the `MarketMaker` trading strategy, we saw that it only makes trading decisions on order book updates and does nothing on trade updates. The `LiquidityTaker` strategy does the opposite – it takes trading decisions in the `onTradeUpdate()` method and does nothing in the `onOrderBookUpdate()` method. We will start by looking at the implementation of the `LiquidityTaker::onTradeUpdate()` method first in the next code block:

```cpp
    auto onTradeUpdate(const Exchange::MEMarketUpdate
      *market_update, MarketOrderBook *book) noexcept -> void {
      logger_->log("%:% %() % %\n", __FILE__, __LINE__,
        __FUNCTION__, Common::
        getCurrentTimeStr(&time_str_),
              market_update->toString().c_str());
```

We will fetch and save BBO using the `getBBO()` method in the `bbo` local variable. For this trading strategy, we will fetch the aggressive trade quantity ratio feature from the feature engine by calling the `FeatureEngine::getAggTradeQtyRatio()` method and saving it in the `agg_qty_ratio` variable:

```cpp
const auto bbo = book->getBBO();
const auto agg_qty_ratio = feature_engine_->
  getAggTradeQtyRatio();
```

As we saw before, we will check to make sure that `bid_price_`, `ask_price_`, and `agg_qty_ratio` are valid values before we decide to take an order action:

```cpp
if (LIKELY(bbo->bid_price_ != Price_INVALID && bbo->
  ask_price_ != Price_INVALID && agg_qty_ratio !=
    Feature_INVALID)) {
logger_->log("%:% %() % % agg-qty-ratio:%\n",
  __FILE__, __LINE__, __FUNCTION__,
    Common::getCurrentTimeStr(&time_str_),
    bbo->toString().c_str(),
      agg_qty_ratio);
```

If the validity check passes, we first need to fetch the `clip_` member from the `ticker_cfg_` object for the `TickerId` of this trade message, as shown in the following code block, and save it in the `clip` local variable. Similarly, we will fetch and save the `threshold_` member from the `ticker_cfg_` configuration object for that `TickerId`:

```cpp
const auto clip = ticker_cfg_.at(market_update->
  ticker_id_).clip_;
const auto threshold = ticker_cfg_
  .at(market_update->ticker_id_).threshold_;
```

To decide whether we send or adjust active orders for this algorithm, we will check whether the `agg_qty_ratio` exceeds the threshold we previously fetched:

```cpp
if (agg_qty_ratio >= threshold) {
```

To send orders using the `OrderManager::moveOrders()` method, we will check whether the aggressive trade was a buy trade or a sell trade. If it was a buy trade, we will send an aggressive buy order to take liquidity at the best BBO `ask_price_` and no sell order by specifying a sell price of `Price_INVALID`. Conversely, if it was a sell trade and we wanted to send an aggressive sell order to take liquidity, we would specify a sell price to be `bid_price_` in the BBO object and no buy order by specifying a `Price_INVALID` buy price. Remember that this trading strategy takes a direction in the market by aggressively sending a buy or sell order one at a time, but not both like the `MarketMaker` algorithm:

```
              if (market_update->side_ == Side::BUY)
                order_manager_->moveOrders(market_update->
                  ticker_id_, bbo->ask_price_, Price_INVALID,
                    clip);
              else
                order_manager_->moveOrders(market_update->
                  ticker_id_, Price_INVALID, bbo->bid_price_,
                    clip);
          }
       }
    }
```

As mentioned before and as shown in the following code block, this `LiquidityTaker` trading strategy does not take any action on order updates in the `onOrderBookUpdate()` method:

```
auto onOrderBookUpdate(TickerId ticker_id, Price price,
  Side side, MarketOrderBook *) noexcept -> void {
  logger_->log("%:% %() % ticker:% price:% side:%\n",
    __FILE__, __LINE__, __FUNCTION__,
              Common::getCurrentTimeStr(&time_str_),
                ticker_id, Common::
                  priceToString(price).c_str(),
              Common::sideToString(side).c_str());
}
```

The next concluding section related to `LiquidityTaker` adds handling to the order updates for the strategy's orders.

Handling order updates in the LiquidityTaker algorithm

The `LiquidityTaker::onOrderUpdate()` method, as shown in the following code block, has an identical implementation to the `MarketMaker::onOrderUpdate()` method and simply forwards the order update to the order manager using the `OrderManager::onOrderUpdate()` method:

```
auto onOrderUpdate(const Exchange::MEClientResponse
   *client_response) noexcept -> void {
  logger_->log("%:% %() % %\n", __FILE__, __LINE__,
     __FUNCTION__, Common::
       getCurrentTimeStr(&time_str_),
             client_response->toString().c_str());
  order_manager_->onOrderUpdate(client_response);
}
```

That concludes our implementation of the `LiquidityTaker` trading strategy. In the next section, we will shift the discussion to building the final form of our trading application so that we can build and run these actual trading strategies in our electronic trading ecosystem.

Building the trade engine framework

In this section, we will build the trade engine framework in the `TradeEngine` class. This framework ties all the different components we built together – the `OrderGateway`, `MarketDataConsumer`, `MarketOrderBook`, `FeatureEngine`, `PositionKeeper`, `OrderManager`, `RiskManager`, `MarketMaker`, and `LiquidityTaker` components. As a reminder of the trading engine component, we present a diagram of all the sub-components here. We have built all the sub-components; now, we will just build the trading engine framework in which these sub-components exist.

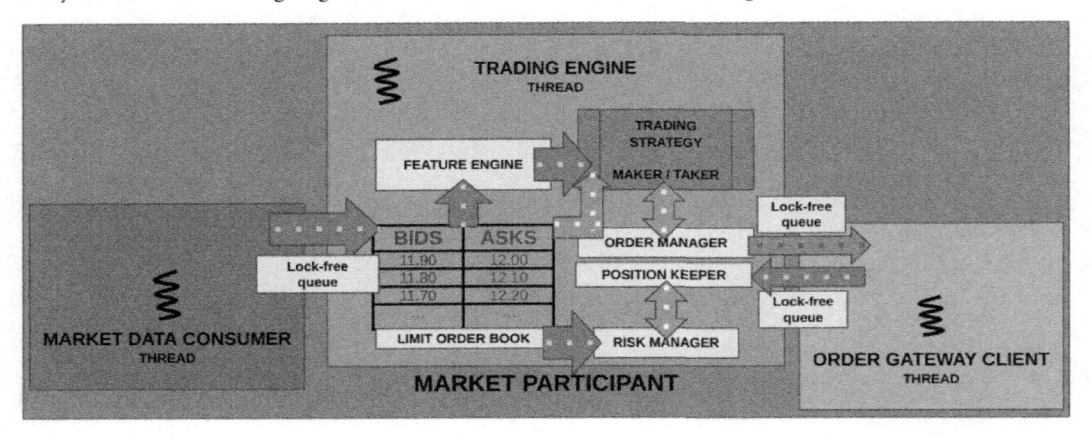

Figure 10.8 – The components of the trading engine in the client's trading system

We will start this section by defining the data members of our class, as usual. All the source code for the basic `TradeEngine` framework is in the `Chapter10/trading/strategy/trade_engine.h` and `Chapter10/trading/strategy/trade_engine.cpp` source files.

Defining the data members in the trade engine

Before we define the data members in the `TradeEngine` class, we present the header files that the `trade_engine.h` source file needs to include:

```
#pragma once

#include <functional>

#include "common/thread_utils.h"
```

```cpp
#include "common/time_utils.h"
#include "common/lf_queue.h"
#include "common/macros.h"
#include "common/logging.h"

#include "exchange/order_server/client_request.h"
#include "exchange/order_server/client_response.h"
#include "exchange/market_data/market_update.h"

#include "market_order_book.h"

#include "feature_engine.h"
#include "position_keeper.h"
#include "order_manager.h"
#include "risk_manager.h"

#include "market_maker.h"
#include "liquidity_taker.h"
```

The `TradeEngine` class needs the following basic data members:

- It has a `client_id_` variable of type `ClientId` to represent the unique trading application instance.

- We create a `ticker_order_book_` instance of type `MarketOrderBookHashMap`, which, as a reminder, is `std::array` of `MarketOrderBook` objects to represent a hash map from `TickerId` to `MarketOrderBook` for that instrument.

- We have three lock-free queues to receive market data updates, send order requests, and receive order responses from the `MarketDataConsumer` and `OrderGateway` components. We receive market data updates using the `incoming_md_updates_` variable, which is a pointer to type `MEMarketUpdateLFQueue` (LFQueue of `MEMarketUpdate` messages). We send client order requests using the `outgoing_ogw_requests_` variable, which is a pointer to type `ClientRequestLFQueue` (LFQueue of `MEClientRequest` messages). We receive client order responses using the `incoming_ogw_responses_` variable, which is a pointer to type `ClientResponseLFQueue` (LFQueue of `MEClientResponse` messages).

- We have the usual Boolean `run_` variable, which will control the execution of the main `TradeEngine` thread and is marked `volatile`.

- We have a `last_event_time_` variable of type `Nanos` to keep track of the time when the last message from the exchange was received.

- We will also have a `Logger` variable called `logger_` to create a log file for `TradeEngine` to use:

```
namespace Trading {
  class TradeEngine {
  private:
    const ClientId client_id_;

    MarketOrderBookHashMap ticker_order_book_;

    Exchange::ClientRequestLFQueue *outgoing_ogw_requests_
      = nullptr;
    Exchange::ClientResponseLFQueue
      *incoming_ogw_responses_ = nullptr;
    Exchange::MEMarketUpdateLFQueue *incoming_md_updates_ =
      nullptr;

    Nanos last_event_time_ = 0;
    volatile bool run_ = false;

    std::string time_str_;
    Logger logger_;
```

We also need instances of each of our components from the previous chapter, namely the following:

- A variable of type `FeatureEngine` called `feature_engine_` to compute complex feature values
- A `position_keeper_` variable of type `PositionKeeper` to track trading strategy positions and Profits and Losses (**PnLs**) money made or lost from our trading
- An instance of type `OrderManager` called `order_manager_`, which will be used by the trading strategies to send and manage live orders
- A `RiskManager` object named `risk_manager_` to manage the trading strategy's risk
- A pointer to a `MarketMaker` object called `mm_algo_`, which will be initialized if we configure `TradeEngine` to run a MM trading algorithm
- Similarly, a pointer to a `LiquidityTaker` object called `taker_algo_`, which will be initialized if we configure `TradeEngine` to run a liquidity taking trading strategy:

```
FeatureEngine feature_engine_;
PositionKeeper position_keeper_;
OrderManager order_manager_;
RiskManager risk_manager_;

MarketMaker *mm_algo_ = nullptr;
LiquidityTaker *taker_algo_ = nullptr;
```

We will also add three `std::function` member variables, which `TradeEngine` will use to forward market data and order updates to the trading strategy that it instantiates. These are explained as follows:

- `algoOnOrderBookUpdate_ std::function` has the same signature as the `TradeEngine::onOrderBookUpdate()` method and is used to forward order book updates to the trading strategy
- `algoOnTradeUpdate_ std::function` has the same signature as the `TradeEngine::onTradeUpdate()` method and is used to forward trade events to the trading strategy
- `algoOnOrderUpdate_ std::function` has the same signature as the `TradeEngine::onOrderUpdate()` method and is used to forward order updates/responses to the trading strategy:

```
std::function<void(TickerId ticker_id, Price price,
  Side side, MarketOrderBook *book)>
    algoOnOrderBookUpdate_;
std::function<void(const Exchange::MEMarketUpdate
  *market_update, MarketOrderBook *book)>
    algoOnTradeUpdate_;
std::function<void(const Exchange::MEClientResponse
  *client_response)> algoOnOrderUpdate_;
```

To default-initialize these three `std::function` data members, we will create three new methods that simply log the parameters they are passed. They are shown here:

```
auto defaultAlgoOnOrderBookUpdate(TickerId ticker_id,
  Price price, Side side, MarketOrderBook *) noexcept
  -> void {
  logger_.log("%:% %() % ticker:% price:% side:%\n",
    __FILE__, __LINE__, __FUNCTION__,
      Common::getCurrentTimeStr(&time_str_),
        ticker_id, Common::
          priceToString(price).c_str(),
        Common::sideToString(side).c_str());
}
auto defaultAlgoOnTradeUpdate(const
  Exchange::MEMarketUpdate *market_update,
    MarketOrderBook *) noexcept -> void {
  logger_.log("%:% %() % %\n", __FILE__, __LINE__,
    __FUNCTION__, Common::
      getCurrentTimeStr(&time_str_),
        market_update->toString().c_str());
}
```

```cpp
  auto defaultAlgoOnOrderUpdate(const
    Exchange::MEClientResponse *client_response) noexcept
    -> void {
  logger_.log("%:% %() % %\n", __FILE__, __LINE__,
    __FUNCTION__, Common::
      getCurrentTimeStr(&time_str_),
        client_response->toString().c_str());
}
```

Next, we will discuss the code for some methods to initialize the `TradeEngine` class and its member variables.

Initializing the trade engine

The constructor for the `TradeEngine` class requires a `ClientId` argument to identify the trading application used in the client order requests. It also needs pointers to the three `LFQueue` of types `ClientRequestLFQueue`, `ClientResponseLFQueue`, and `MEMarketUpdateLFQueue` to initialize the `outgoing_ogw_requests_`, `incoming_ogw_responses_` and `incoming_md_updates_` data members, respectively. It also needs an `algo_type` argument of type `AlgoType` to specify the type of trading strategy and a `ticker_cfg` argument of type reference-to `const TradeEngineCfgHashMap`, which contains the configuration parameters for the risk manager and the trading strategy.

The constructor also initializes the `Logger logger_` member variable with a log file and creates a `MarketOrderBook` component for each possible `TickerId` value, holding them in the `ticker_order_book_` container. It calls the `setTradeEngine()` method on each `MarketOrderBook` component so that callbacks from the book can be received in `TradeEngine`. We also initialize the data members corresponding to the trading sub-components – `feature_engine_`, `position_keeper_`, `order_manager_`, and `risk_manager_`:

```cpp
  TradeEngine::TradeEngine(Common::ClientId client_id,
    AlgoType algo_type,

const TradeEngineCfgHashMap &ticker_cfg,
Exchange::ClientRequestLFQueue *client_requests,
Exchange::ClientResponseLFQueue *client_responses,
Exchange::MEMarketUpdateLFQueue *market_updates)
    : client_id_(client_id),
      outgoing_ogw_requests_(client_requests),
        incoming_ogw_responses_(client_responses),
      incoming_md_updates_(market_updates),
        logger_("trading_engine_" + std::
          to_string(client_id) + ".log"),
      feature_engine_(&logger_),
```

```
      position_keeper_(&logger_),
      order_manager_(&logger_, this, risk_manager_),
      risk_manager_(&logger_, &position_keeper_,
        ticker_cfg) {
  for (size_t i = 0; i < ticker_order_book_.size(); ++i) {
    ticker_order_book_[i] = new MarketOrderBook(i, &logger_);
    ticker_order_book_[i]->setTradeEngine(this);
  }
```

In the body of the constructor, in addition to the order books we previously created, we will initialize our new std::function members – algoOnOrderBookUpdate_, algoOnTradeUpdate_, and algoOnOrderUpdate_ – with the defaults – the defaultAlgoOnOrderBookUpdate(), defaultAlgoOnTradeUpdate(), and defaultAlgoOnOrderUpdate() methods:

```
  algoOnOrderBookUpdate_ = [this](auto ticker_id, auto
    price, auto side, auto book) {
    defaultAlgoOnOrderBookUpdate(ticker_id, price, side,
      book);
  };
  algoOnTradeUpdate_ = [this](auto market_update, auto
    book) { defaultAlgoOnTradeUpdate(market_update,
      book); };
  algoOnOrderUpdate_ = [this](auto client_response) {
    defaultAlgoOnOrderUpdate(client_response); };
```

Finally, we will initialize a trading strategy instance, either mm_algo_ of type MarketMaker or taker_algo_ of the LiquidityTaker type trading strategy. This initialization is shown as follows; remember that the MarketMaker or LiquidityTaker object will update/override the members – algoOnOrderBookUpdate_, algoOnTradeUpdate_, and algoOnOrderUpdate_ – to point to their own method implementations:

```
  if (algo_type == AlgoType::MAKER) {
    mm_algo_ = new MarketMaker(&logger_, this,
      &feature_engine_, &order_manager_, ticker_cfg);
  } else if (algo_type == AlgoType::TAKER) {
    taker_algo_ = new LiquidityTaker(&logger_, this,
      &feature_engine_, &order_manager_, ticker_cfg);
  }

  for (TickerId i = 0; i < ticker_cfg.size(); ++i) {
    logger_.log("%:% %() % Initialized % Ticker:% %.\n",
      __FILE__, __LINE__, __FUNCTION__,
        Common::getCurrentTimeStr(&time_str_),
        algoTypeToString(algo_type), i,
```

```
            ticker_cfg.at(i).toString());
    }
}
```

We have a `start()` method, as we saw for other components. Again, it sets the `run_` flag to `true` to allow the `run()` method to execute and creates and launches a thread to execute the `run()` method:

```
auto start() -> void {
  run_ = true;
  ASSERT(Common::createAndStartThread(-1,
    "Trading/TradeEngine", [this] { run(); }) !=
      nullptr, "Failed to start TradeEngine thread.");
}
```

The destructor does some simple de-initialization of the variables. First, it sets the `run_` flag to `false` and waits a little bit to let the main thread exit, then it proceeds to delete each `MarketOrderBook` instance and clear out the `ticker_order_book_` container, and finally, it resets the `LFQueue` pointers it holds. It also deletes the `mm_algo_` and `taker_algo_` members corresponding to the trading strategies:

```
TradeEngine::~TradeEngine() {
  run_ = false;

  using namespace std::literals::chrono_literals;
  std::this_thread::sleep_for(1s);

  delete mm_algo_; mm_algo_ = nullptr;
  delete taker_algo_; taker_algo_ = nullptr;

  for (auto &order_book: ticker_order_book_) {
    delete order_book;
    order_book = nullptr;
  }

  outgoing_ogw_requests_ = nullptr;
  incoming_ogw_responses_ = nullptr;
  incoming_md_updates_ = nullptr;
}
```

The familiar `stop()` method for this class first waits until all the incoming `MEClientResponse` and `MEMarketUpdate` messages are drained from the `incoming_ogw_responses_` and `incoming_md_updates_` `LFQueue` objects. Then, it resets the `run_` flag to stop the main `run()` thread and returns from the function:

```cpp
  auto stop() -> void {
    while(incoming_ogw_responses_->size() ||
      incoming_md_updates_->size()) {
      logger_.log("%:% %() % Sleeping till all updates
        are consumed ogw-size:% md-size:%\n", __FILE__,
          __LINE__, __FUNCTION__,
                Common::getCurrentTimeStr(&time_str_),
                  incoming_ogw_responses_->size(),
                    incoming_md_updates_->size());

      using namespace std::literals::chrono_literals;
      std::this_thread::sleep_for(10ms);
    }

    logger_.log("%:% %() % POSITIONS\n%\n", __FILE__,
      __LINE__, __FUNCTION__, Common::
        getCurrentTimeStr(&time_str_),
            position_keeper_.toString());

    run_ = false;
  }
```

The next method we will add to this basic framework is meant to be used to send `MEClientRequest` messages to the exchange.

Sending client requests

The `sendClientRequest()` method in the trading engine framework is extremely simple. It receives a `MEClientRequest` object and simply writes it to the `outgoing_ogw_requests_` lock-free queue so that the `OrderGateway` component can pick this up and send it out to the trading exchange:

```cpp
  auto TradeEngine::sendClientRequest(const
    Exchange::MEClientRequest *client_request) noexcept ->
    void {
    logger_.log("%:% %() % Sending %\n", __FILE__,
      __LINE__, __FUNCTION__, Common::
        getCurrentTimeStr(&time_str_),
            client_request->toString().c_str());
    auto next_write = outgoing_ogw_requests_->
      getNextToWriteTo();
    *next_write = std::move(*client_request);
    outgoing_ogw_requests_->updateWriteIndex();
  }
```

The next subsection presents the main `run()` loop and shows how we handle incoming data from the exchange.

Processing market data updates and client responses

The main thread for `TradeEngine` executes the `run()` method, which simply checks the incoming data `LFQueue` and reads and processes any available updates.

First, we check and drain the `incoming_ogw_responses_` queue. For each `MEClientResponse` message we read here, we call the `TradeEngine::onOrderUpdate()` method and pass the response message from `OrderGateway` to it:

```
auto TradeEngine::run() noexcept -> void {
  logger_.log("%:% %() %\n", __FILE__, __LINE__,
    __FUNCTION__, Common::getCurrentTimeStr(&time_str_));
  while (run_) {
    for (auto client_response = incoming_ogw_responses_->
      getNextToRead(); client_response; client_response =
        incoming_ogw_responses_->getNextToRead()) {
      logger_.log("%:% %() % Processing %\n", __FILE__,
        __LINE__, __FUNCTION__, Common::
          getCurrentTimeStr(&time_str_),
              client_response->toString().c_str());
      onOrderUpdate(client_response);
      incoming_ogw_responses_->updateReadIndex();
      last_event_time_ = Common::getCurrentNanos();
    }
```

We perform a similar task with the `incoming_md_updates_` lock-free queue. We read any available `MEMarketUpdate` messages and pass them to the correct `MarketOrderBook` instance by calling the `MarketOrderBook::onMarketUpdate()` method and passing the market update to it:

```
    for (auto market_update = incoming_md_updates_->
      getNextToRead(); market_update; market_update =
        incoming_md_updates_->getNextToRead()) {
      logger_.log("%:% %() % Processing %\n", __FILE__,
        __LINE__, __FUNCTION__, Common::
          getCurrentTimeStr(&time_str_),
              market_update->toString().c_str());
      ASSERT(market_update->ticker_id_ <
        ticker_order_book_.size(),
          "Unknown ticker-id on update:" +
            market_update->toString());
      ticker_order_book_[market_update->ticker_id_]->
```

```
            onMarketUpdate(market_update);
        incoming_md_updates_->updateReadIndex();
        last_event_time_ = Common::getCurrentNanos();
      }
    }
  }
```

Note that in both of the preceding code blocks, when we successfully read and dispatch a market data update or an order response, we update the `last_event_time_` variable to track the time of the event, as we described earlier in this section. We will see some minor miscellaneous placeholder methods in the next subsection.

Handling order book, trade, and order response updates

The `TradeEngine::onOrderBookUpdate()` method performs a couple of tasks. First, it fetches BBO from `MarketOrderBook`, which it receives in the method's arguments by calling the `MarketOrderBook::getBBO()` method. It provides the updated BBO to the `position_keeper_` and `feature_engine_` data members. For the `FeatureEngine` member, it calls the `FeatureEngine::onOrderBookUpdate()` method to notify the feature engine to update its feature values. The method also needs to call `algoOnOrderBookUpdate_()` so that the trading strategy can receive the notification about the order book update:

```
  auto TradeEngine::onOrderBookUpdate(TickerId ticker_id,
    Price price, Side side, MarketOrderBook *book) noexcept
      -> void {
    logger_.log("%:% %() % ticker:% price:% side:%\n",
      __FILE__, __LINE__, __FUNCTION__,
          Common::getCurrentTimeStr(&time_str_),
            ticker_id, Common::priceToString
              (price).c_str(),
          Common::sideToString(side).c_str());

    const auto bbo = book->getBBO();
    position_keeper_.updateBBO(ticker_id, bbo);
    feature_engine_.onOrderBookUpdate(ticker_id, price,
      side, book);
    algoOnOrderBookUpdate_(ticker_id, price, side, book);
  }
```

The `TradeEngine::onTradeUpdate()` method that is called on trade events also performs a couple of tasks, which are like the ones in the `onOrderBookUpdate()` method we just saw. It passes the trade event to `FeatureEngine` by calling the `onTradeUpdate()` method so that the feature engine can update the features it computes. It also passes the trade event to the trading strategy by invoking the `algoOnTradeUpdate_()` `std::function` member:

```cpp
auto TradeEngine::onTradeUpdate(const
  Exchange::MEMarketUpdate *market_update,
    MarketOrderBook *book) noexcept -> void {
  logger_.log("%:% %() % %\n", __FILE__, __LINE__,
    __FUNCTION__, Common::getCurrentTimeStr(&time_str_),
          market_update->toString().c_str());

  feature_engine_.onTradeUpdate(market_update, book);
  algoOnTradeUpdate_(market_update, book);
}
```

Finally, `TradeEngine::onOrderUpdate()` does two things. It checks whether `MEClientResponse` corresponds to an execution (`ClientResponseType::FILLED`) and calls the `PositionKeeper::addFill()` method to update the position and PnLs. It also invokes the `algoOnOrderUpdate_()` `std::function` member so that the trading strategy can process the `MEClientResponse`:

```cpp
auto TradeEngine::onOrderUpdate(const
  Exchange::MEClientResponse *client_response) noexcept
    -> void {
  logger_.log("%:% %() % %\n", __FILE__, __LINE__,
    __FUNCTION__, Common::getCurrentTimeStr(&time_str_),
          client_response->toString().c_str());

  if (UNLIKELY(client_response->type_ ==
   Exchange::ClientResponseType::FILLED))
     position_keeper_.addFill(client_response);

  algoOnOrderUpdate_(client_response);
}
```

Now, we can conclude the design and implementation of the `TradeEngine` framework in the next subsection by defining some miscellaneous methods we require.

Adding some miscellaneous methods

This section defines some miscellaneous methods for the `TradeEngine` class. The first method, `initLastEventTime()`, simply initializes the `last_event_time_` variable with the current time, which is obtained by calling the `getCurrentNanos()` method:

```cpp
auto initLastEventTime() {
  last_event_time_ = Common::getCurrentNanos();
}
```

The `silentSeconds()` method returns the time elapsed (in seconds) since the last event was received:

```
auto silentSeconds() {
  return (Common::getCurrentNanos() - last_event_time_)
    / NANOS_TO_SECS;
}
```

The `clientId()` method is a simple getter method that returns `client_id_` for this `TradeEngine` instance:

```
auto clientId() const {
  return client_id_;
}
```

That concludes the design and implementation of our trading engine framework. In the next section, we will build the main trading application binary.

Building and running the main trading application

In the last section of this chapter, we will finally build the main trading application using all the components we built in this chapter, as well as the previous two chapters. First, we will discuss the implementation of the `trading_main` binary application, which combines the `MarketDataConsumer`, `OrderGateway`, `MarketOrderBook`, and `TradeEngine` components. After that, we will run our complete electronic trading ecosystem – the electronic trading exchange (the `exchange_main` application) from the *Communicating with Market Participants* chapter and a few instances of the market participants (the `trading_main` application), which we will build next.

Building the main trading application

Now, let us build the executable `trading_main` binary that will initialize and run all the components on the market participant's trading system. The source code for this application is in the `Chapter10/trading/trading_main.cpp` source file.

First, we will include the necessary header files and create some basic variables to represent the different components we need. Specifically, we will have a `Logger` object pointer to be used for logging purposes, a `TradeEngine` object pointer for the basic trading engine framework, a `MarketDataConsumer` object pointer to consumer market data, and an `OrderGateway` object pointer to connect to and communicate with the exchange's order server:

```
#include <csignal>

#include "strategy/trade_engine.h"
#include "order_gw/order_gateway.h"
#include "market_data/market_data_consumer.h"
```

```cpp
#include "common/logging.h"

Common::Logger *logger = nullptr;
Trading::TradeEngine *trade_engine = nullptr;
Trading::MarketDataConsumer *market_data_consumer = nullptr;
Trading::OrderGateway *order_gateway = nullptr;
```

Now, we start the entry point – the `main()` method. On the command line, we will accept arguments of the following form – `trading_main CLIENT_ID ALGO_TYPE [CLIP_1 THRESH_1 MAX_ORDER_SIZE_1 MAX_POS_1 MAX_LOSS_1] [CLIP_2 THRESH_2 MAX_ORDER_SIZE_2 MAX_POS_2 MAX_LOSS_2]` …

The first argument represents `ClientId` for this trading application instance. We will also accept `AlgoType` as the second parameter, and configurations for each trading algorithm instance for each `TickerId` as the remaining parameters. We will source the random number generator by calling the `srand()` method and passing it `client_id` for this specific instance:

```cpp
int main(int argc, char **argv) {
  const Common::ClientId client_id = atoi(argv[1]);
  srand(client_id);
```

We will extract `AlgoType`, as shown here:

```cpp
  const auto algo_type = stringToAlgoType(argv[2]);
```

We will also initialize an object of type `TradeEngineCfgHashMap` from the remaining command-line arguments, as shown in the following code block:

```cpp
  TradeEngineCfgHashMap ticker_cfg;
  size_t next_ticker_id = 0;
  for (int i = 3; i < argc; i += 5, ++next_ticker_id) {
    ticker_cfg.at(next_ticker_id) =
      {static_cast<Qty>(std::atoi(argv[i])),
        std::atof(argv[i + 1]),
                                  {static_cast<Qty>(std:
                                  :atoi(argv[i + 2])),
                                   static_cast<Qty>(std:
                                  :atoi(argv[i + 3])),
                                   std::atof(argv[i +
                                   4])}};
}
```

We will initialize the component variables we declared before – `Logger`, the `client_requests` LFQueue, the `client_responses` LFQueue, and the `market_updates` LFQueue. We will also define a `sleep_time` variable and set it to 20 microseconds. We will use this value to pause between consecutive order requests we send to the trading exchange's `OrderGatewayServer` component, only in the random trading strategy:

```
logger = new Common::Logger("trading_main_" +
  std::to_string(client_id) + ".log");

const int sleep_time = 20 * 1000;

Exchange::ClientRequestLFQueue
  client_requests(ME_MAX_CLIENT_UPDATES);
Exchange::ClientResponseLFQueue
  client_responses(ME_MAX_CLIENT_UPDATES);
Exchange::MEMarketUpdateLFQueue
  market_updates(ME_MAX_MARKET_UPDATES);

std::string time_str;
```

The first component we will initialize and start will be `TradeEngine`. We will pass `client_id`, `algo_type`, the strategy configurations in the `ticker_cfg` object, and the lock-free queues that `TradeEngine` needs in the constructor. We then call the `start()` method to get the main thread to start executing, as shown in the following code block:

```
logger->log("%:% %() % Starting Trade Engine...\n",
  __FILE__, __LINE__, __FUNCTION__,
  Common::getCurrentTimeStr(&time_str));
trade_engine = new Trading::TradeEngine(client_id,
  algo_type, ticker_cfg, &client_requests,
    &client_responses, &market_updates);
trade_engine->start();
```

We perform a similar initialization of the `OrderGateway` component next by passing it the IP and port information of `exchange_main`'s `OrderGateway` server component. We also pass it the `client_requests` and `client_responses` LFQueue variables to consume `MEClientRequest` messages from and write `MEClientResponse` messages to, and then we use `start()` on the main thread:

```
const std::string order_gw_ip = "127.0.0.1";
const std::string order_gw_iface = "lo";
const int order_gw_port = 12345;

logger->log("%:% %() % Starting Order Gateway...\n",
  __FILE__, __LINE__, __FUNCTION__,
  Common::getCurrentTimeStr(&time_str));
```

```cpp
order_gateway = new Trading::OrderGateway(client_id,
  &client_requests, &client_responses, order_gw_ip,
    order_gw_iface, order_gw_port);
order_gateway->start();
```

Finally, we initialize and start the `MarketDataConsumer` component. It needs the IP and port information of the snapshot stream and the incremental stream on which the exchange's `MarketDataPublisher` publishes market data. It also needs the `market_updates` LFQueue variable, which it will write decoded market data updates to. Finally, since all the components are ready, we will start `market_data_consumer` so that we can process any market data updates available:

```cpp
const std::string mkt_data_iface = "lo";
const std::string snapshot_ip = "233.252.14.1";
const int snapshot_port = 20000;
const std::string incremental_ip = "233.252.14.3";
const int incremental_port = 20001;

logger->log("%:% %() % Starting Market Data
  Consumer...\n", __FILE__, __LINE__, __FUNCTION__,
    Common::getCurrentTimeStr(&time_str));
market_data_consumer = new
  Trading::MarketDataConsumer(client_id, &market_updates,
    mkt_data_iface, snapshot_ip, snapshot_port,
      incremental_ip, incremental_port);
market_data_consumer->start();
```

Now, we are almost ready to start sending orders to the exchange; we just need to perform a few more minor tasks first. First, the `main()` application will sleep briefly so that the threads we just created and started in each of our components can run for a few seconds:

```cpp
usleep(10 * 1000 * 1000);
```

We will also initialize the first event time in `TradeEngine` by calling the `TradeEngine::initLastEventTime()` method. We intentionally delayed this member's initialization until we were ready to start trading:

```cpp
trade_engine->initLastEventTime();
```

If `AlgoType` is `AlgoType::RANDOM`, we will implement the trading logic right here, since it is super simple. First, we will check the `algo_type` variable, and branch if the `algo_type` argument specifies the random trading strategy:

```cpp
if (algo_type == AlgoType::RANDOM) {
```

For this random trading algorithm, we will create a starting `OrderId` value unique to this trading application's instance, using the `client_id` we received from the command-line argument:

```
Common::OrderId order_id = client_id * 1000;
```

Since we send orders with a random price, quantity, and side in our current test setup, we will initialize a random reference price for each instrument, for which we will send orders. We will send orders with prices that are randomly distributed around this reference price value shortly. We do this purely so that different trading instruments have orders of slightly different and random prices. The random reference price for each instrument is held in the `ticker_base_price` variable. We will also create `std::vector` of `MEClientRequest` messages to store the order requests we send to the exchange. We will also send cancellations for some of these orders to exercise that functionality; hence, we will save them for when we try to cancel them:

```
std::vector<Exchange::MEClientRequest>
  client_requests_vec;
std::array<Price, ME_MAX_TICKERS> ticker_base_price;
for(size_t i = 0; i < ME_MAX_TICKERS; ++i)
  ticker_base_price[i] = (rand() % 100) + 100;
```

Now, we can start sending some orders to the exchange, but first, we will initialize `TradeEngine`'s `last_event_time_` variable before we get started:

```
trade_engine->initLastEventTime();
```

In the following loop, which executes 10,000 times, we will perform a few tasks, described as follows.

We will pick a random `TickerId`, generate a random `Price` close to the `ticker_base_price` reference price value for that instrument, generate a random `Qty`, and generate a random `Side` for the order we will send:

```
for (size_t i = 0; i < 10000; ++i) {
    const Common::TickerId ticker_id = rand() %
      Common::ME_MAX_TICKERS;
    const Price price = ticker_base_price[ticker_id] +
      (rand() % 10) + 1;
    const Qty qty = 1 + (rand() % 100) + 1;
    const Side side = (rand() % 2 ? Common::Side::BUY :
      Common::Side::SELL);
```

We will create an `MEClientRequest` message of type `ClientRequestType::NEW` with these attributes and pass it along to `TradeEngine` using the `sendClientRequest()` method call. We will pause for `sleep_time` (20 microseconds) after we send the order request, and we will also save the `MEClientRequest` message we just sent out in the `client_requests_vec` container:

```cpp
      Exchange::MEClientRequest
        new_request{Exchange::ClientRequestType::NEW,
          client_id, ticker_id, order_id++, side, price,
            qty};
      trade_engine->sendClientRequest(&new_request);
      usleep(sleep_time);

      client_requests_vec.push_back(new_request);
```

After the pause, we randomly pick a client request we sent from our container of client requests. We change the request type to `ClientRequestType::CANCEL` and send it through to `TradeEngine`. Then, we pause again and continue with the loop iteration:

```cpp
      const auto cxl_index = rand() %
        client_requests_vec.size();
      auto cxl_request = client_requests_vec[cxl_index];
      cxl_request.type_ =
        Exchange::ClientRequestType::CANCEL;
      trade_engine->sendClientRequest(&cxl_request);
      usleep(sleep_time);
    }
  }
```

After we have sent out all of the order flow, we wait until we encounter a 60-second period where no market update and no order response have been received by `TradeEngine`. This is a simple method of detecting when there is no market activity due to this client or any other trading client being connected to the exchange:

```cpp
  while (trade_engine->silentSeconds() < 60) {
    logger->log("%:% %() % Waiting till no activity, been
      silent for % seconds...\n", __FILE__, __LINE__,
        __FUNCTION__,
           Common::getCurrentTimeStr(&time_str),
              trade_engine->silentSeconds());

    using namespace std::literals::chrono_literals;
    std::this_thread::sleep_for(10s);
  }
```

After a period of inactivity, this application exits. We first stop each of our components and pause for a brief period, before de-initializing and exiting the application:

```cpp
  trade_engine->stop();
  market_data_consumer->stop();
  order_gateway->stop();
```

```
  using namespace std::literals::chrono_literals;
  std::this_thread::sleep_for(10s);

  delete logger;
  logger = nullptr;
  delete trade_engine;
  trade_engine = nullptr;
  delete market_data_consumer;
  market_data_consumer = nullptr;
  delete order_gateway;
  order_gateway = nullptr;

  std::this_thread::sleep_for(10s);

  exit(EXIT_SUCCESS);
}
```

This concludes the implementation of the `trading_main` application. We have included a build script in `Chapter10/scripts/build.sh`, which uses CMake and Ninja to build the libraries and the `trading_main` application, in addition to the `exchange_main` application that we built before. You will have to edit this script to point to the correct binaries on your system or switch to a different build system if you wish. The `scripts/build.sh` script is expected to be run from the `Chapter10` root directory, and it simply configures the build files, which in this case use `Ninja`, and cleans and rebuilds the build for the release and debug versions. We want to clarify that the choice of `Ninja` is completely arbitrary; we do not depend on anything that is `Ninja`-specific for our system to build and run. The build process generates binaries in the `Chapter10/cmake-build-release` and `Chapter10/cmake-build-debug` directories. The scripts to run the trading binaries use the binaries from the `Chapter10/cmake-build-release` directory.

Running the final trading ecosystem

We are finally at the point where we can run our entire electronic trading ecosystem, admittedly with a random trading strategy for now. We will present two scripts – one is `Chapter10/scripts/run_clients.sh`, which is configured to launch five instances of the `trading_main` application with client IDs of 1 to 5. The second script is `Chapter10/scripts/run_exchange_and_clients.sh`, which first builds the libraries and the binaries using the `build.sh` script. Then, it launches the `exchange_main` application and proceeds to launch the trading client instances using the `run_clients.sh` script. Finally, it waits for all the trading client instances to finish execution, then terminates the exchange instance, and exits.

We will not look at the full `run_clients.sh` script, but an example of the first trading client that creates a `MarketMaker` algorithm is shown here:

```
./cmake-build-release/trading_main  1 MAKER 100 0.6 150 300 -100 60
0.6 150 300 -100 150 0.5 250 600 -100 200 0.4 500 3000 -100 1000 0.9
5000 4000 -100 300 0.8 1500 3000 -100 50 0.7 150 300 -100 100 0.3 250
300 -100 &
```

In this script, the 1 and 2 client IDs are MM trading algorithms, the 3 and 4 client IDs are liquidity taking trading algorithms, and the last client ID, 5, is a random trading algorithm. The random trading algorithm instance exists to simulate all trades made by the rest of the market participants for any reason. We do this because, in our ecosystem, we only run five trading clients (due to limited resources on our workstation). However, we encourage those interested among you with access to a lot more CPU resources to run as many trading clients as the system can handle. Remember that, in practice, the market is composed of orders and trades from thousands of market participants (if not more).

First, we have the output of the build process, which is generated by running the `scripts/run_exchange_and_clients.sh` script that internally calls the `scripts/build.sh` script to first build everything. Note that you need to be in the `Chapter10` root directory, as shown here, for this script to work correctly:

```
sghosh@sghosh-ThinkPad-X1-Carbon-3rd:~/Building-Low-Latency-
Applications-with-CPP/Chapter10$ bash scripts/run_exchange_and_
clients.sh
...
-- Build files have been written to: /home/sghosh/Building-Low-
Latency-Applications-with-CPP/Chapter10/cmake-build-release
...
[36/37] Linking CXX executable trading_main
[37/37] Linking CXX executable exchange_main
```

Then, we have the output of the `exchange_main` application starting up:

```
-----------------------------------------
Starting Exchange...
-----------------------------------------
Set core affinity for Common/Logger exchange_main.log 140716464399936
to -1
Set core affinity for Common/Logger exchange_matching_engine.log
140716293985856 to -1
...
```

Then, the output of the `trading_main` instances launching is produced:

```
-----------------------------------------
Starting TradingClient 1...
-----------------------------------------
Set core affinity for Common/Logger trading_main_1.log 139636947019328
to -1
...
```

```
------------------------------------------
Starting TradingClient 5...
------------------------------------------
Set core affinity for Common/Logger trading_main_5.log 139837285852736
to -1
...
```

Finally, we have the output from the trading clients that shut down, and then the exchange exits:

```
Set core affinity for Trading/MarketDataConsumer 139836325348928 to -1
...
Thu Apr  6 12:37:04 2023 Flushing and closing Logger for trading_
main_1.log
...
Thu Apr  6 12:37:21 2023 Logger for trading_order_gateway_5.log
exiting.
------------------------------------------
Stopping Exchange...
------------------------------------------
...
Thu Apr  6 12:38:09 2023 Logger for exchange_order_server.log exiting.
```

Note that this is just the output displayed on screen. The interesting details are in the log files, which we will inspect and discuss in the next subsection.

One other important note is that the `exchange_main` application has 10 threads, and each `trading_main` application has 8 threads. The `Logger` threads, which are many of these threads (five for `exchange_main` and four for `trading_main`), as well as the thread for the `main()` method (one each for `exchange_main` and `trading_main`), are not CPU-intensive and sleep for most of their runtime. The optimal setup would need a lot of cores for the entire ecosystem, which is common for production trading servers used for electronic trading. On these production-grade trading servers, we would be able to assign a CPU core to each of the remaining critical threads (four for `exchange_main` and three for `trading_main`). Since we are not sure which server we run on, we intentionally avoid setting affinity on those threads. If CPU and/or memory resources are limited on your system, our advice would be to reduce the number of trading clients launched in the `run_clients.sh` script.

Inspecting the output of a run

In this concluding section, we will look at the log files generated by running the `run_exchange_and_clients.sh` script. We know that the trading strategy we ran in this chapter is not interesting since it sends random orders to the exchange, but there are some important observations in these log files. Running the `run_exchange_and_clients.sh` script should generate log files similar to the following:

```
exchange_main.log  exchange_market_data_publisher.log  exchange_
matching_engine.log  exchange_order_server.log  exchange_snapshot_
synthesizer.log
trading_engine_1.log  trading_main_1.log  trading_market_data_
consumer_1.log  trading_order_gateway_1.log
… trading_order_gateway_5.log
```

To understand and follow the events, our advice would be to correlate the log lines we generate from our calls to `Logger::log()` from various components and sub-components and then find them in the log files.

As an example, let us follow the path of a client sending an order to the exchange receiving the request, and generating a client response and a market update for that order request. Let us say, for this example, that we want to find the path followed by **OrderId=1445** and **MarketOrderId=53**; the path which this order follows is laid out as follows from the log files. Note that this is just an example that was generated from this specific run and might not be reproducible; the goal here is to understand how to track the events in our ecosystem:

1. `MEClientRequest` for the new order gets sent by the `TradeEngine` component for the `trading_main` instance with `ClientId=1`:

   ```
   trading_engine_5.log:trade_engine.cpp:33 sendClientRequest() Thu
   Apr  6 12:26:47 2023 Sending MEClientRequest [type:NEW client:1
   ticker:0 oid:1445 side:BUY qty:10 price:184]
   ```

2. The `OrderGateway` component picks up that request from the lock-free queue and sends it out on the TCP connection to the exchange, as shown here:

   ```
   trading_order_gateway_5.log:order_gateway.cpp:19 run() Thu
   Apr  6 12:26:47 2023 Sending cid:1 seq:891 MEClientRequest
   [type:NEW client:1 ticker:0 oid:1445 side:BUY qty:10 price:184]
   ```

3. The `OrderServer` component inside the `exchange_main` application receives it from the `TCPServer` socket, as shown here:

   ```
   exchange_order_server.log:order_server.h:55 recvCallback()
   Thu Apr  6 12:26:47 2023 Received OMClientRequest [seq:891
   MEClientRequest [type:NEW client:1 ticker:0 oid:1445 side:BUY
   qty:10 price:184]]
   ```

4. The `FifoSequencer` sub-component inside `OrderServer` sequences the client order request (`MEClientRequest`) based on the software receive time, and publishes it to the `MatchingEngine` lock-free queue:

   ```
   exchange_order_server.log:fifo_sequencer.h:38
   sequenceAndPublish() Thu Apr  6 12:26:47 2023 Writing
   RX:1680802007777361000 Req:MEClientRequest [type:NEW client:1
   ticker:0 oid:1445 side:BUY qty:10 price:184] to FIFO.
   ```

5. The `MatchingEngine` component finally receives this request from `LFQueue` and processes it, as displayed in the following log file:

   ```
   exchange_matching_engine.log:matching_engine.h:66 run() Thu
     Apr  6 12:26:47 2023 Processing MEClientRequest [type:NEW
     client:1 ticker:0 oid:1445 side:BUY qty:10 price:184]
   ```

6. In response to the order request it received, the `MatchingEngine` component generates a `MEClientResponse` message meant for the client to be published by the `OrderServer` component:

   ```
   exchange_matching_engine.log:matching_engine.h:48
     sendClientResponse() Thu Apr  6 12:26:47 2023 Sending
     MEClientResponse [type:ACCEPTED client:1 ticker:0 coid:1445
     moid:53 side:BUY exec_qty:0 leaves_qty:10 price:184]
   ```

7. Corresponding to the new order that is added to the limit order book, `MatchingEngine` also generates an `MEMarketUpdate` message, as shown here. This is meant for the `MarketDataPublisher` component to publish and update the snapshot it maintains:

   ```
   exchange_matching_engine.log:matching_engine.h:55
     sendMarketUpdate() Thu Apr  6 12:26:47 2023 Sending
     MEMarketUpdate [ type:ADD ticker:0 oid:53 side:BUY qty:10
     price:184 priority:2]
   ```

8. The `OrderServer` component picks up the `MEClientResponse` message from `LFQueue`, sending out an `OMClientResponse` message to the client on the correct TCP connection with the trading client:

   ```
   exchange_order_server.log:order_server.h:32 run() Thu Apr  6
     12:26:47 2023 Processing cid:1 seq:1343 MEClientResponse
     [type:ACCEPTED client:1 ticker:0 coid:1445 moid:53 side:BUY
     exec_qty:0 leaves_qty:10 price:184]
   ```

9. The `MarketDataPublisher` component picks up the `MEMarketUpdate` message sent by `MatchingEngine`, sending out an `MDPMarketUpdate` message on the incremental market data multicast stream:

   ```
   exchange_market_data_publisher.log:market_data_publisher.cpp:19
     run() Thu Apr  6 12:26:47 2023 Sending seq:902 MEMarketUpdate [
     type:ADD ticker:0 oid:53 side:BUY qty:10 price:184 priority:2]
   ```

10. The `SnapshotSynthesizer` sub-component inside the `MarketDataPublisher` component also receives this incremental `MEMarketUpdate` message, adding it to the snapshot it maintains:

    ```
    exchange_snapshot_synthesizer.log:snapshot_synthesizer.cpp:107
      run() Thu Apr  6 12:26:47 2023 Processing MDPMarketUpdate [
      seq:902 MEMarketUpdate [ type:ADD ticker:0 oid:53 side:BUY
      qty:10 price:184 priority:2]]
    ```

11. At some point, `SnapshotSynthesizer` publishes a snapshot of the `MDPMarketUpdate` messages on the snapshot multicast market data stream, including this market update:

    ```
    exchange_snapshot_synthesizer.log:snapshot_synthesizer.cpp:88
    publishSnapshot() Thu Apr  6 12:27:40 2023 MDPMarketUpdate [
    seq:7 MEMarketUpdate [ type:ADD ticker:0 oid:53 side:BUY qty:10
    price:184 priority:2]]
    ```

12. The `OrderGateway` component inside the `trading_main` application receives the `OMClientResponse` response for the order request, from the `TCPSocket` that is connected to the exchange:

    ```
    trading_order_gateway_5.log:order_gateway.cpp:37 recvCallback()
    Thu Apr  6 12:26:47 2023 Received OMClientResponse [seq:1343
    MEClientResponse [type:ACCEPTED client:1 ticker:0 coid:1445
    moid:53 side:BUY exec_qty:0 leaves_qty:10 price:184]]
    ```

13. The `MarketDataConsumer` component inside the `trading_main` application receives the `MDPMarketUpdate` message on the incremental market data stream:

    ```
    trading_market_data_consumer_5.log:market_data_consumer.cpp:177
    recvCallback() Thu Apr  6 12:26:47 2023 Received incremental
    socket len:42 MDPMarketUpdate [ seq:902 MEMarketUpdate [
    type:ADD ticker:0 oid:53 side:BUY qty:10 price:184 priority:2]]
    trading_market_data_consumer_5.log:market_data_consumer.
    cpp:193 recvCallback() Thu Apr  6 12:26:47 2023 MDPMarketUpdate
    [ seq:902 MEMarketUpdate [ type:ADD ticker:0 oid:53 side:BUY
    qty:10 price:184 priority:2]]
    ```

14. The `TradeEngine` component finally receives the `MEClientResponse` message from the `OrderGateway` component over the lock-free queue. It also forwards the `MEClientResponse` message via the `onOrderUpdate()` callback:

    ```
    trading_engine_5.log:trade_engine.cpp:44 run() Thu Apr  6
    12:26:47 2023 Processing MEClientResponse [type:ACCEPTED
    client:1 ticker:0 coid:1445 moid:53 side:BUY exec_qty:0 leaves_
    qty:10 price:184]
    trading_engine_5.log:trade_engine.cpp:75 onOrderUpdate() Thu
    Apr  6 12:26:47 2023 MEClientResponse [type:ACCEPTED client:1
    ticker:0 coid:1445 moid:53 side:BUY exec_qty:0 leaves_qty:10
    price:184]
    ```

15. `TradeEngine` also receives the `MEMarketUpdate` message, updates `MarketOrderBook`, and, in turn, receives `onOrderBookUpdate()` from the order book back in `TradeEngine`:

    ```
    trading_engine_5.log:trade_engine.cpp:52 run() Thu Apr  6
    12:26:47 2023 Processing MEMarketUpdate [ type:ADD ticker:0
    oid:53 side:BUY qty:10 price:184 priority:2]
    trading_engine_5.log:trade_engine.cpp:64 onOrderBookUpdate() Thu
    Apr  6 12:26:47 2023 ticker:0 price:184 side:BUY
    ```

Hopefully, this example provided you with good insight into what the different components in our trading ecosystem do. This should also serve as an example of how to investigate different events in the various applications, components, and sub-components of our electronic trading universe.

Now, let us focus on the entries generated by our other components – `FeatureEngine`, `RiskManager`, `PositionKeeper`, and `OrderManager` – and the strategies – the `MarketMaker` and `LiquidityTaker` algorithms:

1. The following log lines display the feature values that are updated by `FeatureEngine` as the order book updates or new trade events occur in market data:

   ```
   trading_engine_1.log:feature_engine.h:23 onOrderBookUpdate()
   Thu May 11 16:10:45 2023 ticker:7 price:152 side:BUY
   mkt-price:152.394 agg-trade-ratio:0.0994475
   trading_engine_1.log:feature_engine.h:34 onTradeUpdate() Thu
   May 11 16:10:45 2023 MEMarketUpdate [ type:TRADE ticker:1
   oid:INVALID side:SELL qty:50 price:170 priority:INVALID]
   mkt-price:170.071 agg-trade-ratio:1
   trading_engine_1.log:feature_engine.h:23 onOrderBookUpdate()
   Thu May 11 16:10:45 2023 ticker:2 price:119 side:SELL
   mkt-price:115.299 agg-trade-ratio:0.262712
   trading_engine_1.log:feature_engine.h:34 onTradeUpdate() Thu
   May 11 16:10:45 2023 MEMarketUpdate [ type:TRADE ticker:3
   oid:INVALID side:BUY qty:18 price:180 priority:INVALID]
   mkt-price:115.299 agg-trade-ratio:0.00628931
   trading_engine_1.log:feature_engine.h:23 onOrderBookUpdate()
   Thu May 11 16:10:45 2023 ticker:3 price:180 side:SELL
   mkt-price:178.716 agg-trade-ratio:0.00628931
   trading_engine_1.log:feature_engine.h:34 onTradeUpdate() Thu
   May 11 16:10:45 2023 MEMarketUpdate [ type:TRADE ticker:3
   oid:INVALID side:BUY qty:30 price:180 priority:INVALID]
   mkt-price:178.716 agg-trade-ratio:0.0105485
   ```

2. The following log lines correspond to `PositionKeeper` being updated as BBO changes or additional executions are processed:

   ```
   trading_engine_1.log:position_keeper.h:75 addFill() Thu May
   11 16:10:38 2023 Position{pos:476 u-pnl:-120.715 r-pnl:6248.71
   t-pnl:6128 vol:8654 vwaps:[114.254X0] BBO{21@115X116@296}}
   MEClientResponse [type:FILLED client:1 ticker:2 coid:962
   moid:1384 side:BUY exec_qty:25 leaves_qty:102 price:114]
   trading_engine_1.log:position_keeper.h:98 updateBBO() Thu May
   11 16:10:42 2023 Position{pos:194 u-pnl:15.8965 r-pnl:311.103
   t-pnl:327 vol:802 vwaps:[180.918X0] BBO{730@180X182@100}}
   BBO{730@180X182@100}
   trading_engine_1.log:position_keeper.h:75 addFill() Thu May
   11 16:10:42 2023 Position{pos:392 u-pnl:688.98 r-pnl:6435.02
   t-pnl:7124 vol:8782 vwaps:[114.242X0] BBO{44@114X116@150}}
   MEClientResponse [type:FILLED client:1 ticker:2 coid:970
   moid:1394 side:SELL exec_qty:83 leaves_qty:44 price:116]
   trading_engine_1.log:position_keeper.h:98 updateBBO() Thu May
   ```

```
11 16:10:44 2023 Position{pos:373 u-pnl:282.585 r-pnl:6468.41
t-pnl:6751 vol:8801 vwaps:[114.242X0] BBO{19@114X116@131}}
BBO{19@114X116@131}
```

3. Failures in `RiskManager`, due to several reasons we discussed in the *Building the C++ trading algorithm building blocks* chapter in the *Computing and managing risk* section, show up in the log files as something like the following:

```
trading_engine_1.log:order_manager.h:69 moveOrder() Thu May 11
16:10:41 2023 Ticker:1 Side:BUY Qty:60 RiskCheckResult:POSITION_
TOO_LARGE
trading_engine_1.log:order_manager.h:69 moveOrder() Thu May 11
16:10:41 2023 Ticker:4 Side:SELL Qty:1000 RiskCheckResult:LOSS_
TOO_LARGE
trading_engine_1.log:order_manager.h:69 moveOrder()
Thu May 11 16:10:42 2023 Ticker:2 Side:BUY Qty:150
RiskCheckResult:POSITION_TOO_LARGE
```

4. Events in `OrderManager` appear as follows in the log files, as attempts are made to send order requests and responses are processed:

```
trading_engine_1.log:order_manager.h:26 onOrderUpdate() Thu
May 11 16:10:36 2023 OMOrder[tid:6 oid:965 side:SELL price:125
qty:15 state:PENDING_CANCEL]
trading_engine_1.log:order_manager.cpp:13 newOrder() Thu May 11
16:10:37 2023 Sent new order MEClientRequest [type:NEW client:1
ticker:6 oid:966 side:SELL qty:50 price:126] for OMOrder[tid:6
oid:966 side:SELL price:126 qty:50 state:PENDING_NEW]
trading_engine_1.log:order_manager.h:23 onOrderUpdate() Thu
May 11 16:10:37 2023 MEClientResponse [type:ACCEPTED client:1
ticker:6 coid:966 moid:1806 side:SELL exec_qty:0 leaves_qty:50
price:126]
trading_engine_1.log:order_manager.h:26 onOrderUpdate() Thu
May 11 16:10:37 2023 OMOrder[tid:6 oid:966 side:SELL price:126
qty:50 state:PENDING_NEW]
trading_engine_1.log:order_manager.cpp:26 cancelOrder() Thu
May 11 16:10:37 2023 Sent cancel MEClientRequest [type:CANCEL
client:1 ticker:1 oid:927 side:SELL qty:60 price:170] for
OMOrder[tid:1 oid:927 side:SELL price:170 qty:60 state:PENDING_
CANCEL]
trading_engine_1.log:order_manager.h:23 onOrderUpdate() Thu
May 11 16:10:37 2023 MEClientResponse [type:CANCELED client:1
ticker:1 coid:927 moid:1826 side:SELL exec_qty:INVALID leaves_
qty:60 price:170]
```

5. Events in the `LiquidityTaker` trading strategy appear as shown here. These correspond to order book updates, trade events, and updates to strategy orders:

```
trading_engine_1.log:liquidity_taker.h:19 onOrderBookUpdate()
Thu May 11 16:07:48 2023 ticker:4 price:183 side:SELL
trading_engine_1.log:liquidity_taker.h:19 onOrderBookUpdate()
```

```
Thu May 11 16:07:48 2023 ticker:7 price:153 side:BUY
trading_engine_1.log:liquidity_taker.h:25 onTradeUpdate() Thu
May 11 16:07:48 2023 MEMarketUpdate [ type:TRADE ticker:7
oid:INVALID side:SELL qty:90 price:154 priority:INVALID]
trading_engine_1.log:liquidity_taker.h:32 onTradeUpdate()
Thu May 11 16:07:48 2023 BBO{368@154X155@2095} agg-qty-
ratio:0.244565
trading_engine_1.log:liquidity_taker.h:19 onOrderBookUpdate()
Thu May 11 16:07:48 2023 ticker:7 price:154 side:BUY
trading_engine_1.log:liquidity_taker.h:49 onOrderUpdate() Thu
May 11 16:07:48 2023 MEClientResponse [type:FILLED client:3
ticker:7 coid:202 moid:792 side:BUY exec_qty:90 leaves_qty:183
price:154]
trading_engine_1.log:liquidity_taker.h:19 onOrderBookUpdate()
Thu May 11 16:07:48 2023 ticker:0 price:180 side:BUY
```

6. Similarly, events in the `MarketMaker` trading algorithm appear in the log files, as shown here:

```
trading_engine_1.log:market_maker.h:47 onOrderUpdate() Thu May
11 16:06:12 2023 MEClientResponse [type:FILLED client:1 ticker:5
coid:418 moid:552 side:BUY exec_qty:62 leaves_qty:160 price:137]
trading_engine_1.log:market_maker.h:42 onTradeUpdate() Thu
May 11 16:06:12 2023 MEMarketUpdate [ type:TRADE ticker:3
oid:INVALID side:BUY qty:47 price:180 priority:INVALID]
trading_engine_1.log:market_maker.h:19 onOrderBookUpdate() Thu
May 11 16:06:12 2023 ticker:3 price:180 side:SELL
trading_engine_1.log:market_maker.h:27 onOrderBookUpdate() Thu
May 11 16:06:12 2023 BBO{2759@178X180@2409} fair-price:179.068
trading_engine_1.log:market_maker.h:19 onOrderBookUpdate() Thu
May 11 16:06:12 2023 ticker:0 price:183 side:SELL
trading_engine_1.log:market_maker.h:27 onOrderBookUpdate() Thu
May 11 16:06:12 2023 BBO{4395@181X182@534} fair-price:181.892
trading_engine_1.log:market_maker.h:42 onTradeUpdate() Thu
May 11 16:06:12 2023 MEMarketUpdate [ type:TRADE ticker:5
oid:INVALID side:SELL qty:62 price:137 priority:INVALID]
trading_engine_1.log:market_maker.h:19 onOrderBookUpdate() Thu
May 11 16:06:12 2023 ticker:5 price:137 side:BUY
```

We encourage you to inspect the various log files in more detail to understand the processing that occurs in the different components and how our entire electronic trading ecosystem functions.

Summary

This chapter focused on using all the components we have built over the last two chapters and leveraging them to build our intelligent trading strategies – the MM trading strategy and the liquidity taking trading algorithm. We spent some time understanding the theory, motivation, and behavior of these two trading algorithms with some examples.

In the next two sections, we implemented the C++ MM trading algorithm, which manages passive orders, and the liquidity taking algorithm, which sends aggressive orders to the market.

Then, we built the trading engine framework that ties together the market data consumer, the order gateway, the feature engine, the position keeper, the order manager, and the risk manager together with the two trading algorithms. This framework is what we use to join all these components together and facilitate the flow of incoming and outgoing data streams and trading intelligence.

Finally, we built the main trading application, `trading_main`, which is the complement of the `exchange_main` application on the market participant's side. We then ran a few different instances of the trading application to run instances of the random trading algorithm, the MM algorithm, and the liquidity taking algorithm in our ecosystem. We inspected the log files generated by running our electronic trading ecosystem as the different trading client systems and strategies interacted with each other through the electronic exchange.

In the next chapter, we will add an instrumentation system to measure the performance of our entire electronic trading ecosystem. We mentioned throughout this book that the first step to optimizing something is measuring the performance of a system and its components individually, and we will start by doing that in the next chapter.

Part 4: Analyzing and Improving Performance

In this part, we will measure the performance of all the different C++ components in our trading ecosystem. We will analyze the latency profile of the different components individually, as well as measuring the performance of the end-to-end round-trip path. From there, we will discuss further optimization techniques and see the impact of our C++ optimization efforts. We will also discuss some future enhancements that can be made to our electronic trading ecosystem.

This part contains the following chapters:

- *Chapter 11, Adding Instrumentation and Measuring Performance*
- *Chapter 12, Analyzing and Optimizing the Performance of Our C++ System*

11
Adding Instrumentation and Measuring Performance

In this chapter, we will add a system to measure the performance of the C++ components we have built so far in this book. We will measure the latencies in the trading exchange system we built in *Part 2* and the latencies in the client's trading system built in the previous section. Finally, we will measure and analyze the performance of the end-to-end system by running the different algorithms we built in the previous section. In this chapter, we will cover the following topics:

- Adding an instrumentation system to measure system performance
- Measuring latencies in the exchange
- Measuring latencies in the trading engine
- Running the entire ecosystem with the new instrumentation system

Technical requirements

All the code for this book can be found in the book's GitHub repository at https://github.com/PacktPublishing/Building-Low-Latency-Applications-with-CPP. The source for this chapter is in the Chapter11 directory in the repository.

This chapter relies on a lot of the previous chapters since we will be measuring the performance of all the different components and subcomponents in the electronic trading ecosystem. So, we expect you to be familiar with the code base we have built so far, specifically, the *Building the C++ Matching Engine, Communicating with Market Participants, Processing Market Data and Sending Orders to the Exchange in C++, Building the C++ Trading Algorithm Building Blocks*, and finally, *Building the C++ Market Making and Liquidity Taking Algorithms* chapters.

The specifications of the environment in which the source code for this book was developed are shown next. We present the details of this environment since all the C++ code presented in this book is not necessarily portable and might require some minor changes to work in your environment:

- OS – `Linux 5.19.0-41-generic #42~22.04.1-Ubuntu SMP PREEMPT_DYNAMIC Tue Apr 18 17:40:00 UTC 2 x86_64 x86_64 x86_64 GNU/Linux`
- GCC – `g++ (Ubuntu 11.3.0-1ubuntu1~22.04.1) 11.3.0`
- CMake – `cmake version 3.23.2`
- Ninja – `1.10.2`

Adding an instrumentation system to measure system performance

The first task we need to tackle is to add a few utility methods that will serve as the base of our performance measurement system. These are meant to be used to measure the latencies of internal components and subcomponents for processes running on the same server. These are also meant to be used to measure latencies between the different components, which are unlikely to be on the same server in practice, such as the trading exchange and the trading clients, which are on different servers. Note, however, that in this book, we run the trading exchange and the trading clients on the same server for simplicity. Now, let us start by adding these utilities in the next section.

Adding utilities for performance measurement using RDTSC

The first performance measurement utility we add does not directly measure the time itself but, instead, measures how many CPU clock cycles elapse between two spots in our code base. This is achieved by reading the value of the **Time Stamp Counter** (**TSC**), a 64-bit register containing the number of CPU cycles. We will execute an assembly instruction, `rdtsc`, to fetch and return this value, which returns this in the form of two 32-bit values that we will convert into a single 64-bit value. We can use these `rdtsc` values as is to measure/compare performance if we do not really care about converting them into time units. The other option is to convert this `rdtsc` value into time units, which is achieved by dividing this value by the system's clock frequency, which is specified as the number of CPU clock cycles per second. For instance, on my system, the CPU clock frequency comes out to be around 2.6 GHz, as shown here:

```
sghosh@sghosh-ThinkPad-X1-Carbon-3rd:~/Building-Low-Latency-
Applications-with-CPP/Chapter11$ cat /proc/cpuinfo | grep MHz
cpu MHz          : 2645.048
cpu MHz          : 2645.035
cpu MHz          : 2645.033
cpu MHz          : 2645.050
```

What this means is that if we measure the `rdtsc` value before and after the execution of a code block and the difference between the two values is 26 clock cycles, on my system, that translates to approximately 26 / 2.6 = a 10-nanosecond execution time. We will talk about this more in the last subsection of this section, *Understanding some issues with measurement systems in practice*. So, without any more delay, let us look at the code for this measurement implementation. All the code for this section can be found in the `Chapter11/common/perf_utils.h` source file.

First, we implement an `rdtsc()` C++ method, which internally calls the `rdtsc` assembly instruction and provides it with two variables, `lo` and `hi`, to read the lower and higher 32-bits that make up the final `rdtsc` value. The `__asm__` instruction tells the compiler that what follows it is an assembly instruction. The `__volatile__` instruction exists to prevent the compiler from optimizing the instructions so that it is executed as is to make sure we read the TSC register every time this is called. We save the output into the `lo` and `hi` variables and, finally, using a bit shift operation, create a 64-bit value from them and return it:

```
#pragma once

namespace Common {
  inline auto rdtsc() noexcept {
    unsigned int lo, hi;
    __asm__ __volatile__ ("rdtsc" : "=a" (lo), "=d" (hi));
    return ((uint64_t) hi << 32) | lo;
  }
}
```

Next, we will define a simple preprocessor macro, `START_MEASURE`, which accepts an argument called `TAG`, and all it does is create a variable with that name and saves the value of the `rdtsc()` method we just built in it. In other words, this macro simply creates a variable with the name provided and saves the `rdtsc()` value in it:

```
#define START_MEASURE(TAG) const auto TAG = Common::rdtsc()
```

We define another complimentary macro called `END_MEASURE`, which accepts an argument called `TAG` as well as an argument called `LOGGER`, which it expects to be of our `Common::Logger` type. It takes another measurement using the `rdtsc()` method we built previously and uses the `LOGGER` object to log the difference between the two. The only reason this code block is enclosed in a `do { }  while(false)` loop (without a terminating semi-colon) is to make sure that the compiler catches missing semi-colons when this method is invoked. In other words, `END_MEASURE(example, logger_);` is a valid use but `END_MEASURE(example, logger_)` (missing semi-colon) causes a compilation error to maintain symmetry with `START_MEASURE`. This is not strictly necessary, just a preference on our part:

```
#define END_MEASURE(TAG, LOGGER) \
    do { \
```

```
        const auto end = Common::rdtsc(); \
        LOGGER.log("% RDTSC "#TAG" %\n", \
          Common::getCurrentTimeStr(&time_str_), (end - 
            TAG)); \
      } while(false)
```

Finally, we will define a similar macro called `TTT_MEASURE` that takes similar arguments (i.e., `TAG` and `LOGGER`), This macro simply logs the current time in nanoseconds, which it obtains by calling our `Common::getCurrentNanos()` method that we saw before:

```
#define TTT_MEASURE(TAG, LOGGER) \
    do { \
      const auto TAG = Common::getCurrentNanos(); \
      LOGGER.log("% TTT "#TAG" %\n", Common::
        getCurrentTimeStr(&time_str_), TAG); \
    } while(false)
```

We will use these macros throughout this chapter, but before we do that, we need to make some minor changes to the time utilities we built before and have seen many uses of already.

Updating our previous time utilities

In this section, we will make a minor change to the time utility `Common::getCurrentTimeStr()` method to make the output more informative and granular. The goal here is to change our previous output, which looked like this:

```
onMarketUpdate() Sat Jun  3 09:46:34 2023 MEMarketUpdate
```

We want to change it to this format, which drops the date and year from the output and changes the time output from just having seconds to having seconds and nanoseconds to add granularity:

```
onMarketUpdate() 09:46:34.645778416 MEMarketUpdate
```

This will help us inspect, order, and analyze events that happen in the same second even more closely. These changes can be found in the `Chapter11/common/time_utils.h` source file.

Note that the other change is the inclusion of the `perf_utils.h` header file containing the measurement methods we built in the previous section:

```
#include "perf_utils.h"
```

We saw this before in the *Building the C++ Building Blocks for Low-Latency Applications* chapter in the *Designing utility methods for time* section. We call `std::chrono::system_clock::now()` to extract the current `time_point` value and save it in the `clock` variable. We also extract and save the `time_t` object from it into the `time` variable using the `std::chrono::system_clock::to_time_t()` method, as shown:

```
namespace Common {
  inline auto& getCurrentTimeStr(std::string* time_str) {
    const auto clock = std::chrono::system_clock::now();
    const auto time = std::chrono::
      system_clock::to_time_t(clock);
```

We use a combination of `sprintf()`, `ctime()`, and the previously seen `std::chrono::duration_cast<std::chrono::nanoseconds>(clock.time_since_epoch()).count()` method to extract and format the current time in the `HH:MM:SS.nnnnnnnnn` format. Finally, we assign it to the `time_str` object of the `std::string` type, which is passed to this method, as well as return it:

```
    char nanos_str[24];
    sprintf(nanos_str, "%.8s.%09ld", ctime(&time) + 11,
      std::chrono::duration_cast<std::chrono::nanoseconds>
        (clock.time_since_epoch()).count() % NANOS_TO_SECS);
    time_str->assign(nanos_str);

    return *time_str;
  }
}
```

Before we move on to using these new methods, we will discuss a few more points regarding measuring performance in practice.

Understanding some issues with measurement systems in practice

In this section, we will discuss a few important considerations when it comes to measuring performance in practice. This is important to understand because performance measurement is not always as easy as it seems and it requires you to understand some nuances.

Adding overhead due to instrumentation

The first key point we want to make about measuring performance in practice is that it is important to consider that the measurement system itself is not zero-latency. What this means is that adding instrumentation into the path of the critical code base adds some extra latency. It is important to make sure that the instrumentation system/routine itself is extremely low-latency relative to the latency of the system it's measuring. A hypothetical example is that if we are measuring something that takes a few microseconds, we need to make sure that the measurement routines take a few nanoseconds to not add too much overhead. One of the reasons we have the option of using `rdtsc()` to measure performance is that it is significantly faster than calling something such as `std::chrono::system_` `clock::now()` or `clock_gettime()`. That gives us the option of using `rdtsc()` if we are measuring a code block that has extremely low latency to add minimal overhead.

Understanding the limitations and reliability of RDTSC

The second key point is regarding `rdtsc()`, which is not always very portable and can have reliability concerns depending on the platform. Another consideration with `rdtsc()` when converting it into time units is that CPU clock frequency can vary from core to core on a system, and using a static CPU clock frequency for the conversion is not always accurate.

Setting up the correct measurement environment

The third point regarding measuring performance on trading servers is that a lot of tuning needs to be done to facilitate accurate measurements. This involves techniques such as disabling interrupts, making sure unnecessary processes are not running, making sure the NUMA setup is correct, tweaking CPU power settings, setting up CPU isolation, pinning threads to specific cores, and so on. Discussing all these considerations when it comes to electronic trading is beyond the scope of this book, nor is it the focus of this book. We just wanted to mention that there are additional considerations when it comes to performance measurement. We refer interested readers to the book *Developing High-Frequency Trading Systems: Learn how to implement high-frequency trading from scratch with C++ or Java basics*, which discusses **High-Frequency electronic Trading** (**HFT**) specific considerations.

Now we can move on to using the performance measurement system we built in this section in our electronic trading ecosystem, starting with the exchange in the next section.

Measuring latencies at the exchange

First, we will add instrumentation to the components on the electronic trading exchange side – the market data publisher, the matching engine, and the order server. Our approach to measuring performance will comprise two forms; let us understand those first before we look at the code.

Understanding how to measure internally

The first approach is to measure the latency of internal components – for example, how long does a call to the `Exchange::MatchingEngine::processClientRequest()` method take or how long does a call to the `Exchange::MEOrderBook::add()` method take? For these cases, we will use a pair of `START_MEASURE()` and `END_MEASURE()` macros, which, in turn, use the `rdtsc()` method to measure the performance of each such call. There is nothing here that prevents us from using the `TTT_MEASURE()` macro in place of `rdtsc()` or as a supplement. But we will use `rdtsc()` for these, for the sake of providing examples of how to use the two different instrumentation systems. Additionally, we use the rationale that a call to a function such as the one we mentioned previously should be very quick and it might be better to use the lower overhead `rdtsc()` methods for that. The complete list of internal measurements we will take is listed next, but interested readers should use similar techniques to add even more points of measurement as they see fit. We will see the code for how to measure these familiar methods shortly, but for now, the methods we will measure on the exchange side are the following:

- `Common::McastSocket::send()`
- `Exchange::MEOrderBook::add()`
- `Exchange::MEOrderBook::cancel()`
- `Exchange::MatchingEngine::processClientRequest()`
- `Exchange::MEOrderBook::removeOrder()`
- `Exchange::MEOrderBook::match()`
- `Exchange::MEOrderBook::match()`
- `Exchange::MEOrderBook::checkForMatch()`
- `Exchange::MEOrderBook::addOrder()`
- `Exchange::MEOrderBook::removeOrder()`
- `Common::TCPSocket::send()`
- `Exchange::FIFOSequencer::addClientRequest()`
- `Exchange::FIFOSequencer::sequenceAndPublish()`

Next, let us take a few steps back and understand which high-level spots/hops we will timestamp in the electronic trading exchange.

Understanding key hops at the exchange

In addition to measuring the functioning of internal components, exchanges can record performance data, especially timestamps, to track how events (client requests) propagate through the different components and subcomponents. We mean tracking and, often, publishing metrics such as when an order reached the order server, when it reached the matching engine, when the response to that request left the order server, when market updates corresponding to that request left the market data publisher, and so on. By recording these metrics, exchanges can understand and investigate their performance under different market/load conditions, track per-participant performance, and so on. By publishing these metrics to the market participants, the participants can understand and investigate their own performance and consider ways to improve them.

In our electronic trading exchange, we will take timestamps of the following events:

- `T1_OrderServer_TCP_read` – the time when a client request is first read at the TCP socket in `OrderServer`

- `T2_OrderServer_LFQueue_write` – the time when a client request is written to `LFQueue` that connects to `MatchingEngine`
- `T3_MatchingEngine_LFQueue_read` – the time when `MatchingEngine` reads a client request from `LFQueue`
- `T4_MatchingEngine_LFQueue_write` – the time when the market update is written to the `LFQueue` connected to `MarketDataPublisher`
- `T4t_MatchingEngine_LFQueue_write` – the time when the client response is written to the `LFQueue` connected to `OrderServer`
- `T5_MarketDataPublisher_LFQueue_read` – the time when the market update is read from `LFQueue`
- `T5t_OrderServer_LFQueue_read` – the time when the client response is read from `LFQueue`
- `T6_MarketDataPublisher_UDP_write` – the time when the market update is written to the UDP socket in `MarketDataPublisher`
- `T6t_OrderServer_TCP_write` – the time when the client response is written to the TCP socket in `OrderServer`

The exact locations of these timestamps are shown in the following figure:

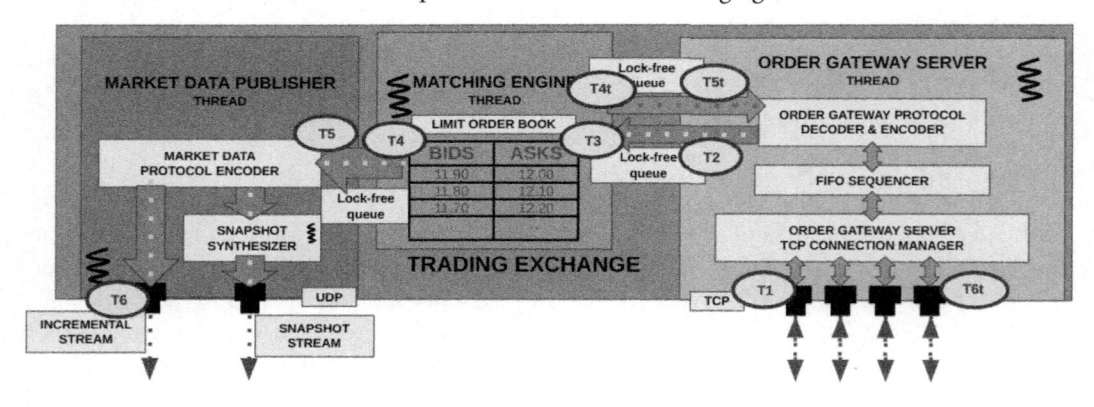

Figure 11.1 – The topology of the electronic trading exchange with the key hops to timestamp

Now, starting in the next section, we can start looking at the code changes we need to add to these two forms of measurement.

Measuring the latencies inside the market data publisher

First, we will add performance measurement and timestamping code to the market data publisher. For the sake of brevity, we will only show the code blocks where we make these changes instead of including the source code for the entire source file or full code blocks in the case of large code blocks. All the changes, as well as the full, updated source code for the market data publisher-related changes, are in the `Chapter11/exchange/market_data/market_data_publisher.cpp` source file.

First, in the `MarketDataPublisher::run()` method, we will add a timestamp using the `TTT_MEASURE` macro and the `T5_MarketDataPublisher_LFQueue_read` tag right after reading from `outgoing_md_updates_ LFQueue`, as shown here:

```
auto MarketDataPublisher::run() noexcept -> void {
  ...
  while (run_) {
    for (auto market_update = outgoing_md_updates_->
      getNextToRead();
        outgoing_md_updates_->size() && market_update;
          market_update = outgoing_md_updates_->
            getNextToRead()) {
      TTT_MEASURE(T5_MarketDataPublisher_LFQueue_read,
        logger_);
```

Next, we will measure the time taken to call `MCastSocket::send()` on `incremental_socket_` using the `START_MEASURE` and `END_MEASURE` macros and the `Exchange_McastSocket_send` tag:

```
      START_MEASURE(Exchange_McastSocket_send);
      incremental_socket_.send(&next_inc_seq_num_,
        sizeof(next_inc_seq_num_));
      incremental_socket_.send(market_update,
        sizeof(MEMarketUpdate));
      END_MEASURE(Exchange_McastSocket_send, logger_);
```

Finally, we will take another timestamp using the `TTT_MEASURE` macro and the `T6_MarketDataPublisher_UDP_write` tag right after the socket write is finished:

```
      outgoing_md_updates_->updateReadIndex();
      TTT_MEASURE(T6_MarketDataPublisher_UDP_write,
        logger_);
  ...
```

Next, let us look at the changes in the `OrderServer` component for performance measurement and timestamping.

Measuring the latencies inside the order server

All the changes for performance measurement and timestamping, as well as the full source code for `OrderServer`, are in the `Chapter11/exchange/order_server/order_server.h` source file. As before, we will only show minimal code blocks where the changes are made for the sake of brevity and to avoid repetition.

First, we will make changes to the `OrderServer::run()` method, right after reading an entry from `outgoing_responses_ LFQueue`. We use the `TTT_MEASURE` macro with the `T5t_OrderServer_LFQueue_read` tag, as shown here:

```
auto run() noexcept {
  ...
  while (run_) {
    ...
    for (auto client_response = outgoing_responses_->
      getNextToRead(); outgoing_responses_->size() &&
        client_response; client_response =
          outgoing_responses_->getNextToRead()) {
      TTT_MEASURE(T5t_OrderServer_LFQueue_read,
        logger_);
```

Next, we will measure the call to the `TCPSocket::send()` method using the `START_MEASURE` and `END_MEASURE` macros and the `Exchange_TCPSocket_send` tag. Note that we measure the call to send out the full client response message, which, in our implementation, results in two calls to the `TCPSocket::send()` methods:

```
START_MEASURE(Exchange_TCPSocket_send);
cid_tcp_socket_[client_response->client_id_]->
  send(&next_outgoing_seq_num,
    sizeof(next_outgoing_seq_num));
cid_tcp_socket_[client_response->client_id_]->
  send(client_response,
    sizeof(MEClientResponse));
END_MEASURE(Exchange_TCPSocket_send, logger_);
```

Finally, after the TCP socket send operations finish, we take another timestamp using the `TTT_MEASURE` method and the `T6t_OrderServer_TCP_write` tag:

```
outgoing_responses_->updateReadIndex();
TTT_MEASURE(T6t_OrderServer_TCP_write, logger_);
...
```

The next set of changes is in the `OrderServer::recvCallback()` method. Right as soon as we enter the method, we take a timestamp with the `TTT_MEASURE` macro with the `T1_OrderServer_TCP_read` tag:

```
auto recvCallback(TCPSocket *socket, Nanos rx_time)
  noexcept {
  TTT_MEASURE(T1_OrderServer_TCP_read, logger_);
  ...
```

Finally, at the end of this method, we measure the call to `FIFOSequencer::addClientRequest()`, using the `START_MEASURE` and `END_MEASURE` macros with the `Exchange_FIFOSequencer_addClientRequest` tag:

```
START_MEASURE(Exchange_FIFOSequencer_addClientRequest);
       fifo_sequencer_.addClientRequest(rx_time,
         request->me_client_request_);
           END_MEASURE(Exchange_FIFOSequencer_
             addClientRequest, logger_);
    ...
```

Finally, for `OrderServer`, we need to update the `OrderServer::recvFinishedCallback()` method. We measure the call to the `FIFOSequencer::sequenceAndPublish()` method using the `START_MEASURE` and `END_MEASURE` macros with the `Exchange_FIFOSequencer_sequenceAndPublish` tag:

```
auto recvFinishedCallback() noexcept {
  START_MEASURE(Exchange_FIFOSequencer_sequenceAndPublis)
;
   fifo_sequencer_.sequenceAndPublish();
   END_MEASURE(Exchange_FIFOSequencer_
     sequenceAndPublish, logger_);
}
```

In the next subsection, we will add instrumentation to the `FIFOSequencer` subcomponent.

Measuring the latencies inside FIFOSequencer

All the instrumentation changes, as well as the full, updated source for the `FIFOSequencer` subcomponent, can be found in the `Chapter11/exchange/order_server/fifo_sequencer.h` source file. The only changes we will make are in the `FIFOSequencer::sequenceAndPublish()` method. Here, all we do is add a timestamp after we write a client request to `incoming_requests_LFQueue`, which we do by using the `TTT_MEASURE` macro and using the `T2_OrderServer_LFQueue_write` tag value, as shown here:

```
auto sequenceAndPublish() {
   for (size_t i = 0; i < pending_size_; ++i) {
```

```
    ...
    auto next_write = incoming_requests_->
      getNextToWriteTo();
    *next_write = std::move(client_request.request_);
    incoming_requests_->updateWriteIndex();
    TTT_MEASURE(T2_OrderServer_LFQueue_write,
      (*logger_));
    ...
```

Next, we move on to the task of adding instrumentation and timestamps to the core matching engine component as well as its subcomponents.

Measuring the latencies inside the matching engine and order book

First, we will update `MatchingEngine`; all the changes and the full, updated source for `MatchingEngine` can be found in the `Chapter11/exchange/matcher/matching_engine.h` source file.

In the `MatchingEngine::processClientRequest()` method, we will measure the time it takes for the `MEOrderBook::add()` and `MEOrderBook::cancel()` methods. First, we show the changes for the `MEOrderBook::add()` method using the `START_MEASURE` and `END_MEASURE` macros and the `Exchange_MEOrderBook_add` tag:

```
    auto processClientRequest(const MEClientRequest
      *client_request) noexcept {
    ...
    switch (client_request->type_) {
      case ClientRequestType::NEW: {
        START_MEASURE(Exchange_MEOrderBook_add);
        order_book->add(client_request->client_id_,
          client_request->order_id_, client_request->
            ticker_id_,
                      client_request->side_,
                        client_request->price_,
                          client_request->qty_);
        END_MEASURE(Exchange_MEOrderBook_add, logger_);
        ...
```

Then, we have the changes for `MEOrderBook::cancel()` using the `START_MEASURE` and `END_MEASURE` macros and the `Exchange_MEOrderBook_cancel` tag, as shown here:

```
      case ClientRequestType::CANCEL: {
        START_MEASURE(Exchange_MEOrderBook_cancel);
```

```
        order_book->cancel(client_request->client_id_,
          client_request->order_id_, client_request->
            ticker_id_);
        END_MEASURE(Exchange_MEOrderBook_cancel,
          logger_);
        ...
```

The next method we need to update is `MatchingEngine::sendClientResponse()`. We will use the `TTT_MEASURE` macro with the `T4t_MatchingEngine_LFQueue_write` tag right after we write the client response to `outgoing_ogw_responses_ LFQueue`, as shown here:

```
    auto sendClientResponse(const MEClientResponse
      *client_response) noexcept {
      ...
      auto next_write = outgoing_ogw_responses_->
        getNextToWriteTo();
      *next_write = std::move(*client_response);
      outgoing_ogw_responses_->updateWriteIndex();
      TTT_MEASURE(T4t_MatchingEngine_LFQueue_write,
        logger_);
    }
```

We also need to update the `MatchingEngine::sendMarketUpdate()` method by adding a timestamp after writing the market update to `outgoing_md_updates_ LFQueue` using the `TTT_MEASURE` macro and the `T4_MatchingEngine_LFQueue_write` tag:

```
    auto sendMarketUpdate(const MEMarketUpdate
      *market_update) noexcept {
      ...
      auto next_write = outgoing_md_updates_->
        getNextToWriteTo();
      *next_write = *market_update;
      outgoing_md_updates_->updateWriteIndex();
      TTT_MEASURE(T4_MatchingEngine_LFQueue_write,
        logger_);
    }
```

The final method we need to update in `MatchingEngine` is the `run()` method itself. We take a timestamp right after reading from `incoming_requests_ LFQueue`, using the `TTT_MEASURE` macro and the `T3_MatchingEngine_LFQueue_read` tag, as shown here:

```
    auto run() noexcept {
      while (run_) {
        const auto me_client_request = incoming_requests_->
          getNextToRead();
```

```
            if (LIKELY(me_client_request)) {
              TTT_MEASURE(T3_MatchingEngine_LFQueue_read,
                logger_);
```

And we measure the call to the `MatchingEngine::processClientRequest()` method with the `START_MEASURE` and `END_MEASURE` macros with the `Exchange_MatchingEngine_processClientRequest` tag:

```
START_MEASURE(Exchange_MatchingEngine_
processClientRequest);           processClientRequest(me_client_
request);
END_MEASURE(Exchange_MatchingEngine_processClientRequest,
  logger_);
    ...
```

The final component on the exchange side that we need to update is the `MEOrderBook` subcomponent in `MatchingEngine`.

Measuring the latencies inside MEOrderBook

We will discuss the instrumentation changes to the `MEOrderBook` component in this subsection, which can be found in the `Chapter11/exchange/matcher/me_order_book.cpp` source file.

The first method we will update is `MEOrderBook::match()`. We want to measure the call to `MEOrderBook::removeOrder()` with the `START_MEASURE` and `END_MEASURE` macros and the `Exchange_MEOrderBook_removeOrder` tag, as shown here:

```
auto MEOrderBook::match(TickerId ticker_id, ClientId
  client_id, Side side, OrderId client_order_id, OrderId
    new_market_order_id, MEOrder* itr, Qty* leaves_qty)
      noexcept {
  ...
  if (!order->qty_) {
    ...
    START_MEASURE(Exchange_MEOrderBook_removeOrder);
    removeOrder(order);
    END_MEASURE(Exchange_MEOrderBook_removeOrder,
      (*logger_));
    ...
```

We also need to update the `MEOrderBook::checkForMatch()` method to measure the calls to `MEOrderBook::match()`. We use the `START_MEASURE` and `END_MEASURE` macros with the `Exchange_MEOrderBook_match` tag for the two branches of execution, as shown here:

```
auto MEOrderBook::checkForMatch(ClientId client_id,
  OrderId client_order_id, TickerId ticker_id, Side side,
```

```
    Price price, Qty qty, Qty new_market_order_id)
      noexcept {
  ...
  if (side == Side::BUY) {
    while (leaves_qty && asks_by_price_) {
      ...
      START_MEASURE(Exchange_MEOrderBook_match);
      match(ticker_id, client_id, side, client_order_id,
        new_market_order_id, ask_itr, &leaves_qty);
      END_MEASURE(Exchange_MEOrderBook_match,
        (*logger_));
    }
  }
  if (side == Side::SELL) {
    while (leaves_qty && bids_by_price_) {
      ...
      START_MEASURE(Exchange_MEOrderBook_match);
      match(ticker_id, client_id, side, client_order_id,
        new_market_order_id, bid_itr, &leaves_qty);
      END_MEASURE(Exchange_MEOrderBook_match,
        (*logger_));
    }
  }
  ...
```

We will add additional instrumentation within the `MEOrderBook::add()` method to measure a few different calls. The first one is the call to `MEOrderBook::checkForMatch()`, for which we will use the `Exchange_MEOrderBook_checkForMatch` tag:

```
auto MEOrderBook::add(ClientId client_id, OrderId
  client_order_id, TickerId ticker_id, Side side, Price
    price, Qty qty) noexcept -> void {
  ...
  START_MEASURE(Exchange_MEOrderBook_checkForMatch);
  const auto leaves_qty = checkForMatch(client_id,
    client_order_id, ticker_id, side, price, qty,
      new_market_order_id);
  END_MEASURE(Exchange_MEOrderBook_checkForMatch,
    (*logger_));
  ...
```

The next one is the call to `MEOrderBook::addOrder()`, for which we will use the `Exchange_MEOrderBook_addOrder` tag:

```
START_MEASURE(Exchange_MEOrderBook_addOrder);
addOrder(order);
END_MEASURE(Exchange_MEOrderBook_addOrder,
  (*logger_));
...
```

The last `MEOrderBook` method we need to add more granular instrumentation to is the `cancel()` method. In this method, we want to measure the call to the `MEOrderBook::removeOrder()` method, as shown next, with the `START_MEASURE` and `END_MEASURE` macros and the `Exchange_MEOrderBook_removeOrder` tag:

```
auto MEOrderBook::cancel(ClientId client_id, OrderId
  order_id, TickerId ticker_id) noexcept -> void {
    ...
    START_MEASURE(Exchange_MEOrderBook_removeOrder);
    removeOrder(exchange_order);
    END_MEASURE(Exchange_MEOrderBook_removeOrder,
      (*logger_));
    ...
```

This concludes all the measurements we wanted to add on the side of the electronic exchange, and in the next section, we will add similar instrumentation on the other side: that is, the trading client system.

Measuring latencies in the trading engine

In this section, we will focus on adding performance measurement and timestamps to the trading client's system – the market data consumer, the order gateway, and the trade engine and its subcomponents. Here too, we will measure the performance of internal components as well as add timestamps to help with a higher-level analysis of incoming and outgoing events latencies.

Understanding how to measure internally

The motivation and approach toward measuring the performance of internal components for the trading clients' systems are identical to those on the exchange side. The complete list of internal measurements we will take is listed next, but interested readers should use similar techniques to add even more points of measurement as they see fit. We will see the code for how to measure these familiar methods shortly, but for now, the methods we will measure on the client's side are the following:

- `Trading::MarketDataConsumer::recvCallback()`
- `Common::TCPSocket::send()`

- `Trading::OrderGateway::recvCallback()`
- `Trading::OrderManager::moveOrders()`
- `Trading::OrderManager::onOrderUpdate()`
- `Trading::OrderManager::moveOrders()`
- `Trading::OrderManager::onOrderUpdate()`
- `Trading::MarketOrderBook::addOrder()`
- `Trading::MarketOrderBook::removeOrder()`
- `Trading::MarketOrderBook::updateBBO()`
- `Trading::OrderManager::cancelOrder()`
- `Trading::RiskManager::checkPreTradeRisk()`
- `Trading::OrderManager::newOrder()`
- `Trading::OrderManager::moveOrder()`
- `Trading::OrderManager::moveOrder()`
- `Trading::PositionKeeper::updateBBO()`
- `Trading::FeatureEngine::onOrderBookUpdate()`
- `Trading::TradeEngine::algoOnOrderBookUpdate()`
- `Trading::FeatureEngine::onTradeUpdate()`
- `Trading::TradeEngine::algoOnTradeUpdate()`
- `Trading::PositionKeeper::addFill()`
- `Trading::TradeEngine::algoOnOrderUpdate()`

As we did with the electronic trading exchange, we will understand the key hops that we will timestamp in the trading client's system.

Understanding key hops in the trading client's system

Market participants also have similar reasons for timestamping the flow of events through each of the components and subcomponents. By recording and analyzing the timings of these events, participants can seek to improve their systems as well as analyze how to increase profitability.

In our electronic trading client's system, we will take timestamps of the following events:

- `T7_MarketDataConsumer_UDP_read` – the time when a market data update is read from the UDP socket in `MarketDataConsumer`

- `T7t_OrderGateway_TCP_read` – the time when a client response is read from the TCP socket in `OrderGateway`
- `T8_MarketDataConsumer_LFQueue_write` – the time when a market data update is written to the `LFQueue` connected to `TradeEngine`
- `T8t_OrderGateway_LFQueue_write` – the time when a client response is written to the `LFQueue` connected to `TradeEngine`
- `T9_TradeEngine_LFQueue_read` – the time when a market data update is read from the `LFQueue` from `MarketDataConsumer`
- `T9t_TradeEngine_LFQueue_read` – the time when a client response is read from the `LFQueue` from `OrderGateway`
- `T10_TradeEngine_LFQueue_write` – the time when a client request is written to the `LFQueue` connected to `OrderGateway`
- `T11_OrderGateway_LFQueue_read` – the time when `OrderGateway` reads a client request from the `LFQueue` from `TradeEngine`
- `T12_OrderGateway_TCP_write` – the time when `OrderGateway` writes a client request to the TCP socket

The exact locations of these timestamps are shown in the following figure:

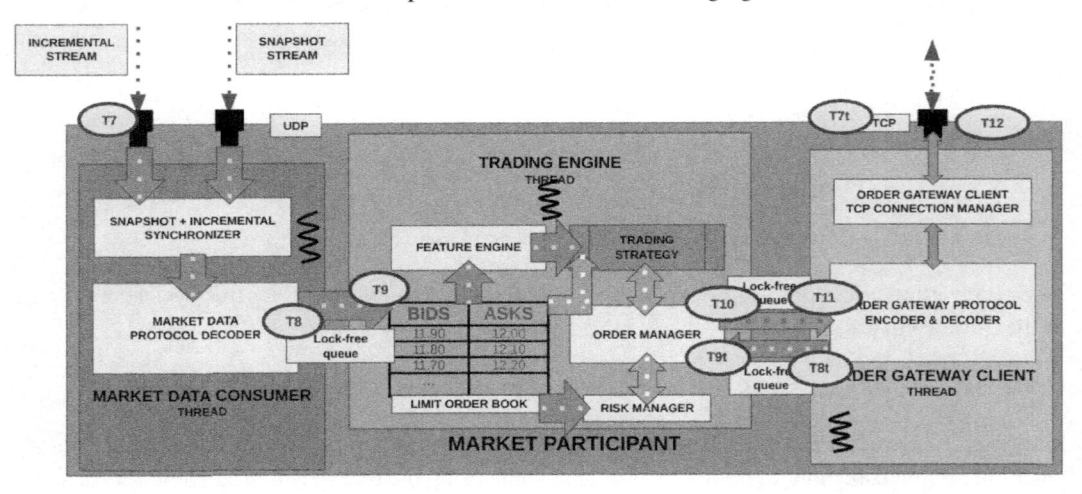

Figure 11.2 – The topology of the electronic trading client's system with the key hops to timestamp

Now, starting in the next section, we can start looking at the code changes we need to add to these two forms of measurement.

Measuring the latencies inside the market data consumer

We will start with the `MarketDataConsumer` component and, as we discussed before, we will only show the changes to the code here and omit repeating the full source code. The changes, as well as the full source code, are in the `Chapter11/trading/market_data/market_data_consumer.cpp` source file.

The first timestamp we take is as soon as we enter `MarketDataConsumer::recvCallback()`, where we use the `TTT_MEASURE` macro with the `T7_MarketDataConsumer_UDP_read` tag:

```
auto MarketDataConsumer::recvCallback(McastSocket
  *socket) noexcept -> void {
  TTT_MEASURE(T7_MarketDataConsumer_UDP_read, logger_);
```

We will also enclose the entire method using the `START_MEASURE` and `END_MEASURE` macros with the `Trading_MarketDataConsumer_recvCallback` tag to measure the latency of the entire method:

```
START_MEASURE(Trading_MarketDataConsumer_recvCallback);
...
END_MEASURE(Trading_MarketDataConsumer_recvCallback,
  logger_);
}
```

We will add a timestamp right after writing the decoded market update to `incoming_md_updates_LFQueue`, using the `TTT_MEASURE` macro and the `T8_MarketDataConsumer_LFQueue_write` tag:

```
        auto next_write = incoming_md_updates_->
          getNextToWriteTo();
        *next_write = std::move(request->
          me_market_update_);
        incoming_md_updates_->updateWriteIndex();
        TTT_MEASURE(T8_MarketDataConsumer_LFQueue_write,
          logger_);
```

In the next section, we move on to adding performance measurement to the `OrderGateway` component.

Measuring the latencies inside the order gateway

We will update the `OrderGateway` component in this subsection; all the changes and the updated full source code are available in the `Chapter11/trading/order_gw/order_gateway.cpp` source file.

The first method we will update is the `OrderGateway::run()` method, and the first timestamp we take is when we read a client request from `outgoing_requests_ LFQueue`. We accomplish this by using the `TTT_MEASURE` macro and the `T11_OrderGateway_LFQueue_read` tag:

```
auto OrderGateway::run() noexcept -> void {
  ...
  for(auto client_request = outgoing_requests_->
   getNextToRead(); client_request; client_request =
    outgoing_requests_->getNextToRead()) {
   TTT_MEASURE(T11_OrderGateway_LFQueue_read,
     logger_);
```

The next thing we will measure is the time it takes to execute the `Common::TCPSocket::send()` method, which we accomplish, as shown next, using the `Trading_TCPSocket_send` tag:

```
START_MEASURE(Trading_TCPSocket_send);
tcp_socket_.send(&next_outgoing_seq_num_,
  sizeof(next_outgoing_seq_num_));
tcp_socket_.send(client_request,
  sizeof(Exchange::MEClientRequest));
END_MEASURE(Trading_TCPSocket_send, logger_);
```

Finally, we also timestamp right after `TCPSocket::send()` finishes using the `TTT_MEASURE` macro and the `T12_OrderGateway_TCP_write` tag:

```
outgoing_requests_->updateReadIndex();
TTT_MEASURE(T12_OrderGateway_TCP_write, logger_);
```

The next method we will update in the `OrderGateway` component is the `recvCallback()` method. As soon as we enter the `recvCallback()` method, we take a timestamp using the `TTT_MEASURE` macro and the `T7t_OrderGateway_TCP_read` tag:

```
auto OrderGateway::recvCallback(TCPSocket *socket, Nanos
  rx_time) noexcept -> void {
  TTT_MEASURE(T7t_OrderGateway_TCP_read, logger_);
```

As with `MarketDataConsumer::recvCallback()`, we will enclose the entire `OrderGateway::recvCallback()` method using the `START_MEASURE` and `END_MEASURE` macros and the `Trading_OrderGateway_recvCallback` tag:

```
START_MEASURE(Trading_OrderGateway_recvCallback);
...
END_MEASURE(Trading_OrderGateway_recvCallback,
  logger_);
}
```

We also take a timestamp right after writing the client response to `incoming_responses_LFQueue` using the `TTT_MEASURE` macro and the `T8t_OrderGateway_LFQueue_write` tag:

```
auto next_write = incoming_responses_->
  getNextToWriteTo();
*next_write = std::move(response->
  me_client_response_);
incoming_responses_->updateWriteIndex();
TTT_MEASURE(T8t_OrderGateway_LFQueue_write,
  logger_);
```

In the next and final subsection of this section, we will add the instrumentation code to the trade engine and all the subcomponents in the trade engine.

Measuring the latencies inside the trading engine

First, we will start by updating the `TradeEngine` class itself, and the changes and the full updated source code for this can be found in the `Chapter11/trading/strategy/trade_engine.cpp` source file.

The `TradeEngine::sendClientRequest()` method is first on our list, and here, we take a timestamp after writing the client request to `outgoing_ogw_requests_` LFQueue with the `T10_TradeEngine_LFQueue_write` tag:

```
auto TradeEngine::sendClientRequest(const
  Exchange::MEClientRequest *client_request) noexcept -> void {
  auto next_write = outgoing_ogw_requests_->
   getNextToWriteTo();
  *next_write = std::move(*client_request);
  outgoing_ogw_requests_->updateWriteIndex();
  TTT_MEASURE(T10_TradeEngine_LFQueue_write, logger_);
```

The next method on our list is the `TradeEngine::run()` method, where the first task is to take a timestamp right after reading a client response from `incoming_ogw_responses_` LFQueue, with the `TTT_MEASURE` macro and the `T9t_TradeEngine_LFQueue_read` tag:

```
auto TradeEngine::run() noexcept -> void {
  while (run_) {
    for (auto client_response = incoming_ogw_responses_->
      getNextToRead(); client_response; client_response =
        incoming_ogw_responses_->getNextToRead()) {
      TTT_MEASURE(T9t_TradeEngine_LFQueue_read, logger_);
```

We will also take a timestamp measurement right after reading a market update from `incoming_md_updates_` LFQueue with the `T9_TradeEngine_LFQueue_read` tag:

```
for (auto market_update = incoming_md_updates_->
  getNextToRead(); market_update; market_update =
    incoming_md_updates_->getNextToRead()) {
  TTT_MEASURE(T9_TradeEngine_LFQueue_read, logger_);
```

The next method we need to update is the `TradeEngine::onOrderBookUpdate()` method, where the first thing we will do is measure the call to `PositionKeeper::updateBBO()`, using the `START_MEASURE` and `END_MEASURE` macros and the `Trading_PositionKeeper_updateBBO` tag:

```
auto TradeEngine::onOrderBookUpdate(TickerId ticker_id,
  Price price, Side side, MarketOrderBook *book) noexcept
  -> void {
  ...
  START_MEASURE(Trading_PositionKeeper_updateBBO);
  position_keeper_.updateBBO(ticker_id, bbo);
  END_MEASURE(Trading_PositionKeeper_updateBBO, logger_);
```

We also need to measure the call to the `FeatureEngine::onOrderBookUpdate()` method, for which we use the `Trading_FeatureEngine_onOrderBookUpdate` tag:

```
START_MEASURE(Trading_FeatureEngine_onOrderBookUpdate);
feature_engine_.onOrderBookUpdate(ticker_id, price,
  side, book);
END_MEASURE(Trading_FeatureEngine_onOrderBookUpdate,
  logger_);
```

We also need to measure the call to `TradeEngine::algoOnOrderBookUpdate_ std::function`, which calls `onOrderBookUpdate()` in either the `MarketMaker` or `LiquidityTaker` algorithm instance. We use the `START_MEASURE` and `END_MEASURE` macros and use the `Trading_TradeEngine_algoOnOrderBookUpdate_` tag:

```
START_MEASURE(Trading_TradeEngine_algoOnOrderBookUpdate_);
  algoOnOrderBookUpdate_(ticker_id, price, side, book);
  END_MEASURE(Trading_TradeEngine_algoOnOrderBookUpdate_,
    logger_);
```

The next method is the `TradeEngine::onTradeUpdate()` method. Here, the first call we measure is the call to `FeatureEngine::onTradeUpdate()`, to which we assign the `Trading_FeatureEngine_onTradeUpdate` tag:

```
auto TradeEngine::onTradeUpdate(const
  Exchange::MEMarketUpdate *market_update,
    MarketOrderBook *book) noexcept -> void {
  ...
  START_MEASURE(Trading_FeatureEngine_onTradeUpdate);
  feature_engine_.onTradeUpdate(market_update, book);
  END_MEASURE(Trading_FeatureEngine_onTradeUpdate,
    logger_);
```

The other call we will measure is the call using the `TradeEngine::algoOnTradeUpdate_` standard function, which will forward it to the `MarketMaker` or `LiquidityTaker` instance. We use the START_MEASURE and END_MEASURE macros using the tag of `Trading_TradeEngine_algoOnTradeUpdate_`:

```
START_MEASURE(Trading_TradeEngine_algoOnTradeUpdate_);
algoOnTradeUpdate_(market_update, book);
END_MEASURE(Trading_TradeEngine_algoOnTradeUpdate_,
  logger_);
```

The final method we have left to add instrumentation to is `TradeEngine::onOrderUpdate()`. Here, the first function call that we measure will be the call to `PositionKeeper::addFill()` using the `Trading_PositionKeeper_addFill` tag:

```
auto TradeEngine::onOrderUpdate(const
  Exchange::MEClientResponse *client_response) noexcept -
  > void {
  if (UNLIKELY(client_response->type_ ==
    Exchange::ClientResponseType::FILLED)) {
    START_MEASURE(Trading_PositionKeeper_addFill);
    position_keeper_.addFill(client_response);
    END_MEASURE(Trading_PositionKeeper_addFill, logger_);
  }
```

Finally, we add the START_MEASURE and END_MEASURE macros with the `Trading_TradeEngine_algoOnOrderUpdate_` tag around the invocation of the `algoOnOrderUpdate_` std::function object:

```
START_MEASURE(Trading_TradeEngine_algoOnOrderUpdate_);
algoOnOrderUpdate_(client_response);
END_MEASURE(Trading_TradeEngine_algoOnOrderUpdate_,
  logger_);
```

We will add some internal measurement code to each of the subcomponents that work with each other inside `TradeEngine`, starting with the `OrderManager` component next.

Measuring the latencies inside OrderManager

The changes to add performance measurement in `OrderManager` are the focus of this subsection, and all the code can be found in the `Chapter11/trading/strategy/order_manager.h` source file.

First, we will add measurements to the `OrderManager::moveOrder()` method. The first thing we will measure is the call to the `OrderManager::cancelOrder()` method using the `Trading_OrderManager_cancelOrder` tag:

```
auto moveOrder(OMOrder *order, TickerId ticker_id,
  Price price, Side side, Qty qty) noexcept {
  switch (order->order_state_) {
    case OMOrderState::LIVE: {
      if(order->price_ != price) {
        START_MEASURE(Trading_OrderManager_cancelOrder);
        cancelOrder(order);
        END_MEASURE(Trading_OrderManager_cancelOrder,
          (*logger_));
```

We will also measure the call to the `RiskManager` component, specifically the `checkPreTradeRisk()` call. We will use the START_MEASURE and END_MEASURE macros with the `Trading_RiskManager_checkPreTradeRisk` tag around the risk check, as shown next:

```
      case OMOrderState::DEAD: {
        if(LIKELY(price != Price_INVALID)) {
          START_MEASURE(Trading_RiskManager_checkPreTradeRisk);
          const auto risk_result =
            risk_manager_.checkPreTradeRisk(ticker_id,
              side, qty);
          END_MEASURE(Trading_RiskManager_checkPreTradeRisk,
            (*logger_));
```

Another thing to measure is the call to `OrderManager::newOrder()` if the risk check succeeds, and we will assign the measurement the `Trading_OrderManager_newOrder` tag, as shown here:

```
          if(LIKELY(risk_result ==
            RiskCheckResult::ALLOWED)) {
            START_MEASURE(Trading_OrderManager_newOrder);
            newOrder(order, ticker_id, price, side, qty);
```

```
        END_MEASURE(Trading_OrderManager_newOrder,
          (*logger_));
```

The other method in `OrderManager` to which we will add measurements is the `moveOrders()` method, and there we will enclose the calls to `OrderManager::moveOrder()` with `START_MEASURE` and `END_MEASURE` and the `Trading_OrderManager_moveOrder` tag:

```
    auto moveOrders(TickerId ticker_id, Price bid_price,
      Price ask_price, Qty clip) noexcept {
      ...
      START_MEASURE(Trading_OrderManager_moveOrder);
      moveOrder(bid_order, ticker_id, bid_price,
        Side::BUY, clip);
      END_MEASURE(Trading_OrderManager_moveOrder,
        (*logger_));
      ...
      START_MEASURE(Trading_OrderManager_moveOrder);
      moveOrder(ask_order, ticker_id, ask_price,
        Side::SELL, clip);
      END_MEASURE(Trading_OrderManager_moveOrder,
        (*logger_));
```

The next subcomponent in the `TradeEngine` class that we need to update is `MarketOrderBook`.

Measuring the latencies inside MarketOrderBook

The changes and full source for `MarketOrderBook` can be found in the `Chapter11/trading/strategy/market_order_book.cpp` source file.

First, in the `MarketOrderBook::onMarketUpdate()` method and the case for the `MarketUpdateType::ADD` message, we will measure the call to `MarketOrderBook::addOrder()`. This is achieved as usual by using the `START_MEASURE` and `END_MEASURE` macros with the `Trading_MarketOrderBook_addOrder` tag:

```
  auto MarketOrderBook::onMarketUpdate(const
    Exchange::MEMarketUpdate *market_update) noexcept ->
void {
    ...
    switch (market_update->type_) {
      case Exchange::MarketUpdateType::ADD: {
        auto order = order_pool_.allocate(market_update->
          order_id_, market_update->side_, market_update->
            price_,
                                          market_update->
                                            qty_,
```

```
                                        market_update-
                                          >priority_, nullptr,
                                          nullptr);
    START_MEASURE(Trading_MarketOrderBook_addOrder);
    addOrder(order);
    END_MEASURE(Trading_MarketOrderBook_addOrder,
      (*logger_));
```

To measure the call to `MarketOrderBook::removeOrder()` in the `MarketUpdateType::CANCEL` case, we will use the `Trading_MarketOrderBook_removeOrder` tag in the `START_MEASURE` and `END_MEASURE` macros:

```
case Exchange::MarketUpdateType::CANCEL: {
  auto order = oid_to_order_.at(market_update-
    >order_id_);
  START_MEASURE(Trading_MarketOrderBook_removeOrder);
  removeOrder(order);
  END_MEASURE(Trading_MarketOrderBook_removeOrder,
    (*logger_));
```

Finally, we will add a measurement around the call to `MarketOrderBook::updateBBO()` and assign it the `Trading_MarketOrderBook_updateBBO` tag:

```
START_MEASURE(Trading_MarketOrderBook_updateBBO);
updateBBO(bid_updated, ask_updated);
END_MEASURE(Trading_MarketOrderBook_updateBBO,
  (*logger_));
```

The next component to measure is one of the trading algorithms – the `LiquidityTaker` algorithm.

Measuring the latencies inside the LiquidityTaker algorithm

The changes we discuss here, as well as the full source code, are in the `Chapter11/trading/strategy/liquidity_taker.h` source file.

Our first measurement is in the `onTradeUpdate()` method for the `LiquidityTaker` class. When the signal initiates a trade, we measure the call to `OrderManager::moveOrders()` and assign it the `OrderManager_moveOrders` tag, as shown here:

```
    auto onTradeUpdate(const Exchange::MEMarketUpdate
      *market_update, MarketOrderBook *book) noexcept ->
 void {
        ...
        if (agg_qty_ratio >= threshold) {
          START_MEASURE(OrderManager_moveOrders);
```

```cpp
      if (market_update->side_ == Side::BUY)
        order_manager_->moveOrders(market_update->
          ticker_id_, bbo->ask_price_, Price_INVALID,
            clip);
      else
        order_manager_->moveOrders(market_update->
          ticker_id_, Price_INVALID, bbo->bid_price_,
            clip);
      END_MEASURE(OrderManager_moveOrders, (*logger_));
    }
```

The other call we want to measure is in the `onOrderUpdate()` method and measures the call to `OrderManager::onOrderUpdate()` using the `START_MEASURE` and `END_MEASURE` macros and the `Trading_OrderManager_onOrderUpdate` tag:

```cpp
    auto onOrderUpdate(const Exchange::MEClientResponse
      *client_response) noexcept -> void {
      START_MEASURE(Trading_OrderManager_onOrderUpdate);
      order_manager_->onOrderUpdate(client_response);
      END_MEASURE(Trading_OrderManager_onOrderUpdate,
        (*logger_));
```

Finally, we are down to our last component for this chapter, updating the `MarketMaker` algorithm.

Measuring the latencies inside the MarketMaker algorithm

The changes and the full source code for `MarketMaker` are in the `Chapter11/trading/strategy/market_maker.h` source file.

The `MarketMaker::onOrderBookUpdate()` method contains the call to `OrderManager::moveOrders()`, which is what we measure in the next code block with the `Trading_OrderManager_moveOrders` tag:

```cpp
    auto onOrderBookUpdate(TickerId ticker_id, Price price,
      Side side, const MarketOrderBook *book) noexcept ->
 void {
        ...
        START_MEASURE(Trading_OrderManager_moveOrders);
        order_manager_->moveOrders(ticker_id, bid_price,
          ask_price, clip);
        END_MEASURE(Trading_OrderManager_moveOrders,
          (*logger_));
```

The other method, `MarketMaker::onOrderUpdate()`, contains the call to `OrderManager::onOrderUpdate()`, which we also measure and to which we will assign the `Trading_OrderManager_onOrderUpdate` tag:

```
    auto onOrderUpdate(const Exchange::MEClientResponse
      *client_response) noexcept -> void {
      ...
      START_MEASURE(Trading_OrderManager_onOrderUpdate);
      order_manager_->onOrderUpdate(client_response);
      END_MEASURE(Trading_OrderManager_onOrderUpdate,
        (*logger_));
```

This concludes all the performance measurement and timestamping-related changes across our entire electronic trading ecosystem. We will very quickly look at how to run the ecosystem with all the changes we made so far and what differences we find in the log files.

Running the entire ecosystem with the new instrumentation system

Running the updated electronic trading ecosystem remains the same as before and is launched by running the following script:

```
sghosh@sghosh-ThinkPad-X1-Carbon-3rd:~/Building-Low-Latency-
Applications-with-CPP/Chapter11$ bash scripts/run_exchange_and_
clients.sh
```

Once the new ecosystem is done running, you can notice performance measurement log entries such as the following for the RDTSC measurements:

```
sghosh@sghosh-ThinkPad-X1-Carbon-3rd:~/Building-Low-Latency-
Applications-with-CPP/Chapter11$ grep Exchange_MEOrderBook_match *.log
exchange_matching_engine.log:02:42:59.980424597 RDTSC Exchange_
MEOrderBook_match 205247
exchange_matching_engine.log:02:43:00.022326352 RDTSC Exchange_
MEOrderBook_match 216239
```

There are also entries such as the following for the RDTSC measurements:

```
sghosh@sghosh-ThinkPad-X1-Carbon-3rd:~/Building-Low-Latency-
Applications-with-CPP/Chapter11$ grep Trading_MarketOrderBook_addOrder
*.log
trading_engine_1.log:02:44:18.894251975 RDTSC Trading_MarketOrderBook_
addOrder 204
trading_engine_1.log:02:44:18.904221378 RDTSC Trading_MarketOrderBook_
addOrder 971
```

There are entries such as the following for the TTT measurements:

```
sghosh@sghosh-ThinkPad-X1-Carbon-3rd:~/Building-Low-Latency-
Applications-with-CPP/Chapter11$ grep T6_MarketDataPublisher_UDP_write
*.log
exchange_market_data_publisher.log:02:40:13.596201293 TTT T6_
MarketDataPublisher_UDP_write 1685864413596201240
exchange_market_data_publisher.log:02:40:13.624236967 TTT T6_
MarketDataPublisher_UDP_write 1685864413624236907
```

And there are also entries such as the following for the TTT measurements:

```
sghosh@sghosh-ThinkPad-X1-Carbon-3rd:~/Building-Low-Latency-
Applications-with-CPP/Chapter11$ grep T8t_OrderGateway_LFQueue_write
*.log
trading_order_gateway_1.log:02:40:14.524401434 TTT T8t_OrderGateway_
LFQueue_write 1685864414524401386
trading_order_gateway_1.log:02:40:14.524425862 TTT T8t_OrderGateway_
LFQueue_write 1685864414524425811
```

We will revisit this performance data in the next chapter, but we have now finished this chapter.

Summary

This chapter was dedicated completely to measuring the performance of our electronic trading ecosystem. First, we built a system to measure and compare the latency incurred due to the execution of any arbitrary code block. We also built a system to generate nanosecond-level timestamps when notable events occur. We also discussed the motivation behind the design of these systems as well as various important points to keep in mind when using these performance measurement techniques.

The next section was dedicated to understanding the design and motivation of performance measurements within the various components and subcomponents on the electronic exchange's end. We then built and updated all the source code in the exchange to add the performance measurement and timestamping code.

After we finished the discussion and implementation of performance measurement within the electronic exchange, we performed similar measurements in the trading system. Finally, we concluded the chapter by running this updated ecosystem and observing the new log entries from the performance measurement system.

In the next and concluding chapter, we will analyze this performance data in detail, discuss our findings, and discuss how to optimize the performance.

12
Analyzing and Optimizing the Performance of Our C++ System

In this chapter, we will analyze the performance of our electronic trading ecosystem based on the measurements we added in the previous chapter, *Adding instrumentation and measuring performance*. Using the insights we develop about the performance of our trading systems based on this analysis, we will learn what areas to focus on in terms of potential performance bottlenecks and what areas we can improve. We will discuss tips and techniques for optimizing our C++ trading ecosystem. Finally, we will think about the future of our electronic trading ecosystem and what enhancements can be made in the future.

In this chapter, we will cover the following topics:

- Analyzing the performance of our trading ecosystem
- Discussing tips and techniques for optimizing our C++ trading system
- Thinking about the future of our trading ecosystem

Technical requirements

All the book's code can be found in the GitHub repository for this book at https://github.com/PacktPublishing/Building-Low-Latency-Applications-with-CPP. The source code for this chapter is in the Chapter12 directory in the repository.

Since this is the concluding chapter of this book and we will discuss tips for improving the performance of the full electronic trading ecosystem as well as future enhancements, we expect you to have gone through all the preceding chapters.

The specifications of the environment in which the source code for this book was developed are listed as follows. We have presented the details of this environment since all the C++ code presented in this book is not necessarily portable and might require some minor changes to work in your environment:

- OS: `Linux 5.19.0-41-generic #42~22.04.1-Ubuntu SMP PREEMPT_DYNAMIC Tue Apr 18 17:40:00 UTC 2 x86_64 x86_64 x86_64 GNU/Linux`
- GCC: `g++ (Ubuntu 11.3.0-1ubuntu1~22.04.1) 11.3.0`
- CMake: `cmake version 3.23.2`
- Ninja: `1.10.2`

Additionally, for those who are interested in running the *optional* Python Jupyter notebook included with this chapter, the following environment was used. We will not discuss the installation process for Python, Jupyter, and these libraries and assume that you will figure it out on your own:

```
-----
Python 3.10.6 (main, Mar 10 2023, 10:55:28) [GCC 11.3.0]
Linux-5.19.0-43-generic-x86_64-with-glibc2.35
-----
IPython              8.13.2
jupyter_client       8.2.0
jupyter_core         5.3.0
notebook             6.5.4
-----
hvplot               0.8.3
numpy                1.24.3
pandas               2.0.1
plotly               5.14.1
-----
```

Analyzing the performance of our trading ecosystem

Before we analyze the performance of our electronic trading ecosystem, let us quickly recap the measurements we added in the previous chapter.

Revisiting the latencies we measure

We added two forms of measurement. The first one measures the performance of internal components and the second one generates timestamps at key points in our entire system.

The first form, which measures the latencies of internal components, generates differences in `RDTSC` values before and after calls to different functions, and generates log entries such as the following:

```
exchange_order_server.log:18:48:29.452140238 RDTSC Exchange_
FIFOSequencer_addClientRequest 26
trading_engine_1.log:18:48:29.480664387 RDTSC Trading_FeatureEngine_
onOrderBookUpdate 39272
trading_engine_1.log:18:48:29.480584410 RDTSC Trading_MarketOrderBook_
```

```
addOrder 176
trading_engine_1.log:18:48:29.480712854 RDTSC Trading_OrderManager_
moveOrder 32
trading_engine_1.log:18:48:29.254832602 RDTSC Trading_PositionKeeper_
addFill 94350
trading_engine_1.log:18:48:29.480492650 RDTSC Trading_RiskManager_
checkPreTradeRisk 1036
...
```

The second form, which measures the latencies at key points in the trading ecosystem, generates absolute timestamp values and generates log entries such as the following:

```
trading_engine_1.log:18:48:29.440526826 TTT T10_TradeEngine_LFQueue_
write 1686008909440526763
exchange_order_server.log:18:48:29.452087295 TTT T1_OrderServer_TCP_
read 1686008909452087219
exchange_market_data_publisher.log:18:48:29.467680305 TTT T5_
MarketDataPublisher_LFQueue_read 1686008909467680251
trading_market_data_consumer_1.log:18:48:29.478030090 TTT T8_
MarketDataConsumer_LFQueue_write 1686008909478029956
trading_engine_1.log:18:48:29.480552551 TTT T9_TradeEngine_LFQueue_
read 1686008909480552495
...
```

Now, let us move forward and analyze these latency measurements.

Analyzing the performance

To analyze these performance metrics, we have built a Python Jupyter notebook, which is available at Chapter12/notebooks/perf_analysis.ipynb. Note that since this is a book about C++ and low-latency applications, we will not discuss the source code in this notebook, but instead describe the analysis. Running the notebook is optional, so we also included an HTML file with the results of this analysis, which is available at Chapter12/notebooks/perf_analysis.html. To run this notebook, you will first have to launch the `jupyter notebook` server from the Chapter12 root directory (where the log files exist) using the following command:

```
sghosh@sghosh-ThinkPad-X1-Carbon-3rd:~/Building-Low-Latency-
Applications-with-CPP/Chapter12$ jupyter notebook
...
    To access the notebook, open this file in a browser:
        file:///home/sghosh/.local/share/jupyter/runtime/nbserver-
182382-open.html
    Or copy and paste one of these URLs:
        http://
localhost:8888/?token=d28e3bd3b1f8109b12afe1210ae8c494c7
7a4128e23bdae7
     or
```

```
http://127.0.0.1:8888/?token=d28e3bd3b1f8109b12afe1210ae8c494c7
7a4128e23bdae7
```

If your browser does not already launch the web page for this notebook, you can copy and paste the URL you receive and navigate to and open the notebooks/perf_analysis.ipynb notebook. Note that the preceding addresses are just examples for this specific run; you will receive a different address, which you should use. Once you open the notebook, you can run it using **Cell | Run All**, or the closest equivalent in your notebook instance, as shown in the following screenshot.

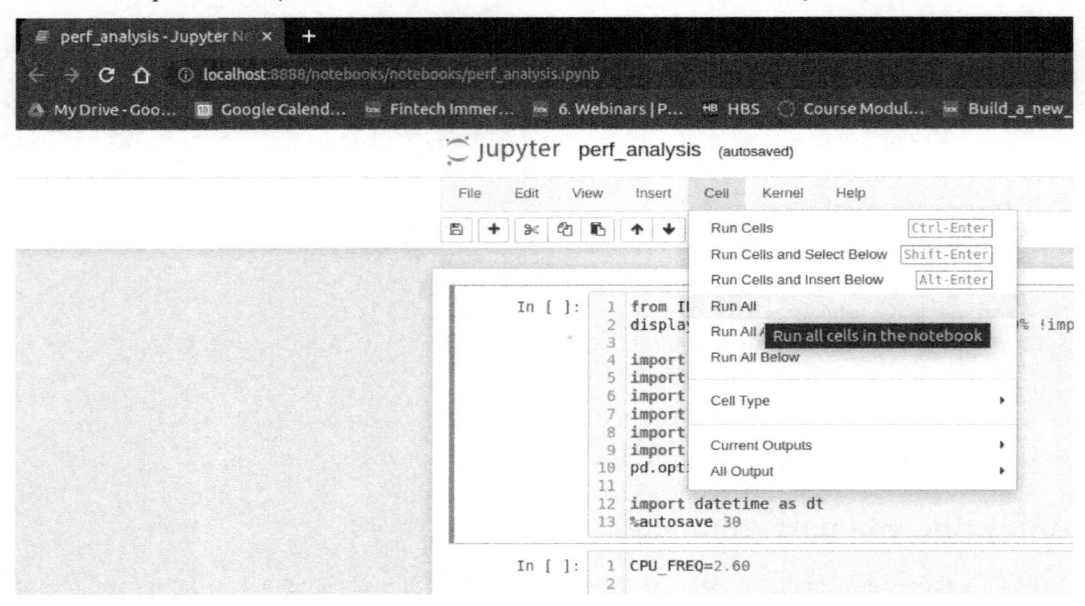

Figure 12.1 – Screenshot of the perf_analysis.ipynb notebook

Since we will not discuss the details of this notebook, we will briefly describe the analysis performed in it. This notebook performs the following steps in the order presented here:

1. First, it looks for the log files generated by running the electronic trading ecosystem in the current working directory. Specifically, it looks for log files from the trading exchange; in the case of this notebook, we look for log files from the trading client with ClientId=1.

2. It opens each log file and looks for log entries that contain the `RDTSC` and `TTT` tokens in them to find the log entries corresponding to the measurements we discussed in the previous chapter and revisited in the preceding sub-section.

3. It then creates two `pandas DataFrame` instances containing each of the measurements it extracts from the log files.

4. For the measurement entries corresponding to the measurement of internal functions, which are tagged with the `RDTSC` token, we generate a scatter plot of those measurements as well as a rolling mean of those plots (to smooth the overall latency measurements). One crucial point here is that the measurement values in the log files represent the difference in `RDTSC` values, that is, the number of CPU cycles elapsed for a function call. In this notebook, we convert the CPU cycles into nanoseconds using a constant factor of 2.6 GHz, which is specific to our system and will differ based on your hardware; it will need to be adjusted. We will look at a few examples of these plots in the next sub-section.

5. For the measurement entries corresponding to the timestamps at key spots in our electronic trading ecosystem, which are tagged with the `TTT` token, we also generate a scatter plot and a plot of the rolling mean values. The difference here is that we display the transit times from one hop to the other. For instance, we will plot the time it takes from the hop at `T1_OrderServer_TCP_read` to the hop at `T2_OrderServer_LFQueue_write`, from `T2_OrderServer_LFQueue_write` to `T3_MatchingEngine_LFQueue_read`, from `T3_MatchingEngine_LFQueue_read` to `T4_MatchingEngine_LFQueue_write`, and so forth.

Each of these inter-hop transits on the side of the exchange is shown in the following diagram.

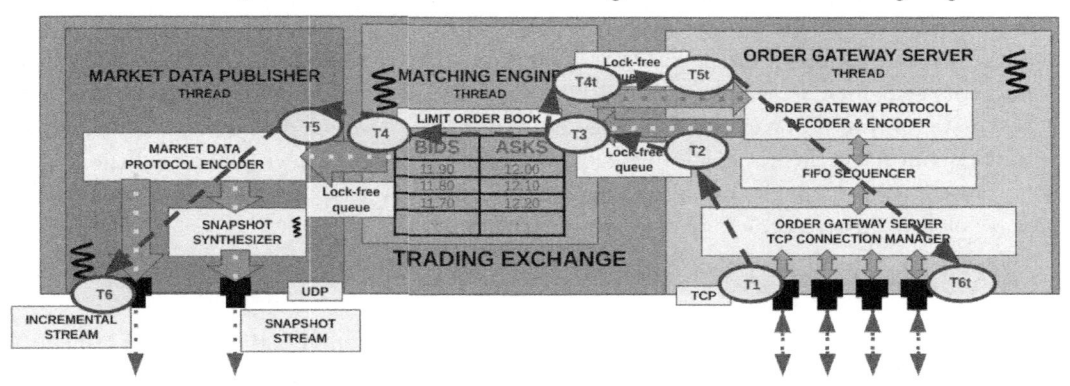

Figure 12.2 – Flow of data between different hops at the electronic exchange

Each of these inter-hop transits on the side of the trading client is shown in the following diagram.

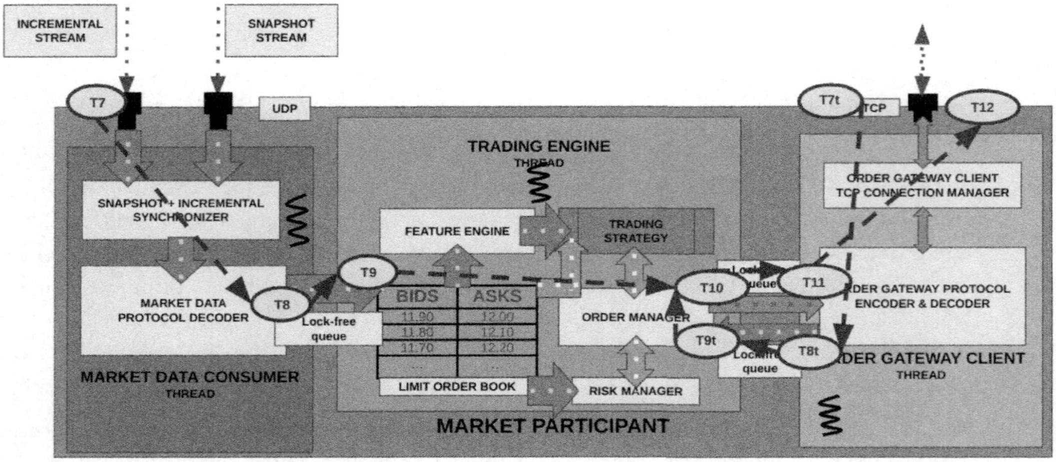

Figure 12.3 – Flow of data between different hops on the electronic trading client

In the next sub-section, we will observe the distribution of a few of these different latency metrics from both groups (`RDTSC` and `TTT`) and see what we can learn from them.

Understanding the output of our analysis

In this section, we will present the distribution of the latencies for a subset of the measurements we added in the previous chapter and analyzed using the notebook presented in the previous sub-section. Our objective here is to gain some insight into the performance of different components and sub-components in our ecosystem. First, we will start with a few examples of latencies for internal function calls in the next sub-section. One thing to note is that for the sake of brevity, we will present and discuss a subset of all the performance plots available in the Python notebook in this chapter. Also, note that these are not arranged in any particular order; we simply picked some of the more interesting ones and left all possible plots in the notebook for you to inspect further.

Observing the latencies for internal function calls

The first performance plot we present in this chapter is the distribution of the latency of calling the `Exchange::MEOrderBook::removeOrder()` method in the matching engine inside the trading exchange. That is presented as follows, but our key takeaway here is that this is a very well-behaved function; that is, the minimum and maximum latencies are within a tight range between 0.4 and 3.5 microseconds and the mean is relatively stable around the 1-to-1.5-microsecond range. There might be the possibility to make this faster, of course, but this seems quite well behaved for now and has low-performance latencies; we should evaluate whether this method is a bottleneck before trying to optimize it any further.

performance Exchange_MEOrderBook_removeOrder microseconds

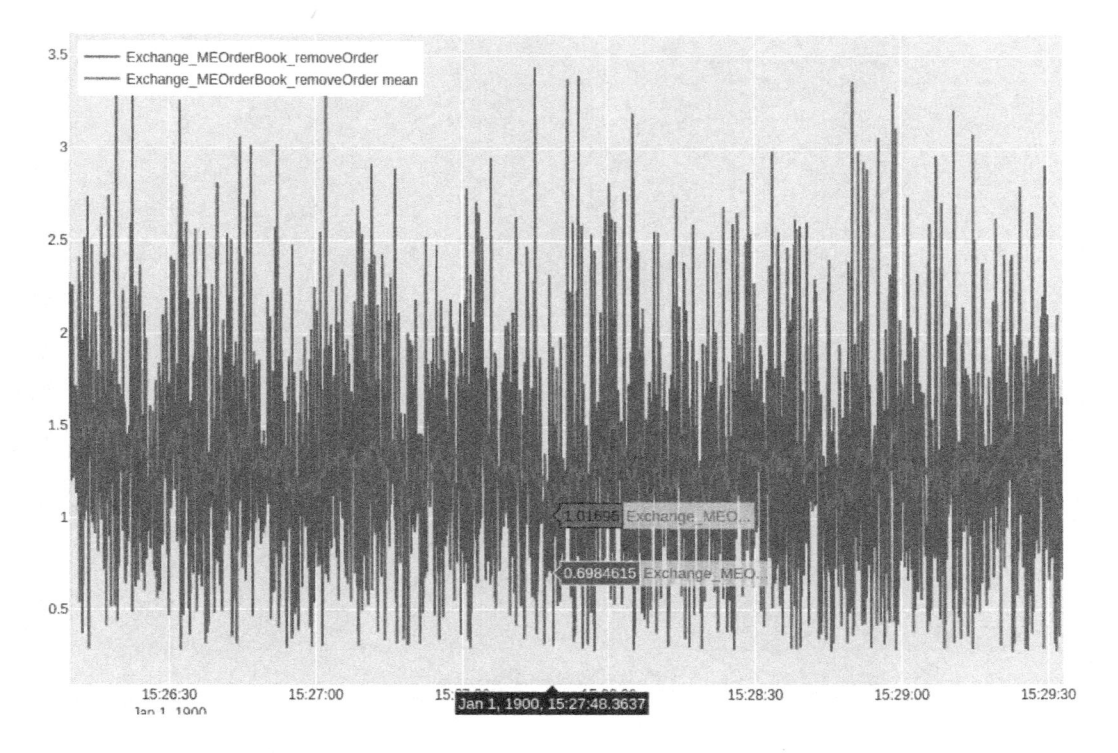

Figure 12.4 – Latency distribution for the removeOrder() method in MEOrderBook for the matching engine

The next plot presents the distribution of latencies for the `Exchange::FIFOSequencer::sequenceAndPublish()` method. This instance is more interesting because here we see that while this method has low average latencies in the 90 microseconds range, it experiences many spikes in latencies spiking up to values in the 500 to 1,200 microseconds range. This behavior will result in jitter in the `OrderServer` component's performance when it comes to processing client order requests and is something we might need to investigate.

performance Exchange_FIFOSequencer_sequenceAndPublish microseconds

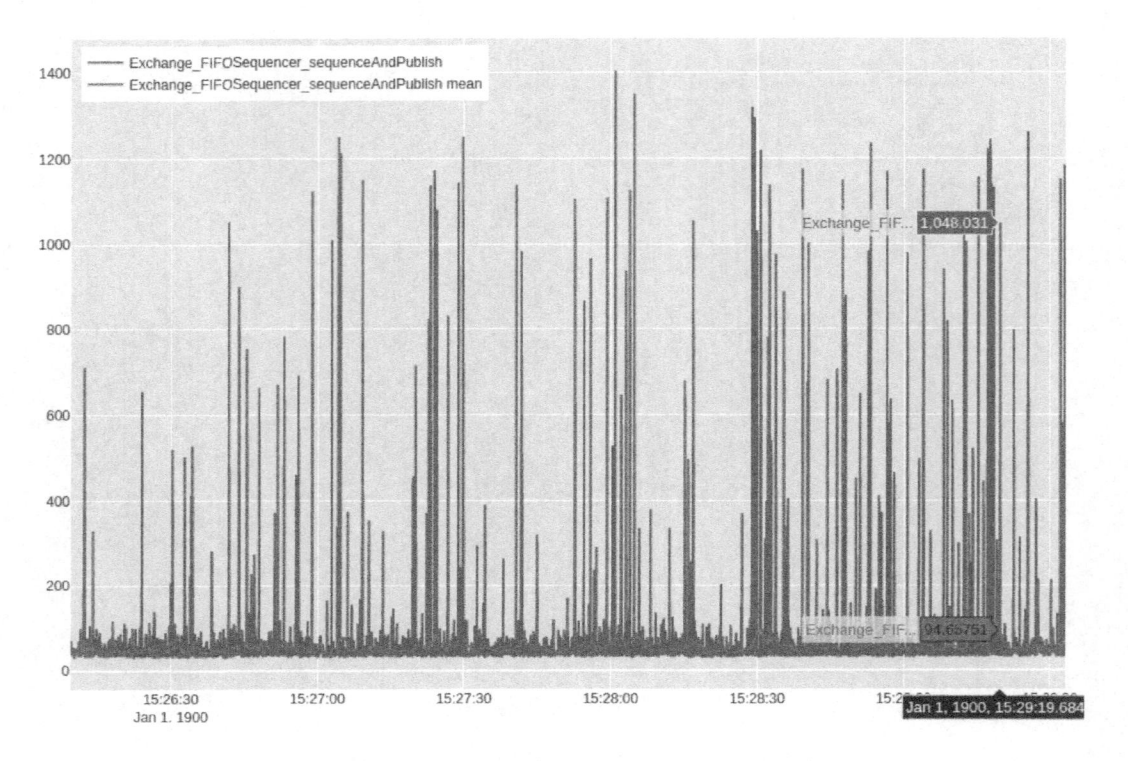

Figure 12.5 – Latency distribution of the sequenceAndPublish() method in FIFOSequencer for the matching engine

The next plot shows another interesting distribution of latency values for the `Trading::PositionKeeper::addFill()` method. In this case, the average performance latency remains stable around the 50 microseconds range. However, between **15:28:00** and **15:29:00**, there are a few spikes in latency that warrant a closer look. The difference here compared to *Figure 12.4* is that there the spikes were distributed evenly, but in this case, there appears to be a small patch of spikes.

performance Trading_PositionKeeper_addFill microseconds

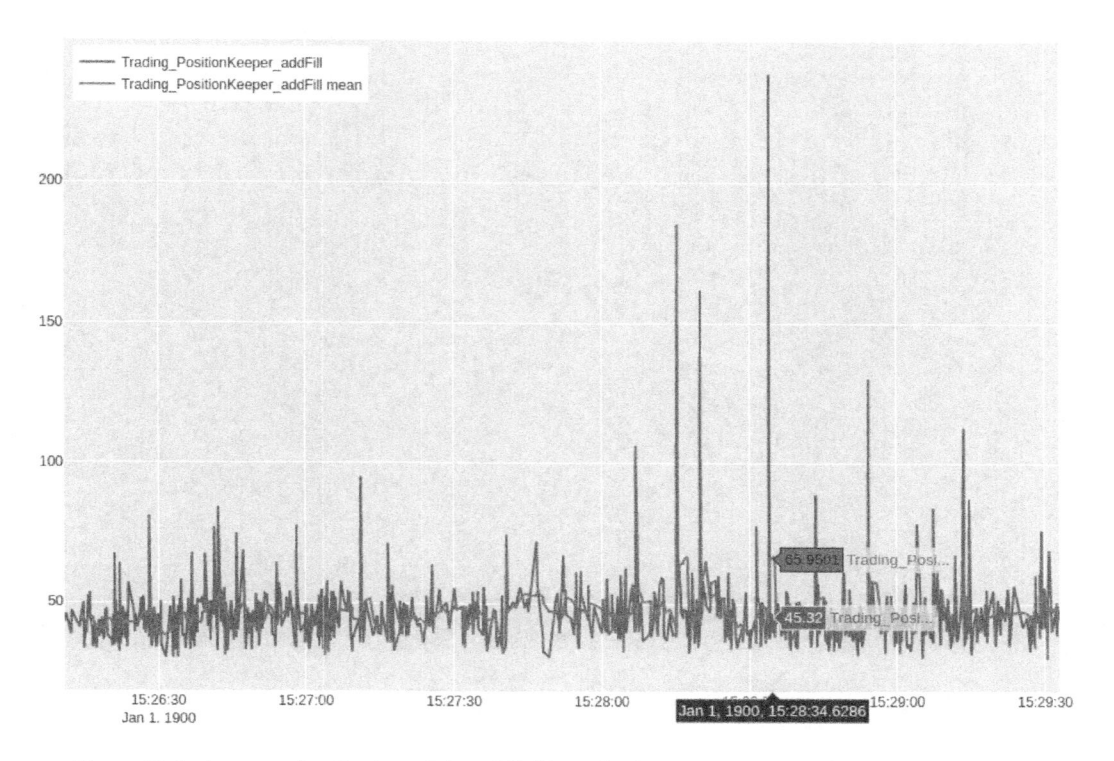

Figure 12.6 – Latency distribution of the addFill() method in PositionKeeper for the trade engine

We conclude this sub-section by presenting one more plot, this time of the `Trading::PositionKeeper::updateBBO()` method, which updates the PnL for open positions. This is another well-behaved method with an average performance latency of 10 microseconds, and there seem to be many measurements close to 0 microseconds, which is slightly different from *Figure 12.3*, where the minimum latency value was never remarkably close to 0.

performance Trading_PositionKeeper_updateBBO microseconds

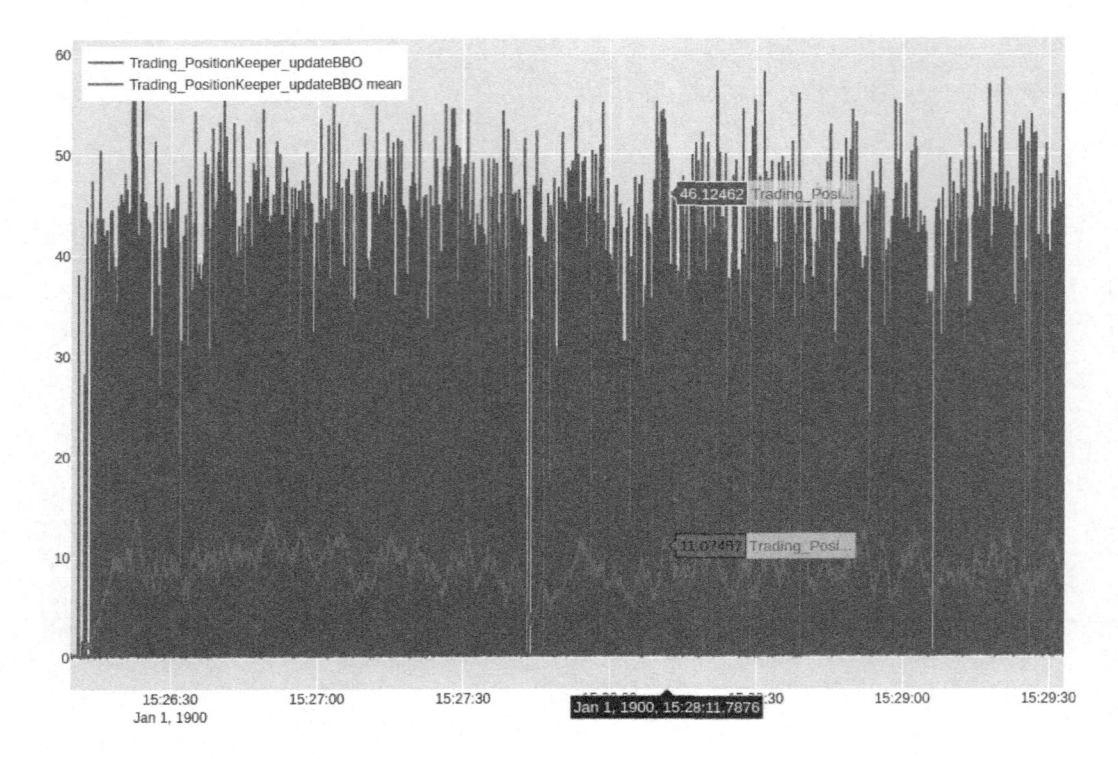

Figure 12.7 – Latency distribution of the updateBBO() method in PositionKeeper for the trade engine

In the next sub-section, we will look at a few similar examples, but this time pertaining to the latencies between the different hops in our ecosystem.

Observing the latencies between hops in the ecosystem

The first plot we will look at is the time difference between when a trading client's `OrderGateway` component writes a client request to the TCP socket (`T12`) up to the point when the exchange's `OrderServer` component reads that client request from the TCP socket (`T1`). This represents the network transit time from the trading client to the trading exchange on the TCP connection. The average latency in this case is around 15 to 20 microseconds and the distribution is evenly distributed.

performance T12_OrderGateway_TCP_write -> T1_OrderServer_TCP_read milliseconds

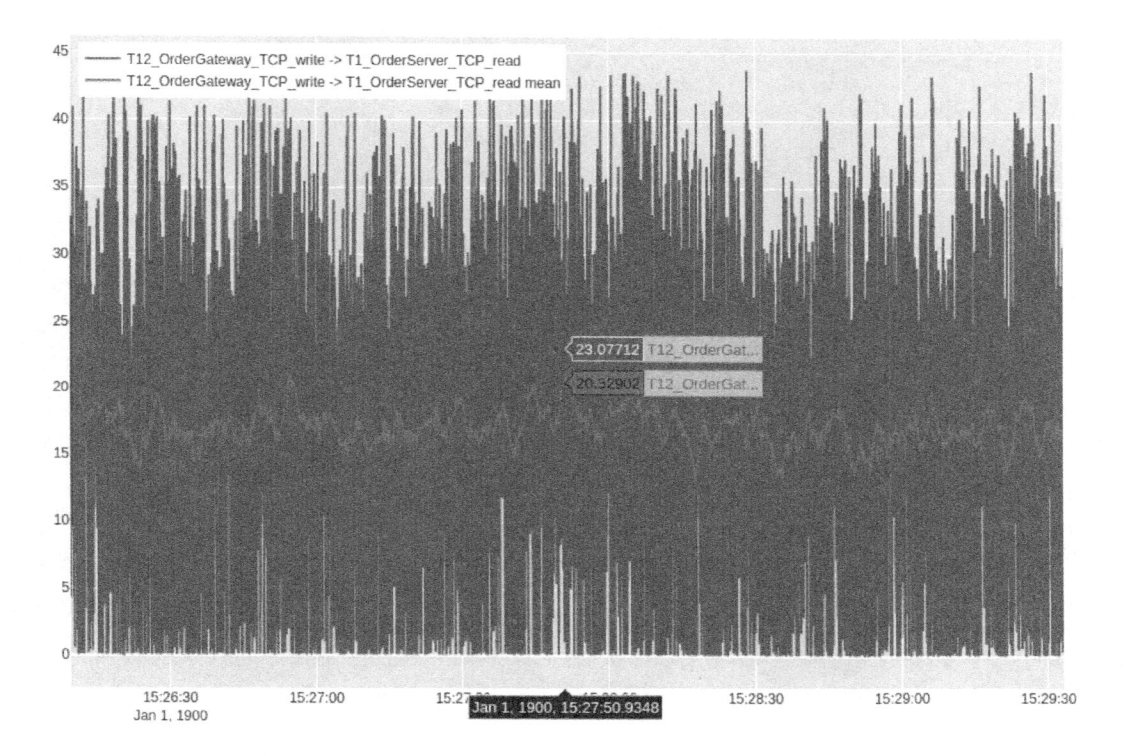

Figure 12.8 – Latency distribution between the T12_OrderGateway_
TCP_write and T1_OrderServer_TCP_read hops

The next plot displays the distribution of the network transit time for the market data updates, from when the market data updates are written to the UDP socket by MarketDataPublisher (T6) to when they are read from the UDP socket by MarketDataConsumer (T7). There seems to be a great amount of variance in the latencies for this measurement, as the plot shows; however, this has lower overall latencies than the TCP path.

440 Analyzing and Optimizing the Performance of Our C++ System

performance T6_MarketDataPublisher_UDP_write -> T7_MarketDataConsumer_UDP_read milliseconds

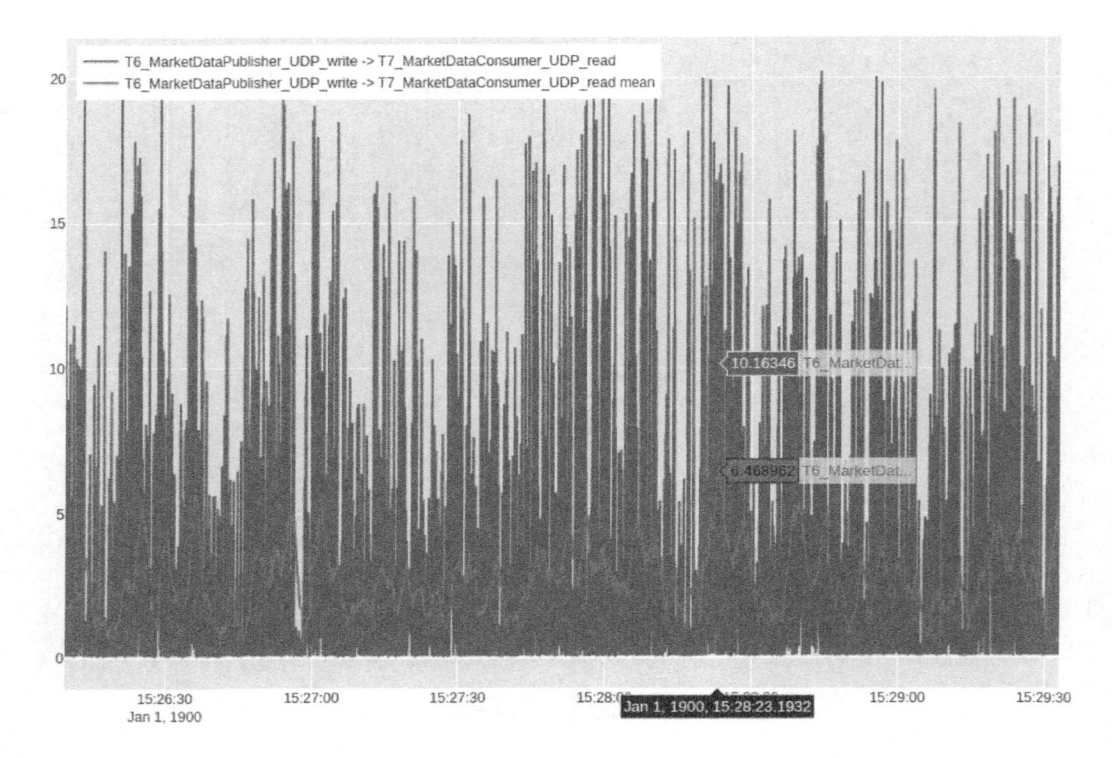

Figure 12.9 – Latency distribution between the T6_MarketDataPublisher_UDP_write and T7_MarketDataConsumer_UDP_read hops

The next diagram shows the distribution of latencies measured from `MarketDataConsumer` reading a market update from the UDP socket (T7) to the time when the market update is written to `LFQueue` connected to `TradeEngine` (T8). This path experiences huge spikes in latencies (up to 2,000 microseconds) compared to its average performance of around 100 microseconds, so this is something we need to investigate.

performance T7_MarketDataConsumer_UDP_read -> T8_MarketDataConsumer_LFQueue_write microseconds

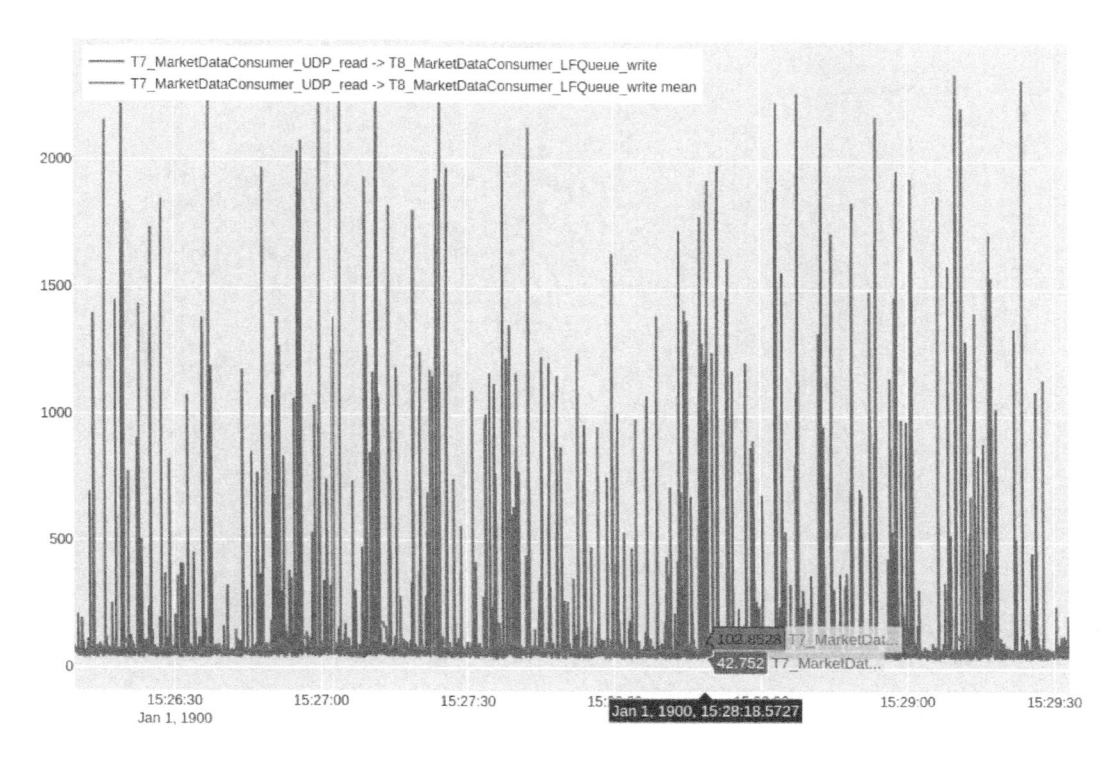

Figure 12.10 – Latency distribution between the T7_MarketDataConsumer_UDP_read and T8_MarketDataConsumer_LFQueue_write hops

The next plot displays the distribution of the latencies between `MatchingEngine` reading a client request from `LFQueue` attached to `OrderServer` (T3) and the time `MatchingEngine` processes it and writes the client response to `LFQueue` back to `OrderServer` (T4t). This path also appears to be experiencing large latency spikes and should be investigated.

performance T3_MatchingEngine_LFQueue_read -> T4t_MatchingEngine_LFQueue_write microseconds

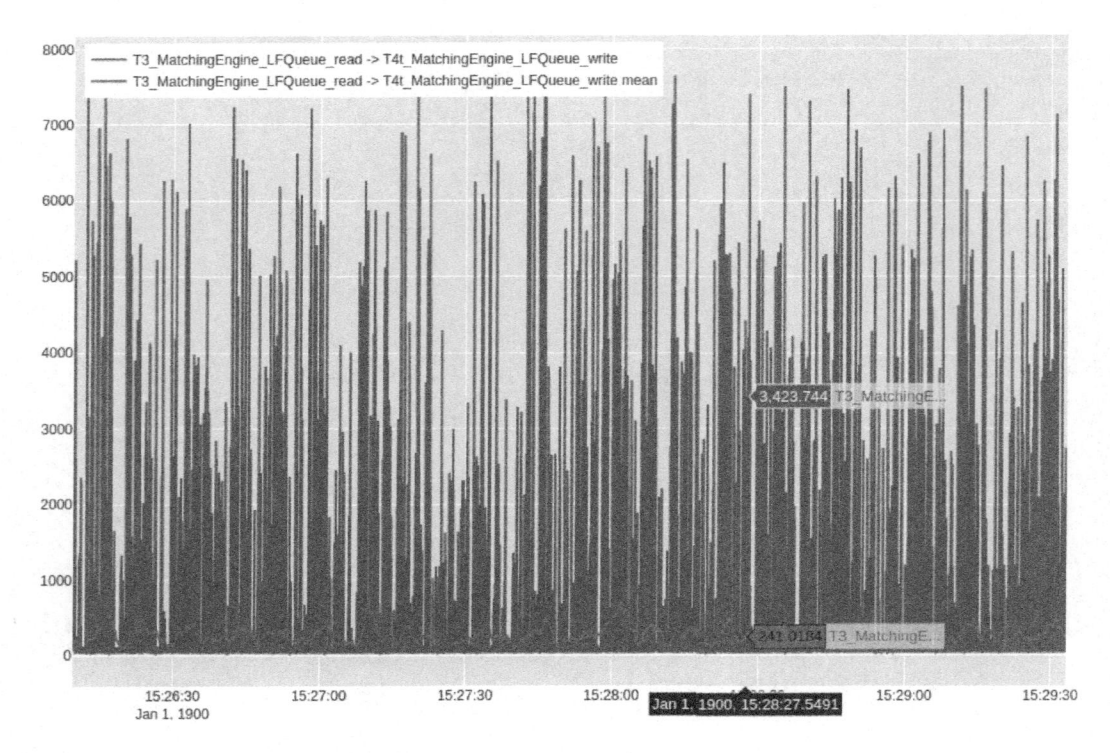

Figure 12.11 – Latency distribution between the T3_MatchingEngine_LFQueue_read and T4t_MatchingEngine_LFQueue_write hops

This section was dedicated to the analysis of the different latency measurements in our ecosystem. In the next section, we will discuss some tips and techniques that we can use to optimize the design and implementation of the different components in our electronic trading ecosystem.

Discussing tips and techniques for optimizing our C++ trading system

In this section, we will present a few possible areas where we can optimize our C++ trading ecosystem. Note that these are only some examples and a lot more is possible, but we will leave you to measure and discover those inefficiencies, as well as improve on them. To reiterate what we have mentioned a few times before, you should measure the performance of various parts of your system with everything we learned in the previous chapter, *Adding instrumentation and measuring performance*. You should analyze them using the approach we discussed in this chapter and use the C++ discussions we had in the chapter *Exploring C++ Concepts from a Low-Latency Application's Perspective* to improve on them further. Now, let us discuss some areas of improvement next. We have tried to arrange these loosely in order from least to most effort.

Optimizing the release build

The first suggestion would be to try and optimize the release build we run for our system. Some simple things we can do in the code itself is remove the calls to `ASSERT()` from the release binaries. The motivation behind this is to remove the extra `if` condition this macro introduces in our code base wherever it gets used. However, this can be dangerous since we might allow exceptional conditions through. The optimal middle ground is to remove the use of this macro only from the critical code path wherever it is safe to do so.

Another suggestion would be to reduce logging in the release build. We have made a decent amount of effort to make logging efficient and low-latency. Additionally, it is not wise to eliminate all logging since it makes troubleshooting difficult, if not impossible. However, logging is not free, so we should try to reduce logging on the critical path for release builds as much as possible.

The most common method to perform optimizations, as we suggested here, that only apply to release builds is to define the NDEBUG (No Debug) preprocessor flag and check for its existence in our code base. If the flag is defined, we build a release build and skip non-essential code such as asserts and logging.

An example of this for the `MemoryPool::deallocate()` method is shown here:

```cpp
    auto deallocate(const T *elem) noexcept {
      const auto elem_index = (reinterpret_cast<const
        ObjectBlock *>(elem) - &store_[0]);
#if !defined(NDEBUG)
      ASSERT(elem_index >= 0 && static_cast<size_t>
        (elem_index) < store_.size(), "Element being
      deallocated does not belong to this Memory pool.");
      ASSERT(!store_[elem_index].is_free_, "Expected in-use
        ObjectBlock at index:" + std::
          to_string(elem_index));
#endif
      store_[elem_index].is_free_ = true;
    }
```

Another example for the `FIFOSequencer::sequenceAndPublish()` method is shown here:

```cpp
    auto sequenceAndPublish() {
      ...
#if !defined(NDEBUG)
      logger_->log("%:% %() % Processing % requests.\n",
          __FILE__, __LINE__, __FUNCTION__, Common::
```

```cpp
                getCurrentTimeStr(&time_str_), pending_size_);
#endif
    ...
      for (size_t i = 0; i < pending_size_; ++i) {
        const auto &client_request =
          pending_client_requests_.at(i);

#if !defined(NDEBUG)
        logger_->log("%:% %() % Writing RX:% Req:% to
          FIFO.\n", __FILE__, __LINE__, __FUNCTION__,
          Common::getCurrentTimeStr(&time_str_),
                  client_request.recv_time_,
                    client_request.request_.toString());
#endif
    ...
    }
```

Another thing to think about is whether the actual entries being logged can be output in a more optimal method. For instance, `Common:: getCurrentTimeStr()`, which gets called in each of our log lines in the current code base state itself, is quite expensive. This is because it performs string formatting operations using `sprintf()`, which is quite expensive, like most string formatting operations. Here, we have another optimization where in release builds, we can output a simple integer value representing time, instead of a formatted string, which, while more readable, is less efficient.

Let us move on to the next possible optimization area – managing thread affinity.

Setting thread affinity correctly

So far, in all the instances of creating and launching threads, we have passed the `core_id` parameter to be `-1` in the call to the `Common::createAndStartThread()` method; that is, the threads were not pinned to any specific core. This was done intentionally since, as we mentioned before, the `exchange_main` application instance creates and runs 10 threads and each `trading_main` application instance creates and runs 8 threads. Unless you are executing the source code for this book on a production-grade trading server, it is unlikely to have too many CPU cores. Our system, for example, has only four cores. In practice, however, each of the following performance-critical threads would be assigned a CPU core all to themselves. We present a sample core assignment next; however, this will change from server to server and might also depend on the NUMA architecture – but that is beyond the scope of this book. Note that these names refer to the names we passed to the method in the `name` string parameter:

- `core_id=0`: `Exchange/MarketDataPublisher`
- `core_id=1`: `Exchange/MatchingEngine`

- `core_id=2`: Exchange/OrderServer
- `core_id=3`: Trading/MarketDataConsumer
- `core_id=4`: Trading/OrderGateway
- `core_id=5`: Trading/TradeEngine
- Any additional performance critical threads get assigned the remaining core ids in a similar fashion

The remaining non-critical threads, as well as any Linux processes running on the server, would be given a block of CPU cores to be run on without any affinity settings. Specifically, in our system, they would be the following non-critical threads:

- `core_id=-1`: Exchange/SnapshotSynthesizer
- `core_id=-1`: Common/Logger exchange_main.log
- `core_id=-1`: Common/Logger exchange_matching_engine.log
- `core_id=-1`: Common/Logger exchange_market_data_publisher.log
- `core_id=-1`: Common/Logger exchange_snapshot_synthesizer.log
- `core_id=-1`: Common/Logger exchange_order_server.log
- `core_id=-1`: Common/Logger trading_main_1.log
- `core_id=-1`: Common/Logger trading_engine_1.log
- `core_id=-1`: Common/Logger trading_order_gateway_1.log
- `core_id=-1`: Common/Logger trading_market_data_consumer_1.log
- Any other non-critical threads would also be assigned core id -1 i.e. these threads will not be pinned to any specific CPU code

Note one additional detail: for this setup to be as optimized as possible, we need to make sure that the Linux process scheduler does not assign any OS processes to the CPU cores being used by the critical threads. This is achieved on Linux using the `isolcpus` kernel parameter, which we will not discuss in detail here. The `isolcpus` parameter tells the process scheduler which cores to ignore when deciding where to schedule a process.

Optimizing Logger for strings

There is an opportunity to optimize our `Logger` class to handle parameters of the `char*` type better. Remember that our implementation for logging `char*` parameters consists of calling the `Logger::pushValue(const char value)` method on each of the characters iteratively, as shown:

```
auto pushValue(const char *value) noexcept {
  while (*value) {
```

```
      pushValue(*value);
      ++value;
    }
  }
```

One option here is to introduce a new enumeration value to the `LogType` enumeration. Let's call it `STRING`, like so:

```
enum class LogType : int8_t {
  ...
  DOUBLE = 8,
  STRING = 9
};
```

We'll update the `LogElement` type to have a fixed-size `char*` array of *some* size, as shown. We are vague on the size of this array on purpose since this is pseudo-code and we want to focus more on the design and the idea and less on the implementation details:

```
struct LogElement {
  LogType type_ = LogType::CHAR;
  union {
    ...
    double d;
    char str[SOME_SIZE];
  } u_;
};
```

Then, finally, update `Logger::pushValue(const char *value)` and `Logger::flushQueue()` to copy and write the strings in blocks of characters rather than a single character at a time.

Eliminating the use of std::function instances

In our code base, we used the `std::function<>` function wrapper in a couple of places, as listed here:

- Common::McastSocket:

    ```
    std::function<void(McastSocket *s)> recv_callback_;
    ```

- Common::TCPServer:

    ```
    std::function<void(TCPSocket *s, Nanos rx_time)> recv_callback_;
    std::function<void()> recv_finished_callback_;
    ```

- Common::TCPSocket:

    ```
    std::function<void(TCPSocket *s, Nanos rx_time)> recv_callback_;
    ```

- `Trading::TradeEngine`:

```
std::function<void(TickerId ticker_id, Price price, Side side,
MarketOrderBook *book)> algoOnOrderBookUpdate_;
std::function<void(const Exchange::MEMarketUpdate *market_
update, MarketOrderBook *book)> algoOnTradeUpdate_;
std::function<void(const Exchange::MEClientResponse *client_
response)> algoOnOrderUpdate_;
```

Calling functions through these objects is slower than directly calling functions, and these incur similar costs as `virtual` functions. This mechanism of calling methods using the `std::function<>` objects can be replaced with templates. To refresh your memory on the drawbacks of calling functions indirectly, please revisit the chapter *Exploring C++ Concepts from a Low-Latency Application's Perspective*, specifically the *Avoiding function pointers* sub-section of the *Calling functions efficiently* section. Additionally, revisit the *Using compile-time polymorphism* section in the same chapter, reviewing the discussion on the **Curiously Recurring Template Pattern** (**CRTP**), to see an example of how to do this. For the sake of brevity, we will not discuss the details of how to replace the `std::function<>` instances in our code base, but we encourage those who are interested to attempt that improvement.

Inspecting the impact of these optimizations

We will not be able to investigate every optimization opportunity in detail, but before we finish this section, we will discuss the details of two optimizations that we discussed in this section. First, let us discuss the implementation and impact of the optimization on our `Logger` class for logging strings.

Benchmarking Logger string optimization

To implement the Logger string optimization, we will change the `pushValue()` method for `char*` arguments as discussed before. For the sake of brevity, we will not look at the full class, which we implement in an alternate `OptLogger` class available in the `Chapter12/common/opt_logging.h` source file. The most important change is shown here, but please refer to the full source file to see the other minor changes:

```
auto pushValue(const char *value) noexcept {
  LogElement l{LogType::STRING, {.s = {}}};
  strncpy(l.u_.s, value, sizeof(l.u_.s) - 1);
  pushValue(l);
}
```

To benchmark this and compare it against the original `Logger` implementation, we will create a simple standalone binary called `logger_benchmark`. We do this so that we can check the performance impact in a controlled environment. Remember that running the full trading ecosystem introduces a lot of variance due to the number of processes and threads, the network activity, the trading activity, and so on, and it can be difficult to properly assess the impact of the `Logger` optimization. The source code for this benchmark application can be found in the `Chapter12/benchmarks/logger_benchmark.cpp` source file. Let us look at the implementation of this source file quickly before looking at the results.

First, we will include the header files corresponding to the original `Logger` and the new `OptLogger` classes:

```
#include "common/logging.h"
#include "common/opt_logging.h"
```

Next, we will define a `random_string()` method, which simply generates random strings of a specified length. We will use this to generate random strings for the two loggers to log to compare the performance difference when it comes to strings. This uses a `charset()` lambda method, which returns a random alphanumeric (0-9, a-z, or A-Z) character. It then uses the `std::generate_n()` method to generate a `std::string` with a length specified in the length argument by calling the `charset()` lambda method repeatedly:

```
std::string random_string(size_t length) {
  auto randchar = []() -> char {
    const char charset[] =
        "0123456789"
        "ABCDEFGHIJKLMNOPQRSTUVWXYZ"
        "abcdefghijklmnopqrstuvwxyz";
    const size_t max_index = (sizeof(charset) - 1);
    return charset[rand() % max_index];
  };
  std::string str(length, 0);
  std::generate_n(str.begin(), length, randchar);
  return str;
}
```

Next, we will define a `benchmarkLogging()` method, which accepts a template parameter, `T`, which it expects to be an instance of one of the two loggers we are comparing here. It runs a loop 100,000 times and uses the `random_string()` method we built previously and the logger's `log()` method to log 100,000 random strings. For each call to the `log()` method, it records and sums up the difference in clock cycles, using the `Common::rdtsc()` method we built in the previous chapter. Finally, it returns the average clock cycles by dividing the sum of each RDTSC difference by the loop count:

```
template<typename T>
size_t benchmarkLogging(T *logger) {
  constexpr size_t loop_count = 100000;
  size_t total_rdtsc = 0;
  for (size_t i = 0; i < loop_count; ++i) {
    const auto s = random_string(128);
```

```cpp
    const auto start = Common::rdtsc();
    logger->log("%\n", s);
    total_rdtsc += (Common::rdtsc() - start);
  }

  return (total_rdtsc / loop_count);
}
```

Now, we can finally build the `main()` method, which is quite simple. It creates an instance of the old logger – `Common::Logger()` – calls the `benchmarkLogging()` method on it, and outputs the average clock cycle count to the screen. Then, it does exactly the same thing again, except this time it uses the new logger – `OptCommon::OptLogger()`:

```cpp
int main(int, char **) {
  using namespace std::literals::chrono_literals;

  {
    Common::Logger logger("logger_benchmark_original.log");
    const auto cycles = benchmarkLogging(&logger);
    std::cout << "ORIGINAL LOGGER " << cycles << " CLOCK
      CYCLES PER OPERATION." << std::endl;
    std::this_thread::sleep_for(10s);
  }

  {
    OptCommon::OptLogger opt_logger
      ("logger_benchmark_optimized.log");
    const auto cycles = benchmarkLogging(&opt_logger);
    std::cout << "OPTIMIZED LOGGER " << cycles << " CLOCK
      CYCLES PER OPERATION." << std::endl;
    std::this_thread::sleep_for(10s);
  }

  exit(EXIT_SUCCESS);
}
```

This binary can be built using the same script as before, that is, by running `scripts/build.sh` from the `Chapter12` root directory. To run the binary, you can call it directly from the command line, as shown here, and, among other output, you will see the following two lines displaying the results of the benchmarking:

```
sghosh@sghosh-ThinkPad-X1-Carbon-3rd:~/Building-Low-Latency-
Applications-with-CPP/Chapter12$ ./cmake-build-release/logger_
benchmark
ORIGINAL LOGGER 25757 CLOCK CYCLES PER OPERATION.
OPTIMIZED LOGGER 466 CLOCK CYCLES PER OPERATION.
```

Note that there will be some variance in the output for each run, and the results you get will likely be different due to system-dependent reasons, but amount the optimization has sped things up, should be somewhat similar to what we have shown. In this case, it seems like our optimization efforts have sped up the `log()` method for strings to be roughly 50 times faster. Next, let us look at another example of the optimization tips we discussed before, which is optimizing the binary for release builds.

Benchmarking release build optimization

To benchmark an example of leaving out non-essential code from the release build, we picked the `MemPool` class. Note that this principle applies to all the components we built, but we arbitrarily picked a single one to limit the scope of our discussion. Similar to what we did for the `Logger` class, we create a new class called `OptMemPool`, which you will find in the `Chapter12/common/opt_mem_pool.h` source file. The primary change in this file compared to the `MemPool` class is that the calls to `ASSERT()` are only built for non-release builds. This is achieved by checking for the `NDEBUG` preprocessor flag, as shown in the following two examples. You can check out the full source code in the file we mentioned previously:

```cpp
    template<typename... Args>
    T *allocate(Args... args) noexcept {
      auto obj_block = &(store_[next_free_index_]);
#if !defined(NDEBUG)
      ASSERT(obj_block->is_free_, "Expected free
        ObjectBlock at index:" + std::to_string
          (next_free_index_));
#endif
      ...
    }
    auto deallocate(const T *elem) noexcept {
      const auto elem_index = (reinterpret_cast<const
        ObjectBlock *>(elem) - &store_[0]);
#if !defined(NDEBUG)
      ASSERT(elem_index >= 0 && static_cast
        <size_t>(elem_index) < store_.size(), "Element
          being deallocated does not belong to this Memory
            pool.");
      ASSERT(!store_[elem_index].is_free_, "Expected in-use
        ObjectBlock at index:" + std::to_string
          (elem_index));
#endif
      ...
    }
```

To benchmark this optimization, we will build a `release_benchmark` binary, and the code for that is available in the `Chapter12/benchmarks/release_benchmark.cpp` source file. First, let us look at the header files we need to include, most importantly the `mem_pool.h` and `opt_mem_pool.h` files. Since memory pools store structures, we will use `Exchange::MDPMarketUpdate` as an example, so we include the `market_update.h` header file for that as well:

```
#include "common/mem_pool.h"
#include "common/opt_mem_pool.h"
#include "common/perf_utils.h"

#include "exchange/market_data/market_update.h"
```

Similar to what we did with the `logger_benchmark.cpp` file, we will create a `benchmarkMemPool()` method, which accepts a template parameter, T, and expects it to be one of the two memory pools we are comparing. In this method, we will first allocate and save 256 `MDPMarketUpdate` objects from the memory pool, using the `allocate()` method. Then, we will deallocate each of these objects and return them to the memory pool, using the `deallocate()` method. We will run this loop 100,000 times to find a reliable average over many iterations. We will measure and sum up the clock cycles elapsed for each call to `allocate()` and `deallocate()` as we did before with the logger benchmark. Finally, we return the average clock cycles by dividing the sum of elapsed clock cycles by the loop count:

```
template<typename T>
size_t benchmarkMemPool(T *mem_pool) {
  constexpr size_t loop_count = 100000;
  size_t total_rdtsc = 0;
  std::array<Exchange::MDPMarketUpdate*, 256>
    allocated_objs;

  for (size_t i = 0; i < loop_count; ++i) {
    for(size_t j = 0; j < allocated_objs.size(); ++j) {
      const auto start = Common::rdtsc();
      allocated_objs[j] = mem_pool->allocate();
      total_rdtsc += (Common::rdtsc() - start);
    }
    for(size_t j = 0; j < allocated_objs.size(); ++j) {
      const auto start = Common::rdtsc();
      mem_pool->deallocate(allocated_objs[j]);
      total_rdtsc += (Common::rdtsc() - start);
    }
  }

  return (total_rdtsc / (loop_count *
    allocated_objs.size()));
}
```

Finally, we build the `main()` method, which again is quite simple. It calls the `benchmarkMemPool()` method twice, once with an object of the `Common::MemPool` type and next with an object of the `OptCommon::OptMemPool` type, and outputs the average clock cycles elapsed for the `allocate()` and `deallocate()` methods:

```
int main(int, char **) {
  {
    Common::MemPool<Exchange::MDPMarketUpdate>
      mem_pool(512);
    const auto cycles = benchmarkMemPool(&mem_pool);
    std::cout << "ORIGINAL MEMPOOL " << cycles << " CLOCK
      CYCLES PER OPERATION." << std::endl;
  }

  {
    OptCommon::OptMemPool<Exchange::MDPMarketUpdate>
      opt_mem_pool(512);
    const auto cycles = benchmarkMemPool(&opt_mem_pool);
    std::cout << "OPTIMIZED MEMPOOL " << cycles << " CLOCK
      CYCLES PER OPERATION." << std::endl;
  }

  exit(EXIT_SUCCESS);
}
```

The process to build this benchmark binary remains the same, so we will not repeat it. Running the binary will yield something that resembles the following:

```
sghosh@sghosh-ThinkPad-X1-Carbon-3rd:~/Building-Low-Latency-
Applications-with-CPP/Chapter12$ ./cmake-build-release/release_
benchmark
ORIGINAL MEMPOOL 343 CLOCK CYCLES PER OPERATION.
OPTIMIZED MEMPOOL 44 CLOCK CYCLES PER OPERATION.
```

In this case, our optimization efforts yielded a speed up of around 7 to 8 times for the `allocate()` and `deallocate()` methods.

In this section, we presented and explained a subset of optimization areas/ideas in our electronic trading ecosystem. The goal here is to get you to understand what these optimization areas can look like and how to approach them with the goal of optimizing performance. In the next section, we'll discuss some more future improvements and enhancements that can be made to our electronic trading ecosystem.

Thinking about the future of our trading ecosystem

Before we conclude this chapter and this book, we will discuss a few possible enhancements to our electronic trading ecosystem. In the previous section, we discussed some examples of things that can be optimized for those interested in maximizing the performance of the electronic trading system we built in this book. In this section, we will discuss some examples of how this ecosystem can be enhanced, not necessarily to reduce latency but to make the system more feature-rich and add functionality.

Growing containers dynamically

We built and used a few containers in this book, as listed here:

- The lock-free queue – `LFQueue` – which is used in multiple components for various object types, such as `MEMarketUpdate`, `MDPMarketUpdate`, `MEClientRequest`, and `MEClientResponse`
- The memory pool – `MemPool` – which was used for multiple object types, such as instances of `MEMarketUpdate`, `MEOrder`, `MEOrdersAtPrice`, `MarketOrder`, and `MarketOrdersAtPrice`

In all these cases, we assumed a safe maximum size value. In practice, that still leaves us open to the possibility that under some circumstances, we might exceed these limits and get in trouble. One enhancement we can make to this system is to improve our handling of this unlikely edge case.

One option would be to fail/exit if we encounter a scenario where `LFQueue` is full or `MemPool` is out of memory. Another option would be to fall back to dynamic memory allocation or a secondary inefficient container for this unlikely event; that is, we will be inefficient and slow in this extremely rare case that we run out of memory or space in our containers, but we will continue to function until it is resolved. Yet another option is to make these containers flexible where they can be grown if needed even though the task of growing these containers when needed will be extremely slow, since in practice we do not expect to encounter that condition.

Growing and enhancing the hash maps

In this book, we used `std::array` in many contexts as a hash map by assuming a safe upper bound. For instance, by assuming that valid `TickerId` values fall in the range of 0 and `ME_MAX_TICKERS`, we used `std::array` instances of size `ME_MAX_TICKERS` as hash maps with `TickerId` keys. A similar design was used for containers such as `TradeEngineCfgHashMap`, `OrderHashMap`, `ClientOrderHashMap`, `OrdersAtPriceHashMap`, `OrderBookHashMap`, `MarketOrderBookHashMap`, and `OMOrderTickerSideHashMap`. While in practice, some of these can continue to exist, that is, valid and reasonable upper bounds can be decided and used, for some of these, this design will not scale up elegantly.

There are several different hash map implementations available – `std::unordered_map`, `absl::flat_hash_map`, `boost::` hash maps, `emhash7::HashMap`, `folly::AtomicHashmap`, `robin_hood::unordered_map`, `tsl::hopscotch_map`, and many more. Additionally, it is common to optimize and tweak these containers so that they perform best under our specific use cases. We'll leave those of you who are interested with the task of exploring these and deciding which ones can replace the `std::array`-based hash maps in our system.

For the sake of demonstrating an example, we will replace the `std::array`-based hash maps in the limit order book that the matching engine builds and maintains (`MEOrderBook`) with `std::unordered_map` hash maps. We will then benchmark the two implementations to see how much of a difference it makes. Following the same pattern as we used in the benchmarking we performed earlier in this chapter, we will introduce a new `MEOrderBook` class, `UnorderedMapMEOrderBook`, where the only difference is the use of the `std::unordered_map` containers instead of the `std::array` containers. All the source code for this new class is available in the `Chapter12/exchange/matcher/unordered_map_me_order_book.h` and `Chapter12/exchange/matcher/unordered_map_me_order_book.cpp` source files. For the sake of brevity, we will not repeat the entire class implementation here, but we will discuss the important changes. The first important and obvious change is the inclusion of the `unordered_map` header file in the `unordered_map_me_order_book.h` header file:

```
#include <unordered_map>
```

We change the `cid_oid_to_order_` data member to be `std::unordered_map<ClientId, std::unordered_map<OrderId, MEOrder *>>` instead of `ClientOrderHashMap`, which is a `typedef` for `std::array<OrderHashMap, ME_MAX_NUM_CLIENTS>`. This data member is a hash map from `ClientId` to `OrderId` to `MEOrder` objects. Remember that `ClientOrderHashMap` is actually a hash map of hash maps, that is, a `std::array` whose elements are also `std::array` objects. The other data member we change is the `price_orders_at_price_` member, which we change to `std::unordered_map<Price, MEOrdersAtPrice *>` instead of the `OrdersAtPriceHashMap` type. This data member is a hash map from `Price` to `MEOrdersAtPrice` objects. If you have forgotten what `MEOrder` and `MEOrdersAtPrice` are, please revisit the *Designing the exchange order book* sub-section in the *Defining the operations and interactions in our matching engine* section of the chapter *Building the C++ Matching Engine*. These changes are shown here:

```
namespace Exchange {
  class UnorderedMapMEOrderBook final {
  private:
    ...
    std::unordered_map<ClientId, std::
      unordered_map<OrderId, MEOrder *>> cid_oid_to_order_;
    std::unordered_map<Price, MEOrdersAtPrice *>
      price_orders_at_price_;
    ...
```

```
    };
  }
```

We will need to remove the following lines from the destructor since the `fill()` method does not apply to `std::unordered_map` objects:

```
MEOrderBook::~MEOrderBook() {
  ...
  for (auto &itr: cid_oid_to_order_) {
    itr.fill(nullptr);
  }
}
```

In terms of accessing these modified containers, we replace the calls to the `std::array::at()` method for `cid_oid_to_order_` and `price_orders_at_price_` with the `std::unordered_map::operator[]` method. These changes for `cid_oid_to_order_` are shown here:

```
    auto removeOrder(MEOrder *order) noexcept {
      ...
      cid_oid_to_order_[order->client_id_][order->
        client_order_id_] = nullptr;
      order_pool_.deallocate(order);
    }

    auto addOrder(MEOrder *order) noexcept {
      ...
      cid_oid_to_order_[order->client_id_][order->
        client_order_id_] = order;
    }

    auto UnorderedMapMEOrderBook::cancel(ClientId client_id,
      OrderId order_id, TickerId ticker_id) noexcept -> void {
      auto is_cancelable = (client_id <
        cid_oid_to_order_.size());
      MEOrder *exchange_order = nullptr;
      if (LIKELY(is_cancelable)) {
        auto &co_itr = cid_oid_to_order_[client_id];
        exchange_order = co_itr[order_id];
        is_cancelable = (exchange_order != nullptr);
      }
      ...
    }
```

We need to make similar changes in spots where we access the `price_orders_at_price_` container, which is shown here:

```cpp
    auto getOrdersAtPrice(Price price) const noexcept ->
      MEOrdersAtPrice * {
      if (price_orders_at_price_.find(priceToIndex(price))
        == price_orders_at_price_.end())
        return nullptr;

      return price_orders_at_price_
        .at(priceToIndex(price));
    }

    auto addOrdersAtPrice(MEOrdersAtPrice
      *new_orders_at_price) noexcept {
      price_orders_at_price_
        [priceToIndex(new_orders_at_price->price_)] =
          new_orders_at_price;
      ...
    }

    auto removeOrdersAtPrice(Side side, Price price)
      noexcept {
      ...
      price_orders_at_price_[priceToIndex(price)] =
        nullptr;
      orders_at_price_pool_.deallocate(orders_at_price);
    }
```

Finally, we present the `hash_benchmark` binary to measure the performance differences because of these changes. The source code for this binary can be found in the `Chapter12/benchmarks/hash_benchmark.cpp` source file. First, we include the header files shown as follows and also define a global `loop_count` variable as we have done in our previous benchmarks:

```cpp
#include "matcher/matching_engine.h"
#include "matcher/unordered_map_me_order_book.h"

static constexpr size_t loop_count = 100000;
```

As we have done before, we will define a `benchmarkHashMap()` method, which accepts a template parameter, T, to represent either `MEOrderBook` or `UnorderedMapMEOrderBook`. It also accepts a vector of `Exchange::MEClientRequest` messages, which will be processed in the benchmark. The actual processing is quite simple. It checks the type of `MEClientRequest` and then calls the `add()` method for `ClientRequestType::NEW` and the `cancel()` method for

`ClientRequestType::CANCEL`. We use `Common::rdtsc()` to measure and sum up the clock cycles elapsed for each of these calls and then return the average at the end of this method:

```
template<typename T>
size_t benchmarkHashMap(T *order_book, const
   std::vector<Exchange::MEClientRequest>& client_requests) {
  size_t total_rdtsc = 0;

  for (size_t i = 0; i < loop_count; ++i) {
    const auto& client_request = client_requests[i];
    switch (client_request.type_) {
      case Exchange::ClientRequestType::NEW: {
        const auto start = Common::rdtsc();
        order_book->add(client_request.client_id_,
          client_request.order_id_,
            client_request.ticker_id_,
                    client_request.side_,
                      client_request.price_,
                        client_request.qty_);
        total_rdtsc += (Common::rdtsc() - start);
      }
        break;

      case Exchange::ClientRequestType::CANCEL: {
        const auto start = Common::rdtsc();
        order_book->cancel(client_request.client_id_,
          client_request.order_id_,
            client_request.ticker_id_);
        total_rdtsc += (Common::rdtsc() - start);
      }
        break;

      default:
        break;
    }
  }

  return (total_rdtsc / (loop_count * 2));
}
```

Now we can look at the `main()` method. We need `Logger` and a `MatchingEngine` object to create the `MEOrderBook` or `UnorderedMapMEOrderBook` object, but to create the `MatchingEngine` object, we need three lock-free queues as we have seen in the implementation of the `exchange_main` binary. So, we create these objects as shown here, even though we are not measuring the performance of any of these components:

```cpp
int main(int, char **) {
  srand(0);

  Common::Logger logger("hash_benchmark.log");
  Exchange::ClientRequestLFQueue
    client_requests(ME_MAX_CLIENT_UPDATES);
  Exchange::ClientResponseLFQueue
    client_responses(ME_MAX_CLIENT_UPDATES);
  Exchange::MEMarketUpdateLFQueue
    market_updates(ME_MAX_MARKET_UPDATES);
  auto matching_engine = new Exchange::
    MatchingEngine(&client_requests, &client_responses,
      &market_updates);
```

Next, we will create a vector of 100,000 (`loop_count`) `MEClientRequest` objects, which will be composed of new order requests as well as requests to cancel these orders. We have seen similar code in the `trading_main` application for the random trading algorithm:

```cpp
Common::OrderId order_id = 1000;
std::vector<Exchange::MEClientRequest>
  client_requests_vec;
Price base_price = (rand() % 100) + 100;
while (client_requests_vec.size() < loop_count) {
  const Price price = base_price + (rand() % 10) + 1;
  const Qty qty = 1 + (rand() % 100) + 1;
  const Side side = (rand() % 2 ? Common::Side::BUY :
    Common::Side::SELL);

  Exchange::MEClientRequest new_request
    {Exchange::ClientRequestType::NEW, 0, 0, order_id++,
      side, price, qty};
  client_requests_vec.push_back(new_request);

  const auto cxl_index = rand() %
    client_requests_vec.size();
  auto cxl_request = client_requests_vec[cxl_index];
  cxl_request.type_ =
    Exchange::ClientRequestType::CANCEL;

  client_requests_vec.push_back(cxl_request);
}
```

Finally, we end the `main()` method by calling the `benchmarkHashMap()` method twice – once with an instance of `MEOrderBook` and once with an instance of `UnorderedMapMEOrderBook`, as shown:

```cpp
{
  auto me_order_book = new Exchange::MEOrderBook(0,
    &logger, matching_engine);
  const auto cycles = benchmarkHashMap(me_order_book,
    client_requests_vec);
  std::cout << "ARRAY HASHMAP " << cycles << " CLOCK
    CYCLES PER OPERATION." << std::endl;
}

{
  auto me_order_book = new Exchange::
    UnorderedMapMEOrderBook(0, &logger, matching_engine);
  const auto cycles = benchmarkHashMap(me_order_book,
    client_requests_vec);
  std::cout << "UNORDERED-MAP HASHMAP " << cycles << "
    CLOCK CYCLES PER OPERATION." << std::endl;
}

  exit(EXIT_SUCCESS);
}
```

The process to build this application remains the same, which is by calling the `scripts/build.sh` script from the `Chapter12` root directory. Running the application by calling the `hash_benchmark` binary will yield output like what is shown here, with some variance between independent runs and depending on the system:

```
sghosh@sghosh-ThinkPad-X1-Carbon-3rd:~/Building-Low-Latency-
Applications-with-CPP/Chapter12$ ./cmake-build-release/hash_benchmark
Set core affinity for Common/Logger hash_benchmark.log 140327631447616
to -1
Set core affinity for Common/Logger exchange_matching_engine.log
140327461033536 to -1
ARRAY HASHMAP 142650 CLOCK CYCLES PER OPERATION.
UNORDERED-MAP HASHMAP 152457 CLOCK CYCLES PER OPERATION.
```

Based on the output of this run, it appears that switching from a `std::array` hash map implementation to a `std::unordered_map` hash map implementation adds an approximate 6 to 7% extra overhead to the `MEOrderBook` `add()` and `cancel()` performance.

Optimizing snapshot messages

In our design of the snapshot messages in the `MarketDataPublisher` component at the trading exchange, a full cycle of snapshot messages between the START_SNAPSHOT and END_SNAPSHOT messages contains the snapshot for all trading instruments, as shown in the following diagram (which we have seen before). In our `SnapshotSynthesizer`, this full snapshot for all trading instruments is published once every 60 seconds. What this means is that if the order books for each of these trading instruments have a lot of orders, then every 60 seconds, there is a huge spike in network traffic on the snapshot multicast channels followed by silence in the remaining 60 seconds.

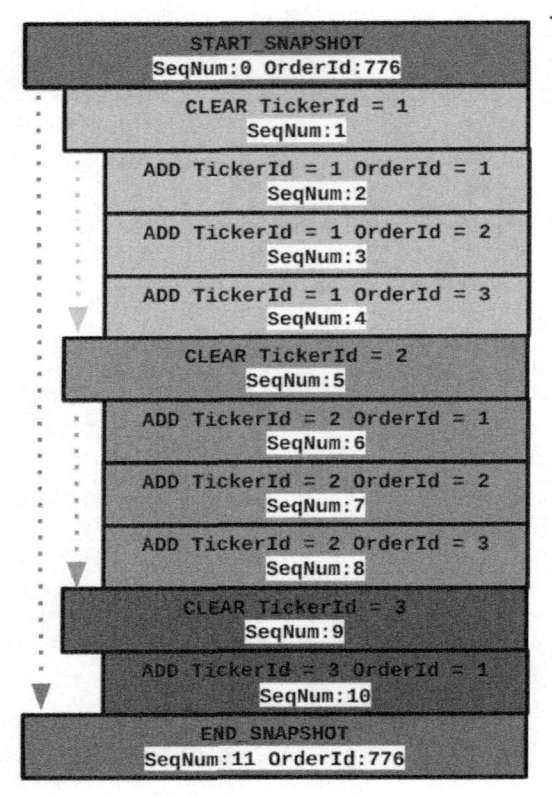

Figure 12.12 – Current composition of snapshot messages

It would be an enhancement to this design if we changed this such that these snapshots are spaced out more evenly and each snapshot cycle contained the snapshot messages corresponding to only one `TickerId`. As a simple example, instead of sending a snapshot message cycle for 6 instruments every 60 seconds, we can send 6 snapshots each containing information for a single instrument, and each of these snapshots is spaced out with 10 seconds in between them. This hypothetical proposal is represented in the following diagram.

```
                START_SNAPSHOT
         SeqNum:0 OrderId:476              T = 0 secs, 60 secs, 120 secs, 180 secs, ...
              CLEAR TickerId = 1
                   SeqNum:1
           ADD TickerId = 1 OrderId = 1
                   SeqNum:2
           ADD TickerId = 1 OrderId = 2
                   SeqNum:3
           ADD TickerId = 1 OrderId = 3
                   SeqNum:4
                 END_SNAPSHOT
         SeqNum:11 OrderId:476

                START_SNAPSHOT
         SeqNum:0 OrderId:656              T = 10 secs, 70 secs, 130 secs, 190 secs, ...
              CLEAR TickerId = 2
                   SeqNum:1
           ADD TickerId = 2 OrderId = 1
                   SeqNum:2
           ADD TickerId = 2 OrderId = 2
                   SeqNum:3
           ADD TickerId = 2 OrderId = 3
                   SeqNum:4
                 END_SNAPSHOT
         SeqNum:11 OrderId:656
```

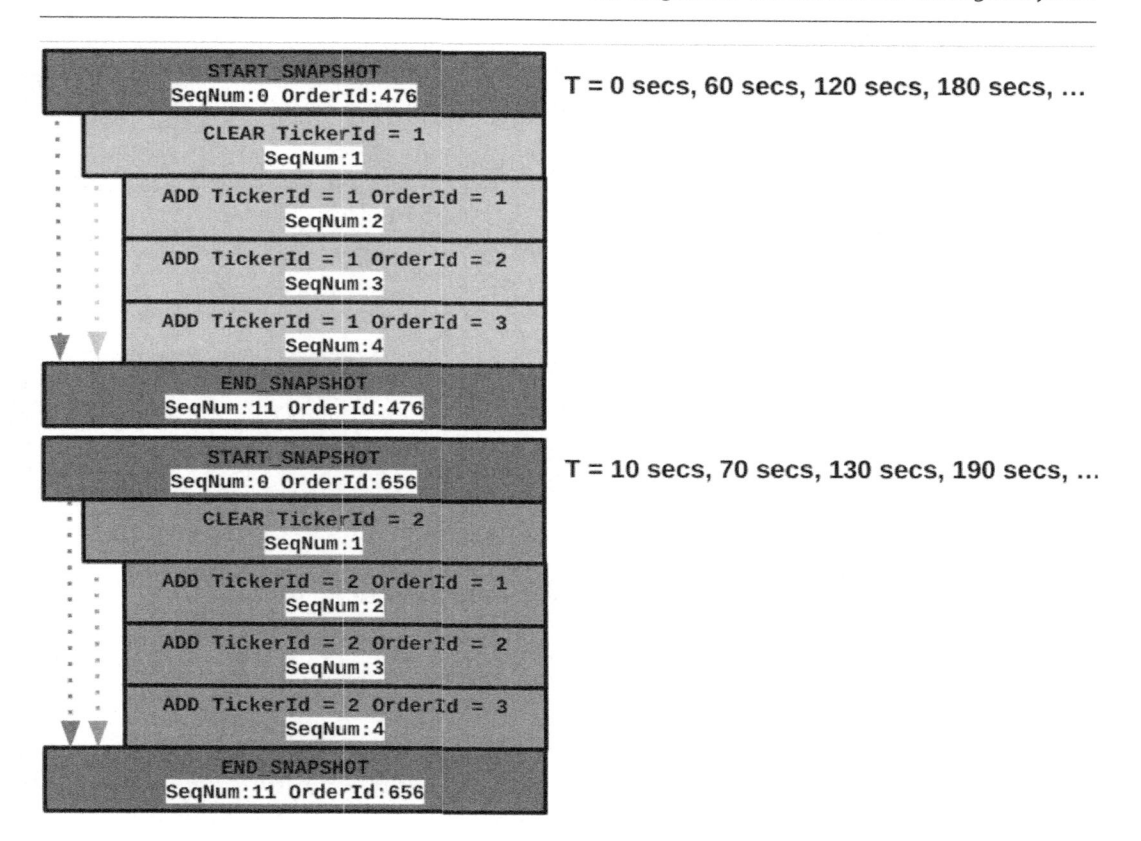

Figure 12.13 – A proposal for an optimized snapshot messaging format

In this new proposal, as we mentioned, there are fewer spikes in network traffic since the full snapshot is distributed over time. This leads to a lower chance of dropping packets on the snapshot multicast stream for the `MarketDataConsumer` components in the trading client's systems. This also leads to the client's system synchronizing or catching up with the snapshot stream for each trading instrument faster, since it does not need to wait for the full snapshot across all trading instruments before it can mark some of the instruments as *recovered*.

Adding authentication and rejection messages to the Order protocol

Our electronic trading exchange right now has no concept of user authentication and is missing a lot of error checking and handling. By this, we mean that it does not check whether clients log in with the correct credentials and are authorized to trade the instruments they try to trade. Additionally, if the `ClientId` and `TCPSocket` instances do not match or there is a sequence number gap in the `ClientRequest` messages that a client sends, we quietly ignore it in `Exchange::OrderServer`.

This is shown in the following code block from the exchange/order_server/order_server.h source file, which we have already discussed in detail:

```
auto recvCallback(TCPSocket *socket, Nanos rx_time)
  noexcept {
  ...
  if (socket->next_rcv_valid_index_ >=
    sizeof(OMClientRequest)) {
    ...
    if (cid_tcp_socket_[request->
      me_client_request_.client_id_] != socket) {
      ...
      continue;
    }

    auto &next_exp_seq_num =
      cid_next_exp_seq_num_[request->
        me_client_request_.client_id_];
    if (request->seq_num_ != next_exp_seq_num) {
      ...
      continue;
    }
    ...
  }
  ...
  }
}
```

Silently ignoring errors like these is not ideal since the clients are not notified about these errors. An enhancement to this workflow would be to add a rejection message to the `ClientResponse` message protocol, which the `OrderServer` component can use to notify the clients about these errors. This enhancement is in addition to the enhancements we suggested to the order protocol to facilitate the authentication of the trading clients.

Supporting modify messages in the Order protocol

Our current order protocol for `ClientRequest` messages only supports `ClientRequestType::NEW` and `ClientRequestType::CANCEL` requests. An enhancement to this protocol would be to add a `ClientRequestType::MODIFY` message type so that client trading systems can modify their order's price or quantity attributes. We would need to update the `OrderServer`, `MatchingEngine`, `MEOrderBook`, and other components on the exchange's side and update the `OrderGateway`, `OrderManager`, `MarketMaker`, `TradeEngine`, and other components on the trading client's side.

Enhancing trade engine components

The trade engine has several components that can be improved and/or enhanced. In this section, we provide brief descriptions of these improvements for each of the components with potential future enhancements.

Adding risk metrics to RiskManager

In the chapter *Designing Our Trading Ecosystem*, in the *Understanding the risk management systems* section, we described a couple of different risk metrics. `RiskManager` was built only with a small subset of those risk metrics and can be enhanced by adding additional risk measures, as described in that section.

Enhancing OrderManager

`OrderManager` was built extremely simply – it supports a maximum of one active order on each side, that is, at most one buy order and one sell order. Obviously, this is an extremely simplified version and `OrderManager` can be enhanced to support much more complex order management.

Enriching FeatureEngine

`FeatureEngine` was set up with two hardcoded features built into it. It can be enriched a lot to support complex configurations of features, a library of diverse types of features, complex interactions between these features, and so on.

Enhancing the trading algorithms

`LiquidityTaker` and `MarketMaker` in this book were also extremely simple representations of realistic trading strategies. These can be enhanced/improved in many ways – improvements in terms of feature compositions, order management, efficient execution, and so on.

This concludes our discussion of future enhancement possibilities for our electronic trading ecosystem.

Summary

The first section of this chapter focused on analyzing the latency metrics we added to our electronic trading systems in the previous chapter. We discussed a few examples of latency measurements for internal functions, as well as a few examples of latency measurements between critical hops in our system. The goal was to understand the distribution of latencies in different cases so that you understand how to identify and investigate areas of potential problems or optimization opportunities.

In the second section of this chapter, we discussed a few tips and techniques regarding how to approach potential performance optimization possibilities. We presented a few examples of what could be improved and discussed the performance problems that exist in the current design and solutions to those problems.

In the concluding section, we described a roadmap for the future of the electronic trading ecosystem we built in this book. We discussed several different components, sub-components, and workflows that can be enriched to build a more mature electronic trading ecosystem.

The approach and principles we discussed in this book pertaining to latency-sensitive applications developed in C++ should guide you on your journey. The full end-to-end electronic trading ecosystem we built is a prime example of a low-latency application and hopefully provided a good practical example of how to build a low-latency application from scratch. Hopefully, this chapter added to the experience by providing you with tools to analyze the performance and iteratively improve the system. We wish you all the best as you continue your low-latency application development journey!

Index

Symbols

-l library option 95
-march parameter 95
-Werror parameter 95

A

Active Template Library (ATL) 14
adaptive bitrate (ABR) 27
adaptive sync 36
aggressive orders 159
   matching 228-232
anonymous namespace 68
anti-aliasing 43
Ant Media Server 33
Application Enablement Platform (AEP) 45
artificial intelligence (AI) 45
asynchronous input/output (asio) 14
augmented reality (AR)
   challenges 19

B

banking applications 20
Best Bid Offer (BBO) 178, 299, 321
   structure, defining 299

bids 201
bitfields
   using 70
bitwise operations
   optimizing 63, 64
boolean operations
   optimizing 63, 64
Boost 13
BoxCaster 27

C

C++
   evolution 15
   threading, for multi-threaded low latency applications 98
C++, characteristics
   community support 15
   compiled language 10
   language constructs and features 11
   language development 15, 16
   low-level language 10
   speed and high performance 11
   usage of resources 11
C++ compiler
   leveraging 59

Index

C++ compiler optimization parameters
  maximizing 78
C++ features
  leveraging, to minimize
    application latency 60
  pitfalls, avoiding to minimize
    application latency 60
C++ features, to minimize application latency
  bitfields, using 70
  bitwise operations, optimizing 63, 64
  boolean operations, optimizing 63, 64
  cache and memory, access 74
  calling functions, efficiently 67
  casting and conversion
    operations, using 61, 62
  compile-time polymorphism, using 71
  compile-time processing, using 73
  data types, selecting 61
  dynamically allocated memory 77
  exceptions, handling 74
  jumps and branches, optimizing 66, 67
  multi-threading 78
  numerical operations, optimizing 62
  objects, copying 64
  objects, destroying 64
  objects, initializing 64
  objects, moving 64
  pointers, using 64, 65
  references, using 64, 65
  runtime polymorphism, using 70, 71
  storage, selecting 60, 61
C++ language, constructs and features
  compiler optimizations 12
  libraries 13
  multiple programming paradigms 13
  portability 12
  statically typed languages 12
  suitable projects 15
C++ matching engine
  designing, in trading exchange 159
C++ network programming
  with sockets 126, 127
C++ trading system
  tips and techniques, for optimizing 442, 443
cache and memory access optimization
  data, accessing 76
  data, aligning 74-76
  functions, grouping 77
  large data structures, using 77
  variables, grouping 77
CacheFly 34
calling functions
  considerations 67-70
capped peak latency 9
chunked encoding 31
chunked transfer encoding 31
clapperboard application 27
ClientId type 190
ClientOrderHashMap types
  defining 202-204
ClientRequestLFQueue types
  defining 193-195
ClientResponseLFQueue types
  defining 195-198
Common Media Application Format (CMAF) 31
Common Subexpression Elimination (CSE) 83
compiler optimization
  failure, scenarios 89, 90
compiler optimization flags 90
  approaching 91
  GCC optimization flags 91

compiler optimization techniques
  algebraic reductions 87
  common cases, optimizing 78
  constant folding 83
  constant propagation 83
  CSE 83
  DCE 83
  devirtualization 88
  induction variable 87
  inlining 83
  instructions, reordering 80
  instructions, scheduling 80
  live range 86
  loop invariant code movement 87
  loop unrolling 85
  peephole optimization 84
  reduce branching 79, 80
  register variables 86
  rematerialization 87
  special instructions, using 81
  Static Single Assignment (SSA) based optimizations 88
  strength reduction 82
  tail call optimization 84, 85
  vectorization 81, 82
compile-time polymorphism
  implementing, with CRTP 72
  polymorphic methods, invoking 73
  using 71
Compile time Polymorphism 67
Component Object Model (COM) 14
Composition paradigm
  using 71
constant folding 83
constant propagation 83
content delivery network (CDN) 24
contention 37

continuation stream 31
CPU clock cycles 6, 7
Crypto++ 15
Curiously Recurring Template Pattern (CRTP) 14, 72, 447

D

Dacast 33
data members
  defining, in FIFO sequencer 248
  defining, in LiquidityTaker algorithm 365, 366
  defining, in market data publisher 254, 255
  defining, in MarketMaker algorithm 360, 361
  defining, in order gateway server 242, 243
  defining, in snapshot synthesizer 259
Dead Code Elimination (DCE) 83
Dead Store Elimination (DSE) 92
defragmentation 44
devirtualization 70, 88
DirectX 44
DirectX 12 Ultimate
  installing 44
Dynamic Adaptive Streaming over HTTP (DASH) 31
dynamically allocated memory 77
  disadvantages 77
dynamically typed language 12
dynamic linking 52
dynamic memory allocations 103

E

edge computing 45, 46
  and 5G 46
  and AI 47

edge computing systems
  buying 47
  deploying 47
ef_vi 51
Eigen 14
electronic trading client's system
  hops 415, 416
electronic trading ecosystem
  layout 156
  running 387-389
  running, with instrumentation system 426, 427
  topology 156, 157
electronic trading ecosystem, components 157
  market data consumer, at market participant level 158
  market data publisher 157
  matching engine 157
  order gateway encoder and decoder client 158
  order gateway server at exchange 158
  trading engine, in the market participants' systems 158
Enhanced Order Book Interface (EOBI) 165
Evercast 33
Exablaze 51
exchange
  connecting to 309
  order requests, sending to 312, 313
  order responses, processing from 314, 315
exchange_main application
  running 215
exchange market data streams
  incremental market data stream 174
  snapshot market data streams 174
exchange, market updates
  instrument update messages 166, 167
  market state changes messages 166
  market statistics messages 167
  order updates messages 167
  trade messages 167
exchange order book
  ClientOrderHashMap types, defining 202-204
  designing 201, 202
  MEOrdersAtPrice types, defining 204-206
  MEOrder types, defining 202-204
  OrderHashMap types, defining 202-204
  OrdersAtPriceHashMap types, defining 204-206
exchange side components 157
external data
  exchanging 206

F

Fast Sync 36
Fat Finger errors 180
feature engine 183
  building 320
  complex features, computing 320
  computing, on order book changes 321
  computing, on trade events 322
  data members, defining 320
  initializing 321
Field Programmable Gate Arrays (FPGAs) 50
FIFO sequencer
  client requests publishing in order 249-251
  data members, defining in 248
  initializing 249
  requests processing 248
financial applications 20
First In First Out (FIFO) order 201
first-person shooters (FPS) 35

Index 469

FIX Adapted for STreaming (FAST) 165
Flash 30
flight software 18
frames per second (FPS) 35
framework, for low-latency C++ trading algorithms
  execution logic, developing 179
  feature engine, building 179
  order book, building 178
  risk management systems 179
FreeSync 36
frustum 39
frustum culling 39

G

gaming application optimization, approaching from developer's perspective 38
  cache access, optimizing 39
  calculations, caching 39
  CPU idle time, leveraging 40
  critical tasks, prioritizing 40
  draw calls, ordering considerations 40
  frustum culling 39
  hot path, optimizing 39
  mathematical approximations 39
  memory, managing 38
gaming application optimization, approaching from gamer's perspective 40
  automatic updates, delaying 42
  background services, turning off 42
  game mode, enabling 42
  game settings, optimizing for low-latency and high frame rate 43
  game settings, tweaking 42
  gaming monitor refresh rates 41
  graphics card, overclocking 41
  graphics card, upgrading 41
  hardware, tweaking 42
  hardware, upgrading 41
  high-performance mode, using 42
  OS, tweaking 42
  RAM, upgrading 42
  refresh rates, exceeding 43
  refresh rates, meeting 43
  triple buffering and V-Sync, disabling 43
gaming applications
  performance, improving 38
GCC optimization flags 91
  -ffast-math parameter 95, 96
  -l library option 95
  -march parameter 95
  -Wall parameter 95
  -Wextra parameter 95
  -Wpendantic parameter 95
  optimization level -O1 92
  optimization level -O2 93
  optimization level -O3 94, 95
ghosting 37
glass-to-glass latency 24-26
Global Common Subexpression Elimination (GCSE) 93
GNU compiler (GCC) 78
GNU Scientific Library (GSL) 14
graphics applications 19
G-Sync 36

H

Hard Disk Drives (HDD) 44
heads-up display (HUD) 40
High-Efficiency Stream Protocol (HESP) 31, 32

Index

higher-level low latency applications
  augmented reality (AR) 19
  banking applications 20
  financial applications 20
  graphics applications 19
  Internet of Things (IoT) applications 21
  libraries 20
  machine-to-machine (M2M) applications 21
  mobile phone applications 21
  search engines 20
  video game applications 19
  virtual reality (VR) 19
  web browsers 20
high-frequency trading (HFT) 10
high latencies, in low latency video streaming applications 26
  capture equipment and hardware 26
  decoding 27
  encoding 27
  internet quality 26
  jitter buffer 27
  physical distance 26
  server load 26
  streaming protocol 26
  transmission 26
HTTP-based protocols 30
  Common Media Application Format (CMAF) 31
  Dynamic Adaptive Streaming over HTTP (DASH) 31
  examples 30
  High-Efficiency Stream Protocol (HESP) 31, 32
HTTP Live Streaming (HLS) 31

I

iceberg orders 178
id Software 39

incremental market data stream 174
induction variables 86, 87
initialization stream 31
inline functions 68
inline keyword 68
input lag 35, 36
instrumentation system
  adding, to measure system performance 400
  electronic trading ecosystem, running with 426, 427
internal data structures
  building 216-219
Internet of Things (IoT) 21, 44
interpreted languages 10
Inter-Process Communication (IPC) 111

J

jitter 37
jitter buffer 27

K

kernel bypass 51

L

lag 24
laptop cooling 44
latencies
  measuring, in low latency video streaming 27, 28
latencies, measuring at exchange 404
  hops 405, 406
  in FIFOSequencer 409
  in market data publisher 407
  in matching engine 410-412
  in MEOrderBook 412-414
  in order book 410-412

in order server 408, 409
internally 404, 405
latencies, measuring in trading engine 414-422
  hops, in electronic trading clients's system 415, 416
  in LiquidityTaker algorithm 424, 425
  in market data consumer 417
  in MarketMaker algorithm 425, 426
  in MarketOrderBook 423, 424
  in order gateway 417, 418
  in OrderManager 422, 423
  internally 414, 415
latency 4
  in video streaming 24
  versus throughput 7
latency-critical applications 5
latency metrics
  differentiating 7
latency-sensitive applications
  requirements 4
  versus latency-critical applications 5
latency-sensitive applications, requirements 8
  capped peak latency 9
  correctness and robustness 8
  high throughput 9
  low latencies on average 8
  low latency variance 9
latency variance 8
libraries 20
limit order book 182, 183
  data members 216
limit orders 159
Linear Algebra Package (LAPACK) 14
Link Time Optimization (LTO) 68
LiquidityTaker algorithm
  data members, defining 365, 366

initializing 366, 367
latencies, measuring 424, 425
order book updates, handling 367-369
order updates, handling 369, 370
trade events, handling 367-369
liquidity taking strategies 183
liquidity taking trading algorithm 357
  mechanics, inspecting with example 357-359
liquidity taking trading strategies 354
live range 86
live video streaming applications
  low latency performance 23, 24
lock-free queue
  communicating, between threads and processes 111
  elements, adding to 113, 114
  elements, consuming from 114, 115
  initializing 113
  storage, designing 112, 113
  used, for transferring data 111
  using 115-117
log function
  adding 124, 125
logger
  creating 120-122
  launching 120
  using, with example 125, 126
logger data structures
  initializing 120
logger queue
  data, pushing to 122-124
logger structures 118, 119
logger thread
  creating 120-122
  launching 120-122
logical AND (&&) 63
logical OR (||) 63
loop fission 85

loop fusion 86
loop interchange 86
loop inversion 86
loop unrolling 66, 85
lower-level low latency applications 17
  cloud/distributed systems 18
  compilers 17
  databases 18
  embedded systems 17
  flight software 18
  operating systems 18
  telecommunications 17
  traffic control software 18
lowest latencies, achieving in electronic trading 50
  context switches 52
  CPU scheduling 52
  dynamic memory allocation 52
  kernel bypass 51
  linking 52
  locks 51
  memory management 52
  multithreading 51
  Network Interface Cards (NICs) 51
  switches 51
  trading server hardware, optimizing 51
low latency
  in modern electronic trading 49, 50
low latency applications 4, 17
  approaches, for development 55-59
  example, building 102, 103
  functions 98, 99
  higher-level low latency applications 19
  macros 98, 99
  thread affinity, setting 101, 102
  thread, creating 100, 101
  thread, launching 100, 101

low-latency C++ trading algorithms
  framework, designing for 178
low latency constraints
  in gaming applications 34, 35
low latency electronic trading 49
low latency, ensuring in IoT devices 45
  cloud costs, reducing 48
  edge computing 46
  fifth-generation wireless (5G), using 45
  P2P connectivity 45
  proximity, leveraging 47
low latency gaming applications, concepts 35
  frames per second (FPS) 35, 36
  input lag 36
  jitter 37
  network bandwidth 37
  networking protocols 37
  network packet loss 37
  ping 35
  refresh rate 36
  response time 37
Low Latency HLS (LL-HLS) 31
low latency logger
  designing 118
low latency logging framework
  building 117
  utility methods, designing to fetch current system time 117, 118
low latency performance
  in live video streaming applications 23, 24
low latency streaming 24
low latency streaming, platforms and solutions 32
  Ant Media Server 33
  CacheFly 34
  Dacast 33
  Evercast 33

Open Broadcast Software (OBS) 34
Twitch 32
Vimeo 33
Vonage Video API 34
Wowza 33
Zoom 33
low latency video streaming
  latencies, measuring in 27, 28
low latency video streaming, technologies 29
  HTTP-based protocols 30
  non-HTTP-based protocols 29
  WebRTC 32

M

machine-to-machine (M2M) 21
macro expressions 68
main exchange application
  building 268-272
main trading application
  building 381-387
  output, inspecting from run_exchange_
    and_clients.sh script 389-395
  running 381
market data
  order books, building from 295
  subscribing to 278, 279
market data consumer
  at market participant level 158
  data members, defining 279-281
  designing 174, 175
  incremental stream synchronizer 175
  initializing 281-283
  latencies, measuring 417
  market data protocol decoder 176
  snapshot stream synchronizer 175
  synchronizing, on startup and
    packet drops 173

market data consumer infrastructure 172
  decoding from, exchange protocol 173
  normalizing from, exchange protocol 173
  subscribing, to UDP multicast traffic 173
  UDP multicast traffic, consuming 173
market data consumer main loop
  running 284
market data protocol
  decoding 278, 279
  defining 236
  designing 236-238
market data protocol encoder 168, 169
market data publisher 157
  building 253, 254
  data members, defining in 254, 255
  designing 168
  initializing 255-257
  latencies, measuring 407
  market data protocol encoder 168, 169
  order book updates, publishing 257-259
  snapshots, publishing 259
  snapshots, synthesizing 259
  snapshot synthesizer 169, 170
market data publisher queue
  publishing to 212
market data updates
  processing 284-287
market events
  communicating, through markets data 165
MarketMaker algorithm
  data members, defining 360, 361
  initializing 361, 362
  latencies, measuring 425, 426
  order book updates, handling 363-365
  order updates, handling 365
  trade events, handling 363-365
market-making strategies 183

Index

market making trading algorithm 354
  mechanics, inspecting with example 355, 356
MarketOrderBook
  data members, defining 300-302
  initializing 302, 303
  latencies, measuring 423, 424
  structures, defining for 295, 296
MarketOrdersAtPrice structure
  defining 298, 299
MarketOrder structure
  defining 297, 298
market participants
  notifying, through order gateway interfaces 170
market participants interface
  building, to exchange 172
market updates
  processing 303-307
massive multiplayer online (MMO) games 35
matching engine 158
  building 206-210
  ClientRequestLFQueue types, defining 193-195
  ClientResponseLFQueue types, defining 195-198
  communication between threads 164
  constant limits, defining 192
  designing 163, 193
  exchange order book 159-161
  exchange order book, defining 201, 202
  latencies, measuring 410-412
  limit order book 164
  MEClientRequest types, defining 193-198
  MEMarketUpdateLFQueue types, defining 198-200
  MEMarketUpdate types, defining 198-200
  operations and interactions, defining 188
  participant orders, matching 162, 163
  purpose 159
  threading model 163
  types, defining 188-192
matching orders
  building 215
mean latency 7
MEClientRequest types
  defining 193-195
MEClientResponse types
  defining 195-198
median latency 7
MEMarketUpdateLFQueue types
  defining 198-200
MEMarketUpdate types
  defining 198-200
memory pools 103
  allocation requests serving 108, 109
  deallocations, handling 109
  designing, to avoid dynamic memory allocations 103
  initializing 107
  storage, designing 104-107
  use cases 104
  using, with example 110, 111
MEOrdersAtPrice types
  defining 204-206
MEOrder types
  defining 202-204
methods, of measuring latency 5
  CPU clock cycles 6, 7
  Round-trip time (RTT) 6
  tick-to-trade (TTT) 6
  time to first byte 6
Microsoft Foundation Classes (MFC) 14
minimum price increment 166

Index   475

mlpack 14
mobile phone applications 21
modern electronic trading
   low latency 49, 50
Moving Picture Experts Group (MPEG) 31
multi-threaded low latency applications
   C++, threading for 98

N

Nagles algorithm 130
natural language processing (NLP) 47
negative impacts, of real-time video
      streaming applications due to latency
   audio-video synchronization issues 28
   buffering pauses and delays 28
   low audio-video quality 28
   playback 29
network bandwidth 37
networking protocols 37
Network Interface Cards (NICs) 51, 127, 169
network packet loss 37
network protocols
   difference 170
non-HTTP-based protocols 29
   Flash 30
   Real-Time Messaging Protocol
      (RTMP) 29, 30
   Real-Time Streaming Protocol
      (RTSP) 29, 30
Non-Uniform Memory Access (NUMA) 51
numerical operations
   optimizing 62
NVIDIA Reflex low latency technology
   using 44

O

object-oriented programming (OOP) 13
OMOrder struct
   defining 334
   key fields 335, 336
   states 334, 335
Open Broadcast Software (OBS) 34
OpenOnload 51
Open Source Computer Vision
      (OpenCV) 14
operating systems (OSs) 15
optimization impact
   Logger string optimization,
      benchmarking 447-449
   release build optimization,
      benchmarking 450-452
optimization techniques, C++ trading system
   Logger for strings, optimizing 445, 446
   release build, optimizing 443, 444
   std**function instances, eliminating 446
   thread affinity, setting 444, 445
order book
   building 215
   building, from market data 295
   latencies, measuring 410-412
   passive liquidity, managing 360
   updating 228- 307
order book management
   generic utility methods, revisiting for 308
order book snapshot
   publishing 264, 266
   synthesizing 262- 264
order book updates
   handling 363-369
order cancellation requests
   handling 225-228

order data protocol
 defining 236
 designing 239-241
order flow
 receiving 309
 sending 309
order gateway
 latencies, measuring 417, 418
order gateway client
 data members, defining 309-311
 initializing 311, 312
order gateway client infrastructure 176
 designing 177
 order gateway protocol encoder
  and decoder 177, 178
 TCP connection manager 177
**order gateway encoder and
 decoder client 158**
order gateway interface
 network protocols, differences 170
 order requests, sending for
  participants' orders 171
 public information, versus
  private information 170
order gateway queue
 consuming from 211, 212
 publishing to 211, 212
order gateway server
 at exchange 158
 building 241, 242
 client responses, sending 251-253
 data members, defining 242, 243
 incoming client requests handling 245-247
 initializing 243-245
 requests processing with FIFO
  sequencer 248

order gateway server infrastructure
 designing 171
 exchange messaging protocol
  decoder and encoder 172
 FIFO sequencer 172
 TCP connection server/manager 171, 172
OrderHashMap types
 defining 202-204, 297, 298
OrderId type 189
OrderManager 318, 334
 data members, defining 337, 338
 designing 337
 initializing 338
 latencies, measuring 422, 423
 methods, adding to simplify order
  management 341-343
 orders, cancelling from 340
 orders, sending from 339
 orders, updating 343-345
 order updates, handling 343-345
Order protocol
 authentication and rejection
  messages, adding 461, 462
 modify messages, supporting 462
order requests
 sending, to exchange 312, 313
order responses
 processing, from exchange 313-315
orders 159
 managing 334
 sending 334
OrdersAtPriceHashMap type
 defining 204-206, 298, 299
order server
 latencies, measuring 408, 409

Index   477

order updates
   handling, in LiquidityTaker
      algorithm 369, 370
   handling, in MarketMaker algorithm 365
order updates messages
   Order Add 167
   Order Delete 167
   Order Modify 167
overclocking 41

P

packet drops
   handling 284-287
passive liquidity
   managing, in order book 360
passive orders 159
   handling 219- 225
peak latency 8
peephole optimization 84
Peer-to-Peer (P2P) protocol 31
performance measurement
   utilities, adding with RDTSC 400-402
**performance measurement
      systems, considerations**
   accurate measurement, setting up 404
   limtations, of RDTSC 404
   overhead, adding due to
      instrumentation 403
   reliability of RDTSC 404
ping 35
PITCH 165
Pointer Aliasing 65
PositionInfo
   data members, declaring 323, 324
   order book changes, handling 330-332
   order executions, handling 325-330
   variables 325

PositionKeeper 318
   designing 332, 333
   initializing 333
   market updates 333
   order executions, handling 333
positions and PnLs
   updating, with executions 323
price level aggregated order book 355
Price type 190
Priority type 191
Profile-Guided Optimization (PGO) 91
Pro Rata 160
public information
   versus private information 170
putting it on the wire 6

Q

QT 15
Qty type 190

R

RDTSC
   using, to add utilities for performance
      measurement 400-402
**Real-Time Messaging Protocol
      (RTMP) 29, 30**
real-time strategy (RTS) games 35
**Real-Time Streaming Protocol
      (RTSP) 29, 30**
Red Black Tree 280
refresh rate 35, 36
registers 86
register variables 86
regular expressions (regex) 13
rematerialization 87

Resource Acquisition is
    Initialization (RAII) 65
response time 35, 37
Return Value Optimization (RVO) 69
RiskCfg structure
    defining 345, 346
RiskCheckResult enumeration
    declaring 347, 348, 349
RiskInfo structure
    defining 349
    risk checks, performing 350
risk management systems 179, 180
    metrics 180-182
RiskManager 318, 345
    data members, designing 351
    initializing 351
    risk checks, performing 351
    risk, computing 345
    risk, managing 345
round-trip time (RTT) 6
RTT latency
    components 6
runtime polymorphism
    implementing, with virtual functions 72
    using 70
Run-Time Type Information (RTTI) 62

S

screen tearing 36
search engines 20
Secure Reliable Transport (SRT) 34
self-match prevention (SMP) 178
sender/receiver TCP socket
    constructing 136, 137
    data members 134, 135
    data, receiving 137-139
    data, sending 137-139
    destroying 136, 137
    implementing 134
    TCP connections, establishing 137
short-circuiting 63
Side type 191
Simple Binary Encoding (SBE) 165, 278
Single Producer Single Consumer
    (SPSC) 112
singular value decomposition (SVD) 14
Small String Optimization (SSO) 60
snapshot market data streams 174
snapshot stream
    synchronizing with 288-295
snapshot synthesizer 169, 170
    data members, defining in 259
    initializing 261
    main loop, running 267, 268
socket API
    additional parameters, setting up 130, 131
    building 127, 128
    interface information, obtaining 128, 129
    Nagle's algorithm, disabling 130
    setting, to be non-blocking 129
sockets
    C++ network programming,
        using with 126, 127
Solarflare 51
Solid State Drives (SSD) 44
spatial locality 57
stack unwinding 74
Standard Template Library (STL) 13, 280
statically typed language 12
    benefits 12
static keyword 68
static linking 52, 53
Static Single Assignment (SSA)-
    based optimizations 88
std::atomic 112

stop orders 178
strength reduction 82
structures
   defining, for market order book 295, 296
switching latency 51
system performance
   instrumentation system, adding to measure 400

T

tail call optimization 84, 85
TCPDirect 51
TCP server and clients
   example, building 147-150
TCP server component
   building 139
   data members, defining 140, 141
   data, receiving 146, 147
   data, sending 146, 147
   de-initializing 141, 142
   initializing 141, 142
   initializing, for connections 142
   listener socket, initializing 142
   monitored sockets, adding 142-146
   monitored sockets, removing 142-146
template metaprogramming 68, 73
temporal locality 57
Teradek 27
thread
   and processes, communicating between 111
   creating 100, 101
   launching 100, 101
thread affinity
   setting 101, 102
throughput
   versus latency 7

TickerId type 189
tick-to-trade (TTT) 6
Time Stamp Counter (TSC) 400
time to first byte 6
Time to Live (TTL) 130
time utilities
   updating 402, 403
TokBox 34
Top Of Book (TOB) 178
TradeEngineCfg structure
   defining 346, 347
trade engine components, enhancing
   FeatureEngine, enriching 463
   OrderManager, enhancing 463
   risk metrics, adding to RiskManager 463
   trading algorithms, enhancing 463
trade engine framework
   building 370
   client requests, sending 377
   client responses, processing 378, 379
   data members, defining 370-374
   initializing 374-377
   market data updates, processing 378
   miscellaneous methods, adding 380
   order book update, handling 379, 380
   order response update, handling 379, 380
   trade update, handling 379, 380
trade events
   handling 363-369
trade messages 167
trading algorithms
   behavior 354
   enumeration, adding to define type of algorithm 359, 360
   liquidity taking trading algorithm 357
   market making trading algorithm 354
trading client-side components 157

trading ecosystem
  analysis output 434
  latencies 430, 431
  latencies for internal function calls, observing 434-438
  latencies, observing between hops 438-442
  performance, analyzing 430-434
trading ecosystem future 453
  authentication and rejection messages, adding to Order protocol 461, 462
  containers, growing 453
  hash maps, enhancing 453-459
  hash maps, growing 453-455
  snapshot messages, optimizing 460, 461
  trade engine components, enhancing 463
trading engine
  components 319
  in market participants' systems 158
trading exchange binary
  building 213-215
trading strategy framework, design 182
  feature engine 183
  limit order book 182, 183
  order manager 183
  risk manager 184
  trading strategy 183
traffic control software 18
transcoding 24
Transmission Control Protocol (TCP) 29, 37
transmuxing 24
transrating 24
triple buffering 43
Twitch 32

U

Unix sockets
  creating 131-134
User Datagram Protocol (UDP) 29, 37

V

variable refresh rate (VRR) 36
vertical synchronization (V-Sync) 36
video distribution service (VDS) 24
video game applications 19
video streaming 24
  latency 24
video streaming applications
  sources of latency 25
Vimeo 33
virtual reality (VR) 19
  challenges 19
Virtual Table (vtable) 88
volume-weighted average price (VWAP) 324
Vonage Video API 34

W

web browsers 20
Web Real-Time Communication (WebRTC) 31, 32
Whole Program Optimization (WPO) 68
word size 74
Wowza 33

Z

Zoom 33

<packt>

www.packtpub.com

Subscribe to our online digital library for full access to over 7,000 books and videos, as well as industry leading tools to help you plan your personal development and advance your career. For more information, please visit our website.

Why subscribe?

- Spend less time learning and more time coding with practical eBooks and Videos from over 4,000 industry professionals
- Improve your learning with Skill Plans built especially for you
- Get a free eBook or video every month
- Fully searchable for easy access to vital information
- Copy and paste, print, and bookmark content

Did you know that Packt offers eBook versions of every book published, with PDF and ePub files available? You can upgrade to the eBook version at packtpub.com and as a print book customer, you are entitled to a discount on the eBook copy. Get in touch with us at customercare@packtpub.com for more details.

At www.packtpub.com, you can also read a collection of free technical articles, sign up for a range of free newsletters, and receive exclusive discounts and offers on Packt books and eBooks.

Other Books You May Enjoy

If you enjoyed this book, you may be interested in these other books by Packt:

Software Architecture with C++

Adrian Ostrowski, Piotr Gaczkowski

ISBN: 9781838554590

- Understand how to apply the principles of software architecture
- Apply design patterns and best practices to meet your architectural goals
- Write elegant, safe, and performant code using the latest C++ features
- Build applications that are easy to maintain and deploy
- Explore the different architectural approaches and learn to apply them as per your requirement
- Simplify development and operations using application containers
- Discover various techniques to solve common problems in software design and development

Developing High-Frequency Trading Systems

Sebastien Donadio, Sourav Ghosh, Romain Rossier

ISBN: 9781803242811

- Understand the architecture of high-frequency trading systems
- Boost system performance to achieve the lowest possible latency
- Leverage the power of Python programming, C++, and Java to build your trading systems
- Bypass your kernel and optimize your operating system
- Use static analysis to improve code development
- Use C++ templates and Java multithreading for ultra-low latency
- Apply your knowledge to cryptocurrency trading

Packt is searching for authors like you

If you're interested in becoming an author for Packt, please visit `authors.packtpub.com` and apply today. We have worked with thousands of developers and tech professionals, just like you, to help them share their insight with the global tech community. You can make a general application, apply for a specific hot topic that we are recruiting an author for, or submit your own idea.

Share Your Thoughts

Now you've finished *Building Low Latency Applications with C++*, we'd love to hear your thoughts! Scan the QR code below to go straight to the Amazon review page for this book and share your feedback or leave a review on the site that you purchased it from.

`https://packt.link/r/1837639353`

Your review is important to us and the tech community and will help us make sure we're delivering excellent quality content.

Download a free PDF copy of this book

Thanks for purchasing this book!

Do you like to read on the go but are unable to carry your print books everywhere? Is your eBook purchase not compatible with the device of your choice?

Don't worry, now with every Packt book you get a DRM-free PDF version of that book at no cost.

Read anywhere, any place, on any device. Search, copy, and paste code from your favorite technical books directly into your application.

The perks don't stop there, you can get exclusive access to discounts, newsletters, and great free content in your inbox daily

Follow these simple steps to get the benefits:

1. Scan the QR code or visit the link below

```
https://packt.link/free-ebook/9781837639359
```

1. Submit your proof of purchase
2. That's it! We'll send your free PDF and other benefits to your email directly

Printed in Great Britain
by Amazon